Until his death in 1993, Belfast-based writer and broadcaster W.D. FLACKES specialised in politics for more than forty years. He was associated with all three main broadcasting organisations in Ireland: in the early 1960s he contributed political commentaries to UTV; from 1964 to 1982 he was the BBC's Northern Ireland political correspondent; and he was a member of the RTE Authority, 1985–90.

Born in County Donegal in 1921, he began his journalistic career in 1939 as a freelance press correspondent in south Antrim. He reported for the *Armagh Guardian* (1942–3), the *Derry Standard* (1943), and the *Northern Constitution* (1943–4), and he was editor of the *Fermanagh Times* (1944–5). He covered the Northern Ireland Parliament for the *Belfast News-Letter* (1945–7), and then moved to Westminster as a parliamentary reporter of the Press Association (1947–57). On his return to Belfast in 1957, he was successively chief leader writer and news editor of the *Belfast Telegraph* before joining the BBC. In 1981 he was awarded an OBE for services to journalism.

He was co-author, with M.C. McGill, of *Montgomery, Field-Marshal* (Quota Press, Belfast, 1945), and he also wrote some science fiction.

SYDNEY ELLIOTT was born in Donaghadee, County Down, in 1943. He was educated at Regent House School, Newtownards, and Queen's University Belfast, where he was awarded a Ph.D. in Political Science in 1971. He taught at Belfast Royal Academy from 1966 to 1967, and since 1972 has taught in the Department of Political Science at Queen's, where he has been a senior lecturer since 1979. He is a regular contributor on BBC television and radio, covering election results in Northern Ireland, and has also broadcast on RTE, UTV, and London Weekend Television. Since 1973 he has published several books dealing with Northern Ireland elections; his most recent publication (with F.J. Smith) is *Northern Ireland: The District Council Elections of 1989* (Queen's University, Belfast, 1992).

£14-99

NORTHERN IRELAND
A Political Directory
1968–1993

W.D.FLACKES &
SYDNEY ELLIOTT

THE
BLACKSTAFF
PRESS

BELFAST

First edition published in 1980 by
Gill and Macmillan Limited
Second edition published in 1983 by
British Broadcasting Corporation
Third edition published in 1989 by
The Blackstaff Press Limited

This fully revised and updated edition published in 1994 by
The Blackstaff Press Limited
3 Galway Park, Dundonald, Belfast BT16 0AN, Northern Ireland

This book has received support from the Cultural Traditions Programme
of the Community Relations Council, which aims to encourage
acceptance and understanding of cultural diversity.

Index compiled by Helen Litton

Typeset by Paragon Typesetters, Queensferry, Clwyd

Printed in England by The Cromwell Press Limited

A CIP catalogue record for this book
is available from the British Library

ISBN 0-85640-527-2

CONTENTS

in memoriam
W.D. Flackes
1921–1993

PREFACE

A quarter of a century on from the start of the current Northern Ireland Troubles, the record of politicians, parties, policies, pressure groups, paramilitaries and the agencies of law and order becomes ever more complex and the tide of events ever more bewildering. This directory started out in 1980 as a quick and neutral guide to the conflict and the varied elements at home and abroad that influence it. The personalities have multiplied, but the objectives remain the same. The format of this fourth edition is unchanged except that an index has been added. Twenty years after Sunningdale, the nature of British-Irish relations is clearer, with the Anglo-Irish Agreement and the British-Irish Parliamentary Body, but the shape of any devolved system of government, including an assembly for Northern Ireland, to fill the 'democratic deficit', and any formal links North–South, are still a matter of debate. The Brooke–Mayhew Talks failed to restart in 1993 despite the brokerage of other ministers. The whispers of peace gradually grew to a crescendo in 1993 and Prime Minister John Major and Taoiseach Albert Reynolds mounted their initiative in the Downing Street Declaration of December in an attempt to attract the paramilitaries into politics. However, it is all too apparent that the forces of nationalism and ethnicity no longer seem just a local problem. In the former Yugoslavia, and from the Baltic to Siberia, very similar arguments about the pros and cons of constitutional change engage mediators, commentators and public opinion. It is no longer unusual to have members of the international media corps, in Bosnia or wherever, turn to Northern Ireland for comparisons. In reverse, the term 'ethnic cleansing' threatens to replace 'sectarian killing' in the local political vocabulary.

Over the years, we have been heartened by comments from many parts of the world on the range of information within the directory. It has become an established reference source across the Atlantic and in many other areas. We have tried to adopt as many as possible of the constructive suggestions from reviewers and readers about individual entries. Although we have relied heavily on our personal research, we are greatly indebted to a host of people and organisations for their help. The resources of the Linen Hall Library's Political Collection (*see* the entry in the dictionary section) have been invaluable, and we have also drawn on material in the Belfast Central Reference Library, the Northern Ireland Public Record Office, Queen's University Library, and the local BBC and newspaper libraries. Our thanks are also due to the information offices of the Northern Ireland Office, the European Commission, the Royal Ulster Constabulary, and army headquarters. Other key points of reference were the three-volume *Northern Ireland, 1968-74: A Chronology of Events* (Richard Deutsch and Vivien Magowan), and the chronology published in each issue of *Fortnight* magazine.

Finally, mention is due to senior BBC executives who were helpful to the project at the outset: the late Sir Richard Francis, a former Northern Ireland Controller, and his successor, James Hawthorne CBE. Brum Henderson CBE, former chairman of UTV, has also shown a close interest, as has Robin Walsh, the current BBC Northern Ireland Controller. In the USA we remain indebted to the Rockefeller Foundation for hosting a breakfast reception in New York for the first edition.

W.D. FLACKES and SYDNEY ELLIOTT
BELFAST, MAY 1993

The originator of *Northern Ireland: A Political Directory*, W.D. Flackes OBE, and the sole author of the first two editions, died suddenly on 1 August 1993. It was a pleasure to work with Billy and experience his skills as a journalist and editor on the third and fourth editions. In many ways it represented his values of personal integrity and factual reporting. He made it a standard work for his colleagues in broadcasting, journalism and politics. His legacy remains not only for the news industry and academia but also for the wider community, where he contributed so much to the understanding of events in Northern Ireland, especially during the past difficult twenty-five years.

SYDNEY ELLIOTT
BELFAST, MAY 1994

LIST OF ABBREVIATIONS

AAOH	American Ancient Order of Hibernians
ABD	Apprentice Boys of Derry
ACE	Action for Community Employment
ADC	aide-de-camp
AIA	Anglo-Irish Agreement
AIIC	Anglo-Irish Intergovernmental Council
ALJ	Association for Legal Justice
All.	Alliance Party
AOH	Ancient Order of Hibernians
ASU	Active Service Unit
b.	born
BA	Bachelor of Arts
B.Agr.	Bachelor of Agriculture
BAO	Bachelor of Art of Obstetrics
BAOR	British Army of the Rhine
BBC	British Broadcasting Corporation
B.Ch.	Bachelor of Surgery
B.Comm.	Bachelor of Commerce
BD	Bachelor of Divinity
BDS	Bachelor of Dental Surgery
B.Ed.	Bachelor of Education
BIA	British Irish Association
BIPB	British-Irish Parliamentary Body
BL	Bachelor of Law
B.Litt.	Bachelor of Letters
BMA	British Medical Association
B.Sc.	Bachelor of Science
B.Sc.(Econ.)	Bachelor of Economic Science
BUDP	British Ulster Dominion Party
Cantab.	Cambridge University
Capt.	Captain
CBI	Confederation of British Industry
CCDC	Central Citizens' Defence Committee
CEC	Campaign for Equal Citizenship
CESA	Catholic Ex-Servicemen's Association
CIA	Central Intelligence Agency
CLMC	Combined Loyalist Military Command
Com.	Communist
Cons.	Conservative Party
CPI	Communist Party of Ireland
CPLS	Certificate in Professional Legal Studies
CRC	Community Relations Council
CSO	Central Statistical Office
d.	died
DASS	Diploma of Applied Social Services
DCDC	Derry Citizens' Defence Committee
DCL	Doctor of Civil Law
DED	Department of Economic Development
Dem. L.	Democratic Left
Dip.Ed.	Diploma in Education
Dip.H.E.	Diploma of Higher Education
Dip.Obst.	Diploma in Obstetrics
DL	Deputy Lieutenant
D.Lit.	Doctor of Literature
D.Litt.	Doctor of Letters
DNA	deoxyribonucleic acid (genetic code)
DOE	Department of the Environment
DPH	Diploma in Public Health
DPP	Director of Public Prosecutions
DULC	Democratic Unionist Loyalist Coalition
DUP	Democratic Unionist Party
E.	east
EC	European Community
ECHR	European Convention on Human Rights
Ecol.	Ecology Party
EDG	European Democratic Group
Elec.	electorate
EOC	Equal Opportunities Commission
EPA	Emergency Provisions Act
ERG	European Right Group
FBI	Federal Bureau of Investigation
FEA	Fair Employment Agency
FEC	Fair Employment Commission
FF	Fianna Fáil
FG	Fine Gael
FRCP	Fellow of the Royal College of Physicians
FRCS	Fellow of the Royal College of Surgeons
FRS	Fellow of the Royal Society
GAA	Gaelic Athletic Association
GB	Great Britain
GDP	gross domestic product
GEC	General Electric Company
Gen.	General

GHQ	general headquarters	MA	Master of Arts
GLC	Greater London Council	MAFF	Ministry of Agriculture, Fisheries, and Food
GOC	General Officer Commanding		
HAA	heavy anti-aircraft	maj.	majority
H.Dip.Ed.	Honorary Diploma in Education	MB	Bachelor of Medicine
HQ	headquarters	MBA	Master of Business Administration
IAAG	improvised anti-armour grenade		
IBA	Independent Broadcasting Authority	MD	Doctor of Medicine
		MEP	Member of the European Parliament
ICTU	Irish Congress of Trade Unions		
IDB	Industrial Development Board	M.o.D.	Ministry of Defence
IFI	International Fund for Ireland	MORI	Mass Opinion Research Institute
IIP	Irish Independence Party	MP	Member of Parliament
IMF	International Monetary Fund	MPA	Member of Parliamentary Assembly (1982)
INC	Irish National Caucus		
Ind.	Independent	MRBI	Market Research Bureau, Ireland
Ind. Lab.	Independent Labour	MRCGP	Member of the Royal College of General Practitioners
Ind. N.	Independent Nationalist		
Ind. Soc.	Independent Socialist	M.Sc.	Master of Science
Ind. U.	Independent Unionist	N.	north
INLA	Irish National Liberation Army	NA	New Agenda
IONA	Islands of the North Atlantic	Nat.	Nationalist Party
IPLO	Irish People's Liberation Organisation	Nat. Dem.	National Democratic Party
		NATO	North Atlantic Treaty Organisation
IPS	Independent Progressive Socialist		
IRA	Irish Republican Army	NCCL	National Council for Civil Liberties
IRLOFP	Independent Raving Looney Ozone Friendly Party		
		NCO	non-commissioned officer
IRSP	Irish Republican Socialist Party	NEC	National Executive Committee
ITGWU	Irish Transport and General Workers' Union	NI	Northern Ireland
		NICRA	Northern Ireland Civil Rights Association
ITN	Independent Television News		
ITV	Independent Television	NICVA	Northern Ireland Council for Voluntary Action
JP	Justice of the Peace		
Lab.	Labour Party	NIE	Northern Ireland Electricity
Lab. and TU	Labour and Trade Union Group	NIF	New Ireland Forum
Lab. '87	Labour '87	NILP	Northern Ireland Labour Party
LAW	Loyalist Association of Workers	NIO	Northern Ireland Office
LCI	Labour Committee on Ireland	NIVT	Northern Ireland Voluntary Trust
LCU	Loyal Citizens of Ulster	NLP	Natural Law Party
Lib.	Liberal Party	NORAID	Irish Northern Aid Committee
Lib. Dem.	Liberal Democrat	NPF	National Political Front
LLB	Bachelor of Laws	NUI	National University of Ireland
LLD	Doctor of Laws	NUJ	National Union of Journalists
LLM	Master of Laws	NUM	National Union of Mineworkers
LOL	Loyal Orange Lodge	NUM	New Ulster Movement
Loy.	Loyalist	NUPRG	New Ulster Political Research Group
Loy. Coal.	Loyalist Coalition		
LPNI	Labour Party of Northern Ireland	NUU	New University of Ulster now UU
LRG	Labour Representation Group		
Lt.	Lieutenant	Off. Rep.	Official Republican
LTU	Labour and Trade Union	Off. U.	Official Unionist

OIRA	Official Irish Republican Army	TD	Teachta Dála (member of the
OU	Open University		Dáil)
Oxon.	Oxford University	U.	Unionist Party
PC	Privy Councillor	u/a	unavailable
PD	People's Democracy	UAC	Ulster Army Council
PESC	Public Expenditure Survey Cycle	UCA	Ulster Citizen Army
Ph.D.	Doctor of Philosophy	UCC	University College Cork
PIRA	Provisional Irish Republican	UCD	University College Dublin
	Army	UCDC	Ulster Constitution Defence
PLO	Palestine Liberation Army		Committee
PM	Prime Minister	UCG	University College Galway
POW	prisoner of war	UDA	Ulster Defence Association
PP	Peace People	UDI	Unilateral Declaration of
PPP	People's Progressive Party		Independence
PPS	Parliamentary Private Secretary	UDP	Ulster Democratic Party
PR	proportional representation	UDR	Ulster Defence Regiment
PRO	public relations officer	UFF	Ulster Freedom Fighters
Prog. D.	Progressive Democrats	UIC	Ulster Independence Committee
Prot. U.	Protestant Unionist Party	UIP	Ulster Independence Party
PSF	Provisional Sinn Féin	UK	United Kingdom
PTA	Prevention of Terrorism Act	ULA	Ulster Loyalist Association
PTF	Protestant Task Force	ULCCC	Ulster Loyalist Central
PUP	Progresssive Unionist Party		Co-ordinating Committee
QC	Queen's Counsel	ULDP	Ulster Loyalist Democratic Party
QUB	Queen's University Belfast	U. Lib.	Ulster Liberal Party
RAF	Royal Air Force	ULP	United Labour Party
RCOG	Royal College of Obstetricians	UN	United Nations
	and Gynaecologists	Unoff.	Unofficial
RDC	Rural District Council	Unoff. U.	Unofficial Unionist
Rep. C.	Republican Clubs	UPNI	Unionist Party of
Rep. Lab.	Republican Labour Party		Northern Ireland
RHC	Red Hand Commando	U. Pro-A	Pro-Assembly Unionist
RIR	Royal Irish Regiment	UPUP	Ulster Popular Unionist Party
RM	Resident Magistrate	UPV	Ulster Protestant Volunteers
RSF	Republican Sinn Féin	US	United States of America
RTE	Radio Telefís Éireann	USC	Ulster Special Constabulary
RU	Real Unionist		(B Specials)
RUC	Royal Ulster Constabulary	USCA	Ulster Special Constabulary
RUCR	Royal Ulster Constabulary		Association
	Reserve Force	USSR	Union of Soviet Socialist
S.	south		Republics
SACHR	Standing Advisory Commission	Utd.	United
	on Human Rights	Utd. Loy.	United Loyalist
SAS	Special Air Service	UTV	Ulster Television
SDA	Shankill Defence Association	UU	University of Ulster
SDLP	Social Democratic and Labour	UUAC	United Unionist Action Council
	Party	UUP	Ulster Unionist Party
SDP	Social Democratic Party	UUUC	United Ulster Unionist Council
SLD	Social and Liberal Democrats		(or Coalition)
Soc.	Socialist	UUUM	United Ulster Unionist
STV	single transferable vote		Movement
TCD	Trinity College Dublin	UUUP	United Ulster Unionist Party

UVF	Ulster Volunteer Force	VUPP	Vanguard Unionist Progressive Party
UWC	Ulster Workers' Council		
VCR	video cassette recorder	W.	west
VHF	very high frequency	WBLC	West Belfast Loyalist Coalition
VPP	Volunteer Political Party	WP	Workers' Party
VSC	Vanguard Service Corps	WPRC	Workers' Party Republican Clubs
VULC	Vanguard Unionist Loyalist Coalition	WT	Women Together
		WUUC	West Ulster Unionist Council
		YTP	Youth Training Programme

CHRONOLOGY OF MAJOR EVENTS

1921-93

1921 First NI Parliament opened by George V on 7 June.

1922 Widespread violence in NI, in which 232 people killed and about 1,000 wounded.

1925 Irish Free State Government confirmed the border in the 1920 Act and registered it with the League of Nations.

1931 IRA declared illegal in Irish Free State.

1932 De Valera's Fianna Fáil party secured power in Irish Free State. In Belfast new Stormont Parliament Buildings opened by Prince of Wales.

1937 New Southern Irish Constitution claimed sovereignty over island of Ireland.

1941 German air raids on Belfast – 949 killed and more than 2,000 injured.

1942 US troops arrived in NI on way to second front in Europe.

1943 Sir Basil Brooke (later Lord Brookeborough) became NI PM, amid demands for more vigorous local war effort.

1949 Southern Ireland became a full Republic and British Government gave new constitutional guarantee to Stormont Parliament.

1956 IRA launched border campaign which led to introduction of internment without trial both in Republic and in NI.

1962 IRA called off its campaign.

1963 Terence O'Neill became NI PM.

1965 Sean Lemass visited Stormont for talks, the first Taoiseach of Republic to do so. The visit and its secrecy were attacked by many Unionists.

1966 UVF declared illegal.

1967 NICRA formed. Republican Clubs declared illegal.

1968

25 March Terence O'Neill television interview on his fifth anniversary as Prime Minister reviewed improved community relations and the need to remove the legacy of hate.

27 April NICRA rally protested at Armagh Republican Easter parade ban.

20 May Terence O'Neill pelted with stones, eggs and flour after Woodvale Unionist Association meeting.

20 June Austin Currie began squat in Caledon house allocated by Dungannon RDC to an unmarried Protestant woman.

21 June Nationalist Party conference unanimously approved the Currie squat.

1 July Belfast Corporation voted for Sunday opening of play centres.

31 July Sir Ralph Grey appointed Governor.

22 August Society of Labour Lawyers documented discrimination in NI and sought comments from parties.

24 August	First civil rights march in NI held from Coalisland to Dungannon.
5 October	Banned Derry civil rights march broken up by RUC batons in presence of Gerry Fitt MP, three British Labour MPs and an RTE television crew. Rioting ensued on two succeeding evenings.
9 October	QUB students marched to Belfast City Hall. People's Democracy formed.
15 October	Nationalist Party withdrew from role as official Stormont opposition.
21 October	Labour Party NI Committee formed.
24 October	PD demonstration at Stormont.
30 October	Taoiseach Jack Lynch met Harold Wilson in London.
4 November	PM O'Neill, Craig (Home Affairs Minister) and Faulkner (Minister of Commerce) had talks at 10 Downing Street with PM Wilson and Home Secretary Callaghan.
8 November	Londonderry Corporation accepted a Nationalist motion for housing allocation to be by a points system.
17 November	Nationalist Party conference adopted a policy of civil disobedience.
22 November	PM O'Neill announced a five-point reform plan: for housing allocation by points, an Ombudsman, an end to company votes in council elections, a review of the Special Powers Act, and a Londonderry Development Commission.
28 November	Electoral Law (Amendment) Act abolished university representation and the business vote in Stormont elections; it created four new constituencies and a permanent Boundary Commission.
30 November	NICRA march in Armagh faced a demonstration led by Rev. Ian Paisley.
9 December	Terence O'Neill's 'Ulster at the Crossroads' speech gained 150,000 letters of support.
11 December	PM O'Neill required Craig to resign because of differing interpretations of the legality of Westminster intervention on devolved matters.
12 December	Unionist Parliamentary Party gave O'Neill vote of confidence with four abstentions.

1969

4 January	PD march to Derry attacked by mob at Burntollet bridge. RUC Reserve broke doors and windows in the Bogside, Derry, that evening, resulting in the creation of a local citizens' army and a no-go area.
7 January	RUC Inspector Harry Baillie appointed to investigate misconduct by the RUC in the Bogside.
9 January	In London, PM O'Neill met PM Wilson and Home Secretary Callaghan, and later Heath, the leader of the Opposition.
11 January	Newry civil rights march erupted into violence.
15 January	PM O'Neill and Cabinet agreed to an independent inquiry into the causes of violence since October 1968. Brian Faulkner resigned from the O'Neill Government.
20 January	PM Wilson said on BBC TV that reform had not gone far enough and his Government might intervene in NI.

30 January	A group of twelve Unionist MPs signed a document calling for a change of leadership. Londonderry Development Commission named to replace Corporation.
6 February	New Ulster Movement formed to support pro-O'Neill candidates in forthcoming Stormont general election.
26 February	Stormont general election results showed Unionists gaining two seats (total thirty-nine), the Nationalist Party losing three (total six). Independent civil rights candidates gained three and the National Democrats and Liberals lost one each.
28 February	Unionist Parliamentary Party confirmed O'Neill as leader by twenty-three votes to one with one abstention.
11 March	Parliamentary Commissioner Bill introduced to enable appointment of an Ombudsman to investigate complaints against Stormont Departments.
12 March	Announcement made that RUC were to carry arms on daytime routine duties in border areas for first time since 1965.
16 March	Four NICRA founding members resigned over PD 'infiltration'.
25 March	Rev. Ian Paisley and Major Bunting began prison sentences of three months for unlawful assembly at Armagh counter-demonstration.
30 March	Castlereagh electricity sub-station damaged by explosion caused by loyalist extremists. USC called up for guard duty.
31 March	Ulster Unionist Council voted by 338 to 263 for O'Neill's leadership.
4 April	Explosion, caused by loyalist extremists, at water installation at Dunadry.
18 April	Bernadette Devlin (Unity) won Mid-Ulster by-election.
19 April	Banned NICRA march in Derry erupted into serious rioting after clashes with opponents.
20 April	Explosion, caused by loyalist extremists, damaged Silent Valley water pipeline to Belfast.
23 April	Unionist Parliamentary Party supported universal adult suffrage in council elections by twenty-eight votes to twenty-two. Major James Chichester-Clark resigned from O'Neill Government.
24 April	Explosion damaged water pipeline from Lough Neagh to Belfast.
25 April	Annalong explosion, caused by loyalist extremists, hit Belfast water supply. Five hundred British troops sent to NI.
28 April	Terence O'Neill resigned as Prime Minister.
29 April	NI Boundary Commission appointed under Justice Lowry.
1 May	Major James Chichester-Clark elected Unionist leader and PM by seventeen votes to sixteen over Brian Faulkner.
4 May	NICRA announced a civil disobedience plan.
9 May	UUP endorsed Chichester-Clark as leader and 'one man, one vote' principle.
21 May	PM Chichester-Clark and colleagues met PM Wilson and Home Secretary Callaghan at Downing Street.
22 May	Harold Wilson announced 'one man, one vote' franchise for 1971 in Commons.
28 June	NICRA renewed demonstrations in Strabane.
1 July	The Parliamentary Commissioner (Ombudsman), Sir Edmund Compton, began work.
2 July	White Paper on Local Government Reorganisation proposed

	seventeen councils and 400 councillors to replace the existing seventy-three councils and 1,200 councillors.
15 July	More USC (B Specials) called up as rioting broke out in some Nationalist towns and parts of Belfast.
12 August	Serious violence occurred after Apprentice Boys' parade in Derry. Taoiseach Jack Lynch sent 'field hospitals' to border areas. RUC stations were attacked in Nationalist areas in NI.
14 August	Continued serious rioting resulted in the call-up of B Specials, and finally PM Chichester-Clark requested army assistance to maintain law and order. Troops began to arrive on the streets.
19 August	Downing Street Declaration issued after PM Chichester-Clark met PM Wilson at Downing Street.
21 August	Hunt inquiry into structure of RUC and USC announced.
22 August	Two senior UK civil servants, Oliver Wright and Alec Baker, appointed to personal office of NI PM and to Ministry of Home Affairs.
27 August	James Callaghan visited Belfast and Derry. A joint communiqué by Callaghan and NI Government promised to speed the implementation of reforms.
29 August	Justice Scarman appointed to inquire into disturbances of the summer.
10 September	Army completed Peace Line in Belfast.
25 September	Ministry for Community Relations created.
30 September	Paisley rally outside Stormont attended by 5,000 people.
8 October	James Callaghan began a four-day visit.
10 October	Sir Arthur Young appointed head of RUC.
12 October	Loyalists clashed with army on Shankill, after abolition of USC and disarming of RUC. Three people killed, including one RUC man, and sixty-six were injured, including two RUC and fourteen soldiers.
12 November	White Paper on reorganisation of RUC and formation of UDR.
17 November	PM Chichester-Clark met PM Wilson and James Callaghan in London.
25 November	Electoral Law Act, making council franchise the same as that in Britain, became law.
27 November	Commissioner for Complaints, John Benn, appointed.

1970

1 January	UDR came into existence.
11 January	Sinn Féin Ard Fheis failed to amend policy on abstentionism and split into Officials and Provisionals, mirroring the split in the IRA at the end of 1969.
14 January	RUC patrols returned to Falls for first time since August.
31 January	NILP conference voted to merge with Labour Party, but the latter refused to accept it as a region.
1 February	PM Chichester-Clark and Minister of Development Faulkner met Callaghan in London on economic issues.
10 March	Stormont MPs given police protection.
14 March	Communist Party of Ireland founded.
18 March	Five Unionist MPs, Boal, McQuade, Craig, West and Laird, expelled from Unionist Parliamentary Party.

1 April	Roy Hattersley, Minister of Defence, visited Northern Ireland as UDR became operational.
17 April	Rev. Ian Paisley and Rev. William Beattie (Prot. U.) won Bannside and South Antrim by-elections.
21 April	Alliance Party of Northern Ireland formed.
30 April	USC formally disbanded.
6 May	Taoiseach Lynch won vote of confidence after sacking Haughey and Blaney over import of arms.
19 June	In Westminster general election, Unionists lost two seats, N. Antrim to Rev. Ian Paisley (Prot. U.) and Fermanagh–S. Tyrone to Frank McManus (Unity), and retained eight.
23 June	Five-year economic plan published.
25 June	Macrory review of local government published.
26 June	Bernadette Devlin MP jailed for role in Bogside disturbances.
27 June	Rioting in Belfast and Derry.
30 June	Reginald Maudling, Conservative Home Secretary, visited Northern Ireland.
3–5 July	Curfew imposed on lower Falls.
6 July	Dr Patrick Hillery, Irish Minister for External Affairs, unofficially visited the Falls Road area.
17 July	PM Chichester-Clark and Robert Porter met Home Secretary Maudling in London.
23 July	Parades banned for six months.
2 August	Army introduced rubber bullets.
10 August	Maudling threatened direct rule if reforms backtracked.
21 August	SDLP formed under leadership of Gerry Fitt.
26 August	Robert Porter resigned as Minister of Home Affairs in Stormont Government.
15 September	One-hundredth explosion in 1970 occurred. Some 70 per cent had occurred in west.
23 September	Sir Arthur Young announced resignation from 23 November.
2 October	Local government elections postponed until October 1972.
8 October	SDLP proposed PR for elections.
11 October	Commissioner for Complaints upheld claim of maladministration in a housing allocation by Dungannon RDC.
23 October	Dublin arms conspiracy trial found Charles Haughey, Neil Blaney and two others not guilty of the illegal import of arms.
29 October	Electoral Reform Society pressed Home Office to introduce PR for NI.
30 October	PM Chichester-Clark met Home Secretary Maudling on reforms and security.
19 November	Commissioner for Complaints announced he had had 970 complaints in first ten months, 74 alleging discrimination.
17 December	NI Government accepted Macrory reforms of local government. Legislation promised for structural reform and elections by autumn 1972.
23 December	Father Robert Murphy of Newtownards named first Catholic parliamentary chaplain to Stormont.
30 December	Cost of disturbances in 1969–70 put at £5.5 million.

1971

17 January	Official Sinn Féin Ard Fheis in Dublin ended sixty-five-year policy of abstention from Dáil, Stormont and Westminster.
18 January	PM Chichester-Clark met Home Secretary Maudling in London.
20 January	Independent commissioner to define boundaries of twenty-six new District Councils.
27 January	Ombudsman upheld two out of thirty-three complaints.
6 February	Gunner Robert Curtis became the first soldier to die in NI since August 1969.
25 February	PM Chichester-Clark's meeting with Cardinal Conway reported as a first since 1921.
4 March	Home Secretary Maudling addressed MPs and Senators at Stormont.
10 March	Three Royal Highland Fusiliers found dead at Ligoniel – murders later attributed to PIRA.
12 March	Four thousand shipyard workers marched in Belfast seeking internment of PIRA leaders.
16 March	PM Chichester-Clark met Prime Minister Heath and security chiefs at his own request.
20 March	Chichester-Clark resigned because he saw 'no other way' to bring home 'the realities of the present constitutional, political and security situation'.
23 March	Brian Faulkner defeated William Craig by twenty-six votes to four in Unionist leadership election.
25 March	James Callaghan addressed a rally of the Labour movement at the Ulster Hall but refused regional party status to NILP.
2 April	Newtownabbey held first by-election under the new local government franchise.
6 April	Westminster debate on NI heard Harold Wilson say a Bill for direct rule existed.
6 May	NILP conference sought list form of PR.
13 May	NI Housing Executive met for first time.
6 June	Alliance proposed PR for elections.
8 June	Army GOC Sir Harry Tuzo said a permanent solution could not be achieved by military means.
18 June	SDLP and Nationalist MPs refused to attend state opening of Stormont.
22 June	Faulkner outlined new Stormont committee system chaired by members of opposition.
8 July	Riots in Derry for fourth day; two shot dead – Seamus Cusack and Desmond Beattie.
16 July	Hume and others withdrew from Stormont after the refusal of an inquiry into the deaths of two Derry men, and announced their intention of setting up a separate assembly.
23 July	Dawn raids by security forces arrested forty-eight people in ten hours.
3 August	Official Sinn Féin registered in Dublin as a party.
5 August	Westminster debate on NI. PM Faulkner met PM Heath and GOC Tuzo in London.
9 August	Internment dawn swoop lifted over three hundred people. Violence in Belfast and Derry.

11 August	Seven thousand 'refugees' said to have moved South.
15 August	Gerry Fitt (SDLP) announced campaign of civil disobedience and resignations from public bodies.
22 August	Some 130 non-Unionist councillors on twenty local authorities announced withdrawal.
23 August	Sixteen abstentionist MPs and Senators attended talks in Dublin with Taoiseach Lynch.
25 August	Gerry Fitt met U Thant at UN on brutality claims.
31 August	Compton inquiry set up into alleged brutality against detainees.
3 September	Ulster Liberals advocated PR.
6 September	PM Heath met Taoiseach Lynch at Chequers for eight and a half hours.
8 September	Harold Wilson put forward a twelve-point plan for a united Ireland.
12 September	Cardinal Conway and six Catholic bishops issued statement on violence, internment and ill-treatment.
16 September	Unionist resignations over agreement to tripartite talks including the Republic.
27–28 September	Tripartite talks at Chequers involving Edward Heath, Jack Lynch and Brian Faulkner as violence and PIRA strength increased.
30 September	Rev. Ian Paisley and Desmond Boal announced intention to form a new party, the Ulster Loyalist Party.
5 October	Stormont opened, with the opposition formed by Rev. Ian Paisley, Desmond Boal, Rev. William Beattie and John McQuade. John Hume elected president of the alternative assembly to meet in Strabane town hall.
7 October	Faulkner met PM Heath and Cabinet.
17 October	Some 16,000 were said to be withholding rent and rates for council homes in protest at internment.
19 October	Five Northern Ireland MPs began a forty-eight-hour hunger strike outside 10 Downing Street to protest at internment and treatment of internees.
20 October	In US Congress Senator Edward Kennedy called for withdrawal of troops and a united Ireland.
24 October	PSF Ard Fheis in Dublin heard Ó Brádaigh set aim of an ungovernable North as a prelude to a united thirty-two-county republic.
26 October	The alternative Nationalist Assembly of the Northern Irish People, proposed in July, met in Dungiven Castle.
27 October	G.B. Newe, a Catholic, was appointed to Faulkner's Cabinet.
30 October	DUP formed at Ulster Hall rally. Paisley predicted direct rule.
4 November	PM Faulkner met Wilson and Callaghan in London.
16 November	Compton report claimed there had been ill-treatment of internees, but rejected brutality claims.
21 November	Cardinal Conway and five Northern Catholic bishops condemned 'interrogation in depth'.
25 November	Harold Wilson, after a four-day visit, put forward fifteen-point plan of transition to a united Ireland.
30 November	Republic announced it would take 'brutality' case to European Court of Human Rights.
4 December	McGurk's Bar bomb left by the UVF killed fifteen.
6 December	PM Faulkner met Maudling in London.

12 December	Senator Jack Barnhill killed at home in Strabane by IRA.
15 December	Home Secretary Maudling, after a two-day visit, said he could foresee a time when violence would be reduced to an 'acceptable level'.
23 December	PM Heath on visit gave televised Christmas message about his determination to end violence.
31 December	John Benn replaced Sir Edmund Compton as Ombudsman.

1972

30 January	Thirteen men shot dead by army in Derry ('Bloody Sunday').
2 February	British Embassy in Dublin burned down.
22 February	Seven killed by bomb at Aldershot military barracks; OIRA claimed responsibility.
23 February	Legislation rushed through Westminster to validate army actions in NI, after the High Court ruled that the armed forces could not operate under Stormont laws.
25 February	John Taylor, Minister of State, survived OIRA assassination attempt in Armagh.
4 March	Abercorn restaurant bombed; 2 killed, 130 injured.
24 March	British Government announced direct rule in NI after Faulkner Government said it would not accept loss of law-and-order powers.
30 March	NI Temporary Provisions Act became law, providing the legal basis for direct rule.
26 May	SDLP urged those who had withdrawn from public offices to return.
29 May	In situation of growing violence, OIRA called a ceasefire.
26 June	PIRA began what it called a 'bilateral truce'.
1 July	UDA set up no-go areas in Belfast.
7 July	William Whitelaw, Secretary of State, met PIRA leaders in secret in London.
9 July	PIRA claimed that British army had broken ceasefire in Lenadoon area of W. Belfast.
21 July	Nine people killed when twenty-two bombs exploded in Belfast ('Bloody Friday').
31 July	Army entered W. Belfast and Bogside no-go areas in 'Operation Motorman'. Eight people killed by car bombs in Claudy, Co. Derry.
24 September	Darlington conference on political options.
30 October	British Government published discussion paper on NI's political future, repeating guarantee of constitutional position but recognising 'Irish dimension'.
16–17 November	Edward Heath visited NI and said that UDI would lead to a 'bloodbath'.
1 December	Two people killed and eighty injured in Dublin when two bombs exploded while Dáil was debating tougher anti-subversion laws. Both wings of IRA and the UDA denied responsibility.

1973

1 January	NI, like the rest of the UK, became part of the EC.

8 March	Voting in border poll. In London two car bombs exploded, one man killed and 180 injured; PIRA later claimed responsibility.
20 March	British Government published White Paper, proposing an Assembly elected by PR and with Westminster retaining law-and-order powers.
28 March	Shipment of arms for PIRA found on vessel *Claudia*, off Waterford.
30 May	First elections for the new District Councils – voting by PR for first time since 1920.
28 June	Polling for the new seventy-eight-member Assembly.
31 July	Noisy scenes at first meeting of new Assembly.
18 September	PM Edward Heath told BBC that if the NI Assembly parties failed to set up an Executive by March 1974 it would be better to integrate NI within UK.
21 November	Agreement reached on setting up power-sharing Executive.
6–9 December	Sunningdale Conference on NI attended by British and Irish Ministers and NI power-sharing parties.

1974

1 January	NI Executive takes office.
4 January	Ulster Unionist Council rejected the Council of Ireland proposed in the Sunningdale Agreement.
7 January	Brian Faulkner (Chief Executive in power-sharing administration) resigned as UUP leader.
16 January	Brian Faulkner flew to Dublin for talks with Taoiseach Liam Cosgrave.
22 January	Loyalist disruption of Assembly proceedings led to police forcibly ejecting eighteen members, including the Rev. Ian Paisley. Harry West appointed UUP leader.
1 February	Cosgrave and seven of his Ministers flew to Hillsborough, Co. Down, for a meeting with NI Executive Ministers.
28 February	In Westminster general election eleven seats won by UUUC candidates and SDLP held W. Belfast.
5 March	With Labour forming a Government, Merlyn Rees became NI Secretary of State.
26 April	UUUC, after a conference in Portrush, Co. Antrim, called for an NI regional parliament in a federal UK.
14 May	The power-sharing Executive won by forty-four to twenty-eight an Assembly vote on Sunningdale Agreement. The loyalist UWC immediately threatened power cuts in protest.
15 May	Power cuts forced the closure of several factories, and many workers, including those in Belfast shipyard, went on strike.
16 May	As the stoppage developed, the Secretary of State accused the organisers of intimidation, and said it was a political, not an industrial, strike.
17 May	In Dublin twenty-two killed by car bombs which exploded without warning, and five people killed by a car bomb in Monaghan town. Two of three cars used in Dublin bombing had been hi-jacked earlier in Protestant areas of Belfast; UDA and UVF denied responsibility. (Three more people died later from injuries received in the explosions.)

25 May	Harold Wilson, in a broadcast, said the strike was being run by 'thugs and bullies'.
28 May	In face of the strike, the Unionist members of the Executive resigned and the Executive collapsed. Direct rule resumed.
29 May	UWC called off its strike.
31 May	Merlyn Rees said that the rise of 'Ulster nationalism' was a major factor which the Government would have to take into account.
4 July	British Government announced the setting up of an elected Constitutional Convention to seek a political settlement.
1 August	Meeting between representatives of SDLP and UDA.
4 September	Brian Faulkner launched UPNI.
5 October	Five people killed and fifty-four injured when bombs exploded without warning in Guildford, Surrey, in two pubs popular with off-duty army personnel.
10 October	In Westminster general election, UUUC got ten of the twelve seats, the SDLP retaining W. Belfast and Frank Maguire, Independent, unseating UUP leader Harry West in Fermanagh–S. Tyrone. Enoch Powell returned in S. Down.
15 October	Republican convicted prisoners in the Maze Prison set fire to a large number of huts, and troops were brought in to suppress a riot.
16 October	Secretary of State Rees revealed that nine Maze prisoners were in hospital after disturbances, while fifteen prison officers had been injured and sixteen soldiers hurt, nine seriously. At Magilligan Prison Republican prisoners burned cookhouse, prison shop and a hut. In Armagh Women's Prison the governor and three women prison officers were held captive overnight in an attic, and were only released after they had got an assurance through clergymen that prisoners in the Maze were safe.
21 October	John Hume, deputy leader of SDLP, said Rees had lost all credibility and that they saw little point in talking to him.
22 October	UUUC MPs elected James Molyneaux as their leader.
30 October	Rees said riot and burnings at Maze Prison had caused £1.5 million of damage, and at Magilligan, £200,000.
6 November	In the early hours of the morning thirty-three Republican prisoners escaped through a tunnel from the Maze Prison; twenty-nine recaptured a few hours later and three in Andersonstown in the evening. During the escape, a 24-year-old detainee was shot dead by a sentry.
9 November	Defence Ministry ruled that names of soldiers killed in NI not to be added to war memorials since it was not classed as war zone.
18 November	Plans announced for £30-million high-security prison at Maghaberry, Co. Antrim.
21 November	Nineteen killed and 182 injured when bombs exploded in two Birmingham pubs.
22 November	PIRA denied responsibility for Birmingham bombings.
25 November	Home Secretary Roy Jenkins announced that IRA was to be declared illegal in GB and tougher anti-terrorist laws would be introduced.
28 November	In Dublin the Government introduced Bill to allow people to be tried for terrorist offences committed outside the jurisdiction.
5 December	Parliament extended the new Prevention of Terrorism Act to NI,

allowing, among other things, persons to be held without charge for up to seven days.

10 December	At Feakle, Co. Clare, a group of Protestant Churchmen met members of PSF and PIRA.
18 December	Churchmen met Rees to report on their talks in Feakle.
20 December	PIRA announced ceasefire from midnight on 22 December to midnight on 2 January 1975.
23 December	Edward Heath, during a visit to Stormont, said he believed there was majority support in NI for power-sharing.
29 December	PIRA prisoners at Portlaoise top-security prison in the Republic caused serious damage and held fourteen warders hostage in a bid for better conditions. The officers were freed unhurt when troops stormed the jail.
31 December	Rees said Government would not be wanting in its response if 'a genuine and sustained cessation of violence' occurred.

1975

2 January	PIRA extended its Christmas ceasefire.
16 January	PIRA called off ceasefire.
9 February	PIRA announced new ceasefire.
12 February	Incident centres, manned by PSF, set up to monitor ceasefire in liaison with Government officials.
18 February	Airey Neave MP appointed Conservative NI spokesman.
18 March	Two Price sisters, Marion and Dolours, convicted for London car bombings in 1973, transferred from Durham Prison to Armagh, following long campaign for their transfer.
25 March	Harold Wilson visited Stormont and announced 1 May as Convention election polling day.
5 April	Secretary of State Rees said loyalist gunman had tried to murder him in 1974.
1 May	Convention polling day.
8 May	First meeting of Convention.
5 June	Common Market referendum showed narrow majority in NI for membership.
24 July	Rees promised to release all detainees by Christmas.
31 July	Three members of Miami Showband killed and one seriously injured in UVF gun attack. Two UVF men also died, blowing themselves up during the attack.
8 September	William Craig cast the only vote for voluntary coalition with SDLP during UUUC meeting at Stormont.
2 October	In a series of UVF attacks twelve people killed, including three women and four UVF men, and forty-six injured.
3 October	UVF declared illegal.
12 October	Split in VUPP after Craig's support for voluntary coalition.
14 November	Conservative leader Margaret Thatcher visited Belfast.
5 December	Last detainees released.
18 December	Harold Wilson visited Derry, where two soldiers were killed by PIRA soon after he left.
22 December	US authorities broke up gang of PIRA gun-runners.

1976

4 January	Five Catholics killed in two shooting incidents; one was at Whitecross, S. Armagh, and the second at Ballydugan, Co. Down.
5 January	Ten Protestant workers shot dead at Kingsmills, S. Armagh. Republican Action Force claimed responsibility.
7 January	SAS unit moved into S. Armagh.
15 January	PM Wilson presided at first all-party security meeting on NI, held at 10 Downing Street.
21 January	Government said 25,000 houses damaged in violence.
3 February	Convention recalled in bid to secure agreement.
12 February	UUUC and SDLP inter-party talks broke down after an hour.
1 March	Persons committing terrorist-type offences no longer entitled to special category status.
3 March	Final sitting of Convention ended in uproar.
9 March	Convention formally dissolved.
18 March	Rees came out against any increase in the number of NI MPs.
30 March	NICRA called off rent and rates strike, originally started in 1971.
5 May	Nine members of IRSP escaped from Maze Prison through tunnel.
15 May	Three RUC men killed in explosion at Belcoo, Co. Fermanagh.
22 May	UVF announced three-month ceasefire.
25 May	Loyalist vigilante group, Ulster Service Corps, announced that it was mounting patrols in view of 'deteriorating security situation'.
4 June	Rev. Ian Paisley leaked news of private talks between UUP and SDLP.
7 June	UUUC vote opposing UUP–SDLP talks.
3 August	Extensive damage caused in Portrush, Co. Antrim, by six explosions for which PIRA claimed responsibility.
8 August	Gerry Fitt fought off, with a gun, Republican demonstrators who broke into his Belfast home.
10 August	Two Maguire children killed in Andersonstown by a car whose driver had been shot dead by troops.
11 August	A third child from the Maguire family died as a result of Andersonstown accident.
12 August	Women demonstrated in favour of peace in Andersonstown and sparked off the women's peace movement (later the Peace People).
18 August	Brian Faulkner announced his resignation from active politics.
21 August	Some 20,000 attended peace rally in Belfast.
1 September	Republic's Government declared a state of emergency which allowed people to be held for seven days without charge.
2 September	European Commission of Human Rights decided that Britain had a case to answer before the European Court concerning its treatment of internees in 1971.
9 September	Leaders of main Churches supported women's peace movement.
10 September	Roy Mason succeeded Merlyn Rees as Secretary of State.
13 September	Anne Dickson became leader of UPNI.
28 October	Maire Drumm, vice-president of PSF, shot dead in Mater Hospital, Belfast, where she was a patient.
11 November	ULCCC put forward plan for NI independence with title 'Ulster Can Survive Unfettered'.
26 November	Mason said NI in danger of being left behind by 'the tide of devolution'.

1 December	Fair Employment Act, making it an offence to discriminate in employment on religious or political grounds, became effective.
4 December	SDLP annual conference rejected by 158 to 111 a motion calling on Britain to declare its intention to withdraw from NI.
9 December	PIRA fire bombs caused more than £1 million damage to Derry shops.
12 December	ULCCC claimed that some loyalist politicians, who were not named, had been involved in the past in gun-running, in selecting targets for bombs, and in promising money to buy arms and explosives.
25–27 December	PIRA had Christmas ceasefire.

1977

19 January	PIRA in S. Derry claimed it had carried out wave of booby-trap bomb attacks on members of security forces.
15 February	Rhodesia's Ian Smith thanked Portadown DUP for message of support.
21 February	Conservative leader Margaret Thatcher visited Belfast and Derry.
3 March	Lord Faulkner of Downpatrick killed in hunting accident.
8 March	In a Dublin court eight SAS men, who were found on the Republic side of the border, were each fined £100 for carrying guns without a certificate.
11 March	Twenty-six UVF men sentenced to a total of 700 years' imprisonment.
12 March	Mason denied reports that his officials were involved in 'black propaganda'.
29 March	It was disclosed that UUP was boycotting UUUC.
1 April	Government backed the idea of NI as one constituency, with three seats, for direct elections to European Parliament. It also supported PR. UUP and DUP attacked the plan, and SDLP and Alliance supported it.
17 April	Catholic Primate Cardinal William Conway died in Armagh, and there was praise for his efforts for peace and reconciliation.
23 April	UUAC said it would call a loyalist strike in May to protest against security policy and demand a return of majority government.
3 May	UUAC strike began, but many factories stayed open, although the port of Larne was closed.
4 May	As a result of the stoppage, supported by Rev. Ian Paisley and Ernest Baird, the UUUC Parliamentary Coalition was dissolved.
6 May	UUAC failed to get support of Ballylumford power-station workers for strike.
9 May	Demonstrations and roadblocks in many places in support of strike, and Paisley joined farmers who blocked roads in Ballymena, Co. Antrim, with tractors.
13 May	UUAC called off its strike, which had failed to stop industry and commerce. Critics of the strike praised the Government for refusing to make concessions, but Paisley claimed the stoppage had been a success.
23 May	Mason began a new round of talks with political parties.
25 May	In a Labour switch of policy, PM James Callaghan announced that

	an all-party Speaker's conference would be set up to consider the possibility of more NI MPs.
8 June	Mason announced that more troops would be used on SAS-type activity and that RUC and UDR strength would be increased. UUAC claimed the move was in response to the strike, but UUP, which had opposed strike, said it arose from constitutional politics.
14 June	Lord Melchett announced that the eleven-plus examination would be scrapped and comprehensive education promoted.
16 June	In the Republic, Jack Lynch's Fianna Fáil party regained power by defeating the Coalition by a record margin of twenty seats.
19 June	New Zealand Premier Robert Muldoon discussed with Peace People leaders in Belfast the possibility of ex-terrorists being permitted to emigrate to New Zealand.
21 June	Unemployment in NI reached 60,000, the highest June total for thirty-seven years.
12 July	PIRA threatened disruption during Queen's jubilee visit in August.
16 July	SDLP deputy leader John Hume appointed adviser on consumer affairs by EC Commissioner Richard Burke.
27 July	Four killed and eighteen injured in Belfast in feud between OIRA and PIRA. US naval communications base in Derry closed.
9–10 August	Queen's jubilee visit. On second day PIRA caused some minor explosions at edge of campus of NUU, but royal programme unaffected.
30 August	US President Carter, in a special statement, said that his administration supported a form of government in NI which would have widespread acceptance throughout both parts of the community. He also urged Americans not to support violence and said that if NI people could resolve their differences, the US would be prepared, with others, to see how additional jobs could be created for the benefit of all the people.
12 September	Mason, after a year as Secretary of State, said the 'myth of British withdrawal from NI' was now dead for ever.
20 September	SDLP defined its policy as 'an agreed Ireland'.
28 September	James Callaghan and Jack Lynch met in Downing Street; cross-border economic co-operation one of main topics.
5 October	Seamus Costello, leader of IRSP, shot dead in Dublin.
7 October	Irish Independence Party launched.
10 October	Betty Williams and Mairead Corrigan, founders of the Peace People, awarded 1976 Nobel Peace Prize.
14 October	Dr Tomás Ó Fiaich appointed new Catholic Primate.
18 October	William Craig MP, a member of Council of Europe, appointed by Council to carry out research aimed at updating European Convention on Human Rights.
20 October	Roy Jenkins, EC president, on a visit to Belfast, confirmed that EC would open NI information office.
6 November	SDLP, at its annual conference, rejected call for British withdrawal from NI.
21 November	Mason suggested the setting up of a Stormont Assembly without legislative powers to run local departments.
26 November	Craig announced that VUPP would cease to be a political party.
3 December	Seamus Twomey, former PIRA chief of staff, arrested in Dublin.
21 December	Five hotels throughout NI damaged by PIRA fire-bombs.

22 December   PIRA said there would be no Christmas ceasefire.

1978

11 January   Fair Employment Agency report stated that Catholics suffered more from unemployment than Protestants.

18 January   European Court of Human Rights in Strasbourg held that interrogation techniques used on internees in 1971 did not amount to torture, but had been 'inhuman and degrading'.

17 February   Twelve people killed and twenty-three injured when La Mon House Hotel in Co. Down destroyed by PIRA fire bombs.

25 February   Standing Committee of Irish Catholic Bishops conference said the overwhelming majority of Irish people wanted the campaign of violence to end immediately.

6 March   UUP turned down idea of talks with the Rev. Ian Paisley and Ernest Baird.

12 March   Comments by Mason about the role of the Republic in terrorism brought angry retorts from Government and opposition in Dublin.

26 March   Speakers at PIRA celebrations of Easter Rising said that their campaign of violence would be stepped up.

7 April   Conservative spokesman Airey Neave said power-sharing was no longer practical politics. James Callaghan and Jack Lynch, at Copenhagen EC summit, had talks which apparently helped to heal the breach between London and Dublin on security issues.

19 April   James Callaghan announced that legislation would be introduced to increase NI's representation to between sixteen and eighteen seats.

2 May   Belfast appointed its first non-Unionist Lord Mayor, David Cook (Alliance). Mason had talks in Dublin with Irish Ministers.

1 August   Catholic Primate, Dr Ó Fiaich, after visit to Maze Prison, said Republican prisoners engaged in 'no wash – no toilet' protest were living in 'inhuman' conditions.

2 August   Mason announced 2,000-job sports car factory for W. Belfast, a project hailed as a breakthrough in securing US investment.

28 August – 1 September   Visit to NI by US Congressmen Joshua Eilberg (Democrat) and Hamilton Fish (Republican), who later urged that the US should seek to assist in a political solution in NI.

21 September   PIRA bomb attack on Eglinton airfield, Co. Derry, destroyed terminal building, two hangars and four planes.

22 September   Mason and Conservative spokesman Airey Neave issued simultaneous statements attacking calls in GB for British withdrawal from NI.

24 September   Paisley held his first religious service in Dublin, at the Mansion House.

8 October   Sixty-nine RUC men injured in Derry when PSF and a number of other organisations held a march to celebrate the 5 October 1968 civil rights march, and the DUP staged a counter-demonstration. Sixty-seven of the police were injured in a clash with loyalists, and two were hurt by Republicans.

14 October   DUP march in Derry to protest against Republican march on previous Sunday. Thirty-two RUC men injured when trouble broke out near Guildhall Square, and loyalists caused much damage to property.

4 November	With only two dissenting votes, SDLP annual conference voted that British withdrawal was 'desirable and inevitable', and called for fresh conference involving British and Irish Governments and two communities in NI.
14 November	PIRA bomb attacks caused serious damage in Belfast, Armagh, Dungannon, Enniskillen, Cookstown and Castlederg.
26 November	Albert Miles, deputy governor of Crumlin Road Prison, shot dead by PIRA.
28 November	Commons passed by 350 votes to 49 the Bill to give NI five more MPs.
30 November	PIRA warned that it was 'preparing for a long war', after admitting to setting off explosives and fire bombs in fourteen towns and villages, with the most serious damage in Armagh city.

1979

20 February	Eleven Protestants, known as the 'Shankill butchers', were sentenced to life imprisonment for a wide variety of offences including nineteen murders.
28 March	Votes of NI MPs decisive in defeat of Labour Government by 311 votes to 310, thus precipitating a general election. Eight Unionists voted with Conservative opposition and two UUPs, John Carson and Harold McCusker, voted with the Government. Gerry Fitt (SDLP) and Frank Maguire (Ind.) abstained.
30 March	Conservative NI spokesman Airey Neave killed when bomb exploded in his car at House of Commons car park. INLA claimed responsibility.
17 April	Four RUC men killed by PIRA at Bessbrook, Co. Armagh, when 1,000-lb bomb exploded in a van.
3 May	In Westminster general election DUP gained two seats from UUP, E. Belfast and N. Belfast.
5 May	Humphrey Atkins (Conservative) succeeded Mason as NI Secretary of State.
7 June	In first European election Rev. Ian Paisley, John Hume and John Taylor elected to fill the three NI seats.
2 July	INLA declared illegal throughout the UK.
17 July	Rev. Ian Paisley, at opening session of European Parliament in Strasbourg, was first MEP to speak, apart from the acting president, when he protested that the Union flag was flying the wrong way up on the Parliament Buildings.
18 July	Paisley shouted down in European Parliament when he sought to interrupt Jack Lynch as European Council president.
21 July	Visit of Pope John Paul II to Ireland was announced for 29 September. Paisley and Orange Order warned that NI must not be included in itinerary.
31 July	US State Department stopped private arms shipments to NI, including supplies to RUC.
11 August	Irish National Caucus deputations said in Belfast that it planned to make NI a major issue in 1980 US presidential election.
22 August	Secretary of State Humphrey Atkins rejected proposal from New York Governor Hugh Carey that he (the Governor) should preside

	at New York talks involving the NI Secretary of State and Irish Foreign Minister Michael O'Kennedy.
27 August	PIRA bombers killed eighteen soldiers near Warrenpoint, Co. Down; biggest death toll in a single incident in NI in ten years of violence. Lord Mountbatten of Burma was murdered by PIRA at Mullaghmore, Co. Sligo, when his boat was blown to pieces in a radio-triggered explosion. His fourteen-year-old grandson, Nicholas, and crew member Paul Maxwell, aged fourteen, also died instantly, and the Dowager Lady Brabourne died later from her injuries.
29 August	PM Margaret Thatcher flew to NI to discuss tightening of security. It was announced in Rome that, because of the recent violence, the Pope would not now visit Armagh.
30 August	British Cabinet decided to increase RUC by 1,000.
2 September	UFF threatened to strike back at PIRA.
5 September	Thatcher and Taoiseach Jack Lynch met in London for security talks.
29 September	The Pope, speaking in Drogheda, Co. Louth, appealed 'on [his] bended knees' for an end to violence.
2 October	PIRA rejected the Pope's appeal and declared that it had widespread support, and that only force could remove the British presence.
5 October	British and Irish Governments agreed to tighten up the anti-terrorist drive. British Labour Party conference rejected a call for withdrawal from NI.
15 October	Opinion poll published by Dublin-based Economic and Social Research Institute, based on questioning in July–September 1978, showed 21 per cent of people in Republic giving some degree of support to PIRA activities, with under 3 per cent expressing strong support.
25 October	Atkins announced that he was inviting four main parties – UUP, DUP, SDLP and Alliance – to a Stormont conference to discuss a possible political settlement. The UUP immediately rejected the invitation and said the Government should proceed with two-tier local government. PIRA denied that it had planned to assassinate Princess Margaret during her recent US visit.
1 November	Jack Lynch said the NI problem 'continues to be as intractable as at any stage in the last ten years'. One hundred and fifty-six guns, including a powerful M-60 machine gun, seized at Dublin docks. They were believed to have been sent from the US for use by PIRA.
3 November	SDLP, at its annual conference, urged a joint approach by the British and Irish Governments to the NI problem. It also rejected a proposal for talks with PIRA.
22 November	SDLP leader Gerry Fitt MP resigned from the party because of its initial refusal to attend Atkins conference.
28 November	John Hume MEP became SDLP leader.
5 December	Jack Lynch resigned as Republic's Taoiseach.
7 December	Charles Haughey TD appointed to succeed Lynch by forty-four votes to thirty-eight of Fianna Fáil parliamentary party.
15 December	SDLP decided to attend Atkins conference.
16 December	Four soldiers killed by PIRA landmine in Co. Tyrone and another by a booby-trap bomb in S. Armagh.

1980

7 January	Constitutional Conference opened at Stormont.
17 January	Three people killed in terrorist train explosion at Dunmurry, near Belfast.
8 February	Leonard Kaitcer, Belfast antiques dealer, murdered after kidnap linked with £1 million ransom demand.
11 February	Serious differences emerge within Peace People.
16 February	Charles Haughey at Fianna Fáil conference in Dublin urged joint British–Irish initiative on NI.
5 March	Cardinal Ó Fiaich and Dr Edward Daly met Secretary of State Atkins to voice concern about conditions within H-Blocks.
11 March	Body of German industrialist Thomas Niedermayer found at Colinglen Road, W. Belfast. He had disappeared in December 1973.
24 March	Stormont Constitutional Conference adjourned indefinitely with no sign of agreement.
26 March	It was announced that as from 1 April there would be no entitlement to special category status for terrorist offenders.
15 April	Atkins in Dublin for talks with Haughey Government.
30 April	Marion Price, convicted with sister Dolours for their part in London car bombing in 1973, released from Armagh Prison on humanitarian grounds. She was suffering from anorexia nervosa.
5 May	PIRA blew up pylon at Crossmaglen, part of North–South power link, which both Governments were seeking to re-establish.
13 May	SDLP leader John Hume met Thatcher at 10 Downing Street.
21 May	Thatcher and Haughey had meeting at 10 Downing Street. Communiqué promised closer political co-operation and referred to 'unique relationship' between the two countries.
4 June	John Turnly, Protestant joint chairman of IIP, shot dead in his car at Carnlough, Co. Antrim, in front of his family.
5 June	Presbyterian General Assembly voted 443 to 322 to take Church out of World Council of Churches on the basis that the council supported terrorist groups.
9 June	Haughey appealed to Britain to accept that withdrawal was in the best interests of UK and Ireland. On BBC *Panorama* programme he also mentioned the possibility of some form of federation and separate social laws for NI.
11 June	PIRA threatened to renew attacks on prison officers, suspended since March.
12 June	Markethill town centre seriously damaged by PIRA car bomb.
19 June	European Commission of Human Rights rejected the case of protesting H-Block prisoners, finding that the debasement arising from the 'dirty protest' was self-inflicted. The Commission also criticised British Government for 'inflexibility'.
25 June	US Democratic Party adopted Senator Edward Kennedy's policy, calling for 'an end to the divisions of the Irish people', and a solution to the conflict based on the consent of all the parties.
26 June	Dr Miriam Daly, prominent Republican member of National H-Block/Armagh Committee, shot dead at her home in Andersonstown.
2 July	British Government published two-option document on NI

devolution. It produced no agreement – Unionists rejected the option with a large element of power-sharing and anti-Unionists turned down the option of majority rule.

20 July	Car bomb in Lisnaskea, Co. Fermanagh, caused extensive damage.
6 August	Extra Government spending of £48 million in NI announced after ICTU delegation had met Thatcher to protest at 14.7 per cent unemployment.
8 August	Three killed and eighteen injured in widespread violence on ninth anniversary of internment.
24 September	Cardinal Ó Fiaich 'hopeful of progress' on H-Block issue.
27 October	Seven H-Block prisoners began hunger strike in support of demand for, among other things, the right to wear their own clothing.
8 December	Thatcher, accompanied by three Cabinet Ministers – Lord Carrington (Foreign Secretary), Sir Geoffrey Howe (Chancellor of Exchequer) and Humphrey Atkins – had talks in Dublin with Haughey and senior colleagues. The meeting agreed to joint studies on a wide range of subjects and Haughey called it 'a historic breakthrough'.
18 December	H-Block hunger strike called off with one PIRA prisoner critically ill.

1981

16 January	Bernadette McAliskey and husband shot and seriously wounded by gunmen at their home near Coalisland, Co. Tyrone.
21 January	Two leading Unionists – Sir Norman Stronge and son James – shot dead by PIRA gunmen at their home, Tynan Abbey.
6 February	British coal boat, *Nellie M,* sunk by PIRA off Moville, Co. Donegal.
9 February	Paisley launched 'Ulster Declaration' against Anglo-Irish talks.
12 February	Paisley suspended from Commons when he persisted in calling Humphrey Atkins a 'liar'.
19 February	James Molyneaux, UUP leader, described as 'ludicrous' an allegation by Paisley that there was a UUP plot to kill him.
21 February	Eight stores in Belfast and three in Derry damaged by PIRA fire bombs.
27 February	Three-hundred-pound van bomb damaged forty premises in Limavady, Co. Derry.
1 March	New H-Block hunger strike in support of political status began when PIRA prisoner Bobby Sands refused food.
3 March	In Commons Humphrey Atkins said there would be no political status for prisoners, regardless of protests inside or outside the prison.
5 March	Frank Maguire, Ind. MP for Fermanagh–S. Tyrone, died. Thatcher, on a visit to NI, again denied that Anglo-Irish talks threatened NI's constitutional position.
21 March	Cardinal Ó Fiaich called on PIRA to end violence.
22 March	Republic's Foreign Minister, Brian Lenihan, said Anglo-Irish talks could lead to Irish unity in ten years.
28 March	Paisley attracted large attendance at Stormont rally against Anglo-Irish talks. RUC estimated 30,000 audience.
1 April	DUP held three late-night rallies on hillsides near Gortin, Newry and Armagh. At Gortin two RUC vehicles were overturned.

9 April	Hunger-striker Bobby Sands won the Fermanagh–S. Tyrone by-election.
11 April	Riots in Belfast, Lurgan and Cookstown after celebrations of Sands's election.
19 April	On fifth successive night of rioting in Derry, two nineteen-year-old youths were killed when struck by army landrover.
22 April	Dolours Price released from Armagh Prison since her life was said to be in danger from anorexia nervosa; her sister Marion had been released in 1980 for the same reason.
28 April	President Reagan said US would not intervene in NI, but he was 'deeply concerned at the tragic situation'.
5 May	Bobby Sands MP died on sixty-sixth day of his fast. There was rioting in Belfast and Derry, and also in Dublin.
6 May	Six hundred extra troops sent to NI as sporadic violence continued.
7 May	Massive attendance at Bobby Sands's funeral in Milltown cemetery, Belfast.
9 May	PIRA claimed they had planted a bomb at the Sullom Voe oil terminal in the Shetlands to explode during the Queen's visit there.
12 May	Hunger-striker Francis Hughes died, and blast and petrol bombs were thrown at security forces during riots in Belfast and Derry.
13 May	John Hume met Thatcher and unsuccessfully urged concessions to hunger-strikers on clothing and free association.
19 May	Five soldiers killed when their Saracen armoured car was blown up by landmine near Bessbrook, Co. Armagh.
20 May	Polling in council elections.
21 May	Cardinal Ó Fiaich criticised 'rigid stance' of Government on hunger strike.
26 May	Arms found in RUC raid on UDA HQ in Belfast.
11 June	Eight PIRA men awaiting sentence escaped from Crumlin Road Prison. Two H-Block prisoners elected to Dáil in general election which resulted in return to power of Fine Gael–Labour Coalition.
2 July	Atkins suggested an advisory council of already elected representatives; the idea was later dropped because of lack of support.
4 July	H-Block hunger-strikers said they would be happy that any concessions granted to them should apply to all prisoners.
14 July	Irish Government asked US to intervene with Britain over the hunger strike.
18 July	In Dublin over 200 people were injured during a riot when an H-Block march was prevented by Gardaí from passing British Embassy.
2 August	Hunger-striker Kieran Doherty TD died.
5 August	Concentrated PIRA car-bomb and incendiary attacks in seven centres, including Belfast, Derry and Lisburn, caused widespread damage, but no serious injuries.
8 August	Two people died during violence in Belfast; more than 1,000 petrol bombs were thrown at security forces.
20 August	Owen Carron won Fermanagh–S. Tyrone by-election.
2 September	Paisley called for Third Force on lines of former B Specials.
7 September	Two RUC men killed by PIRA landmine near Pomeroy, Co. Tyrone.

13 September	James Prior became NI Secretary of State and Humphrey Atkins deputy Foreign Secretary.
17 September	Prior visited Maze Prison for three hours, with growing signs that the hunger strike was collapsing.
29 September	British Labour conference voted to 'campaign actively' for united Ireland by consent.
3 October	H-Block hunger strike, which had led to deaths of ten Republican prisoners, called off.
6 October	Prior announced that all prisoners would now be allowed to wear their own clothes.
8 October	Belfast Independent councillor Lawrence Kennedy shot dead in Ardoyne, apparently by loyalist gunman.
10 October	PIRA set off remote-controlled nail bomb outside Chelsea Barracks in London. One woman killed and twenty-three soldiers and seventeen civilians injured.
22 October	European Court of Human Rights ruled that NI law banning male homosexuality was a breach of European Convention.
6 November	Margaret Thatcher and Irish Taoiseach Dr Garret FitzGerald decided in London talks to set up Anglo-Irish Intergovernmental Council.
14 November	Rev. Robert Bradford MP assassinated by PIRA gunmen at Finaghy, Belfast.
16 November	Three DUP MPs suspended from Commons after protests on security. Third Force march in Enniskillen, Co. Fermanagh.
17 November	Prior faced barrage of verbal abuse at Robert Bradford's funeral at Dundonald near Belfast. RUC leave cancelled.
23 November	Loyalist 'Day of Action' to protest against security policy marked by rallies and stoppages of work in Protestant areas. Both UUP and DUP had separate rallies at Belfast City Hall. Some 5,000 men paraded at a DUP rally in Newtownards, Co. Down, addressed by Paisley.
25 November	INLA bomb exploded at British army camp at Herford, West Germany, but caused no injuries.
30 November	Several Unionist-controlled councils adjourned in protest at the security situation.
3 December	Paisley claimed Third Force had 15,000–20,000 members. Prior said private armies would not be tolerated.
21 December	Revealed that US State Department had revoked Paisley's visa.

1982

29 January	A prominent E. Belfast loyalist, John McKeague, shot dead in his shop, apparently by INLA.
1 February	UUP delegation met Prior to tell him it was opposed to his 'rolling devolution' plan and reaffirmed support for Convention report. Labour leader Michael Foot arrived in NI for three-day visit and said more jobs was the top priority.
8 February	Five Belfast men arrested when they tried to enter US from Canada with lists of firearms.
18 February	General election in Republic returned Fianna Fáil to power when the party secured the backing of Sinn Féin the Workers' Party and Independent TDs. None of PSF's seven candidates returned.

23 February	PIRA used bombs to sink coal boat *St Bedan* in Lough Foyle. At European security conference in Madrid, Poland alleged Britain was using torture in NI.
24 February	Government said it would bring homosexual laws in NI into line with rest of UK, following European Court of Human Rights ruling against existing laws. Catholic Bishops and DUP opposed reforms.
4 March	Rev. Martin Smyth, UUP, returned in S. Belfast by-election.
6 March	Gerard Tuite, who escaped from prison in London, was charged in Dublin with causing explosions in London. He was the first person charged in the Republic with a crime committed in GB.
14 March	SDLP leader John Hume called the new devolution plan 'unworkable'.
16 March	Eleven-year-old boy killed and thirty-four people injured, some seriously, by a bomb which exploded without warning in Banbridge, Co. Down.
17 March	On a St Patrick's Day visit to the US, Taoiseach Charles Haughey said US Government should bring more pressure on Britain to adopt a more positive attitude to Irish unity. President Reagan said any solution must come from NI people themselves.
25 March	Three soldiers killed in PIRA ambush in Crocus Street, W. Belfast. M-60 machine gun used. British Cabinet approved 'rolling devolution' plan.
26 March	PIRA offered 'amnesty' to informers if they retracted their evidence.
28 March	RUC Inspector Norman Duddy shot dead by PIRA in Derry.
1 April	Two plain-clothes soldiers killed in Derry in PIRA machine-gun attack.
14 April	Four leading members of UDA arrested after ammunition and some gun parts found in Belfast HQ during police raid.
16 April	Prior said he had no plans to proscribe UDA. He also said Falklands crisis would not delay devolution plans.
17 April	A soldier who rammed 'Free Derry Wall' in a personnel carrier was taken into military custody.
19 April	James Molyneaux MP said the Falklands crisis had vindicated the Unionist position and his suspicion of the Foreign Office.
20 April	Two killed, twelve injured and £1 million damage caused by PIRA bomb attacks in Belfast, Derry, Armagh, Strabane, Ballymena, Bessbrook and Magherafelt.
22 April	Sinn Féin the Workers' Party in Dublin denied a claim in *Magill* magazine that OIRA was still active and involved in murders and armed robberies.
24 April	Alliance leader Oliver Napier told his party's conference that devolution plan might be last chance for NI to solve its own problems.
25 April	Sinn Féin the Workers' Party decided to call itself simply the 'Workers' Party'.
3 May	Republic's Defence Minister Paddy Power described Britain as the 'aggressor' over the Falklands.
10 May	Haughey appointed Seamus Mallon, SDLP deputy leader, and John Robb of New Ireland Group to Republic's Senate.

13 May	European Parliament called for ban on use of plastic bullets throughout EC.
20 May	INLA bomb defused at home of Rev. William Beattie, DUP.
24 May	Closure of DeLorean car plant at Dunmurry announced, with loss of 1,500 jobs.
28 May	British and Irish Governments said NI would get natural gas from Republic in about two years' time.
29 May	Friends of Ireland Group in US Congress on fact-finding visit to NI.
18 June	Former RUC Inspector Albert White shot dead near his home in Newry, Co. Down.
21 June	FBI arrested four men in New York who were said to have tried to buy 'Redeye' surface-to-air missiles for PIRA.
25 June	Devolution Bill amended to ensure that both Commons and Lords must be satisfied about 'cross-community support' before transfer of powers.
1 July	Gardaí found large cache of bombs at Castlefin, Co. Donegal.
19 July	Prior on short visit to US to explain his devolution scheme.
20 July	Eight soldiers died and fifty-one people were injured by two PIRA bombs in London – one near the Household Cavalry barracks at Knightsbridge and the other at the Regent's Park bandstand, where an army band was playing. Three people died later.
27 July	Disclosed that British Government had told Irish ambassador in London that it was under no obligation to consult Republic about NI matters.
8 August	Representatives of NORAID and PLO spoke at internment anniversary demonstrations in W. Belfast.
15 August	In the US Rev. Martin Smyth MP claimed that he knew who killed the Rev. Robert Bradford, and he alleged the CIA was involved in NI.
25 August	SDLP decided to contest Assembly elections, but not to take seats.
28 August	PIRA was believed to have suffered one of its biggest setbacks through seizures of arms and explosives. The RUC found about one and a half tons of gelignite hidden in a lorry near Banbridge, Co. Down; the Gardaí seized a smaller quantity of gelignite and 10,000 rounds of ammunition at Glencree, Co. Wicklow.
1 September	Merger of departments of Commerce and Manpower took effect to create new Department of Economic Development. Belfast DUP councillor Billy Dickson wounded in INLA gun attack at his home.
16 September	INLA bomb at Divis Flats in W. Belfast killed a soldier and two boys of eleven and fourteen.
20 September	INLA blew up radar station at Schull, Co. Cork.
23 September	RUC Chief Constable Sir John Hermon said PIRA and INLA 'reeling' from arrests arising from evidence of informers.
2 October	British Labour Party conference call for ban on use of plastic bullets throughout UK.
20 October	Polling day in Assembly election. John DeLorean charged in California with drug-smuggling offences.
27 October	Three RUC men killed in booby-trap landmine explosion near Lurgan, Co. Armagh.
2 November	SDLP delegation told Prior the party would continue its boycott of the Assembly.

3 November	Queen's Speech at opening of Parliament reaffirmed Government's intention to carry on with Assembly.
9 November	RUC constable and woman leisure-centre worker died in Enniskillen, Co. Fermanagh, in booby-trapped car.
11 November	At Assembly's first session James Kilfedder MP was elected Speaker. Three PIRA men shot dead by RUC when they were alleged to have driven through checkpoint near Lurgan, Co. Armagh.
16 November	Two RUC constables shot dead in Markethill, Co. Armagh. Leonard Murphy, reputed to have been leader of the notorious 'Shankill butchers', shot dead.
25 November	In Republic's general election Fine Gael and Labour secured overall majority, paving the way for a coalition.
30 November	Prior addressed Assembly, and announced increase in RUC strength.
6 December	Seventeen people, including eleven soldiers, died in INLA bombing of the Droppin' Well pub disco in Ballykelly, Co. Derry.
16 December	Election Petition Court in Armagh deprived SDLP deputy leader Seamus Mallon of his Assembly seat on the grounds that he was a member of the Republic's Senate.
23 December	Thatcher made one-day visit to NI, mainly to meet members of security forces.

1983

5 January	INLA declared illegal in Irish Republic.
6 January	Two RUC men shot dead by PIRA in Rostrevor, Co. Down.
16 January	County Court judge William Doyle shot dead by PIRA as he left Catholic church in S. Belfast.
28 January	Republic's Government announced that it would give full voting rights to 20,000 British citizens.
30 January	SDLP annual conference reaffirmed Assembly boycott.
1 February	Irish Foreign Minister Peter Barry met Prior in London and expressed doubts as to whether the Assembly had a useful future.
17 February	At Westminster Labour Party decided to oppose Prevention of Terrorism Act in its present form.
23 February	European Parliament's political committee voted for an inquiry as to whether EC could help solve NI's economic and political problems, despite opposition by British Government and Conservative and Unionist MEPs.
26 February	GLC leader Ken Livingstone flew to Belfast for two-day visit at the invitation of PSF – a visit strongly attacked by Unionists.
27 February	Haughey at Fianna Fáil conference in Dublin urged British and Irish Governments to organise a constitutional conference as a prelude to final British withdrawal from NI.
2 March	NI Assembly voted unanimously for a halt to European Parliament inquiry.
7 March	Home Secretary announced new anti-terrorism Bill with five-year life, subject to annual renewal.
11 March	Republic's Government announced it would set up an all-Ireland Forum on lines suggested by SDLP.
17 March	President Reagan said those who supported terrorism were no friends of Ireland. Senator Edward Kennedy called for Irish unity in a Senate motion.

21 March   Thatcher's meeting with Garret FitzGerald at Brussels EC summit was her first with an Irish Taoiseach for nearly sixteen months.

24 March   UUP, DUP and Alliance Party rejected Garret FitzGerald's invitation to take part in all-Ireland Forum.

3 April   Statements at Republican Easter Rising celebrations indicated that PIRA was dropping punishment shootings, commonly known as 'kneecappings'.

8 April   Prior announced an inquiry into working of Emergency Provisions Act.

11 April   Fourteen UVF men jailed, two for life, on evidence of supergrass Joseph Bennett, former UVF battalion commander, who had been granted immunity from prosecution in respect of two murders and other terrorist offences.

25 April   Republic's Coalition Government suffered first Parliamentary defeat when its proposed wording for anti-abortion referendum was defeated by twenty-two votes.

5 May   Prior in Dublin for talks with the Government. But occasion overshadowed by Irish Government protest to London about remarks in NI by Defence Secretary Michael Heseltine that small neutral countries allowed NATO 'to carry responsibility for the whole area'.

10–11 May   NI Assembly had all-night sitting on devolution, but failed to agree on any clear-cut approach.

24 May   A 1,000-lb PIRA bomb outside Andersonstown police station in W. Belfast caused £1 million damage.

30 May   New Ireland Forum, comprising the main constitutional Nationalist parties in Ireland, held initial meeting in Dublin to pursue structures and processes to achieve a new Ireland.

9 June   In Westminster election Unionists took fifteen of the seventeen NI seats, with SDLP and PSF getting one each.

11 June   Prior reappointed NI Secretary of State in Thatcher's new Cabinet.

28 June   SDLP leader John Hume in maiden Commons speech spoke of Britain's 'psychological withdrawal' from NI.

3 July   Unoccupied Belfast home of ex-MP Gerry Fitt set alight by youths from nearby New Lodge Road.

4 July   Catholic Bishops in NI warned against reintroduction of death penalty and called for ban on use of plastic bullets.

8 July   NI Assembly voted thirty-five to eleven for death penalty for terrorist murders.

10 July   Prior said return of capital punishment would increase terrorism and lead to 'violent disorders' in NI.

13 July   Commons rejected death penalty for terrorist murders by majority of 116. Four UDR soldiers killed by PIRA landmine in Co. Tyrone – the regiment's heaviest loss in a single incident.

17 July   Former NI Secretary of State Merlyn Rees said a Cabinet subcommittee had considered withdrawal from NI between 1974 and 1976 but no Minister had favoured it.

21 July   Ex-MP Gerry Fitt became life peer; former NI Secretary of State Humphrey Atkins was knighted; and UUP leader James Molyneaux was appointed Privy Councillor.

26 July   Irish Foreign Minister Peter Barry told MPs at Westminster that democracy in NI was being undermined by increased PSF vote.

	Gerry Adams, PSF MP for W. Belfast, in London as guest of GLC leader Ken Livingstone, said Britain had erected 'wall of misinformation' around NI.
5 August	One-hundred-and-twenty-day trial of thirty-eight people implicated in terrorism by PIRA supergrass Christopher Black ended in Belfast. Mr Justice Kelly jailed twenty-two of the accused, with sentences totalling more than 4,000 years. Four were acquitted and the others got mainly suspended sentences. (In 1986 eighteen of the twenty-two jailed had their convictions quashed by Court of Appeal.)
25 August	Elizabeth Kirkpatrick, wife of an informer, freed in Belfast after being held captive for two months by INLA.
8 September	Unionists said 67 per cent vote for pro-life amendment in Republic's Constitution underlined the sectarian nature of Southern society.
13 September	Prior defended use of supergrasses.
23 September	FEA said it would be monitoring recruitment at Short Brothers aircraft factory after allegations of anti-Catholic bias.
25 September	Thirty-eight PIRA prisoners escaped from Maze Prison – the biggest escape in British prison history. During the escape a prison officer was stabbed and died. Within a few days nineteen escapees had been recaptured, but the others got away.
26 September	An NIF group on a visit to Derry was attacked by DUP demonstrators.
6 October	Two RUC Reservists shot dead by PIRA in Downpatrick, Co. Down.
28 October	Sir George Terry (former Sussex Chief Constable), in report on Kincora boys' home sex allegations, said he had found no evidence that civil servants, RUC or military intelligence were involved in homosexual activities at the home or had tried to suppress information about them.
4 November	PIRA bomb at Ulster Polytechnic at Jordanstown, Co. Antrim, killed RUC inspector and a sergeant and injured thirty-three others.
10 November	Prior said a PSF takeover in NI could lead to the whole of Ireland becoming another Cuba.
13 November	Big changes in PSF leadership, with Gerry Adams MP being elected president at Ard Fheis.
21 November	Three elders shot dead during service in Darkley Pentecostal Church, Co. Armagh. Seven others were injured. Shooting claimed by 'Catholic Reaction Force'.
27 November	Dominic McGlinchey, said to be INLA chief of staff, admitted his organisation had been indirectly involved in Darkley killings.
4 December	SAS undercover soldiers shot dead two PIRA members near Coalisland, Co. Tyrone.
7 December	UUP Assembly member Edgar Graham shot dead by PIRA at QUB.
8 December	FEA found Catholics under-represented at policy-making levels in NI civil service.
16 December	Irish soldier and a Garda cadet killed in gun battle with PIRA when Dublin supermarket executive Don Tidey, kidnapped three weeks earlier, was rescued at Ballinamore, Co. Leitrim.
17 December	Five people killed and eighty injured when PIRA car bomb exploded outside Harrods in London.

24 December   Thatcher made six-hour NI tour, including meeting with Christmas shoppers in Newtownards, Co. Down, and visit to security forces in counties Armagh and Tyrone.

1984

15 January   Cardinal Ó Fiaich described Thatcher's visit to Armagh UDR base, where several UDR men were accused of murder of Catholics, as 'disgusting'. He also said that, because of its work on housing and other community issues, it was not morally wrong to join PSF.

16 January   Irish Government said it could not identify with Cardinal Ó Fiaich's remarks.

25 February   Two thousand loyalists staged protest at Stormont against proposal to change Londonderry District Council's name to 'Derry'.

29 February   NI Assembly voted twenty to one against extending 1967 Abortion Act to NI.

6 March   PIRA shot dead Maze Prison assistant governor outside his E. Belfast home.

14 March   PSF president Gerry Adams was shot and wounded in Belfast; UFF admitted responsibility.

15 March   Garret FitzGerald, addressing US Congress, urged US politicians to call for British acceptance of NIF proposals.

17 March   Alleged INLA leader Dominic McGlinchey, extradited from Republic to NI to face murder charge, was claimed as first in North–South extradition of a member of Republican paramilitary organisation.

22 March   PIRA bombed three buildings in Belfast city centre.

29 March   RUC Constable John Robinson, on trial for murdering Armagh INLA man Seamus Grew in December 1982 (he was later acquitted), claimed senior RUC officers had ordered him to tell lies about events leading to the shooting so as to protect Special Branch officers and an RUC informer operating inside the Republic.

4 April   British Government apologised to Irish Government for RUC undercover action in Republic in December 1982.

7 April   RUC Chief Constable denied a cover-up in Armagh killing of two INLA men, but said two unarmed RUC men had gone into Republic for observation purposes in December 1982.

8 April   PIRA shot dead Mary Travers, and seriously wounded her father, magistrate Tom Travers, as they left Mass in S. Belfast.

19 April   FEA chairman said Belfast shipyard, Harland and Wolff plc, had agreed to recruit more Catholic workers.

26 April   UUP proposed NI should have regional council with strictly administrative powers.

2 May   NIF report issued.

6 May   Riots in Belfast and several towns on third anniversary of death of hunger-striker Bobby Sands.

17 May   *Sunday World* Northern editor Jim Campbell shot and seriously injured by UVF at his N. Belfast home.

18 May   Two RUC men killed and another seriously injured in PIRA landmine explosion at Camlough, S. Armagh.

25 May   Security forces made large hauls of explosives at Carrickmore,

	Co. Tyrone, and Castlewellan in S. Down. Both Houses of US Congress unanimously backed NIF report.
1 June	President Reagan began four-day visit to Republic.
4 June	President Reagan told Dáil and Senate in Dublin that current US policy was not to interfere in Irish matters. But he praised the NIF and strongly criticised violence in NI.
5 June	Assembly member George Seawright lost DUP Whip after commenting at a meeting of Belfast Education and Library Board that Catholics and their priests should be incinerated.
14 June	European election poll.
18 June	In European election count Ian Paisley, John Taylor and John Hume retained seats.
20 June	British Labour leader Neil Kinnock voiced support for NIF report and united Ireland by consent.
2 July	Prior, speaking in Commons, rejected the unitary state, federal Ireland, and joint authority options of the NIF report.
12 July	Orange Order demonstration resolutions condemned NIF report. Violence after parades included attacks on security forces and shops in Derry, and on Catholic families in Limavady, Ballymena and Ballynahinch.
14 July	Two UDR soldiers killed by PIRA landmine at Castlederg, Co. Tyrone.
18 July	Public Accounts Committee at Westminster said loss of £77 million public money in DeLorean project was 'one of the gravest cases of misuse of public resources in recent years'.
9 August	NORAID leader Martin Galvin, banned from UK, appeared in Derry.
12 August	Sean Downes of Andersonstown died when hit by plastic bullet as RUC tried to arrest Martin Galvin at a W. Belfast rally.
13 August	W. Belfast march in honour of Sean Downes was followed by serious rioting in area.
14 August	Prior admitted ban on Galvin was 'a bad mistake'.
16 August	RUC came under sniper fire in riots on Belfast's Shankill Road.
22 August	Armagh coroner Gerry Curran resigned after finding 'grave irregularities' in RUC files relating to shooting by RUC of two INLA men in 1982.
10 September	Douglas Hurd appointed NI Secretary of State in succession to James Prior, who left the Government. Rhodes Boyson became NI Minister of State.
20 September	DUP suggested devolution scheme involving majority cabinet government with a Bill of Rights and minority having strong role in departmental committees.
24 September	Oliver Napier resigned as Alliance Party leader; succeeded by party Chief Whip John Cushnahan.
27 September	Eight Maze Prison officers and five prisoners injured in clash between loyalist and Republican prisoners.
28 September	Seven tons of arms and ammunition intended for PIRA seized on trawler *Marita Ann* off Kerry coast. Five men arrested. It was biggest capture of PIRA arms since *Claudia* was intercepted off Waterford coast in 1973.
5 October	British Labour Party conference in Blackpool opposed Diplock courts, and the use of supergrass evidence, and also called for ban

	on plastic bullets and an end to strip-searching of prisoners.
12 October	PIRA set off bomb inside Grand Hotel, Brighton, HQ of the Conservative conference, in a bid to kill Margaret Thatcher and senior Government figures. No member of the Government died, but the four killed (a fifth died later) included Sir Anthony Berry MP and Roberta Wakeham, wife of Government Chief Whip Robert Wakeham. Secretary for Trade and Industry Norman Tebbit and his wife Margaret were among the thirty-four injured.
16 October	Thatcher rejected idea of any 'sudden new initiative' on NI.
17 October	In Boston, US, trawler *Valhalla* seized on suspicion of being ship which transferred arms to trawler *Marita Ann* off Kerry coast eighteen days earlier.
22 October	European Commission of Human Rights held that use of plastic bullets was justified in riot situation.
25 October	Nineteen Maze prisoners, recaptured after the 1983 escape, appeared in court on charge of murdering a prison officer and firearms charges.
1 November	Kilbrandon report published; the unofficial committee, set up by the British Irish Association, suggested in majority report that NI should be run by five-member executive, including an Irish Government Minister.
6 November	New anti-personation measures announced for NI elections.
19 November	Thatcher, after Anglo-Irish summit at Chequers, ruled out three options of NIF report.
21 November	Garret FitzGerald reported to have told his backbenchers that Thatcher's behaviour after the summit had been 'gratuitously offensive'.
2 December	SAS soldier and a PIRA member died in exchange of shots at Drumrush, Co. Fermanagh.
4 December	Hurd warned NI Assembly that Unionists would have to make a significant move to accommodate Nationalists. Thatcher, in Dublin for EC summit, suggested that misunderstandings after the London summit had been due to her weakness 'for giving a direct answer at a press conference to a direct question'.
6 December	Two PIRA members shot dead by SAS in Derry.
14 December	Private Ian Thain became first soldier to be convicted for murdering a civilian while on duty in NI.
18 December	In Derry thirty-five local people held on 180 charges were cleared by Lord Chief Justice Lord Lowry in the Raymond Gilmour informer trial.
23 December	Cardinal Ó Fiaich said alienation among NI Catholics was at an 'unprecedented level'.
24 December	Court of Appeal quashed convictions of fourteen men jailed on evidence of UVF supergrass Joseph Bennett.

1985

30 January	Hurd rejected Nationalist demands for disbandment of UDR.
1 February	John Hume accepted PIRA invitation to talks, but said he would be urging it to end its campaign of violence. Unionists said such a meeting would be an obstacle to SDLP–Unionist dialogue.

3 February	Garret FitzGerald said SDLP–PIRA meeting could be used by PIRA for propaganda purposes, but Charles Haughey supported the exchange. Hurd said it could only give credibility to PIRA.
16 February	US State Department refused PSF president Gerry Adams a visa to address meeting of Congressmen.
19 February	Republic's Government pushed through legislation to freeze £1.75 million in bank account said to be held by PIRA nominees.
20 February	Thatcher, in address to US Congress, asked Americans not to give money to NORAID.
23 February	Meeting between SDLP leader John Hume and PIRA at secret venue lasted only a few minutes because Hume refused to have part of meeting recorded on video. Three members of PIRA shot dead by soldiers in Strabane, Co. Tyrone.
27 February	INLA threatened lives of visiting British sports teams after leaving bomb near Windsor Park, Belfast, during World Cup match between England and NI.
28 February	Nine RUC members killed in PIRA mortar attack on Newry, Co. Down, RUC station.
23 March	At DUP conference Paisley accused Irish Government, SDLP and Catholic hierarchy of having vested interest in PIRA atrocities.
5 April	Government announced it was not prepared to put up funds to save NI's gas industry and some 1,000 jobs.
11 April	Hurd announced new RUC complaints procedure.
20 April	Four senior PIRA men expelled after internal row.
15 May	District Council elections – PSF took fifty-nine seats.
20 May	Four RUC officers killed by PIRA bomb at Killeen on the border.
26 May	US Lear Fan aircraft company announced closure of its NI plant with loss of £57 million in Government grants.
23 June	Scotland Yard said it had uncovered a PIRA plan to bomb English seaside resorts.
3 July	Thousands of loyalists demonstrated in Portadown, Co. Armagh, against any ban on Orangemen walking through Catholic areas.
7 July	Clashes in Portadown between Nationalist protesters and RUC after police allowed Orange Church parade through Catholic Obins Street.
12–13 July	Sporadic rioting in Portadown as police prevented Orange and Royal Black Institution parades passing through Obins Street/'Tunnel' area, with fifty-two RUC men injured and extensive damage to property.
21 July	Cardinal Ó Fiaich, in interview with the *Universe* newspaper, said he believed 90 per cent of religious bigotry in NI was found among Protestants.
29 July	Belfast Magistrates' Court among buildings damaged by PIRA van bomb.
30 July	BBC governors stopped transmission, after Government representations, of a TV documentary which featured PSF Assembly member Martin McGuinness of Derry. (It was later broadcast, with slight amendments, after protest strikes by BBC and ITN journalists and a threat of resignation by the BBC's NI controller, James Hawthorne.)
16 August	Some shops in Portadown, Co. Armagh, looted and set alight in disturbances which followed a band parade.

30 August	Two Unionist leaders, James Molyneaux and Ian Paisley, met Margaret Thatcher at Downing Street to protest at continuing Anglo-Irish talks.
2 September	Tom King succeeded Douglas Hurd as NI Secretary of State.
4 September	RUC training depot in Enniskillen, Co. Fermanagh, seriously damaged in PIRA mortar attack.
8 September	PIRA shot dead husband and wife, Gerard and Catherine Mahon, in E. Belfast, claiming they were RUC informers.
5 October	Charles Haughey said Fianna Fáil would not stand for any departure from the principle of Irish unity set out in NIF report and enshrined in 1937 Constitution.
8 October	NI Court of Appeal quashed a murder conviction against former INLA leader Dominic McGlinchey. (Three days later he was re-extradited to the Republic.)
14 October	Study by Irish Information Partnership said more than half the 2,400 killings in NI since 1969 were carried out by Republican paramilitaries, and that more than a quarter of their victims were Catholic civilians.
30 October	Paisley and Molyneaux met Thatcher and warned that a consultative role for Republic in NI affairs would result in loyalist backlash.
2 November	Campaign launched to set up loyalist Ulster Clubs in every District Council area.
15 November	Margaret Thatcher and Taoiseach Garret FitzGerald signed AIA at Hillsborough, Co. Down.
16 November	NI Assembly called for a referendum on the AIA, and Unionists disclosed that all fifteen UUP and DUP MPs would resign their seats in protest at the agreement, and so create by-elections on the issue.
20 November	Tom King attacked by angry loyalists as he arrived at Belfast City Hall.
21 November	Dáil approved AIA by eighty-eight votes to seventy-five, with Fianna Fáil opposing, although its leader, Charles Haughey, said it would not oppose developments that would benefit Northern Nationalists.
23 November	Massive loyalist demonstration against AIA in Belfast city centre.
25 November	High Court in London refused leave to Unionists to challenge the legality of AIA.
27 November	Commons backed AIA by 473 votes to 47, with Thatcher declaring that her Government would not give way to threats or violence.
3 December	King expressed regret for a speech in Brussels in which he said he believed that the Irish Government now accepted that there would never be a united Ireland – a remark which embarrassed Thatcher and brought protests from Dublin.

1986

14 January	King said coming by-election results would not change Westminster support for the AIA, and Unionist attitude to it was misconceived and negative.
16 January	Police who raided an Amsterdam flat arrested Maze escapees Brendan McFarlane and Gerard Kelly, who were later extradited conditionally to UK.

23 January   In the fifteen by-elections on the AIA Unionists increased their vote on the 1983 general election, but lost Newry and Armagh to SDLP.

24 January   King said he was encouraged by swing of 5 per cent in Nationalist vote against PSF.

30 January   Fianna Fáil welcomed suggestion by UUP deputy leader Harold McCusker MP of a conference of British, Irish and NI politicians to discuss the 'totality of relationships' in the two islands.
Unemployment in NI reached 21.6 per cent.

18 February   Republic's Government announced its intention to sign the European Convention on the Suppression of Terrorism.

25 February   Paisley and Molyneaux met Thatcher on the AIA, and said afterwards that they welcomed her promise to consider their ideas for round-table talks on devolution. Later, after talks in Belfast with a variety of Unionist representatives, including spokesmen for power and shipyard workers, they said they would be discharging their electoral mandate and withdrawing consent from the Government and there would be no further discussions with Thatcher unless the AIA was abandoned.

26 February   Unionist leaders announced a general strike on 3 March against the AIA, and urged a peaceful protest without paramilitary involvement.

3 March   The Unionist strike, or 'Day of Action', against the AIA halted most of industry and commerce, disrupted public services and transport, including air travel, and led to extensive power cuts. In many areas masked loyalists manned barricades, and during riots at night in Belfast, shots were fired at the RUC in loyalist districts. The Government and the RUC were criticised for not keeping roads open and failing to prevent intimidation.

4 March   Molyneaux and Paisley, in a joint statement, condemned the violence and intimidation of the previous day and said these were not acts of loyalty. In the Commons King accused Unionist MPs of making common cause with people in paramilitary uniform.

7 March   Garret FitzGerald accused Charles Haughey of trying to sabotage the AIA during a visit to the US. In a New York speech Haughey had suggested that his own opposition to the AIA had been vindicated by King's remarks that the agreement meant that there would not be a united Ireland.

9 March   Chief Constable Sir John Hermon defended the RUC's behaviour during the loyalist strike, but admitted that it had not always been in sufficient strength to deal with particular situations.

10 March   Unionist leaders offered to reopen talks with British Government if AIA suspended, but King ruled out suspension.

11 March   Three DUP Assembly members arrested when they tried to cut through barbed wire surrounding Stormont Castle, where Anglo-Irish Intergovernmental Conference was meeting.

13 March   Extra battalion of troops brought in to support RUC.

17 March   Garret FitzGerald told President Reagan he believed there was a desire among Unionists opposed to the AIA to 'get off the hook' and to begin discussions on devolution.

18 March   Women prisoners from Armagh Women's Prison became first occupants of new £30 million prison at Maghaberry.

20 March	NIO, in a press advertisement, denounced the Unionist anti-AIA campaign as one of 'lies, deceit, distortion and half-truths'.
24 March	Thatcher, in letter to Unionist leaders, rejected the idea of suspension of AIA as a prelude to devolution talks.
31 March	Serious clashes occurred between loyalists and RUC in Portadown, Co. Armagh, after banning of an Apprentice Boys' parade. Eleven Catholic homes petrol-bombed in Lisburn, Co. Antrim.
1 April	More rioting in Portadown, with a twenty-year-old Protestant fatally wounded by plastic bullet.
3 April	SDLP leader John Hume praised RUC action in Portadown.
4 April	Main Protestant Churches condemned loyalists involved in attacks on Catholic-owned property and RUC members' homes, fourteen of which were attacked during previous night.
8 April	Rioting in Belfast and more petrol-bombing of policemen's homes.
23 April	A rates strike was among anti-AIA measures announced by Unionist leaders.
25 April	UUP executive voted to end special relationship with Conservative Party, dating from the nineteenth-century Home Rule crisis.
1 May	Sir Charles Carter warned Government of further violence without state action to help industry.
2 May	Chief Constable Sir John Hermon condemned intimidation of police officers and Catholics (fifty RUC and seventy-nine Catholic families were fire-bombed in their homes from 1 to 26 April). He accused politicians of 'consorting with paramilitary elements'.
6 May	Belfast City Council voted twenty-seven to twenty-three to resume normal business and end adjournment policy imposed in protest at AIA.
11 May	King recommended release of UVF supergrass William 'Budgie' Allen after serving only two years of fourteen-year sentence.
14 May	In Assembly several Unionists warned of sectarian 'bloodbath' unless AIA suspended.
15 May	Six months of AIA marked by loyalist demonstration in Hillsborough, Co. Down, DUP takeover of telephone switchboard at Stormont, a short work stoppage at Ballylumford power station and a renewed poster campaign.
16 May	At seminar on NI in Amsterdam PSF president Gerry Adams said AIA copper-fastened partition and insulated British Government from international criticism.
21 May	Ulster Young Unionist Council advocated integration with an NI Grand Committee.
29 May	King tells Commons of decision to dissolve NI Assembly.
2 June	James Molyneaux claimed that AIA was beginning to 'totter' and 'crumble'.
4 June	Ian Gow and others launched Friends of the Union Group.
5 June	John Stalker replaced in investigation of RUC alleged 'shoot to kill' policy in 1982.
11 June	Five Irish people, including Patrick Magee (Brighton hotel bomber), found guilty at the Old Bailey of conspiring to cause explosions in Britain.
12 June	Five people arrested in France after major arms seizure.
13 June	Loyalist Workers' Committee '86 warned Southern delegates to ICTU conference in Belfast to 'stay at home'.

17 June	Deputy Libyan leader Ahmed Jalloud told German MEPs that his country planned to resume aid to PIRA.
20 June	Chief Constable Sir John Hermon threatened legal action against accusations by media of his involvement in the removal of John Stalker.
23 June	NI Assembly dissolved. Police baton-charged 200 loyalist protesters outside Stormont. Twenty-two Assembly members, mainly DUP, refused to leave the chamber and were removed physically by the RUC early next day.
30 June	Referendum in Republic rejected divorce.
2 July	Loyalist politicians continued their own version of Assembly in Belfast City Hall.
3 July	RUC permitted Orange Church parade to pass through the Catholic Obins Street area in Portadown, Co. Armagh, but banned 12–13 July parades.
6 July	Rioting as RUC barred George Seawright from 'Tunnel' area of Portadown.
7 July	NCCL report opposed prison strip-searching.
10 July	Ian Paisley and Peter Robinson and 4,000 loyalists took over Hillsborough, Co. Down, in early-morning protest against AIA.
11 July	Portadown Orangemen accepted compromise Garvaghy Road route. Later at a bonfire, the RUC fired over 200 plastic bullets to disperse loyalist crowds. The twenty-six-day-old loyalist hunger strike at Magilligan Prison ended after visit by Paisley.
13 July	Chief Constable Sir John Hermon suspended two senior officers after investigations into alleged 'shoot to kill' policy in 1982. Weekend violence resulted in 128 police and 66 civilian injuries and 127 arrests; 281 plastic bullets fired and 79 reported cases of intimidation.
15 July	Peter Barry shared 'deep resentment' of Nationalists about the RUC decision on Garvaghy Road route.
16 July	Sixth consecutive night of riots in parts of Belfast and Portadown. RUC said 167 police and 125 civilians injured since 11 July; 300 plastic bullets fired and 200 people arrested; 111 cases of intimidation reported, including 11 against the homes of police officers.
17 July	Court of Appeal quashed convictions of eighteen sentenced in 1983 on the evidence of Republican supergrass Christopher Black; convictions of four others confirmed.
18 July	Orange Order inquiry into rioting in Portadown blamed RUC.
22 July	A report on recruitment and promotion trends in the NI civil service revealed more Catholic recruits in the last five years but that Catholics and women were still under-represented in top grades.
5 August	PIRA issued new warning to contractors servicing the security forces, and extended list of 'legitimate targets'.
7 August	Peter Robinson arrested when 500 loyalists converged on Clontibret, Co. Monaghan.
15 August	In Dundalk Robinson remanded to Ballybay; supporters stoned and petrol-bombed.
22 August	John Stalker cleared of allegations of misconduct and reinstated as deputy Chief Constable in Manchester. Short Brothers

management ordered removal of flags and emblems from their premises following claims of intimidation of Catholics.

2 September SDLP-controlled Newry and Mourne District Council instructed its workers not to collect refuse from local RUC station.

3 September Harold McCusker called for new relationship between Britain and NI, arguing that under the AIA the Union was not worth fighting for, much less dying for.

10 September NIO reshuffle. Nicholas Scott promoted to Minister of State and deputy Secretary of State; Peter Viggers replaced Rhodes Boyson at Economic Development.

16 September UUP and DUP politicians attended funeral of UVF member John Bingham.

19 September Sir Frederick Catherwood MEP (Conservative) at QUB urged a round-table conference of main parties to get devolution under AIA.

23 September UUP and DUP councillors separately decided to continue anti-AIA protest in council chambers but opposed full-blooded boycott or mass resignations.

24 September Paisley and Molyneaux advised AIA rate-protesters to pay the amount in full now.

25 September Molyneaux revealed Department of Environment (NI) confidential document on policy changes on Irish language and use of Irish street names.

29 September Amnesty International renewed its call for judicial inquiry into disputed killings in NI.

2 October George Seawright given nine-month sentence for protest at Belfast City Hall, November 1985, during visit by Tom King.

6 October Anglo-Irish Intergovernmental Conference's first meeting in Dublin discussed border security and agreed that non-NI-born Irish citizens resident in NI could vote in District Council elections.

12 October Charles Haughey at Bodenstown said position of Northern minority had 'seriously worsened' since AIA; in office his party would seek to renegotiate it.

13 October NIO agreed progressively to demolish Divis Flats in Belfast and Rossville Flats in Derry.

16 October Unemployment rose to new peak of almost 135,000, 23.1 per cent – up 11,500 on 1985.

24 October Richard Needham announced legislation to allow pubs to open on Sundays.

1 November Paisley and Molyneaux launched anti-AIA campaign in Britain at Orange rally in Glasgow.

2 November PSF's Ard Fheis voted to allow successful candidates in future Dáil elections to take their seats. Former PSF leader Ruairí Ó Brádaigh, and a hundred others, walked out.

4 November The demand that the trial of scheduled offences in a Diplock court should be heard by three judges rather than one, as at present, was rejected by Thatcher in a confidential letter to Taoiseach FitzGerald.

7 November Lord Mayor Sammy Wilson barred NIO Ministers from Remembrance Day service at Belfast City Hall.

8 November UFF planted four bombs in Dublin city centre.

10 November Ulster Resistance formed to 'take direct action as and when required' to defeat AIA at Ulster Hall closed meeting.

12 November	Queen's Speech reiterated Government's commitment to AIA.
15 November	Huge anti-AIA demonstration outside Belfast City Hall. City-centre shops damaged afterwards when RUC confronted a section of the crowd.
18 November	Paisley and Molyneaux met Labour leader Neil Kinnock in London.
20 November	Sir Geoffrey Howe reaffirmed Government's commitment to AIA and criticised its opponents.
21 November	SDLP annual conference in Newcastle, Co. Down, rejected suspension or abrogation of AIA.
26 November	UUP councillors voted not to resign from District Councils despite party leadership support for the option. SACHR recommended three judges in Diplock courts but rejected return to jury trial of scheduled offences.
28 November	FEA report on geographical distribution of Government-sponsored employment said it did not disadvantage Catholics, even before 1972.
1 December	King announced proposed changes in laws affecting demonstrations, incitement and the repeal of the Flags and Emblems Act.
3 December	Maze escapees Brendan McFarlane and Gerard Kelly extradited from Netherlands.
9 December	Paisley expelled from European Parliament after repeatedly interrupting address by Thatcher, in protest against AIA.
10 December	PSF president Gerry Adams, at the launch of his book *Politics of Irish Freedom,* said he had never been a member of IRA.
16 December	Lisburn Road police station in Belfast destroyed by proxy bomb and 700 homes and scores of businesses damaged.
21 December	Cardinal Ó Fiaich said on RTE that morale of Nationalists had improved since AIA, but time was not right to join RUC.
23 December	Thatcher visited NI and reaffirmed Government's commitment to AIA and stated that a change of Government in the Republic would not alter it.

1987

3 January	At Belfast City Hall UUP and DUP leaders launched petition to the Queen for referendum on the AIA.
6 January	NI Housing Executive revealed it dealt with 1,118 cases of intimidation in 1986.
8 January	David Calvert (DUP) shot and wounded by INLA gunman at Craigavon shopping centre, Co. Armagh. Molyneaux warned against another Day of Action against AIA.
14 January	Cardinal Ó Fiaich 'appalled' by Lord Brookeborough's description of him in the Lords as an 'evil prelate'.
16 January	Peter Robinson pleaded guilty in Dublin to unlawful assembly; freed after paying £17,500 in fines and compensation.
18 January	Charles Haughey said NI and AIA would not be election issues.
19 January	Nicholas Scott contradicted Haughey view that Article 1 of AIA might be open to renegotiation.
20 January	Two members of INLA shot dead in a Drogheda hotel in an internal feud. John Taylor (UUP) MEP left European Democratic

	Group in European Parliament to join European Right Group.
21 January	INLA said it would disband in its present form.
24 January	Neil Kinnock visited border security bases; defended Labour meetings with PSF but said 'not productive' for him to meet PSF in person.
29 January	UDA published 'Common Sense' document proposing constitutional conference, devolved assembly and coalition government based on party strengths.
7 February	UFF planted eighteen incendiary devices in Dublin and Co. Donegal.
10 February	Report of SACHR recommended end of excessive remands and of exclusion orders under PTA, more flexibility on transfer of prisoners from GB, three judges in Diplock courts, and reforms in strip-searching procedures. PTA renewed by Commons. *Daily Express* poll found 61 per cent of British in favour of withdrawal from NI.
12 February	Unionist MPs deliver 400,000-signature petition to Buckingham Palace calling for referendum in NI on AIA.
17 February	Richard Needham announced extra £28 million for projects over three years as part of the Belfast programme.
19 February	In Republic's election Fianna Fáil won eighty-one seats – three short of a majority.
23 February	Outgoing Presbyterian Moderator, Dr John Thompson, described Unionist anti-AIA campaign as 'counter-productive and morally questionable'. Belfast City Council fined £25,000 by High Court for contempt in failing to resume normal business; DOE appointed a commissioner to strike a rate in loyalist-controlled councils.
24 February	US Police Foundation cancelled invitation to Chief Constable Sir John Hermon after Irish National Caucus protests.
26 February	Nicholas Scott rejected Enoch Powell amendment to EPA to proscribe PSF.
2 March	Ulster Clubs announced plan to set up alternative system of government run by Unionist political and paramilitary groups.
9 March	Thirty-one RUC women awarded £240,000 compensation in sex-discrimination case against Chief Constable, who later agreed to offer women equal access to all training and employment opportunities.
10 March	Charles Haughey elected Taoiseach on the casting vote of Speaker. NIO approved a £300 million development plan for Laganbank in Belfast.
11 March	Garret FitzGerald resigned as Fine Gael leader.
17 March	President Reagan authorised first $50 million grant for International Fund for Ireland.
21 March	Alan Dukes elected leader of Fine Gael.
22 March	Former MI5 agent James Miller claimed British intelligence had helped promote the 1974 UWC strike to destabilise Wilson Government.
23 March	PIRA car bomb at officers' club in joint army/RAF base at Rheindalen, West Germany; thirty-one people, mostly German, injured.
24 March	Molyneaux and Paisley called for 'peaceful' demonstrations on 11 April against new Public Order Order.

25 March	SACHR asked Government to strengthen fair employment law, claiming 'serious problems of inequality' between Catholics and Protestants.
26 March	End of INLA feud announced by two W. Belfast priests.
1 April	RUC statement said 'provocative' flying of Union flag could be illegal under new Public Order Order.
8 April	The Lawrence Marley Republican funeral with around 5,000–6,000 mourners was largest since hunger strike.
10 April	Ten Unionist MPs, including Molyneaux and Paisley, protested at the new Public Order laws by an illegal march through Belfast.
11 April	Low turnout for loyalist Day of Defiance.
15 April	PIRA letter bombs franked 'Students' Union, University of Ulster' sent to Thatcher's press secretary, a deputy secretary in the Cabinet Office, and the head of the Cabinet Office economic secretariat. Colonel Gaddafi announced that he would open centres for the PIRA and the PLO.
16 April	PIRA said it would no longer fire volleys of shots over dead members' coffins in Church grounds.
23 April	Labour spokesman on NI Peter Archer wrote letter supporting MacBride Principles circulated in the US by Fair Employment Trust.
25 April	Lord Justice Maurice Gibson and his wife Cecily killed by PIRA car bomb at Killeen, Co. Down. He was fifth member of NI judiciary killed by PIRA.
28 April	Unionists launched anti-AIA campaign in Britain with press conference and £15,000-advertisement in *The Times*.
30 April	SDLP criticised NIO pamphlet, 'Northern Ireland: Fair Treatment For All' (for distribution in the US), for implying that the SDLP sided with the NIO against the MacBride Principles.
1 May	PSF issued 'Scenario for Peace', demanding British withdrawal and calling for all-Ireland constitutional conference.
4 May	SDLP fund-raising poker game in a Cookstown hotel, Co. Tyrone, robbed of £15,000–£20,000 by armed gang.
5 May	Paisley said his party would have no part in power-sharing arrangement after rumours that Unionist Task Force might propose a form of devolution with an executive based on proportion of party support.
6 May	King announced that several hundred full-time RUC Reservists would be recruited.
8 May	Eight PIRA men shot dead by SAS in Loughgall, Co. Armagh.
9 May	Chief Constable Sir John Hermon in statement on paramilitary funerals said RUC would liaise with family and clergy of the dead.
13 May	US State Department warned that application of the MacBride Principles to US companies in NI could leave them 'possibly contravening UK law, or losing access to the UK market'.
19 May	Robert McCartney expelled from UUP because of his presidency of the Campaign for Equal Citizenship and comments about UUP leadership.
21 May	Molyneaux and Paisley launched joint general election manifesto which offered Unionist MPs' 'consent' to a new government committed to a suspension of AIA.

4 June	Presbyterian General Assembly urged Unionist MPs to return to Westminster.
5 June	RUC figures showed more punishment beatings and shootings by paramilitaries in first four months of 1987 than whole of 1986.
9 June	Lord Fitt attacked SDLP and said that if he had a vote, it would go to the WP.
12 June	Conservatives returned to power with 375 seats. The only change in NI was defeat of Enoch Powell (UUP) by Eddie McGrady (SDLP) in S. Down.
15 June	King returned as Secretary of State for NI. Nicholas Scott replaced by former Armed Forces Minister, John Stanley.
25 June	Queen's Speech at the opening of Parliament expressed a commitment to seeking devolution in NI.
30 June	Three men jailed in Boston for *Marita Ann* (1984) arms smuggling to PIRA.
1 July	Short Brothers management threatened closure of sections of plant over display of loyalist flags.
3 July	Short Brothers closed three of its main production areas.
5 July	Protest march at Glasdrummond, S. Armagh, at takeover of lands and building of observation posts by army.
6 July	Production resumed at the three Short Brothers plants.
7 July	Legislation for NI included provisions for Sunday pub opening and the abolition of jurors in civil injury cases.
8 July	Paisley and Molyneaux announced they would use the Task Force report in low-level introductory talks with Government.
22 July	FEA draft inquiry into Derry City Council cleared it of Unionist allegations of discrimination against Protestants.
1 August	Fifty-strong NORAID group from the US on an NI 'fact-finding' mission.
2 August	Jim McAllister (PSF) led march to protest at a 'spy camera' monitoring cross-border traffic at an army base near Crossmaglen, Co. Armagh.
3 August	SDLP claimed PSF used hundreds of forged medical cards in W. Belfast during June election; PSF dismissed the claim.
4 August	Planning Appeals Commission refused permission for the 'Belfast Says No' banner at the City Hall.
12 August	Paisley rejected Archbishop Robin Eames's attempts to set up informal talks between the four main constitutional party leaders.
14 August	Unionists called for end to cross-border RUC–Garda intelligence co-operation after a Garda memo fell into PIRA hands.
2 September	John Taylor claimed that PIRA campaign united Protestants and, ironically, benefited their commercial rebuilding plans; he urged Unionists to accept the challenge of devolution and improved links with Dublin.
5 September	Two men and one woman, with Dublin and Kildare addresses, charged with conspiracy to murder King in Wiltshire (later convicted, and in 1988 freed on appeal). Eleven Unionist MPs, including Molyneaux and Paisley, summoned under new Public Order laws for an illegal march on 10 April and the loyalist Day of Defiance on 11 April.
6 September	Chris Mullin, Labour MP, claimed to have interviewed the 'real' Birmingham pub bombers.

7 September	John Cushnahan, Alliance leader, announced he was going to resign.
9 September	Government proposed that electoral candidates be required to 'declare opposition to the use of violence for political ends'.
10 September	US Ambassador to UK, Charles Price, supported UK Government's stand against the MacBride Principles.
12 September	WP leader Tomás Mac Giolla announced his resignation. Cardinal Ó Fiaich described the AIA as 'a shot in the arm for Catholics in the North'.
14 September	Unionist leaders Molyneaux and Paisley ended nineteen-month boycott of Government Ministers to meet Tom King at Stormont for 'talks about talks'.
15 September	King launched 'Religious Equality of Opportunity in Employment: An Employer's Guide to Fair Employment'.
16 September	European Commission of Human Rights held that provisions of PTA for seven-day detention breached requirement that suspects be charged 'promptly'.
29 September	Strabane DUP councillor Ronald Brolly jailed for two years for sectarian arson attacks.
3 October	Dr John Alderdice elected new Alliance Party leader.
4 October	Peter Barry claim of a British undertaking to reform Diplock courts denied by Sir Geoffrey Howe in Denmark.
7 October	Peter Robinson resigned as deputy leader of DUP.
8 October	Lord Hailsham, former Lord Chancellor, rejected need for reform of Diplock courts.
9 October	Chief Constable Sir John Hermon approved new RUC code of conduct.
11 October	Charles Haughey at Bodenstown expressed disappointment at AIA results.
15 October	DPP Sir Barry Shaw denied Garret FitzGerald's claim that supergrass trials ended in NI due to AIA.
20 October	Belfast Unionist councillors agreed to pay £25,000 fine and £11,000 in costs imposed by the High Court over AIA protest.
21 October	King met Brian Lenihan for four hours and warned of 'serious implications' if no extradition after 1 December.
22 October	Thatcher told MPs: 'The future of courts in NI is a matter for the UK Government and it is not a bargaining point.'
23 October	PSF won Belfast City Council by-elections in Upper and Lower Falls.
27 October	Republic's Government expressed concern at lobbying of opposition politicians on extradition by senior British Embassy staff in Dublin.
1 November	One hundred and fifty tons of arms and ammunition for PIRA seized on French coaster *Eksund*.
7 November	UUP conference in Belfast opposed devolved government with minority veto arising from AIA. At SDLP conference John Hume called on Unionists to negotiate.
8 November	Eleven killed and sixty-three injured when PIRA bomb went off at Enniskillen Remembrance Day ceremony.
11 November	Charles Haughey met British Labour leader, Neil Kinnock, to discuss extradition.
12 November	Molyneaux and Paisley led 2,000 Unionists through London to

mark their opposition to AIA. Unemployment total fell by 5,283 to 124,707 – 18.2 per cent of workforce.

14 November   Paisley and Molyneaux attended Hillsborough rally against AIA.

15 November   Republic observed one minute's silence over Enniskillen bombing.

16 November   Anglo-Irish Intergovernmental Conference met in Dublin and agreed 'a very positive response' to security post-Enniskillen.

17 November   DOE published 'Belfast Urban Area Plan 2001', which met widespread criticism.

18 November   Fianna Fáil backbenchers demanded prima-facie evidence requirement in Extradition Bill.

19 November   George Seawright shot and fatally injured by IPLO.

22 November   Thatcher joined 7,000 for rearranged Remembrance Day service at Enniskillen.

23 November   Massive arms search in Republic and NI after claims of three successful arms runs before the *Eksund*. Republic's Bill published amending 1965 Extradition Act to require the Attorney-General to satisfy himself of a case to answer before endorsing an extradition warrant.

24 November   Forty PSF activists arrested in Belfast, Derry and border counties.

25 November   King disagreed with Republic's proposed extradition safeguards.

30 November   Republic's Extradition Act effective at midnight.

1 December   Thatcher claimed Britain was 'least-favoured nation' in new extradition arrangements.

2 December   Molyneaux and Paisley met Tom King for fifth of series of 'talks about talks'.

5 December   Thatcher met Taoiseach Haughey at EC summit in Copenhagen and re-established 'working relationship'.

12 December   Chief Constable Sir John Hermon confirmed cross-border co-operation between bomb disposal teams.

14 December   Tony Benn published draft Bill sponsored by Labour Campaign Group setting a date for British withdrawal from NI.

17 December   PIRA bomb exploded outside Belfast home of Judge Donald Murray.

18 December   County Court judge Andrew Donaldson resigned after a dispute with the RUC Chief Constable over his security arrangements.

22 December   UDA deputy leader John McMichael killed by PIRA booby-trap car bomb outside his Lisburn home.

1988

1 January   Chief Constable Sir John Hermon warned that PIRA had SAM-7 missiles.

8 January   Police intercepted 100 guns and ammunition, destined for loyalists, in cars near Portadown, Co. Armagh. Peter Robinson re-elected as DUP deputy leader at annual meeting.

11 January   John Hume met Gerry Adams for talks in Belfast at request of a third party; both parties denied PIRA ceasefire on agenda.

14 January   Unemployment 120,588 (17.6 per cent) – 8,200 fewer than December 1986. Recorder of Belfast upheld FEA finding of discrimination by Ministry of Defence against W. Belfast Catholic.

20 January   UK opposed inclusion of NI with poorest EC regions to gain increased structural funds. NI MPs united to support David Alton's Bill to reduce the abortion time limit to eighteen weeks.

21 January	King announced more control by army over border security.
24 January	SDLP constituency representatives endorsed Hume/Adams talks.
25 January	Sir Patrick Mayhew (Attorney-General) announced that eleven RUC officers investigated by Stalker/Sampson inquiry would not be prosecuted for reasons of 'national security'; Republic expressed 'deep dismay'.
26 January	Molyneaux and Paisley met King with plan for administrative devolution with committee system in which chairmanships would be allocated in proportion to party share of the vote.
27 January	Gardaí discovered PIRA arms dump at Malin Head, Co. Donegal.
28 January	Court of Appeal in London rejected plea by Birmingham Six.
5 February	NIO confirmed new draft fair employment legislation.
6 February	Five thousand attended Dublin anti-extradition rally.
7 February	Molyneaux wanted AIA rewritten to cover 'totality of relationships' between Britain and Ireland.
9 February	European Parliament asked Britain to reconsider non-prosecution decision on Stalker/Sampson findings.
13 February	PSF executive permitted Adams to resume talks with SDLP.
14 February	Republic said Britain had sent extradition warrants without new evidence required by it.
15 February	Thatcher met Haughey after EC summit in Brussels.
17 February	King announced two disciplinary inquiries into the RUC over Stalker/Sampson investigation.
18 February	Unemployment rose to 121,778. SACHR again recommended three-judge Diplock courts.
20 February	Haughey spoke about 'historic inability in Britain to comprehend Irish feelings and sensitivities'; willing to travel North to talk to Unionists.
21 February	Aidan McAnespie shot dead at Aughnacloy, Co. Tyrone, border checkpoint.
23 February	Private Ian Thain, the first British soldier convicted of murder while on duty in NI, released from life sentence after twenty-six months to rejoin his regiment.
24 February	FEA annual report published: Catholic share of public-sector employment increased.
25 February	John Hume accepted King's invitation to talks on devolution.
1 March	John Stanley (NIO), on the PTA renewal debate, said SAM-7 missiles were 'in the island of Ireland'. Belfast City Council refused an invitation to Dublin millennium celebrations.
2 March	Haughey said devolution proposals neither 'workable nor beneficial' at present.
6 March	Mairead Farrell, Sean Savage and Daniel McCann (all PIRA) shot dead by SAS in Gibraltar.
8 March	Spanish police found car packed with explosives in Marbella, Spain.
10 March	Sixty British Labour MPs denounced Gibraltar shootings as 'capital punishment without trial'.
11 March	Andy Tyrie (UDA) resigned as leader after no-confidence motion in inner council of the organisation.
16 March	Loyalist Michael Stone attacked Gibraltar funerals at Milltown cemetery in Belfast, killing three and injuring several.
19 March	Two army corporals killed by mob at W. Belfast funeral.

23 March	After temporary resistance, BBC, ITN and RTE handed over film of the killing of two army corporals to RUC.
28 March	Tony Benn published Bill to end British rule in NI by 1990.
29 March	SDLP presented to King a strategy document on political progress.
1 April	Colonel Gaddafi of Libya pledged support for PIRA.
12 April	RUC annual report said 1987 worst year for violence since 1981.
16 April	Proinsias De Rossa replaced Tomás Mac Giolla as leader of WP.
21 April	Brian Donnelly (Dem.) introduced Fair Employment Incentives Bill in US Congress.
26 April	King met SDLP delegation at Stormont.
28 April	King said AIA 'an end in itself' not 'part of a process sliding to something else'.
1 May	PIRA killed two RAF men at Niew Bergen and one at Roermond, the Netherlands.
3 May	Nigel Dodds (DUP) elected youngest-ever Lord Mayor of Belfast.
15 May	UVF gun attack on Belfast bar kills three. Molyneaux told *Weekend World* that UUP officials could exchange position papers with Haughey.
19 May	Unemployment rose by 733, but 8,938 lower than April 1987.
26 May	Paisley and Molyneaux met King for last of 'talks about talks'.
27 May	Seamus Mallon (SDLP) asked Government not to deploy Royal Irish Rangers in NI.
7 June	Police Federation asked for simultaneous internment in NI and Republic.
10 June	Conservative Association launched in Bangor, Co. Down.
13 June	SDLP and PSF met in Belfast for on-going discussions.
14 June	The McGimpsey brothers' action challenging the AIA began in Dublin High Court.
15 June	Six soldiers killed by bomb at Lisburn, Co. Antrim, fun run.
16 June	King refused to rule out internment as security response.
22 June	Chief Constable Sir John Hermon said he would retire in 1989. Catholic Bishops attacked proposed educational reforms.
23 June	PIRA shot down helicopter at Crossmaglen, Co. Armagh.
27 June	Amnesty International sought judicial inquiry into disputed killings by police and army since 1982.
28 June	Government said Harland and Wolff to be privatised. PM Thatcher and Taoiseach Haughey met at EC Hanover summit and discussed security.
29 June	Police Authority decision (by one vote) not to inquire further into senior officers' role in 'shoot to kill' cases criticised by Republic.
30 June	King said new Police Authority included substantial representation of Catholics. Labour hard-left supporters launched Time to Go campaign for British withdrawal from NI.
1 July	The Department of Economic Development said Short Brothers would 'ultimately return to the private sector'.
3 July	Eddie McGrady, SDLP MP, expressed disquiet at continuation of his party's talks with PSF.
4 July	Twenty RUC men to be subject to disciplinary proceedings as result of Kelly inquiry arising from Stalker/Sampson investigations. Belfast City Council meeting abandoned after PSF and Unionists came to blows.
11 July	King said he was willing to remain in any reshuffle of Cabinet.

13 July	Duisburg (West Germany) British army base damaged by two PIRA bombs.
14 July	Harland and Wolff announced loss of £17.3 million, lowest since 1970s. Criminal Justice Bill published which would permit RUC to take mouth and saliva swabs from suspects.
15 July	NIO said Northern Ireland Electricity would be privatised as a unit.
18 July	It was announced that Gerry Adams and John Hume met in private on 11 July. Attorney-General Sir Patrick Mayhew met Dublin counterpart on extradition.
19 July	£10 million extra aid for W. Belfast from Government.
20 July	Molyneaux rejected Anglo-Irish inter-parliamentary tier.
22 July	NI trade unionists lobbied Westminster over privatisation of Short Brothers and Harland and Wolff.
23 July	Border bomb (1,000 lbs), intended for Mr Justice Higgins, killed Robert and Maureen Hanna and their son David; they were among the seventeen civilians to die in PIRA 'mistakes' since November 1987.
25 July	John Stanley replaced by Ian Stewart in Cabinet reshuffle and returned to back benches.
28 July	All NI parties opposed privatisation of Short Brothers and Harland and Wolff in Commons debate.
29 July	Ed Koch, Mayor of New York, withdrew favourable comments on British army role in NI under the pressure of his re-election campaign.
1 August	First PIRA bomb in GB since 1984 killed soldier at Inglis barracks, N. London.
4 August	The McGimpsey brothers decided to appeal the rejection by the High Court in Dublin of their constitutional challenge to AIA.
5 August	Police Federation and UUP urged reintroduction of internment. PIRA bomb at British army base at Düsseldorf. WP and Prog. D. urged SDLP to end PSF contacts.
8 August	Mr Justice Brian Hutton succeeded Lord Lowry as Lord Chief Justice.
11 August	NIO confirmed three helicopter overflights into Republic in previous two weeks.
12 August	IPLO exploded proxy bomb outside Belfast Law Courts. Republic denied overflight agreement.
14 August	Martin McGuinness (PSF) praised the 'Continental battalion' of PIRA.
15 August	John Hume defended his latest meeting with Gerry Adams. Charter Group warned Molyneaux of challenge to his leadership.
16 August	Coopers and Lybrand review of the economy criticised absence of political stability and urged caution on privatisation of Short Brothers and Harland and Wolff.
17 August	Robert Russell failed to have his extradition order set aside by the Dublin High Court. British and Irish Governments denied overflight agreement. Unemployment rose 2,500 to 118,239.
20 August	Eight British soldiers killed by bomb attack on service bus at Ballygawley, Co. Tyrone. (Most soldiers killed in a single attack since 1979 attack at Warrenpoint.)
21 August	King announced major security review.
22 August	Royal Navy recruiting officer in Belfast killed by bomb attached to his car.

23 August	Gerard Harte extradited from the Republic. PIRA exploded massive car bomb in Belfast city centre.
27 August	Robert Russell transferred by Garda to RUC at border.
30 August	Three PIRA members shot by SAS near Drumnakilly, Co. Tyrone.
31 August	Two PIRA suspects arrested by West German police near Dutch border.
1 September	Committee on Administration of Justice urged a stronger Police Authority.
2 September	SDLP/PSF talks broke down.
5 September	SDLP and PSF formally announced end of talks. NIO blocked FEA investigation of NIE contract on grounds of national security.
6 September	Gibraltar inquest opened into deaths of three PIRA members.
7 September	IPLO shot dead William Quee (UDA) in Belfast.
8 September	Marketing Research Consultancy poll for UTV supported requirement that politicians sign an 'anti-violence' declaration. International Fund for Ireland to devote more funds to disadvantaged areas.
9 September	PIRA shot dead Colin Abernethy, treasurer of Ulster Clubs movement.
13 September	Seamus Mallon said SDLP would talk to Unionists irrespective of whether the AIA was in operation or not.
19 September	David Owen (SDP leader) said that the AIA should be 'recast'.
20 September	Home Secretary Douglas Hurd announced plans to attack funds raised by paramilitary groups.
21 September	Labour document proposed harmonisation of policies on economy, security, currency, and social security as a prelude to united Ireland by consent.
26 September	DPP announced he would not proceed with charges in the Aidan McAnespie case.
27 September	Ian Stewart (NIO) confirmed an agreement on border overflying to 200 metres had existed for two years.
28 September	PM Thatcher visited NI.
29 September	Republic's Foreign Minister Brian Lenihan addressed UN Assembly on AIA.
2 October	Molyneaux criticised King for saying that Unionists had made no proposals for political development. BBC postponed *Panorama* documentary on SAS in NI.
3 October	Alliance Party urged a devolved government with power-sharing and an input into the Anglo-Irish Intergovernmental Conference.
5 October	Brian Mawhinney (NIO) published educational reforms for NI, which followed those in GB and boosted integrated education locally.
6 October	Trial opened at Winchester of three charged with conspiracy to murder King.
7 October	Patrick McVeigh arrested in Dundalk but released by Gardaí despite being wanted in Britain. Tom Hartley (PSF) refuted SDLP claim that Britain was neutral on NI since AIA.
8 October	Corrymeela conference at Ballycastle, Co. Antrim, brought Ken Maginnis (UUP) and Eddie McGrady (SDLP) together on devolution. Derry civil rights march marked twentieth anniversary.
10 October	Molyneaux rejected King's invitation to talks on security.

Conservative Party conference opened in Brighton for first time since 1984 PIRA bomb.

11 October Paisley ejected from European Parliament after interrupting an address by Pope John Paul II. King invited general submissions to the review of the workings of the Anglo-Irish Intergovernmental Conference.

13 October Unionist joint policy group formally rejected any involvement in the review of AIA. Monsignor Colm McCaughan said Catholic parents sending children to integrated schools were breaking canon law. Unemployment fell to 115,743 (16.6 per cent).

14 October In Brighton Thatcher praised SAS action in Gibraltar. Taoiseach Haughey admitted to hospital with a respiratory illness. Talks in Duisburg, West Germany, aimed at finding formula for inter-party negotiations in NI.

15 October James Craig (UDA) killed by UFF.

18 October MRBI/*Irish Times* opinion survey in Republic revealed that support for extradition had fallen from 40 to 31 per cent.

19 October Home Secretary Douglas Hurd announced a ban on 'direct statements' on radio and television by spokesmen and supporters of paramilitary and other organisations advocating the use of violence.

20 October King announced that the law would be changed on the right to silence of people facing terrorist charges.

22 October RSF Ard Fheis in Dublin condemned extradition from the Republic.

28 October Three Irish defendants in King conspiracy case were sentenced to twenty-five years each after a ten to two verdict.

29 October Molyneaux told a Friends of the Union conference in London that the 1980 Anglo-Irish Intergovernmental Council might be an acceptable alternative to AIA.

1 November Mr Justice Nicholson called on loyalists to reject the UDA, when he sentenced three of its members for possessing the largest haul of loyalist arms uncovered during the Troubles, found at Portadown in January 1988.

2 November Anglo-Irish Intergovernmental Conference met at Stormont and decided to widen review of AIA. Public spending of £5,468 million announced for 1989-90.

4 November AIA inter-parliamentary body of fifty members proposed, but Unionists indicated they would not take part while AIA operated.

7 November British and Irish Foreign Ministers Sir Geoffrey Howe and Brian Lenihan met in Dublin: agreement on continental shelf exploitation and discussion of AIA matters.

8 November King attacked right to silence in Criminal Evidence (NI) Order debate.

10 November Conservative National Union rejected application by N. Down Model Conservative Association; political reasons cited were that it split pro-Union vote and was critical of Conservative policies. Settlement of £900,000 for 310 RUC women Reservists in Equal Opportunities Commission case.

14 November Inquest opened on three S. Armagh deaths in 1982 – the subject of the Stalker/Sampson inquiries. Five-hundred-job Korean investment in VCR plant for Antrim. Friends of the Union published proposed replacement for AIA. Lagan Valley Model Conservative Association formed.

15 November	Small protests marked third anniversary of AIA. Molyneaux said proposals that had been with King for eight months may be withdrawn. King said he was uncertain of their status.
16 November	President Reagan renewed pledge on AIA and promised extra funds.
17 November	Ulster Independence Committee (leader Rev. Hugh Ross) formed network of eleven branches after fifteen public meetings in NI. Unemployment 110,445 (15.9 per cent).
18 November	Loyalist arms find in Co. Armagh linked with Ulster Resistance.
19 November	Plans to close six RUC stations and five police posts announced to save £2 million. UUP conference at Portrush, Co. Antrim, called for referendum on AIA. DUP said it had severed all connections with Ulster Resistance some time ago.
22 November	Queen's Speech promised stronger fair employment legislation, anti-violence oath for council candidates and 'votes in local elections for Irish citizens resident in NI', and a new PTA. Princess Royal visited NI.
24 November	Bomb explosion at Benburb, Co. Tyrone, RUC station killed two civilians.
25 November	New PTA Bill published.
26 November	SDLP annual conference attacked changes in right to silence and councillors' oath.
28 November	Unionists studied letter from Thatcher on their proposals.
29 November	European Court of Human Rights ruled against detention without charge beyond four days – affecting PTA seven-day provision.
30 November	Law officers admitted errors in original Father Patrick Ryan extradition warrant. Thatcher statement strongly critical of Belgium and Republic on Ryan case. E. Londonderry Model Conservative Association set up at Coleraine meeting.
1 December	Commons row over Ryan; chronology of crisis set out. Paddy Ashdown (SLD) visited NI.
3 December	Irish Attorney-General posed twenty new questions on Ryan extradition. British Labour Party split on whether to abstain on second reading of new PTA: Clare Short and Andrew Bennett resigned over abstention policy.
6 December	Dáil debate approved Extradition Act 1987 amid public protests. Forty-two Labour backbenchers revolted on PTA.
7 December	US Ambassador Charles Price urged NI businessmen to get involved in politics.
8 December	Joint European approach to extradition suggested by EC. FEA twelfth annual report criticised private employers.
10 December	EC ordered review of extradition between members. Denmark ended cross-border shopping restrictions on its citizens, leaving Republic isolated as only EC state with such measures.
12 December	Danny Morrison (PSF) left to visit Belgium for four days. Haughey stance on Ryan boosted public support for Taoiseach by 8 per cent to 62 per cent.
13 December	Irish Attorney-General rejected British request for extradition of Ryan. Labour '87 published plan for devolution.
14 December	Anglo-Irish Intergovernmental Conference meeting at Stormont heard King express dissatisfaction on extradition. Thatcher described Irish decision on Ryan as an 'insult to the British people'.

	John Taylor (UUP) urged Unionists to apply for funds to the International Fund for Ireland.
15 December	Second report of International Fund for Ireland showed 858 projects, supported by £26.5 million, created 4,500 jobs. Unemployment fell 1,400 to 108,981 (15.7 per cent). PLO formally denied any links with PIRA.
16 December	Fair Employment Bill published.
17 December	Apprentice Boys launched tercentenary celebrations of the Siege of Derry.
19 December	Visit by Neil Kinnock, Labour leader, to Fermanagh, army families and trade unionists.
20 December	Court of Appeal ruled RUC witnesses could be compelled to give evidence in court and ordered a fresh inquest into three 1982 deaths in Co. Armagh.
21 December	IDB secured biggest inward investment, of £90 million and 1,000 jobs by French-owned Montupet company to make aluminium cylinder heads for Ford on former DeLorean site. Police discovered PIRA bomb factory in N. London.
22 December	Government decided to retain seven-day detention of suspects despite European Court of Human Rights decision and to seek temporary derogation from European Convention.
27 December	It was announced that the Harland and Wolff management buyout was lodged on 23 December.
28 December	The *Independent* newspaper revealed that NI judges had informed King of their disquiet over the effects of changes in the right to silence and a proposed role for them in detention under the PTA.
30 December	PIRA end-of-year message explicitly warned British politicians and the royal family.

1989

7 January	Mary McSorley (SDLP) disowned by party meeting for accepting MBE for services to tourism.
13 January	Hume invited Unionists to talks with Nationalists and Irish Government to transcend the AIA.
16 January	Guildford Four case referred to Court of Appeal.
17 January	Three UUP councillors joined N. Down Model Conservatives.
29 January	Gerry Adams told the PSF Ard Fheis that PIRA had to be 'careful and careful again' to avoid civilian casualties.
1 February	BBC disclosed Duisburg meeting of four NI parties in October 1988 and claimed 'historic breakthrough'.
3 February	PSF announced a legal challenge to limitations on access to media imposed by Home Secretary in October 1988.
12 February	Pat Finucane, solicitor, shot dead by loyalist gunmen in his N. Belfast home.
14 February	Magherafelt councillor John Davey (PSF) shot dead by loyalist gunmen. Tom King proposed to sound parties out on the scope for political progress.
16 February	Figures released showing unemployment rose to 111,000, 16 per cent, in January.
19 February	A *Sunday Life* poll showed 63 per cent supported Duisburg Talks; 71 per cent supported power-sharing devolution within UK.

22 February	Lord Colville reported on NI emergency legislation.
23 February	NI Police Authority appointed Hugh Annesley (forty-nine), Assistant Commissioner at the Metropolitan Police, to be the next Chief Constable of the RUC.
26 February	*Sunday Life* poll showed over 50 per cent welcomed chance to vote for British party in an election.
27 February	Twelve Unionist councillors from Craigavon lost High Court appeal against a £225,000 surcharge imposed for their delay in granting lease to a GAA club, but the sum was reduced to £100,000.
5 March	Gerry Adams stated he sought a 'non-armed political movement to work for self-determination' in Ireland.
8 March	Emergency Provisions Act renewed in House of Commons by 239 votes to 121.
9 March	Hurd said PIRA must be 'extirpated': political solutions were not enough.
14 March	Stevens inquiry reprimanded eighteen and cautioned one of the twenty RUC men it had investigated.
17 March	Conservative Party agreed to hold debate at autumn conference on affiliation motion put by N. Down Model Conservatives.
22 March	The new PTA became law, enabling bank accounts to be examined in a search for paramilitary funds.
27 March	Eight thousand Apprentice Boys celebrated the 300th anniversary of the siege of Derry.
4 April	British Council of Churches called for a 'fundamental review' of the AIA.
5 April	Anglo-Irish Intergovernmental Conference meeting at Stormont agreed to 'deepen and widen' its work.
10 April	Sir Alasdair Fraser succeeded Sir Barry Shaw as Director of Public Prosecutions.
11 April	Reporting restrictions on PSF were lifted for the District Council elections.
13 April	Paul A. Kane, a Maze escaper, was extradited North.
18 April	John Hume and Dr Godfrey Brown, Presbyterian Moderator, had a 'frank and constructive' meeting.
22 April	Three Ulster Resistance members were detained in Paris with a South African diplomat and an arms dealer.
27 April	Gerry Adams was refused NIO compensation for gunshot injuries inflicted by loyalists in 1984.
9 May	Meeting of British–Irish Interparliamentary Body delayed until the autumn.
11 May	Christopher Neeson (PSF), a Cookstown councillor, was jailed for three years on arms charge.
17 May	District Councils election polling day.
24 May	Review of the working of the AIA published in a 3,000-word document.
26 May	Patrick Corr, an unsuccessful PSF election candidate, charged with kidnapping in Cookstown.
31 May	Sir John Hermon retired as Chief Constable; succeeded by Hugh Annesley.
7 June	The aircraft manufacturer Shorts sold to Bombardier (Canada). Presbyterian General Assembly called for scrapping of AIA.

12 June	*Cook Report* on Central TV claimed a network of legitimate businesses helped to fund PIRA.
13 June	Mawhinney announced major education reforms, including financial support for integrated education.
15 June	European Parliament election and Dáil election.
12 July	Charles Haughey re-elected Taoiseach with PD support – first-ever Fianna Fáil coalition.
24 July	Cabinet reshuffle moved Tom King to Defence and Peter Brooke, Conservative Party chairman, to Secretary of State for NI. Subsequently John Cope replaced Ian Stewart, and the Government's team was completed by Peter Bottomley and Lord Skelmersdale.
6 August	NI allocated £535 million sterling from EC structural funds; Republic allowed £3 million sterling.
9 August	Merlyn Rees called for the suspension of the AIA.
13 August	Twentieth anniversary of the arrival of British troops in NI.
14 August	Brooke met Molyneaux and Paisley for talks. James Callaghan called for the conditional suspension of the AIA.
22 August	Lord Skelmersdale replaced three Unionist council nominees to health boards by two SDLP and one Alliance.
29 August	UFF produced confidential security forces files on PIRA suspects four days after its shooting of Loughlin McGinn in Rathfriland.
6 September	Unionist leaders rejected Kilfedder's offer to chair talks.
11 September	Another security forces document went missing and a chorus began for the disbandment of UDR.
12 September	Margaret Thatcher, visiting NI, described the UDR as 'a very, very, very brave group of men'. The Irish National Congress was launched in Dublin as part of PSF's 'broad front' strategy.
14 September	Anglo–Irish Intergovernmental Conference met in Dublin for seven hours.
19 September	International Fund for Ireland proposed to spend £4 million on urban development grants in thirty 'disadvantaged' towns.
21 September	Ray Burke said the Republic's Government wanted Britain to justify 'the very existence of the UDR'.
22 September	Ten killed by PIRA bomb at Royal Marines School of Music, Deal, Kent.
25 September	It was revealed that fifty-eight motions to the forthcoming Conservative Party conference advocated organising in NI. SDP's Scarborough conference permitted members to stand for election in NI.
27 September	Lord Colville appointed to review Emergency Provisions Act. John Taylor MP proposed a devolved assembly, with a committee structure based on proportionality and an institution with members drawn from Assembly and Dáil to replace the AIA.
2 October	Speaking at Labour Party conference fringe event, Gerry Adams, PSF president, supported 'IRA's right to engage in armed struggle'.
3 October	Confirmation given that UDR were in future to be armed with plastic bullets.
5 October	Anglo–Irish Intergovernmental Conference meeting in London broke up after eight hours and the shortest communiqué so far. Paisley postered Dublin with 'Hands off the UDR' posters and launched a petition to save the UDR at Stormont.

8 October	Twenty-eight UDR men arrested by RUC in dawn swoop on instruction from Stevens inquiry team.
10 October	Conservative Party conference voted to organise in NI.
11 October	Dick Spring called for suspension of AIA.
18 October	Anglo-Irish Intergovernmental Conference met at Stormont for record nine hours.
19 October	Guildford Four released by Court of Appeal and campaign pressure mounted to have the Birmingham Six released.
21 October	UUP conference at Enniskillen passed motion in favour of integration.
27 October	NI Civil Service Equal Opportunities Unit found a religious balance in the workforce but that the religious composition of the NIO was 78 per cent Protestant.
3 November	Brooke in an interview admitted PIRA could not be defeated militarily, and said he would not rule out talks with PSF if violence ended. He used Cyprus as an analogy to explain that he would not say 'never', but four days later expressed regret over the analogy.
4 November	SDLP at its Newcastle conference appealed to Unionists to talk to Dublin, and asked PIRA to lay down its guns.
9 November	Conservative National Union Executive unanimously accepted the affiliation of N. Down, Lagan Valley, E. Belfast and E. Londonderry.
15 November	The Unionist 'human chain' protest drew hundreds of anti-AIA protesters, not 300,000 as predicted.
16 November	PSF relaunched 'Scenario for Peace' document.
21 November	NUJ appealed in London High Court against broadcasting ban.
25 November	DUP annual conference decided to contest all safe Unionist seats, ending the electoral pact with the UUP.
30 November	Anglo-Irish Intergovernmental Conference meeting in Dublin agreed that ten meetings would take place in 1990.
8 December	Hume told Brooke he opposed suspension of AIA.
13 December	Alderdice accepted 'gap in conferences' method in order to enable talks to begin without suspension of AIA.
17 December	Molyneaux denied ending UUP boycott of ministers; they could meet on issues of 'very special importance'.
18 December	NI Minister Needham announced £65 million investment in Derry, half from a Boston developer.
21 December	Molyneaux dismissed 'gap in conferences' strategy without possibility of change in AIA. Neil Kinnock visited NI and supported devolution in the short term with Irish unity the goal.
22 December	EC announced £100 million grant for transport in NI.
31 December	*Observer* poll showed 51 per cent of people of Britain wanted withdrawal of troops; 36 per cent thought they should stay.

1990

1 January	New Fair Employment Act became law.
4 January	Community Relations Council launched.
9 January	Brooke speech in Bangor detected 'common ground' between NI parties on devolution. Ards became first Unionist council to end boycott of NIO Ministers.
13 January	Three men killed by army in raid on bookmaker's in W. Belfast.

16 January	UDA leader Tommy Lyttle appeared in court on charges resulting from the Stevens inquiry.
19 January	Hume met Brooke about possible talks.
22 January	Inaugural meeting held of Young Conservatives in NI.
29 January	Joint *Belfast Telegraph*/BBC *Newsnight* poll said 41 per cent of Catholics and 8 per cent of Protestants in NI supported AIA.
31 January	Anglo-Irish Intergovernmental Conference postponed by Dáil crisis. Irish Supreme Court appeal begun by McGimpsey brothers against 1988 decision on AIA.
2 February	PSF Ard Fheis rejected ceasefire as a 'precondition' of talks.
10 February	Hugh Annesley issued strategy document for RUC.
12 February	Green Party launched in NI at meeting in QUB.
19 February	Unionist leaders met Brooke at Stormont. BBC programme on UDR, highlighting the criminal record of its former members, produced an extensive reaction.
20 February	Brooke met Hume on talks.
21 February	'Hands off the UDR' petition handed to Downing Street by Paisley and McCrea.
23 February	Conservatives approved three more NI constituency associations, but deferred decision on Upper Bann, where a by-election was pending owing to the death of Harold McCusker, UUP MP.
24 February	UUP announced that its councillors would in future meet NIO Ministers on issues of 'special importance' to their area.
26 February	British-Irish Interparliamentary Body met for the first time in London and agreed that its deliberations would be secret for one year. DUP councillor Garry Haggan joined Conservatives.
1 March	Irish Supreme Court rejected McGimpsey appeal: Articles 2 and 3 were a 'claim of legal right' over the 'national territory'.
2 March	Anglo-Irish Intergovernmental Conference met in London.
8 March	Law Lords held that RUC officers in 1982 'shoot to kill' case could not be compelled to appear as witnesses at the dead men's inquests.
9 March	EC approved allocation of £112 million for training in NI until 1993.
13 March	Irish Supreme Court upheld two appeals against extradition; Thatcher was said to be 'hopping mad'.
23 March	Molyneaux told Ulster Unionist Council that McGimpsey case ruled out agreement on talks while Articles 2 and 3 remained. Brooke in Ballymena said there was 'no question' over the future of the UDR.
30 March	It was announced that Stevens report was not to be published. Fifty-eight files sent to DPP – thirty-four alleging possession of information likely to be of use to paramilitaries.
1 April	Brooke described UDR on its twentieth birthday as an essential element in anti-terrorist strategy, committed to 'justice, decency and democracy'.
5 April	Stevens report presented to Chief Constable of the RUC.
6 April	Application for extradition of Owen Carron quashed by Republic's Supreme Court.
7 April	John Alderdice told Alliance conference that AIA without extradition by Republic or devolution from UK was in danger of becoming a 'cynical masquerade'.
9 April	Four UDR men killed by landmine near Downpatrick. EC

	announced £113 million for transport infrastructure in NI.
11 April	Four hundred loyalists protested at Haughey visit to Institute of Directors conference in Belfast.
15 April	Adams told Easter Rising commemoration that the Republican struggle would last as long as a British presence in Ireland.
19 April	Anglo-Irish Intergovernmental Conference in London agreed to review extradition.
26 April	Home Office rescinded ban on Martin Galvin of NORAID.
27 April	The convictions of the Winchester Three, sentenced for conspiracy to murder Tom King, were quashed but exclusion orders were invoked against the three.
4 May	Brooke told Unionist leaders he would consider in principle alternatives to AIA.
11 May	Unionist leaders met Brooke; agreed on a gap in Anglo-Irish Intergovernmental Conference meetings as a device to enable talks to begin without suspension of AIA.
17 May	Summary of Stevens report published.
18 May	David Trimble won Upper Bann by-election for UUP.
22 May	Bank of Ireland said annual cost of Troubles to British and Irish Governments was £410 million. Molyneaux and Paisley stated they were 'well satisfied' with Brooke meeting.
24 May	Hume met Brooke in London.
28 May	Brooke met Taoiseach Haughey and Foreign Minister Collins in Dublin.
29 May	Police Federation passed vote of 'no confidence' in NIO and Secretary of State.
6 June	Catholic Hierarchy challenged Education Reform Order in Belfast High Court, alleging discrimination in favour of integrated schools.
8 June	Banbridge Council instituted power-sharing.
13 June	Lord O'Neill of the Maine died in Hampshire.
15 June	Brooke met SDLP and planned talks to begin after the summer holidays.
27 June	Brooke met Collins but the formula already agreed by Unionists – 'substantial progress' on devolution before North–South talks – was not accepted.
5 July	Brooke told Commons, on renewal of direct rule, that he was unable to report a schedule for talks.
11 July	Colville review of Emergency Provisions Act published.
17 July	Anglo-Irish Intergovernmental Conference in Belfast failed to find talks formula.
23 July	Peter Bottomley dropped from NIO in reshuffle.
24 July	A 1,000-lb command-wire bomb outside Armagh killed three RUC men and a nun, Sister Catherine Dunne.
26 July	Brooke told Commons he had not yet secured agreement on a basis for talks but would renew his initiative in September.
30 July	Ian Gow MP killed by PIRA bomb attached to his car at home in Sussex.
21 August	SDLP celebrated its twentieth birthday.
23 August	Molyneaux said he wanted UN to address Republic's constitutional claim to NI in light of Iraq's invasion of Kuwait.
24 August	Belfast man Brian Keenan released in Damascus after 1,574 days' captivity in Beirut.

28 August	NIO withdrew funding from Irish-language group Glór na nGael.
30 August	European Court of Human Rights judgment against UK, on grounds that arrests in 1986 breached the 'reasonable suspicion' requirement.
7 September	Brooke relaunched talks initiative in Ballymena. High Court in Belfast rejected appeal by Derry councillor Mitchel McLaughlin (PSF) against broadcasting ban.
14 September	Anglo-Irish Intergovernmental Conference meeting held in Dublin.
19 September	PM Thatcher in Budapest referred to PIRA conducting 'guerilla warfare' against Britain. Her remarks provoked annoyance in Dublin.
26 September	Brooke told reporters he might produce his own proposals for new political institutions in NI.
5 October	Catholic Bishops lost 'discrimination' case in Belfast High Court against Education Reform Order. British Labour Party voted against organising in NI.
9 October	Two PIRA activists were shot dead by army in Loughgall and three others were arrested. Fifty delegates from NI attended Conservative Party conference in Bournemouth.
11 October	Loophole in Fair Employment Act discovered, preventing an employer from disclosing religion of an employee.
24 October	Five soldiers killed at Cashquin near Derry and one soldier and a civilian killed at Cloghogue, Newry.
25 October	Anglo-Irish Intergovernmental Conference meeting in London failed to find formula for talks.
27 October	UUP conference in Newcastle, Co. Down, heard Molyneaux attack the Republic's territorial claim to NI.
31 October	Brooke said talks initiative was now 'on hold'.
5 November	Belfast City Council reviewed its anti-AIA ban on NIO Ministers attending Remembrance Day service.
7 November	Polling for presidency of Irish Republic. Mary Robinson elected.
9 November	Brooke told his constituency party that Britain had no selfish economic or strategic interest in NI and would accept unification by consent.
14 November	NI Social Attitudes survey said 56 per cent of NI Catholics favoured unification.
16 November	PM Thatcher visited security forces in Fermanagh. SDLP annual conference in Derry told by Alban Maginness to convert 10 per cent of Unionists to unity.
20 November	John Bruton, the new FG leader, endorsed proposals for change in Articles 2 and 3 of Republic's Constitution to include consent.
22 November	Margaret Thatcher resigned as Conservative Party leader and PM.
24 November	DUP annual conference heard Paisley reject power-sharing and any place for Dublin at devolution (internal) talks.
27 November	John Major elected Conservative leader and PM. Brigadier Angus Ramsay appointed new head of UDR.
29 November	Brian Mawhinney was promoted to Minister of State, and Lord Belstead replaced John Cope.
30 November	Seamus Mallon of SDLP argued for 'quasi-constitutional' changes in NI. Anglo-Irish Intergovenmental Conference meeting in Belfast sought movement on talks.

3 December	Ken Maginnis (UUP) attended inauguration of President Robinson. Jeremy Hanley appointed to NIO, replacing Lord Skelmersdale.
10 December	British-Irish Interparliamentary Body met in Dublin.
11 December	Mawhinney said OIRA was still active.
3 December	Needham draft order for privatisation and compulsory competitive tendering in District Councils.
16 December	In Armagh, Dr Cahal Daly installed as Catholic Primate.
19 December	Kenneth Baker, Home Secretary, retained the broadcasting ban, and extended it to cable and satellite.
20 December	Neil Kinnock visited NI.
23 December	PIRA declared a three-day ceasefire – the first for fifteen years.
28 December	Brooke article in *Belfast Telegraph* claimed 'real advances' and 'notable achievements' had been made in 1990.

1991

2 January	Belfast City Council rejected proposed invitation to President Mary Robinson.
7 January	Needham attacked Gerry Adams of PSF on PIRA fire-bomb campaign and its effects on jobs and investment.
14 January	Tom King, Defence Minister, visited NI.
17 January	Brooke heard SDLP objections at Westminster to a new talks formula enabling him to determine the timing of the Dublin government's entry into talks.
26 January	RUC raided offices of the Republican newspaper *An Phoblacht* in Belfast and removed computer and discs.
29 January	Tom Hartley confirmed that PSF would no longer comment on actions of PIRA. Rhonda Paisley called for a ban on the UDA.
31 January	After Anglo-Irish Intergovernmental Conference meeting in Dublin, Brooke said talks were 'a possibility, not a probability'.
1 February	Reports of moves towards a ceasefire, current since Christmas, were described by Adams as 'unfounded speculation'.
5 February	Brooke told reporters he might have to 'put up the shutters for the time being' on the talks.
7 February	PIRA launched three mortars at 10 Downing Street while Ministers were in session. House of Lords upheld the broadcasting ban on PSF and other named groups.
8 February	Republic agreed to allow Brooke to decide when it should enter talks.
14 February	PIRA spokesman denied reports of internal or PSF pressure for a ceasefire. Brooke told the Commons it was not yet possible to 'bridge the gap' to begin talks between NI parties, the NIO and Dublin ministers.
21 February	The High Court in Belfast ruled that 'gagging' of PSF by Belfast City Council in January was illegal.
22 February	John Major visited NI and praised the skill of Peter Brooke.
1 March	European Court of Human Rights agreed to hear a complaint against the UK's derogation from the European Convention over the power of seven-day detention of suspects allowed under the PTA.
5 March	Haughey told the Dáil that devolution did not commend itself to most NI parties.

13 March	A *Guardian*/International Communications and Marketing poll in Britain on NI said 43 per cent of people supported army withdrawal; on long-term solutions, 43 per cent supported Irish unity, whilst 30 per cent wanted NI to remain in UK.
14 March	Brooke told Commons of Easter deadline for a new talks formula. It was promptly accepted by Irish Government.
23 March	Major endorsed NI Conservatives at Southport.
25 March	DUP, UUP, Alliance and SDLP agreed on a formula for talks. Needham became the first NIO Minister to visit Belfast City Hall since AIA.
31 March	Seventy-fifth anniversary of the 1916 Easter Rising.
9 April	Anglo-Irish Intergovernmental Conference in Belfast announced ten-week gap after its next meeting on 26 April to allow for talks.
14 April	Bishop Desmond Tutu, at an Anglican conference in Newcastle, Co. Down, said PSF should be at the talks.
15 April	Brooke left for a week to promote the talks in US. Sir Kenneth Bloomfield retired as head of NI civil service, succeeded by David Fell.
22 April	Loyalist ceasefire announced for duration of the talks. Fair Employment Commission published religious composition of workforce showing a 65:35 ratio of Protestants to Catholics compared to 62:38 in population at large.
26 April	Anglo-Irish Intergovernmental Conference met in London, then was suspended for eleven weeks until 16 July to allow talks to take place.
30 April	Bilateral party meetings with Brooke began.
1 May	British Government accepted principle of an NI Select Committee, stating that it 'may be desirable', but rejected the timing of the Procedure Committee suggestion.
7 May	Bilateral talks at Stormont failed to resolve the impasse over the venue for North–South talks.
15 May	Unionist leaders refused Brooke Talks deadline and met PM Major instead on issues of venue and the independent chairman.
20 May	SDLP left talks until procedures agreed by others.
22 May	Venues for Strand Two of the talks, the North–South stage, agreed. Brooke was still looking for a chairman of sufficient standing.
25 May	PSF councillor Eddie Fullerton shot dead by UFF at his home in Buncrana, Co. Donegal.
28 May	Denis Haughey (SDLP) attended business committee meeting on Strand One talks at Stormont.
5 June	Parties agreed on a 17 June start to talks.
15 June	The independent chairman for the North–South strand of the talks was named as Sir Ninian Stephen, former Governor-General of Australia and Australian High Court judge.
17 June	Stormont talks began with opening statements.
25 June	Paisley said preparations by Maryfield for Anglo-Irish Intergovernmental Conference would end the talks.
26 June	Court of Appeal in London quashed the convictions of the Maguire Seven for the Guildford and Woolwich bombs.
28 June	Archbishop Cahal Daly elevated to Cardinal.
29 June	Queen presented colours to four UDR battalions in NI.

3 July	Brooke told the Commons that he had ended the talks. Unionists were not willing to talk beyond 9 July and the SDLP refused to present specific proposals.
4 July	The Combined Loyalist Military Command said its ceasefire would end at midnight.
12 July	A Gallup/Irish Marketing Surveys/Ulster Marketing Surveys opinion poll found massive support for resumption of Brooke Talks – 73 per cent in NI, 87 per cent in Republic and 79 per cent in GB.
16 July	Anglo-Irish Intergovernmental Conference met in Dublin for six hours.
17 July	David Blatherwick replaced Sir Nicholas Fenn as Ambassador to Republic.
23 July	Defence White Paper announced army cuts, including plans for the Royal Irish Rangers and UDR to merge. The military origin of the decision was asserted, and any 'political' consideration denied.
25 July	Brooke referred case of UDR Four, convicted of murder of Adrian Carroll, to Court of Appeal.
26 July	Preliminary report of 1991 census put population of NI at 1,569,971.
9 August	Gary Lynch, an Ulster Democratic Party election worker, was shot dead by PIRA in Derry.
11 August	PSF rally held to mark twentieth anniversary of internment and tenth of hunger strike.
12 August	Patrick Shanaghan, a PSF election worker, shot dead by UFF in Killen, Co. Tyrone.
21 August	Adams letter to British and Irish Governments and political and Church leaders sought 'open-ended discussions'.
26 August	NI Emergency Provisions Act came into force.
1 September	Democrat Tom Foley, Speaker of the US House of Representatives, led a delegation to NI. He urged Americans not to give to NORAID and refused to meet PSF until it renounced violence.
10 September	Brooke claimed NI parties' enthusiasm for talks but said, with an election looming, the timetable was 'against us'.
13 September	Anglo-Irish Intergovernmental Conference met at Stormont. Brooke again mentioned problem of election timetable.
16 September	Bernard O'Hagan, PSF councillor on Magherafelt council, was shot dead by UFF.
21 September	Brooke left for five-day visit to US.
27 September	Brooke, interviewed in *Irish Times*, said Articles 2 and 3 were 'not helpful' and warned that AIA could overturn itself if asked to carry too much.
1 October	Labour Party conference in Brighton heavily defeated a motion committing party to organise in NI.
2 October	Channel 4 *Dispatches* programme claimed that an 'inner circle' in RUC and UDR colluded with loyalists.
9 October	Conservative Party conference at Blackpool praised Brooke, recognised 'Irish dimension', reaffirmed constitutional position of NI and pledged full support for Tory candidates in NI in the general election.
15 October	Northern Ireland Centre in Europe opened in Brussels by EC president Jacques Delors.

16 October	At the Anglo-Irish Intergovernmental Conference meeting in London, the British Government reassured Collins that the Conservative conference debate did not signify any change in policy.
21 October	A BBC *Panorama* programme blamed Unionists for the breakdown of talks.
26 October	At UUP conference in Derry, Molyneaux advocated talks at Westminster with MPs only involved.
29 October	Peter Robinson said Unionists were being 'edged into a united Ireland'.
2 November	PIRA bombed Musgrave Park Hospital; two died, eighteen injured.
6 November	Public expenditure in NI during 1992–3 planned to be £7,030 million, an increase of 8.4 per cent.
13 November	UN Committee on Torture criticised British Government's refusal to videotape interviews with paramilitary suspects.
14 November	Fourteen hundred part-time UDR members called up.
18 November	Belfast City Council decide to take part in a community relations project.
20 November	Anglo-Irish Intergovernmental Conference met in Dublin. Ray Burke confirmed changes to extradition law.
21 November	British Social Attitudes survey showed 60 per cent favouring the withdrawal of troops and 56 per cent favouring Irish reunification (NI figures were 30 per cent and 25 per cent).
24 November	Explosion in Crumlin Road Prison killed two loyalist prisoners and injured seven others.
27 November	Four INLA members arrested at home of Laurence Kennedy, leader of NI Conservatives.
2 December	British-Irish Parliamentary Body met in Dublin and called for a single rail authority in Ireland.
4 December	Major met Haughey in Dublin and agreed to biannual meetings. It was first visit by a British PM since Thatcher in 1980.
9 December	Brooke announced a freeze on capital projects due to increased cost of bomb damage.
18 December	Anglo-Irish Intergovernmental Conference met in London. Brooke claimed there was a sea-change in the attitude of NI parties to talks.
19 December	Initiative '92 launched.
23 December	PIRA announced three-day ceasefire over Christmas.

1992

2 January	A new formula emerged for political talks.
3 January	Labour pledged to continue talks after election.
4 January	An 800-lb bomb left by PIRA in Belfast city centre caused extensive damage.
5 January	A 500-lb PIRA bomb exploded in Belfast city centre.
10 January	A 5-lb PIRA bomb in a briefcase exploded 300 yards from Downing Street.
13 January	DUP issued a document advocating security changes.
17 January	PIRA bomb killed seven Protestant workmen in a minibus at Teebane crossroads near Cookstown (an eighth died four days

later). Peter Brooke appeared on RTE's *Late, Late Show* and sang 'My Darling Clementine'.

20 January   John Major visited NI and met security chiefs.

22 January   Brian Nelson, former army agent and UDA intelligence officer, pleaded guilty to charges of conspiracy.

27 January   Brooke announced that it was not possible to launch 'fresh substantive talks'.

30 January   Charles Haughey announced his resignation.

2 February   On television, Brooke refused to rule out a post-election deal with Unionists; he warned if talks were exhausted a solution might be imposed that was more integrationist than devolutionist.

4 February   Three men shot dead at PSF Falls Road office by off-duty RUC man who later shot himself. President Mary Robinson visited women's groups in Belfast at the invitation of the EOC.

5 February   Five Catholics were murdered by loyalist gunmen at a bookmaker's on the Ormeau Road, Belfast.

6 February   Albert Reynolds elected leader of Fianna Fáil.

10 February   An extra battalion of troops was posted to NI.

11 February   PM Major and Brooke met the NI party leaders about security policy.

15 February   A 250-lb car bomb exploded in Belfast city centre.

16 February   Four PIRA members were shot dead by undercover soldiers at Clonoe, after an attack on Coalisland RUC station.

17 February   PSF published 'Towards a Lasting Peace in Ireland'.

19 February   Joe Doherty (PIRA) was deported from the US to NI.

22 February   Proinsias De Rossa and five other Workers' Party TDs left a party meeting in Dublin and formed a new organisation, initially called New Agenda and later Democratic Left.

24 February   The four main party leaders in NI were briefed by Brian Mawhinney on the running of NI.

26 February   The Taoiseach met John Major at Downing Street and later the Labour leader Neil Kinnock.

28 February   Leaders of the four main constitutional parties agreed to renew talks after the next Anglo-Irish Intergovernmental Conference meeting.

3 March   Paddy Ashdown opened Alliance election HQ in Bangor.

5 March   A 1,000-lb PIRA bomb devastated commercial centre of Lurgan, Co. Armagh. Another bomb caused extensive damage to Belfast city centre offices.

9 March   Delegates from the four parties met at Stormont for what was called 'the first plenary meeting of the first strand of the new political talks'. They agreed to meet after the election and a further Anglo-Irish Intergovernmental Conference meeting.

11 March   Major announced general election on 9 April.

20 March   BBC Radio Four debate took place between Adams and Hume.

24 March   A 500-lb PIRA bomb near Donegall Pass RUC station in Belfast caused extensive damage to the area.

25 March   An *Irish Times*/MORI poll on British attitudes towards NI found 31 per cent supported NI becoming independent, 29 per cent favoured NI remaining in the UK and 23 per cent favoured a united Ireland.

28 March   New Agenda held its first conference in Dublin and adopted the name Democratic Left.

3 April	Molyneaux advised UUP voters to support Robinson (DUP) in E. Belfast and Jim Kilfedder (PUP) in N. Down.
5 April	Bill Clinton told the American-Irish Presidential Forum in Manhattan that he would reverse the ban on Adams entering the US, back the MacBride Principles, appoint a peace envoy to NI, explore possibilities for UN involvement and raise human rights violations with the British government.
10 April	Conservatives won the UK general election with a majority of twenty-one. In NI the only seat change was in W. Belfast where Joe Hendron (SDLP) defeated Gerry Adams (PSF).
11 April	Former Attorney-General Sir Patrick Mayhew replaced Peter Brooke as Secretary of State for NI.
23 April	Two former Presbyterian Moderators, who had spoken to the UDA, revealed that they had had talks with Gerry Adams and Tom Hartley of PSF.
27 April	The Anglo-Irish Intergovernmental Conference in London agreed a three-month suspension of meetings for political talks in NI to recommence.
29 April	Political talks reconvened at Stormont with statements from the four parties.
8 May	To counter PIRA actions in GB, Home Secretary Kenneth Baker moved responsibility for intelligence-gathering from the Metropolitan Police to the Security Service (MI5).
1 June	Derry City Council elected a DUP mayor for the first time.
12 June	Deadlock reached on Strand One talks, on institutions and relations within NI, but parties agreed to move to the next stages.
19 June	Sir Ninian Stephen chaired a discussion in London on a provisional agenda for Strand Two talks on the North–South relationship.
25 June	Molyneaux/Paisley motion in Commons for an NI select committee was supported by Liberal Democrats, Scots and Welsh Nationalists, but opposed by the Government.
1 July	Royal Irish Regiment came into existence with the amalgamation of the UDR and the RIR.
6 July	Strand Two of the talks process began at Lancaster House in London.
24 July	Strand Two talks adjourned until 2 September.
29 July	Three of the UDR Four had their convictions quashed by the Appeal Court in Belfast, but Neil Latimer was not released.
2 August	Two bombs of over 200 lbs exploded in Bedford Street, Belfast, causing extensive damage there for the second time in 1992.
10 August	Sir Patrick Mayhew banned the UDA from midnight.
27 August	Hugh McKibben, aged 21, became the 3,000th 'official' victim of the Troubles. The figure did not include 113 people killed in Britain, 110 killed in the Republic and 18 killed in Europe.
2 September	Strand Two talks recommenced at Stormont.
7 September	President Mary Robinson visited Derry and Enniskillen.
9 September	Ian Paisley and Peter Robinson walked out of the Strand Two talks at Stormont.
21 September	UUP delegation led by Molyneaux began three days of Strand Two talks at Dublin Castle, their first formal discussions there since 1922.
23 September	A 2,000-lb PIRA bomb destroyed the NI forensic science

laboratories in S. Belfast, damaging 700 homes and injuring twenty persons.

25 September Meeting between John Major and Albert Reynolds in London set 16 November as the date for the next Anglo-Irish Intergovernmental Conference meeting and a limit to the talks.

30 September DUP returned to talks to discuss Articles 2 and 3.

12 October Election Court began hearing petition against the election of Joe Hendron (SDLP) in W. Belfast.

16 October Sheena Campbell, a law student and PSF candidate in the Upper Bann by-election in 1990, was shot dead by UVF in Belfast.

20 October Robert Irvine became the first member of the new RIR to be shot dead by PIRA.

21 October A 200-lb PIRA bomb destroyed main street of Bangor, Co. Down.

3 November Belfast Brigade of IPLO disbanded after PIRA action killed one and injured eight members in feud.

4 November NIO offered Catholic schools 100 per cent capital funding.

6 November UFF extended its campaign to 'the entire Republican community' after attacks on Protestant homes and housing estates. Irish Government Coalition collapsed.

7 November Dublin-based Army Council faction of the IPLO announced that it was disbanding.

9 November UUP tabled series of proposals to stop the talks collapsing.

10 November Maryfield secretariat began work for the Anglo-Irish Intergovernmental Conference meeting and Unionists withdrew from the talks process.

13 November Massive van bomb blitzed commercial heart of Coleraine.

14 November PSF won High Court action against Belfast City Council's anti-AIA committee structure, which retained power in Unionist hands. Three men shot dead by UFF at Oldpark bookmaker's shop.

16 November Anglo-Irish Intergovernmental Conference in Dublin reviewed talks procedures and favoured bilateral talks over the previous large conference and three-strand process.

23 November SACHR chairman Charles Hill sought a Bill of Rights and an enlarged role for the organisation to promote human rights issues.

1 December Bomb in shopping area of central Belfast injured twenty-seven people.

8 December NI Public Expenditure figures for 1993–4 announced, showing a planned total of £7,460 million, an increase of 5.3 per cent. 'Safety net' negotiated with Treasury for Compensation Agency to meet larger-than-expected property damage claims. Unionists on Belfast City Council proposed power-sharing deal whereby chairmanships and committee membership would be based on party share of the vote.

9 December Republic signed deal for a gas link with Scotland.

15 December A story alleging the tapping of John Hume's phone broke in the press.

16 December Sir Patrick Mayhew's Coleraine speech interpreted by Unionists as giving 'wrong signal' to PSF.

17 December Sir Louis Blom-Cooper QC appointed to oversee conditions at the three holding centres.

18 December John Smith, Labour Party leader, visited NI.

22 December Adams, in reply to Mayhew's speech, urged a UN and EC role in peace-making and criticised the exclusion of PSF from talks as undemocratic.

24 December   PIRA declared a three-day ceasefire over Christmas.

1993

1 January   Irish National Congress reopened twelve border roads from Donegal to Dundalk to mark the end of EC internal boundaries.

4 January   SDLP reject proportional power-sharing on Belfast City Council in talks on rotation of offices.

6 January   Incendiaries detonated in four Oxford Street stores in London.

7 January   Fianna Fáil-Labour Government formed by Albert Reynolds; its policy on NI was criticised as 'vague' by opposition parties.

10 January   Major-General Roger Neil Wheeler was named as GOC (NI) in succession to Lieutenant-General Sir John Wilsey.

11 January   Sir Patrick Mayhew told BBC that Articles 2 and 3 of the Irish Constitution were 'unhelpful' and were central to future talks.

12 January   *The Times* reported that the UDA planned to target the 'pan-Nationalist front' – defined to include the SDLP, PSF, the Irish Government, PIRA and the GAA.

13 January   Spring promised 'openness and flexibility' in new talks which he said he wanted urgently.

17 January   John Alderdice told BBC that Sir Patrick Mayhew saw his role as similar to that of Chris Patten in Hong Kong – of unity by consent but in the medium term.

19 January   The Opsahl commission began its hearings in Belfast.

22 January   Sir Patrick Mayhew met Dick Spring for informal talks in Dublin and agreed to an Anglo-Irish Intergovernmental Conference meeting early in February and informal party talks before any resumed talks process.

25 January   Cardinal Daly told the BBC programme *Songs of Praise* that there could be peace 'by the end of the year'.

27 January   Irish Cabinet created a new committee to monitor NI policy.

30 January   Bloody Sunday rally attended by 5,000 people in Derry.

2 February   UDA planted incendiaries outside homes of two SDLP councillors.

3 February   The Anglo-Irish Intergovernmental Conference meeting in London decided to invite the parties to bilateral talks; two PIRA bombs exploded in London, one on a train and one in an underground station.

8 February   Leaders of four main Churches visited the US to appeal for new business investment.

10 February   The Taoiseach nominated Gordon Wilson of Enniskillen to the Irish Senate.

16 February   In an *Irish News* interview PSF president Gerry Adams sought 'inclusive dialogue' and new Irish-British agreement to end partition.

17 February   The SDLP met the Republic's Government in Dublin for a 'wide-ranging review' of the prospects for North–South talks.

22 February   An election court found Joe Hendron MP and his election agent guilty of a number of corrupt and illegal practices in the 1992 W. Belfast election but granted them relief on grounds of 'inadvertence'.

24 February   John Major met President Clinton in Washington and stated afterwards that he did not find the 'peace envoy' idea useful.

28 February   Spring told BBC that Articles 2 and 3 of Irish Constitution were not 'cast in bronze' and that change, if necessary, would be implemented.

3 March   Six UDR men were awarded undisclosed damages against the RUC Chief Constable for their arrest on the instructions of the Stevens inquiry in 1989.

5 March   Spring's speech to the Irish Association, accepting change in the Irish Constitution and a guarantee of minority rights, was welcomed for its different tone.

7 March   Bangor Main Street hit by 500-lb bomb.

8 March   Sir Parick Mayhew welcomed Spring's Irish Association speech as showing someone he could 'do business with'.

10 March   In the Commons, the Prevention of Terrorism Act was renewed by 329 votes to 202.

12 March   The European Parliament, at the request of John Hume, decided to report on how EC institutions could help the NI conflict.

16 March   John Major, in the Commons, ruled out devolved assemblies for UK regions.

20 March   Warrington bomb killed two children and sparked Peace Initiative '93.

23 March   Anglo-Irish Intergovernmental Conference meeting in Belfast agreed to continue to enhance security co-operation.

24 March   Taoiseach Reynolds disciplined backbench comment on Articles 2 and 3 of Constitution.

25 March   UFF killed four Catholic workmen at Castlerock. Republic's Senate held its first debate on NI in eight years.

28 March   Hume advocated an imposed blueprint and referendum device to bypass parties if necessary. *Sunday Telegraph* poll in Britain showed 56 per cent no longer wanted NI to remain in the UK.

30 March   RTE lost Supreme Court challenge to ban PSF access to media in Section 31 of the Broadcasting Authority Act.

1 April   *News Letter* readers' poll said 42 per cent agreed with loyalist paramilitary violence. Dáil debated NI, and Spring met Mayhew in Dublin.

2 April   Spring supported use of a referendum North and South to overcome Unionist refusal to talk. Alliance Party conference called on Governments to resume Stage Three talks.

6 April   John Major, on a two-day visit to NI, said proposals would be presented once talks began.

8 April   Gordon Wilson said he was saddened by his meeting with PIRA.

10 April   John Hume met Gerry Adams for 'extensive discussions' arranged by priests and welcomed by Cardinal Daly.

11 April   Hume and Adams both rejected devolution as a solution to the NI conflict.

16 April   Spring told British Irish Association meeting in Oxford that the solution lay in a 'Europe of the regions'.

17 April   Foreign Secretary Douglas Hurd said the Republic's Government had a 'crucial role' in new talks and that its willingness to change the Constitution was a 'positive context'.

19 April   Mayhew met Alderdice in fresh round of exploratory talks.

20 April	Molyneaux presented his 'Blueprint for Stability' to John Major in London.
21 April	Reynolds made a seven-day visit to US: in Boston he stated that the peace envoy idea was 'not appropriate at present'.
23 April	Mayhew, in a speech to the Institute of Irish Studies, Liverpool, said the Government rejected joint sovereignty and aimed to devolve wide powers; he mentioned a select committee and said the Government saw no realistic prospect of change in the constitutional status of Northern Ireland.
24 April	The Bishopsgate bomb in London caused £350 million damage. Hume and Adams issued a joint statement on their talks, excluding an internal settlement and asserting the right to 'national self-determination' of the Irish people as a whole.
25 April	An interview in *Die Zeit* by Mayhew, in which he tried to argue a 'disinterested' case by remarking on the £3,000 million per year subsidy, and on the effect of a settlement on the issue of sovereignty, provoked controversy among Unionists.
28 April	Paisley refused to enter talks that many expected after the District Council elections. The previous day Molyneaux had rejected talks while the SDLP talked to PSF.
5 May	Gerry Adams (PSF) was refused a US visitor's visa.
9 May	UVF threatened to kill politicians in the Republic if Republican violence increased.
10 May	Mayhew promised proposals for new talks; the initiative would be a British plan without prior consultations with the Republic. A Belgian MEP began a three-day inquiry for the European Parliament into fair employment.
12 May	A PIRA bomb exploded in Oxford.
17 May	The Combined Loyalist Military Command said it would study the election results for evidence of 'pan-Nationalist candidates' co-operating together.
19 May	District Council elections were held for the 582 seats on twenty-six District Councils. The new boundaries were drawn by the Independent Boundary Commissioner.
20 May	A 1,000-lb bomb exploded in Glengall Street, Belfast, causing damage estimated at £6.5 million.
21 May	The election results showed increased representation for PSF, the SDLP, Alliance and UUP.
22 May	PIRA exploded a 1,000-lb bomb in Portadown and a 1,500-lb bomb in Magherafelt.
25 May	The Anglo-Irish Intergovernmental Conference met in Dublin.
26 May	The European Commission of Human Rights rejected an appeal against seven-day detention under the Prevention of Terrorism Act.
27 May	Queen met Irish President Mary Robinson at Buckingham Palace. Jeremy Hanley returned to London to the Ministry of Defence and was succeeded at Stormont as Minister for Political Affairs and Education by Michael Ancram.
1 June	Reg Empey was elected Lord Mayor of Belfast, with Hugh Smyth as Deputy.
6 June	It was announced that women soldiers would be armed with SA80 rifles from October.

8 June	Mayhew met Molyneaux in London to start a new round of bilateral talks.
9 June	The Opsahl commission report was published, containing twenty-five main recommendations.
10 June	Jean Kennedy Smith was confirmed as US Ambassador to the Republic.
11 June	Amnesty International criticised emergency powers in NI. John Smith met Dublin party leaders. Queen visited NI. Hume met Adams for further talks.
15 June	SACHR requested changes in the method of legislating for NI away from the Order-in-Council procedure.
16 June	PM Major and Taoiseach Reynolds met in London and called for talks to resume.
18 June	President Mary Robinson paid an unofficial visit, against British Government advice, to community groups in Belfast, where she met Gerry Adams, and to Coalisland, where PSF councillors were present.
24 June	NIO Minister Michael Mates resigned as a result of increasing pressure arising from his links with Asil Nadir, the fugitive former head of Polly Peck, revealed the previous month.
25 June	Sir John Wheeler replaced Mates at the NIO.
26 June	PM Major paid a two-day visit to NI. Rioting broke out when the RUC stopped the Whiterock Orange march.
28 June	A Labour discussion document, 'Options for a Labour Government', proposed joint authority with the Republic for twenty years.
30 June	The British-Irish Parliamentary Body met in Cork.
1 July	The annual report of the SACHR advocated a review of the law on lethal force and the videorecording of RUC interviews.
2 July	The RUC decided not to attend police liaison committees where PSF councillors were present.
5 July	A 1,500-lb bomb exploded in the centre of Newtownards.
8 July	In a *Guardian* interview, published on the morning of an Anglo-Irish Intergovernmental Conference meeting, Dick Spring advocated that Dublin and London set out a framework settlement and use the device of a referendum to appeal directly to the public over the heads of objecting politicians.
11 July	Molyneaux claimed that peace proposals had been put to PIRA at the end of 1992 by the NIO.
18 July	On the same day as Sir Patrick Mayhew said it was 'damaging' to suggest that PIRA was winning, Sir Edward Heath said he would talk to PIRA at the 'right moment'.
23 July	PM Major told the Commons that there had been no deal with the Ulster Unionists in return for support on the Social Chapter vote on the Maastricht Treaty, but speculation was rife.
27 July	Taoiseach Reynolds warned that an NI select committee could undermine the AIA. Laurence Kennedy (Cons.) resigned his seat on N. Down Borough Council in protest at the Conservative/UUP 'understanding'.
2 August	Molyneaux told the *Belfast Telegraph* that he had proposed to John Major in April a devolved administration with powers extending to the main local government services, centralised since 1973, and that he expected it to be effective by 1995.

5 August	Hugh Brady, a PSF councillor in Derry, resigned after being fined for possession of cannabis.
11 August	The RUC Chief Constable announced that women members of the force would be armed from April 1994.
12 August	RUC intercepted a 3,000-lb van bomb in Portadown, Co. Armagh. RUC figures showed thirty-seven killed in the first seven months of 1993, fifteen fewer than the same period in 1992, despite the sustained level of loyalist paramilitary activity.
13 August	PIRA fire-bombed Bournemouth pier and four shops.
14 August	ETA delegation from Basque country in Spain visited Belfast to support PSF and PIRA.
16 August	Strabane town centre bombed by PIRA.
19 August	Jean Kennedy Smith, US Ambassador to Ireland, made an unofficial two-day visit to Fermanagh and Derry.
23 August	NIO denied *Sunday Times* claim that it had put fifty-point ceasefire plan to PIRA at Christmas 1992.
26 August	Sir John Wheeler told BBC that 'the IRA is already defeated' and that it was 'fossilised in a campaign that simply cannot win, cannot succeed'.
27 August	PIRA reply to Wheeler said it would meet 'head-on any British persistence with the failed policies of the past'.
1 September	Belfast City Council banned President Mary Robinson from council property.
2 September	Prison officer Jim Peacock shot dead by loyalist paramilitaries.
6 September	European Commission of Human Rights accepted a case brought by relatives of the Gibraltar Three under Article 2 (Right to Life).
7 September	Labour Party conference motions published, with six on organising in NI. Ken Maginnis claimed Irish border security costs were exaggerated – more like £2.1 million a year than £1 million a day.
8 September	Initiative '92 promoters appealed to Secretary of State Mayhew to break the deadlocked talks by acting on the main findings of the Opsahl report.
10 September	Three detectives from the UDR Four case sent for trial. Anglo-Irish Intergovernmental Conference met in London and Mayhew repeated the assurance that there was no deal with Unionists and that the three-strand process for talks would continue. Cardinal Daly criticised the use of the phrase 'pan-Nationalist'.
11 September	September Conservative conference resolutions published and showed thirty-seven advocating integration. There were reports of a secret bid to end loyalist violence.
12 September	Mayhew speech to British Irish Association meeting in Cambridge advocated urgency, patience and flexibility in the talks process. He said an NIO document was 'no blueprint' but it would provide 'focus and direction'. DUP announced their 'Breaking the Log-Jam' document.
14 September	Jean Kennedy Smith, US Ambassador to Ireland, visited Belfast as part of a week-long fact-finding visit.
16 September	Major met Hume at Downing Street. At press conference afterwards Hume said he hoped for renewed talks in six months and that he did not care 'two balls of roasted snow' about the reaction to the talks with Adams.
17 September	Major met Paisley at Downing Street and received the DUP

document 'Breaking the Log-Jam'. Afterwards he criticised Hume as the voice of 'pan-Nationalism'.

18 September   RUC denied PSF claims of a policy of refusing licensed weapons to its members, stating that five councillors already had personal weapons. Martin McGuinness interview in the *Guardian* spoke of the 'right to self-determination of the Irish people' and any new structure of Government would be up to the people of Ireland.

20 September   Adams feared that pressure from SDLP members might end talks with Hume. Joe Hendron spoke about his position as MP being undermined.

21 September   UFF placed bombs at the homes of four SDLP councillors. After a few days of doubts, the top SDLP members expressed full support for the Hume–Adams talks. Reynolds said he had received 'very positive signals' from the British Government about the prospects of talks.

22 September   David Trimble (UUP) attacked the Hume–Adams talks as 'misconceived and bound to fail'. He said the talks 'create a distance between the SDLP and constitutional parties' and criticised the language of the documents as '1920s Republicanism'. Sir John Wheeler said the first priority was to end terrorism – just four weeks after he had said that the IRA were defeated.

23 September   Campaign for Labour Representation dissolved after sixteen years. SDLP met Ancram on future talks.

24 September   Paisley selected by DUP as candidate for the European Parliamentary election in 1994 at party meeting in Portadown.

25 September   A joint statement from John Hume and Gerry Adams reported considerable progress on a peace process, which they forwarded to Dublin.

27 September   Rumours appeared in the press doubting the existence of a Hume–Adams report.

28 September   Unionists rejected calls by the UDA for the boycott of Government.

29 September   Mayhew asserted the right of 'self-determination of the people living in NI' and said that violence had to end 'for real' before PSF could sit at the conference table.

30 September   It was revealed that thirty PSF officials had been briefed on the Hume–Adams document while few SDLP members or MPs were informed of its content.

1 October   DUP delegation met Michael Ancram but refused to discuss their 'Breaking the Log-Jam' document until he undertook to ignore the Hume–Adams initiative.

2 October   PIRA bombs injured six people in London. Dick Spring addressed the UN on Ireland.

4 October   PIRA statement welcomed the Hume–Adams initiative.

6 October   James Molyneaux told a Conservative Party conference fringe meeting in Blackpool that the Hume–Adams initiative had wrecked any chance of renewed inter-party talks. Rev. Ian Paisley wrote to John Major, claiming Hume–Adams 'aimed at Ulster's destruction'. Taoiseach Reynolds repeated that in an 'overall settlement' a referendum would change Articles 2 and 3 of the Irish Constitution.

7 October   John Hume met Taoiseach Reynolds and Tánaiste Spring in Dublin and provided a document containing the broad principles on which he and Adams had agreed a peace process could be established. Dáil opposition parties criticised the secrecy surrounding the initiative. Adams, speaking in Dublin, said a declaration by the British Government on the right of the Irish people to self-determination would end PIRA violence.

8 October PM Major's keynote address to his 'Conservative and Unionist' Party conference said the only message he wanted from PIRA was that it was finished with violence for good. After a series of sectarian attacks, the Church of Ireland Primate, Dr Robin Eames, condemned the UFF threat to the Catholic community.

9 October Sir Patrick Mayhew, speaking on Radio Ulster, stated that the people of NI had a right of self-determination and that PSF could only be involved in talks after PIRA violence had ended and a 'sufficient period' had shown this was 'for real'. John Taylor (UUP) said loyalist paramilitaries should end their murder campaign.

10 October A *Sunday Independent* poll revealed 72 per cent in the Republic supported the Hume–Adams talks. Taoiseach Reynolds met Nelson Mandela of the African National Congress, who endorsed the Hume–Adams initiative. The *Sunday Times* serialisation of Margaret Thatcher's memoirs revealed her disappointment at the AIA and the need for an alternative approach. President Mary Robinson launched a peace project in Warrington.

11 October Rev. Martin Smyth (UUP) told BBC that PSF could be included in talks on what was best for 'Northern Ireland within the United Kingdom' if they stopped trying to impose their will by acts of violence on the Northern majority. Next day Peter Robinson described this comment as 'monumental folly'.

12 October Taoiseach Reynolds and Tánaiste Spring briefed Irish Cabinet on meeting with Hume. Mary Harney, the new leader of the Progressive Democrats, said good relations with all 'constitutional' parties in the North was 'extremely important' to her.

13 October Reynolds refused opposition request in the Dáil for a debate on NI, claiming the issue was too delicate. Adams said peace would be the result of 'total demilitarisation' and was not a 'prerequisite' for a peace process.

15 October *Ulster News Letter* telephone poll found 62 per cent opposed to PSF involvement in talks, even after a genuine ceasefire. NIO Equal Opportunities Unit found Catholics were fairly represented in the NI civil service, except at senior level. Around 1,000 people, including Shorts workers, attended a protest meeting after the UFF killing of Joseph Reynolds and the wounding of five others on their way to work in the factory.

16 October Molyneaux told the UUP conference in Craigavon, Co. Armagh, that the Hume–Adams initiative sought NI's future outside the UK. He proposed a lengthy period of 'quarantine' after any PIRA cessation of violence before they could participate in talks. Kevin McNamara, in Cork, opposed the unilateral abandonment of the constitutional claim.

17 October Taoiseach Reynolds said at Bodenstown that there would be 'no secret agreement' with 'organisations supporting violence' in order to achieve peace.

19 October PM Major told the Commons he 'knew nothing' of the details of

Hume–Adams talks. Home Secretary Michael Howard signed an exclusion order against Gerry Adams, who had been invited by Tony Benn (Lab.) to address a meeting at Westminster.

20 October After a meeting with Michael Ancram, John Alderdice (All.) said the Hume–Adams initiative had thrown a shadow over efforts to revive talks. The Institute for Public Policy Research advocated shared authority in NI 'by its peoples and the British and Irish Governments'.

21 October Sir Patrick Mayhew told the Commons that bilateral discussions were taking place but round-table talks at the moment would be 'counter-productive'. Alliance won the N. Down–Holywood by-election vacated by Laurence Kennedy (Cons.).

22 October PSF retained the Derry–Cityside seat vacated on the resignation of Hugh Brady. The day after killing John Gibson, PIRA threatened five firms alleged to be supplying building materials to the security forces.

23 October A PIRA bomb at a fish shop on the Shankill Road killed nine (ultimately ten) and injured fifty-eight. One bomber killed, and another injured.

24 October Anglo-Irish Intergovernmental Conference meeting of 27 October postponed as mark of respect for Shankill victims. UUP on Belfast City Council decided to break relations with SDLP until Hume–Adams initiative ended.

25 October Thousands of workers from Harland and Wolff and Shorts walked to scene of Shankill bombing.

26 October UFF killed two Catholic workmen and injured five others at refuse depot at Kennedy Way in W. Belfast. Gerry Adams carried coffin of Shankill bomber, Thomas Begley.

27 October Spring outlined in Dáil six 'democratic principles' for a sustainable peace, including the principle of consent and the right to withhold it. Peace rallies were held in Dublin, Limerick, Galway and other venues.

28 October UVF killed two Catholic brothers near Waringstown, Co. Down.

29 October Major met Reynolds at the EC summit in Brussels, and issued a statement saying that initiatives could only come from Governments; there would be no secret deals with supporters of violence as the price for its cessation; if violence ended, the two Governments would respond imaginatively.

30 October Seven killed – six Catholic and one Protestant – and thirteen injured in UFF gun attack inside Rising Sun bar at Greysteel, Co. Derry, making October the worst month for casualties in seventeen years.

1 November Major told Hume, after having been informed of his proposals by Reynolds, that they were 'not the right way to proceed'. He would intensify efforts at inter-party talks.

2 November Major proposed to meet the leaders of the four main constitutional parties to clear the way for talks. DUP and UUP refuse to talk to SDLP until Hume–Adams talks are ended. Major ordered review of the broadcasting restrictions on PSF.

3 November ICTU organised peace rallies in Belfast and Derry. Anglo-Irish Intergovernmental Conference meeting in Belfast agreed to work on 'a framework for peace, stability and reconciliation'. Reynolds met John Hume and John Alderdice in separate meetings.

4 November	Senator Gordon Wilson revealed that he and two others had met three loyalist paramilitary leaders earlier in the week and planned a further meeting. Major met Alderdice, then Hume, at Downing Street.
6 November	Reynolds told FF Ard Fheis that peace could begin at the end of the year. Adams rejected Spring's six principles as 'the basis for a peace process'.
7 November	Greysteel peace rally attracted 3,000 people.
9 November	Paisley and Molyneaux met Major separately.
11 November	Michael Ancram completed his bilateral talks with parties after meeting UUP in London. DUP published 'Breaking the Log-Jam' document suggesting a new Assembly.
12 November	*Irish Press* reported that Reynolds was prepared to 'walk away' and pursue his own proposals.
15 November	PM Major's Guildhall speech said there was a 'better opportunity for peace in Northern Ireland than for many years'.
16 November	Spring met President Clinton in Washington.
18 November	Sixteen peace rallies organised by ICTU. Phone-in for *Ulster News Letter* and *Irish News* registered 157,457 calls for peace.
19 November	The *Irish Press* published a draft paper from the Republic's Department of Foreign Affairs that anticipated UK recognition of 'the full legitimacy and value of the goal of Irish unity by agreement'.
20 November	Hume met Adams and they issued a third joint statement, emphasising that the British response was crucial.
21 November	Rally for Hume–Adams initiative attended by 2,000 people on Falls Road in W. Belfast.
22 November	Sir Patrick Mayhew told QUB audience there could be no talks with PSF until PIRA violence ended.
24 November	A UVF arms shipment from Poland was seized at Teesport. DUP delegation met Major at Downing Street.
25 November	A PIRA spokesperson told the *Irish Times* there would be no unilateral cessation of violence. US Congress debate heard criticism of British policy from Irish-American lobby and support for Hume–Adams talks.
27 November	SDLP conference in Cookstown, Co. Tyrone, told by Hume that PM Major held 'the key to peace'. DUP conference at Castlereagh in Belfast warned by Paisley of 'the greatest threat to the Union since the Home Rule Crisis'.
28 November	*Observer* revealed that a channel of communication had existed between British Government and PIRA for years.
29 November	Documents, published by PSF, of their recent contacts with the Government pointed up differences from those later laid in Commons by Sir Patrick Mayhew. Paisley was suspended from Commons for accusing Mayhew of lying.
1 December	Mayhew admitted there were twenty-two errors in documents about contacts with Republican movement. Cardinal Cahal Daly addressed Catholic parliamentarians at Westminster.
2 December	PSF released more documents on its contacts with the Government.
3 December	*Irish Times*/Coopers and Lybrand poll found 33 per cent of Catholics favoured joint authority, 32 per cent, Irish unity;

35 per cent of Protestants favoured integration. 'Power-sharing' devolution had 26 per cent support and most cross-community support. John Major met Albert Reynolds in Dublin. Paisley delivered a protest letter to Dublin Castle.

5 December	Around 1,000 people attended an inter-denominational service in Keady, Co. Armagh, where a soldier had been shot dead three days before.
8 December	Visit of Diana, Princess of Wales, to NI.
10 December	Reynolds and Major met in margins of EC heads of states summit in Brussels. John Smith, visiting Derry, said PSF could be admitted to talks if PIRA violence ended.
11 December	*Irish Times*/Coopers and Lybrand poll found 59 per cent support in NI for Reynolds–Major talks (88 per cent of Catholics, 37 per cent of Protestants). A further Reynolds–Major meeting failed to resolve differences. Two RUC men were shot dead in Fivemiletown, Co. Tyrone.
12 December	*Sunday Press* revealed that Reynolds planned an all-Ireland convention, including PSF, when PIRA violence ended. Reynolds told RTE that 70 per cent of a draft declaration had been agreed.
14 December	Mayhew announced that he had offered to resign over the twenty-two 'transcription and typographical errors' in documents placed in Commons.
15 December	Downing Street Declaration published. In Commons, Major emphasised the items that were *not* included in the declaration in order to reassure Unionists.
17 December	Press and media sought to gauge public reaction to declaration. A UTV phone-in attracted 50,090 calls, of which 51.3 per cent were pro-declaration. Paisley called for a referendum in NI. Major announced decision to create an NI Select Committee.
18 December	Paisley promised series of province-wide rallies.
20 December	Hume met Adams and arranged to meet again when PSF concluded its analysis of the declaration.
21 December	Molyneaux said he aimed for an NI Assembly in 1994.
22 December	PM Major visited NI and met the constitutional party leaders at Hillsborough. PSF called for 'direct and unconditional dialogue'. Ulster Marketing Surveys/ITN poll found 56 per cent in favour of the declaration; 61 per cent wanted to remain in the UK, 25 per cent wanted a united Ireland and 14 per cent did not know or failed to reply.
23 December	Acquittal of two marines on grounds of 'reasonable doubt' in the Caraher murder case attracted criticism. Paisley article in the *Belfast Telegraph* entitled 'The Great Sell Out'.
24 December	PIRA was widely criticised for having only three-day ceasefire at Christmas.
25 December	Queen's Christmas message mentioned NI.
27 December	Fintona police station in Co. Tyrone attacked by mortars.
28 December	Two hundred influential Irish-Americans praise British and Irish Governments in *New York Times*. Republican meeting at Loughmacrory, Co. Tyrone, attended by 300 expressed negative views on the declaration.
30 December	Soldier shot by sniper in Crossmaglen, Co. Armagh. PIRA

New Year message spoke of twenty-six years of unbroken struggle and of 'lasting peace' inextricably linked to the 'right of the Irish people to national self-determination'.

31 December Permanent Secretary, NIO, John Chilcot, was knighted in the New Year's honours.

DICTIONARY
OF NORTHERN IRELAND POLITICS

A

ABERCORN, DUKE OF
Unionist MP for Fermanagh-S. Tyrone,
1964–70. Sat in Parliament as Marquess of
Hamilton, succeeding to Dukedom in
June 1979. b. 4 July 1934. Member,
Council of Europe, 1966–70; European
Economic and Social Committee,
1973–8. Conservative. Served in UDR,
1974–8. Wide business interests include
chairmanship of North West Exploration,
a mining company exploring in Co.
Tyrone and other sites in Ireland;
chairmanship of the Laganside
Corporation, set up in 1987 to develop
the River Lagan frontage in Belfast; and
chairmanship of TVNI, which made an
unsuccessful bid for the NI ITV franchise
in 1991. NI Industrial Development
Board, 1982–. Her Majesty's Lieutenant
for Co. Tyrone, 1986–.

**ABERCORN RESTAURANT
BOMBING**
The explosion of a bomb in the crowded
central Belfast restaurant, the Abercorn,
on 4 March 1972, was one of the most
horrific incidents of the NI violence. Two
women were killed and some 130 people
injured. There was no warning and the
casualties were mainly women and
children having a break from Saturday
afternoon shopping. Many suffered severe
mutilation. Two sisters out shopping
were among the most seriously affected;
each lost both legs, and one of them, who
was buying her wedding dress, also lost an
arm and an eye.

ACTIVE SERVICE UNIT *see*
Provisional Irish Republican Army

ADAMS, GERARD (GERRY)
PSF MP for W. Belfast, 1983–92. Assembly
member for W. Belfast, 1982–6. Vice-
president, PSF, 1978–83; president, PSF,
1983–. b. Belfast, 5 October 1948.

Barman in Belfast when he became
involved in what Republicans describe as
'defence work during the pogroms', and
he was believed by the security forces to
be head of the PIRA in the Ballymurphy
area of W. Belfast when he was interned
in 1971. Released in July 1972 to take
part in secret London talks between PIRA
and Secretary of State William Whitelaw,
which gave rise to a brief ceasefire. In the
resumed campaign he was believed by
British intelligence sources to be the
Belfast brigade commander of PIRA, and
in 1973 one of three-man group running
PIRA after arrest of Seán Mac Stiofáin,
chief of staff. After arrest with other
leading Republicans in Belfast in 1973, he
tried to escape from the Maze Prison. For
this, he was sentenced to eighteen
months' imprisonment; he was released in
1976. Both as an internee and as a
convicted prisoner, he was in the PIRA
compound at the Maze, but he has
repeatedly denied that he has been a
member of PIRA. In February 1978 he
was charged with membership of PIRA,
but after being remanded in custody for
seven months, he was freed after the Lord
Chief Justice, Lord Lowry, ruled that
there was not sufficient evidence for a
conviction. In June 1979 he told a Wolfe
Tone commemoration ceremony at
Bodenstown, Co. Kildare, that the aims
of Republicans could not be achieved
simply by military means, and their failure
to develop an alternative to constitutional
politics had to be continually analysed. At
the 1980 PSF Ard Fheis he said that the
British now realised that there could not
be a military victory, and it was time that
Republicans realised it too. He had a
leading role in deciding policy on the
1981 H-Block hunger strike, and when
he topped the poll in W. Belfast in the
1982 Assembly election, he became the
dominant NI personality in PSF. Tim Pat

Coogan, an authority on the IRA, called him a 'Shogun-like figure' in Northern republicanism. When the party dropped federalism from its policy in 1982, it was a further triumph for Adams and his supporters, and it put him at odds with some leading Southern PSF figures such as Dáithí Ó Conaill. In December 1982 he was banned by Home Secretary William Whitelaw, under the Prevention of Terrorism Act, from entering GB to speak to Labour MPs and councillors at the invitation of GLC leader Ken Livingstone. But the ban was lifted by the Home Office in June 1983 when he took W. Belfast in the general election with a majority of more than 5,000, unseating veteran MP Gerry Fitt. In July 1983 he provoked controversy with a visit to London, where he met some Labour MPs, but his efforts to explain his policies in the US and Canada have been frustrated by the denial of a visa, although Bill Clinton, during his campaign for the US presidency, supported Adams's entry to the US. Within PSF, Adams's influence developed steadily and he became president in a Northern coup in 1983. He moved PSF towards further political participation and the 1986 Ard Fheis took the radical step of dropping abstention from the Dáil. This provoked a split in the movement and division from former associates. Public prominence brought dangers and in March 1984 Adams and three PSF colleagues were shot as they travelled by car through Belfast city centre from the Magistrates' Court. The loyalist gun gang was captured by a UDR patrol. In May 1987 PSF published 'Scenario for Peace', which envisaged a British withdrawal followed by an all-Ireland constitutional conference. Adams retained his W. Belfast constituency in the June 1987 general election despite a determined campaign against him led by the SDLP; he increased his majority and his share of the vote. Early in 1988 he engaged in private talks with SDLP leader John Hume, which were later widened to include other prominent members of both parties. The discussions created some puzzlement in political circles in view of the previous tensions between PSF and the SDLP. Most Dublin politicians

suppressed their doubts out of regard for Hume; the British Government saw no value in the exchanges, while Unionists declared them an insuperable obstacle to dialogue between themselves and the SDLP. Repeated statements by PSF figures discounted the idea that they could satisfy Hume's hope for an end to the PIRA campaign, even if it were to be the ticket to all-Ireland round-table negotiations. But the exchanges, which broke down after six months with some recriminations, fitted in with an increased trend towards self-examination within PSF, which was reflected in Adams's own mild criticism of some PIRA killings in 1987 and 1988. In what he himself described as an 'unprecedented' intervention at the PSF Ard Fheis in January 1989, he said accidental killings of civilians by PIRA must stop because they 'retarded' the Republican struggle. But he reiterated support for the PIRA campaign generally. The late 1980s and early 1990s proved a difficult period for Adams. In 1989, PSF lost ground electorally both North and South. He had admitted that PIRA 'mistakes' could cost PSF votes, adding, 'Sinn Fein does not claim to be the conscience of the IRA – neither is Sinn Fein going to be a scapegoat for the IRA.' In June 1989, he was in England on a 'peace mission', and Labour MP Tony Benn, who shared his platform in Sheffield, remarked: 'The history of Britain is of terrorists ending up having tea with the Queen at Buckingham Palace.' At that time Adams's efforts were largely directed to getting into talks with the British Government, no doubt encouraged by comments by NI Secretary of State Peter Brooke that this need not be ruled out if PIRA abandoned violence. In April 1990 Adams put forward a formula for talks, but it was summarily rejected by Britain. Adams's idea was that PIRA would call off its campaign if the British Government and PSF met to seek a solution; there would be no public declaration of a ceasefire and PIRA must reserve the right to continue the armed struggle. Adams dismissed the Brooke talks as 'a game of deceit'. In February 1992 he was urging the UN and EC to help resolve local problems, and once more stressing that PSF and PIRA were not as one, that he did not agree with everything that PIRA did, and that 'if PIRA ceased to operate, another organisation would continue the armed struggle'. During the April 1992 general election campaign, Adams commented that 'the ballot paper in one hand and the Armalite in the other' policy was 'outdated'. But a vigorous campaign by the SDLP's Joe Hendron, plus tactical anti-Adams voting by a few thousand loyalists across the Peace Line, ended his MP status. It was clear that these Protestant votes had been decisive, since Adams's poll was only 56 short of the 1987 figure. Adams said he would be back, and Peter Brooke, who had been dropped in the post-election reshuffle, admitted that he would have liked to meet Adams 'as a matter of history' and because of Adams's 'significant role' in events. In 1992 Adams had informal talks with senior Presbyterian clergymen, but he deplored the refusal of the major Churches to have official contacts with PSF. He was at the same time developing his writing career, and the decision of RTE to ban an advertisement for one of his books sparked controversy. In April 1993 he began a series of meetings with SDLP leader John Hume in Derry, which had been arranged by Catholic clergy. Many Unionists attacked the exchanges as a means of getting PSF into inter-party dialogue, but they were given a cautious welcome by the Irish Government and praised by Cardinal Daly and some Protestant Church leaders. Adams told the PSF executive that suggestions that a ceasefire was being discussed were misleading, since he was not speaking for PIRA. With a rise in the PSF vote in the 1993 council elections, he renewed his call for a voice in inter-party negotiations. In May 1993 he was disappointed by the continued refusal of the US authorities to grant him a visa. The following month, the Irish President Mary Robinson was criticised for agreeing to meet him at a W. Belfast reception. In July Dublin High Court threw out an appeal made by Brandon, his publishers, against a ban under the 'Section 31' broadcasting restrictions on his personal 20-second

sound advert for his latest book. He welcomed the visit from the US of Bruce Morrison and associates and the clear Irish agenda that President Clinton had espoused in the election campaign. During September his talks process with John Hume came to occupy a dominant position. On a visit to Derry he asked the Dublin and London Governments for a 'new and imaginative initiative' restoring Irish self-determination. He affirmed the PIRA commitment to the armed struggle but stated that they were more willing than ever to 'explore new avenues towards a settlement'. As pressure mounted within the SDLP about the talks, Adams feared the consequences. The joint statement issued on 25 September reported 'considerable progress on a peace process'. Hume then left for the US for ten days, and in his absence Adams became the focus of media attention as journalists sought elaboration on the statement. When Secretary of State Mayhew had not commented by 28 September, Adams described him as rude for not offering talks. The lack of detail on the statement provoked speculation and criticism which Adams dismissed as 'narrow and negative'. During October a number of speeches set out his conditions for an end to violence. He told a Dublin audience that it required a declaration by the British Government of the right of the Irish people to self-determination. Later he stated that Unionists had no right to preserve the Union against the wish of the British Government. By 25 October he was 'absolutely confident' of an end to violence if the Government 'responded positively' to the Hume–Adams document. He also rejected calls for a ceasefire, for he regarded peace as the result of 'total demilitarisation' and not as a 'prerequisite for a process'. The Shankill bombing on 23 October and his carrying of the coffin of bomber Thomas Begley was a reminder of Adams's ambivalent role, for which Home Secretary Michael Howard had renewed the exclusion order against him on 19 October. While the British and Irish Governments struggled to accommodate a peace process, evidenced by the Brussels joint declaration on 29 October, Dick Spring's six principles and even the disclaimed Department of Foreign Affairs document, Adams's rejection of them all made it clear that his commitment was exclusively to the Hume–Adams document. Further, his claim of 'protracted contact' between the Government and PSF, made on 15 November, resulted in revelations in the *Observer* on 28 November of contacts over the past twenty years and regular contact over the past three years. The frenetic initial publication of documents by PSF and Sir Patrick Mayhew, seeking to establish the credibility of their respective versions of events, influenced British-Irish relations only temporarily and the joint declaration was published at Downing Street on 15 December. Adams made no immediate formal response to the declaration but, after a further meeting with Hume on 20 December, he asked for 'unconditioned dialogue' and for the British Government to join the 'persuaders'. Amid rumours that he had a viral illness requiring rest, he and PSF went into a consultations procedure with the Republican movement. Early in 1994 he stated that he could not take the document to PIRA in its present form and sought 'clarification'. He issued a thirteen-page document relating the declaration to the PSF peace process and concluding that a stalemate existed. Despite 'clarification' from the Irish Government and a lifting of the broadcasting ban in the Republic, Adams switched the emphasis to the reluctant British. At the end of January the granting of a visa, however restricted, by President Clinton enabled Adams to attend a conference in New York, organised by the National Committee on American Foreign Policy, Inc. He received coast-to-coast television coverage, which swamped that for fellow participants John Hume and Dr John Alderdice. However, the ceasefire announcement, which some had anticipated, did not occur and as he left after his forty-eight-hour visit, President Clinton was declaring his support for the 'astonishing peace initiative' – the declaration of Prime Ministers Major and Reynolds. On his return to Dublin

Adams was met by protesters who had suffered directly at the hands of PIRA. His interview with Brian Walden on London Weekend Television in February reopened the arguments about the direct broadcast ban. As the PSF Ard Fheis approached, Sir Patrick Mayhew provided public 'clarification' in an interview in the *Irish Times* but PSF had attempted to divert attention away from it by organising further peace commissions consultations beyond the end of February.

ADVISORY COMMISSION
An eleven-member body set up by William Whitelaw, Secretary of State soon after direct rule in 1972, to advise him on local legislation and matters generally. It first met on 25 May 1972 and subsequently twenty-five times that year. It continued until the setting up of the Assembly, and was controversial from the start. Both Unionists and the SDLP boycotted it. Members: Sir Robin Kinahan, businessman and one-time Unionist MP; Sheelagh Murnaghan, former Liberal MP for QUB; Professor Norman Gibson of NUU; R.D. Rolston, president of the Confederation of British Industry Council in NI; Ada Malone, headmistress of Enniskillen Collegiate School for Girls; Norman Kennedy, trade-union leader; Tom Conaty, businessman and chairman of the Falls-Road-based CCDC; R.B. Price of Ballymoney; James O'Hara, a member (later chairman) of the Housing Executive and the first Catholic appointed to the former Housing Trust; A.E. Gibson, former president Ulster Farmers' Union; and John H. Nicholl, vice-chairman of Londonderry County Council, to which he was elected as a Nationalist.

AGNEW, FRASER
UUP Assembly member for S. Antrim, 1982–6. Served on committees on Economic Development and Environment. b. 1942. Newtownabbey Council, 1981–. Mayor, 1990. Resigned from UUP, June 1992. In the early days of the AIA he appeared to have inside information on the date, place and agenda of the ministerial conference meetings.

ALDERDICE, DR JOHN

Leader of the the Alliance Party, 1987–. Belfast City Council, 1989–. b. 1955. Educated Ballymena Academy and QUB. Consultant psychiatrist at Belfast City Hospital. Alderdice was an unexpected choice to succeed John Cushnahan. He had joined the party in 1978 and although he had been on the party council since 1979 and had been a vice-chairman, he had never held elected office. He had failed to win a council seat in Lisburn in 1981. But in 1987 he produced the best-ever Alliance showing in a Westminster election by polling 32 per cent against Peter Robinson, DUP MP for E. Belfast. In the Alliance leadership election in October he defeated Seamus Close by 117 votes to 77. In January 1988 he began a series of meetings with party leaders in the Republic, GB and NI. On the AIA he expressed the view that Unionist demands for its suspension were unrealistic; he called for a constructive review of its operation in 1988 through wide consultation, and for efforts to allay Unionist fears. He unsuccessfully contested the 1989 European election. In 1990 he was active in pressing for serious inter-party negotiations and urged the British and Irish Governments to use their influence in this direction. He was pessimistic, however, about Peter Brooke's extended 'talks about talks' with the parties, and in January 1991 dubbed them 'burlesque'. In the substantive talks that began a few months later, he led the party delegation and as the negotiations neared an end in November 1992, he confirmed that Alliance had reached 'broad agreement' on a system of NI devolution with the UUP and DUP. Reflecting a party view that the SDLP had failed to move during the talks, he told a meeting of European Liberals in Prague in November 1992 that it would be wrong to assume that Unionists were to blame for their breakdown earlier that month. In the 1992 general election, he maintained his strong position in E. Belfast, taking nearly 30 per cent of the votes despite the presence for the first time of a Conservative candidate. That was Alliance's best result in the contest, in which the party's overall vote dropped

1.3 per cent from its 1987 level despite a strong 'vote for peace' campaign. Meantime, he strengthened links with the Liberal Democrats in Britain and the Progressive Democrats in the Republic, where he also enjoyed good relations with Fine Gael, one of whose MEPs was former Alliance leader John Cushnahan. (In his professional capacity, Dr Alderdice attracted interest with a comment at a Dublin conference, in July 1992, that psychiatrists in NI were seeing people in their twenties and thirties who could not suppress the horrors of childhood in the bloodshed and violence of the 1960s and 1970s.) In January 1993, he suggested that Sir Patrick Mayhew saw his role in NI as 'relatively similar to that of his colleague Chris Patten in Hong Kong'. At the end of September he warned that if the core of the Hume–Adams peace process was Irish self-determination then the SDLP had been detached from Article 1 of the AIA in favour of a traditional PSF position. In October, after a meeting with Michael Ancram, he said that the Hume–Adams initiative was casting a shadow over prospects for renewed talks. He met Taoiseach Albert Reynolds in Dublin early in December and again early in January 1994, after he had expressed interest in the forum idea in the Downing Street Declaration. In the third week of January he urged the Westminster Government to produce its plans for governing Northern Ireland; he wanted fresh talks, stating that they could not wait for PSF. He attended the New York conference organised by the National Committee on American Foreign Policy, Inc., with Adams and Hume and criticised the Unionist abstention as a 'huge mistake'. Although he refused to share the same press conference platform as Adams, his contribution was described as 'probably the most important input by a non-Nationalist politician from Northern Ireland'.

ALISON, MICHAEL JAMES HUGH

Minister of State, NIO, 1979–81. b. 27 June 1926. At the NIO he was deputy to Secretary of State Humphrey Atkins, and his most arduous period at Stormont was in 1981 when he was responsible for handling the prison situation during most of the H-Block hunger stike. He left NI, however, a month or so before the protest ended. Conservative MP for Barkston Ash, 1964–83; Selby, 1983–. Conservative Research Department, 1958–64; Parliamentary Under-Secretary, Health and Social Security, 1970–4; Minister of State, Employment, 1981–3; PPS to PM Margaret Thatcher, 1983–7.

ALL CHILDREN TOGETHER

An organisation aimed at bringing together Protestant and Catholic children in shared schools, with the co-operation of the Churches and where parents have expressed a wish to have their children educated together. It promoted a parliamentary Bill to achieve this object, which was introduced in the House of Lords in June 1977 by the Alliance peer Lord Dunleath. In Parliament, the Government supported its general aims, but suggested its withdrawal. It was, however, passed, and got the royal assent on 26 May 1978. Education proposals published in 1988 pleased the organisation because they gave extra Government encouragement to integrated schools.

ALLEN, DAVID

VUPP Convention member for N. Antrim, 1975–6. b. 1937. Ballymena Borough Council, 1973–7. A former teacher and active educationist, he became general secretary of the Ulster Teachers' Union in 1977.

ALLEN, JOHN ALEXANDER (JACK)

UUP Assembly member for Londonderry, 1982–6; chaired committees on Economic Development and Devolution, member of Environment Committee. b. 1943. Londonderry Corporation, 1967–9. Londonderry City Council, 1973–85. Mayor, 1974–5. Chairman, NI Housing Association, 1983–. Chairman, UUP executive, 1988–90. Chairman, local government Staff Commission, 1985–. Hon. Treasurer, Ulster Unionist Council, 1990–. Delegate at Brooke–Mayhew Talks, 1991–2, and Duisburg Talks, 1988.

ALLIANCE PARTY

One of NI's main political parties, it prides itself on giving priority to attracting support from both sides of the community. The party was launched in April 1970, and although its initial leadership was drawn largely from people previously unknown in politics, it quickly gained support from a section of Unionists who had backed the PM Terence O'Neill, and who felt that Alliance, rather than the UUP, represented their outlook. Although its main base, to start with, appeared to be middle-class, it also absorbed many people who had formerly backed the NILP. It got an early boost in 1972, when three sitting MPs joined it: Phelim O'Neill, ex-Unionist Minister; pro-O'Neill member Bertie McConnell, and Tom Gormley, Nationalist. In its first electoral test, the May 1973 District Council elections, it got 13.6 per cent of the vote. This should have secured it more than seventy seats, under the newly introduced PR system, but in fact it got sixty-three. In the hard-fought Assembly election, which followed the next month, it secured 9.2 per cent of the total vote and eight seats. Many of its supporters had hoped for more, but it went on to take part in the crucial negotiations on the power-sharing scheme and in the Sunningdale Conference. Two of its members – Oliver Napier, the party leader, and Bob Cooper, the deputy leader – were included in the short-lived Executive Government. In the 1975 Convention election its share of the vote rose slightly to 9.8 per cent and it again got eight seats. In the Convention campaign it called for a strong legislative assembly. It said that both sides of the divided community must be involved at all levels in the government of NI, although it indicated in the convention itself that it would not object to majority government eventually if the atmosphere improved. It dropped the idea of a Council of Ireland, as envisaged at Sunningdale, saying that it was unnecessary to have such a formal body to achieve practical co-operation with the Republic. Its main policy contribution in the Convention was to outline a scheme for government by committees, elected in proportion to the strength of parties in the Assembly. In the District Council elections in 1977 it improved its poll to 14.4 per cent of the total and secured seventy seats. It benefited from transfers, notably from the UUP and SDLP. In the 1979 Westminster election the party fought all twelve seats, but failed to gain a single one, despite its prediction that it would take E. Belfast. Its share of the poll was 11.9 per cent. In the 1979 European election its candidate was Oliver Napier, and his share of first preferences was only 6.8 per cent. In the 1980 Constitutional Conference, it continued to press the case for partnership government. But this did not bring it any dividends in the 1981 council elections when it suffered from the polarisation produced by the H-Block hunger strike. Its 9 per cent vote was more than 5 per cent down on the previous council contests. In 1982 it emerged as the party showing most enthusiasm for the 'rolling devolution' initiative. However, its vote in the October Assembly election stayed at 9 per cent, but PR worked very appreciably to its advantage, so that it took ten Assembly seats – or twice as many as PSF, which had 10 per cent of the vote. But its share of the poll in the 1983 Westminster election fell to 8 per cent, and its hope of taking one or more seats was disappointed. Partly for tactical reasons, it contested only twelve of the seventeen seats. In the second European election in 1984 David Cook polled only 5 per cent of the vote and lost his deposit. The District Council elections of 1985 saw Alliance lose further ground to become largely a party of the Greater Belfast area. It won thirty-four seats, four fewer than in the highly polarised 1981 election, and only 7.1 per cent of the vote compared with 8.9 per cent. The pressure had fallen largely on one section of the party support as the SDLP sought to counter-balance losses to PSF. In November 1985 the conditional acceptance of the AIA by Alliance threatened its support from the Protestant section of the community. This was evident in the January 1986 Westminster by-elections when it fought its five best seats but lost 17 per cent of its

1983 vote in the same constituencies. In June 1987 Alliance fielded sixteen candidates to capitalise on Unionists' discontent with their party leaders' adjournment policy against the AIA. They polled 10 per cent of the vote, recovered their 1983 position and produced good performances in E. Belfast and N. Antrim. In contrast party leader John Cushnahan was pushed into third place in N. Down and in September he resigned from politics for 'family reasons'. He was replaced in October by Dr John Alderdice, who early in 1988 began a round of meetings with party leaders in the Republic, GB and NI. By March he was not hopeful about devolution. However, the launch of the Social and Liberal Democrats brought the prospect of links between them and the Progressive Democrats in the Republic, and Alliance in NI. The aim was to fight the 1989 European election on the same platform and manifesto. David Steel (SLD) and Des O'Malley (Prog. D.) attended the Alliance Party conference in April 1988. A new policy statement in October 1988 called for devolved power-sharing government which would have an equal role with Republic in a new tripartite AIA conference. In the late 1980s and early 1990s, the party faced new problems and opportunities. The entry of the Conservative Party into NI electoral politics created new competition for the middle ground, notably in N. Down where Alliance had previously polled strongly. In the 1992 general election, it obtained just 15 per cent of votes in that constituency, less than half the Tory showing. Its overall vote in 1992, at 8.7 per cent, was 1.3 per cent down on 1987, despite a vigorous 'vote for peace' campaign. In the 1989 council elections, Alliance's 6.8 per cent vote compared with 7.1 per cent in 1985, partly due to Conservative successes in N. Down, but its vote also eroded slightly in Belfast, although it advanced in Ards, Newtownabbey and Castlereagh. The party was active throughout the 1991 and 1992 phases of the Brooke–Mayhew Talks, and was in 'broad agreement' with the UUP and DUP on a scheme for devolution. But its old link with the SDLP through a common interest in power-sharing was broken by SDLP rejection of the principle in favour of a more radical approach. Dr Alderdice criticised the SDLP for failing to move during the negotiations. In April 1991 Seamus Close became deputy leader when Gordon Mawhinney resigned for 'health and business reasons'. Former NILP MP David Bleakley joined the Alliance team in the final stages of the Brooke-Mayhew Talks. The party's showing in the 1993 council elections was its best since 1977, with forty-four seats and 7.6 per cent of the vote. For the first time it provided mayors for Lisburn and Carrickfergus. In October 1993 it won the N. Down-Holywood by-election for the seat vacated by Dr Laurence Kennedy (Cons.). The call by John Hume in January 1994 for 'clarification' of the December Downing Street Declaration was described by Alliance as 'perverse' while he refused to publish the Hume-Adams document.

ALLISTER, JAMES HUGH (JIM)
DUP Assembly Whip and member for N. Antrim, 1982–6. Served on committees on Finance and Personnel, and Devolution. b. 1953. Educated Regent House School, Newtownards; LLB (QUB). Barrister. European Parliament personal assistant to Rev. Ian Paisley and DUP press officer, 1980–2. Joint organiser of UUP–DUP 'Operation USA' publicity campaign in the US, January 1982. In the 1983 Westminster election, he was only 367 votes behind the UUP winner in the new E. Antrim seat. The decision of the two Unionist parties not to oppose one another in the 1987 election in furtherance of their drive against the AIA prevented his standing for the seat, and soon afterwards he announced that he was leaving active politics.

ALTON, DAVID PATRICK
Liberal and later SLD spokesman on NI, January 1987–8. b. 1951. MP for Mossley Hill, Liverpool, a constituency with a significant Irish community, 1979–. Britain's youngest councillor (Liverpool) in 1972. As Liberal Chief Whip he sought, during 1987, to increase contacts with Alliance Party in NI and Progressive Democrats in Republic, which resulted in an SLD–All.–Prog. D. common front for the 1989 European election. Critical of Unionist MPs' boycott of Westminster in their anti-AIA campaign. Urged SDLP to give full support to RUC. In 1988 promoted a parliamentary Bill to outlaw abortions after eighteen weeks, which had support of all NI MPs.

AMERICAN ANCIENT ORDER OF HIBERNIANS
This Irish-American organisation, with some 30,000 members, organises the huge annual New York St Patrick's Day parade. In 1978 spokesmen for the AOH in Ireland stressed that the US organisation was entirely autonomous. This arose from controversy, going back to 1972, about the precise attitude of the US body to NI affairs. In 1972 Judge James Comerford, a former president of the AAOH, declared that it 'unequivocally supports the Provisional IRA campaign'. But this was denied by the US National Secretary, William Bartnett, who said that the organisation neither granted financial aid to PIRA nor maintained goodwill contacts with its leadership. When the AAOH held its annual convention in Killarney in July 1978, a resolution that repudiated violence in NI and praised the Irish Government's stand on the North was ruled out of order. The motion was stated to have been backed by Senator Edward Kennedy. Later a spokesman for AAOH stressed that the conference decision was stictly procedural, since the organisation could not support any foreign government. And the spokesman said it was totally opposed to the use of violence as a solution to the NI problem. Argument also arose from a comment by the then deputy leader of the SDLP, John Hume, that the AAOH had been writing to US firms, opposing the idea of investment in NI. George Clough, a director of the AAOH, said it did not want to stop US investment in NI, but it wanted equal opportunities in employment there. Its 1983 St Patrick's Day parade in New York provoked controversy because a PIRA supporter, Michael Flannery, founder of NORAID,

was chosen to head the parade. By 1985 there were some signs that leaders of the Order were anxious to present a more moderate image. But in 1988 Nick Murphy, leader of the AAOH, was among Irish-Americans who criticised the Republic's Government for its new extradition arrangements. He also said that a ten-day search for arms was turning the South into 'a banana republic'. Early in 1989 the chairman, M.J. Coogan, lobbied to have Joe Doherty (PIRA), then in a New York prison and fighting extradition to GB on murder charges, made grand marshal of the St Patrick's Day parade. (Doherty was extradited to Belfast in 1992.) In June 1992 the organisation called on the US Congress to stop funding 'the IFI gravy train'.

AMNESTY INTERNATIONAL

The London-based human rights body which has taken a close interest in NI issues since the start of the Troubles. Its intervention in the late 1970s persuaded the Labour Government to set up the Bennett inquiry into allegations of ill-treatment of terrorist suspects by the RUC. In 1988 its call for a judicial inquiry into disputed killings by the security forces since 1982 was rejected by the Government, although it attracted support from the Labour opposition, the Irish Government, and the SDLP. It also took up the SAS killings of three unarmed PIRA members in Gibraltar in 1988, and suggested that there was evidence of 'extra-judicial executions'. PM Margaret Thatcher dismissed the claim as 'utterly disgraceful'. The organisation has also criticised the operation of non-jury courts, the supergrass system, and strip-searching. In a 1992 report, it listed allegations of ill-treatment of people at the Castlereagh interrogation centre. After claims of partiality, made by Ken Maginnis MP, it began to spotlight 'deliberate and arbitrary' killings by paramilitaries. Its report in July 1993 accused the UK of being one of the worst human rights offenders in Europe. It cited collusion, army/public relations, the Diplock courts and the number of people convicted in the Corporals Wood and Howes murder case as specific causes for

concern. A report on political killings in NI was published on 9 February 1994. It sought a new inquiry into allegations of collusion and criticised the level of protection of Nationalist areas. While it condemned paramilitary violence, the report was criticised for not condemning explicitly the killing of police officers.

ANCIENT ORDER OF HIBERNIANS

An organisation often regarded as the Catholic equivalent of the Orange Order. It has always been associated with defence of the Catholic faith and promotion of Irish nationalism. Its present title dates from the 1830s, but its origins are traceable from the Catholic insurrection of 1641 through the Whiteboys and the Ribbonmen of the eighteenth and nineteenth centuries. A formidable AOH personality was Joe Devlin, the Belfast Nationalist MP who was active in the early years of the twentieth century and became national president. In the 1960s the national vice-president, the late Gerry Lennon of Armagh, a Nationalist Senator, had talks with the then leader of the Orange Order, Sir George Clark, about a possible political settlement. The discussions, known as the 'Orange–Green talks' were unsuccessful. The Order has declined somewhat, a trend evidently linked with the eclipse of the Nationalist Party. It still has a substantial membership, however, and the AOH hall remains a familiar landmark in many parts of rural Ulster. It is organised in divisions, and its public parades, with bands, banners and sashes, superficially resemble those of the Orange Order. They are held on 15 August (the Feast of the Assumption) and sometimes on St Patrick's Day. The leadership decided not to hold any parades between 1971 and 1974 because of the violence. Its national vice-president, Hugh News of Lurgan, defined its aims in 1976 as 'faith, unity and true Christian charity'. In 1978 he criticised the AAOH, which, he said, had no connection with the Irish organisation. His statement followed claims that the AAOH had been discouraging investment in NI, a claim denied by spokesmen for the US organisation. In 1991 its national secretary, Frank Kiernan, offered to mediate in the NI Troubles.

ANCRAM, MICHAEL (EARL OF)

Parliamentary Under-Secretary, NIO, 1993-. b. 1946. Barrister. Edinburgh University and Oxford. Heir to Marquess of Lothian, prominent Scottish Catholic peer, but does not use the title Earl. Wife is daughter of Duke of Norfolk. Cons. MP for Devizes, 1992-. Earlier Scottish MP, 1974-87, when he lost Edinburgh S. while Scottish Under-Secretary. In Scotland, he was an early advocate of the Poll Tax and a firm supporter of the Union. Has been chairman of the Scottish Conservatives and a member of the Public Accounts Committee. At Stormont, he succeeded Jeremy Hanley as Minister for Political Affairs and Education. At the September meeting of the Anglo-Irish Intergovernmental Conference he was asked to explore and identify the 'extent and degree of flexibility' of the NI political parties with a view to restarting the talks on the three-strand basis. After a meeting with UUP in London, he completed the round of bilateral talks in the second week of November. In January 1994 he wrote to the main parties seeking further meetings, with the implication that PSF would be left behind. Early in February he met a WP delegation at Stormont.

ANDERSON, ALBERT WESLEY

Unionist MP for Londonderry at Stormont, 1968-72. b. 23 July 1907; d. 1981. Mayor of Londonderry, 1963-8. Senior Parliamentary Secretary, Home Affairs, 1971-2.

ANDERSONSTOWN

The district on the western fringe of W. Belfast that has been one of the main strongholds of PIRA, and where the Peace People movement was born in 1976. There is a strong Republican tradition, so that it became an area of intense confrontation between the PIRA and the security forces, particularly after the introduction of internment. The area has been heavily scarred by the violence, and troops and police have operated from strongly fortified stations. The former RUC station has become a joint police and army centre, and is heavily protected. There is heavy unemployment, but the Government has set up several factories at Kennedy Way in an effort to provide local employment. There has been Government support for other job-creation projects and in 1992 local MP Dr Joe Hendron visited the US in a bid to attract new investment. The local SDLP Convention member, Vincent McCloskey, wrote in May 1976: 'More than any other area, Andersonstown has suffered all the horrors of this undeclared civil war. There is not a street that has not suffered its own private tragedies. There is not a child that cannot recognise the sound of gunfire or the type of weapon being used. The people have been battered from all sides with the propaganda of the various forces but have managed in spite of all to maintain their civilised standards of behaviour.' Loyalists have tended to see it as the heartland of republicanism. Before the launching of the Peace People, after the incident in which three young children died, there were several moves by women in the area to organise peace meetings, and on some occasions they clashed with women supporting the PIRA. In the 1981 hunger strike it was the venue of many rallies in support of the anti-H-Block cause, and there were emotional scenes as the funerals of hunger-strikers paused on the way to Milltown cemetery. The area became more quiet in the next few years but in 1988 two incidents put it again in the world spotlight. On 16 March three men, among thousands of mourners at the funeral in Milltown cemetery of three PIRA members shot dead by the security forces in Gibraltar, died in a loyalist gun and grenade attack. (*See also* Gibraltar Shootings.) The RUC, who had come under criticism from Nationalists for their strong presence at PIRA funerals, had kept their distance and a lone loyalist attacker, Michael Stone, created panic by his assault on the mourners. Just three days later, as the cortege of one of the victims of the cemetery attack moved towards Milltown cemetery, two British soldiers in plain clothes, who had suddenly driven close to the procession, were dragged from their car, beaten and shot dead. The soldiers, Derek Wood and David Howes, both corporals in their early twenties, were said by the army to have been on the scene quite innocently as they were attached to the Royal Signals and returning to their base at Lisburn. With the security forces again absent, apart from having a helicopter overhead, the incident sparked fresh controversy about their tactics. Since the mob attack on the soldiers was projected worldwide on TV, the killings aroused much wider condemnation than is usually attached to deaths in NI. The Nationalist *Irish News* commented: 'While one must make allowances for the understandable initial fear that some kind of repetition of the Milltown cemetery killings was imminent, such concessions do not lessen the sense of collective guilt that all decent citizens in the Nationalist sector are now experiencing.' Three men received life sentences for the killings, and four years after the attack charges were still being brought. Up to mid-1992, thirty-four people had been convicted for a variety of offences. While PIRA admitted the killings, up to that time no one had been convicted of PIRA membership in relation to the incident. In November 1990 local priest Father Tom Toner said the local community had been 'persecuted' over the deaths and that more police effort had been put into the investigation than into the 210 murders that had occurred since. In May 1992 the Belfast-based Committee on the Administration of Justice sent a report to the British and Irish Governments, urging a retrial of those given life sentences. In 1992 the security forces rejected the suggestion in a book by local author Martin Dillon that they had not taken prompt enough action to rescue the two soldiers. Dillon also claimed the men were members of a hitherto unknown intelligence unit. In June 1992 the Haldane Society of Socialist Lawyers urged that the convictions should be overturned and pending charges withdrawn.

ANDREW, SIR ROBERT (JOHN)
Permanent Secretary, NIO, 1984-7. b. 25 October 1928. MA (Oxon.). Served with Intelligence Corps, 1947-9, and joined Civil Service, 1952. Defence counsellor, UK NATO delegation, 1967-70. Served with three NI Secretaries of State in his first twenty-one months at NIO and had crucial role in negotiations leading to AIA.

ANDREWS, DAVID
Foreign Minister of the Irish Republic and co-chairman of the Anglo-Irish Intergovernmental Conference, February 1992-January 1993. Minister for Defence and Marine, 1993-. b. Dublin, 1935. UCD and King's Inns, Dublin. Barrister. FF TD (Dun Laoghaire), 1965-. He was well qualified by previous experience for his NI responsibilities since he had been Foreign Affairs Minister of State, 1977-9, and Justice Minister of State, 1979, and a member of the 1967 Committee on the Constitution and of the New Ireland Forum. On his appointment as Foreign Minister by Taoiseach Albert Reynolds, he quickly made clear his full support for the talks on NI initiated by NI Secretary of State Peter Brooke. While he conceded that Unionist views were vital in the process, Unionists were angry that he also stressed that the Government of Ireland Act, 1920, would be on the table as well as the articles in the Republic's Constitution laying claim to NI. When Sir Patrick Mayhew succeeded Peter Brooke as NI Secretary of State after the April 1992 general election, Andrews readily gave his support to suspension of the Anglo-Irish Intergovernmental Conference meetings to allow inter-party talks to resume, and he took part in the negotiations between July and November 1992. When the talks then broke up without agreement, he said he regarded this as simply an 'intermission' in the exchanges. But when the outcome of the November 1992 election was a FF-Labour coalition, he had to make way for Dick Spring, the Labour leader, who became both Tánaiste and Foreign Minister. In May 1992 he made a strong plea for the removal of the Parachute Regiment from E. Tyrone.

ANDREWS, SIR JOHN LAWSON ORMROD
Minister and leader, NI Senate, 1964-72,

in which capacity he frequently acted as deputy PM. b. Comber, Co. Down, 15 July 1903; d. 1986. Son of second PM of NI, John Miller Andrews. Unionist MP for Mid-Down, 1953–64, holding office successively as Minister of Health and Local Government, Minister of Commerce and Minister of Finance, before being elected to the Senate. Took part in Downing Street talks immediately prior to direct rule, 1972. Sided with Faulkner in the 1974 split and went out of politics in the late 1970s.

ANGLO-IRISH AGREEMENT

The AIA, signed at Hillsborough by PM Margaret Thatcher and Taoiseach Garret FitzGerald on 15 November 1985, was arguably the most far-reaching political development since 1920 and the creation of NI. In it the UK and Irish Governments committed themselves to much closer working on NI, and the agreement was later registered at the UN. The communiqué issued after the signing said the aims were to promote peace and stability in NI, the reconciliation of the two traditions in Ireland, the creation of a new climate of friendship, and co-operation in combating terrorism. The radical feature of the agreement was that it set up a joint ministerial conference of British and Irish Ministers, backed by a permanent secretariat at Maryfield, close to the Stormont estate, to monitor political, security, legal and other issues of concern to the Nationalist minority. Thus, while the agreement was not formally a joint authority, since the UK Government had the final word on matters affecting NI, it represented a major change of attitude by the British PM. In July 1982 Thatcher had forcibly pointed out that no commitment existed for her Government to consult the Irish Government on matters affecting NI. The new role of the Irish Government in the Anglo-Irish Intergovernmental Conference (which first met in Belfast on 11 December 1985), and the commitment that 'determined efforts shall be made . . . to resolve any differences' meant that in practice it was something more than consultation. The

main points of the AIA may be summarised as follows:

ARTICLE 1, on the status of NI, recognised that any change could only occur with the consent of a majority in NI; it further recognised that there was no present wish for change but if there were a swing in the future, legislative change would give it effect.

ARTICLE 2 stated that the Anglo-Irish Intergovernmental Conference existed within the frame-work of the 1981 BIIC, and that it was concerned with NI, and relations North and South; that the Irish Government would put forward proposals; that 'determined efforts' would be made to 'resolve any differences', but that there would be no derogation of sovereignty.

ARTICLE 3 said that the conference could meet, regularly and frequently, at ministerial or official level, and that a secretariat would service the conference.

ARTICLE 4 set out the aims for the conference as a framework to accommodate the rights and identities of the two traditions in NI, and to promote peace, stability and prosperity in Ireland. It recognised that Government policy was to devolve power on a 'widespread acceptance' basis; that the conference would be the framework for proposals on the 'modalities' of bringing devolution about and that the Irish Government would propose schemes on behalf of the interests of the minority community.

Articles 5–10 set out the functions and concerns of the conference:

ARTICLE 5 stated that on political matters the Irish Government could put forward proposals on behalf of the minority where major legislation or policy was involved. It listed as examples the protection of human rights and the prevention of discrimination in areas such as cultural heritage, electoral arrangements, flags and emblems; the avoidance of social and economic discrimination; and a possible Bill of Rights.

ARTICLE 6 accepted that the Irish Government could make proposals on the role and composition of various public bodies, including the SACHR, FEA, EOC, Policy Authority, and Police Complaints Board.

ARTICLE 7 concerned security and related matters: the conference could consider security policy, the relationship of security forces to the community, and prisons policy.

ARTICLE 8 concerned legal matters, including the administration of justice, policy aspects of extradition and the possibility of mixed courts in both jurisdictions (that is, additional judges drawn from the other jurisdiction). (*See also* Diplock report.)

ARTICLES 9 AND 10 concerned cross-border co-operation in security and practical economic and social matters.

ARTICLE 11 provided for a review of the working of the agreement after three years, or earlier, if requested.

ARTICLE 12 reiterated the possibility of an inter-parliamentary link between London and Dublin, first suggested in 1981.

The response inside NI to the AIA was an immediate welcome by Nationalists on the one hand and, on the other, a series of protests by Unionists against the role given to the Republic in the internal affairs of part of the UK. The Unionist protests took the form of mass demonstrations, the simultaneous resignation of fifteen MPs and the subsequent holding of by-elections, protests at Maryfield, and other methods of visibly showing the withdrawal of consent. Indeed, the existence of the NI Assembly as a representative body became itself a platform for protest against the AIA. It suspended its scrutiny function, the Devolution Committee was wound up, and a new Committee on the Government of NI was set up to examine the effects of the AIA on the government of NI, the 1973 Constitution Act and the 1982 NI Assembly Act. But as a consequence of the Assembly neglecting its scrutiny role, the Alliance members withdrew from the Assembly, leaving only forty-nine members attending, and the NIO cut off access to civil servants and departmental papers. Even though the committee issued three reports, the Assembly had become preoccupied with its assault on the AIA across a wide front, and around the time when arrangements for new elections to the Assembly were due, it was dissolved on 23 June 1986. In the summer of 1988 two brothers, Christopher and Michael McGimpsey of the UUP, challenged the legality of the AIA in the Dublin High Court. Although the case was not successful, costs were awarded and the path was opened to appeal to the Supreme Court, which gave its findings in March 1990. To the surprise of politicians North and South, the Supreme Court, having held that it could not overturn the AIA, went on to rule that Article 2 represented not simply an aspiration, but a 'constitutional imperative'. UUP leader James Molyneaux commented that the finding would 'damage the prospects of agreement between Unionists and Nationalists', and the issue was to dominate much of the debate that preceded the setting up of the Brooke–Mayhew Talks (*see* separate entry) and the discussions within that framework. The commitment to devolution in Article 4 proved elusive. Secretary of State Tom King engaged in 'talks about talks' with the local parties from 1987 but it was not until 1991, under his successor Peter Brooke, that a basis for comprehensive negotiations was found. Meanwhile, a review of the AIA carried out by the two Governments and published in 1989 recommended that a wider range of Ministers and issues should be included in the proceedings of the Anglo-Irish Intergovernmental Conference, and it promised to act on complaints about excessive secrecy by giving more information to the public on conference business. It said the twenty-seven sessions of the conference so far held had proved a 'valuable forum' and the aim would be to hold ten meetings a year. Fewer meetings were held in 1991 and 1992 because of the decision to suspend conference meetings to allow for the Brooke–Mayhew Talks. By November 1993 there had been fifty-four meetings of the conference. The extent of influence of the conference was an issue, with Garret FitzGerald making wide claims. Tom King, however, emphasised that whilst the Irish Government submitted nominations for appointments to some public bodies in NI, membership was decided by the British Government. Peter Brooke was co-chairman of the conference from 1989 to 1992, when Sir Patrick Mayhew took over. The Irish co-chairmen were Peter Barry (1985–7), Brian Lenihan (1987–9), Gerry Collins (1989–92), David Andrews (1992–3) and Dick Spring (1993–). The British–Irish Parliamentary Body (*see* separate entry), envisaged in Article 12, was launched in 1990.

ANGLO-IRISH INTERGOVERNMENTAL COUNCIL

The structure for Anglo-Irish consultations which developed from the Thatcher–Haughey summit in Dublin in December 1980. The idea was finally approved at the Downing Street meeting between Margaret Thatcher and Garret FitzGerald in November 1981, and the plan envisaged a four-tier structure – ministerial, official, parliamentary, with an advisory committee. The London meeting in January 1982 between NI Secretary of State James Prior and Irish Foreign Minister James Dooge was the first ministerial get-together under the council. Initially there seemed to be more enthusiasm for the parliamentary tier in Dublin than in London. There was the possibility, however, that members of an NI Assembly might be involved, although Unionists continued to say that they would have nothing to do with such a body. In July 1983 both Governments agreed to sponsor an 'Encounter Organisation' to organise high-level Anglo-Irish conferences, an arrangement that continued into the era of the AIA, which effectively replaced the AIIC. During the AIA controversy some Unionists said they would be prepared to work the AIIC if the AIA were abandoned.

ANNESLEY, SIR HUGH

Chief Constable of RUC, June 1989 –. b. 1939. Although he was Assistant Commissioner of the Metropolitan Police when he was appointed by the Police Authority to succeed Sir John Hermon, his appointment came as a surprise and was attributed in some quarters to a more independent stance by the authority. Born and educated in Dublin – his father was from NI and his mother from the Republic – he joined the Metropolitan Police in 1958, and rose through the ranks to Chief Superintendent by 1976, when he became Assistant Chief Constable of Sussex. In 1979 he began an intensive course with the Royal College of Defence Studies, which involved extensive travel in the Far East. In 1981 he returned to the 'Met' as deputy Assistant Commissioner, and was appointed Assistant Commissioner in 1985. It was his responsibility for specialist operations since 1987, including the Special Branch and anti-terrorist work in GB, that obviously impressed the authority. In this post he was in regular contact with both RUC and Gardaí. He was also on the executive committee of Interpol. Most NI politicians welcomed his appointment, and there were hopes in Dublin Government circles that he would be able to improve relations between the RUC and the Nationalist community. On 13 August 1989 he surprised people on the Falls Road by appearing at a demonstration to mark twenty years of the army on the streets and the anniversary of internment. He praised stewarding of the parade, which passed off quietly. But PSF called his presence 'provocative'. Two months later, he described as 'arrant nonsense' reports of a pro-loyalist 'inner circle' within the RUC. At the same time, there were growing complaints about the leaking of security documents identifying terrorist suspects and their use by loyalists in the selection of Catholics for assassination. But he had the satisfaction of finding the RUC cleared of complicity in an inquiry conducted by John Stevens, deputy Chief Constable of Cambridgeshire, although several UDR members faced charges in 1990. He issued a statement of RUC aims in 1990 in a bid to secure wider acceptance of the force, and in an effort to step up recruitment of Catholics he made several appeals to the Catholic community. In 1991, when overall RUC membership was about 8 per cent Catholic, although higher in senior posts, he ran into criticism from Archbishop Cahal Daly and the SDLP for using schools in the recruiting campaign. At that time, he was facing what proved to be an extended period of loyalist killings. In November 1991 he briefed PM John Major at 10 Downing Street on the general security situation. The meeting occurred at a time when many Unionists were calling for internment without trial, and when fresh allegations of ill-treatment of suspects at the Castlereagh holding centre were being looked at by a UN sub-committee. PM Major was also considering the future of anti-PIRA intelligence-gathering, prior to his decision to increase the role of MI5 in this field. The Government later decided that there should be an official to monitor conditions at interrogation centres. The Chief Constable faced questions on this issue and on the big increase in complaints against the RUC in 1991 at meetings of the Anglo–Irish Intergovernmental Conference. In August 1992 NI Secretary Sir Patrick Mayhew accepted Annesley's recommendation that the UDA should be banned – a move widely welcomed in the Nationalist community. Whilst speculation that he would be appointed Metropolitan Police Commissioner in 1992 proved inaccurate, an address that he gave to a major policing conference in July 1992, in which he urged a national anti-terrorism supremo, clearly impressed Government Ministers. In the 1990s he has directed strong efforts to counter racketeering by paramilitaries, some of which were linked with similar operations south of the border. In May 1993 he angered Nationalists and human rights bodies with a call for sweeping changes in anti-terrorist laws, which he claimed were allowing paramilitary figures to walk free. He argued that in certain circumstances, the burden of proof should rest on the accused, that

silence under questioning should become an offence, and that phone intercepts should be admissible as evidence. In August a leaked memo expressed 'grave reservations' about aspects of the Sheehy report on police pay and conditions, especially the effect on morale. On 2 August he approved the request from the DPP, Alasdair Fraser, that John Stevens, now Chief Constable of Northumbria, reopen his inquiries into collusion to investigate the new evidence revealed by the Nelson trial and convictions. Early in September the rise in loyalist violence brought stinging criticism from Dr Joe Hendron MP about the vigour of pursuit. Annesley replied that 166 loyalists and 93 Republicans had been charged with serious offences. In an interview with the *Belfast Telegraph* on 22 September he admitted that the Brian Nelson case had damaged intelligence information on loyalists.

ANNON, WILLIAM
DUP Convention member for N. Belfast, 1975–6. b. 1912; d. 1983. Before his adoption as DUP candidate for the Convention, he was chairman of the UUP's Sydenham (Belfast) branch; he returned to the UUP in 1983. Belfast City Council, 1977–83.

APPRENTICE BOYS OF DERRY
One of the Protestant 'Loyal Orders', which is based on the 'no surrender' action of the thirteen apprentice boys in slamming the gates of Derry on the army of King James II at the start of the siege of 1689. Its main parade in the city is held on 12 August to celebrate the relief of the city and the end of the siege, and up to 10,000 members take part, drawn from all parts of NI and sometimes accompanied by members from GB and overseas. There is a lesser demonstration on 18 December to mark the shutting of the gates. On that occasion an effigy of Colonel Lundy, an officer who tried to negotiate the surrender of the city at the start of the siege, is burned. This is the origin of the term 'Lundy', frequently used by extreme loyalists to describe someone whom they regard as having betrayed their cause. Members of the ABD can be initiated only

within the city walls, and such ceremonies are held in August and December. There were serious riots in the city after the August march in 1969, and parades were banned in 1970 and 1971. In 1972 the ABD's general committee decided to call off its parade when it was limited to the Waterside area – that is, the predominantly Protestant east side of the River Foyle. But many Apprentice Boys rallied on the Waterside and were addressed by one of their number, the Rev. Ian Paisley. The then NI PM Brian Faulkner was expelled from the Order in 1971 for being associated with the parades' ban. Members of the organisation were permitted to parade again within the old walled city in 1975. But they were not allowed to walk round the walls, which had been part of their traditional route, because these overlook the mainly Catholic Bogside. In 1985 the Order dropped two of its main office bearers because, as local councillors, they had refused to support a Unionist boycott of the council over the changing of the council name from Londonderry to Derry. James Guy was replaced as 'Lieut.-Governor' and David Davis as chief marshal. Guy became Mayor of Derry, 1987–8. The order celebrated the 300th anniversary of the siege in 1989, but this was marked by one of the bitterest internal disputes in the Order's history. Its leaders decided to apply for an IFI grant to help finance a proposed £500,000 cultural centre. They stressed that this did not mean they had dropped opposition to the AIA. The move caused an outcry among a section of the membership, including the Rev. Ian Paisley, who denounced any idea of taking 'blood money'. Hundreds of members were expelled during 1990, and in November 1990 the IFI offered a £250,000 grant. But the money was refused because, it was said, of 'the strings attached', which were apparently related to cross-community staffing and flags and emblems. In March 1991 a plan was put forward for alternative financing, including a £10-a-head contribution by the Order's 10,000 members.

ARCHER, LORD (OF SANDWELL)

As Peter Archer, Labour front-bench spokesman on NI, 1983–7. MP for Warley W., 1974–92. b. 20 November 1926. QC. Solicitor-General, 1974–9. As Labour spokesman he maintained close touch with parties in the Republic and NI, including PSF. Gave strong support to the AIA, but was critical of secrecy surrounding its drafting and held open the possibility that a Labour Government would enter into talks on it without preconditions. Supported Irish Government's call for three judges in Diplock courts and was a strong critic of the supergrass system. Resigned as MP, 1992, and became a life peer.

ARDILL, CAPTAIN ROBERT AUSTIN

UUP Whip in Assembly, 1974, and in Constitutional Convention, 1975–6. b. 1917. As MP for Carrick, 1965–9, and Secretary of the '66 Committee (Unionist backbench committee), he was opposed to leadership of Terence O'Neill. He was chairman of the Ulster Loyalist Association in 1971 and deputy leader of the Vanguard movement in 1972. Before Harry West took over as leader of the UUP in 1974 he was Whip of the Unionist Assembly members who did not accept Brian Faulkner as leader. In the Convention he was one of the UUUC team of negotiators with the SDLP, and after the Convention was dissolved he and the Rev. Martin Smyth had private talks with John Hume and Paddy Devlin of the SDLP. The talks did not lead to any agreement. Joint Honorary Secretary of Ulster Unionist Council, 1978. He has been associated with the strongly devolutionist wing of the UUP and was a leading member of the Charter Group when it was launched in 1986.

ARDOYNE

A mainly Catholic area of N. Belfast, adjoining the upper Crumlin Road. There was serious rioting in the district in August 1969, and there has been considerable burning of homes, many explosions, and a variety of violent incidents in the area over the years. In the early 1970s the PIRA was extremely active in the district. In August 1969 there were clashes between local people and the RUC, and with Protestants from the nearby Shankill area. Some of the initial violence in August 1969 was attributed by the Scarman tribunal to efforts to tie up the RUC, and so prevent police reinforcements being sent to the Bogside in Derry. The Scarman report mentioned that stones, petrol bombs, and explosive devices made from copper tubing had been used in assaults on the police. Scarman also held that Protestants had been responsible for the burning of several Catholic-owned pubs in the area on 15 August and for the burning of about twenty houses in Brookfield Street which had been occupied by Catholics before the riots. On the night of 15–16 August twenty-six civilians suffered gunshot injuries and one man was killed. The army moved into the area on 16 August. The Scarman report rejected suggestions that the Ardoyne monastery had been used as an arsenal and the priests had been handing out bullets. Referring to the RUC's use of the Browning machine gun, Scarman said these incidents illustrated the unsuitability of this weapon for riot control, and that it was a merciful chance that there was no fatal casualty from Browning fire. In October 1981 local city councillor Lawrence Kennedy, thirty-five, an Ind. Republican, was shot dead in a local social club, apparently by loyalist gunmen. PIRA was active in the area during the 1981 hunger strike and there were several shootings and riots. A report produced for the local Flax Trust in January 1983 said support for PIRA and INLA was high in the area, which had been 'abused and abandoned by Government and industry alike'. The report added that male unemployment was over 54 per cent among the 8,000 residents, with poverty rampant, 28 per cent of families living in overcrowded conditions and 35 per cent of homes lacking basic amenities. In the 1990s much deprivation has remained, along with unemployment of over 30 per cent, despite efforts to promote jobs. And increased activity by paramilitaries has raised tension. The area's summer *fleadh*, which had to be abandoned at the height

of the Troubles, has flourished in recent years. Five of the Birmingham Six, released in 1991, came from Ardoyne.

ARMAGH

Ireland's ecclesiastical capital, which was mentioned as a possible venue for a Council of Ireland if it had come into being after the 1973 Sunningdale Agreement. With fairly well-defined Protestant and Catholic areas, it has always had a reputation for intense political rivalries. One of the major incidents involving loyalists and civil rights supporters occurred here on 30 November 1968. The police had given permission to the civil rights supporters to have a march through the city centre, but at 2 a.m. the Rev. Ian Paisley and his supporters began to arrive in the central area. By the time the civil rights march had moved off from the fringes of the town, the loyalists had effectively occupied the key junction. Many of them carried walking sticks and clubs, and although they were warned by the police that it was an illegal assembly, they were able to prevent the civil rights march getting into the main thoroughfare. Later Paisley and one of his supporters, Major Ronald Bunting, were each sentenced to three months' imprisonment for illegal assembly, but they were released early as part of an amnesty. Armagh's main shopping streets have suffered heavily during the PIRA bombing campaign, and there have been many murders in the area, which in the 1970s became known, together with adjoining areas of Co. Tyrone, as the 'murder triangle'. In December 1972 an Armagh Unionist councillor and member of the Police Authority, William Johnston, was kidnapped and murdered. In 1982 Cardinal Ó Fiaich and Church of Ireland Archbishop John Armstrong co-operated in promoting a one-day 'at home' festival aimed at improving inter-community relations. Soon afterwards the shooting dead by the RUC of two local INLA members who had driven through a checkpoint provoked angry controversy. In November 1983 council chairman Charles Armstrong (UUP) was killed by a PIRA car bomb as he left a council meeting. In 1986 the long-established women's prison closed and prisoners moved to the new Maghaberry Prison. In 1988 the local Drumadd barracks became base of revived 3 Brigade of army given responsibility for border operations. In the 1990s Armagh has been frequently in the news. In August 1990 a nun and three police officers died in a PIRA landmine attack, and during the same year two RUC officers and an IPLO member died in separate shootings. Also in 1990, EC aid was announced for the city, with hopes it could become a 'tourist Mecca'. The IFI has provided £1 million for development of the ancient Navan Fort complex. With an element of power-sharing in the loyalist-controlled council, that authority got good marks in 1990 for having its workforce exactly reflect the religious composition of the local community. In 1991 the council was represented at the 200th anniversary celebrations of Armagh, Pennsylvania. In 1992 the Appeal Court cleared three of four local UDR soldiers who had been convicted of the murder of a 24-year-old Catholic in 1984. There had been a widespread campaign on behalf of the UDR Four, and it continued in respect of the fourth man, Neil Latimer, whose appeal failed. After the local elections in May 1993 Unionists retained overall control but power-sharing continued, with Pat Brannigan (SDLP) elected chairman. The council planned a major festival, Armagh Together, for 1994–5. Early in September 1993 a 1,000-lb bomb shattered the courthouse and damaged property on the Mall.

ARMSTRONG, MICHAEL

UUP Convention member for Armagh, 1975–6. b. France, 1924. Fatally injured in car accident, 1982. LLB (Cantab.). Barrister. With a strong military background (Captain in Irish Guards, 1939–45, and for a time in Allied military Government in West Germany; district commandant in USC at disbandment; commander in Armagh company UDR, 1970–4), he had been UUP spokesman on security and Honorary Secretary of the Ulster Unionist Council.

ARMY *see* Security System section, pp. 443–51

ARRAN, EARL OF

(Arthur Desmond Colquhoun Gore, whose eighteenth-century title is linked to Aran Islands, Co. Galway.) Parliamentary Under-Secretary, NIO, 1992–4. b. 14 July 1938. Former newspaper manager and publisher, he was Government Whip, 1987–9, and Parliamentary Under-Secretary, Defence, 1989–92. Given responsibility at Stormont for agriculture and health and social services. His arrival at the NIO coincided with sharp controversy over the creation of self-governing hospitals and other health units – a policy opposed locally by politicians, trade unions and doctors. Early in 1993 he attracted criticism from the farming community for failure to support potato producers and for the restrictive use of beef intervention. In July he presided over the introduction of new child-care legislation. He was appointed, in a straight exchange with Baroness Denton, Under-Secretary in the Department of Trade and Industry from 11 January 1994.

ASHDOWN, JEREMY JOHN DURHAM (PADDY)

Leader of Liberal Democrats, July 1988–. MP for Yeovil, 1983–. b. 27 February 1941. Although born in India, he spent his boyhood in NI. In the early years of the Troubles he served in NI with the Royal Marine commandos and for a period was commander of Special Boat Section; served in Crumlin Road area of Belfast and in Derry, where he arrested John Hume for obstruction in February 1972. Diplomat attached to UN, 1971–6. Throughout his leadership of Liberal Democrats, he has sought to strengthen ties with the Alliance Party, whose candidates he supported on the ground in the Upper Bann by-election in 1990 and in the 1992 general election, in which he warned PM John Major that any election pact with the Unionists would be 'a threat to peace'.

ASSEMBLY *see* Election Results section, pp. 369–72 *and* 389–92, *and* Systems of Government section, pp. 415–21

ASSOCIATION FOR LEGAL JUSTICE

A body set up in 1971, it has been active in investigating allegations of ill-treatment against the security forces and in monitoring the reform programme. In 1971 it published a booklet, *Know Your Legal Rights,* setting out procedures to be adopted by persons if they were arrested, subjected to search, or approached to give evidence. It campaigned for an end to political appointments to the judiciary. It strongly opposed internment, and in 1971 co-operated with NICRA in protesting that detainees had been ill-treated by the security forces. In 1974 it opposed the system of extra-territorial courts in NI and the Republic, and in a report in 1974 accused NI courts of showing an anti-Catholic bias in terms of longer sentences for Catholics. In 1974 it also complained that the RUC was using torture to extract confessions of PIRA membership. In 1982 it complained that shootings by the security forces of suspected terrorists represented 'summary executions'.

ATKINS, HUMPHREY *see* Colnbrook, Lord

ATKINS, ROBERT JAMES

Minister of State, NIO, 1992–4. Cons. MP for S. Ribble, 1983–. b. 5 February 1946. Had held several junior ministerial posts before moving to Stormont, at departments of Trade and Industry, Transport, and Education and Science (Minister of Sport, 1990–2). Known as a keen cricketer. A close friend of PM John Major, he insisted that Major had made NI his 'top political priority'. At Stormont responsible for the environment and the economy, and in the latter post was seen as having 'a difficult act to follow' in succeeding long-serving minister Richard Needham. From late 1992 some worthwhile inward investments, including a 900-job textile plant in Antrim and a 600-job rechargeable battery plant from California, seemed to justify his strategy and that of the IDB. He proved a good publicist for departmental campaigns on trading standards and renewable energy. In January 1993 he weathered the embarrassment of being convicted for speeding in his constituency while responsible for road safety in NI. Appointed Minister for the Environment and the Countryside on the resignation of Tim Yeo on 5 January 1994. He lists ecclesiology (church building and decoration) as one of his interests.

ATKINS CONFERENCE *see* Colnbrook, Lord *and* Constitutional Conference

B

BABINGTON, ROBERT JOHN

Unionist MP for N. Down, 1969–72. b. Dublin, 9 April 1920. QC. County Court judge, 1974–. In his 1969 election address he called for one man, one vote, and in 1970 urged the expulsion from the Unionist Party of those who refused to support Government policy. He frequently warned against the dangers of UDI for NI, and advised Unionists not to get involved in violence. He complained in 1972 that the PIRA ceasefire had resulted in gunmen finding NI a safer haven than the Republic. In 1973 he resigned from the Orange Order 'for personal reasons'.

BAILIE, ROBIN JOHN

Minister of Commerce, NI, 1971–2. b. 6 March 1937. Unionist MP for Newtownabbey, 1969–72. LLB (QUB). Solicitor, NI Supreme Court, 1961. On the liberal wing of the Unionist Party, he gave up active politics and resigned from Brian Faulkner's 'shadow cabinet' soon after direct rule in 1972. As Minister of Commerce he had been interested in the possibilities offered to NI by EC membership, and was among the earliest to urge a cross-border development plan for the north-west, with Common Market support. In 1973 he joined the Alliance Party for a brief period.

BAIRD, ERNEST AUSTIN

Leader of the UUUP, 1977–84.

b. Ballycampsie, Co. Donegal, 1930. A
founder and the first chairman of the
Vanguard movement in 1972, he was
closely associated with William Craig
until 1976, when as deputy leader of the
VUPP, he disagreed with Craig's advocacy
of voluntary coalition with the SDLP, and
established the UUUM, dedicated to
promoting Unionist unity. In this it
failed, and became the UUUP to fight the
local government elections in 1977. He
polled surprisingly strongly in the
Assembly elections in Fermanagh–S.
Tyrone in 1973, securing more first-
preference votes than either Harry West,
who was shortly to become Unionist
leader, or John D. Taylor, who had been
MP for S. Tyrone in the former Stormont
Parliament. He was also returned there in
the Convention election, but this time he
lagged behind West. He was extremely
active in the UWC strike in 1974, and was
associated with the Rev. Ian Paisley in the
UUAC strike in May 1977, which secured
much less support. Unsuccessfully
contested Fermanagh–S. Tyrone in 1979
Westminster election, and the 1982
Assembly election.

BAKER REPORT
Sir George Baker, in a review of working
of Emergency Provisions Act,
recommended in April 1984 the
retention of single-judge Diplock courts,
with the continuing use of supergrass
evidence and the non-proscription of the
UDA. He also suggested that victms of
PIRA violence should have legal aid so
that they could sue PSF, as its political
wing, for damages.

BALLYGAWLEY BUS BOMBING see
Provisional Irish Republican Army

BALLYKELLY BOMBING see
Derry/Londonderry

BALLYMURPHY
The W. Belfast Catholic housing estate
which was the centre of serious rioting in
1971 and 1972. In January 1971 trouble
on a serious scale continued for five
consecutive nights and the NI PM Major
Chichester-Clark declared that the army
would not be forced out of its main base

there, the Henry Taggart Memorial Hall,
by either physical or political pressure.
The hall had been repeatedly attacked by
crowds with stones and bottles. The
security forces claimed that the rioting
had been orchestrated by the PIRA, and
Dr William Philbin, the Catholic bishop
of Down and Connor, said in
Ballymurphy that members of secret
organisations had no obligation to obey
immoral orders. A group of Ballymurphy
women demonstrated at the bishop's
home in protest against the sermon. In
October 1971 an arms haul by the
security forces included seven Thompson
sub-machine-guns and a number of rifles
and revolvers. Mother Teresa of
Calcutta set up a mission in Ballymurphy
in late 1971 and stayed there until 1972.
The area has continued to suffer from
heavy unemployment.

BANNISTER, GRACE
First woman Lord Mayor of Belfast
(UUP), 1981–2. b. 1924; d. 1986. Left
school at fourteen years of age. Served as
deputy Lord Mayor in 1975 and High
Sheriff in 1979.

BARNHILL, JOHN (JACK)
UUP member of the NI Senate, 1958–71.
b. 1904. Assassinated in his home at
Brickfield, near Strabane, Co. Tyrone, on
12 December 1971. He was the first
politician to be assassinated in the
violence which began in 1969, and his
death was claimed by the OIRA. They
claimed that they had not intended to kill
him, but only to destroy his home 'in
reprisal for the destruction of working-
class homes by the British army'. The
OIRA said they had shot him during a
struggle. Bernadette Devlin MP asked the
Army Council to discipline those
involved. The NI PM Brian Faulkner
blamed an OIRA gang which, he said, had
been able to operate from a safe haven in
nearby Donegal in the Republic, and he
said this gang might have killed five
people in the Strabane area in the
previous three months. Jack Barnhill was
remembered by his fellow Senators as a
speaker who laced his speeches with
poetic quotations.

BARR, GLENN

Vanguard Unionist Progressive Party, Assembly, 1973–4, and Convention, 1975–6, member for Londonderry. b. Derry, 1932. He was in the LAW and the UDA in 1971, and in 1974 he had the key post of chairman of the Co-ordinating Committee which ran the loyalist strike. The committee included loyalist politicians, the UWC and representatives of Protestant paramilitary groups. During the strike he commented that it would have been perfectly possible to set up a provisional government. After the stoppage he led paramilitary spokesmen in talks with Secretary of State Merlyn Rees. In October 1974 he was suspended from the UUUC for three months for supporting the VPP candidate in W. Belfast in the Westminster election. In November 1974, as political adviser to the UDA, he took a UDA deputation to Libya for talks with the Libyan Government. A PSF delegation was there at the same time and there was apparently some contact between them, although both sides denied that there had been any negotiations. Barr said on his return that the possibility of Libyan financial aid to an independent NI, and the prospect of Libyan orders for NI firms, had been discussed. (He was involved later in negotiations for the sale of NI beef to Libya.) A UDA spokesman said they had been trying to stop Libyan aid for the PIRA. The VUPP executive at first decided to expel Glenn Barr over the visit, but later changed its mind, and in the end took no action. In the Convention he stood by William Craig when VUPP split over the idea of a voluntary coalition, and he was joint leader of the VUPP until February 1978, when it reverted to the status of the Vanguard movement, and ceased to be a political party. He did not follow Craig into the UUP, but took up an independent stance. Involved with UDA again in 1978–9 when he took part in a body known as New Ulster Political Research Group, which produced a plan for an independent NI, and he visited the US in 1979 with UDA leaders for talks in Washington with leading politicians. In June 1981 he withdrew from politics when the UDA set up the Ulster Loyalist Democratic Party. He then became head of a Derry training centre for unemployed youths drawn from both sides of the community. In 1988 he was associated with a project to attract US investment and the development of leisure and other facilities in Derry as a result of a link-up between the city and Boston. In 1990 he was appointed to the Community Relations Council. In 1993, concerned at the extent of Protestant alienation, whereby young people were 'queueing up to join the UFF', he considered returning to politics. In August Ulster Community Action Network, which he had chaired since 1992, asked Amnesty International to investigate claims of 'ethnic cleansing' against Protestants.

BARRY, PETER

Foreign Minister of Irish Republic, 1982–7. b. Cork, August 1928. He was deputy leader of Fine Gael, 1979–87, when he took over as Foreign Minister, and shared responsibility with the Taoiseach Dr Garret FitzGerald for NI matters. Formerly served as Transport Minister and Education Minister. TD, 1969–. Alderman, Cork City Council, 1967–73 (Lord Mayor, 1970–1). In January 1983 he visited NI for talks with local political parties. In March 1983 he declared that a long-term British presence in Ireland was a barrier to peace. As Foreign Minister he had a key role in negotiation of the AIA, and became the first co-chairman of the ministerial conference set up in November 1985, a post which he held until the defeat of the FitzGerald Government in 1987. In that year he was briefly Tánaiste (deputy Taoiseach) when Labour pulled out of the coalition. In early 1988 he said Unionists had been excluded from consultation on the AIA because it was feared they would sabotage it. At the same time he suggested a confederal system in Ireland. In 1991, he again became deputy leader of FG and said PIRA should be at the negotiating table if it renounced violence. Ceased to be deputy leader, FG, 1993.

BAXTER, JOHN LAWSON

Head of the Office of Information Service in NI Executive, 1974. b. Coleraine, Co. Derry, 1940. BA (TCD), LLM (Tulane University, New Orleans); qualified as solicitor, 1964 (QUB). He was chairman of N. Antrim Unionist Association, and member of committee which had drawn up Unionist election manifesto, when he was returned from N. Antrim to Assembly in 1973. Strong supporter of Brian Faulkner.

BEATTIE, REVEREND WILLIAM JOHN

DUP Assembly member for S. Antrim, 1982-6. Deputy chairman, Economic Development Committee; member, Devolution Committee. b. 1942. Deputy leader of DUP, 1971-80; party secretary, 1980-3. Chairman, party's social/economic research unit. Minister, Dunmurry Free Presbyterian Church. In April 1970, as a Protestant Unionist, he gained the S. Antrim seat at Stormont from the UUP by a majority of 958 votes in a by-election. He headed the poll in S. Antrim in the Assembly election, 1973, with 10,126 first-preference votes. Deputy Chief Whip of the United Unionists in Assembly, 1973-4. Re-elected in S. Antrim in Convention election, 1975, and one of UUUC negotiators in talks with the SDLP in the Convention. Lisburn Borough Council, 1977-. Candidate, Westminster general elections, for N. Belfast in 1970 and Lagan Valley in 1983. In 1982 INLA placed a bomb at his home near Lisburn but it was discovered in time and defused. Active in seeking to attract jobs to Lisburn area, and in 1992 was on council delegation to Canada to meet potential investors. He has campaigned on behalf of local investors in several failed investment companies.

BEGGS, JOHN ROBERT (ROY)

UUP MP for E. Antrim, 1983-. Assembly member for N. Antrim, 1982-6. Larne Council, 1973-. Mayor of Larne, 1977-. b. 20 February 1936. Originally DUP, but joined UUP in 1982 after being suspended by the DUP for visiting the council at Dun Laoghaire in the Republic in 1981 in defiance of DUP policy. First chairman of Assembly's Economic Development Committee, 1983-4. In 1983 his majority in E. Antrim was only 367 over Jim Allister of DUP, but in 1987 he raised it to over 15,000 as agreed Unionist candidate. (In 1992, he had a majority of more than 7,000 over Nigel Dodds of the DUP.) In 1987 he resigned as chairman of North Eastern Education and Library Board in protest at AIA, and attacked the idea of power-sharing with SDLP. In January 1994 he supported the electricity supply link to Scotland, despite claims of possible job losses and environmental effects in his constituency.

BELFAST see Andersonstown, Ardoyne, Ballymurphy, Europa Hotel, Falls Road, Markets, New Lodge Road, Peace Line, Sandy Row, Shankill Road, Short Strand, Stormont, Tiger Bay and Population

BELL, EILEEN

Alliance Party's general secretary, 1985-90, spokeswoman on women's affairs, 1988-93, education, 1993-, and delegate to Brooke-Mayhew Talks, 1991-2. b. 15 August 1943. BA Hons., history and politics (NUU). Before becoming party general secretary, she was active in the organisation as a member of the W. Belfast executive, 1981-4. In 1992 she became administrator of the Peace Train organisation. Unsuccessfully contested Newry and Armagh in 1992 general election. N. Down Council, 1993-.

BELL, STUART

Labour spokesman on NI, 1984-7. b. 16 May 1938. MP for Middlesbrough, 1983-. Barrister. In 1986 attended special NI Assembly committee on AIA to give Labour views. In March 1987 his comments on AIA were widely interpreted as an offer to Unionists to bring forward the review of AIA in return for Unionist support in Parliament, but party chiefs, including Neil Kinnock, denied any change of policy on AIA. Deputy chairman, BIPB.

BELL, WILLIAM BRADSHAW

UUP Assembly member for S. Antrim,

1982–6. b. Belfast, 1935. Served as N. Belfast Convention member, 1975–6. Chairman, N. Belfast Unionist Association, 1973–5. Belfast City Council, 1977–85. Lord Mayor of Belfast, 1979–80. Lisburn Borough Council, 1989–.

BELL, SIR WILLIAM EWART

Head of the NI civil service, 1979–84. b. 13 November 1924. MA (Oxon.). Joined NI civil service, 1948. Assistant Secretary, Commerce, 1963–70; deputy Secretary, 1970–3. Permanent Secretary, 1973–6. Permanent Secretary, Finance, 1976–9. On retirement from civil service, headed a group aiming to develop locally lignite power. He became a Senator and Honorary Treasurer of QUB. Active in Co-operation North. Former Irish rugby international.

BELSTEAD, LORD

Only Minister to serve for two periods at NIO – Parliamentary Under-Secretary, 1973–4 and Minister of State, 1990–2. b. 30 September 1930. MA (Oxon.). Was House of Lords NIO spokesman during both his terms at Stormont, and maintained his interest in NI affairs as an opposition front-bencher, 1974–9. Home Office Under-Secretary, 1979–82. After periods as Minister of State at the Foreign Office and Agriculture, he succeeded Lord Whitelaw as Leader of the Lords in 1988. Following John Major's arrival as PM in 1990, he was dropped from the Cabinet but given the largely nominal post of Paymaster-General, with the substantive job of deputy at Stormont to Peter Brooke, with responsibility for security and education. In November 1991 he strongly resisted any formal segregation within Crumlin Road Prison, where two loyalist prisoners died in an explosion. Soon afterwards security responsibility was transferred to Brian Mawhinney, while Lord Belstead took over Finance. He was dropped from the Government in April 1992.

BENN, JOHN NEWTON

NI Ombudsman, 1972–4. Commissioner of Complaints, 1968–74. b. Burnley, Lancashire, 16 July 1908; d. 16 September 1992. Before becoming Ombudsman (Parliamentary Commissioner dealing with grievances channelled through MPs about administration) he was Permanent Secretary, NI Ministry of Education. Hon. LLD (QUB), 1972; QUB Senate, 1973–86; Pro-Chancellor, 1979.

BENNETT REPORT

The report produced by a three-man committee, headed by Judge Harry Bennett QC, an English Crown Court judge, on the interrogation procedures of the RUC, and the operation of the machinery for dealing with complaints. The committee was set up by NI Secretary of State Roy Mason in June 1978 in response to many demands for an official inquiry after an Amnesty International team had inquired into seventy-eight complaints of ill-treatment by persons who had been held at the Castlereagh interrogation centre in Belfast and other centres. The committee, which reported in 1979, went outside its terms of reference to mention that there had been cases where medical evidence had been produced concerning injuries sustained while in police custody which were not self-inflicted. Two of the main recommendations of the committee – that closed-circuit TV should be installed in interview rooms and that terrorist suspects should have access to a solicitor after forty-eight hours – were accepted by the Labour Government, and virtually all the remaining forty recommendations were endorsed by the Conservative Government. But one Government Minister stressed in Parliament in May 1979 that only fifteen cases had fallen into the category of injuries sustained while in police custody, and not self-inflicted, out of a total of some 3,000 people who were detained in 1977–8. The publication of the report was accompanied by angry controversy and two doctors involved at the interrogation centres voiced their concern about ill-treatment.

BETTING SHOP MURDERS (ORMEAU/OLDPARK)

Five Catholics, one a fifteen-year-old boy, were shot dead in a betting shop on the Lower Ormeau Road, Belfast, on

5 February 1992. They died at the hands of two gunmen from the UFF. The killings, which brought widespread condemnation, were in retaliation for the PIRA bombing at Teebane, Co. Tyrone, the previous month, which resulted in the deaths of eight Protestant workers. The UFF repeated this tactic on 14 November 1992, when it shot dead three Catholic men in a bookmaker's shop on Oldpark Road, Belfast, in response to the PIRA bombing of Coleraine town centre. A few days after the Ormeau Road attack, two Presbyterian ex-Moderators, Dr Jack Weir and Dr Godfrey Brown, had a meeting with the UDA, but the UDA's Inner Council banned further meetings with the Churchmen when they discovered that they had also had meetings with PSF.

BIAGGI, MARIO

Democratic Congressman for New York and chairman of the *ad hoc* Congressional Committee on Irish Affairs, 1978–88. b. New York, 26 October 1917. LLB (New York Law School). First New York policeman elected to US National Police Hall of Fame. Despite an Italian background, he took up the Irish cause in 1970 when he co-signed a letter urging President Nixon to act on claims about the deprivation of human rights and discrimination in NI. He made several visits to Ireland. Biaggi was in Newry for a protest march held after 'Bloody Sunday' in 1972. In 1975 he met British officials and representatives of political parties, including PSF. The *ad hoc* Committee on Irish Affairs in 1978 had the objectives of holding Congressional hearings on Ireland, challenging the State Department refusal of visas to PSF members and generally promoting a 'broader' perspective on Ireland. In the same year he also met leaders of the Republican movement to urge a six-month ceasefire to facilitate a peace forum he proposed to hold in Washington DC. This visit, on behalf of the Irish National Caucus, was criticised by Taoiseach Jack Lynch for associating with men of violence and for misrepresenting the Irish Government's view in the US. The peace forum idea

was opposed by Senator Edward Kennedy and invitations were declined by political parties and PIRA. Biaggi reportedly showed interest in schemes for independence proposed by the UDA and the Ulster Independence Committee. In 1979 Biaggi announced the suspension of weapon sales to the RUC pending a review of US policy and subsequently campaigned to retain the suspension. In 1980, after the Democratic Party election platform confirmed its support for Irish unity, Biaggi sought a meeting, under the auspices of the UN, to decide the future of NI. In 1983 he co-sponsored a bill obliging US firms in NI to provide equality of opportunity. In the same year a delegation was sent to examine the employment record of Short Brothers plc and in 1984 he turned his attention to Harland and Wolff plc. In 1987 he was sentenced to two and a half years' imprisonment and fined $500,000 on charges in connection with a Brooklyn ship repairer and in 1988 he was convicted in a corruption scandal involving a New York defence contractor, Wedtech. He was sentenced to eight years' imprisonment for soliciting kickbacks in return for using his influence in the award of defence contracts.

BIGGS-DAVISON, SIR JOHN

Conservative front-bench spokesman on NI, 1976–9, and chairman of party's NI committee, 1979–88. b. 7 June 1918; d. 1988. MA (Oxon.). MP for Chigwell, 1955–74; Epping Forest, 1974–88. He had lengthy association with NI Unionists, and spoke frequently at party meetings. He warned repeatedly of an 'Irish Cuba' on Britain's doorstep. In January 1973 he wrote in the *News Letter*: 'Civil rights have been used as a front by the formenters of civil war; social reform as a stepping stone to social revolution. What civil rights are there in Cuba?' In 1980 he suggested loose linkage of UK, Republic of Ireland, Isle of Man and Channel Islands as Islands of North Atlantic (IONA). Strongly opposed Prior devolution plan in 1982. A Catholic, he said in 1985 that the lesson of the old Stormont was that Catholics were safer under Westminster. A leading

Conservative critic of AIA, but unhappy about Unionist policy of abstention from Westminster in protest against it. In 1986 one of founders of Friends of the Union Group set up to convince people in GB that the union with NI must be maintained. He spoke at a number of CEC meetings. He wrote several books, including *The Cross of St Patrick: The Catholic Unionist Tradition in Ireland* (1985).

BIRMINGHAM SIX

The six NI men sentenced to life imprisonment for the bombing of two Birmingham pubs on 21 November 1974, in which twenty-one people died, were finally freed in March 1991 after the most prolonged and intense campaign in British legal history to demonstrate a miscarriage of justice. After seventeen years in prison, they were told by the Appeal Court that their convictions were 'no longer safe and satisfactory', that fresh evidence cast 'grave doubt' on the scientific evidence, and that some police at the trial in 1975 had deceived the court. The freeing of the men came after the failure of two previous hearings in the Appeal Court and an appeal to the House of Lords. PIRA had been the prime suspect when the bombs exploded, but it issued an immediate denial which was, however, qualified to some extent by later statements promising an inquiry, about which nothing more was heard. In 1977 two priests – Father Denis Faul of Dungannon and Father Raymond Murray of Armagh – argued in a book, *The Birmingham Framework*, that the six men were innocent. Many Catholic clergy, including Bishop Edward Daly of Derry, supported the campaign. Irish Government Ministers including Foreign Minister Peter Barry added their weight and Labour MP Chris Mullin wrote a persuasive book on the case. The Birmingham bombings had led to the Prevention of Terrorism Act being rushed through Parliament in a weekend sitting, and the freeing of the Six also had major consequences. Home Secretary Kenneth Baker, conscious of the damage done to the courts system, announced a Royal Commission on Criminal Justice.

The many human rights groups who had worked on the case were vindicated, and there was a not inconsiderable boost to PIRA and its supporters. Ms Gareth Peirce, defence solicitor in the case, claimed in 1992 that fresh police investigations were aimed at re-establishing the convictions.

BLACK, ALISTAIR

Vanguard Unionist (late UUUM) Convention member for Armagh, 1975–6. b. Lanarkshire, 1913. MA, Dip. Ed. (QUB). Headmaster at Lurgan, Co. Armagh. Chairman of Co. Armagh Committee of UWC, 1974. One of the Vanguard Convention members who refused to support William Craig's idea of voluntary coalition, he became a member of UUUM, later UUUP, led by Ernest Baird. Stood unsuccessfully as UUUP candidate in Armagh in the 1982 Assembly election.

BLACK, SIR HAROLD

Last Secretary to NI Cabinet before direct rule. b. 9 April 1914; d. 1981. As Cabinet Secretary, 1965–72, he accompanied three PMs (O'Neill, Chichester-Clark and Faulkner) to London for talks with British Ministers. He had a key role in reform programme after James Callaghan's October 1969 visit, since he was on three-man steering committee which co-ordinated the work of committees on detailed changes.

BLACKBURN, RONALD HENRY ALBERT

Clerk of the NI Parliament, 1971–2, of Assembly, 1973–4, and of Constitutional Convention, 1975–6. b. 9 February 1924; d. 6 September 1993. LLB (London). Served Foreign Office, 1943–6; Stormont Parliamentary staff, 1946. Planning appeals commissioner, 1980–93.

BLANEY, NEIL

MEP for Connaught–Ulster, 1979–84 and 1989–. Independent Fianna Fáil TD for Donegal, 1977–. Earlier, TD for North-East Donegal, 1948–77. b. 1922. Neil Blaney succeeded his father, an old IRA man, in North-East Donegal, and has made it a strong power base. With his Republican background and his closeness to events in NI, he has regarded himself as a voice of NI nationalism in the Republic. He survived politically his expulsion from the Fianna Fáil party in 1970, following his sacking by the Taoiseach Jack Lynch. Soon after his dismissal from the post of Minister of Agriculture, he was accused of conspiring to import arms illegally into the Republic. But a district court found that he had no case to answer. In the Dáil in 1972 he attacked new anti-terrorist legislation and complained that the PIRA was being smeared, although it had arisen from the needs of the time from local defence committees in NI. He has frequently demanded British withdrawal from NI, and has urged that cross-border co-operation should be withheld until this is achieved. Despite his expulsion from Fianna Fáil, he topped the poll in North-East Donegal in 1973, and in 1976 a supporter, Paddy Keaveney, gained a Donegal seat from Fianna Fáil in a by-election, although he lost it again in the 1977 general election. In earlier years Blaney was one of the most influential figures in Fianna Fáil. He was Minister for Posts and Telegraphs and Minister for Local Government before becoming Minister of Agriculture. His capacity for local political organisation in Donegal led to his supporters being dubbed the 'Donegal Mafia' and his appeal in the north-west was confirmed when he easily won a seat in the first directly elected European Parliament. In Strasbourg he was appointed chairman of a group of independent MEPs. In the Fermanagh-S.Tyrone by-elections in 1981 he supported hunger-striker Bobby Sands, and his successor Owen Carron. After he lost his European seat in 1984 he was the centre of much speculation as to whether he would rejoin Fianna Fáil but he was clearly opposed to Fianna Fáil's acceptance of new extradition arrangements in 1987. He said an Irish person could not get a fair trial in GB or NI. He became longest serving TD in 1987. During the Brooke-Mayhew Talks in 1992, he urged retention of the Republic's constitutional claim to NI.

BLEAKES, WILLIAM GEORGE
UUP Assembly member for N. Down,

1982-6. b. 1934. Lisburn Council, 1977- (Mayor, 1987-9). Chairman, UUP Councillors' Association, 1978. While a member of the UUP Executive, he defied his party's policy of not meeting Government Ministers in protest at the AIA when, as Mayor, he greeted PM Margaret Thatcher in Lisburn in September 1988. He said twenty people had been murdered in the town and he had complained to her about Government security policy. In 1990 he joined the Conservative Party, and became chairman of the Conservative Councillors' Association. After the local elections in May 1993 he admitted that the NI Conservatives would have a struggle to survive.

BLEAKLEY, DAVID
Minister of Community Relations, April-October 1971. b. 11 January 1925. The only NILP member to serve in an NI Government, he was appointed to the Community Relations post by Brian Faulkner. He was not then an MP, so his tenure of office was limited to six months. A former shipyard worker, who through Ruskin College, Oxford, and QUB moved to a distinguished career in education and politics. Best-known NILP personality. MP for Victoria, Belfast, 1958-65, and served as chairman of Stormont Public Accounts Committee. Elected in E. Belfast to Assembly and Convention, in both of which he was the only representative of his party. He unsuccessfully contested E. Belfast in the Westminster elections, February and October 1974, and he was also unsuccessful in the 1979 European election in which he stood as a United Community candidate. Chief Executive, Irish Council of Churches, 1979-92. President, Church Missionary Society, 1983-. Chairman, Standing Commission on Human Rights, 1981-4. Founder member, Peace Pledge Ireland, 1990. In 1992 joined Alliance Party and was on its negotiating team in Brooke-Mayhew Talks. He strongly opposed water privatisation in NI. In July 1993 he appealed for calm after three nights of loyalist rioting on the Shankill following the funeral of Brian McCallum.

BLEASE, LORD

Created Labour life peer, 1978.
Opposition spokesman on NI in House of
Lords and Labour Whip, 1979–83. b.
Cromac, Belfast, 1914. Formerly William
(better known as Billy) Blease, he was
officer of the NI Committee of ICTU,
1959–75. He had a key role in securing
recognition of ICTU by Unionist
Government for the first time under PM
Terence O'Neill. In 1974 he faced an
arduous task when ICTU was unable to
counter the loyalist strike aimed at
bringing down the power-sharing
Executive. Associated over many years
with NILP, and party candidate in four
elections in Belfast. NI member,
Independent Broadcasting Authority,
1975–9. Rapporteur, EC cross-border
communications study on
Derry–Donegal, 1978. Hon. LLD (QUB)
and Hon. D. Litt. (NUU). Active member
of Lords and voted on the Maastricht
Treaty in July 1993. He criticised Kevin
McNamara's document, 'Oranges and
Lemons', opposing Labour Party
organisation in NI, as 'a great error of
judgement' and lacking the authority of
the NEC.

BLELLOCH, SIR JOHN

Permanent Secretary, NIO, 1988–90. b.
1930. In a lengthy civil service career he
served as deputy Secretary at the NIO,
1980–2, before moving to the Defence
Ministry, where he became Second
Permanent Secretary in 1984. Thus he
brought a useful mix of experience to
Stormont at a time when security issues
figured strongly in AIA discussions.

'BLOODY FRIDAY'

Friday 21 July 1972, when PIRA set off
twenty-six explosions in Belfast, which
killed eleven people and injured 130.
Seven people were killed at the Oxford
Street bus station, which had been
crowded at the time, and four at a
shopping centre on the Cavehill Road.
Two soldiers were among the dead. Since
this was the most devastating day of
violence in Belfast up to that time, and
many of the injured suffered serious
mutilation, the impact on public opinion
was enormous, and many observers
regarded it as the point at which PIRA put
itself outside the pale of political
negotiation.

'BLOODY SUNDAY'

The incident in Derry's Bogside on 30
January 1972, in which thirteen people
were shot dead by soldiers of the First
Parachute Regiment. The shootings
occurred on the occasion of an illegal
march organised by the Derry Civil
Rights Association, and they gave rise to
angry controversy. They were denounced
by civil rights leaders as 'another
Sharpeville'; the Republic's Taoiseach
Jack Lynch (FF) said it was 'an
unwarranted attack on unarmed civilians';
the British Embassy in Dublin was burned
down by demonstrators, and in the
Commons, Bernadette Devlin MP struck
the Home Secretary, Reginald Maudling.
The PM Edward Heath announced an
inquiry into the shootings by the Lord
Chief Justice of England, Lord Widgery.
That report did not appear until April
1972, but by then the Stormont
Parliament had been suspended: and the
convulsion caused by the affair was
regarded as the decisive factor in the
decision to impose direct rule from
Westminster. Lord Widgery's verdict was
a complex one. He held that there would
have been no deaths if there had not been
an illegal march, which had created 'a
highly dangerous situation'. But he also
said that it might well be that if the army
had maintained its low-key attitude and
had not launched a large-scale operation
to arrest hooligans, the day might have
passed off without serious incident. Lord
Widgery also found that the soldiers had
been fired on first and he said there was
no reason to suppose that they would
have opened fire otherwise. None of the
dead or wounded had been proven to
have been shot while handling a firearm
or bomb. The verdict was sharply
attacked and Jack Lynch said that it
showed the need for an international
examination of the activities of the British
army. Unionist MP Lawrence Orr said it
'exploded some of the myths surrounding
the so-called Bloody Sunday'. Around
the twentieth anniversary of the shootings
in 1992, there were fresh demands for a

public inquiry. The calls were supported by Derry City Council, but rejected by PM John Major. In January 1993 Major repeated a Government comment that those killed could be regarded as innocent, but this did not satisfy campaigners for a new investigation, including British Labour spokesman Kevin McNamara.

BLOOMFIELD, SIR KENNETH

Head of NI civil service, 1984–91. Permanent Secretary, Department of Economic Development, 1982–4. Earlier Permanent Secretary of Commerce, 1981–2. Environment, 1976–81 and Housing and Local Government, 1975–6. b. 15 April 1931. MA (Oxon.). As deputy Secretary to the NI Cabinet, 1963–72, he was involved in many of the crucial negotiations linked with the reform programme and the period prior to the abolition of the old Stormont Parliament. Under-Secretary, NIO, 1972–3, and Permanent Secretary to the power-sharing Executive, January–May 1974. With the signing of the AIA, he was heavily engaged in the meetings of the ministerial conference, as well as with political parties in 1987–8. In August 1988, after PIRA issued a threat to senior civil servants, his N. Down home was severely damaged by a bomb, but he and his family escaped injury. On his retirement from Stormont, he developed a variety of interests. He was immediately appointed BBC Governor for NI, and soon afterwards joined the Bank of Ireland's NI Advisory Board. In 1992 he headed a national inquiry into dentists' pay and conditions, and was appointed first chairman of the Higher Education Council for NI. Chairman of BBC Children in Need, 1992–. In October 1992 he told a Belfast conference on European affairs that Britain had failed to make good use of the 'huge bonanza' of oil revenues, while the Republic had 'exhibited for many years an even more serious improvidence'. In 1993 he told Initiative '92 inquiry that, in the absence of power-sharing, there should be consideration of a new tier of administration between central government and District Councils.

BOAL, DESMOND

Unionist MP for Shankill, 1960–71; DUP MP, 1971–2. b. Derry, 1929. LLB (TCD). One of NI's leading barristers (QC, 1973), he is also one of its most intriguing political figures. As a Unionist MP, he was frequently at odds with the party leadership. He was deprived of the party Whip for criticism of Lord Brookeborough as PM; he was prominent in the back-bench revolt against Terence O'Neill as Premier, largely because of O'Neill's decision to invite Sean Lemass, Taoiseach of the Republic, to Stormont, for unannounced talks; and he was highly critical of the law-and-order policies of the Chichester-Clark and Faulkner Governments. In 1966 he lost his post as counsel to the Attorney-General after he had defended the right of Free Presbyterians to protest at the General Assembly of the Irish Presbyterian Church. In 1971 he resigned from the Unionist Party after describing the tripartite talks between Brian Faulkner, Jack Lynch and Edward Heath as 'adding a new dimension of dishonesty' to Unionist politics. Soon afterwards he joined the Rev. Ian Paisley in launching the DUP, of which he became the first chairman. He resigned his Shankill seat immediately following the introduction of direct rule in March 1972, as a protest against Westminster's move. In 1974, after he had given up the chairmanship of DUP, he announced support for an Irish federal parliament holding the powers reserved to Westminster under the 1920 Act, and the restoration of the Stormont Parliament with its old powers. The idea attracted some interest in Dublin, but was generally rejected by Unionists. Paisley joined in the denunciation. In 1977 Boal was involved with Sean MacBride in a chain of contacts between PIRA and loyalist paramilitaries aimed at securing a PIRA ceasefire. In 1987 he became a senior counsel in the Republic after he had been admitted to the Dublin Bar to defend Peter Robinson MP on charges arising from loyalist 'invasion' of Clontibret, Co. Monaghan.

BOGSIDE *see* Derry/Londonderry

BOLAND, KEVIN
The Minister for Local Government in the Republic, who resigned from the Lynch Government (FF) as a protest against the sacking in 1970 of two Ministers – Charles Haughey and Neil Blaney – on the grounds that they had been implicated in the illegal importation of arms intended for NI. b. 1917. Boland claimed later that he had originally offered his resignation in August 1969, when he said B Specials in Belfast had led loyalist attacks on Catholic areas, but he had been persuaded by President Eamon de Valera to stay in office. After his split with Fianna Fáil he set up Aontacht Éireann (the Republican Unity Party), and claimed that the major parties in the Republic had abandoned their republicanism. But he failed in a series of efforts to return to the Dáil, and decided to quit active politics in 1976, when he got just over 1,000 votes in a Dublin by-election. In 1974 he sought to have the Sunningdale Agreement, reached by the British and Irish Governments, declared unconstitutional. The paragraph to which he took exception read: 'The Irish government fully accepted and solemnly declared that there could be no change in the status of Northern Ireland until a majority of the people of Northern Ireland desired a change in that status.' But in the High Court, Mr Justice Murnaghan held against Boland. He said that this paragraph did not acknowledge that NI was part of the UK, that it was no more than a statement of policy and that the court should not usurp the functions of the Dáil. Boland's appeal to the Supreme Court was dismissed.

BORDER POLL
The constitutional referendum introduced by Westminster to establish the extent to which support existed for the British link and for a united Ireland. The poll, intended to be taken every ten years, was first held on 8 March 1973. Questions and votes in favour were as follows:

Do you want NI to remain part of the UK? 591,820

Do you want NI to be joined with the Republic of Ireland, outside the UK? 6,463

Other figures: total electorate, 1,030,084; percentage poll, 58.7; spoiled votes, 5,973 (1.0 per cent); percentage of valid poll for UK link, 98.9; percentage of valid poll for united Ireland 1.1; percentage of non-voters, 41.3; percentage of total electorate supporting UK link, 57.5. The SDLP and most Nationalists boycotted the poll. The Secretary of State William Whitelaw said the wishes of the majority would be respected. Unionists welcomed the outcome, and the SDLP said it proved nothing since everyone knew that there was a Protestant majority in NI. The poll could have been repeated in March 1983, but Secretary of State James Prior decided against it. He said it would not tell them anything since recent elections had shown that a large majority wanted to remain within the UK.

BOTTOMLEY, PETER
NIO Under-Secretary, 1989–90, with responsibility for the Environment Department. b. 30 July 1944. MA (Cantab.). Cons. MP for Eltham, 1983–. Husband of Health Secretary Virginia Bottomley. Enthusiastic supporter of newly established Conservative organisation in NI. After he was dropped from the Government he continued briefly as PPS to NI Secretary of State Peter Brooke. In 1992, he was among MPs pressing for a new inquiry into the events of 'Bloody Sunday' in Derry – a plea rejected by PM John Major. His description of the Ulster Farmers' Union as sectarian was rejected by its chairman, J. Mulgrew, a Catholic. Member of the Transport and General Workers' Union.

BOYSON, SIR RHODES
Minister of State and deputy Secretary of State, NIO, 1984–6. b. 11 May 1925. An ex-headmaster on the right wing of the Conservative Party, and with a combative approach to opponents, he hit back at Unionists for their boycott of Ministers and their protests aginst the AIA. In March 1986, as Industry Minister, he said: 'Days of inaction heckling Ministers and generally making a mockery of the political process is deplored by rational

people. It is an abuse of the unemployment situation.' The rate of unemployment was particularly high during his tenure of office and he stepped up job-creation measures, put forward plans for the development of tourism, and raised FEA spending by 26 per cent. Shortly before leaving NI, he drew hostile comment with a suggestion that he would try to ease emigration to US and Canada for unemployed people. Moved to GB Department of Environment and left government in 1987.

BRADFORD, REVEREND ROBERT JOHN

The first NI Westminster MP to be assassinated in the Troubles, he had been UUP MP for S. Belfast for seven years when he was shot dead by a five-man PIRA squad at a community centre in Finaghy, in his constituency, on Saturday 14 November 1981. b. 1941. Formerly Methodist minister at Suffolk, close to the Lenadoon estate in W. Belfast, a flashpoint in the early period of the violence. Resigned from Methodist Church, 1974. In the 1973 Assembly election, he stood unsuccessfully as a Vanguard candidate in S. Antrim. His maiden speech at Westminster broke with tradition since he attacked the Constitution Act, 1973, as undemocratic, and security policy as inadequate. Keen sportsman and played for House of Commons soccer team. He was industry spokesman of the UUP and made a reputation at Westminster as campaigner against pornography. His murder was widely seen as an attempt by PIRA to provoke a loyalist backlash. Some of his friends also regarded it as a bid to silence an MP who had frequently accused Republican paramilitary groups of racketeering. PIRA itself accused him of being 'one of the key people responsible for winding up the loyalist paramilitary sectarian machine'. His death provoked a tense situation and calls by Unionists for better security generally, and a greater effort to protect politicians. Secretary of State James Prior (Cons.) got a hostile reception from a section of the congregation when he attended the funeral service. In 1984 his widow Norah

wrote an account of his career, *A Sword Bathed in Heaven*.

BRADFORD, ROY HAMILTON

Unionist member for E. Belfast in Assembly, 1973–4, and head of Department of the Environment in Executive, 1974. b. Belfast, 7 July 1920. BA (TCD). Unionist MP for Victoria (Belfast), 1965–72. Parliamentary Secretary, Ministry of Education, 1967. Minister of Commerce, 1969–71; Minister of Development, 1971–2. N. Down Council, 1989–. Strongly criticised British Government's initial handling of direct rule. He came into conflict with some Executive colleagues when he suggested that there should be some contact between the British Government and the UWC during the loyalist strike in 1974. In 1975 he was an unsuccessful candidate in the Convention election in E. Belfast. He speaks French and German fluently and was active as a broadcaster for both BBC and ITV before entering politics. Has had a long-standing interest in EC affairs, and was chairman of the European Movement in NI, 1977–87 (president, 1987–). In a novel, *The Last Ditch* (1981), he gave a barely fictionalised account of the inside struggle by NI Cabinet in 1972 against imposition of direct rule.

BRADLEY, PATRICK A.

Chief electoral officer, NI, May 1980–. b. 1935. BA (OU). Has had varied career in civil service both in London and Belfast, including periods at Air Ministry and Local Enterprise Development Unit in NI, and in private industrial management (Chemstrand and Du Pont). Joined electoral office in NI, 1974. Visited various eastern European countries since 1989 to advise on and observe free elections.

BRAY, BRIGADIER MICHAEL

Commander of UDR, 1986–8. b. 1937. His family has an unbroken record of military service going back over 300 years. He moved from NATO HQ to UDR post, but had considerable previous experience of NI. He spent first two years of commissioned service with the Duke of Wellington's Regiment at Holywood in the 1950s and, as a Company Commander in the same regiment, spent sixteen months in Derry in mid-1970s. In 1978–9 he had a four-month tour in Derry as Commanding Officer of a 'Dukes' regiment and was mentioned in despatches. During his career he served in many parts of the world, and was for a time at the Defence Ministry before going to NATO, where he became Chief of Land Operations. In 1988 he rejected suggestions that the UDR had a problem with links with Protestant paramilitaries. He said an internal review at the end of 1987 had shown that only one soldier had faced dismissal because he had taken part in a UDA parade.

BRIGHTON HOTEL BOMBING

On 12 October 1984 five people, including Conservative MP Sir Anthony Berry, died in a PIRA explosion at the Grand Hotel, Brighton, where PM Margaret Thatcher and several leading Ministers were staying during the Conservative conference. The PM was not injured. The judge in sentencing top PIRA bomber Patrick Magee, who placed the delayed-action bomb, to eight life sentences told him: 'You intended to wipe out a large part of the Government, and you very nearly did.' Two of Magee's five accomplices were also sentenced to life imprisonment. The bomb, with a long-delay fuse, had been placed in a sixth-floor bathroom, and went off at 2.54 a.m., while Margaret Thatcher, in a room below, was working on her party conference speech. She later described the bombing as 'an indiscriminate attempt to massacre innocent and unsuspecting men and women . . . to cripple Her Majesty's democratically elected Government'. A PIRA statement said: 'Today we were unlucky . . . but remember we have only to be lucky once; you have to be lucky always.'

BRITISH IRISH ASSOCIATION

An organisation which annually brings together top London, Belfast and Dublin politicians, diplomats, security chiefs, officials, journalists and academics to discuss the current NI situation. The weekend conference is usually held in Oxford, Cambridge or London, and several NI Secretaries of State have spoken at the gatherings as well as leading Irish Ministers. Garret FitzGerald (FG) addressed several meetings as Foreign Minister and Taoiseach. Sir Robin Day has presided at some debates.

BRITISH–IRISH PARLIAMENTARY BODY

The forum of British and Irish parliamentarians, which had its inaugural meeting at Westminster on 26 February 1990. The idea for such a body grew out of the Anglo-Irish Intergovernmental Council, and was given extra impetus by the AIA. The initial meeting was historic in the sense that it brought parliamentarians from the South of Ireland to Westminster for the first time since 1918 to conduct formal business. The membership comprised twenty-five British MPs and twenty-five members of the Dáil, with three of the British seats reserved for NI MPs – two Unionists and one Nationalist. Unionists refused to take part but the SDLP was represented by Seamus Mallon. Lord Dunleath attended for Alliance. The move was welcomed by PM Thatcher and Taoiseach Haughey, and the co-chairmen were Conservative MP Peter Temple-Morris and Fianna Fáil TD Jim Tunney. Austin Currie, Fine Gael TD and ex-SDLP, is a member. The group meets every six months, alternately in London and Dublin, to discuss issues of common concern. The EC figured strongly in early exchanges.

BRITISH ULSTER DOMINION PARTY

A small organisation originally launched in 1975 by Professor Kennedy Lindsay under the title Ulster Dominion Group, which changed its name to BUDP in 1977. Professor Lindsay, who was elected to the Convention on the VUPP ticket, submitted a policy document to that body in September 1975, urging that NI should become a self-governing dominion, with the Queen as monarch and with a resident Governor-General.

BROADCASTING BAN

On 19 October 1988, Home Secretary Douglas Hurd announced a ban on direct broadcasting by twelve organisations which supported violence: OIRA, PIRA, INLA, PSF, RSF, UDA, UFF, UVF, Cumann na mBan, Fianna na hÉireann, RHC, Saor Éire. The restrictions did not apply during elections and guidelines stated that representatives could be interviewed about constituency matters. The practice on television became one of dubbing on an actor's voice rather than using subtitles, sometimes the voice being synchronised to the speaker's lips. John Simpson, giving the Huw Weldon Lecture, said the ban had been used as a justification for the Iraqi restrictions imposed during the Gulf War. In the US 'health warnings' were being used on some BBC programmes. The ban intensified the interest in Gerry Adams, as 'the man Britain could not hear', when he visited New York at the beginning of February 1994. Although the ban was under review since October 1993, the removal of the 'Section 31' broadcasting ban by the Irish Government in January was expected to have an influence on the outcome.

BROADHURST, BRIGADIER JOSEPH CALLENDER

Deputy Speaker, Assembly, 1973–4. b. 24 December 1906; d. January 1987. UPNI member of Assembly for S. Down, 1973–4, unsuccessful candidate there for Constitutional Convention, 1975. A strong supporter of Brian Faulkner in Assembly. Had a distinguished military career in Middle East, and was Chief of Staff in Arab Legion. Expert on Middle East affairs.

BROCKWAY, LORD

Labour life peer, who campaigned over many years for more discussion of NI affairs at Westminster. b. Calcutta, 1888; d. 1988. As Archibald Fenner Brockway, Labour MP (latterly for Eton and Slough, 1950–64), he was among the first Labour members to call for reforms in NI. He was involved with the Campaign for Democracy in Ulster, and in 1971 made the first of several unsuccessful attempts in the House of Lords to have a Bill of Rights in NI. He spoke at one Tyrone anti-internment rally. He was at the centre of the successful campaign to have the Price sisters moved to Armagh Prison.

BROOKE, PETER LEONARD

NI Secretary of State, July 1989–April 1992. b. 3 March 1934, son of Henry Brooke (later Lord Brooke of Cumnor, Home Secretary, 1971–3, who was a descendant of the Rantavan, Co. Cavan, branch of the Brooke family, who were linked to the Brookes of Colebrooke, Co. Fermanagh – the Viscounts Brookeborough). MA (Oxon.), MBA (Harvard Business School). Cons. MP, Cities of London and Westminster S., 1977–. As Conservative Party chairman, 1987–9, he had already attracted attention in NI before he was appointed to succeed the longest-serving NI Secretary of State, Tom King, since he had opposed the idea of the Conservative Party organising in NI. But the involvement of local Conservatives in elections was something he was forced to accept, and they proved less than helpful when he set talks in train with the aim of securing the devolution envisaged in the AIA. Most prominent local Conservatives preferred integration. In 1989, 1990 and early 1991 he worked patiently through 'talks about talks' with the local parties to set up the structured discussions that eventually got under way at Stormont in April 1991. They were soon halted, however (see also Brooke–Mayhew Talks), and by the time they were reactivated in spring 1992, Brooke had been dropped from the Government. In his early days at Stormont, he had strong differences with Irish Ministers over the UDR and alleged leaks of security documents to loyalists. And in the context of the EC, he criticised Dublin for its curb on cross-border shopping. He angered Unionists and some Conservative MPs by saying more than once that Britain had no selfish interest in staying in NI. During the Conservative leadership contest in 1990, he initially urged Margaret Thatcher to stay in office, and later supported Douglas Hurd. In January 1992 he offered to resign as NI Secretary of State when there were protests that he had sung on Gay Byrne's TV show on RTE hours after eight Protestant workmen had been killed by a PIRA bomb in Tyrone. John Major did not accept his offer, but three months later, after the election, Brooke was on the back benches and failed in his attempt to be elected Commons Speaker in the new Parliament. Soon afterwards he admitted that he would have liked to have been able to meet PSF president Gerry Adams as a matter of history and as a 'human reaction' to his 'significant role' in events. By September 1992 Brooke was back in the Cabinet, replacing David Mellor, who had stepped down as Heritage Secretary. In October 1993 he began a review of the direct broadcasting ban on a number of organisations supporting, or committed to, violence.

BROOKEBOROUGH, 2nd VISCOUNT

Son of 1st Viscount Brookeborough, PM of NI, 1943–63, and active as a Conservative peer in the House of Lords and in the old Stormont Commons and Government. b. 9 November 1922; d. March 1987. As Captain John Brooke, he succeeded his father as Unionist MP for Lisnaskea in 1968, and held the seat until the dissolution of the Stormont Parliament in 1972. Parliamentary Secretary, 1969–70, at Ministry of Commerce and to PM James Chichester-Clark, with special responsiblity for Government information services. Government Chief Whip, 1971–2. Represented N. Down in Assembly, 1973–4, and Convention, 1975–6. While the UPNI was in existence, he put forward that party's views in the Lords, where he concentrated on security, farming and EC issues. At home in Fermanagh he was deeply involved in the promotion of tourism and in 1985 became president of Fermanagh Unionist Association. He was a strong opponent of the AIA, and attracted widespread criticism in January 1987 for a remark in the Lords that Cardinal Ó Fiaich was an 'evil prelate'. His son Alan succeeded to the title.

BROOKEBOROUGH, 3rd VISCOUNT

Alan Henry Brooke. b. 30 June 1952. Son of 2nd Viscount (John), whom he succeeded in 1987. Commissioned in 17/21 Lancers and transferred in 1977 to Co. Fermanagh battalion, UDR, in which he became a company commander. On succeeding to the title, he indicated that he would be active in the Lords where, although a member of the UUP, he takes the Conservative Whip. In 1988, he was appointed to the Lords EC Agricultural Subcommittee. Like his father, he is keenly interested in the development of tourism in Fermanagh. Green Park Health and Social Service Trust, 1993–.

BROOKE-MAYHEW TALKS

These unprecedented discussions on NI's political future spanned nineteen months – April 1991 to November 1992. They involved the British and Irish Governments and the four main constitutional parties in NI – UUP, DUP, SDLP and All. In the end, the exchanges did not produce any comprehensive agreement, but their very existence marked a historic milestone. Irish Ministers came to Parliament Buildings, Stormont – for so many years the seat of Unionist power – to talk across the table to the leaders of unionism. UUP leader James Molyneaux took his party to Dublin Castle – Britain's power base in Ireland before partition – to debate North–South relations. And although DUP leader Ian Paisley and his colleagues refused to journey South because Dublin had declined to commit itself in advance of a settlement to holding a referendum on the Republic's constitutional claim to NI, this was the sort of dialogue that SDLP leader John Hume had always claimed was the key to an eventual political deal. Such contacts had not occurred for some seventy years. The exercise had its roots in the many 'talks about talks' between local parties and NI Secretary Tom King and his successor Peter Brooke, held between 1988 and 1991. It fell to Brooke, assisted by Brian Mawhinney, to get an agreed basis for talks and the parties together in formal session in April 1991. The basis for the talks was that a 'new, more broadly based agreement' would be considered during a specified gap in Anglo-Irish Intergovernmental Conference meetings. The talks would involve three sets of relationships – within NI, North–South, and between the UK and the Republic. All strands would begin within weeks, and nothing would be agreed until everything was agreed. However, procedures had not been agreed in advance and there was much wrangling about venues and the choice of an independent chairman for the North–South strand of the discussions. Dublin and London apparently preferred Lord Carrington, but his record in Irish affairs was suspect to Unionists. Eventually Sir Ninian Stephen, former Australian Governor-General, emerged, and chaired talks at Stormont, London and Dublin. In London, the meetings were at the Queen Elizabeth II conference centre and Lancaster House, the latter venue stirring memories of Rhodesian independence negotiations. Peter Brooke presided over the June–July 1991 plenary sessions, which saw opening presentations by the parties and inter-party questioning on possible devolution. But Unionists insisted that they could not continue with the meetings in the shadow of a planned Anglo-Irish Intergovernmental Conference, and the process was halted by Brooke on 3 July 1991. The intervention of PM Major produced a formal restart in March 1992, with agreement to recommence after the April 1992 general election. By then, Sir Patrick Mayhew had replaced Brooke, who was obviously disappointed that he could not resume his role. But there were also changes at the top in Dublin. In early 1992 Charles Haughey stepped down as Taoiseach, to be succeeded by Albert Reynolds. Some Unionists, long hostile to Haughey, felt the change would be beneficial. But Reynolds was adamant that, with the constitutional claim on the table, the Government of Ireland Act, 1920, must be on the table as well. The upshot was that Unionists concentrated on demanding a referendum on the constitutional claim, and the Irish ministerial team – John Wilson (Tánaiste), David Andrews (Foreign

Minister), Padraig Flynn (Justice Minister), and Prog. D. representative Desmond O'Malley (Industry Minister) – were not prepared to go beyond saying that there could be a referendum on the Constitution in the event of an overall agreement. Failure to resolve this point would in itself have blocked a settlement, but on devolution there were also sharp differences. The UUP, DUP and the Alliance delegation headed by Dr John Alderdice found 'broad agreement' on a system of local rule based on Assembly committees. But this fell far short of SDLP expectations. In May 1992 the SDLP suggested that NI should be run by six commissioners with an assembly based on the European Parliament. Three of the commissioners would be elected in NI by PR, while the British and Irish Governments and the EC would each appoint one commissioner. There would also be a North–South council of Ministers which would deal with a wide range of issues, including economic issues and security. The SDLP approach reflected John Hume's view that neither majority rule nor power-sharing would produce stability. This radical approach found no support among Unionists (nor publicly from Jacques Delors), but the UUP was ready to envisage a less ambitious North–South element if Dublin dropped its constitutional claim. In short, Unionists rejected an executive role for Dublin in NI, and seemed set to concentrate in the short term on ending the Order-in-Council system of legislating for NI at Westminster and getting an NI select committee there, as suggested by the Commons Procedure Committee. Sir Patrick Mayhew, in an interview in July 1992, said he wanted to see a system of devolution with 'at least' the wide-ranging powers of the pre-1972 Stormont. And it seemed likely that the British Government would stall on Westminster reforms while any hope of devolution in the medium term remained. Both London and Dublin tried to put a positive slant on the collapse of talks in 1992, and Sir Patrick remarked that 'things will never be the same again'. Two junior Ministers, Dr Brian Mawhinney (1991) and Jeremy Hanley

(1992), assisted the Secretaries of State, and senior NIO and Irish Government officials were also involved. The FF–Labour Coalition, headed by Reynolds, that took office in the Republic in January 1993 shared Mayhew's wish to see the talks restart. SDLP and Alliance also indicated eagerness for fresh exchanges, but Unionists still saw the constitutional claim as the prime obstacle. In any event, it seemed unlikely that the 1991–2 format would be repeated.

BROWN, WILLIAM

UUP Assembly member for S. Down, 1982–6. Deputy chairman, Agriculture Committee, 1985–6. b. 1930. Down Council, 1977–93. Farmer; active in unionism and Orange Order.

BROWNLOW, WILLIAM STEPHEN

Unionist and later UPNI Assembly member for N. Down, 1973–4. b. Winchester, 1921. Down County Council, 1969–73. Unsuccessfully contested N. Down Westminster seat, October 1974, and Convention election, 1975.

BRUGHA, RUAIRÍ

Fianna Fáil spokesman on NI affairs, 1973–7. b. Dublin, 15 October 1917. Fourth son of veteran Republican Cathal Brugha, who was killed in 1922. Senator, 1969–73 and 1977–81; TD, 1973–7. He has described, in Tim Pat Coogan's *The IRA*, how he joined the IRA at sixteen, was interned during the war, and how he came to realise that IRA activities had not helped to end partition. Frequently visited NI as Fianna Fáil spokesman. In 1975 he called on Britain to disarm the loyalist paramilitaries. In 1976 he claimed that it was unrealistic to expect Ulster Unionists to abandon their 'not an inch' attitude while Britain was guaranteeing their position. In 1977 he suggested a federal Ireland, independent of Britain, with autonomy for NI. In the 1979 European election he was an unsuccessful candidate in Dublin. In 1987 he praised the UDA 'Common Sense' plan.

BRUSH, LIEUTENANT-COLONEL EDWARD JAMES AUGUSTUS HOWARD

UUP Convention member for S. Down, 1975–6. b. Fermoy, Co. Cork, 5 March 1901; d. 1984. Had distinguished army career. Wounded and taken POW during the British evacuation from France in 1940. Spent three years as POW. After the war he took up farming in Co. Down, was a leading figure in the Territorial Army and became deputy Lord Lieutenant for Co. Down. He first attracted public attention in 1973, when it was disclosed that over the previous two years he had built up a loyalist paramilitary group known as Down Orange Welfare, which claimed a membership at that time of about 5,000. In the 1974 loyalist strike he was a member of the organising body – the UWC Co-ordinating Committee. In October 1974 he resigned as deputy Lieutenant for Co. Down. In the 1975 Convention he represented S. Down, where he was president of the local UUP Association.

BRUTON, JOHN

Leader of Fine Gael, 1990–. b. Dublin, 1947. UCD and King's Inns, Dublin. TD (Meath), 1969–; the youngest TD (twenty-two) when elected. Minister of Finance in FG–Labour Coalition at a difficult period, 1986–7, and also in 1981–2. Also Industry Minister twice in 1980s. As FG leader has advocated the modification of the constitutional claim to NI, pointing out that the principle of consent figured in both the AIA and the Helsinki Accord in 1975. In March 1991 he visited Derry and had talks with John Hume, and in May 1991 he had talks in Dublin with leading Unionists, including Ken Maginnis. In January 1992 he had wide-ranging discussions in London with PM John Major and other political leaders. A convinced European, he has been on Council of European Movement since 1972, and in May 1992 welcomed the SDLP plan for a six-member Commission to rule NI, with one member drawn from Europe and one from the Republic. In 1992 he faced a major setback when FG lost one-fifth of its seats and its vote share

(19 per cent) was its lowest ever in the November election, thus destroying his hopes of leading a 'rainbow coalition' of FG, Labour and Prog. D. At the end of September 1993 he warned the Irish Government against dialogue with PSF, either directly or indirectly. In January 1994 he expressed doubts about 'clarifying' the Downing Street Declaration for PSF and opposed the removal of the 'Section 31' broadcasting ban. Towards the end of the month he visited UUP headquarters at Glengall Street in Belfast. Survived a leadership challenge from Michael Noonan in February 1994 and immediately reconstructed his front bench, seeking to improve the FG opinion poll position.

B SPECIALS *see* Security System section, pp. 436–7

BUNTING, MAJOR RONALD
A leading loyalist activist in 1968–70. b. 1924; d. 1984. BA (OU), M.Sc. (Manchester). A former regular army officer, he was involved, while a mathematics lecturer, in promoting local government reform. One of his earliest political activities was to help Gerry Fitt in a Belfast election. In 1968 and 1969 he was a leader of the Ulster Protestant Volunteers and the Loyal Citizens of Ulster, and associated with other loyalist groups opposed to the civil rights campaign. In November 1968 he joined the Rev. Ian Paisley in leading a Protestant rally in Armagh which blocked the path of a civil rights march. Like Paisley, he was jailed for this activity, but he was released quickly under the amnesty called by Major Chichester-Clark when he took over as NI PM. Bunting was prominent in harassing the PD march from Belfast to Derry in January 1969. He broke with Paisley in 1970. His son Ronald, who was associated with IRSP, was murdered in Belfast in October 1980.

BURCHILL, JEREMY
UUP Assembly member for E. Belfast, 1982–6. In 1983 resigned from committees on Environment, and Finance and Personnel. Representative of

same constituency in Convention, 1975–6. Belfast City Council, 1981–5. b. Dublin, 1951. Barrister. Former Honorary Secretary, Ulster Unionist Council, and chairman of Young Unionist Council. Conservative Party executive committee, 1973–4. Stood unsuccessfully against the Rev. Ian Paisley in N. Antrim at 1979 Westminster election.

BURKE, RAY
While the Republic's Energy and Communications Minister (FF) in the Haughey Government, he attended meetings of the Anglo-Irish Intergovernmental Conference in 1988–9 during the illness of Foreign Minister Brian Lenihan and when he was Justice Minister, 1989–92. b. Dublin, 1943. TD (Dublin N.), 1973–. Was Minister for the Environment for two periods in the early 1980s. Chairman, Dublin County Council, 1985–. Dropped from Government by Taoiseach Albert Reynolds when he took over from Charles Haughey in 1992.

BURNS, JOSEPH
Parliamentary Secretary, NI Government, 1971–2, and Whip, 1968–9. Unionist MP for N. Derry, 1960–72. b. Belfast, 19 July 1906. Joined USC at fourteen. In the early 1920s he worked on farms in Canada and later as a stocks-and-bonds salesman. Studied at New York University, 1928. Strong traditional loyalist, and prominent in Orange, Black and Apprentice Boys Orders. Chairman of UUAC which organised the loyalist strike of May 1977.

BURNS, THOMAS EDWARD
DUP, Assembly, 1973–4, and Convention, 1975–6, member for S. Belfast. b. Lurgan, Co. Armagh, 1927. Company director, whose firm developed a new building material – rubber concrete – in 1977.

BURNTOLLET
The point in Co. Derry at which the PD Belfast–Derry march was ambushed by militant Protestants on Saturday 4 January 1969. The marchers, then numbering about 70 and accompanied by 80 police, were attacked by about 200 Protestants

using sticks and stones. Several of the marchers were injured and some were driven into the nearby river. The marchers included two prominent PD figures – Bernadette Devlin and Michael Farrell. The incident gave rise to criticism of the RUC by civil rights spokesmen, who said the police had failed to provide adequate protection and had not acted strongly enough against the Protestants involved. The police pointed out that the marchers had continued through Burntollet despite police warnings.

BURROUGHS, RONALD ARTHUR
UK Government representative in NI from March 1970 to April 1971. b. 4 June 1917; d. 1980. His period of office covered the growth of both PIRA and loyalist violence and anxious decisions about marches through sensitive areas. He was also concerned in the security arguments between London and Stormont which culminated in the resignation of Major Chichester-Clark as PM in March 1971.

BUSH, GEORGE
President of US, 1989–93, b. 12 June 1924. Vice-president, 1981–9. Congressman for Texas, 1966–70. US Permanent Representative, UN, 1971–3. Director, CIA, 1976–7. He tended to follow policies he had endorsed as vice-president – that is, support for AIA and for extradition arrangements affecting PIRA suspects, along with opposition to US contributions to pro-PIRA groups. He also continued support for IFI. In 1988 election he made no special effort to attract Irish-American votes, but is believed to have had substantial support from that sector because of emphasis on values likely to appeal to Catholics. One of his first engagements as president-elect was a meeting with PM Margaret Thatcher, and his relations with her proved to be almost as close as those she had had with his predecessor, President Reagan. In March 1992 he was reported to have promised the Republic's Foreign Minister David Andrews that he would be prepared to act as an 'honest broker' in the Anglo-Irish process, but eight months later he had lost office. Many Irish-Americans had preferred his Democratic rival, Bill Clinton. Bush paid an official visit to Dublin in 1983, and said that while the US adopted a 'non-interventionist' policy towards Irish affairs, it would continue to condemn violence. When in the oil industry in the early 1960s, he paid a brief business visit to NI. A Boston genealogist has claimed that some of the President's ancestors named Halliday came from Rathfriland, Co. Down.

BUTLER, SIR ADAM COURTAULD
Minister of State, NI, January 1981–September 1984. b. 11 October 1931. Son of Lord Butler – R.A. Butler. Pembroke College, Cambridge. Took charge initially of the Departments of Commerce and Manpower, and in September 1981 of Agriculture as well. With the recession and the image of NI cutting outside investment, in 1982 he set up a new Industrial Development Board, to spearhead the drive for new industry, and the new Economic Development Department for which he took responsibility. In 1982 he negotiated with Republic's Government a plan (later dropped) for bringing natural gas from Kinsale to Belfast. After the 1983 election, he became deputy Secretary of State, and took charge of Finance and Economic Development. Minister of State at Defence until September 1985. Resigned as MP, 1987. President, British Horse Society.

C

CAHILL, JOSEPH
A member of the PSF executive, who was among the founders of the PIRA. b. Belfast, 1920. A former carpenter and construction foreman, he was reprieved in 1942 after being sentenced to death with four other men for the killing of a policeman in Belfast. He was Belfast commander for the PIRA for a time before moving to Dublin in 1972. In 1973 he was sentenced to three years' penal servitude for illegal gun-running and PIRA membership. In a Dublin court Cahill and four other men were convicted of

attempting to import arms and explosives which had been captured when the ship *Claudia* was intercepted in Waterford Bay on its way from Libya. When the judge described Cahill as the ringleader in the operation, he replied from the dock, 'You do me an honour.' He was in ill-health when released from prison, and turned his attention to PSF work. For a time he handled aid for Republican prisoners and their families, and later became general secretary and treasurer of the party. In July 1984 he was deported from the US for illegal entry. No action was taken by the RUC when he addressed the annual internment rally in W. Belfast in August 1992 – his first visit to the city for twenty-one years.

CALDWELL, THOMAS HADDEN (TOM)

Ind. Unionist MP for Willowfield division of Belfast, 1969–72. b. Uganda, 30 June 1921. He won Willowfield as a pro-O'Neill candidate, and unsuccessfully contested S. Antrim in the 1970 Westminster general election. In 1971 he aroused controversy and criticism from Unionists when he met PIRA leaders in the Republic in a bid 'to stop the killings'. In 1973 he joined the Alliance Party, but resigned a year later.

CALEDON

The Co. Tyrone village where the first protest in the 1968 civil rights campaign occurred. Austin Currie, then a Nationalist MP, took possession of a council house on 20 June which he claimed had been improperly allocated to a young, single Protestant woman by Dungannon Rural Council. He was ejected by police.

CALLAGHAN, LORD (OF CARDIFF)

As James Callaghan, Labour PM 1976–9. Responsible for NI affairs as Home Secretary, 1967–70. b. 27 March 1912. He first became interested in NI affairs in the 1950s, when, with other Labour MPs, he was concerned with studying ways of strengthening the local economy. His tenure at the Home Office saw NI move from being a departmental detail to one of the Government's most pressing

problems. As the civil rights movement gathered pace in the spring of 1968, he also came under pressure from Labour MPs in the Campaign for Democracy in Ulster. They not only demanded changes in line with those urged by the civil rights demonstrators, but argued that it was wrong for NI MPs to have equal voting rights in Parliament when NI issues could not be debated effectively at Westminster. In August 1969, after the serious violence in Derry, Belfast and other towns, he was involved, with PM Harold Wilson, in the decision to send troops to NI to support the RUC. At the end of August 1969 he visited NI for talks with the Government and a wide variety of interests. This was the first major intervention by the British Government in NI affairs. Although Callaghan sought to give the impression that electoral, housing and other reforms were being taken on Stormont's initiative, the Home Secretary was clearly the driving force. He returned for a second visit in October 1969, when the new-style RUC emerged, and the B Specials were abolished, in line with the Hunt report. Although he had drawn up contingency plans for direct rule, it fell to the Heath Government to implement these. In his book *A House Divided,* which he wrote while in opposition, and which was published in 1973, he made a number of points. He asked why the RUC had not tried to gain control of Derry's Bogside from the rear in August 1969. He also wrote that if the majority made the Assembly and Executive unworkable, then the UK would be entitled to reconsider its position and its pledges on all matters. He also said that the unity of Ireland could only come about through a freely negotiated voluntary agreement. 'So at the end of the day I would like to see Ireland come together again. If and when it does, it will be a signal to the world that the people themselves have entered freely into a new compact because they are at peace and at ease with one another and recognise how much they have in common.' The decision of his Government to back extra MPs for NI pleased Unionists and angered the SDLP, who claimed that he was buying Unionist votes to keep his minority Government in office. In May 1979, in his first speech as leader of the opposition, he indicated that his party would seek to keep a bipartisan policy on NI and he offered to co-operate with the Conservatives in seeking a political initiative. In 1981, after he had given up the party leadership, he called for an independent NI. But speaking in August 1989, twenty years after he had authorised deployment of troops on the streets of NI, he described the AIA as 'a bone that stuck in the craw of Protestants', which should be scrapped if something better could be put in its place. He said he believed the eventual political solution could only be found by the Ulster people.

CALVERT, DAVID NORMAN

DUP Assembly member for Armagh, 1982–6. Served on committees on Education, Environment, Finance and Personnel. b. 1945. Craigavon Council, 1973–89. Member, Southern Education and Library Board. He was prominent in the council protest against the AIA, and in January 1987 he was wounded in an assassination attempt by INLA, which claimed it was the start of a campaign against all those 'responsible for the continued oppression of Nationalists'. He was one of several Unionist Councillors in Craigavon who were surcharged and disqualified in 1989 over the refusal, then delay, in granting a lease to St Peter's GAA club. Candidate, NI Convention, 1975, for Fermanagh–S.Tyrone. Fought Armagh in Westminster general election in 1979.

CAMERON COMMISSION

A three-man commission of inquiry announced by PM Terence O'Neill in January 1969. Its terms of reference were to inquire into the violence since 5 October 1968, to trace the causes of the violence and to examine the bodies involved. The chairman was Lord Cameron, and the other members were Professor Sir John Biggart and James Joseph Campbell. It sat in private, and the NI Attorney-General gave an assurance that no prosecutions would be brought on the basis of any written or oral evidence to the inquiry. Brian Faulkner,

Minister of Commerce, resigned from the Government because he disagreed with the decision to establish the inquiry. The commission's findings were believed to be known to the Home Secretary, James Callaghan, when he visited NI in August 1969, but they were published in early September 1969. The commission declared that there had been a failure of leadership on all sides, and that the Stormont Government had been 'hidebound' and 'complacent'. It gave seven main causes for the disorders:

1 A rising sense of continuing injustice and grievance among large sections of the Catholic population, particularly because of the inadequacy of the housing provision of some local authorities and 'unfair methods of allocation' of houses to perpetuate Unionist control.

2 Religious discrimination in appointments by some Unionist-controlled authorities.

3 Deliberate manipulation of local government electoral boundaries to achieve or maintain Unionist control of some local authorities.

4 A growing and powerful sense of resentment and frustration among the Catholic population at the failure of the Government to investigate complaints and provide a remedy for them.

5 Resentment, particularly among Catholics, at the existence of the USC as a partisan paramilitary force recruited exclusively from Protestants.

6 Widespread resentment, among Catholics in particular, about the Special Powers Act.

7 Fears and apprehension among Protestants of a threat to Unionist domination and control of government by the increase of the Catholic population. These feelings were inflamed in particular by the activities of the UCDC and the UPV which had provoked a hostile reaction to civil rights claims as asserted by NICRA and later by the PD. The atmosphere thus created was readily translated into physical violence against civil rights demonstrators. The commission also criticised the RUC, which was said to have been inept on occasions. It said that 'subversive

elements' had used the civil rights platform to stir up trouble in the streets.

CAMPAIGN FOR DEMOCRACY IN ULSTER

A London-based group which monitored civil rights in NI and which was especially prominent in pressing for reforms in 1968-9. Although not confined to parliamentarians, it had the support of up to 100 Labour MPs on occasion, and among those who held office in it were Lord Fenner Brockway, and Labour MPs Stanley Orme, Paul Rose and Kevin McNamara. Gerry Fitt, as W. Belfast MP, was a frequent speaker at its meetings.

CAMPAIGN FOR DEVOLVED PARLIAMENT

A group launched in March 1988 to campaign for a 'strong devolved Parliament' as an initiative to replace the AIA and command 'extensive cross-community support'. Executive responsibility would be exercised by representatives chosen by an agreed method, such as PR or voluntary coalition, and would have responsibility for policing. There would be both legislative and administrative powers, and considerable financial autonomy. There would also be a Bill of Rights and a cross-border dimension. Among those associated with the group were ex-UPNI Assembly member Peter McLachlan, former UUP leader Harry West, Austin Ardill, James Cooper, Christopher McGimpsey, David McNarry, Alex Boyd, Ken Larmour, James Gorman and David Reid.

CAMPAIGN FOR EQUAL CITIZENSHIP

A pressure group headed by Robert McCartney QC, which has campaigned for the main British parties to organise in NI. McCartney stood unsuccessfully in N. Down in the 1987 Westminster election as a 'Real Unionist'. The CEC has attracted some supporters of integration and has argued that the setting up of devolved government under the AIA would hasten a united Ireland. It also claims backing from outside Unionist ranks, and says that members of the

Campaign for Labour Representation, who urge the British Labour Party to be active in NI, have been among its supporters. Some divisions appeared in the organisation in 1988 when McCartney returned as president after a brief absence. In 1988 both the Conservative and Labour parties came out against organisation in NI, but while Labour has maintained this stance, the Conservative conference forced a change of policy in 1989.

CAMPAIGN FOR LABOUR REPRESENTATION

Founded in 1977 to promote Labour Party organisation in NI, its case was regularly presented in the *Workers' Weekly,* later the *Northern Star,* and other publications emanating from 10 Athol Street in Belfast. It lobbied the Labour Party conference annually and members often challenged visiting politicians from Britain on the issue. In April 1986 it supported J.B.H. Black, from NI, as the candidate in the Fulham by-election. Its work paved the way for other groups such as the Campaign for Equal Citizenship. It was disparaging of the tactics of the Model Conservatives but saw them succeed in 1989 while Labour still refused to organise. It endorsed thirteen candidates standing for election in several District Councils in May 1993 but only one, Mark Langhammer, was elected, in Newtownabbey. It decided to dissolve on 23 September 1993 after sixteen years of activity, blaming its decision on the recently formed Democracy Now, claiming that the new body had made the case for organising in NI 'sectarian' rather than 'socialist'.

CAMPAIGN FOR SOCIAL JUSTICE

An organisation based in Dungannon, Co. Tyrone, which began in January 1964, and which over the next five years mounted a strong publicity campaign in Britain and abroad. Its declared aims were to collect data on injusticies in NI and to fight discrimination, especially in employment, housing, electoral practices and boundaries, and public appointments. Its efforts were particularly effective in building up support for the civil rights movement within the British Labour Party. Councillor Patricia McCluskey and her husband Dr Conn McCluskey, of Dungannon, became best known as speakers for the group.

CAMPBELL, GREGORY LLOYD

DUP Assembly member for Derry, 1982-6. Served on committees on Economic Development, Environment, Finance and Personnel, and as deputy chairman of Security Committee. Londonderry City Council, 1977-. b. 1956. Leads DUP group on council. He featured in the controversial *Real Lives* documentary broadcast by BBC in 1985 despite Government opposition arising from inclusion of Martin McGuinness of PSF. Strong opponent of Government decision to change name of City Council from 'Londonderry' to 'Derry' in 1984 and has also campaigned against the admission of PSF to councils and against the AIA. In December 1984 he and his family survived an INLA murder bid when a bomb fell off their car as they were driving away from church. Has criticised FEA for discriminating against Protestants, and one of founders of loyalist-sponsored Anti-Discrimination Association set up in 1988. Has published several booklets on fair employment; in *Discrimination – Where Now!* (July 1993) he claims increased discrimination against Protestants. At the beginning of February 1994 he published a booklet on the Downing Street Declaration, pointing out that it contained twenty-seven references to Irish unity and only two to the Union. He has praised the Garda for arms and explosives finds in Donegal. Chairman, DUP Councillors' Association. Member, Independent Orange Order.

CAMPBELL, ROBERT VICTOR

Unionist member of Assembly for N. Down, 1973-4, and unsuccessful UPNI Convention candidate for the same constituency. b. Coleraine, Co. Derry, 1914; d. 1978. Mayor of Bangor, Co. Down, 1966-70. Member, N. Down District Council, 1973-7.

CANAVAN, DENNIS

Labour MP for Falkirk West, 1983-; West Stirlingshire, October 1974-83. b. 8 August 1942. B.Sc. (Edinburgh University), Dip. Ed. Chairman, Parliamentary Labour Party NI Committee, 1989-. Lists British–Irish relations as one of his many interests.

CANAVAN, MICHAEL

SDLP member for Londonderry in the Assembly, 1973-4, and the Convention, 1975-6. Security spokesman of SDLP, 1974-82. b. Derry, 1924. Prominent in civil rights campaign in Derry. Chairman of Derry Citizens' Central Council in 1970, after holding office in the Derry Citizens' Defence Association and the Derry Citizens' Action Committee. Earlier he was on the executive of the University for Derry Campaign in 1965 and in later years led the successful drive to have full university status for Magee College. He was a founding member of the SDLP, and as security spokesman paid frequent visits to prisons and opposed the use of plastic bullets or any excessive force by the security forces. He expressed his opposition to the 1982 Assembly by refusing to stand as a candidate in Derry. In 1986 he was on the first board of the International Fund for Ireland.

CARDWELL, JOSHUA

Unionist member, Assembly, 1973-4, and UPNI Convention, 1975-6, member for E. Belfast. b. 1910; d. 1982. Belfast City Council, 1952-82. Unionist MP for Pottinger at Stormont, 1969-72.

CAREY, HUGH

Governor of New York, 1974-83. b. 11 April 1919. Associated with Senator Edward Kennedy and other leading Irish-Americans in encouraging US Government interest in NI, and in discouraging Americans from giving money to organisations associated with violence in Ireland. Member of Friends of Ireland Group. Stayed away from New York dinner for British Labour PM James Callaghan in June 1978 because he wished to protest against British slowness in eradicating violence in NI, and in ending discrimination against Catholics in jobs and housing. In 1979 he tried to set up a New York meeting between Britain and Irish Republic on NI. The idea was accepted by the Republic but rejected by Britain. On a visit to Ireland in 1981 he said the British Government's attitude to the hunger strike had increased support for PIRA in the US.

CARRINGTON, LORD

Closely involved with NI as Defence Secretary in the Conservative Heath Government, 1970–4. Leader of opposition, House of Lords, 1974–9. Foreign Secretary, 1979–82. Resigned in the wake of the Falklands crisis. Secretary-General, NATO, 1984–8. b. 6 June 1919. He was responsible for big build-up of UDR, but would not agree to radical changes in security tactics being demanded by NI Government in early 1971. He flew to Stormont in March 1971 in an unsuccessful bid to persuade Major Chichester-Clark to stay as PM. In December 1980 he accompanied Margaret Thatcher at the Dublin summit with Charles Haughey, which proved to have a large impact on Anglo-Irish relations. In 1991 Unionists objected to him as a possible independent chairman in the Brooke–Mayhew Talks, and soon afterwards he was appointed EC mediator in the former Yugoslavia, 1991–2.

CARRON, JOHN

Nationalist MP for S. Fermanagh, 1965–72. b. Kinawley, Co. Fermanagh, 1909. Was Lisnaskea rural councillor when he succeeded veteran Nationalist Cahir Healy in S. Fermanagh in 1965. In 1949 he unsuccessfully contested Lisnaskea, held by the then PM, Lord Brookeborough. During the short-lived opposition alliance at Stormont in 1969, he was spokesman on community relations.

CARRON, OWEN

Republican MP for Fermanagh–S. Tyrone, 1981–3. PSF member of the NI Assembly, 1982–6. b. Macken, Enniskillen, 1953. Trained as teacher at Manchester University and held a variety of teaching posts in Armagh and Fermanagh, 1976–9. Although he had no Republican family background, he was a founder member and chairman of Fermanagh H-Block

committee, and was a member of PSF when he acted as election agent for Bobby Sands in the April 1981 by-election in Fermanagh–S. Tyrone. When Sands died Carron was elected as a 'proxy political prisoner' in the August 1981 by-election. He fought on an abstentionist ticket and said he would operate as a full-time constituency MP. In the 1982 Assembly election he stood as a PSF candidate. In January 1982 he was arrested while trying to enter the US from Canada, along with PSF colleague Danny Morrison. He lost his Westminster seat in the 1983 election when the SDLP intervened to take nearly 10,000 votes and he was succeeded by an Ulster Unionist. In 1985 he denied an accusation in the Assembly that he was PIRA commander in Fermanagh. In January 1986 he was in custody on a firearms charge, but was given bail to fight the Westminster by-election in Fermanagh–S. Tyrone. He went on the run, however, and was only recaptured in the Republic in February 1988. Failure to extradite him to NI brought protests from PM Thatcher and Unionists. It had been claimed that his life would be in danger if he returned to NI, and this argument was accepted by the Dublin Supreme Court. In November 1990 Carron was in a crowd protesting against extradition when NI Secretary of State Peter Brooke attended Co. Cavan ceremony to mark reopening of canal link between Lough Erne and the Shannon.

CARSON, JOHN

UUP Assembly member for N. Belfast, 1982–6. Served on Environment, and Finance and Personnel committee. b. 1933. A Belfast shopkeeper, he was elected to Belfast City Council, 1971–, High Sheriff in 1978 and Lord Mayor, 1980–1 and 1985–6. MP for N. Belfast, February 1974–9. Pushed up majority in N. Belfast between two 1974 general elections from 10,000 to more than 18,000. The UUP lost seat to DUP when he retired for health reasons in 1979. Repeatedly called for tougher security measures in N. Belfast, and also specially active on housing issues. Voted with Labour Government on crucial confidence vote which led to 1979 election. His independent line, particularly in City Hall politics, has often put him at odds with colleagues. His criticism of Unionist boycott of councils over the AIA lost him the party Whip, but it was restored in 1992.

CARTER, JAMES EARL (JIMMY)

US President (Democrat), 1976–80. b. 1 October 1924. In the final stages of his election campaign in October 1976 Carter was widely reported as saying that there should be an international commission on human rights in NI; that the Democratic Party was committed to the unification of Ireland; and that the US could not stand idle on the NI question. His remarks caused the Irish National Caucus (an umbrella group for Irish-American organisations) to call for support for Carter. But there were protests from Unionists in NI, some MPs at Westminster, and the Peace People. There were also demands for clarification from the Irish Republic's Government. Carter then sent a cable to Dr Garret FitzGerald, Irish Foreign Minister, in which he complained that he had been misrepresented in some reports. He stressed that he did not favour violence as a solution to the Irish Question. He believed in negotiations and peaceful means of finding a just solution which would involve the two communities in NI, and protect human rights which had been threatened. In August 1977 he issued a statement which indicated that there would be economic help for NI if a political settlement could be reached. On 16 March 1978 he had a brief meeting at the White House with Mairead Corrigan of the NI Peace People at which he likened the US Government's efforts for peace to those of the peace movement in NI. In a video message to a Derry conference on 'getting beyond hate' in September 1992, he asked, 'How can we ever hope to get beyond hate if the only contact we have with each other is violent?' Also in 1992, he was mentioned as a possible peace envoy to NI when the idea was supported by President Clinton.

CARTER, RAYMOND JOHN (RAY)

Parliamentary Under-Secretary, NIO 1976–9. b. 17 September 1935. Labour MP for Northfield (Birmingham), 1970–9, when he lost his seat in the general election – the only member of the Stormont team of Ministers to do so. Initially responsible at Stormont for assisting the Ministers of State in charge of Commerce, Manpower Services and Education. Later took charge of the Environment Department, which covered housing, planning and local government matters. Ran into controversy in 1977 over his unsuccessful attempt to make the wearing of car seat belts compulsory in NI in advance of GB.

CASTLEREAGH *see* Bennett report

CATHERWOOD, SIR HENRY FREDERICK ROSS

Conservative MEP, June 1979–. Ulster-born industrialist and chairman, 1975–8, of the British Overseas Trade Board. b. 30 January 1925. In January 1972 he first suggested a Stormont Parliament in which the minority would have influence through a system of two-thirds majority voting and offers of Government posts to individual members of opposition parties. He repeated the proposal in 1974, when he came out strongly against an independent NI, which he said would be 'catastrophic'. In 1985 he assisted the NI Assembly devolution committee in the preparation of an agreed report, published before the AIA. In 1986 he urged a round-table political conference, but the idea foundered because Unionists insisted on the prior suspension of the AIA.

CATHOLIC ANTI-DISCRIMINATION

A body active between 1969 and 1974 in opposing prejudice against Catholics in private firms, Government departments, and institutions generally. It was also involved in pressing for reform of the RUC.

CATHOLIC EX-SERVICEMEN'S ASSOCIATION

Catholic paramilitary organisation formed after the introduction of internment without trial in the summer of 1971. Its organiser Phil Curran quickly claimed to have 8,000 registered members, and it was very active during 1972. It was described as a 'people's army' for the defence of Catholic areas, and although it was unarmed, it claimed to be able to get arms if necessary.

CENTRAL CITIZENS' DEFENCE COMMITTEE

This organisation, based on the Catholic Falls Road in Belfast, brought together in 1969 the various W. Belfast defence and community groups operating in Catholic areas. Its first chairman Jim Sullivan was a leading Republican, who was succeeded by businessman Tom Conaty. It also brought together local politicians such as Paddy Devlin MP (NILP) and Paddy Kennedy MP (Rep. Lab.), and the local priest, Canon Pádraig Murphy. Its first major crisis was over the Government demands for removal of the barricades set up during the violent summer of 1969. This entailed talks with the Home Secretary, James Callaghan, and many contacts with the army. There were repeated rows over the RUC and the extent to which the troops could prevent any loyalist attack. In July 1970 the CCDC was engaged in the angry controversy over the thirty-four-hour curfew imposed by the army on a large section of the Lower Falls. It argued that the army operation was unjustified, and particularly criticised the tactics which had led to the deaths of five men during the curfew. It claimed that hundreds of complaints had been filed with the CCDC over the behaviour of the troops, and that any ammunition seized did not begin to compare with arms supplies held in Protestant areas. The CCDC published a special book, *Law (?) and Orders, 1970,* itemising its case against the army, but official spokesmen denied an excess of force. During 1970 the CCDC took a strong line against violence. It called for a halt to the throwing of missiles at the army, attacked the shooting of RUC men, and said violence could harm the cause of justice. With the introduction of internment in 1971, it became involved in the organising of visits to Long Kesh,

and in arranging parcels for internees and prisoners. In June 1973 the committee made a bid to persuade the PIRA to call a ceasefire. The PIRA replied eventually that it could not agree to peace at any price. It set out a series of demands – an amnesty for all imprisoned because of the Troubles, withdrawal of troops from sensitive areas, declaration of intent to withdraw from Ireland, and agreement by Britain that the Irish people should decide their own future. The CCDC replied that PIRA should show maturity and recognise that peace was the first priority. The general theme of CCDC policy was that Catholics had been treated unfairly by the security forces in comparison with Protestants. In 1973 it put out a 'Black Paper' calling for replacement of the RUC by an 'impartial police force'. William Whitelaw, as Secretary of State, retorted that there was little point in looking back and rehearsing old grievances. The CCDC HQ was among Falls Road premises bombed in November 1973. (*See also* Falls Road.)

CHANNON, HENRY PAUL GUINNESS

Minister of State, NIO, 1972. b. 9 October 1935. Has Irish family associations – his mother was a daughter of the 2nd Lord Iveagh, head of the Guinness family. His London home was the venue of the secret meeting between Secretary of State William Whitelaw and PIRA leaders in July 1972. Conservative MP for Southend W., 1959–. Secretary for Trade and Industry, 1986–7. Secretary for Transport 1987–9. Chairman, Commons Finance and Services Committee, 1992–.

CHARTER GROUP

Group established in 1986 and drawn from UUP to campaign for the return of devolved government to NI. Headed by ex-UUP leader Harry West. Its policy document issued in 1987 was signed by West, ex-UUP MP Austin Ardill, and David McNarry, who claimed the group had about 200 supporters. But UUP leader James Molyneaux stressed that the group did not speak for the party. In 1991 the group said it was an 'error of judgement' to hold inter-party talks at Stormont, and at the same time suggested a Unionist convention to sort out policy issues. In November 1991 it said Molyneaux and Hume should make way for younger men. In September 1993 the group was concerned that the Hume–Adams talks had rejected a power-sharing devolved government for 'unity or bust'. It asked the 'Catholic establishment' to state their acceptance of the ramifications of the constitutional status of NI.

CHICHESTER-CLARK, MAJOR JAMES *see* Moyola, Lord

CHICHESTER-CLARK, SIR ROBERT (ROBIN)

Unionist MP for Londonderry, 1955–February 1974. Announced decision not to seek renomination in January 1973. Unsuccessful in contesting nomination for Lewes in Sussex. b. 10 January 1928. Brother of Lord Moyola, PM NI, 1969–71. Chief Conservative spokesman, NI, 1964–70. Minister of State, Employment, 1972–4. Chairman of the Unionist MPs at Westminster, 1971–4. He kept closely in touch with his brother as PM, and in January 1971 he voted against the Conservative Government as a protest against what he called the 'ineffectiveness' of the Government's security policy in NI. In July 1971, a few weeks before internment was introduced, he threatened to withdraw support altogether unless there was a tougher anti-terrorist policy. Patron of Friends of the Union, 1986–.

CHILCOT, SIR JOHN

Permanent Under-Secretary, NIO, 1990–. b. 22 April 1939. MA (Cantab.). Civil service career began in 1963 in Home Office, where he was private secretary to three Home Secretaries – Jenkins, Whitelaw and Rees. Has also served in Cabinet Office and was deputy Under-Secretary in Home Office before moving to NIO. In 1991–2, he was involved in the Brooke–Mayhew Talks. Knighted in January 1994.

CITY OF LONDON BOMBINGS

On 10 April 1992 PIRA set off its largest bomb in GB, in a van in the City of London, killing three people and causing some £800 million damage. Another large device was exploded almost simultaneously in N. London, damaging an important flyover and nearby flats. The blasts came as counting ended in the general election, and were accompanied by a PIRA threat to continue such attacks. Almost exactly a year later – 24 April 1993 – PIRA struck again at the City, with a huge van bomb causing £350 million damage in Bishopsgate and killing one man. The cost of damage led to the passage of the Reinsurance (Acts of Terrorism) Act in May and the setting up of security checks on roads into the City of London from 3 July.

CLARK, SIR GEORGE

Patron of Ulster Unionist Council, 1990–1; President, 1979–90. b. 1914; d. 1991. NI Senator, 1951–72. Grand master, Grand Orange Lodge of Ireland, 1957–67. Chairman of standing committee of Ulster Unionist Council, 1967–72. Sir George, who had started out in politics as Stormont MP for Dock division of Belfast, attracted interest in the early 1960s when he had talks with the late Gerry Lennon, a Nationalist Senator, about the possibility of improving relations between both sections of the community. The discussions, known as the 'Orange–Green talks' did not have any tangible result. As chairman of the Unionist standing committee, he presided at a series of crucial meetings which preceded the resignation of Terence O'Neill from the premiership. He was a member of the party delegation that made clear to Secretary of State James Prior in 1982 its opposition to 'rolling devolution'.

CLARK-GLASS, MARY

Alliance Party spokeswoman on European affairs, 1992–. Member, Social and Economic Committe of EC, 1978–82. b. S. Wales, 1940. BA (University of London); FRS. Joined Alliance Party in 1976 when she was a law lecturer at the Belfast College of Business Studies (1974–9), and was on National Consumer Council, 1978–91. Chair and chief executive of NI

Consumer Council, 1984–92, after presenting a regular programme on consumer affairs on BBC NI for seven years. In October 1992 she joined the Alliance negotiating team in the Brooke–Mayhew Talks and at the same time was co-opted to the party's Strategy Committee and to the Executive of the European Liberals. SACHR, 1990–. Chair of Extern Organisation, 1988–. Former chair of Local National Insurance and Supplementary Benefits Appeals Tribunal (Lisburn). Wife of Basil Glass, founder member and former deputy leader of Alliance. Party candidate in 1994 European election.

CLINTON, WILLIAM JEFFERSON (BILL)

US President (Democrat), 1993–. Governor of Arkansas, 1977–80 and 1982–93. Lawyer. b. Hope, Arkansas, 19 August 1946. Law graduate of Georgetown University and Rhodes Scholar at Oxford. In defeating George Bush, he won back many Irish-American voters who had gone over to Ronald Reagan and who had stayed with Bush in 1988. He expressed sympathy with many issues of concern to Irish-Americans, including fair employment in NI and the MacBride Principles. During his campaign he also voiced concern about the 'wanton use of lethal force' by the security forces in NI, and supported the idea of issuing a visa to PSF president Gerry Adams. He also proposed sending a presidential peace envoy to NI – an idea opposed by the British Government and Unionists. Some Washington reports said that such an appointment would be conditional on the agreement of all the parties involved. Taoiseach Albert Reynolds told Clinton that he was sure the Irish could count on his 'unremitting efforts' to help deal with the 'tragic problem' of NI. A prominent Irish-American, Mayor Ray Flynn of Boston, who was national co-chairman of the Clinton campaign (now Ambassador to the Vatican), claimed Clinton was 'very, very knowledgeable' about NI affairs. On St Patrick's Day 1993 the President disclosed that he would not be going ahead with the appointment of a peace envoy or fact-finding mission 'for the time being' but stressed that he would be supportive of local talks and keeping in close touch with the situation. He also announced the appointment of Jean Kennedy Smith, sister of late President John F. Kennedy, as Ambassador to Ireland. This was seen as a means of strengthening US monitoring of Irish affairs. Clinton had been urged by many Congressmen and Senators, as well as Irish-American groups, to press on with his envoy plan, but he was also conscious of warnings against it from many quarters. PM Major had indicated opposition to any mediation effort, whilst the influential Tom Foley, Speaker of the House of Representatives, had suggested that a special US envoy might be 'disruptive and damaging' to NI inter-party talks. After talks between Clinton and Taoiseach Albert Reynolds, also on 17 March 1993, Reynolds welcomed Clinton's approach to NI. It also emerged that the President would back the maintenance of the $20 million per year grant to the IFI. SDLP leader John Hume told Clinton at a Washington lunch that he hoped he would become the first President in office to visit NI, particularly since some of his mother's (Cassidy) ancestors had come from Fermanagh. There was speculation in Fermanagh that her forebears might have been linked with Ballycassidy. Shortly before the St Patrick's Day meetings, the House of Representatives in Clinton's home state of Arkansas had described NI as a 'sectarian state', and in the wake of the meetings there were calls for new hearings on NI before the Senate Foreign Relations Committee. In May 1993 Clinton said he did not want to create an NI-type problem in Bosnia. In September, during a visit by a delegation led by former Congressman Bruce Morrison, a letter from Clinton was published which indicated his agenda. It urged UK action on job discrimination, citing a 2.5:1 unemployment ratio, more effective safeguards against the 'wanton use of lethal force' and against 'further collusion' between the security forces and Protestant paramilitaries. It repeated that the 'special envoy' idea could be a catalyst for peace. In the wake of the Shankill bomb at the end of October 1993 he condemned violence and supported talks between the parties. He informed David Dinkins, Mayor of New York, in the second week of November that he would not change his previous decision of May to refuse Gerry Adams a visa because of 'his involvement in terrorist activity'. However, Clinton changed his mind at the end of January 1994, in what appeared to be almost a personal decision and contrary to most official advice. Adams was granted a visa limited to forty-eight hours' duration and to within twenty-five miles of New York City; fund-raising, directly or indirectly, was forbidden. Clinton said that this course of action seemed the appropriate thing to do to 'advance the cause of peace'. However, any anticipated ceasefire was frustrated and the coast-to-coast television coverage seemed to mock the physical restrictions placed on the visit. When Adams left the US, Clinton gave his full backing to the joint declaration of Premiers Major and Reynolds and dropped any plans for a peace envoy.

CLOSE, SEAMUS

Deputy leader of the Alliance Party, 1991–. b. 1948. Assembly member for S. Antrim, 1982–6 (served on economic and finance committees). Lisburn Council, 1973–. Its first non-Unionist Mayor, 1993–. Chairman, Alliance Party, 1981, and economic spokesman, 1982–91; deputy chairman, 1991–. Member of party delegation at Atkins conference, 1980. Unsuccessfully contested Fermanagh–S. Tyrone by-election, August 1981; and 1983, 1987 and 1992 general elections in Lagan Valley. In 1986 he was among Alliance councillors who mounted a High Court challenge to Unionist anti-AIA tactic of council adjournments. Contender for Alliance leadership in 1987. A key delegate in Brooke–Mayhew Talks; in a break in discussion in January 1992, he complained that the intransigence of 'yesterday's men' was blocking success.

COALISLAND

A village a few miles from Dungannon, Co. Tyrone, with a mainly Catholic population, and suffering heavily from unemployment, from which the first civil rights march set off for Dungannon on 24 August 1968. The Scarman tribunal mentioned in its report that it had been told that 400 men were without employment out of a total population of 3,000. 'It is not without significance,' said Scarman, 'that the first of the events of the 1968–9 sequence of disturbances began in this little place.' In 1990 a £2 million regeneration plan for the town was announced by Environment Minister Richard Needham, who visited the town despite a security leak on his movements. The IFI was involved in the scheme. Local unemployment was then around 50 per cent. In February 1992 four PIRA members were shot dead by the SAS after they had attacked the RUC station. In May 1992 the behaviour of members of the Parachute Regiment in the town gave rise to widespread protests by Nationalists and Catholic clergy, which were supported by the Irish Government. A senior officer was moved, disciplinary action was taken by the army, and some members of the regiment were brought to court.

COLLINS, JAMES GERARD (GERRY)

Foreign Minister of Irish Republic, 1989–92. b. 1938. BA (UCD). Former schoolteacher, he succeeded his father James as TD for W. Limerick in 1967. Minister for Posts and Telegraphs, 1970–3. Council of Europe, 1973. As Minister for Justice, 1977–81, he became closely involved with NI issues such as cross-border security and extradition. In the short-lived Fianna Fáil administration of 1982, he was strongly critical as Foreign Minister of James Prior's 'rolling devolution' scheme, which he found lacking any Anglo-Irish dimension and a retreat from power-sharing. As Justice Minister, 1987–9, he regularly accompanied Foreign Minister Brian Lenihan at Anglo-Irish Intergovernmental Conference meetings and was prominent in the security and extradition discussions that provoked intense controversy in London–Dublin relations at this period. On taking over Foreign Affairs in 1989, as co-chairman of the conference he was critical of the UDR and concerned about allegations of 'leaks' of security documents to loyalist paramilitaries. In September 1990 he spoke at the UN of his hopes for a 'durable solution' in NI, and in 1991 he expressed 'cautious optimism' about the first stage of the inter-party talks. In the leadership battle at the end of 1991, he criticised Albert Reynolds for his challenge to Charles Haughey, and Reynolds dropped him from the Government when he became Taoiseach in February 1992.

COLNBROOK, LORD
As Humphrey Atkins, Secretary of State for NI, May 1979–September 1981. b. 12 August 1922. After service in Royal Navy, 1940–8, he developed an interest in politics, and became Conservative MP for Merton and Morden, 1955–70, and Spelthorne, 1970–87. He was Parliamentary Private Secretary to Civil Lord of the Admiralty, 1959–62, and Honorary Secretary of the Conservative Defence Committee, 1965–7. From 1967 to 1979 he served either as an opposition or Government Whip, and was Government Chief Whip, 1973–4. He was the third former Conservative Chief Whip to become NI Secretary of State, the others being William Whitelaw and Francis Pym. His appointment as NI Secretary was one of the few surprises in Margaret Thatcher's first Cabinet. It became necessary because of the assassination of the party's NI spokesman Airey Neave. Like Neave, he was a very close adviser of the new PM. The upsurge of PIRA violence in August 1979 led to his policy of increasing RUC strength by 1,000. His most severe test came with the Republican hunger strikes in 1980 and 1981 – the latter resulting in the deaths of ten prisoners, including Bobby Sands MP. He reflected Thatcher's uncompromising opposition to the protest, which was still under way when he left office. He tried two unsuccessful political initiatives. The first was a Constitutional Conference at Stormont, January–March 1980, attended by the DUP, SDLP and Alliance. The UUP boycotted it. And in 1981 he proposed a fifty-member Advisory Council which would consist of nominated members. On leaving NI he became deputy Foreign Secretary, but he resigned along with the Foreign Secretary at the start of the Falklands crisis in 1982. He was knighted in 1983 and created life peer in 1987. Chairman of Conservative Peers. Press Complaints Commission, 1990–.

COLVILLE, LORD (OF CULROSS)
Conservative peer initially appointed by Home Secretary Douglas Hurd to independently review emergency legislation. QC. b. 1933. Lord Colville, who visits NI periodically, had some of his recommendations included in the new PTA brought forward in 1988. The Government accepted that the legislation, formerly limited to five years, should have greater permanence, but it rejected his idea of dropping annual renewal by Parliament. It also failed to adopt his proposal that exclusion orders should be replaced by tighter immigration procedures. This change, Lord Colville argued, would be 'more acceptable than a system of internal exile'. When the European Court of Human Rights ruled in 1988 against seven-day detention under the PTA, he opposed calls for a special tribunal to consider such cases. He said this would raise expectations that reasons for detention would be made public when this could not be done. In June 1992 he called for urgent action to deal with allegations of ill-treatment of suspects at the Castlereagh holding centre – a plea that brought an almost immediate announcement by NI Secretary of State Mayhew of an independent commissioner for RUC holding centres. Lord Colville also wanted some sort of lay presence in the centres. His proposal in 1990 that the power of internment should be dropped was not accepted.

COMBINED LOYALIST MILITARY COMMAND
Umbrella body of the loyalist paramilitaries, UVF, UFF and Red Hand Commando, which emerged in April 1991 to call a ceasefire to coincide with the start of the inter-party talks at Stormont; the ceasefire ended at midnight, 4 July, when the Stormont

discussions ended. The CLMC linked the ceasefire to a successful outcome of the talks, but it broke the ceasefire in June when the UFF killed Buncrana (Co. Donegal) PSF councillor Eddie Fullerton. On 30 June PIRA murdered UDP chairman Cecil McKnight in Derry and claimed he was one of seven members of CLMC. The ceasefire was not repeated during the second stage of the Brooke–Mayhew Talks in 1992, and the CLMC was believed to have a role in the upsurge of loyalist violence in 1991–2. In December 1992 it authorised the firing of a rocket at Crumlin Road Prison. Early in November 1993 CLMC rejected a PIRA offer that it would stop targeting loyalists; in response, they required a complete cessation of PIRA violence before their campaign against nationalists could end. On 22 November they warned that in the event of peace being 'bought at any price' they were 'preparing for war'. On 10 December they again warned of violence if the Union was tampered with but they also defended the democratic purusit of change and endorsed the principle of North–South structures. After the Downing Street Declaration on 15 December they made no immediate statement, preferring to await a PIRA response.

COMMISSIONER OF COMPLAINTS
The officer who deals with complaints of maladministration against local authorities and public bodies. First created in 1969. (*See* McIvor, [Frances] Jill.)

COMMITTEE ON THE ADMINISTRATION OF JUSTICE
Broadly based group formed in 1980 to monitor the administration of justice. Has issued frequent comments on legal developments and was particularly critical of the supergrass system. Its chairman, Stephen McBride, in 1988 deplored 'the efforts of sectarian supporters of violence to hi-jack the mantle of successors to the civil rights movement'. In May 1992 it urged the return of jury trials.

COMMON MARKET *see* European Community

COMMON MARKET REFERENDUM
In the Common Market poll in June 1975 NI recorded a narrow majority in favour of remaining in the EC. The result was a surprise, since there had been a strong lobby against membership, involving a large section of unionism, including MPs like Enoch Powell and the Rev. Ian Paisley. The Northern Ireland Committee of the Irish Congress of Trade Unions had also campaigned against membership. The turnout of 48.2 per cent of the 1,030,534 electors was low by local standards. The figures were:

YES	259,251	52.1 per cent
NO	237,911	47.9 per cent
YES MAJORITY	21,340	4.2 per cent

COMMUNIST PARTY OF IRELAND
The party was originally founded on an all-Ireland basis in 1933, but it split during World War II into the Communist Party of Northern Ireland, and the Irish Workers' Party in the South. In 1970 the party was reunited at a Belfast conference, with separate area committees North and South. The NI executive members at the time of the merger were: Andrew Barr, Hugh Moore, James Graham, Brian Graham, Edwina Stewart, James Stewart, Betty Sinclair, Hugh Murphy, Sean Morrissey, and Bill Somerset. Barr and Graham were leading trade unionists, and Sinclair was secretary of Belfast trade-union council and first secretary of NICRA, of which Edwina Stewart later became secretary. Membership of the CPI at the time of the merger was probably between 400 and 500. The CPI has taken the line that there must be a declaration of independence by the whole of Ireland and that 'it is not in the interests of the Irish people to be part of the monopoly capitalist system'. In 1975 the party called on all paramilitary groups to order a ceasefire, and it also urged the withdrawal to barracks of British troops. No Communist candidate has been returned in any Stormont election, although candidates have stood in Belfast on several occasions. In the 1982 Assembly election two CPI candidates appeared in S. Antrim and

S. Belfast; they polled about 400 votes between them and lost their deposits. The Communists have been credited, by some writers, with exercising a large background influence in the Troubles but there is evidence that party members in London, Belfast and Dublin have often been at odds on the NI situation. External broadcasts from Communist countries, notably the USSR, China and Albania, during the 1970s frequently attacked British policy in Ireland, but Russian authorities always rejected suggestions that they had supplied arms to the PIRA. In March 1987 CPI had a visit from a member of the Soviet International Department, and later that year rejected suggestions that the Workers' Party was being given more attention in Moscow than the CPI. *Pravda* had mentioned a WP speech at the seventieth anniversary of the October Revolution, while ignoring the CPI. The party has been generally critical of the operation of the AIA. In 1988 it put forward a development plan for W. Belfast. In September 1990, despite the retreat of Communism in Eastern Europe, the party decided to continue in existence and to retain its name.

COMMUNITY RELATIONS COUNCIL

The CRC was established by the British Government in January 1990 as an independent organisation to promote better community relations and the recognition of cultural diversity in NI. Its membership was widely based, and it represented a less centralised approach to community relations than the idea of a separate Minister, adopted by the NI Government in 1969 on the urging of Home Secretary James Callaghan. In recent times, community relations have been part of the remit of the Education Minister (Brian Mawhinney when the council was set up). Government influence is exercised through the Central Community Relations Unit at Stormont (set up in 1987); the CRC incorporated the Cultural Traditions Group formed in 1988. James Hawthorne, former Controller of BBC NI and earlier head of broadcasting in Hong Kong, was appointed first chairman of the council, and Mari Fitzduff director. Other members of council are Maurice Hayes, Vivienne Anderson, Paul Arthur, Jonathan Bardon, Glenn Barr, Geraldine Donaghy, Ronnie Buchanan, Terence Donaghy, Caroline Ferguson, Hugh Frazer, Anne Graham, Chris Ryder, Jackie Hewitt, Anne McCorkell, Donal McFerran, Maura Maginn, Alasdair MacLaughlin, Christopher Napier, Quintin Oliver, David Stevens and Paul Sweeney. The Cultural Traditions Group is chaired by Ronnie Buchanan and contains five other CRC members, together with John Darby, Brian Ferran, Eamonn Fitzgerald, Imelda Foley, Carmel Gallagher, David Harkness, Myrtle Hill, Gordon Lucy, Geraldine McAteer, Vivian McIver, Martin McLoone, Aodán Mac Póilin, Sean Nolan and Brian Turner.

COMPTON REPORT

The report of the committee set up to investigate allegations that men being interrogated after their arrest on 9 August 1971 – the date of the introduction of internment without trial – had been subjected to brutal treatment. The inquiry was conducted by Sir Edmund Compton, Edgar Fay QC, Recorder of Plymouth, and Dr Ronald Gibson, former chairman of the BMA Council. The commission, in its report issued in November 1971, found that there had been physical ill-treatment of detainees, but it dismissed charges of brutality. The methods which had been investigated were hooding, exposure to continuous noise, standing against a wall leaning on fingertips, and deprivation of food and sleep. Apart from one man, the detainees involved refused to give evidence, on the grounds that the commission was sitting in private, and that there would be no opportunity to cross-examine official witnesses. The report was widely criticised both in Britain and in NI, and Home Secretary Reginald Maudling announced a new inquiry, under Lord Parker, to consider whether interrogation methods should be changed. Most of the cases before the Compton inquiry eventually went to the European Court of Human Rights.

CONATY, THOMAS (TOM)
Chairman of the Central Citizens' Defence Committee (based on Falls Road, Belfast), 1969–74. b. 1930. In 1969, while serving as an ordinary member of the CCDC, he flew to London with a deputation for talks with Home Secretary James Callaghan about plans to protect Catholic areas if the barricades were taken down. He also served on the Peace Committee, a short-lived Government-sponsored body set up in 1969. In 1970 he was highly critical of the army curfew imposed over two days on an area of the Falls Road, and in 1971 he was a leading opponent of internment without trial. His decision to join the Secretary of State's Advisory Commission after direct rule was attacked by Republicans, some of whom demonstrated at his home. In 1974 he issued a strong appeal to the PIRA to call off its campaign of violence. In 1975 he stood unsuccessfully in W. Belfast in the Convention election.

CONCANNON, JOHN DENNIS (DON)
Minister of State, NIO, 1976–9. b. 16 May 1930. After period as branch official of National Union of Mineworkers, became Labour MP for Mansfield, 1966–87. Labour Whip, 1968–74. Parliamentary Under-Secretary, NIO, 1974–6. As Minister of State, NI, he was responsible for Commerce and Manpower Services. Also acted as deputy Secretary of State. Active in seeking new industrial investment, notably through trips to US, Germany and Scandinavia. When he left NIO with defeat of the Labour Government in May 1979, he was longest-serving Minister ever in NIO – over five years. (Later, Nicholas Scott set new record.) Gave strong backing to Conservative Government during H-Block hunger strikes, 1981, and also encouraged 'rolling devolution' initiative in 1982, although pressing for larger Irish dimension. At the 1982 party conference he was critical of a decision to call for a ban on the use of plastic bullets throughout the UK. He dropped out of politics at the 1987 election because of injuries suffered in a road accident.

CONN, SHENA E.
UUP Assembly, 1973–4, and Convention, 1975–6, member for Londonderry. b. Belfast. BDS (QUB).

CONSERVATIVE PARTY, BRITISH
The British Conservative Party has greatly altered its attitude to NI affairs since 1969. In earlier years the UUP was considered an integral part of the Conservative Party. The link went back to the Home Rule controversies of the nineteenth century when Conservatives aligned themselves with the Unionists against the Liberals and Home Rule. Edward Heath's attitude was decisive in bringing about a change. He veered away from positive defence of the Union above all else, and infuriated Unionists with his suspension of the Stormont Parliament in 1972. The break became all but complete when Heath supported the Sunningdale Agreement and the great majority in the UUP came out against power-sharing. After the February 1974 election, Unionist MPs were not offered the Conservative Whip and they adopted a neutral stance in Parliament. In 1977 UUP MPs used their bargaining power to secure support from the Labour Government for extra NI MPs. Meantime, the Conservatives moved close to Unionist policy by urging that priority should be given to local government reform. Clearly, Margaret Thatcher was initially more appealing to Unionists as Conservative leader than Edward Heath – her frequent references to support for the Union were particularly acceptable to Unionists, but the SDLP became highly suspicious of Conservative intentions. In its 1979 election manifesto, the Conservative Party suggested a regional council or councils in the absence of devolved government. But this approach was quickly dropped as first Humphrey Atkins and then James Prior tried to get devolved government established. The right wing of the party strongly opposed Prior's Assembly plan in 1982. In April

1983 the UUP executive voted narrowly to seek restoration of its links with the Conservative Party. The Unionists clearly had in mind the possibility of Tory backing for the return of majority government at Stormont. The Conservative 1983 election manifesto, however, said NI would continue to be offered devolution through the Assembly, but only on the basis of cross-community support. The manifesto also urged a practical working relationship with the Republic without threatening in any way the majority community in NI. But when the AIA was signed in 1985, only a small group of Tory MPs rallied to the support of the Unionists, and only one Government Minister, Ian Gow, felt strongly enough to resign his post. The firmness of the party in support of the AIA was very welcome, however, to the SDLP and the Irish Government. Serious division seemed to be confined to the Young Tories, whose 1987 conference showed 300 delegates, or 40 per cent, critical of the AIA. In April 1987 Norman Tebbit, then party chairman, disappointed the CEC by turning down the idea of the party organising in NI. In 1988, the party's National Union rejected the affiliation of a 'model' N. Down Association. The then party chairman, Peter Brooke, endorsed this line. But in the 1989 council poll, Conservatives took six seats in N. Down; the 1989 party conference voted for the principle of organising in NI, and early in November the N. Down association and three others were admitted. In May 1990 local Conservatives decided to stand a candidate in the Upper Bann by-election created by the death of Harold McCusker. There was a touch of irony about the campaign. Peter Brooke, now NI Secretary of State, was among Conservative personalities who visited the constituency, which had still to be adopted, and some local politicians pointed out that this was a departure from the normally non-partisan stance of NI Secretaries of State. The candidate, Colette Jones, took just over 1,000 votes in a poll of 35,000, and David Trimble (UUP) had a large majority. Even three minor candidates – PSF, WP and an

Independent – attracted more votes than the Conservative. But the party in NI, clearly enjoying considerable encouragement from grassroots Tories in GB, fought on a wide front in the 1992 Westminster general election, with its main hopes centred on N. Down, where its best-known personality, Dr Laurence Kennedy, stood. But N. Down remained loyal to its veteran UPUP MP, Sir James Kilfedder, partly because of UUP support, although Kennedy cut the UPUP majority to 5,000 by taking 32 per cent of the vote. Oddly enough, the Conservatives were targeting the one NI MP who was frequently found in the Conservative division lobby. Overall, they took 5.7 per cent of the vote in eleven constituencies. Local Conservatives have tended to be strongly integrationist and thus in conflict with Government attempts to secure devolution. Leonard Fee, who became NI party chairman in 1992, backed integration and 'no holds barred' relations with NI Ministers. In April 1993, John Major became first PM to address a meeting of officers of the party in NI, to which he pledged full support. He looked forward to the day when a local MP would be Conservative Secretary of State. But the May 1993 council elections saw the party's strength in town halls cut from twelve to six – a situation blamed on the Government's attitude to NI and the unpopularity of Conservative policies. The 'understanding' with UUP in July over the Maastricht Treaty vote emphasised differences between the party nationally and in NI. Dr Laurence Kennedy resigned as a N. Down councillor in July in protest at the UUP understanding. The motions for the party conference called for integration not devolution.

CONSTITUTIONAL CONFERENCE
A conference organised by Secretary of State Humphrey Atkins and held at Parliament Buildings, Stormont, between January and March 1980. All four main parties were invited, but the UUP declined the invitation. The DUP, SDLP and Alliance delegates met privately under the chairmanship of the Secretary of State. They agreed that there should be

devolved government, but while the SDLP and Alliance maintained their position that there should be power-sharing government, the DUP stuck to its demand for majority rule, although it conceded that the minority should have a 'meaningful role'. From outside the conference, the UUP also supported majority government, with no entrenched powers or privileges for any group. The three parties in the conference were against local government reform without devolved government, and in this they differed from the UUP, who believed that such reform should be pursued in the absence of devolved government – a move to invoke the Government's general election pledge. Since the conference did not deal with security or relations with the Republic, these matters were examined in a parallel conference. With the conference failing to point to any agreed solution, Atkins, in July 1980, put forward fresh options for study. One involved an executive made up of parties achieving a certain measure of popular support and in proportion to their strength. Another envisaged a majority cabinet balanced by an assembly council which would include opposition parties. Again, there was no common ground, and a further proposal by Atkins for an advisory council composed of already-elected representatives was abandoned in 1981.

CONSTITUTIONAL CONVENTION
The elected Convention of NI parties established by the British Government in 1975 to consider, as the Government White Paper put it, 'What provision for the government of Northern Ireland is likely to command the most wide-spread acceptance throughout the community there?' It comprised seventy-eight members elected by PR on the same basis as the former assembly, which had been abolished when the power-sharing Executive fell in 1974. (*See* Election Results section, pp. 377–80.) The Convention chairman was Sir Robert Lowry, Lord Chief Justice of NI (now Lord Lowry), and he had two special advisers, Dr John A. Oliver and Maurice N. Hayes. The Clerk of the Convention

was Ronald Blackburn. The fact that forty-seven of the convention seats were held by supporters of the UUUC indicated that agreement would prove elusive. They were committed to the rejection of power-sharing on the 1973 model. At the same time, the parties of the former Executive – SDLP, Alliance and UPNI – still pressed for partnership. Although the public debates simply underlined these facts, an elaborate programme of inter-party discussions was mounted. The UUUC made it clear that they wanted restoration to a new devolved government of the powers conferred on Stormont by the original 1920 Act, including law-and-order powers. They also saw minority participation in Government as something which would be achieved by inclusion in departmental committees rather than the Cabinet. This approach was firmly opposed by the power-sharing parties. The Vanguard Unionist leader William Craig MP made an attempt to break the deadlock by suggesting a voluntary coalition during the emergency – he used the analogy of a wartime coalition at Westminster – but he got no support from his coalition partners and very little within his own party, which split on the issue. Westminster refused to accept the majority report of the convention as meeting the criteria of the White Paper. But Secretary of State Merlyn Rees recalled the Convention for a further month at the start of 1976 to allow it to think again. He also told the Convention that the Government would not agree to extra NI seats at Westminster until a local political settlement had been reached (this attitude was reversed by the Labour Government in 1977). The Government also held that a formal Council of Ireland was not essential to cross-border co-operation, and that any transfer of law-and-order powers from Westminster (excluding judicial appointments and control of courts) would have to be gradual. The Convention ended its sittings in March 1976, without finding any agreement acceptable to Westminster.

COOK, DAVID
Deputy leader of Alliance Party, 1980–4.

Assembly member for S. Belfast, 1982–6. Served on committees on Environment and Security. b. 1944. Lord Mayor of Belfast, 1978–9, and first non-Unionist to hold that office. His election as Lord Mayor was a major political surprise and arose because two UPNI councillors opposed the outgoing UUP Lord Mayor James Stewart, and gave Cook a two-vote margin. Leader of Alliance group on Belfast City Council, 1973–80, but lost council seat in 1985. Unsuccessfully contested S. Belfast in the 1974, 1983 and 1987 general elections, and in the 1982 and 1986 by-elections. Lost deposit in 1984 European election. Stood down in 1984 as party deputy leader so as to devote more time to his business as a solicitor. Involved in court action against Unionist adjournment policy in Belfast City Council directed against AIA. As president of the Alliance Party, he told its 1992 conference that modernisation of the Republic's Constitution was essential to any NI settlement. Chairman, NIVT. His appointment in 1994 to chair the Southern Area Trust at the same time as his wife Fionnuala chaired its watchdog body, the Southern Area Health Council, was queried by David Trimble MP in Parliament and defended by Michael Ancram, who praised Cook's 'skills and experience' and expected 'strong leadership'.

COONEY, PATRICK MARK

Minister for Justice, Irish Republic, 1973–7, and Defence Minister, 1982–6. b. 2 March 1931. BA, LLB (UCD). Solicitor. Cooney was a Fine Gael member of the Dáil from 1970 to 1977, when he lost his seat and was elected to the Senate, where he was Fine Gael leader, 1977–81. As Justice Minister in the Cosgrave administration, he took a strong stand against the IRA, and strengthened cross-border security co-operation, notably by improving communications between the Gardaí and the RUC. He also negotiated with the British Government the reciprocal legislation to enable a person accused of terrorism to be brought to trial on whichever side of the border he was arrested, and after the assassination of the British Ambassador to Dublin in 1976, he

introduced the power to hold without charge for seven days. He was an unsuccessful candidate in the European election of June 1979. In 1990 he suggested the setting aside of the AIA by the British and Irish Governments and said the Republic should end its neutrality policy. In 1991 he urged the internment of terrorist suspects on both sides of the border. In March 1992 the Catholic hierarchy rejected a call by him that it should urge Catholics not to vote for PSF in the British general election; hierarchy spokesman Bishop Joseph Duffy of Clogher said it would not wish to get involved in the political process at election time.

COOPER, SIR FRANK

Permanent Under-Secretary, NIO, 1973–6. b. 2 December 1922. Head of the civil service in the NIO during a critical period, which extended from the Sunningdale Conference through the five-month life of the NI Executive, the loyalist strike of 1974, and over the period of the Convention. He worked under three Secretaries of State – Whitelaw, Pym and Rees. He was no desk-bound administrator, and through a great variety of political and other contacts was usually aware of the smallest intrigue. He knew in advance of the talks at Feakle, Co. Clare, between leading Churchmen and PIRA. In 1976 he moved to the Defence Ministry as Permanent Secretary. When he retired in 1982, he talked of 'organising' the people who had talked to PSF. He also said he did not expect an NI solution for a long time, and that the British and the loyalists had never understood each other.

COOPER, IVAN AVERILL

Minister of Community Relations in NI Executive, 1974, SDLP Assembly member, 1973–4, and Convention member, 1975–6, for Mid-Ulster. b. Killaloo, Co. Derry, 1944. First experience in politics as a Young Unionist; member NILP, 1965–8; prominent in civil rights movement from earliest days, and president of the Derry Citizens' Action Committee, 1968–9. MP for Mid-Derry at Stormont, 1969–72; Independent until

1970, then SDLP, of which he was a founder member. Unsuccessfully contested Mid-Ulster in both the February and October 1974 Westminster elections.

COOPER, ROBERT GEORGE (BOB)

Head of the Department of Manpower Services in the NI Executive, 1974. b. Donegal, 24 June 1936. LLB (QUB). Gave up his job in industrial relations to become Alliance Party's first full-time general secretary, and later deputy leader. Elected from W. Belfast to Assembly, 1973–4, and Constitutional Convention, 1975–6. Head of the FEA, set up to investigate allegations of political and religious discrimination in employment, 1976–90. In 1987 and 1988 he strongly defended the FEA against a variety of charges, and welcomed the Government's proposals for tougher anti-discrimination laws. In the US he was active in countering the campaign for the rival MacBride Principles. In 1988 he answered Unionists who alleged that the FEA was only interested in anti-Catholic discrimination by saying that the important fact was that Catholics were still two and a half times as likely to be unemployed as Protestants. In 1990, he became head of the Fair Employment Commission – successor to the FEA – which has operated with much stronger sanctions against employers introduced by a 1989 Act. With official statistics up to 1992 indicating a continuing higher level of unemployment among Catholics than among Protestants, and with outside institutions as diverse as the European Parliament and US state legislatures keeping watch on the local situation, he has frequently had to defend the FEC's approach.

CO-OPERATION NORTH

An organisation based in Dublin and aimed at fostering friendship and co-operation with NI. Launched in June 1978 with the support of a large number of voluntary bodies, trade unions, commercial companies, professional organisations and state-sponsored companies. Dr T.K. Whitaker, an Ulsterman who was largely responsible for organising the historic Stormont meeting between Sean Lemass and Terence O'Neill in 1965, presided at the inaugural meeting. The organisation has steadily expanded its activities, notably in promoting North–South sporting events and in working through schools. A peace campaign that it promoted in 1991 had the support of the leaders of the four main Churches.

COPE, SIR JOHN

Minister of State and deputy Secretary of State, NIO, July 1989–December 1990. b. 13 May 1937. Deputy Chief Whip, 1983–7. Minister for Small Business, 1988–9. Handled security and finance at NIO. His early period at Stormont included major disputes with Dublin over alleged leaks of security documents to loyalist groups and over the role of the UDR. In the summer of 1990, he opposed loyalist and Republican demands for segregation in Crumlin Road Prison, but agreed measures 'to reduce confrontation'. As Conservative Party deputy chairman, he was strongly sympathetic to NI Conservatives and canvassed for them in 1992 Westminster election. Paymaster General, 1992–.

CORRIGAN-MAGUIRE, MAIREAD

As Mairead Corrigan, one of the three founders of the Peace People, she was joint recipient, with Betty Williams, of the Nobel Peace Prize for 1976. b. 1944. Aunt of the three Maguire children whose deaths, when they were struck by a gunman's getaway car in W. Belfast, led to the formation of the PP. In September 1981 she married Jackie Maguire, husband of her sister Anne, who 'died of heartbreak' in a suicide in 1980, when she was said to have been seriously depressed by the death of her children and the continuing violence. Has travelled widely in the US and in Europe to advance the movement, and in 1978 she had a brief meeting with President Carter, who later sent her a personal message wishing the movement well. She disclosed in 1977 that she had almost joined the PIRA in 1973 because of the behaviour of troops in W. Belfast. She became chairwoman of the PP in 1980, when it was affected by internal rows, but in 1981 she returned to the role of an executive member. In 1986, when the movement was said to have 200 members, she said in a TV programme that the split had occurred because the German support organisation planned to provide money on condition that they avoided controversy, and they could not do that. In the 1990s she continued to promote the aims of the PP, and her Nobel prizewinner status makes her a welcome figure at international peace gatherings. In 1990 she made a twelve-day visit to Japan. She was active in opposing war in the Gulf. In January 1994 she spoke about a 'crisis of identity in NI' at a Peace People conference. In the wake of the publicity surrounding the visit of Gerry Adams to a conference in New York in February, she appealed to the organisers to provide a similar platform for Unionist leaders.

CORRYMEELA

The community centre at Ballycastle, Co. Antrim, set up in 1965 to promote reconciliation by bringing together people of differing backgrounds from both sides of the community. The project was the idea of Rev. Ray Davey as Presbyterian chaplain at QUB, and it now has a complex of buildings on an eight-acre site. In April 1966 PM Terence O'Neill caught attention when he spoke about the need for better community relations to an audience of about fifty leading Protestants and Catholics. In 1993 Rev. Trevor Williams succeeded Dr John Morrow as leader of the community.

COSGRAVE, LIAM

Taoiseach of the Irish Republic, 1973-7. b. 13 April 1920. Son of William T. Cosgrave, former Taoiseach of Irish Free State. TD, 1943-81. Leader of Fine Gael, 1965-77. Cosgrave's ministerial career began as a Parliamentary Secretary in the Inter-Party Government of 1948-51, which took the Republic out of the Commonwealth, and he was Minister for External Affairs, 1954-7. Chairman of Council of Ministers, Council of Europe, 1955. Chairman, first Irish delegation, UN General Assembly, 1956. His most crucial involvement with NI affairs was as head of

the Irish Government delegation at the Sunningdale Conference in December 1973. His comments afterwards suggested that he believed that this get-together of British and Irish Ministers and representatives of the pro-power-sharing parties in NI would provide the basis for a permanent settlement. He was personally acquainted with the Chief Executive designate of the NI Executive, Brian Faulkner, both as a politician and as a lover of horses and hunting. And while Cosgrave did not concede that there was any need for amendment of the Republic's Constitution (unlike some of his Ministers, particularly Garret FitzGerald and Conor Cruise O'Brien), he did agree to the clause in the Sunningdale Agreement which stated that there could be no change in the status of NI unless the people there desired it. Although Britain would have preferred the Republic to agree to straight extradition of suspected terrorists who had entered the Republic, a compromise was reached, with the joint legislation providing that such a person could be tried on whichever side of the border he was arrested. And broadly, the Cosgrave Government's security policies were welcomed by Britain. Cosgrave pressed for British initiatives to secure partnership government in NI, and what he regarded as fair representation of the minority in NI in the new directly elected European Parliament. His proposal that there should be three NI seats filled on the PR system was eventually adopted by Westminster.

COSGROVE, GERRY

Party administrator of the SDLP, January 1992-. b. 23 June 1952. She was assistant general secretary of the party, 1985-91.

COSTELLO, SEAMUS

Leader and founder of the Irish Republican Socialist Party until he was shot dead in Dublin in October 1977. b. Bray, Co. Wicklow, 1939. Active in his early years in the Republican movement, he was the leader, according to J. Bowyer Bell, in his history of the IRA, *The Secret Army*, of an IRA flying column which was active in NI during the 1956 campaign. He was said to have been responsible for burning down the courthouse in Magherafelt, Co. Derry. During the campaign, he was interned at the Curragh for two years. He opposed the OIRA ceasefire in 1972, and after his expulsion from the IRA, he established the IRSP. From 1967 he had been active in council politics in Co. Wicklow. In 1975, during the feud between the Official Republicans and the IRSP, he survived an assassination bid in Waterford. In 1977 both the PIRA and OIRA denied that they had been responsible for his murder. In 1982 INLA accused OIRA of carrying it out. It was the first assassination of a party leader in the history of the Republic.

COULTER, JEAN
UUP Assembly member for W. Belfast, 1973–4, and Convention member for the same constituency, 1975–6. b. 6 July 1930.

COUNCIL FOR THE UNION *see* Molyneaux, James

COUSLEY, CECIL JAMES
DUP Assembly member for N. Antrim, 1982–6. Served on Agriculture Committee. Ballymoney Borough Council, 1981–; Mayor 1993–4. b. 1932. One of several DUP councillors to resign the Whip in the wake of the James Allister resignation in 1987. Farmer.

CRAIG, JAMES
DUP Assembly member for N. Antrim, 1973–4. Chief Whip, 1973–4. Unofficial Unionist candidate in the Carrick constituency in the Stormont parliamentary election, 1969. Founder member DUP and executive member, September 1971–4. Chairman, Carrickfergus DUP Association. b. December 1931; d. 2 November 1974. Educated at Larne Grammar School. Foreman engineer at Courtaulds. Member, Carrickfergus District Council, and deputy Mayor, 1973–4. Carrickfergus Borough Council 1962–73. NI Housing Council, 1973–4.

CRAIG, WILLIAM
MP for E. Belfast at Westminster, February 1974–9. b. 2 December 1924.

One of Northern Ireland's most controversial politicians, he began as an orthodox Ulster Unionist, notably active in the Young Unionist movement. He became MP for Larne in 1960, and as Government Chief Whip, 1962–3, had a key role in the choice of Captain Terence O'Neill as PM in 1963. He became Minister of Home Affairs in the O'Neill Government, and then Minister of Health and Local Government in July 1964. When O'Neill set up a new Ministry of Development to look after local government reform and establishment of the new city of Craigavon in 1965, Craig took charge of it. He returned to the post of Minister of Home Affairs in October 1966. He became the centre of intense controversy in October 1968, when he restricted a civil rights march in Duke Street, Derry – a march which went ahead on 5 October and led to a bitter clash between police and civil rights supporters, who included several Westminster and Stormont MPs, among them Gerry Fitt MP and Eddie McAteer, then leader of the Nationalist Party. Batons and water cannon were used by the RUC, and the scenes transmitted on TV focused world attention on the NI situation. Craig was sharply attacked by anti-Unionists on all sides but he defended himself vigorously. He denied police brutality and claimed that the IRA had been involved in the Derry march. He also accused the British Government of bringing pressure on the NI Government to introduce reforms. He said there had been financial pressure which amounted to blackmail. In December 1968 Captain O'Neill sacked Craig from the Cabinet. He said Craig had been attracted by ideas of a UDI nature, and a 'go it alone' NI was a delusion. Craig now hit out strongly at O'Neill's tactics, and as a backbencher was a steady critic of what he regarded as the 'appeasement' of the enemies of unionism. He also assailed the security policies of Westminster and the Chichester-Clark and Faulkner Governments. The disbandment of B Specials he considered to be one of the major blunders in this field. Although he was frequently at odds with the Rev. Ian

Paisley, they often came together on loyalist platforms. He headed the Ulster Loyalist Association from 1969 to 1972, and on various occasions mentioned that force might have to be used to achieve 'normality'. He led the Unionist pressure group, Ulster Vanguard, which was in the forefront of the opposition to the Heath Government's suspension of Stormont and introduction of direct rule in 1972. It helped organise a forty-eight-hour loyalist strike against the move. At that period, Craig became familiar as the leading speaker at massive rallies. One of these was held at Parliament Buildings to coincide with the last sitting of the local Parliament; Brian Faulkner, as PM, appeared on the balcony beside Craig – much to Faulkner's embarrassment, it emerged later. In the Assembly election in 1973 he was returned in N. Antrim some 6,000 votes behind the Rev. Ian Paisley. He forcefully attacked the Sunningdale Agreement, and the power-sharing Executive, and converted Vanguard into a full political party (VUPP). In February 1974 he won the E. Belfast seat at Westminster, and with the other two leaders of what had now become the UUUC – the Rev. Ian Paisley and Harry West – he was among the top planners of the May 1974 loyalist strike which brought down the three-party Executive. In the October 1974 Westminster election he strengthened his hold on E. Belfast – his majority was up about 10,000. He headed the poll in E. Belfast in the Convention election in 1975. In the Convention he caused a major surprise by advocating the idea of a voluntary coalition, including the SDLP, for a limited period. He claimed that this was not power-sharing, which he had attacked in the Assembly. But he got no support from his coalition partners – the UUP and the DUP – and the majority of his own party deserted him on the issue. The breakaway group, under the leadership of Ernest Baird, now called themselves the United Ulster Unionist Movement. When Paisley and Baird backed the loyalist strike in May 1977, Craig stood aside. In 1977 he was appointed to the Council of Europe on the nomination of the British

Government, and as a member of the legal committee he was appointed by the council to report on human rights legislation in Europe – an assignment which was criticised by some of those associated with the original civil rights campaign. Then, in February 1978, the VUPP ceased to exist as a political party. It reverted to the title Ulster Vanguard, as a pressure group, and Craig remained at its head. In more than one sense his career had turned full circle. But in the general election of May 1979, when he stood for UUP, he lost E. Belfast to the DUP by sixty-four votes. Six months after the election, he was threatening to resign from the UUP because of its refusal to attend the Atkins conference, and in 1980 there were hints that Vanguard might reappear as a political party. In July 1981 he urged that James Callaghan's plea for an independent NI should be carefully examined, and soon afterwards he criticised the UUP for failing to respond to Dr Garret FitzGerald's constitutional 'crusade' which he described as 'very significant'. In November 1981 he had talks in Dublin with Dr FitzGerald who, he believed, wanted to be helpful. And the next month he called for a decision to take NI out of the UK by 1983 if the Convention report was not implemented. But the 1982 Assembly election showed that his power-base in E. Belfast had all but vanished and he failed to secure election. He stood as a Vanguard Unionist. In 1985, on the eve of the AIA, he warned Unionists that Margaret Thatcher was 'sailing close to a policy of condominium'. But he opposed abstention from Westminster by Unionists in face of the agreement. In 1987 he suggested that force would be used ultimately to end the AIA.

CRAIGAVON

The new city in Co. Armagh which embraced the two old-established boroughs of Lurgan and Portadown, both of which have suffered seriously in the PIRA bombing campaign. The Craigavon project was the focus of sharp controversy when it was launched by the O'Neill Government in the early 1960s, with a population target of 100,000 by 1981.

The opposition parties accused the Government of neglecting W. Ulster, and especially Derry, and of providing a new centre for incoming industry at Craigavon, with its mainly Protestant population. In the event it proved difficult to persuade people to move from Greater Belfast to the new city, despite special grants for new occupiers of public authority and private housing. Apart from bombings in the shopping streets, the area has had many attacks on members of the security forces and sectarian assassinations. In July 1979 a plan to have a twinning scheme between Craigavon and Santa Rosa, California, was abandoned after protests by Irish-American groups, including the Irish National Caucus. In the 1981 H-Block hunger strike tension was high in the Lurgan area and there was a row over Republican attempts to rename streets after hunger-strikers. At the end of 1982 three policemen were killed by a booby-trap landmine near Lurgan, and soon afterwards a row developed over the shooting dead by the RUC of three PIRA members who were said to have driven through a checkpoint. In the 1980s the council was accused by the FEA of anti-Catholic bias. In March–April 1986 there were serious clashes in Portadown between loyalists and RUC after the banning of an Apprentice Boys' parade. A Protestant, Keith White, was fatally wounded by a plastic bullet. UUP and DUP councillors were among the most determined in obstructing council business as a protest against the AIA. Both Republican and loyalist gunmen were active in the area in the early 1990s and PIRA bombings in late 1991 and early 1992 caused serious damage to an RUC station and the main shopping area. In December 1992 Mayor Fred Crowe said compensation for damage in that year would total £30 million. On 22 May 1993 Portadown town centre was severely damaged by a bomb.

CREASEY, LIEUTENANT-GENERAL SIR TIMOTHY

Army GOC, NI, November 1977–9. b. 1923. After wartime service with Indian troops, he joined the Royal Norfolk Regiment in 1947. His later career included a period as Military Secretary to the Defence Ministry in 1967–8. He acquired special expertise in anti-guerilla operations as commander of the Sultan's forces in Oman, 1972–5. He was Director of Infantry, 1975–7. In December 1977 he commented that the PIRA was being 'suppressed, contained and isolated'. In August 1979 he drew criticism from both Unionists and the SDLP when he called in at the Falls Road, Belfast, shop of PSF with an army patrol. In a BBC programme in January 1980 he said they were faced in NI with an organised revolutionary force of some 500 hard-core terrorists. But he did not subscribe to the view that they could not be defeated – 'given the national will' and using all the resources of a modern state.

CROSSMAGLEN

The S. Armagh village regarded as one of the main strongholds of the PIRA. With a population of about 1,000, and situated six kilometres from the border, it has taken on a legendary quality for Republicans, and is more widely identified as defying authority through the lines 'From Carrickmacross to Crossmaglen, there are more rogues than honest men.' To locals, it is known simply as 'The Cross'. The area has a long history of support for the Republican cause, and more than thirty British soldiers were killed by local PIRA units in the three years after internment, mainly through culvert bombs and booby traps on the twisting roads which criss-cross the border. There have been several attacks on the RUC and the army post, and the use by the army of part of the Gaelic football pitch as a helicopter landing pad has particularly angered villagers. In August 1979 Margaret Thatcher visited the army base during a border tour following the Mountbatten and Warrenpoint killings. In the same year a memorial to dead Republicans was unveiled in the village and attracted protests from Unionists. On a visit to Crossmaglen in March 1981 Cardinal Ó Fiaich urged PIRA to end violence. The Cardinal was a native of the district and in 1991 the central area was named

Ó Fiaich Square. Around that time local and Church authorities sought to give a new image to S. Armagh but the police and army continued to regard it as territory important to PIRA, which in 1992 dumped the bodies there of three of its members who it claimed were informers for the security forces. In 1992 the NIO and the IFI put up £1 million for improvement schemes. On 30 December 1993 a soldier was shot dead in the village, the eighth victim of a PIRA sniper in the border area within the previous two years.

CUBBON, SIR BRIAN CROSSLAND
Permanent Secretary, NIO, 1976–9. b. 9 April 1928. Sir Brian first became familiar with NI problems as Private Secretary to Home Secretary James Callaghan in 1968–9. Soon after taking up his Stormont post, he narrowly escaped death when he was travelling in the same car as the British Ambassador to Dublin *en route* to the Embassy, when it was blown up by a landmine and the Ambassador and a woman civil servant were killed. Before going to Stormont, he had been deputy Secretary at the Home Office and earlier deputy Secretary to the Cabinet.

CUMANN NA MBAN
The women's section of the IRA, which has always had a significant part in IRA activities. It is illegal in both NI and the Republic. In the PIRA campaign its members have been used as couriers for the gathering of intelligence, reporting on the movements of army and police, and in finding shelter for PIRA men. Women have also had a role in the placing of fire bombs. The exact strength of the section is uncertain, since it has always relied on the support of sympathisers and relatives of PIRA activists.

CUNNINGHAM, LIEUTENANT-COLONEL JAMES GLENCAIRN
Patron of Ulster Unionist Council, governing body of UUP, since 1979 after five years as president. b. 1904. Served in World War II with 8th (Belfast) Regiment, HAA, and with 14th Army in Burma. NI Senate, 1958–72.

CUNNINGHAM, JOSIAS
President of Ulster Unionist Council, 1990–. Chairman of UUP Executive, 1976–9. b. 20 January 1934. MA (Cantab.). Chairman, S. Antrim Unionist Association, 1974. Irish deputy grand master in Orange Order. Chairman of Belfast unit of Stock Exchange. Party delegate in Brooke–Mayhew Talks, 1991–2.

CURRIE, AUSTIN
SDLP Assembly member for Fermanagh–S. Tyrone, 1982–6. Head of the department of housing, planning and local government in the power-sharing Executive, 1974. b. Coalisland, Co. Tyrone, 11 October 1939. BA (QUB). Youngest MP ever returned to Stormont when he was elected as Nationalist in 1964 by-election in E. Tyrone (a seat he held until 1972), and he was active, in association with Nationalist leader Eddie McAteer, in a bid to give the Nationalist Party a more progressive image and a stronger organisational base. In June 1968 he was engaged in the first direct action of the civil rights çampaign when he staged a sit-in in a council house at Caledon, Co. Tyrone, as a protest against its allocation to an unmarried Protestant woman. He was a regular speaker at civil rights demonstrations and helped organise the first civil rights march at Dungannon, Co. Tyrone, in August 1968. A founder member of the SDLP, he was returned as a member for Fermanagh–S. Tyrone to both the Assembly, 1973–4, and the Convention, 1975–6. Chief Whip of the SDLP from 1974 to 1979, when he resigned the post to fight Fermanagh–S. Tyrone unsuccessfully as Independent SDLP in the 1979 Westminster election. He was defying a party decision not to contest the seat, but he retained his SDLP membership and was the prospective candidate of the party when it decided to opt out of the 1981 by-election in the constituency. SDLP North–South spokesman, 1979–82. In the 1986 by-elections he polled some 12,000 votes in Fermanagh–S. Tyrone – one of the constituencies where the results showed a swing away from PSF. In 1987 he argued for a new power-sharing administration

with security powers. During the Troubles, his home has been attacked on some thirty occasions, and his wife was injured in one attack. Participant in Duisburg Talks, October 1988. In 1989 he was elected Fine Gael TD for Dublin W. and made an easy transition to Southern politics. Most observers felt that his failure as his party's nominee in the 1990 presidential election enhanced rather than damaged his standing, for his transfers ensured the election of Mary Robinson. In 1991 he was appointed FG front-bench spokesman on communications. He angered the FG leadership, however, when he suggested Labour leader Dick Spring as Taoiseach after the 1992 election rather than his own leader, John Bruton. Appointed front-bench spokesman on equality and law reform after the FG leadership challenge reshuffle in February 1994.

CUSHNAHAN, JOHN

Leader of Alliance Party, 1984–7. Party Whip in Assembly, 1982–4. Assembly member for N. Down, 1982–6. b. 1948. B.Ed. (QUB). Alliance general secretary, 1974–82. Belfast City Council, 1977–85. Chairman of 1982 Assembly's Education Committee. Member, Devolution Committee. Unsuccessfully contested Westminster elections: N. Belfast, 1979; N. Down, 1983; 1986 by-election, and 1987. As party leader, developed strong contacts with British Liberals and the Liberal–SDP Alliance. Also kept lines open to major politicians in Britain, including Thatcher, and to Dublin parties. Under his leadership, Alliance gave general support to AIA and initiated court actions against councils adjourning in protest, but he said at one point that he would have preferred the Government to impose power-sharing rather than the agreement. He stood down as leader in 1987 because he saw little prospect of early devolved government and could not support his family as unpaid party leader. In 1989 he joined Fine Gael and was elected MEP for Munster. In 1990 he carried out a study on cross-border trade for the European Parliament.

DÁIL ULADH

The name given to a proposed new nine-county Ulster parliament, which was promoted energetically by PSF and PIRA during 1972. A council was set up to promote the idea, and among those also associated with it were Frank McManus, the Unity MP for Fermanagh–S. Tyrone, and Patrick Kennedy, Republican Labour MP at Stormont, as well as some members of the NICRA.

DALY, THOMAS

SDLP Assembly, 1973–4, and Convention, 1975–6, member for Fermanagh–S. Tyrone. b. Belleek, Co. Fermanagh, 1938. BA (QUB). Irvinestown Rural District Council, 1963–8. Fermanagh County Council, 1968–73. Fermanagh District Council, 1973–9 (chairman, 1975–9). Joined SDLP from Nationalist Party in 1973, and announced resignation from public life in February 1979. Brother of Dr Edward Daly, Catholic Bishop of Derry.

DARLINGTON CONFERENCE

A three-day conference on NI affairs held at Darlington, 25–27 September 1972. It was called by William Whitelaw, as Secretary of State, in a bid to find inter-party agreement on a future form of government for NI. It achieved very little, since only three parties agreed to attend – UUP, Alliance and NILP. Four other parties – SDLP, Nationalist, DUP and Republican Labour – rejected the invitation for a variety of reasons, and the politicians who did attend could not agree on the form of a top tier of government.

DAVIS, IVAN

DUP Assembly member for S. Antrim, 1982–6. Served on Education Committee. b. 1937. Lisburn Council, 1973–. Mayor, 1991–3. Joined UUP in 1987.

DEAL BOMBING

In September 1989 PIRA killed eleven Royal Marines bandsmen at a barracks in Deal, Kent, with a 50-lb bomb. It was

134

the biggest PIRA operation in GB since the 1984 bombing of the Brighton hotel HQ of the Conservative conference. Former PM Edward Heath was among those who criticised the use of private security guards at the barracks. The attack led to an extended red alert at military installations in GB.

DEMOCRATIC LEFT
The party that resulted from the split in the Workers' Party in February 1992. It was set up by six TDs, including WP leader Prionsias De Rossa; the remaining WP TD, Tomás Mac Giolla, stayed with the WP. The emergence of Dem. L. followed serious dissension in WP centred on allegations that some elements in the party had links with OIRA – still claimed to be active by political and security sources on both sides of the border. There were also claims that WP had received cash aid from the USSR, and differences over internment. De Rossa got majority backing for reforms in January 1992, but his critics refused to leave, and he and five Dáil colleagues then withdrew. Initially the group was known as New Agenda, but at its first conference, in Dublin on 28 March, the name Democratic Left was adopted. These developments were mirrored in NI, where Seamus Lynch, who had been Northern chairman of WP, went over to the new party. His vote in N. Belfast in 1992 under the new party label was down by more than 1,500, with a WP candidate taking 419. There were claims that the majority of WP members in NI had not joined the new group. In the November 1992 Dáil election, Dem. L. strength was cut to four, and the WP was deprived of representation with the defeat of Mac Giolla.

DEMOCRACY NOW
The organisation was launched at Westminster on 15 July 1992 to campaign for the Labour Party to organise in NI. Two Labour MPs, Kate Hoey (Vauxhall) and Nick Raynsford (Greenwich) were prominent but the literature claimed the support of twenty-one MPs, a ground swell in the constituencies and unions. Its aim was a change in Labour Party policy, which refused to organise or even accept members from NI. Democracy Now literature pointed out that it was possible to become a member of the Labour Party in 'Baghdad or Bali, but not Belfast'. Its stance was strongly opposed by the shadow NI Secretary, Kevin McNamara, and by the SDLP. It criticised as 'mischievous and scurrilous' the 'Oranges and Lemons' booklet commissioned by McNamara and launched a petition in favour of organising in NI with the objective of gaining 1,000 signatures. By September 1993 some thirty-three Labour MPs, 12 per cent of the total, were said to support a policy change to organise in NI.

DEMOCRATIC UNIONIST PARTY
Founded in September 1971 by the Rev. Ian Paisley and the then MP for Shankill, Desmond Boal (a leading barrister), who had been expelled from the Unionist Parliamentary Party. Boal had been a strong opponent of Terence O'Neill as PM, and his views at that time coincided with Paisley's – the new party, said Boal, would be 'right wing in the sense of being strong on the Constitution, but to the left on social policies'. Boal was the first chairman of the party, which took the place of the Protestant Unionist Party, also led by Paisley. The Protestant Unionist Party's first successes were in the two April 1970 by-elections for the NI Commons. Bannside, seat of Terence O'Neill, was won by Paisley, while the Rev. William Beattie gained the S. Antrim seat from an Ulster Unionist. In the Assembly elections, when it got eight seats (10.8 per cent of first-preference votes), it opposed power-sharing with the SDLP, and fought both the 1974 Westminster general elections as part of the UUUC. In both elections Paisley retained the N. Antrim seat which he had won in 1970. The DUP also contested the 1975 Convention elections in co-operation with UUUC partners. It secured twelve seats (14.7 per cent of first-preference votes). Again in the Convention, it publicly rejected power-sharing, and firmly denied suggestions that it had on occasion privately toyed with some form of partnership with the

SDLP. Paisley strongly attacked William Craig's proposal for a voluntary coalition, which would have included the SDLP. In 1977 the withdrawal of the Ulster Unionists from the UUUC over the issue of an action council, which organised the abortive loyalist strike in May 1977, created a new situation for the DUP. Paisley and Ulster Unionist leaders publicly attacked each other. These exchanges came at the same time as the District Council elections, and undoubtedly robbed the DUP of many UUP second-preference votes. None the less, the DUP, which employed the slogan 'the Unionist Party you can trust' to underline its differences with the Ulster Unionists, got seventy-four seats (12.7 per cent of first-preference votes). In 1978 the DUP tried to get an agreement with the Ulster Unionists and the UUUP on how candidates could best be deployed in the coming Westminster election, but the Ulster Unionists pointed out that they had no control over local associations in the selection of candidates. In the May 1979 Westminster election DUP gained two seats from Ulster Unionists – E. and N. Belfast – by narrow majorities. The successful candidates were Peter Robinson and John McQuade. Its share of the poll in that election was 10.2 per cent (five seats contested). In the 1979 European election Paisley headed the poll with 29.8 per cent of first-preference votes – a triumph which surprised even the most enthusiastic of DUP supporters. The DUP took a firm anti-EC line, and polled strongly even in Fermanagh-S. Tyrone, Mid-Ulster and Londonderry, areas where it had not been active to any extent in previous elections. Its run of success was maintained in the 1981 council elections, when its 142 seats doubled those of the previous council election, and its 26.6 per cent of the vote was even slightly ahead of UUP. But it ran second to UUP in the 1982 Assembly election, getting twenty-one seats and 23 per cent of first preferences. In contrast to the UUP, it welcomed the first stage of the 1982 Assembly with mainly scrutiny powers, and it also angered the UUP by supporting James Kilfedder as Assembly Speaker and not UUP candidate John

Carson. In the 1983 Westminster election, its representation remained at three seats in the redrawn constituencies. It held N. Antrim and E. Belfast; lost N. Belfast and gained Mid-Ulster. It took 20 per cent of the votes, after making a limited agreement with the UUP by which the DUP were not opposed by the UUP in Foyle, while UUP got a clear run on the Unionist side in Fermanagh-S. Tyrone, and Newry and Armagh. In the event, its position was weakened relative to the UUP, which got 34 per cent of the votes and eleven seats. In the 1985 council elections DUP fared less well than in 1981. It was now 5 per cent behind UUP in first preferences and had forty-eight fewer seats. The AIA, however, ushered in a period of co-operation with the UUP in opposing the agreement. In both the Westminster by-elections of 1986, forced in protest at the AIA, and the 1987 general election, the three DUP seats were secure. But in E. Antrim there was dissatisfaction within the DUP that the inter-Unionist pact prevented it contesting the local seat, which had been narrowly won by UUP in 1983. The runner-up at that time, James Allister, had been anxious to stand again and when this was denied, he withdrew from politics. Several party officials and councillors also resigned. The party faced a further problem in October 1987, when Peter Robinson MP resigned as deputy leader, apparently because he was not satisfied with anti-AIA tactics or the weight given to the UUP–DUP Task Force report which he had helped to draft as the party representative. But in January 1988 he was back in his old post after the party conference. In the 'talks about talks' with Tom King and Peter Brooke from 1988 to 1991, which paved the way for the Brooke–Mayhew Talks, Ian Paisley worked closely for the most part with James Molyneaux. Whilst there were occasional inter-party strains, these were often not reflected in the personal contacts between the two leaders. In the substantive discussions, however, the DUP refused to go to Dublin for talks with Irish Ministers unless the latter gave a prior commitment to a referendum on the South's constitutional claim to NI.

The UUP's readiness to talk in Dublin without such an assurance angered the DUP, which also complained of excessive social contacts between the UUP and Dublin delegations. In the event Ian Paisley was deprived of his hoped-for 'eyeball-to-eyeball confrontation' with Charles Haughey, but he and Peter Robinson apparently played the Irish Constitution card with vigour in the North–South exchanges. There was 'broad agreement' with UUP and Alliance on a scheme for devolution. Paisley kept his lead position in the 1989 European election, although his vote was down 4 per cent compared with 1984. But the DUP failed to enlarge its Westminster representation in April 1992 despite a strong challenge in E. Antrim, where the UUP strengthened its hold. On the council front, the 1989 poll gave the party 110 seats – 32 down on 1985. The party's vote in the 1993 council elections, at 17.2 per cent, was down slightly on 1989, and it dropped five seats. With the party attacking the NIO's approach to new political talks and facing a strong UUP challenge, Paisley presented the outcome as a rebuff to the Secretary of State. In September 1993 it presented a document, 'Breaking the Log-Jam', to the PM at Downing Street, and published it two months later. After a delegation met PM Major at Downing Street it was pleased at the language used to reject the Irish Department of Foreign Affairs leaked document. However, its reaction to the Downing Street Declaration was angry, regarding it as a 'sellout'. It organised a series of 'Save Ulster' campaigns in major towns in NI, beginning in Portadown on 17 January 1994. At the end of January the party claimed that the NIO had used a go-between in an attempt to get it to engage loyalist paramilitaries in discussion.

DENTON, BARONESS (OF WAKEFIELD)

Parliamentary Under-Secretary, NIO, 11 January 1994–; responsible for agriculture, and health and social services. She became the first woman appointed to the NIO team, replacing the Earl of Arran in a straight swop after changes resulting from the resignation of the Earl of Caithness. Formerly Jean Denton CBE until created a life peer in 1991. Parliamentary Under-Secretary, Department of Trade and Industry, 1992–4. Baroness-in-waiting (Government Whip), 1991–2. b. 1936. Educated at Rothwell Grammar School and the London School of Economics (B.Sc.Econ.) She was a university lecturer (Surrey) but her career was mainly in marketing and management with public companies and public affairs. She was a racing-car driver, 1969–72, and remains a member of the British Women's Racing Drivers' Club.

DE ROSSA, PROINSIAS

Leader of Democratic Left, 1992–. Leader of Workers' Party, 1988–92. b. 1940. TD for Dublin North West, 1982–. Dublin City Council, 1985–. Interned in 1950s as a member of Fianna na hÉireann and the IRA. As WP leader, he repeatedly denied links between the party and OIRA, Taoiseach Charles Haughey and security forces in the Republic and in NI claiming OIRA was still active. In early 1992 the situation came to a head when De Rossa defeated the old guard in an internal vote. At the time, there was also a split on internment within WP and suggestions that the party had received cash aid from the USSR. In February 1992 De Rossa challenged those who would not accept reforms to leave the party. When they refused, he and five other party TDs left to set up the Democratic Left. In the 1992 general election he retained his Dublin seat, but the Dáil strength of Dem. L. was reduced to four. At his party conference in Dun Laoghaire in October 1993 he said that a realistic peace agenda for NI required democratic institutions, the right to remain in the UK, a Bill of Rights, economic regeneration, and change in the Irish Constitution.

DERRY/LONDONDERRY

The city where the civil rights demonstration in Duke Street on 5 October 1968 put the movement on the TV screens and newspaper front pages throughout the world. The dual name of the city epitomises its eventful history. The name Derry is based on the original Irish, Doire, and tends to be favoured more by nationalists, who sought in the City Council in 1978 and 1983 to have Derry adopted as the official name of the city. The suggestion was bitterly attacked by Unionists, but in 1984 the Government agreed that henceforth the City Council would be known as Derry although the official name of the city would continue to be Londonderry. This NIO concession to nationalists led local Unionists to call, without success, for a separate council for the Waterside area of the city and to impose a ban on attending council meetings. The city's official title denotes the British connection and the role of the City of London companies in the development of the city. It has been symbolic for loyalists since Protestants defied James II in the siege of 1689. Local conditions were a key issue in the civil rights controversy. One of the reforms demanded was the abolition of the corporation, dominated by Unionists because ward boundaries had been drawn in a manner which meant that a Unionist minority was able to secure a majority in the City Council. One of the earliest reforms granted by the O'Neill Government was the replacement of the council by a nine-member Development Commission. This reform was announced only a month or so after the Duke Street demonstration. The march route had been heavily restricted by the Government, but some 200 people, including opposition MPs from Stormont, a few British Labour MPs, civil rights leaders and local civil rights groups, defied the ban. TV film of the event showed the attempts of the RUC to prevent the march and the ensuing confused confrontation in which police batons and placard poles were intermingled with bleeding faces. The publicity spin-off for the civil rights movement was astonishing. It was highly damaging to the NI Government and an embarrassment to the British Labour administration, headed by Harold Wilson, whose sympathies were largely with the marchers. There is no doubt that the event caused Britain to put heavy pressure on Stormont for reforms. But it was not until 1969, and after even larger civil rights demonstrations in the city,

that Derry came to play a decisive role in reducing the power and authority of the NI Government. The riots which blew up on the edge of the Catholic Bogside in the wake of the Protestant Apprentice Boys' 12 August march led to British troops being introduced in the streets. The barricades went up in the Bogside and the adjoining Catholic area, Creggan, and behind them the PIRA planned bombing and other missions which caused substantial damage to the city. The existence of 'Free Derry', as extreme Republicans termed it, raised tensions in loyalist areas, and there were many sectarian killings in the city and county. The refusal by the authorities to agree to an impartial inquiry into the shooting dead by the army of two Derry men – Seamus Cusack and Desmond Beattie – on 8 July 1971 led to the withdrawal of the SDLP from Stormont. The SDLP contested the official explanation that Cusack was shot when he was seen to raise a rifle against troops, and Beattie when he was about to throw a nail bomb. The 'Bloody Sunday' affair, in which thirteen civilians were shot dead by paratroopers on the edge of the Bogside on 30 January 1972, was one of the incidents which precipitated direct rule from Westminster. At the end of July 1972 the security forces mounted 'Operation Motorman' to end the no-go areas and moved in strength into the Bogside and Creggan, with little more than token resistance from PIRA. With the reform of local government in 1973, the Development Commission was replaced by an enlarged District Council, in which PR gave Nationalists a majority of two. In 1978, as a result of a special Derry–Donegal survey, EC money became available to help finance a second bridge across the River Foyle and to improve the harbour, and road and telephone links with Donegal. There was still sporadic violence but by 1978 there was some easing of traffic checks at the approaches to the old walled city. However, tension rose sharply during the 1981 hunger strike, and in that and the following year there were many deaths arising from PIRA and INLA activity. There was also intense controversy over deaths caused by the operations of the security forces, notably through the use of plastic bullets. But 6 December 1982 brought the heaviest death toll in any incident in Co. Derry during the Troubles. Seventeen people died in the bombing of the Droppin' Well pub disco at Ballykelly. Eleven were soldiers stationed nearby, and most of the civilian victims were from Ballykelly itself. INLA claimed the attack, and mentioned that warnings had been given to pubs serving members of the security forces. The SDLP took control of the City Council after the 1981 council elections, but PSF got a boost in the 1982 Assembly election, when its best-known Derry-city figure, Martin McGuinness, was returned. With some 9,000 unemployed in the city, the Government announced in 1982 an 'enterprise zone', with special inducements for investment. Throughout the 1980s considerable effort was put into improving facilities for sport and shopping, and rehousing has changed out of all recognition the city of the early civil rights demonstrations. In 1983 the area got its first non-Unionist MP at Westminster since NI was established when SDLP leader and MEP John Hume took the new Foyle seat. His wide contacts in the US and in Europe have helped to boost outside industrial and other investment, particularly in a link-up with Boston. There has been much cross-community effort to improve the infrastructure, and this has paid off in terms of an impressive £70 million waterfront scheme, deepwater port facilities, the development of electronic links and computer production. The more progressive image was fostered in 1989 by a non-sectarian pageant to mark the 300th anniversary of the siege. In the City Council, the arrival of PSF members in 1985 and the Unionist boycott imposed in the wake of the AIA heightened tension, but divisions in unionism led to an independent unionist, Jim Guy, being installed as Mayor in 1987-8, with the support of the SDLP. (In 1992-3 the city had its first DUP Mayor, William Hay.) In 1990 there was concern about the decline of the Protestant population on the west bank, their concentration in Waterside and desire for separate council status. The remaining 2,000 living in the Fountain Street district had a development scheme implemented in the area. 1992 began with thoughts of 'Bloody Sunday' twenty years earlier, but PM John Major turned down demands for a fresh inquiry which were backed by the City Council. The transfer of Government jobs to the city and local interest in developing cultural and tourist projects, together with heavy EC and local investment in the upgrading of the city's airport, were seen as justifying an Impact '92 promotion. But the city has not been free of violence in the 1990s. PIRA operations included a major proxy bomb attack on the army checkpoint on the Derry–Buncrana Road in October 1990. Patsy Gillespie, a 42-year-old father of three, died along with five soldiers when he drove a 1,000-lb bomb into a search bay in the early morning. His family had been held hostage at their home in Shantallow, and the killings brought condemnation from all sides. The start of the Single European Market in 1993 and the ending of customs controls on the border raised hopes of a trade boom. (*See also* Apprentice Boys of Derry, Derry Citizens' Action Committee, and Derry Citizens' Defence Association.)

DERRY CITIZENS' ACTION COMMITTEE

A body established on 9 October 1968 and made up of five local groups which had helped to organise the civil rights march in Duke Street, Derry, on 5 October 1968. Ivan Cooper was chairman and John Hume deputy chairman. The first move by the committee was a sit-down in the Diamond, Derry, on 19 October, and the committee also sponsored a massive parade from the Waterside across Craigavon Bridge on 2 November 1968, and supported the People's Democracy march from Belfast to Derry in January 1969. They were also concerned with organising patrols in the Bogside after complaints about RUC behaviour there. They took a petition to Downing Street, calling for police and other reforms. (*See also* Derry/Londonderry.)

DERRY CITIZENS' DEFENCE ASSOCIATION

The vigilante group set up in the Bogside area of Derry in July 1969, which took a more militant line than the Derry Citizens' Action Committee. It was involved throughout the period of rioting in August 1969, erecting barricades, mounting patrols, providing first-aid, countering CS-gas attacks, and on 24 August it said it had taken control of administration and security behind the barricades of what became known as 'Free Derry'. (*See also* Derry/ Londonderry.)

DEVLIN, BERNADETTE *see* McAliskey, Josephine Bernadette

DEVLIN, PATRICK JOSEPH (PADDY)

SDLP member of NI Executive, 1974, as head of the Department of Health and Social Services. b. Belfast, 8 March 1925. M.Sc. (1981). A highly individualistic politician, he has switched party several times. He was in the Republican movement from 1936 until 1950, and was interned in Belfast Prison, 1942-5. In 1950 he joined the Irish Labour Party, but moved to the NILP in 1958 and was chairman, 1967-8. In 1970 he became a founder member of the SDLP, and was Chief Whip in the Assembly and chairman in the Convention. But in 1977 he was expelled from the SDLP after he had complained that the party was departing from its previous approach, and reducing the socialist content of its policy. Belfast City Council, 1956-8 and 1973-85. MP at Stormont for Falls, 1969-72. Elected to Assembly, 1973-4, and Convention, 1975-6, from W. Belfast, where he had the largest single vote of any candidate in the 1977 District Council election. He was a founder member of NICRA and was closely involved in dealing with the situation in the Falls Road area in the violence of 1969. When the Convention failed, he joined his then SDLP colleague, John Hume, in private talks with the Rev. Martin Smyth and Captain Austin Ardill of the UUP on a possible political settlement. But the effort was unfruitful.

He has had a lifelong association with the trade-union movement, and became full-time district secretary of the Irish Transport and General Workers' Union in 1976, but left the post in 1985 to devote himself to writing. In 1978 he was among a small group who launched the United Labour Party, and he stood unsuccessfully as the party's candidate in the 1979 European election. In the 1981 council election he narrowly retained his Belfast City Council seat in the west of the city, but had to leave his home in that area because of threats from Republican extremists. In 1985 he failed to win a council seat in N. Belfast as a candidate of the LPNI, which he had helped to form. In 1987 he was first vice-chairman of Labour '87. In that year he campaigned against the MacBride Principles in the US. Housing Executive, 1983-6. Member of Belfast Harbour Commissioners. Prominent in Peace Train organisation. He has written a book on the fall of the NI power-sharing Executive, one on outdoor relief in Belfast in the inter-war years, and his autobiography was published in 1993.

DICKSON, ANNE LETITIA

Leader of UPNI, 1976-81. b. London, 1928. Elected as Unionist MP for Carrick in 1969 and strong supporter of Terence O'Neill as Premier. Vice-chairwoman of Newtownabbey Urban Council, 1967-9. In the Assembly election of 1973 she was elected in S. Antrim without the support of Unionist Party HQ. She supported the power-sharing Executive, and was also elected to the Convention from S. Antrim in 1975. When Brian Faulkner gave up the leadership of UPNI in 1976, she succeeded him as the first woman leader of an NI political party. In 1979 she unsuccessfully contested N. Belfast in the Westminster election. In October 1981 she presided at UPNI's final conference, when it was decided to wind up the party after a series of poor election results. Chairwoman, NI Consumer Council, 1985-90.

DIPLOCK REPORT

The report of the commission, headed by Lord Diplock, which reported in

December 1972 that non-jury trials should be introduced for a wide range of terrorist offences. It argued that trials should be held before judges sitting alone, because of the risks of intimidation, for the period of the emergency. The commission also held that there should be easier admissibility of confessions. The proposals were adopted by the Government and the courts became known as Diplock courts. (*See also* Anglo-Irish Agreement.)

DIRECT RULE *see* Systems of Government section, pp. 422–4

DOBSON, JOHN
Government Chief Whip and leader of the Commons at Stormont, 1969–71. b. Lurgan, 7 May 1929. LLB (TCD). Solicitor. Banbridge Urban District Council, 1961–7. Unionist MP for W. Down, 1965–72. He was one of twelve Unionist MPs who signed a statement in February 1969 saying they would like to see Terence O'Neill replaced as party leader.

DODDS, NIGEL ALEXANDER
Secretary, DUP. b. 1958. MA (Cantab.), CPLS (QUB). Barrister. European Parliamentary Assistant to Rev. Ian Paisley in his role as MEP. Belfast City Council, 1985–. Was youngest person (twenty-nine) ever to hold office of Lord Mayor, which he has held twice – 1988–9 and 1991–2. Vice-president, Association of Local Authorities of NI, 1988–9. Declined to meet Republic's President Mary Robinson when she visited Belfast in February 1992. Unsuccessfully contested E. Antrim in 1992 Westminster election.

DONALDSON, LORD (OF KINGSBRIDGE)
Parliamentary Under-Secretary, NIO (and spokesman of the NIO in the House of Lords), 1974–6. b. 9 October 1907. A Labour life peer (he later switched to the Liberal Democrats), he took charge of three NI departments – Health and Social Services, Agriculture, and Community Relations – after the fall of the NI Executive in May 1974. He was involved in public controversy mainly because he also had responsibility for prison administration.

DONALDSON, JEFFREY
UUP Assembly member for S. Down, 1985–6. b. 1963. Returned in 1985 by-election before Assembly was wound up. Served briefly on Environment, and Health and Social Services committees. Honorary Secretary, UUP council, 1988–. Unsuccessful contender for UUP nomination for 1989 European election. Delegate to Brooke–Mayhew Talks.

DONEGAN, PATRICK SARSFIELD
Defence Minister (Fine Gael) in the Coalition Government in the Republic, 1973–7. b. 29 October 1923. TD for Louth, 1954–7 and 1961–77. Senator, 1957–61. As Defence Minister, Donegan took a strong line against the PIRA. In April 1974 he declared that he would be 'tightening up everything' to beat the PIRA, and pointed out that the Republic's security forces had reached their greatest numbers for twenty years. There were 11,257 in the defence forces and 7,500 in the Garda Síochána. Under his direction the patrolling of the border was intensified, principally by the use of planes and light armoured cars. Communications were also strengthened between the security forces on either side of the border, although he resisted any direct army-to-army link-up.

DONNELLY, MARIAN
Leader of the Workers' Party, 1992–. b. 10 August 1938. A former schoolteacher and a mother of three from Maghera, Co. Derry, she was elected leader at the first Ard Fheis of the party after the major split in the WP in which six of its seven TDs resigned to set up the Democratic Left. First woman to lead an all-Ireland political party. After her election, she denounced violence and said she had never had any links with the IRA. In NI, she presented a plan in May 1992 for a Stormont Assembly with committees, whose chairpersons would form an executive. In November 1992 she said the role of the Reynolds Government in the Brooke–Mayhew Talks had been a negative one and the Irish Government should cease being a 'prop to the SDLP'. She polled 239 votes in Dublin NE in the 1992 general election.

DOOGE, JAMES CLEMENT IGNATIUS

Foreign Minister (Fine Gael) of Republic, 1981–2. b. 7 July 1922. Appointed to the Senate in 1981 by the Taoiseach, Dr Garret FitzGerald, he was a surprise choice as Foreign Minister in the Fine Gael–Labour Coalition which took office in July 1981. Involved with Dr FitzGerald in negotiations with British Government on setting up of Anglo-Irish Intergovernmental Council, and was at first formal meeting of that council in January 1982.

DOUGLAS, WILLIAM ALBERT BOYD

UUP Assembly member for Londonderry, 1982–6. Served on Agriculture, Finance and Personnel, and Security committees. Also served in 1973–4 Assembly and 1975–6 Convention. UUP Whip in 1982 Assembly. b. 1921. Farmer. Flight lieutenant, RAF, during World War II. As Limavady district master of the Orange Order, he was prominent in demonstrations against civil rights meetings in S. Derry in 1969, and in staging loyalist demonstrations in Dungiven, where there were clashes between Orangemen and their opponents on several occasions during 1971. Limavady Rural District Council, 1960–73.

DOWN ORANGE WELFARE

Loyalist paramilitary group based in N. Down and linked with membership of the Orange Order. Formed in 1972, and especially active during the loyalist strike in May 1974, under the leadership of Colonel Brush (d. 1984). Its members were involved in road blocks during the stoppage. The organisation also backed the more limited loyalist strike in May 1977.

DOWNING STREET BOMBINGS

On 7 February 1991 PIRA fired three mortars into the communal garden of 10, 11 and 12 Downing Street, smashing windows of the No. 10 Cabinet Room, where PM John Major was chairing a meeting of Ministers discussing the Gulf War. A Cabinet official, two police officers and a member of the public were injured. The mortars had been fired over Whitehall office buildings from a van parked 200 yards from No. 10, close to the Banqueting Hall in Whitehall and thus breaching the tight security in the area. High gates had been erected at the entrance to Downing Street during Margaret Thatcher's premiership, and the 1991 attack led to extensive structural work during 1992 to increase security. On 30 October 1992 a PIRA car bomb exploded close to the entrance to Downing Street after a cab driver was ordered by PIRA to drive the bomb to the street – the first time this tactic had been employed in London.

DOWNING STREET DECLARATION 1993

The Downing Street Declaration, proclaimed on 15 December 1993, was helped by the quality of the relationship between Taoiseach Albert Reynolds and PM John Major. They had met as Finance Ministers, before Major became party leader and PM in 1990, and Reynolds similarly in 1992. Although both claimed that their contact since February 1992 had aimed at agreement, significant progress only appeared from July 1993. After pushing joint authority hard in the run-up to the Anglo-Irish Inter-governmental Conference meeting early in July, Reynolds sent a framework for a solution to London that contained some of the elements in the final declaration. In September relations between the two Governments were affected by claims of a Conservative deal with the UUP on the Maastricht vote in July and uncertainty arising from the continuing Hume–Adams talks. On 25 September, when John Hume, in a joint report, said there was agreement on a peace process, increased optimism was generated. However, by 12 October the Irish Cabinet had considered the report and decided on their own path to peace. The underlying principles were outlined by Foreign Minister Dick Spring in a special debate in the Dáil on 27 October. He said that six principles, derived from the principle of consent in Article 1 of the AIA, 'could underpin the peace process'. First, the people living in

Ireland, North and South, without coercion or violence, should be free to determine their own future, which 'should ideally lead to the possibility, ultimately, of unity on this island'. Second, this freedom to determine could be expressed in the development of new structures for the governing of NI, for relationships between North and South, and for relationships between the two islands. Third, no agreement could be reached in respect of any change in the present status of NI without the freely expressed consent of a majority of the people of NI. Fourth, that consent would include the recognition of the freedom of Unionists to withhold their consent from change, unless and until they were persuaded by democratic political means only. Fifth, the Irish Government would have to be prepared, at the right time and in the right circumstances, to express its commitment to consent as an integral part of any democratic approach to peace in fundamental law. Sixth, the Irish Government would have to be prepared to say to the men of violence that they could come to the negotiating table, that they could play a peaceful part in the development of Ireland's future – if they stopped the killing, the maiming and hurting. While speculation remained about the contents of the Hume–Adams document, it became clear that the Irish Government saw its interests as broader and wider, leading to the formal statement in Point 4 of the Unionist right to say no. Further, deputy leader of the SDLP Seamus Mallon said that the six Spring principles incorporated three from Hume–Adams. The six principles were the subject of discussion between Major and Reynolds at the EC summit meeting in Brussels on 29 October, where they issued a joint statement that expressed their commitment to restarting the talks process. They condemned terrorism, expressed sympathy for the bereaved and support for the security forces, and stated their determination that violence for political ends would not succeed. The Taoiseach had given an account of the Hume–Adams document and the Irish Government's assessment of it. The joint statement praised Hume's courage and

imagination, but in stating that initiatives were for the two Governments and that the Hume–Adams document had not been passed on to Britain, it was clear that neither endorsed it. Instead, they agreed to work together in their own terms and framework for peace, stability and reconciliation, consistent with their international obligations and responsibility to the wider community. The two leaders said that the situation in NI would never be changed by violence or the threat of it and that any political settlement had to be based on consent freely given in the absence of force or intimidation. Negotiations would be between the Governments and the parties and there would be no talks with those who threatened or exerted violence. There would be no secret agreements or understandings between the Governments. Major and Reynolds committed themselves to the removal of violence and in those circumstances they stressed that 'new doors could open' and they would 'respond imaginatively'. When Major reported progress to the House of Commons, after the Shankill bomb and the massacre at Greysteel, which made October the most violent month for deaths since 1976, agreement was even more urgent. He repeated the main points of the joint statement and emphasised that the renunciation of violence would 'open new doors'. He repeated his call for renewed talks, stressing the principle of consent in Spring's six principles. The leader of the opposition, John Smith, condemned the atrocities, stating that they had to pursue a way forward with 'intensity'. He also sought an early resumption of talks and commended Spring's six principles, which he described as a 'fine balance' between unionism and nationalism which should not be treated selectively. Paddy Ashdown, leader of the Liberal Democrats, also commended the six principles as a 'considerable contribution to the search for peace'. In reply the PM revealed that his object was to restart talks on the three-strand basis. When they resumed he would give them 'focus and direction'. The Anglo-Irish Intergovernmental conference meeting in

Belfast on 3 November agreed to work from the basis of the Irish document for 'a framework for peace, stability and reconciliation' with Spring's principles central. Major's speech at the Guildhall in London on 15 November revealed that he had now given prominence to a push for peace ahead of talks – the path preferred by Reynolds. However, differences remained between the leaders. The *Irish Press* reported an overheard conversation in which Reynolds had said that in certain circumstances he would 'walk away' and pursue his own proposals. The strong reaction to the leaking of a draft Irish Department of Foreign Affairs paper, anticipating British recognition of the 'full legitimacy and value of the goal of Irish unity by agreement', was an indication of the sensitivity, with Major's reported comments to Rev. Ian Paisley that he would have booted it 'over the house tops' had he formally received it. The revelations of long-standing British contacts with PIRA/PSF at the end of November cannot have helped confidence. However, by 5 December Reynolds had told RTE that he was willing to give a written guarantee that the territorial claim in Articles 2 and 3 of the Irish Constitution would be put to a referendum if it would help. Further British-Irish meetings at the EC summit in Brussels on 10 December were said to have revealed differences which were 'a bit more than language'. The declaration was launched at Downing Street on Wednesday 15 December 1993:

1 The Prime Minister and the Taoiseach agreed on the urgency of the problem of conflict in NI. They believed that discussions since February 1992, based on widely accepted principles and a number of key principles over the past twenty years, provided the starting point for a peace process designed to culminate in a political settlement.
2 They agreed on the value of healing divisions and ending conflict by agreement and co-operation of the people North and South. They made a solemn commitment to promote co-operation on the basis of fundamental

principles, international agreements and the NI constitutional guarantee. They aimed to foster agreement and reconciliation, leading to a new political framework founded on consent for arrangements within NI, the whole island and between these islands.
3 They recognised that developments in Europe will require new approaches.
4 The British Government, through the Prime Minister, reaffirmed:

  (a) that they would uphold the democratic wish of a greater number of the people of NI on the issue of support for the Union or a sovereign united Ireland;
  (b) that the British Government had 'no selfish strategic or economic interest in NI';
  (c) that their primary interest was 'peace, stability and reconciliation' by agreement among the people of the island and by working with the Irish Government to embrace the 'totality of relationships'.

He stated that the role of the British Government was to 'encourage, facilitate and enable' the achievement of agreement 'over a period' through dialogue and co-operation and based on full respect for the rights and identities of both traditions in Ireland. He accepted that the form of agreement may be 'structures for the island as a whole, including a united Ireland' achieved by peaceful means. The British Government agreed that the right of self-determination was 'for the people of the island of Ireland alone, by agreement between the two parts respectively . . . on the basis of consent, freely and concurrently given, North and South'. It undertook to legislate for unity, if agreed, or any measure of agreement of future relationships in Ireland freely agreed without external impediment. Finally, he expressed the view that the people of Britain would wish to enable the people of Ireland to reach agreement on living together in harmony and partnership, with respect for diverse traditions and recognising the special links between the peoples of Britain and Ireland.
5 The Irish Government, through the Taoiseach, stated that the lesson of Irish

history was that there could be no stability and well-being where a significant minority refused or rejected allegiance on grounds of identity. He stated that:

(1) it would be wrong to impose unity without 'the freely given consent of a majority of the people of NI';

(2) the democratic right of self-determination by the people of Ireland as a whole must be achieved 'subject to the agreement and consent of a majority of the people of NI' and respect must be given to the democratic dignity and civil rights and religious liberties of both communities;

(3) future political and constitutional arrangements emerging from any new, more broadly based, agreement would include the following rights – free political thought, freedom and expression of religion, the democratic pursuit of national and political aspirations, the right to seek constitutional change by peaceful and legitimate means, the right to live wherever one chooses without hindrance, equal opportunity in all social and economic activity, regardless of class, creed, sex or colour.

6 The Taoiseach promised to work for a new era of trust, recognising that the future of the island depended on relations between the two main traditions. He recognised the fears of the Unionist community and agreed to examine the Irish state for 'any elements in its democratic life and organisation' which could be represented as 'a substantial threat to their way of life and ethos', or 'not fully consistent with a modern democratic and pluralist society' and possible ways of removing them. He aimed to preserve shared inherited values and hoped that a 'meeting of hearts and minds will develop' over time to bring all the people of Ireland together. In the meantime, he hoped that Northern Unionists should not have to fear in future that this ideal would be pursued by either threat or coercion.

7 Both Governments accepted that Irish unity could only come about by those in favour persuading 'peacefully and without coercion or violence' those who were not. The Taoiseach recognised the 'continuing uncertainties and misgivings' of Northern Unionist attitudes to the rest of Ireland, despite the commitment in the AIA on change in the status of NI only by consent. He appealed to both traditions to grasp the opportunity for a fresh start and asked the people of NI to look on the people of the Republic as friends. He acknowledged the presence in the Irish Constitution of elements which were 'deeply resented by Northern Unionists' but in a new era the time had come to consider together how hopes and identities could be 'expressed in more balanced ways'. He confirmed that in the event of an overall settlement, the Irish Government would 'as part of a balanced constitutional accommodation, put forward and support proposals for change in the Irish Constitution which would fully reflect the principle of consent in NI'.

8 The Taoiseach recognised the need to engage in dialogue to address the fears of all traditions through an open, frank and balanced approach.

9 The British and Irish Governments would, with the NI constitutional parties, create institutions and structures, which, while respecting diversity, would 'enable them to work together in all areas of common interest'. The structures would include 'institutional recognition of the special links that exist . . . as part of the totality of relationships, while taking account of newly forged links with the rest of Europe'.

10 The British and Irish Governments reiterated that peace must involve the permanent end to the use of paramilitary violence. They confirmed that joining dialogue on the way ahead was open to 'democratically mandated parties which establish a commitment to exclusively peaceful methods and which have shown that they abide by the democratic process'.

11 The Irish Government also proposed to establish a Forum for Peace and Reconciliation to make recommendations on promoting trust and agreement.

12 The Taoiseach and Prime Minister

were determined to create a 'climate of peace'. They believed that this framework offered the people of Ireland, North and South, the basis to agree that 'differences can be negotiated and resolved exclusively by peaceful political means'. They appealed for the opportunity to be grasped which would 'compromise no position or principle, nor prejudice the future for either community'. They argued that it would break decisively the cycle of violence, allow economic and social co-operation on the island for prosperity and mutual understanding and transform the prospects for building on the talks process between the two Governments and the parties. The two Prime Ministers committed themselves to work, unremittingly, to the objective of a 'peaceful and harmonious future devoid of the violence and bitter divisions of the past generation'.

The declaration was launched at a press conference at midday on Wednesday 15 December. In the Dáil that afternoon Reynolds received a standing ovation and in the House of Commons, Major received an encouraging reaction. During his statement in the House, Major appeared particularly concerned to allay the fears of Unionists, stressing what was *not* included in the declaration. The UUP did not support the document, but its criticism was muted, even laconic. The DUP and Rev. Ian Paisley had delivered a letter to the PM accusing him of being part of a tripartite agreement with Reynolds and the IRA. He said that the PM had 'sold Ulster to buy off the fiendish Republican scum'. Both the Alliance Party and the SDLP welcomed the declaration. In the following days there were many attempts to gauge the strength of public support through phone-in facilities, polls of professional bodies and public opinion polls. On balance, the declaration was supported by around 55 per cent and was clearly ahead of those with decisive negative views by over two to one. In so far as the declaration was a package designed to attract the paramilitaries, and PIRA in particular, into a cessation of violence, their reaction was crucial. The loyalist paramilitaries postponed a reaction until after PIRA's. The Republican movement demanded 'direct unconditional dialogue', clarification of 'self-determination', and an amnesty for prisoners. Their demand for clarification was, in effect, for negotiation, and their process of consultation of supporters extended beyond the PSF Ard Fheis in February 1994. Although it was unclear whether there would ever be a formal response to the declaration, statements by prominent Republicans made it clear that they would not take it to PIRA and ask for a cessation of violence.

DRUMM, MAIRE

Vice-president of PSF, 1972–6, who was shot dead while a patient in the Mater Hospital, Belfast, on 28 October 1976. b. 1920. She was assassinated by two gunmen, dressed as doctors, who burst into the ward. An open verdict was returned at the inquest in 1978, and her husband Jimmy Drumm (also a leading figure in PSF) protested after the inquest that the army had put about suggestions that she had been killed by the PIRA. This was denied by the army. (In 1985 an ex-soldier and former security man at the hospital, who said he was in the UVF, admitted having shown the gunmen the ward in which Maire Drumm was a patient, and he was jailed for life.) Maire Drumm had resigned as vice-president of PSF ten days before her death; she said she had done so strictly for health reasons and supported the leadership. She had been acting president of PSF in 1971–2 when Ruairí Ó Brádaigh was in prison in the Republic. She herself had been to prison several times – the first occasion was in 1970 when she was accused of inciting people to join the PIRA in the Bogside area of Derry. In a speech in Belfast in 1975 she spoke of Republicans 'pulling down Belfast stone by stone' in defence of political status for prisoners. This led Secretary of State Merlyn Rees to describe her as 'a Madame Defarge sitting by the guillotine'. Roy Mason, Secretary of State at the time of her death, spoke of her murder as 'savage' and there was a message of sympathy from the UDA. In

1978 all sections of the Provisional Republican movement were represented at a ceremony in Milltown cemetery, Belfast, when a memorial to her was unveiled. She had previously requested that she should be buried outside the Republican plot. Jimmy Drumm continued to serve on the executive of PSF.

DUFFY, PATRICK ALOYSIUS
SDLP Assembly, 1973–4, and Convention, 1975–6, member for Mid-Ulster. b. Stewartstown, Co. Tyrone, 1934. BA, LLB (QUB). Solicitor, with extensive business interests. Representative, National Political Front, 1964. Secretary of the Assembly of the Northern Irish People, 1971–2. Cookstown District Council, 1973–93. When the NI Executive collapsed in 1974, he urged a joint British–Irish administration as 'the only means of providing a satisfactory form of government in Northern Ireland'. Unsuccessfully contested Mid-Ulster in 1979 Westminster election. At the party's annual conference in November 1980 he said he could support the five individual demands of the H-Block hunger strikers, but not the idea of bringing them together as political status. He caused some surprise when he declined to be a candidate in Mid-Ulster in the 1982 Assembly election. Chairman, NI Law Society, 1991–. On IFI board.

DUISBURG TALKS
Secret talks in Duisburg, West Germany, on 14–15 October 1988 between Jack Allen (UUP), Peter Robinson (DUP), Austin Currie (SDLP) and Gordon Mawhinney (All.) on the possibility of inter-party negotiations. Discussion centred on ways of accommodating the Unionist demand that the workings of the AIA should first be suspended and the insistence of the SDLP that there should be no suspension and that discussions should be held outside the agreement. Disclosure of the Duisburg exchanges in early 1989 produced a confused reaction, but encouraged Secretary of State Tom King to try to set up formal talks.

DUKAKIS, MICHAEL
Democratic candidate for US presidency, 1988. b. 3 November 1933. Governor of Massachusetts, 1974–8 and 1982–. Of Greek origin, he made civil rights for minorities a key issue of his campaign, and was the first Governor to sign into law the MacBride Principles on fair employment in NI. His strong attack on British policy on NI helped him to secure heavy Irish-American support in the vital New York primary, and he visited Gaelic Park in New York in April 1988 to 'throw in the ball'. He was critical of extradition of PIRA suspects from US, and also opposed broadcasting restrictions imposed by UK in 1988.

DUKES, ALAN
Leader of Fine Gael, March 1987–November 1990. b. Dublin, 1945. MA (UCD). As Minister for Justice, 1986–7, in the FitzGerald Government, he was involved in AIA ministerial meetings, and was disappointed at the refusal of British Government to agree to three-judge Diplock courts. But he said the whole process of the agreement has made the British authorities more sensitive in their dealings with the Nationalist community. In 1987 he questioned whether the Fianna Fáil Government was showing enough commitment to the AIA. In 1981, as TD for Kildare, he was appointed Agriculture Minister on his first day in the Dáil; later Finance Minister, 1982–6. Economist. Personal adviser in Brussels to EC Commissioner Richard Burke, 1977–80. Governor, European Investment Bank and IMF, 1982–6. Joined the revolt against Bruton's leadership in February 1994 and as a result lost his opposition post.

DUNGANNON
The S. Tyrone town, with a population almost evenly comprised of Protestants and Catholics, which has figured heavily in events since 1968. The first civil rights march was from Coalisland (a nearby predominantly Catholic village) to Dungannon on 24 August 1968. One of the points of community tension in 1968 was the complaint of Catholics that they were denied their fair share of houses by

the Unionist-controlled local council. In August 1969 riots flared in the town in the wake of events in Derry. The town has suffered greatly from PIRA bombing campaigns, and there have been many attacks on RUC stations in the area, and killings of members of security forces, as well as sectarian murders. In 1988–9 council chairmanship began to be shared between members from both communities as a gesture of reconciliation. In 1993 a major overseas investment located in the area.

DUNLEATH, LORD

Active member of the House of Lords and for many years the voice of the Alliance Party at Westminster. b. London, 23 June 1933; d. 1993. Son of Baron and Lady Dunleath. Represented N. Down in 1973 and 1982 Assemblies and in the Constitutional Convention, 1975–6. Ards Borough Council, 1977–85. In 1977 successfully sponsored legislation in the House of Lords to provide for shared schools (for Protestant and Catholic pupils), wherever there was sufficient demand from parents. He also brought forward a Bill to bring divorce law in NI broadly into line with that in GB, which led to the Government having similar legislation passed in 1978. Had extensive business interests and was president of the Royal Ulster Agricultural Society. BBC National Governor for NI, 1967–73. Resigned from Alliance Party for a period in 1979–80 to make an unsuccessful bid for NI ITV franchise. In 1990, he represented Alliance at the inaugural meeting of the BIPB. Soon afterwards, he resigned from the party on his appointment as DL for Co. Down.

DUNLOP, DOROTHY

UUP Assembly member for E. Belfast, 1982–6. Chairwoman, Health and Social Services Committee; member, Education and Security committees. BA (QUB). Formerly on staff of BBC talks department in Belfast, and later taught in several Belfast schools and in the prison education service. Belfast City Council, 1975–. Deputy Lord Mayor, 1978–9. In 1987 she was one of five Belfast UUP councillors who lost the party Whip for

failing to support the anti-AIA adjournment policy, and later that year she lost her position as chairwoman of E. Belfast Unionist Association. Stood unsuccessfully as Independent in E. Belfast in 1992 election, and shortly afterwards joined the Conservatives 'as a lifelong integrationist'. Granddaughter of Sir Robert Woods, one-time Unionist MP at Westminster for TCD.

DUNLOP, JOHN

MP for Mid-Ulster, February 1974–83. Originally Vanguard–UUUC; UUUP, 1977–83. b. 20 May 1910. Sat in Assembly for Vanguard, 1973–4. Joined Rev. Ian Paisley in support of United Unionist Action Council strike in May 1977, and split from UUP MPs with the break-up of United Ulster Unionist Coalition in 1977. In the 1979 general election, UUP decided not to oppose him in Mid-Ulster. Unsuccessful candidate in 1982 Assembly election.

DUNLOP, STEWART

DUP Convention member for S. Antrim, 1975–6. b. 1946. Founder member of Protestant Unionist Party and DUP. Antrim District Council, 1973–.

DUNN, JAMES ALEXANDER

Parliamentary Under-Secretary, NIO, 1976–9. b. 30 January 1926. Labour MP, Kirkdale (Liverpool), 1964–81; SDP, 1981–3. A prominent figure in the Merseyside Catholic community and especially active in education and soccer circles. At NIO he had special responsibility for Agriculture, Finance, and overseeing of public bodies. Absent from NIO through illness for most of his last year in office. Commons spokesman for SDP during passage of the 1982 devolution measure, to which he gave general support.

DUTCH–NORTHERN IRISH ADVISORY COMMITTEE

This committee, comprising educationists, Churchmen and others in both countries, sponsored trips to Holland to show how the Netherlands had tackled the problems of religious and other divisions. Delegations of NI politicians to Holland have included an inter-party group in 1973, a further party in 1975, including members of the SDLP, Alliance, NILP and UPNI and a twenty-strong UUP deputation, headed by then party leader Harry West. Members of paramilitary groups have attended some of the conferences sponsored by the committee.

E

ECONOMY

Most economic indicators show NI lagging behind GB with lower earnings, higher unemployment and a smaller Gross Domestic Product. This situation has obtained over many years, and has been worsened by the decline in jobs in manufacturing industry, notably shipbuilding, general engineering and textiles, and in farming. Indeed, GDP has declined in recent years. Between 1982 and 1986 it was almost 80 per cent of the UK figure, by 1990 it was down to 75.4 per cent but rose to 81 per cent in 1992. As for earnings, total personal income in 1990 was 81.3 per cent of the national average. In 1991 average weekly earnings for men, including overtime, were £272 against £319 in GB, while women, with £202, were £20 a week below the GB figure. The gap is partly explained by NI having less employment than GB in well-paid, high-skill jobs. The differential in earnings might be even greater but for the large (30 per cent plus) public sector in NI. The Government decision in 1992 to abolish the nine Wages Councils covering 34,000 low-paid workers was condemned as 'exploitation' by trade-union chiefs. Heavy unemployment has been a permanent feature of the local economy, and although Government Ministers took some comfort from the fact that NI had not suffered the same surge in the numbers jobless as GB in the recent recession, the outlook is highly uncertain; moreover, trade unions claim that the many recent changes in methods of computing official unemployment statistics hinder comparison with past performance. At the end of 1993 the total unemployed was 99,947 or 13.3 per cent

– that is, about 4 per cent higher than in GB. In November 1992 the independent NI Economic Council, set up in 1977, cast doubt on Government strategy in attracting outside investment. The council pointed out that between 1980 and 1992, the Industrial Development Board for NI had promoted 9,000 jobs in new, externally owned projects compared with more than 102,000 jobs attracted to the Republic. It also revealed that in 1990 there were just over 200 externally owned (mainly British and US) manufacturing plants in NI, employing 41,000 people. This was 41 per cent fewer plants than in 1973, and represented a loss of 46,000 jobs. The council acknowledged that the IDB's efforts had been adversely affected by the political situation and the continuing violence, but it called for an urgent review of Government policy. However, the IDB, under new leadership, passed its target of 1,800 new jobs in 1992–3 in contrast to its 430 total in 1991–2. From late 1992 there was encouraging news about investment. An Indonesian textile company planned 900 jobs at Antrim, Seagate promised high-tech jobs for Derry and a Californian company promised 600 jobs, making rechargeable batteries, at Glengormley. In 1991–2, the Local Enterprise Development Unit created 2,500 jobs – a shortfall of 650 – and reported some 200 fewer start-ups in business during the year. The Major Government continued the privatisation policy in NI, with NI Electricity sold off in 1993. The international airport was also on the privatisation list, along with water, the latter privatisation attracting widespread local opposition. In 1993–4 extra Government spending was earmarked for NI because of the increased population shown by the 1991 census. It was set at 2.87 per cent of GB spending compared with 2.75 per cent previously. This entailed a £367 million increase to £7,460 million in 1993–4, with spending for 1994–5 at £7,690 million, and for 1995–6 at £7,940 million. Government expenditure per head was 45 per cent higher than in the rest of the UK. Social security benefits for 1993–4 totalled £2,353 million. Law and order (including the RUC) costs for 1993–4 were £902 million. Expenditure arising from the large army presence is not included in the NI estimates, but past statements in Parliament have indicated that it costs less to maintain army units in NI than in Germany. The much-discussed Treasury subvention to NI in 1991–2 was £2,544 million, with locally raised taxes, National Insurance, rates and other revenue totalling £3,905 million against spending of £6,449 million. There have been high hopes in government and business circles that NI will benefit appreciably from the Single European Market. The NI Economic Research Centre has calculated that if cross-border trade in manufactured goods doubled to £2 billion by 1997, more than 3,000 jobs would be created in NI. A survey by Dun and Bradstreet revealed the highest level of bankruptcies in 1993 since 1985. (*See also* European Community.)

'ÉIRE NUA' *see* Provisional Sinn Féin

ELTON, LORD
Parliamentary Under-Secretary, NIO, 1979–81. b. 2 March 1930. MA (Oxon.). Varied teaching career in comprehensive and grammar schools and as college lecturer, 1962–72. Conservative Whip in House of Lords, 1974–6. Front-bench Conservative spokesman in Lords, 1976–9. In NIO, spokesman on all subjects in Lords and responsible for the departments of Agriculture and Education. Held posts in Whitehall at Health Department, Home Office, and Environment between 1981 and 1986. Deputy chairman, Conservative Peers.

EMERGENCY PROVISIONS ACT *see* Security System section, pp. 453–61

EMPEY, REGINALD
VUPP (and later UUUM) Convention member for E. Belfast, 1975–6. b. 1947. B.Sc. (QUB). He had been vice-chairman of the Young Unionist Council (UUP) before he joined VUPP, of which he became chairman in 1975. In the Convention he was secretary of the UUUC's policy committee. Deputy leader,· UUUP, 1977–84. Unsuccessfully contested

E. Belfast in 1982 Assembly election. In 1985 elected as UUP councillor in Belfast. Deputy Lord Mayor, 1988; Lord Mayor, 1989–90, 1993–. Awarded OBE for services to local government in January 1994. He was involved in controversy over a visit to Belfast in April 1990 by Taoiseach Charles Haughey (then holding the EC presidency) to address a conference of business people from NI and the Republic. As Lord Mayor he was invited to welcome the delegates, and insisted on doing so despite strong opposition from Unionist councillors. But he spoke before Haughey arrived, and his remarks were largely critical of the Republic. None the less, he was deprived of the City Hall UUP Whip, which was restored in 1991 after he had been elected an honorary secretary of the Ulster Unionist Council. Active in Brooke–Mayhew Talks, 1991–2. In January 1994 he argued that Paisley's call for a referendum on the Union in GB could end the link with NI. After Gerry Adams's forty-eight-hour visit to New York in February, Empey wrote to President Clinton urging him to refuse Adams a visa that would allow him to spend St Patrick's Day in New York. On board of Laganside Corporation.

ENGLISH, MICHAEL
Chairman of the NI standing committee of MPs at Westminster, 1976–9. b. 24 December 1930. LLB (Liverpool). Has an Ulster family background. Labour MP for Nottingham W., 1964–83.

ENNISKILLEN BOMBING
Eleven civilians – six men and five women – were killed and sixty-three people, including children, were injured when a PIRA bomb exploded close to the Enniskillen war memorial on 8 November 1987, shortly before the annual Remembrance Sunday ceremony was due to begin. The circumstances led to widespread condemnation of the attack, which the PIRA admitted only on the following day in a statement which expressed 'deep regret' and suggested that the bomb could have been triggered by a security forces scanning device – a claim rejected as a 'lie' by the RUC. Margaret

Thatcher, who attended the memorial service in Enniskillen, made a strong plea in the Commons to constitutional parties to come together in the wake of the tragedy. A group, Enniskillen Together, set up after the bombing to develop cross-community contacts, has established an integrated primary school.

ERSKINE, LORD (OF RERRICK)

Governor of NI, 1964–8. b. 14 December 1893; d. 1980. Was jeered by supporters of Rev. Ian Paisley when he attended the General Assembly of the Irish Presbyterian Church in Belfast on 5 June 1966. The protest was said to be against the 'Romeward trend' of the Church. The incident drew condemnation from the then PM, Captain Terence O'Neill, who talked of trends towards Nazism and fascism.

EUROPA HOTEL

The international press corps, who provided much of the business for this centrally situated Belfast hotel at the height of the Troubles, dubbed it 'the world's most bombed hotel'. More than twenty bombs have exploded in or near the building. The hotel has been a popular rendezvous for politicians as well as journalists. For several years it was known as the Forum Hotel, but it reverted to its original title with a change of ownership in 1986. In 1991 a small bomb was found inside and it suffered from an explosion that caused serious damage to the nearby Grand Opera House. Bomb-damaged again in May 1993 while in receivership, it was purchased by the Hastings Group in August 1993 for £7 million.

EUROPEAN COMMUNITY

January 1, 1993 marked not only the completion of the Single European Market and the end of customs checks along the border with the Republic, it also marked the twentieth anniversary of NI's accession to the EC as a region of the UK. Common Market membership was particularly controversial in NI (*see* Common Market Referendum) and the Maastricht Treaty (1992), intended to pave the way for European economic and monetary union, divided NI politicians. All the Unionist MPs, with the exception of Sir James Kilfedder, opposed ratification of Maastricht. They argued that it would erode national sovereignty. By contrast, the SDLP strongly favours European union, and is thus in line with opinion in the Republic, where the June 1992 referendum showed 70 per cent in favour. The debates on Maastricht and the Single Market greatly increased local interest in EC issues, particularly in the business community. In the 1970s and early 1980s there tended to be a general indifference, except perhaps in academic and farming circles. While the future of European union was still uncertain in 1993, EC policy towards regions like NI remained intact. NI was given Objective One, or priority, status for the funding programme 1989–93, which has brought some £600 million to NI for economic development, and this status is to be continued for a new programme, which is likely to run to the end of the century. Since joining the EC in 1973, NI has received aid estimated at £2,000 million. About half has been devoted to economic development. This has gone into areas like transport, industrial development, training, tourism, research, cross-border initiatives and – a novel idea for the EC – the promotion of reconciliation in the community. The other half of the EC funding has gone into support for farm prices. Until December 1992 the attributed contribution to EC funds from NI was £1,016 million. Negotiations began at the end of 1992 on the funding for 1994, and there was much pressure for a big rise in support for the structural funds. Comments by EC Commission President Jacques Delors during a visit to NI in 1992 indicated that the Commission is impressed by the NI case for extra assistance. Delors stressed that the EC had a 'useful role' in tackling the heavy unemployment in NI where, in recent years, unemployment has been double the EC average. The EC has decided that there should be a two-thirds increase in money for the structural funds overall to the end of the century, but how much NI gets will depend on the case presented by the Government. The NIO's initial bid was for £2,000 million. The controversial question of whether or not EC financial assistance to NI is 'additional' to planned Government spending has been raised repeatedly over the years, and remains a matter of debate. Also, there tends to be much local comment on the comparison between the relatively small funding NI receives from the EC and that obtained by the Republic. Also, NI does not benefit from the new Cohesion Fund, which should mean £8,000 million for the Republic by the end of the century. MEP John Hume has suggested that the UK could qualify for Cohesion Fund money which would benefit NI (because of the devaluation arising from Black Wednesday) but EC Finance Ministers have ruled out any extension of the fund. The idea of 'subsidiarity' in Maastricht – that is, decentralistion of decision-making – will also be crucial in NI. 'Subsidiarity' (the term is drawn from Catholic social teaching) could mean wider consultation locally on EC programmes than has occurred in the past and possibly NI representation on the new Committee of the Regions. As the Single Market began, there were, however, many uncertainties as to its impact locally. NI Secretary of State Sir Patrick Mayhew argued that it would bring 'unprecedented opportunities'. Jane Morrice, head of the NI EC office, felt many local businesses had still to face up to the challenge. An independent Northern Ireland Euro-centre in Brussels was launched in 1991. (*See also* European Parliament.)

EUROPEAN COURT/COMMISSION OF HUMAN RIGHTS

Some interesting decisions affecting NI have been handed down by these inter-linked Strasbourg-based bodies. The first of major interest was given in 1978 when, on the application of the Republic's Government, the court dealt with charges of ill-treatment of internees during 'interrogation in depth'. The court found that some internees had been subjected to 'inhuman and degrading treatment', but not to torture. Shortly before the 1981 H-Block hunger strike, the Commission (representing the first

stage of the procedure) turned down a submission by four H-Block prisoners that their treatment was a breach of the European Convention, although it criticised the 'inflexibility' of the British Government. Two members of the Commission visited the Maze Prison when Bobby Sands MP was on hunger strike, but Sands refused to follow up a complaint lodged on his behalf by his sister. This was followed by an unsuccessful move by a group of widows of victims of terrorism in NI to persuade the Commission that the Republic's Government was breaching the Convention by not taking adequate anti-terrorist measures. In October 1981 the court held that the ban on male homosexuality in NI was a breach of the Convention, and in 1982 an Order was introduced to achieve parity in the law with GB. In 1984 the Commission held that the use of plastic bullets was justified in a riot situation. It said 66,000 plastic and rubber bullets had been fired since 1969, causing thirteen deaths, and the weapon was less dangerous than alleged. In May 1988 a spokesman for the Commission criticised the power to detain suspects for up to seven days under the PTA. In December 1988 the Court ruled against seven-day detention, but Home Secretary Douglas Hurd announced that the Government was seeking 'temporary' derogation from the Convention while it decided on its long-term response. The derogation was still effective in 1993. In March 1991 the restrictions on broadcasting interviews with paramilitaries were referred to the ECHR from the NI High Court. In April 1991, however, a move to have the Republic's 'Section 31' broadcasting ban declared in breach of the European Convention on Human Rights was rejected by the Commission. Many threats to take issues to the ECHR do not materialise, and in 1992 the NI SACHR again urged the introduction of a Bill of Rights in NI that would incorporate the Convention, so that cases could be heard locally, thus avoiding the expense and long delay entailed in a Strasbourg hearing. The proposal was put before the Brooke–Mayhew negotiations. In May

1993, the Court pleased the NIO with a ruling that the NI situation justified detention for more than four days and that this was not a breach of the Convention, which required suspects to be brought before a court 'promptly'. In September 1993 the Commission accepted that there was a case to be heard under Article 2 (Right to Life), brought by relatives of the Gibraltar three.

EUROPEAN PARLIAMENT

In the original, appointed European Assembly NI was not entitled to any separate representation, but the late Rafton Pounder, Unionist MP for S. Belfast, was included in the Conservative delegation for some years and he served on the staff of the European Commission for a time in order to draft a report on a Court of Auditors to check financial abuses. When the elected Parliament was planned in 1976, NI was given three seats. On a population basis, it was only entitled to two, but the Irish Republic suggested an extra seat to ensure representation of both communities. The idea was endorsed by James Callaghan for the British Government. In January 1978 the British Government got Parliament's backing for the election of the three MEPs by PR in a single NI constituency – a departure from the GB elections and further guarantee of Nationalist representation. The election on 7 June 1979 resulted in the return of Ian Paisley (DUP), John Hume (SDLP) and John Taylor (UUP) in that order. (*See* Election Results section, pp. 384–6.) Paisley, who had easily topped the poll, made his presence felt at the first session of the Assembly. He interrupted Taoiseach Jack Lynch, then holding the EC presidency, with the words 'In the name of Ulster's dead I indict you for harbouring their murderers.' The interruption brought cries of protest from MEPs. (In 1988 the DUP leader was ejected from the Parliament when he interrupted an address by Pope John Paul II.) Hume serves on the Regional, Agriculture, and African, Caribbean and Pacific committees and is a Socialist front-bencher, whilst Paisley is on the Political Committee and the enlarged Bureau of

the Parliament. Despite their differences, the three MEPs have co-operated in pressing NI's case for special treatment. An early notable example was when Hume, in 1979, put forward a motion calling for a special report on action to boost the NI economy. He was supported by Paisley and Taylor, and a special survey was carried out by a French MEP, Simone Martin, in 1980. The Parliament backed her report, which called, among other things, for tax exemption for new industries for at least five years, special help for Belfast housing, and a common energy price structure throughout the UK. Margaret Thatcher's decision to bring electricity charges in NI broadly into line with those in GB, and special financial aid for Belfast housing could be seen as a reply. The two Unionist MEPs and the SDLP leader have been at odds on occasion on whether the Parliament should concern itself with NI political issues. In the autumn of 1982 Hume sought to have special hearings organised by the Parliament's political affairs committee to find ways in which the Community could help end the political and economic crisis in NI. But both Paisley and Taylor attacked the suggestion, saying that it conflicted with a decision by the Parliament in 1981 that it should not become involved in the political and constitutional affairs of NI. In the event, the proposal gave rise to strong opposition from the British Government, with Thatcher declaring that there would be no co-operation with such an inquiry. But the Bureau of the Parliament authorised the political affairs committee to have a special report prepared by Danish MEP Neils Haagerup. This report, adopted by the Parliament in 1984, called for power-sharing, and an integrated economic plan for NI. In May 1981 the Parliament rejected a motion calling for British 'flexibility' on the H-Block dispute, put forward by two MEPs from the Republic, Neil Blaney and Paddy Lalor, on the grounds that it was not competent to intervene in NI, and regretting the more than 2,000 deaths in the current violence. But in 1982 the Parliament passed a motion calling for a ban throughout the EC on the use of plastic bullets, which were at that time a matter of intense controversy in NI. In December 1985 the Parliament voted decisively for the AIA, by 150 to 28. In 1990 the UUP's Jim Nicholson, who succeeded John Taylor at the 1989 election, presented a report to the Parliament that highlighted the long-standing problem of additionality as it affects NI, that is, whether EC funding is additional to British Government funding or merely replaces it. In recent years the MEPs have worked together on farming and industrial issues and in dealing (in co-operation with MEPs from the Republic) with the threat of submarines to fishing vessels in the Irish Sea. But on the Maastricht Treaty, which proposed major extra powers for the Parliament, Hume is very much in favour and the Unionists are opposed. In November 1992 the Parliament appointed a Belgian lawyer to investigate anti-Catholic job discrimination in NI. This followed the tabling of a resolution by Neil Blaney, MEP for Connaught–Ulster, who got the support of more than fifty MEPs. A month later, it appointed a committee to investigate claims of health risks arising from the use of hi-tech army surveillance equipment in NI. A fomer NI civil servant, Dr Robert Ramsey, is Director-General of Research in the Parliament. (*See also* European Community.)

EWART-BIGGS, CHRISTOPHER

British Ambassador to Dublin, assassinated on 21 July 1976, two weeks after he took up the post. b. 1921. Ewart-Biggs and a young woman civil servant from the NIO, Judith Cook, died when the ambassador's car was blown up by a landmine, a short distance from his official residence. The assassination gave rise to the declaration of a state of emergency in the Republic, and the introduction of additional anti-terrorist measures. In September 1976 Dublin newspapers reported that a PIRA spokesman had admitted responsibility for the murders. Ewart-Biggs was a colourful personality – 'straight out of P.G. Wodehouse' was a common assessment – and had a distinctive appearance, having worn an eye-patch since he lost his right eye in World War II. A novel which he

had written in his early years was still banned in the Republic when he was appointed to Dublin. His wife Jane (created life peer, 1978; d. 1992) declared that she had no bitterness towards the Irish people and she joined the Peace People, and also launched a memorial prize awarded to authors whose works have helped towards peace and reconciliation in Ireland.

EXTRADITION *see* Mayhew, Sir Patrick

F

FAIR EMPLOYMENT

Complaints of anti-Catholic bias featured strongly in the civil rights campaign. In 1976 the Fair Employment act set up the Fair Employment Agency to address the problem of religious or political discrimination. But it outlawed only direct, and not indirect, discrimination, and relied substantially on a voluntary approach by employers. By the late 1980s there were repeated references to the fact that a Catholic man was two and a half times more likely to be unemployed than a Protestant man. Local pressure for stronger legislation, particularly through the SACHR and the Anglo-Irish Intergovernmental Conference, together with a widespread campaign by Irish-Americans in support of the MacBride Principles, led to even tougher anti-discrimination laws which mainly took effect at the start of 1990. The 1989 Fair Employment Act split the functions of the FEA. A Fair Employment Commission was given wide powers, including that of assisting people complaining of discrimination. Indirect discrimination was outlawed. A Fair Employment Tribunal was established to hear complaints. By February 1992 all companies with more than ten employees were required to notify the FEC of the religious composition of their workforces. In May 1992 the FEC reported that while Catholics had a fair share of all jobs in the public service, the situation was different for senior posts. Of these, the percentage held by Catholics varied from 17 per cent in NIE to 40 per cent in education and library boards, and was 21.1 per cent in the civil service and 22 per cent in District Councils, with an overall average of 24.3 per cent. FEC chairman Bob Cooper said he was treating this imbalance 'with a sense of urgency'. In September 1992 a 'leaked' internal civil service report to Industry Minister Robert Atkins said that, in key areas of employment, the unemployment differential between Protestants and Catholics was 'unlikely to alter significantly over the next decade, in spite of the strengthened fair employment legislation'. It emphasised the difficulty of making progress during economic recession, and suggested that it would be necessary to put substantial investment into Catholic areas where there was very high unemployment. Two months later, Minister of State Michael Mates announced that goals and timetables were to be established for female and Catholic representation in the civil service, although he stressed that this did not mean quotas, which would be illegal. International interest in fair employment remained high in 1992. By then, thirteen US states had adopted the MacBride Principles, and President Clinton voiced support for them during his election campaign. In 1992 the European Parliament launched an inquiry into job and other discrimination in NI. In 1992, in the FEC's second monitoring report, Bob Cooper said that while the first monitoring report had shown that Catholics were under-represented by 3 per cent in monitored companies, the second report showed that Catholic representation had risen by 0.4 per cent to 35.3 per cent. He described this as 'a promising start', but added that the FEC's aim was to achieve a situation in which the proportion of Catholics in employment was the same as that in the working population. This meant that the rate of improvement needed to be accelerated. He also pointed to a 'significant increase' in the numbers of Catholic males in managerial and professional occupations.

FALLS ROAD

The main Catholic district of Belfast, centred on the thoroughfare which stretches westwards from the city centre to Andersonstown. It runs parallel to the predominantly Protestant Shankill Road, from which it is separated by the Peace Line, erected after riots and house burnings in 1969. In this area of confrontation there have been many serious incidents during the Troubles, and thousands of people moved out of their homes in the summer of 1969 when Protestant militants invaded the area and burned many homes (there were counter-claims on the Protestant side that loyalist homes had been attacked). The IRA has always looked for support to the Falls area, and it was here in the aftermath of the serious violence of 1969 that the PIRA began to assert itself. It was in the Lower Falls in the summer of 1969 that protests were mounted against RUC action in the Bogside area of Derry, and the Scarman report criticised the RUC for 'unjustified' firing of a Browning machine gun into Divis Flats, which resulted in a young boy's death. The erection of barricades in the area in 1969 gave rise to angry controversy, and delicate negotiations between the Falls Road-based CCDC and the Government and security forces. These involved, at one point, a deputation to London to meet Home Secretary James Callaghan. The barriers were eventually lowered, but their existence had brought repeated protests from loyalists, who sometimes erected their own barricades in the Shankill area as a protest. A major problem for the security forces has been the refusal of people in the area to fully accept the RUC, although by 1978 the police were claiming that co-operation was increasing and people in the area were more willing to give information, particularly by way of the confidential telephone. But the Scarman report showed that the policing problem was there even before 1969. It stated that after 1968, RUC foot patrols did not go into a substantial area of the Falls on foot either late at night or early in the morning. This was the area bounded by the Falls Road, Grosvenor Road, Albert Street and

Cullingtree Road. The police, according to Scarman, had code-named the area 'No-go-land'. This was virtually the area chosen for the army curfew on 3–5 July 1970, which, according to Catholics, marked the end of the 'honeymoon' with the British army as protectors of the minority. During the curfew, which extended over thirty-four hours (apart from a two-hour shopping break), five civilians were killed, and sixty injured, while fifteen soldiers were injured. The army search during the curfew yielded fifty-two pistols, thirty-five rifles, six automatic weapons, fourteen shotguns, one hundred homemade bombs, a grenade, 250 pounds of explosives, about 21,000 rounds of ammunition and eight two-way radio sets. The operation led to strong protests from NICRA and the CCDC, and two local politicians, Gerry Fitt MP and Paddy Devlin MP, flew to London to complain that the troops had abused people, looted, and stolen during the operation – charges broadly denied by the army. Falls Road spokesmen claimed that the army was ignoring much larger supplies of weapons and ammunition in the Shankill area. During the Troubles, the Falls has been the venue of some fierce gun battles between the security forces and the PIRA, and of bitter feuds between the PIRA and the OIRA, and between the OIRA and the IRSP. Several factories in the area were burned in 1969, and over the years there have been numerous riots and demonstrations, in many of which buses have been burned and vehicles hi-jacked. Police and army posts in the area have been attacked frequently. Easter parades to the Republican plot at Milltown cemetery, where many IRA men are buried, and funerals of members of the Republican movement have been occasions of high tension between many residents and the police and army (see Andersonstown). Earlier, the introduction of internment in 1971 and the subsequent civil disobedience campaign alienated many residents from the authorities. But up to the 1981 hunger strike, the SDLP, with its support for constitutional politics, had majority backing in the area, and in 1977 official sources attributed PIRA's decision

to regroup and alter its tactics to the disenchantment of local people with violent methods. But there was undoubtedly strong support for the H-Block protest in the Falls Road area, and in wider W. Belfast. There were many pro-hunger-strike demonstrations, and the vast turn-out for the funeral of Bobby Sands MP to Milltown cemetery testified to the growth of republicanism. PSF's decision to contest W. Belfast at the 1982 Assembly election was a direct challenge to the SDLP, and strong organisational effort and a network of PSF advice centres paid off. Gerry Adams, then vice-president of PSF, headed the poll with 25.5 per cent of first preferences, with the total SDLP vote for three candidates standing at 24.5 per cent. Adams was also returned to Westminster in the 1983 general election, unseating Gerry Fitt, who had held the seat since 1966, and he retained the seat in 1987 despite a major organisational drive by the SDLP and the decision by Alliance to stand aside. PSF also outvoted SDLP in the 1985 council elections, in two 1987 council by-elections, and again in the 1989 poll. In 1990, after many calls from local politicians and Churchmen for an ambitious job-creation plan for the area, Economy Minister Richard Needham announced development of the Springvale project and plans for more advance factories and efforts to attract new firms, which he foresaw as bringing 'many, many jobs to West Belfast'. The IFI also promised money for the area. The Minister warned that violence could threaten new investment, and it soon became clear that recession also reduced hopes of a major employment boost. The deployment, however, of some civil service jobs to the city centre along with new shopping developments there helped employment in the Falls Road area. And the environment was improved by the gradual demolition of the controversial Divis Flats. In the 1990s the area has experienced the killing of Catholics by loyalist paramilitaries, and also several deaths arising from the internal feud in IPLO that, together with PIRA action against alleged drug dealers in IPLO, led to the disbandment of both the 'Belfast

Brigade' and 'Army Council' factions of IPLO in November 1992. In February 1992 an off-duty RUC man shot dead three men in the PSF advice centre on the Falls Road. In the first years of the decade, there were signs of PSF seeking to distance itself from PIRA attacks that killed innocent civilians, and some increase in contacts across the Peace Line. In the 1992 Westminster election, indeed, the surprise defeat of Gerry Adams by local GP Dr Joe Hendron of the SDLP was put down to the decision of a few thousand loyalists in the Shankill area to vote tactically to dislodge the PSF chief. Soon after his election, Hendron joined the N. Belfast UUP MP Cecil Walker on a US trip which raised hopes that the area might secure its own modest 'Silicon Valley'.

FARREN, SEAN NIAL

SDLP Assembly member for N. Antrim, 1982-6. SDLP chairman, 1981-6. b. 1939. Unsuccessfully contested N. Antrim in 1979, 1983, 1987 and 1992 Westminster elections. Lecturer in education at University of Ulster. He was a negotiator in the Brooke–Mayhew Talks, and as they ended in November 1992 he said the SDLP had moved Nationalist attitudes 'away from futile flag-waving and empty rhetoric' and that 'many in the Unionist delegations were genuinely anxious for an honourable accommodation'.

FAUL, FATHER DENIS

A leading campaigner against alleged ill-treatment of persons arrested for interrogation and of detainees during internment. b. Co. Louth, 1932. A teacher at St Patrick's Academy, Dungannon, he first attracted attention in November 1969 when he declared that Catholics felt that NI's judicial system was loaded against them. The statement was attacked by Government Ministers and brought a rebuke from Cardinal Conway, the Catholic Primate of Ireland. He has been strongly critical of the army and the RUC Special Branch, but he has also repeatedly condemned PIRA violence and has repeatedly called on PIRA to declare a ceasefire. In March 1977 he described the PIRA campaign of that period as 'spurious in Republican terms' and 'directly

contrary to Catholic teaching on the sacredness of human life'. As a Maze Prison Chaplain during the H-Block hunger strikes, 1980–1, he strongly opposed the fasts, but at the same time urged Government reforms to defuse the crisis. The meetings of relatives which he organised in the autumn of 1981 were seen as an important element in bringing the protest to an end. PSF accused him of putting pressure on relatives to request medical intervention where hunger-strikers had lapsed into a coma. In 1984 he suggested that only 20 per cent of Catholics would vote for removal of the border in an immediate referendum and that the ending of violence was their priority. In 1988 his repeated demands for a more generous policy of releases of young prisoners seemed to be having an impact on Government practice. In May 1992 he made a strong protest about the use of the Parachute Regiment and the Royal Marines in E. Tyrone, suggesting that 'high-level, assault–combat troops' were unsuited to day-to-day contact with the public.

FAULKNER, LADY LUCY (OF DOWNPATRICK)

Widow of Lord Faulkner (Brian Faulkner), former NI Prime Minister, who died in a hunting accident in 1977. b. 1 July 1925. BA (TCD). After working as a Belfast Telegraph journalist in the 1950s, she was private secretary to NI Prime Minister Sir Basil Brooke (later Viscount Brookeborough). After her husband stood down from active politics in 1976, she was President of UPNI until the party ceased to operate in 1981. NI National Governor of BBC, 1978-85, and first chair of NI Broadcasting Council, 1982-5. Governor of Linen Hall Library, 1982-. NI Tourist Board, 1984-. A member of the Initiative '92 commission, which in 1992-3 heard evidence on NI's political future.

FAULKNER, LORD (OF DOWNPATRICK)

Formerly Brian Faulkner, PM, 1971-2, and Chief Executive in power-sharing administration, 1974. b. 18 February 1921 and killed in a hunting accident near his

Co. Down home in March 1977. His career was the most dramatic and varied of any in NI politics. He was the last PM under the 1920 Constitution, and the first head of a Unionist Government to include a Catholic in the Cabinet. In 1974 he led the brief inter-party Executive which embraced Unionists as well as members of the mainly Catholic SDLP and the Alliance Party. First spotted as a potential politician by British Labour Minister Hugh Dalton, he started out as a traditional Unionist active in the Orange Order (he was a member of the Grand Orange Lodge of Ireland), and he was elected as MP for E. Down in 1949. At twenty-eight he was the youngest MP returned to Stormont up to that time. After three years as Government Chief Whip, he became Minister of Home Affairs in 1959 and was active in countering the IRA border campaign. In March 1963 he became Minister of Commerce in the Terence O'Neill Government, and even political opponents praised his energetic and successful approach to the attraction of new industry, particularly from overseas. He caused a major surprise in January 1969 when he resigned from the O'Neill Government in protest against the setting up of the Cameron Commission to inquire into the causes of the violence. This was obviously a climax to tensions between Faulkner and O'Neill. And when O'Neill resigned as PM in April 1969, Faulkner failed by only one vote to succeed him. Major Chichester-Clark became PM and appointed him Minister of Development, with the task of carrying through local government reform and the setting up of a central housing authority. When Chichester-Clark bowed out as Premier in 1971, he finally achieved his ambition to become PM, easily beating his only challenger, William Craig. In August 1971 he introduced internment without trial, a move which infuriated the opposition, and led to an escalation of violence. And in March 1972, what he had confidently predicted would never happen occurred overnight – the Stormont Parliament was prorogued. He joined militant Unionists in demonstrating against the action of the

Heath Government, and he refused to have anything to do with the Commission set up to advise the Secretary of State. Northern Ireland, he declared, would not be treated like a 'coconut colony'. His biggest test came in 1973 when he joined with the SDLP and Alliance parties in the Sunningdale Conference and the cross-community Executive. But power-sharing and the cross-border Council of Ireland were too much for the Unionist Party. The loyalist strike brought down the Executive in May 1974. In the Convention election he tried to bring mainline unionism behind his UPNI, a break-away group, but it fared badly in the election. In 1976 he announced that he was quitting active politics. In 1977 he became a life peer (he could have had a peerage in 1972), and he confessed that power-sharing had cost him his political life. His autobiography, *Memoirs of a Statesman,* appeared in 1978, fifteen months after his death.

FEAKLE TALKS
Secret discussions between Protestant Churchmen, mainly from NI, and PSF and PIRA representatives in Smyth's Village Hotel, Feakle, Co. Clare, on 9–11 December 1974. The talks were criticised by many Unionists, and the Churches stressed that the clergy taking part had acted only as individuals. The talks were followed by a brief PIRA ceasefire, and later by a more extended ceasefire (or truce according to the PIRA) which petered out in renewed PIRA violence after a few months. The Churchmen involved were: Dr Arthur Butler, Church of Ireland Bishop of Connor; Dr Jack Weir, then Clerk of the Presbyterian Assembly; Rev. Eric Gallagher, former president of the Methodist Church in Ireland; Rev. Ralph Baxter, secretary, and Rev. William Arlow, assistant secretary of the Irish Council of Churches; Dr Harry Morton, secretary, British Council of Churches; Right Rev. Arthur McArthur, moderator of the United Reformed Chuch in England; and Stanley Worrall, former headmaster of Methodist College, Belfast, and chairman of NUM (d. 1991). The PSF spokesmen included the president, Ruairí Ó Brádaigh; Maire

Drumm, vice-president (murdered 1976), and Seamus Loughran, Belfast organiser. The PIRA leaders included Dáithí Ó Conaill, chief of staff and at the time regarded as the most-wanted man in Ireland, Seamus Twomey and Kevin Mallon. There was a touch of drama during the meeting, since men from the Republic's Special Branch entered the hotel, apparently as a result of a tip-off. But the PIRA men had already left. The proposals exchanged between the Churchmen and the Provisionals were as follows:

The Churchmen suggested that the PIRA would consider that its requirements prior to a permanent ceasefire were met if the British Government issued a policy statement which included the following:

1 That the Government stated it had no political or territorial interests in Ireland beyond its obligations to NI citizens.
2 That the Government's prime concern was the achievement of peace and the promotion of such understanding between the various sections in NI as would guarantee to all its people a full participation in the life of the community, whatever be the relationship of NI to the EC, UK or Republic.
3 Contingent on the maintenance of a declared ceasefire and effective policing, the Government would relieve the army as quickly as possible of its internal duties.
4 Until agreements about the future government of NI had been freely negotiated and guaranteed, armed forces would be retained in NI.
5 The Government recognised the right of all those who had political aims to pursue them through the democratic process.

The PIRA's point-by-point reply was sent within a few days:

1 Until the Government clearly stated that it had no claim to sovereignty in any part of Ireland the statement was meaningless. 'We accept that economic commitments must be honoured.'
2 'A noble wish with which we concur but we believe it can only be realised in the full community of the people of Ireland.'
3 No difficulty in maintaining community peace if a bilateral truce was agreed between the army and the PIRA. Discussions with loyalist groups in maintaining peace would be welcomed.
4 If declaration of intent to withdraw, PIRA accepted that there should be a limited army presence during negotiations and implementation of an agreed settlement.
5 'It is meaningless to talk of democratic processes while . . . 2,000 political prisoners are in jail.'

PIRA then sent a number of counter-proposals, including an elected all-Ireland constituent assembly which would draw up a constitution that would have to be approved by a two-thirds majority. There would be a provisional parliament for Ulster (nine counties). It called for British withdrawal within twelve months of the constitution being adopted and an amnesty for all political prisoners in Britain and Ireland. It also offered a temporary ceasefire from midnight on 22 December 1974 until midnight on 2 January 1975 to enable the Government to respond 'favourably', but said this was conditional on the army stopping raids, harassment and arrests for the same period. On 18 December Secretary of State Merlyn Rees received five of the Churchmen involved in the Feakle Talks. Afterwards he issued a statement saying that if there was a genuine cessation of violence there would be 'a new situation to which the British Government would naturally respond'. Rees stated in his memoirs that he believed the 'ignominy of Birmingham' had been a major reason for the PIRA move. On 19 December Mr Arlow, described as a 'chatterbox' by Rees, had a meeting with the PIRA chief of staff, who ordered a ceasefire over the Christmas period. The Secretary of State continued to insist that there should be no deals with PIRA, although Government officials met PSF representatives to 'explain' Government policy. But special incident centres were set up to allow PSF to make quick contact with the authorities so as to safeguard the ceasefire

– a move fiercely denounced by loyalists and regarded with great suspicion by the SDLP. By Easter 1975 the PIRA apparently felt they were not getting anything tangible in political terms and violence crept back steadily. One of the Feakle Talks participants, Dr Jack Weir, engaged in talks with PSF leaders in 1992.

FEELY, FRANCIS (FRANK)

SDLP Assembly member for S. Down, 1982–6. Also represented same constituency in Assembly, 1973–4, and Convention, 1975–6. b. Kiltimagh, Co. Mayo, 1937. BA (UCG); Dip.H.E. (Maynooth). Publican. Active in ALJ and in Newry civil rights committee, 1968–71. Party delegate at Atkins conference, 1980. Party spokesman on energy and transport. Delegate, Brooke–Mayhew Talks, 1991–2.

FELL, DAVID

Head of NI civil service and second Permanent Secretary, NIO, 1991–. b. 20 January, 1943. B.Sc. (QUB). Joined civil service in 1969 and in 1982 became deputy chief executive in the IDB. He was Permanent Secretary at DED, 1984–91. When he became civil service head, he was the youngest holder of that post, and his tenure has been marked by many changes in the structure of the service. He arrived at a time when NI Secretary of State Peter Brooke was embarking on sensitive talks with the local parties, and became heavily involved in the Brooke–Mayhew Talks, 1991–2.

FENIAN

A term sometimes applied to Catholics by extreme loyalists, but strictly referring to members of the Fenian Brotherhood, active in the nineteenth century in Britain and North America in fighting British rule in Ireland.

FERGUSON, RAYMOND

UUP Assembly member for Fermanagh–S. Tyrone, 1982–6. Served on committees on Economic Development, and Education. b. 16 February 1941. Comes from a family long associated with unionism in Fermanagh. Fermanagh Council, 1977–. Chairman of Council,

1981–3. Unsuccessfully contested the Westminster seat in the 1979 general election. After the closing of the 1982 Assembly, he remained a strong advocate of devolved government. Solicitor; ex-Ulster rugby player. In November 1988 he called on Unionists to have dialogue with constitutional Nationalists in NI and Republic, but his approach was rejected by UUP conference. He declined an Irish Senate seat in 1989 because of the AIA. In 1992 he criticised his party for not alternating the Fermanagh Council chairmanship with the SDLP.

FERGUSON, RICHARD

Unionist MP at Stormont for S. Antrim, 1968–70. b. Belfast, 22 August 1935. BA (TCD); LLB Hons. (QUB). Member NI Bar (QC), English Bar, and in March 1983 became first NI barrister called to Republic's Inner Bar. In 1984 he moved to London, where he quickly made a reputation as defence counsel in major criminal cases. On the liberal wing of the Unionist Party, and a supporter of Terence O'Neill, he resigned from the Orange Order in August 1969. In February 1970 he resigned as MP for health reasons, and in April 1970 his home in Lisburn was damaged by a bomb. He joined the Alliance Party in March 1971.

FIANNA FÁIL

One of the two major parties in the Irish Republic, it originated from the wing of old Sinn Féin opposed to the Anglo-Irish Treaty of 1921. It first came to power under Eamon de Valera in 1932, and it has been the governing party for most of the period since. It gave way to inter-party Governments headed by Fine Gael, 1948–51, 1954–7, 1973–7, July 1981–February 1982; and November 1982–March 1987. In the 1930s it took a number of steps to underline separation from Britain – high protective tariffs, and the distinguishing of Irish nationality from British, the abolition of the post of Governor-General. Furthermore, the 1937 Constitution contained articles stating the claim to a united Ireland. These have been regarded by NI Unionists as a threat to NI, although

Southern spokesmen have always insisted that they seek unity only by consent. A Fianna Fáil policy statement in 1975 called for a British declaration of intent to withdraw from NI, but party leader Jack Lynch and his colleagues stressed that it was not comparable with the 'Brits out' demands of PSF. But in March 1990 the Supreme Court ruled that the claim was 'a constitutional imperative'. Jack Lynch, in the early 1960s, as Minister for Industry and Commerce, broke new economic ground by giving preferential tariffs to some NI goods. But he caused anger in Britain and in NI with his criticism of British security policy in NI in 1969. There were also occasional complaints from Britain that his Government was not taking a sufficiently tough line against PIRA, notably after the Mountbatten murder. When Lynch resigned in December 1979, his favoured candidate as successor, George Colley, lost out to Charles Haughey. And Haughey gave a new direction to FF's NI policy. He stressed the need for agreement with Britain on NI's future, and clearly saw his December 1980 summit meeting with Margaret Thatcher in Dublin as a useful step. But FF's relations with Britain worsened as the Thatcher Government felt Haughey had overplayed the Dublin meeting, and when he criticised the Conservative Government's approach to the H-Block hunger strike and failed to back Britain on anti-Argentina sanctions during the Falklands conflict. The 1982 FF Government was also highly critical of Britain's 'rolling devolution' initiative. The party gave full support to the New Ireland Forum, 1983–4, and laid greater stress on the main unitary thirty-two-county-state option than the others set out in the final report. It also questioned the maintenance of the constitutional guarantee for NI in the AIA in 1985. Yet the minority Government led by Haughey, which took office in 1987, worked the AIA and pressed strongly for law-and-order reforms in NI and tougher fair employment laws. But it modified the extradition arrangements with Britain, accepted by the outgoing Fine Gael–Labour Coalition, to provide for

the Irish Attorney-General to check the evidence adduced in a particular case. In 1989 Haughey made a strong bid to secure an overall FF majority, but it eluded him for the fifth time. He was forced to abandon the traditional 'no coalition' policy of the party and to make a deal with the Progressive Democrats, whose six TDs led by Des O'Malley gave him a bare majority. Haughey also tried without success to appoint two Ulster Unionists, Dr Chris McGimpsey and Raymond Ferguson, to the Senate. Then, in 1990, FF lost a presidential election for the first time, with Labour nominee Mary Robinson becoming the first woman head of state. Haughey backed the inter-party talks on NI, but said on several occasions that he did not see much support for devolution. In November 1991 Finance Minister Albert Reynolds backed a challenge to Haughey's leadership, and was sacked from the Government. But in February 1992, faced with an ultimatum from his Prog. D. partners, Haughey stood down and Reynolds succeeded him as Taoiseach. Reynolds dropped eight FF Cabinet Ministers and ten FF Ministers of State from the Government. He enjoyed some initial popularity and got the Maastricht Treaty approved in a referendum. But in the summer and autumn of 1992 his relations with Prog. D. Ministers rapidly deteriorated. He went to the country in November 1992 and the FF poll dropped below 40 per cent, the worst result since 1927, reducing party strength to 68 TDs. But by January 1993 he had joined Labour leader Dick Spring to launch the first FF–Labour Coalition. Labour had more than doubled its Dáil strength to thirty-three, and the new administration had a record thirty-six majority. But Reynolds had to pay a stiff price, including adoption of many of Labour's social policies and six Labour Cabinet seats.

FIANNA NA HÉIREANN
Youth wing of the PIRA, traditionally used to provide communications, to alert terrorists to the approach of security forces, and on occasion to stage incidents that might lure troops or police into ambush positions. The security forces

claimed that after the introduction of internment without trial, the youth wing was employed increasingly in carrying bombs and in moving weapons. The exact strength of the movement is difficult to determine but it probably reached several hundred in Belfast in the 1971-2 period, and then declined as the PIRA switched its effort more to small active service units.

FINE GAEL

One of the two main political parties in the Irish Republic. Derives from the pro-Treaty wing of the old Sinn Féin movement. In the 1920s it was known as Cumann na nGaedheal, and formed the first Government of the Irish Free State. That administration was headed by William T. Cosgrave, whose son Liam Cosgrave was to become Taoiseach, 1973-7. To many people outside the Republic, particularly NI Unionists and the British public, it has been regarded as taking a softer line than the Fianna Fáil party on NI issues and a united Ireland. But the overall records of the two parties on these matters have differed little in practice. Although de Valera and Fianna Fáil rejected the Treaty which led to the setting up of two separate administrations in Ireland, and to the partition of the country, the future Fine Gael party was supported by Republicans like Michael Collins and by the underground Irish Republican Brotherhood. Since losing power to de Valera and Fianna Fáil in 1932, it has been unable to sustain a government from its own ranks. Out of power in the 1930s, it was allied briefly to Eoin O'Duffy's Blueshirts, a fascist-type group. When one of FG's leading figures, James Dillon, urged support for the Allies in World War II, he was expelled. The inter-party Government of 1948-51, made up of Fine Gael, the Irish Labour Party and the small Republican party, Clann na Poblachta, and led by John Costello, broke the last tenuous link with the British Commonwealth. When FG came to power in combination with the Irish Labour Party in 1973, under the leadership of Liam Cosgrave, it had acquired a left-centre image. One of the disappointments of the Fine Gael

leadership in that period was the failure of the Sunningdale Conference in 1973 to provide a lasting solution in NI. And when Dr Garret FitzGerald took over as party leader in 1977, after the defeat of the Coalition, one of his first moves was to launch a fresh appraisal of policy on NI and Irish unity. In 1979 the party published a scheme for an Irish confederation, but it failed to attract any serious interest among Unionists. The party returned to power after the June 1981 election, again in Coalition with Labour, but as a minority administration dependent on the votes of a few independents. The Coalition agreed with the British Government in November 1981 the setting up of the Anglo-Irish Intergovernmental Council, but soon afterwards it was defeated on its Budget and lost office in the February 1982 election. Fine Gael was unhappy about the British Government's 'rolling devolution' initiative on NI in 1982, but less vehement in its denunciation than the Fianna Fáil government. It was also critical of Taoiseach Charles Haughey's all-out assault on sanctions against Argentina during the Falklands conflict; Haughey's attitude had greatly angered the Thatcher Government. When the minority Fianna Fáil Government was defeated in the November 1982 election, Fine Gael returned to power, once more in combination with Labour, and promised a 'radical new approach' to NI. In 1983 Garret FitzGerald launched the New Ireland Forum, and the strong international support for its report in 1984 set the scene for the AIA in 1985. But the February 1987 election saw a new alignment. Labour had opted out of coalition politics, and Fine Gael was now exchanging transfers with the recently launched Progressive Democrats. But FG was down to fifty seats and the Progressive Democrats had only fourteen, so that FF, with eighty-one seats, was able to establish a minority administration. Dr FitzGerald resigned the next month, but party officials insisted that, despite the defeat, FG had greatly improved its organisation and electoral base under his leadership. Former Minister Alan Dukes succeeded FitzGerald as leader, and in

1989 there was a meeting of Young Fine Gael and Young Unionists (UUP), whilst in 1990 FG supported the idea of NI MEPs being able to speak in the Senate. But after Austin Currie's poor showing in the 1990 presidential election, there was pressure on Dukes to resign, and John Bruton became leader in November 1990. In January 1992 Bruton had talks in London with PM John Major, amid suggestions that he was helping Major to secure the entry of British Conservative MEPs to the Christian Democrat European Group. FG lost ground in the November 1992 election, getting forty-five TDs elected, a drop of ten. Bruton urged an FG/Prog. D./Labour 'rainbow coalition' commanding eighty-nine seats. Austin Currie's suggestion that Labour leader Dick Spring should head such a coalition was dubbed 'disloyal' by Bruton and quickly withdrawn. Bruton was confirmed as leader after the FF–Labour Coalition took office in January 1993. The party standing fell further in January 1994 with low poll ratings, and produced a leadership challenge from Michael Noonan. Bruton survived and immediately restructured the opposition front bench.

FISH, HAMILTON

Chairman of US *ad hoc* Congressional Committee on Irish affairs, 1988–. b. 3 June 1926. Lawyer and member of old New York Republican family. US vice-consul in Dublin 1951–3. New York Congressman, 1969–. Member of Congressional delegation that visited NI in 1978 and urged role for US as 'honest broker' in negotiating NI settlement. He was said to be close to President Bush.

FITT, LORD

As Gerard (Gerry) Fitt, MP at Westminster for W. Belfast, 1966–83. Independent Socialist since 1979, when he resigned from the SDLP, which he had led from its foundation in 1970. He broke with the SDLP because of its initial refusal to attend the Constitutional Conference organised by Secretary of State Humphrey Atkins, and his belief that the party was becoming less socialist and 'more green Nationalist'. Earlier, he was Republican Labour and, still earlier,

Irish Labour. b. Belfast, 9 April 1926. He first worked as a soap boy in a barber's shop, and then served with the British merchant navy, 1941–53, and he was in many wartime convoys to the USSR. At sea, he educated himself in law and politics and when he left the navy he devoted himself to grassroots politics in his native Dock ward in Belfast, then a tough and colourful waterfront area. His energy and keen sense of humour – he often referred to his five daughters as the 'Miss Fitts' – soon established him as a personality in local politics. In 1958 he was returned as an Irish Labour member of Belfast City Council, of which he remained a member until 1981, when his anti-hunger-strike stance brought about his defeat. In 1962 he entered the NI Parliament, gaining the Dock seat from the Unionists. In 1966 he also won the W. Belfast seat from a Unionist, and his effective use at Westminster of material provided by the Campaign for Social Justice was an important factor in developing British Labour interest in the NI situation. He organised several trips to NI by sympathetic Labour MPs, notably on the occasion of the Derry civil rights march on 5 October 1968 when he received a head injury. During the five-month power-sharing Executive in 1974, he was the deputy Chief Executive – that is, deputy to Brian Faulkner. He has stood out strongly against PIRA, some of whose supporters attacked his Belfast home in August 1976. On that occasion he defended himself, his wife and some members of his family with a gun. He has been a supporter, for the most part, of the Labour Party at Westminster, and his vote was often important to the Wilson and Callaghan Governments. But he abstained in the crucial confidence vote in 1979 which brought down the Labour administration. He was demonstrating, he said, his 'disillusionment' with Roy Mason as NI Secretary of State. He lost his seat to Gerry Adams, PSF, in the 1983 election, but got over 10,000 votes, many of which were believed to have come from normally Unionist and Alliance voters. He had campaigned on an anti-PIRA ticket and his appointment as a life peer in 1983 was popular at Westminster, but not with Irish Nationalists. In 1985 he was critical of the AIA, saying that London and Dublin had come up with a deal without consulting the Unionists, and a Council of Ireland was being set up in the guise of the conference. He also accused the SDLP of showing cowardice during the hunger strike, and in boycotting the Assembly. In 1987 he angered the SDLP by calling on W. Belfast voters to support the Workers' Party.

FITZGERALD, GARRET

Leader of the Fine Gael party in the Republic, 1977–87. Taoiseach, 1981–March 1982; December 1982–February 1987. b. 9 February 1926. BL, Ph.D. (UCD); Hon LLD (New York and St Louis). Dr FitzGerald has probably visited NI more frequently than any other Dublin-based politician. He has close Northern family connections for, while his father Desmond was the first Foreign Minister of the Irish Free State, his mother was an Ulster Presbyterian. His ministerial responsibility for NI affairs as Foreign Minister in the Cosgrave Government, 1973–7, covered the period of Sunningdale, the Assembly and the Convention, so that he was regularly involved in talks with British Ministers on security and political issues affecting NI. He used his influence as Foreign Minister and as EC president to promote cross-border economic co-operation. After the failure of the Convention in 1976, he tried to encourage fresh thinking on NI devolution and had fairly regular meetings with most of the NI political groups, other than the DUP. While looking to an eventual united Ireland, he has always stressed the need for full consent within NI and reassurance for Northern Protestants. He disclosed in 1978 that he had told loyalist leaders in NI in 1974 that they would be 'bloody fools' to join the Republic under its existing Constitution. Formerly a lecturer in political economy at UCD, he operated extensively as a journalist for British and American publications before going on to the front bench in the Dáil. On taking over the Fine Gael leadership in 1977, he emphasised that he would continue to have personal oversight of his party's

policy on NI. Following a reassessment, Fine Gael produced in 1979 a scheme for an Irish confederation and while Unionists showed no enthusiasm for the idea they conceded for the most part that it was a sincere effort by Dr FitzGerald to meet Northern sensibilities. In February 1980 Dr FitzGerald said most British politicians would prefer not to have to maintain the link with NI and should say so publicly. When he took office as Taoiseach after the June 1981 general election, he quickly announced a 'crusade' to make the Republic's Constitution more attractive to NI Protestants. At his London meeting with Margaret Thatcher in November 1981 the decision to set up an Anglo-Irish Intergovernmental Council was announced. But that Fine Gael–Labour administration was dependent on the backing of a few independents, and their refusal to support the January 1982 Budget led to a further inconclusive election in February and a minority Fianna Fáil Government. In the November 1982 general election he was once more poised for power as Fianna Fáil lost ground, and he took office again in December as head of a Fine Gael–Labour Coalition with an overall majority. During that election campaign he urged the setting up of all-Ireland courts and an all-Ireland police force to counter terrorism – ideas which brought him into sharp collision with Fianna Fáil leader Charles Haughey. Speaking at QUB in January 1983, he said his government wanted a 'new and dynamic relationship' with both NI communities, the British Government and their European friends in creating a tolerant, compassionate and just society in Ireland. He did not want EC 'interference' in NI, but he said there was need for international encouragement for some solution that would end the impasse. In March 1983 he had talks with Margaret Thatcher in a bid to restore Anglo-Irish relations. In April 1983 he launched the New Ireland Forum. But this bid to give Irish nationalism a new cohesion in its approach to NI did not quite succeed, for it was clear that there were differences between himself and Charles Haughey on policy and tactics when the NIF report appeared in 1984. Also, Thatcher summarily dismissed the main option in her 'out, out, out' reply at a London news conference in November 1984, after he had talked with her at a Chequers summit meeting. Dr FitzGerald was reported to have described Thatcher's remarks as 'gratuitously offensive' when he spoke to his parliamentary party. However, he launched a major diplomatic offensive in support of the NIF report, emphasising its point that Nationalists were prepared to consider any ideas put up. President Reagan had praised the NIF report during his 1984 visit to Ireland, and a direct appeal by Dr FitzGerald to the US Congress was sympathetically received. And apart from the international pressure on the British Government, there was clearly support in London, both official and ministerial, and within the opposition, for a new initiative. After numerous negotiating sessions, the AIA was hammered out in close secrecy and signed at Hillsborough in November 1985 by FitzGerald and Thatcher. Although it met with intense hostility from Unionists and did not produce any early progress towards power-sharing government in NI, it was still regarded as the main achievement of the Coalition Government which ended in 1987. When Haughey took over again, FitzGerald quickly stood down as Fine Gael leader. He admitted that the rejection of divorce proposals in the 1986 referendum had been a special disappointment. Out of high office, he remained a major controversialist and retained an intense interest in NI affairs. In May 1990 he angered John Bruton by suggesting a possible coalition involving FG, Labour and the WP. In July 1991 he argued that NI could be within the UK and yet be part of a united Ireland within the EC. And Unionists criticised his suggestion that the Republic should speak for NI in EC negotiations. In 1991, too, his memoirs sparked several disputes. One of his claims was that Haughey had discussed with Thatcher the idea that the Republic would join NATO and that in return Britain would withdraw troops from NI. In March 1992 he told a

conference in Derry that he had miscalculated Unionist opposition to the AIA. He stressed his 'private citizen' role by joining an anti-PIRA picket outside the PSF Ard Fheis in Dublin. Also in 1992, he retired from the Dáil along with his old adversary Charles Haughey. In September 1993 he urged John Hume to set a time limit on his talks with Gerry Adams because of the 'negative impact' on the Unionist population and the 'propaganda advantage to the IRA'. The publication of Margaret Thatcher's memoirs brought consideration of their respective views at the time of the AIA. In the debate after the 1993 Downing Street Declaration he said that an agreement had existed since July 1985 on the future of prisoners if violence ended.

FITZSIMMONS, WILLIAM K.

Minister of Health and Social Services, 1969–72. b. Belfast, 31 January 1909; d. 1992. As Minister of Development in 1967, he drew up a statement on reform of local government. Unionist MP for Duncairn, 1956–72.

FLANAGAN, SIR JAMIE

Chief Constable of the RUC, 1973–6. b. 1914. The first Catholic to be appointed police chief, he had been deputy Chief Constable since November 1970. He had two especially difficult periods as Chief Constable – the UWC strike in 1974 and the PIRA ceasefire in 1975.

FLANNERY, MARTIN

Chairman, Labour backbench group on NI, 1983–92. MP for Hillsborough, Sheffield. b. 2 March 1918. Urged inquiry into SAS shooting of three PIRA members in Gibraltar in 1988. Later that year criticised Labour abstentions on main Commons vote on new PTA. BIPB, 1990–.

FLYNN, PADRAIG

As Minister for Justice in the Republic, 1992, he played a prominent role in the North–South strand of the Brooke–Mayhew Talks. b. 1939. St Patrick's Teachers' Training College, Dublin. Publican and former national school teacher. Mayo County Council, 1967–86. TD for Mayo W., 1977–92. He held a variety of ministerial posts, including Environment, Trade, Commerce and Tourism, and the Gaeltacht. In December 1992 he was appointed the Republic's EC Commissioner.

FOLEY, THOMAS

Speaker (Democrat), US House of Representatives, 1989–. b. 6 March 1929. Lawyer. Like several of his predecessors, notably Tip O'Neill, he has shown a close interest in Irish affairs. In 1991 led a Congressional delegation to Republic and NI for talks with Taoiseach Charles Haughey and NI Secretary of State Peter Brooke. In particular, he welcomed the opening of inter-party talks at Stormont, and promised ongoing support for the IFI, whilst warning people in the US not to give money to PIRA front organisations. In 1993 he expressed strong doubts about President Clinton's idea of sending a peace envoy to NI, which apparently contributed to the President's decision to put off any early implementation of the plan. Unsuccessfully opposed visa application by Gerry Adams (PSF) at the end of January 1994.

FOOT, MICHAEL

Leader of British Labour Party, 1980–3. b. 23 July 1913. Deputy leader, Labour Party, 1976–80. MP for Ebbw Vale, 1960–83; Blaenau Gwent, 1983–92. As leader of the Commons in the Callaghan Government, he pleased Unionists and angered the SDLP when he supported the proposal for a Speaker's Conference on the NI seats, which led to the boundary Commission recommendation of five extra MPs. When he visited NI in February 1982 to talk to politicians and trade unionists, he stressed mainly the need for more jobs rather than pushing his party's new policy of campaigning actively for a united Ireland by consent. He urged Unionist MPs to abandon their initial policy of abstention from Westminster in protest against the AIA. Retired as MP, 1992.

FORD, DAVID

General Secretary, Alliance Party, 1990–. b. 1951. B.Sc. (Econ.) (QUB). Antrim

Borough Council, 1993–. Formerly on staff of Eastern Health and Social Services Board. Community services officer, Carrickfergus Council, 1978–80. Unsuccessful candidate for Antrim council in 1989. Co-ordinated party submissions at Brooke–Mayhew Talks.

FORSYTHE, CLIFFORD

UUP MP for S. Antrim, 1983–. Communications party spokesman. b. 24 August 1929. Assembly member for S. Antrim, 1982–6 (on committees on Environment, Finance and Personnel, and deputy chairman, Health and Social Services). Newtownabbey Council, 1981–3 (Mayor, 1983). Former party spokesman on local government. Strongly opposed merger of UDR and RIR. Former professional footballer with Linfield and Derry City.

FORUM FOR A NEW IRELAND see New Ireland Forum

FORUM HOTEL see Europa Hotel

FOSTER, REVEREND IVAN

DUP Assembly member for Fermanagh–S. Tyrone, 1982–6. Served on committees on Agriculture, Education, and Devolution. b. 1943. Free Presbyterian Church minister, 1967–. Prominent in loyalist street demonstrations since 1960s and active in Vanguard movement in early 1970s. Named local commander in Fermanagh of the Third Force set up by the DUP in early 1982. In 1987 he criticised the Unionist pact for hampering the anti-AIA campaign. Has served several brief prison sentences arising from protests, including one outside the Presbyterian General Assembly in 1966; a loyalist demonstration in Armagh on the occasion of a 1969 civil rights march; and taking part in a banned parade in Castlewellan, Co. Down, in June 1985 (in default of fine). Omagh Council, 1981–5; unsuccessful candidate for Fermanagh Council, 1985. Left active politics in 1989.

FREELAND, LIEUTENANT-GENERAL SIR IAN HENRY

Army GOC and Director of Operations,

NI, 1969–71. b. 14 September 1912. Sir Ian, who had been deputy Chief of the General Staff, 1968–9, was the first GOC to be overall Director of Operations in NI – a situation which arose from talks between the British and NI Governments in August 1969, when troops first went on to the streets in support of the RUC. Sir Ian had to cope with a great variety of problems – the 1969 riots and the development of barricades and no-go areas, the erection of a Peace Line between Catholic and Protestant areas in W. Belfast, and the recurring civil rights marches and loyalist counter-demonstrations. In 1970 he took a tough line with 'trouble-makers' and ran into severe criticism from NICRA and local defence committees in Catholic areas. In April 1970 he warned petrol-bombers that they could be shot, and in June 1970, that anybody carrying a firearm would be shot without warning. His most controversial operation in Belfast was the Falls Road curfew of 3–5 July 1970. From Friday night until Sunday morning a large area was sealed off and houses were searched intensively. A large cache of arms and ammunition was uncovered, but there was severe violence during which five civilians were killed and sixty injured, while fifteen soldiers were injured. The curfew, which was raised for only two hours on Saturday to allow for local shopping, gave rise to allegations by the NICRA and local MPs that there had been looting, theft and abusive behaviour by the troops. General Freeland denied, however, that there had been any excessive force.

FRENCH, THOMAS (TOM)
Vice-chairman of the Workers' Party, 1984–; chairman of the Northern Regional Committee of the WP, 1992–. b. 26 May 1934. Craigavon Borough Council, 1978–93.

FREUD, CLEMENT
British Liberal Party spokesman on NI, 1976–9. b. 1924. A grandson of Sigmund Freud, father of modern psychology, he supported reconciliation in statements on NI, and sought to maintain all-party approach to NI problems. MP for Isle of Ely, 1973–87. Popular journalist and broadcaster.

FRIEL, BRIAN
Senator in Irish Republic, 1987–9. Nominated to Senate by Taoiseach Charles Haughey. Internationally known playwright. b. Derry, 9 January 1929. Hon D. Litt. (NUI).

FRIENDS OF IRELAND
An organisation formally set up in Washington DC on 16 March 1981 by leading Irish-Americans associated with Senator Edward Kennedy and Speaker 'Tip' O'Neill. The politicians reaffirmed support for Irish unity, but said it must have the support of the NI majority. They said the US had a constructive role to play in promoting an NI settlement, and they expressed satisfaction that support in the US for violence in Ireland had diminished since they had issued their first St Patrick's Day message in 1977. In 1982 some leaders of the Church of Ireland and the Presbyterian Church criticised the group for not taking enough account of the Unionist viewpoint. The group was particularly influential in building US support for the AIA and the International Fund for Ireland. In 1987 it called on the EC to back the fund, and its chairman, Congressman Brian Donnelly, on a visit to Belfast in 1989, urged that grants should be targeted more on disadvantaged areas. Congressman Donnelly has been active in recent years in campaigning for more visas for emigrants from the Republic and NI.

FRIENDS OF THE UNION
An organisation set up in June 1986 to 'increase knowledge and understanding of the need to maintain the union of Great Britain and Northern Ireland'. Sixteen Conservative MPs and eight peers were listed as trustees or patrons of the body. Most of those involved were active in opposing the AIA. Prominent were the late Sir John Biggs-Davison MP, and Ian Gow MP, who was the only Minister to resign from Government in protest at the AIA and who was murdered by PIRA in July 1990. Other supporters included former NI PM Lord Moyola, the Marquess

of Salisbury, and the Earl of Caledon. In a document sent to Margaret Thatcher in 1988 the organisation suggested that the AIIC of 1981 should be revived to replace the AIA. At the 1992 conference of the group, Alistair Cooke, director of the Conservative Political Centre, described the Republic's claim to NI as 'intolerable'.

FYFFE, WILLIAM
Unionist MP for N. Tyrone at Stormont, 1969–72. b. Strabane, 1914. A leading local journalist, he strongly argued against the holding of civil rights marches in Strabane, since they tended, he argued, to worsen community relations.

G

GADAFFI, COLONEL *see* Libyan Connection

GARDINER REPORT
The report of the committee of inquiry, headed by former Lord Chancellor Lord Gardiner, which reported in January 1975 on measures to deal with terrorism in NI in the context of civil liberties and human rights. The committee also included Lord MacDermott, former Lord Chief Justice of NI, Alistair Buchan, J.P. Higgins, Kathleen Jones, Michael Morland, and John Whyte. It held that detention without trial was a short-term necessity, and that special category (or political) status for convicted prisoners should be ended, with priority being given to a halt on admission of new prisoners to the status. It also said that non-jury trials for terrorist offences should be continued for the present and that there should be a new offence of terrorism. It recommended that the prison building programme be speeded up and that an independent police complaint procedure be introduced. The committee also said that the normal conventions of majority rule would not work in NI. It said no political framework could endure unless both communities shared in the responsibility of administering, and recognition was given to the different national inheritances of the two communities. Lord MacDermott declined

to subscribe to this second point, however, saying he could not understand what it meant.

GASTON, JOSEPH ALEXANDER
UUP Assembly member for N. Antrim, 1982–6. Served on committees on Agriculture, Education, and Security. b. 1928. Ballymoney Council, 1973–. Chairman, N. Antrim Unionist Association. Was part-time member of UDR for seven years until he lost a leg from IRA booby-trap bomb in 1975.

GIBRALTAR SHOOTINGS
On Sunday 6 March 1988 the SAS shot dead in Gibraltar three unarmed PIRA terrorists who were said to be planning to bomb a changing-of-the-guard ceremony on 8 March. Those who died – all from Belfast – were Mairead Farrell (thirty-one); Daniel McCann (thirty); and Sean Savage (twenty-four). Farrell, a student at QUB, had served ten years for bombing the Conway Hotel, near Belfast. McCann had served two years for possession of explosives. In 1982 Savage had been charged with IRA membership and conspiracy to cause explosions, but the charges were later dropped. PIRA claimed that the SAS would have known that their volunteers were unarmed, and it emerged that British and Spanish intelligence had traced the journey of the three in their car, which had been parked close to where the guard-changing ceremony was due to take place. This car did not contain explosives. Two days after the shootings a car with explosives and a timer was found in the Spanish resort of Marbella and was said to be the actual car bomb. There was considerable controversy over the shootings. Some Labour MPs suggested that the three could have been arrested. SDLP deputy leader Seamus Mallon found a 'striking similarity' with Armagh shootings in 1982. The Irish Government said it was 'gravely perturbed' at what had happened. But British Ministers defended the action and PM Margaret Thatcher thanked the Spanish Government for the co-operation of their police. At the inquest SAS men gave evidence from behind a screen, and the jury returned a

nine to two verdict of 'lawful killing'. In September 1990 Sir Peter Terry, Governor of Gibraltar at the time of the shootings, was shot and seriously injured by PIRA at his home in England. In June 1991 Mr Justice Carswell ruled in the NI High Court that the families of the three PIRA members were not entitled to compensation because a certificate by the Foreign Secretary absolving the Government from liability was not subject to review. In September 1993 relatives of those killed persuaded the Commission of the European Court of Human Rights that the UK had a case to answer under Article 2 (Right to Life). (*See also* Andersonstown.)

GIBSON, SIMPSON

DUP Assembly member for N. Down, 1982–6. Deputy chairman, Agriculture Committee. b. 1946. Ards Borough Council, 1981–. Mayor, 1987. Vice-chairman of DUP and secretary of the Unionist Forum, an umbrella group of the Unionist parties. Member, local government Staff Commission, 1985–.

GILLILAND, DAVID

Chief Information Officer, NIO, at Stormont, 1972–87. b. Derry, 1927. Journalist on the *Londonderry Sentinel* and *Belfast Telegraph* before joining the NI Government Information Service in 1956. Became Principal official spokesman at Stormont when he was appointed press secretary to Lord Moyola as PM in 1969, and when he retired in 1987, he had served under eight Secretaries of State. In 1992 he suggested on BBC radio that the British Government might eventually impose an NI settlement.

GILMOUR, LORD

As Sir Ian Gilmour, Conservative spokesman on NI, 1974–5. b. 8 July 1926. Conservative MP for Norfolk Central, 1962–74; Chesham, 1974–83; Chesham and Amersham, 1983–92. Lord Privy Seal (deputy Foreign Secretary), 1979–81. Sir Ian was closely involved with security policy in NI between 1970 and 1974, as during this period he rose from Under-Secretary in the Defence Ministry to

Secretary for Defence. As opposition spokesman on NI from June 1974 until early 1975 he gave strong support to the Labour Government's Convention initiative, and he warned that if it failed the dangers could be very great. Sacked from Government by Margaret Thatcher in 1981. Life peer, 1992.

GLASS, (JOHN) BASIL (CALDWELL)

Deputy leader of the Alliance Party, 1976–80. b. Co. Leitrim, 1926. LLB (QUB). A leading Belfast solicitor, he was the first chairman of the Alliance Party and president, 1972–4. Represented S. Belfast in both the Assembly, 1973–4, and the Convention, 1975–6, but unsuccessful candidate there in the 1982 Assembly election. Alliance Chief Whip, 1973–6, and deputy Chief Whip of NI Executive, 1974. Unsuccessfully contested S. Belfast in the Westminster elections of October 1974 and 1979. Belfast City Council, 1977–81. Party vice-chairman, 1983–5; party chairman, 1985–7. In 1987 appointed Bankruptcy and Companies Master in High Court.

GLENDINNING, WILLIAM (WILL)

Alliance Assembly member for W. Belfast, 1982–6. Deputy chairman, Environment Committee; member of Health and Social Services Committee. Belfast City Council, 1977–87. Leader of Alliance group in City Council, 1981–7. With the closure of the Assembly he became education officer of the NI Council on Alcohol. In 1987 he and his wife Pip, also a City Councillor, resigned their seats in Lower and Upper Falls respectively, and withdrew from political activity for 'personal reasons', while remaining members of the Alliance Party. When the Community Relations Council was set up in 1990, he was appointed development officer. As chairman of the Citizens' Advice Bureaux, he welcomed new proposals for a District Council contribution to the financing of the organisation.

GOODHART, SIR PHILIP CARTER

Parliamentary Under-Secretary, NIO, 1979–81. b. 3 November 1925. Conservative MP for Bromley,

Beckenham, 1957–92. Former Fleet Street journalist. Has served on many British delegations, including UN General Assembly, NATO Assembly, and Council of Europe. Chairman of Conservative Party's Committee on NI, 1976–9. Responsible in NIO for Department of the Environment. Trustee of Friends of the Union, 1986–. Retired as MP, 1992.

GORMLEY, THOMAS COLUMBA

MP at Stormont for Mid-Tyrone, 1962–72. (Ind. Nationalist until 1972, when he became one of first three members of Alliance Parliamentary Party.) b. Claudy, Co. Derry, 29 July 1916; d. 1984. Strabane Rural Council, 1947. Tyrone County Council, 1950–73. Strabane District Council, 1973–7.

GOULDING, CATHAL

Chief of staff of OIRA, 1969–72. b. Dublin, 1922. Comes of strong Republican family, and his record in IRA goes back to World War II, during which he was interned by the Dublin Government. He was involved in revival of IRA organisation after the war, and in 1953, while working as house painter in England, became associated with Seán Mac Stiofáin, who was later to become chief of staff of PIRA. They, together with another man, were sentenced to eight years' imprisonment for an arms raid on Felstead School in Essex in 1953. By 1967 he had become powerful in the IRA, and in an address at that period put forward the Marxist views which were later to become associated with Official Sinn Féin and the OIRA. In 1972 he led the OIRA in declaring a ceasefire, and he was strongly critical of the PIRA bombing campaign. In an interview with *Pravda* in 1972 he said the PIRA bombings were inhuman acts in moral terms, and provocative in political terms. He made no comment when allegations were made in a Dublin magazine in 1982 that OIRA was still involved in murders and large-scale armed robberies. The Workers' Party (formerly Official Sinn Féin, the political wing of OIRA) dismissed the charges as 'muck'. In 1983, as an executive member of the WP, he attacked PIRA for sectarianism and defended the use of supergrasses against 'undemocratic elements'. In September 1992 he gave the graveside oration for veteran Belfast Republican Jim Sullivan, describing him as 'a heroic figure of our time'. He appealed for an end to violence in January 1994 and for PIRA to follow the political path taken by OIRA.

GOW, IAN

The only Minister to resign from the Thatcher Government in protest at the AIA, he was murdered by PIRA in a car bomb explosion at his Sussex home in July 1990. b. 11 February 1937. Solicitor. Cons. MP for Eastbourne, 1974–90. A close friend of Margaret Thatcher, to whom he was PPS, 1979–83. He was Minister of State at the Treasury when he stepped down, saying that he was 'profoundly opposed' to the AIA because, in his view, it would prolong and not diminish NI's agony. When he spoke to the Assembly Committee at Stormont in 1985, he urged Unionists not to resort to violence in opposing the AIA. He was a founding Trustee of Friends of the Union and in October 1988 said he believed there was a real chance of PM Thatcher having a change of heart on the AIA. At his inquest in May 1991, his widow Dame Jane Gow said that her husband's whole attitude had been 'Bugger the IRA.' A memorial fund was launched in 1991, and up to June 1992 more than £60,000 had been distributed with beneficiaries including Lagan College and the Centre for the Study of Conflict at the University of Ulster.

GOWRIE, LORD

Minister of State and deputy Secretary of State, September 1981–3. b. 26 November 1939. Educated Eton and Oxford. Member of a Southern Irish Protestant family, he came to NI with James Prior, with whom he had served as Minister of State at the Employment Department. As Minister responsible for prisons, he was closely involved in the later talks on the 1981 H-Block hunger strike. He occasionally stirred controversy – for example, by urging joint British and Irish citizenship for Northern Irish people. In 1982 he commented that the

Government's plans for 'rolling devolution' might take twenty or thirty years to mature. In 1983 he described PIRA leadership as 'very intelligent, very sophisticated'. After the 1983 election, he left NI to become Minister for the Arts, and although promoted to the Cabinet in 1984, he left the Government in 1985, saying he could not live on his £33,000 ministerial salary. Chairman of Sotheby's.

GRAHAM, EDGAR SAMUEL DAVID

UUP Assembly member for S. Belfast, 1982–3. b. 1954. Shot dead by PIRA at QUB, 7 December 1983. Barrister and law lecturer, QUB. Chairman, Ulster Young Unionist Council, 1981–2. Honorary Secretary, Ulster Unionist Council, 1982. He wrote two pamphlets for his party's Devolution Group, and was responsible for legal submissions to European Commission of Human Rights on behalf of widows of terrorist victims through special unit set up by Harold McCusker MP. First chairman of Assembly's Finance and Personnel Committee.

GRAHAM, GEORGE

DUP Assembly member for S. Down, 1982–6. Served on committees on Agriculture, Health and Social Services, and Finance and Personnel. b. 1947. Co-opted in 1975, he was the first DUP member of Newry and Mourne council. In 1982 the SDLP-controlled council elected him as chairman, despite his opposition to cross-border co-operation. In 1987 he continued to attend council meetings in defiance of party policy on AIA, and resigned from DUP in January 1989. Re-elected under the label 'Protestant' in May 1989 but resigned in 1991.

GRAHAM, BRIGADIER PETER WALKER

Commander, UDR, May 1982–6. b. 1937. He had considerable army experience in NI before joining UDR: served two years as brigade major with the 39th Infantry Brigade, and later commanded 1st Battalion, Gordon Highlanders, during a two-year stay at Holywood barracks. Has served in Kenya, Borneo and with BAOR.

GREEN, DESMOND GEORGE RENNIE

VUPP (and later UUUM) Convention member for N. Down, 1975–6. b. 1914. Bangor Borough Council, 1971–3. N. Down District Council, 1973–93. Mayor, 1979–81. As chairman of the Ulster Special Constabulary Association (organisation of former B Specials, of which he was former district commandant), he was involved in the loyalist strike in 1974, and in later efforts to set up a new 'home guard'. In 1974 he claimed that more than 30,000 people had registered their names as possible members of such a Third Force, but the claim was never accepted by the Government. Some members of his organisation were believed to be involved in the unofficial Ulster Service Corps, which mounted patrols in some rural areas in early 1977. When VUPP split in 1976, he supported Ernest Baird and UUUP until 1980. Elected N. Down Borough Council in 1981 as UPUP member. Unsuccessful candidate in NI Assembly elections, 1982, when his leader, Jim Kilfedder, transferred only 42 per cent of his surplus to him. He rejoined UUP soon after and in 1985 topped poll in his area as UUP candidate but in 1986 he was expelled for failure to support council adjournment policy. In January 1989 he switched to the then unofficial N. Down Conservative Association. In 1992 he left the council's Conservative group after he backed the UUP candidate for Mayor. He returned to the group before the 1993 District Council elections, when he was one of several defeated members.

GREEN PARTY OF NORTHERN IRELAND

The party was launched in Belfast on 12 February 1990 and was the brainchild of Peter Doran, a Derry journalist and former member of the Green Party/ Comhaontas Glas in Dublin. Doran carried the party colours in the Upper Bann by-election in May 1990, but polled only 576 votes, 1.6 per cent, and was ninth in a field of eleven that was topped by David Trimble (UUP). The party fielded no candidates in the 1992 general election. It only contested the District Council elections in May 1993 in Belfast, where six candidates polled 1.1 per cent of the vote; it had no candidates in Coleraine or Down, where support existed in 1989 for Ecology candidates. The party was relaunched in November 1993 as an autonomous unit of the Green Party in Britain. However, since its launch the party had made little impact in membership or mobilising support in comparison even with the Ecology Party since 1981 and individual efforts of Malcolm Samuel and Peter Emerson. Samuel's 1.2 per cent of the vote in the 1989 European elections remained the target to pass.

GREY, LORD (OF NAUNTON)

The last Governor of NI. b. Wellington, New Zealand, 15 April 1910. LLB (Auckland) and Hon. LLD (QUB). A barrister and solicitor in New Zealand, he entered the British Colonial Service. Deputy Governor-General, Nigeria, 1957–9. Governor, British Guiana, 1959–64. Governor, Bahamas, 1964–8. Governor, NI, 1968–73. The post of Governor was abolished under the legislation which provided for an Assembly elected by PR and the constitutional duties of Governor were absorbed by the Secretary of State. During the initial period of direct rule, he felt that his experience could have been utilised more by the Government. The ending of the office was strongly criticised by Unionists who regarded it as a weakening of the link with the Crown. After leaving, he maintained his interest in NI, notably as chancellor of NUU, later University of Ulster, until 1992.

GREYSTEEL

A village close to Derry where UFF gunmen killed seven people and injured thirteen in the Rising Sun bar on Saturday 30 October 1993. The Saturday evening crowd, drawn from the village and the surrounding area, were surprised by a 'trick or treat' gunman coolly firing and reloading inside the bar. The dead included two women and an eighty-one-year-old man; six were Catholics and one a Protestant. The UFF claimed it as an

attack on the 'nationalist electorate' and described it as a reprisal for the Shankill Road bomb seven days previously. The killings were widely condemned and they made October the worst month for deaths since 1976.

GUILDFORD FOUR

In October 1989 the three men and one woman jailed for life for the Guildford and Woolwich pub bombings carried out by PIRA in 1974 were freed following the announcement by the Director of Public Prosecutions that it would be wrong for the Crown 'to seek to sustain' the convictions of Paul Hill, Gerard Conlon, Carole Richardson and Patrick Armstrong on the basis of confessions that they had later retracted. Their release was welcomed by the Irish Government and by the many politicians, legal figures, Churchmen and journalists who had campaigned on their behalf or pressed for a new appeal. These had included Lord Scarman, Lord Devlin, Cardinal Basil Hume and former NI Secretary Merlyn Rees. The move led to an intensification of the drive to secure the freedom of the Birmingham Six, who were released in 1991.

H

HAILSHAM, LORD (OF SAINT MARYLEBONE)

Formerly Quintin McGarel Hogg, concerned with NI as Shadow Home Secretary, 1966–70, and Lord Chancellor, 1970–4, and 1979–87. b. 9 October 1907. A former Conservative MP for Oxford, he has held a variety of Government posts, including leader of the House of Lords. His father's family were Lowland Scots who were settled for more than a century at Lisburn, Co. Antrim. Lord Hailsham strongly backed James Callaghan as Home Secretary in his efforts to get reforms in NI in 1969. At that time he urged a treaty of perpetual friendship, binding GB, NI and the Republic. Such a treaty, he said, should involve a recognition of the border as a fact of the situation of indefinite duration; a human rights convention placing the rights of minorities in all three territories on a judicially enforceable, and not simply political, footing. In 1971 he created controversy with a suggestion that people accused of serious bombings should be charged with treason, which would carry the death penalty. In 1974 he urged the setting up of a 'Council of the Islands' which would bring together England, Scotland, Wales, NI, the Irish Republic, the Channel Islands, and Orkney and Shetland. He said that unless all these components prospered, none could prosper, and he suggested that it was the failure to recognise this dimension that was largely at the bottom of the 1974 loyalist strike in NI. But he also argued that the extreme Protestant viewpoint in NI had not assisted those who wanted to maintain the Union. As Lord Chancellor in the Thatcher Government he was said to be the most vocal member of the Cabinet committee that considered the issue of NI devolution. In 1986 he resisted demands by the Irish Government that the Diplock courts should be reconstructed to allow for a 'mix' of British and Irish judges or, failing that, the replacement of one-judge courts by a three-judge panel.

HALL-THOMPSON, MAJOR ROBERT LLOYD

Leader of Assembly, 1973–4, and Chief Whip in Executive. b. 9 April 1920; d. 1992. Represented N. Belfast in Assembly, 1973–4, and in the Convention, 1975–6. First elected to Stormont in 1969 as pro-O'Neill Unionist in Clifton. Son of former Stormont Education Minister and grandson of MP for N. Belfast at Westminster. With split in unionism, he joined Brian Faulkner in UPNI and represented the party in the Convention.

HAMILTON, SIR ARCHIBALD (ARCHIE) GAVIN

Minister of State for the Armed Forces, 1988–93. Conservative MP for Epsom and Ewell since 1978 with a 20,000 majority in 1992. b. 30 December 1941. Educated Eton College. He was Under-Secretary of State for Defence Procurement during the Gulf War and afterwards presided

over cuts in spending and manpower at a time when new demands, as in Bosnia, began to be made. He left the Government by choice in the reshuffle of 27 May 1993. In July 1993 he was critical of the extent of commitment in NI and clearly saw it as a candidate for manpower and budget cuts. He described the NI commitment as 'a ratchet operation' that absorbed twelve out of forty army units with two extra battalions sent in 1987 and again in 1992. His views were criticised by UUP security spokesman Ken Maginnis, who said that troop numbers were decided by the Chief Constable and the GOC 'on the basis of the perceived terrorist threat'. Out of office he could devote more time to his farming interests and his membership of Lloyd's. Knighted, January 1994.

HANLEY, JEREMY JAMES

Parliamentary Under-Secretary, NIO, 1990–3. Cons. MP for Richmond and Barnes, 1983–. b. 17 November 1945. Before entering Parliament had accountancy business in Dublin. At NIO responsible initially for health, social security and agriculture, and encountered widespread criticism over health service changes. Set up new Social Security Agency. Only member of Stormont ministerial team to return after 1992 general election, and he accompanied Sir Patrick Mayhew in intensive inter-party talks in 1992. He also took charge of education and community relations. In 1992 he met a long-standing Catholic demand for 100 per cent capital grants for Catholic schools; he apologised to teachers for stress caused by school reforms, some of which he delayed. In 1993, he was reported to be learning Irish. Although promoted to the Defence Ministry on 27 May 1993, he retained his connection with NI as Armed Forces Minister.

HARNEY, MARY

Elected leader of the Progressive Democrats on 12 October 1993, in succession to Des O'Malley, becoming the first woman to lead a political party in the Republic of Ireland. b. Galway, March 1953. Educated Trinity College

Dublin. Former teacher and researcher. When appointed to the Senate in August 1977, by Taoiseach Jack Lynch, she was the youngest ever member. In 1979 she was elected to Dublin County Council and in 1981 became Fianna Fáil TD for Dublin South-West. She left Fianna Fáil with Des O'Malley to found the Progressive Democrats in December 1985, a move that helped her to top the poll in her constituency in 1987, taking votes mainly from Fine Gael. She took a special interest in environmental issues and at the time of the leadership contest in 1993 was deputy leader of the party. Although she was probably O'Malley's choice as successor, he refused to declare it publicly, and she won the poll by seven votes to three (for MEP Pat Cox). Early in 1993 she had appeared to eschew leadership ambitions because, as a single person, she felt she did not have the social and emotional support for the job. However, the weekend before the leadership election, a poll showed her to have the support of two-thirds of respondents compared with less than one-quarter for Cox. As deputy leader she had dismissed the Hume-Adams process and disliked, particularly, the way the talks had increased Adams's credibility. Her general objective was a pluralist Ireland in which the two traditions could be accommodated, and on her election she sought talks and good relations with NI constitutional political parties. When the Downing Street Declaration was published on 15 December 1993 she warmly welcomed it as 'a historic step forward', describing it as 'fair and balanced', enabling the democratic wishes of the Irish people to be 'articulated, developed and pursued, without undermining or threatening each other'.

HARTE, PATRICK DONAL

Fine Gael spokesman on security and NI, 1977-81. b. 1932. Elected to the Dáil as a Donegal TD in 1961, and served on Dáil committee reviewing the Republic's Constitution. Minister of State, 1981-2. Throughout the Troubles he has sought to promote peace in NI, and has maintained close contacts with a wide variety of interests, including

paramilitaries. In early 1982 he complained that Donegal was being used increasingly as a terrorist base by PIRA and INLA, following a number of large seizures of arms and explosives in areas of the county adjoining the border. In 1984 he urged the Republic to assert its claim to the island of Rockall in the Atlantic, which has been claimed by Britain. On the AIA he said in 1986 that it could not work unless the NI Unionist majority gave its consent. At a meeting in Bangor, Co. Down, in December 1988 he urged Protestants to change their attitude to the AIA. In 1992 supported the idea of joint British-Irish sovereignty for NI. In August 1993 he complained about TV references to Donegal being used as a launchpad for PIRA attacks on NI.

HARVEY, CECIL

Chairman of the UUUP, 1977-80, but joined DUP in 1981. Down District Council, 1981-5. b. 1918; d. 1985. Ex-member of the UUP, he was elected in S. Down as a Vanguard Unionist to the Assembly, 1973-4. In the Convention, 1975-6, he was Chief Whip of the VUPP, and represented his party on the business committee. With the split in Vanguard on the issue of a voluntary coalition, he opposed the idea and became member of the UUUM, led by Ernest Baird. When the UUUM became a separate political party as the UUUP in 1977, he was appointed chairman of the new party, and became its prospective candidate for the Westminster S. Down seat held by Enoch Powell MP, whom he backed in the October 1974 election. He did not fight the 1979 election but in 1983 he opposed Powell and lost his deposit. He was active in the Free Presbyterian Church.

HATTERSLEY, ROY SYDNEY GEORGE

Minister of Defence (Administration), 1969-70, and mainly responsible for detailed planning for setting up UDR; b. 28 December 1932. B.Sc. (Econ.) (Hull). Labour MP for Sparkbrook (Birmingham), 1964-. Visited NI for 'Operation Motorman', 1972, as Labour Defence spokesman. In 1978, as Prices Secretary, asked Prices Commission to make informal investigation of higher prices in NI. Shadow Home Secretary, 1980–3. Deputy leader of Labour Party, 1983–92. In 1991 he warned against any election deals with Unionists. When he opposed renewal of the PTA in the Commons in 1992, he urged all-party agreement on anti-terrorist laws.

HAUGHEY, CHARLES JAMES

Taoiseach of Irish Republic, March 1987–February 1992; 1979–June 1981; and March–December 1982. Leader of opposition, July 1981–February 1982. b. Castlebar, Co. Mayo, 16 September 1925. B.Comm., BL (UCD). One of Republic's ablest, wealthiest and most colourful politicians, he has an NI background. His parents came from Swatragh, Co. Derry, and from families with a strong Republican tradition. His father, Sean, was second-in-command of the Northern division of the IRA. He joined Fianna Fáil in Dublin in 1948, and in 1951 married Maureen Lemass, daughter of former Fianna Fáil Taoiseach Sean Lemass. After two years in Dublin Corporation, he was elected to the Dáil at the third attempt in 1957 in Dublin North-East, an area which has provided him with a strong constituency base over the years. He was Minister for Justice, 1961–4, and Minister for Agriculture, 1964–6, when he was a strong contender for the Fianna Fáil leadership, but eventually withdrew from the contest and gave his support to Jack Lynch. He was at the centre of gun-running allegations at the height of the NI Troubles in 1970. As Finance Minister he was sacked by Lynch, and later charged with conspiracy to import arms and ammunition illegally. But he and three others were acquitted. He returned to office in the Lynch Government elected in 1977, taking over the Health Ministry. In December 1979 he succeeded Lynch as Taoiseach and Fianna Fáil leader, but the Parliamentary Party vote was indicative of his inability to win general acceptance within Fianna Fáil at that time. He defeated George Colley (Lynch's deputy and his favourite for the post) by 44 votes to 38. On taking over as head of Government, he voiced his opposition to all the activities of PIRA,

undertook to maintain all existing security measures, and named peaceful reunification of Ireland as his first political priority. At his party's annual conference in Dublin in 1980 he declared that the Stormont Constitutional Conference, then under way, could not provide a conclusive settlement. He envisaged the British and Irish Governments working together to find a solution. 'For over sixty years now,' he said, 'the situation in Northern Ireland has been a source of instability, real or potential, in these islands. It has been so because the very entity itself is artificial. . . In these conditions, violence and repression were inevitable.' This approach dominated his thinking on NI as Taoiseach. Unlike his Fine Gael opposite number, Garret FitzGerald, he was not prepared to modify those parts of the Constitution which were attacked by Unionists, and he saw no merit in an internal settlement in NI. Thus, he considered the Anglo-Irish talks as the key to the situation. His summit talks with Thatcher in Dublin in December 1980 were particularly gratifying, since the British PM and three Cabinet colleagues (Secretaries for Foreign Affairs, Northern Ireland, and the Chancellor of the Exchequer) agreed to a communiqué which he described as 'a historic breakthrough'. There were to be joint studies into a wide range of subjects and the 'totality of relations between the two countries', and the possibilities of new institutions. The ground was laid for the Anglo-Irish Intergovernmental Council, which emerged in late 1981 and, it could be argued, the AIA of 1985. But in the wake of the 1980 summit, Thatcher was obviously worried about the intense anger which the Dublin package aroused among Unionists, many of whom talked of a 'sell-out' and an attempt to revive the Sunningdale plan. This led Thatcher to repeat the NI constitutional guarantee on every possible occasion, and she also rejected any idea of concessions to the H-Block hunger-strikers for which Haughey pressed. In the event it was probably the appearance of anti-H-Block candidates which led to the downfall of the Haughey administration in the June 1981 election. And when he got back to power in 1982 as the leader of a minority government, he had a further policy clash with Britain, since he was opposed to EC sanctions against Argentina over the Falklands. In this situation there was little surprise that NI Secretary of State James Prior went ahead with his 'rolling devolution' initiative in 1982 without consulting the Dublin Government about the details. Indeed, Thatcher rubbed in the point by saying that Britain had no obligation to consult the Republic about NI affairs. So Haughey denounced the initiative as 'unworkable'. London, however, apparently found nothing to complain about in Haughey's anti-terrorist policy. In the November 1982 election campaign he firmly opposed suggestions by FitzGerald that there should be an all-Ireland court and cross-border police force to deal with terrorism, and he sought to portray much of British political opinion and the media as interfering in an Irish election by expressing a preference for FitzGerald. The election was certainly a severe blow to Haughey, since it gave a Fine Gael–Labour Coalition a secure majority and he left office with Anglo-Irish relations extremely strained. Unionists in NI took the change calmly, with some of them saying that they preferred the certainty of Haughey's republicanism to FitzGerald's subtlety. The SDLP looked for the restoration of a strong bipartisan policy on NI in Dublin. This emerged to the extent that Haughey joined FitzGerald in supporting the New Ireland Forum. On the NIF report, published in May 1984, Haughey angered the other participants by insisting that the report meant that only the unitary state option had been accepted and that neither federation nor joint authority would bring peace in the North. When the AIA emerged in 1985, Haughey was critical of Article 1, which provided a constitutional guarantee for NI, and he accused NI Secretary of State Tom King of 'impertinence' in attacking the articles in the Irish Constitution which claim sovereignty over NI. At the Wolfe Tone commemoration at Bodenstown in October 1986 he said his party would

seek to renegotiate the AIA when it took office again. In the event, he just failed to secure an overall majority in the February 1987 election, but he was elected Taoiseach by the casting vote of the Speaker. In power, Haughey demonstrated a new pragmatism. He dropped the renegotiation demand and stressed that he accepted the AIA as an international agreement and would seek to make it work for the benefit of people in NI. But his Government did amend the extradition arrangement with the UK to ensure that the Irish Attorney-General was able to check the evidence related to each application. Thatcher protested that Britain was being treated in this matter less favourably than other European countries and coincidentally there were several clashes between Dublin and London over law-and-order issues. But behind the scenes Haughey seemed to be anxious to get Anglo-Irish relations on a better basis. At the same time he showed anxiety to build contacts with Unionists – a gesture which brought an open response in early 1988 from UUP leader James Molyneaux. In 1989 he mounted a major bid to win an overall majority for FF in a general election, but he failed for the fifth time to do so, and was forced to abandon the historic anti-coalition stance of FF and enter into partnership with the Progressive Democrats led by Des O'Malley, a party which had always displayed more flexibility on NI than FF. The new Government was involved in some sharp exchanges with London over leaks of security documents to loyalist paramilitaries and over the UDR, on which Haughey called for a rethink. Also in 1989, he failed to find a UUP politician to serve in the Senate and was unable to persuade Unionists to enter into economic talks. In April 1990 he travelled to the Europa Hotel in Belfast to give a speech to businessmen to mark his EC presidency. Ian Paisley and supporters protested at the visit, despite Haughey's promise to seek extra EC aid for NI. The visit followed hard on the Dublin Supreme Court ruling that the constitutional claim to NI was 'a constitutional imperative'. In 1990 too, he had to face his party's defeat in the

Irish presidential election – the first such loss in the history of FF. In 1990–1 he insisted on several occasions that he was not to blame for delays in getting the inter-party talks under way, but NI was put to one side in late 1991 when he faced a leadership challenge from Finance Minister Albert Reynolds. Reynolds was sacked from the Government but by February 1992 he had taken over as Taoiseach from Haughey. The Prog. D. Ministers had been unwilling to back him after allegations related to phone tapping. But his resignation pointed to a watershed in Southern politics, illustrated by the decline in support for both FF and FG in the November 1992 general election and the rise of Labour. This election came soon after the ending of the Brooke–Mayhew Talks, in which Reynolds's Ministers and the Northern parties failed to work out a comprehensive settlement. Haughey's political career, which had so often touched NI, ended with the dissolution of the Twenty-sixth Dáil.

HAUGHEY, DENIS

SDLP Assembly member for Mid-Ulster, 1982–6. Cookstown District Council, 1989–. Chairman of SDLP, 1973–8. b. Coalisland, Co. Tyrone, 3 October 1944. BA Hons. in political science and modern history (QUB). Active in university as member of New Ireland Society, and in civil rights movement as first chairman of Tyrone Civil Rights Association. Joined SDLP on its formation, and unsuccessful in four Westminster elections – Fermanagh–S. Tyrone in February 1974 and Mid-Ulster in 1983, 1987 and 1992. Candidate in Convention poll in N. Antrim in 1975. SDLP delegate to Socialist International and bureau of Confederation of Socialist Parties of EC. In 1980 became full-time assistant to party leader John Hume in his work as MEP, and also International Secretary of the party. SDLP's spokesman on agriculture. A delegate in the Brooke–Mayhew Talks, he said in March 1991 that Articles 2 and 3 of the Republic's Constitution must stay. In 1992 he described the SDLP as 'a Republican party in the proper sense of

that word'. In 1994 appointed as one of two representatives from NI to the European Union's Committee of the Regions, which first met in March 1994.

HAYES, MAURICE

Local Boundaries Commissioner for NI, 1991–. Ombudsman and Commissioner of Complaints, 1987–91. b. 8 July 1927. BA Hons.; Hon LLD (QUB). Has had extremely diverse career in public service. As Town Clerk of Downpatrick, 1955–73, he was seconded as first chairman of Community Relations Commission, 1969–72, and director of Ombudsman's Office, 1972–3. During 1973–4, he was Assistant Secretary in office of power-sharing Executive, and after it collapsed, senior adviser to Sir Robert (later Lord) Lowry as Convention chairman, 1974–6. In 1976 he was involved in the setting up of the Fair Employment Agency, and his civil service career between that and 1987 included a period as Head of Personnel, but was mainly in the Department of Health and Social Services, where he was Permanent Secretary, 1984–7. He has been a visiting professor at the University of Ulster, and has served on a great variety of public bodies, including the Arts Council of NI, the BBC Advisory Committee, 1967–73, and the Community Relations Council, 1990–.

H-BLOCKS

The Maze Prison cell blocks – so called because of their shape – which were designed to accommodate terrorist-type prisoners with the ending of special category status. (*See also* Special Category.) The term 'H-Block' went round the world in the spring of 1978 when some 300 Republican prisoners, campaigning for political status or the restoration of special category status, decided to step up their existing campaign of wearing only a blanket. They refused to wash, or leave their cells, or use the toilet facilities, and the walls of many of the cells were covered with excreta. They also smashed up cell furniture. For the PIRA, the protest had the effect of attracting worldwide publicity, and the British Government attempted to counter it by claiming that if the prisoners would only accept the normal prison discipline they would be able to enjoy the facilities of one of the best-equipped prisons in Western Europe. The Catholic archbishop of Armagh, Dr Tomás (later Cardinal) Ó Fiaich, urged the British Government in August 1978 to do something to deal with the 'inhuman conditions' at the Maze, but the then Secretary of State, Roy Mason, ruled out any change of policy. In late 1978 and early 1979, the Government stepped up its publicity drive against the H-Block protesters since they obviously feared that the Republican campaign was making some impact in the US, notably among Irish-Americans, and possibly stimulating financial aid to Republican funds. For the first time, journalists were allowed inside the Maze Prison to describe the conditions, although they were not allowed to talk to the protesters. In 1980 the Republican prison protest took a more dramatic turn, with the arrival of the mass hunger strike. On 27 October seven prisoners – six PIRA and one INLA – at the Maze began fasting in support of the demand that, among other things, they should be allowed to wear their own clothes and be excused prison work. The British Government, through Secretary of State Humphrey Atkins, insisted that there could be no concession which could be regarded as permitting political status, although he argued that the Government was prepared to talk about improvements in conditions on purely humanitarian grounds. In October 1980 the Government announced that all male convicted prisoners would be allowed to wear official-issue, civilian-type clothing, but it emerged quickly that this would not be seen by the protesters as meeting the 'own clothing' demand and many people sympathetic to the prisoners' cause criticised the Government for stopping short of conceding on the clothing issue. This phase of the hunger strike ended in some confusion on 18 December 1980. With one PIRA prisoner, Sean McKenna, close to death, the prisoners said they had abandoned their fast because of a message from Atkins and a thirty-four-page description of prison conditions which had been shown to them. On 25 January 1981, however, Bobby Sands, twenty-six-year-old newly elected leader of the PIRA prisoners, claimed that moves for gradual co-operation between the prisoners and the administration had broken down. On 1 March 1981 – fifth anniversary of the start of phasing out of special category – Sands began fasting on his own, and thus launched a campaign which was to drag on for seven months, provoking a political crisis in both NI and the Republic, and intense controversy in many parts of the world. In the course of the protests ten hunger-strikers died – seven from PIRA and three from INLA. On 5 May Sands, who had been elected MP for Fermanagh–S. Tyrone in the April 1981 by-election, was the first hunger-striker to die, after sixty-six days without food. His funeral from Twinbrook, W. Belfast, to Milltown cemetery was an impressive display of Republican strength, with some 70,000 people attending. The others who died were:

Francis Hughes (twenty-five) PIRA, on 12 May after fifty-nine days.

Raymond McCreesh (twenty-four), PIRA, on 21 May after sixty-one days.

Patsy O'Hara (twenty-three), leader of INLA prisoners, on 21 May after sixty-one days.

Joe McDonnell (thirty), PIRA, on 8 July after sixty-one days.

Martin Hurson (twenty-seven), PIRA, on 13 July after forty-six days.

Kevin Lynch (twenty-five), INLA, on 1 August after seventy-one days.

Kieran Doherty (twenty-five), PIRA, elected TD in Cavan–Monaghan in the June general election, on 2 August after seventy-three days.

Thomas McElwee (twenty-three), PIRA, on 8 August after sixty-five days.

Michael Devine (twenty-three), INLA, on 20 August after sixty-six days.

Basically, it was a battle of wills between the prisoners and the British Government. Outside the prison, the campaign for the 'five demands' (own clothing, no prison work, freedom of association, extra recreational facilities and more visits and letters, and restoration of remission lost on protests) was spearheaded by the National H-Block/Armagh Committee, and strongly backed by PSF. (*See also* National H-Block/Armagh Committee.) But there was much sympathy for the hunger-strikers in the general Nationalist-Catholic sector of the community. This often fell short of support for political status and, in common with much Dublin opinion, concentrated on British 'intransigence'. Certainly Thatcher gave a strong lead against any concessions while the hunger strike continued, and during a visit to Belfast on 28 May, she remarked that the protest 'might well be the last card' of the PIRA campaign. British information services abroad stressed the rejection by the European Commission of Human Rights of a claim by four prisoners that their treatment had breached the European Convention on Human Rights. Britain also argued that prisoners were failing to take advantage of the modern prison facilities. But the recurring deaths, the tense atmosphere and a high level of violence spurred a great variety of individuals and organisations to try their hand at reconciliation. The Catholic Church was involved at many levels. In the early stages, the Papal envoy, Monsignor John Magee, Ulster-born personal secretary to Pope John Paul II, talked with Sands in an unsuccessful bid to persuade him to abandon the protest. Cardinal Ó Fiaich and the Bishop of Derry, Dr Edward Daly, had several meetings with Government Ministers. They urged that prison clothing and work should be optional, and apparently were disappointed at an early stage that the Government did not concede 'own clothing', as they had been led to believe it would. When Raymond McCreesh and Patsy O'Hara died in May, the Cardinal warned that the Government would 'face the wrath of the whole Nationalist population' if it failed to modify its 'rigid stance'. The Irish Commission for Justice and Peace (a sub-committee of the Irish Bishops' Conference) had a series of lengthy talks with Michael Alison, the Minister of State in charge of prisons up to September 1981. The Commission

was optimistic about an end to the protest in July, when it produced an elaborate package of reforms, but it evidently misjudged the Government's attitude. Father Denis Faul, a prison chaplain, was also closely involved, particularly in the final stages of the hunger strike, when he organised meetings of relatives of those still fasting. In Dublin both Charles Haughey and Garret FitzGerald, as successive heads of Government, tried unsuccessfully to persuade Thatcher to soften her approach, as did SDLP leader John Hume at a meeting with the PM. In July the Irish Government also failed in a bid to enlist the support of President Reagan, at least publicly. The European Commission of Human Rights, and the International Red Cross were also briefly involved. The hunger strike had widespread repercussions in terms of violence and a political spin-off both in NI and the Republic. During the protest, sixty-one people died in violent incidents in NI. Fifteen RUC men – twelve regulars and three reservists – along with eight soldiers and seven UDR members died in bombings and shootings. Five of the soldiers died on 19 May in a landmine explosion near Camlough, Co. Armagh, home village of hunger-striker Raymond McCreesh. Thirty-four civilians were killed, including seven people (two of them girls of eleven and fourteen) who died as a result of injuries inflicted by plastic bullets fired by the police or army. In the Republic the most serious violence occurred in Dublin on 18 July, when some two hundred people were injured during a riot, when Gardaí prevented an H-Block march passing the British Embassy. As for the political effects inside NI, the by-election victory of Sands and then of his election agent, Owen Carron, in Fermanagh–S. Tyrone, were a reminder that the passions of an across-the-board nationalism could still be aroused. The by-elections also served to weaken the British argument that the protest enjoyed very little public support. In the council elections of May 1981 the atmosphere also resulted in hardened attitudes, and candidates, from several parties, campaigning directly on the H-Block issue, polled 51,000 votes and won thirty-six seats. The impact on Southern Irish politics was also far-reaching. The return of two Maze prisoners as TDs – hunger-striker Kieran Doherty in Cavan–Monaghan, and Paddy Agnew in Louth – and the substantial vote for H-Block nominees were seen as playing a major part in the defeat of the Fianna Fáil Government in the June 1981 general election. The nine H-Block candidates took nearly 40,000 first-preference votes. In Britain Thatcher had broad support in Parliament for her refusal to make concessions, and a MORI poll in May suggested that 92 per cent of English and Welsh voters rejected political status. Opposition politicians such as Labour's Don Concannon and Liberal leader David Steel visited the Maze, but saw no scope for Government concessions. Only about fourteen Labour backbenchers were sympathetic to the H-Block cause. When James Prior became Secretary of State in mid-September, there were clear signs that the hunger strike had lost its impetus. Already, the relatives of four hunger-strikers had intervened to ensure that they were fed under medical supervision. None the less, Prior's first commitment outside Government offices was a three-hour visit to the Maze Prison within four days of taking over, and he saw two of the hunger-strikers, although he did not talk to them. On 29 September Lord Gowrie, Minister of State and deputy to Prior, who had now taken responsibility for prison matters, repeated that no concessions would be made to prisoners until the protest ended. The six remaining hunger-strikers now became aware that their relatives would intervene to save their lives, and this was the factor which finally brought an end to the long-drawn-out bid to secure political status. On the afternoon of Saturday 3 October, the six men still fasting agreed to take food. Three days later the Secretary of State announced that all prisoners would be allowed to wear their own clothing at all times. At the same time protesters would have 50 per cent of lost remission restored. But the Government refused to meet the demand for an end to prison work and for free association, although it hinted at some improvement on these points. Unionists protested strongly at the clothing and remission moves, and some Republicans who had backed the protest consoled themselves with the claim that the overall result of the hunger strike had been to give international recognition to the prisoners' political status. And in 1982 the demand for segregation of Republican and loyalist prisoners, which had seemed a minor element in 1980–1, suddenly began to be pressed by both sides. The Government showed itself opposed to segregation in principle and hinted at collusion between Republican and loyalist prisoners to achieve separation. The Maze H-Blocks were again in the world headlines when, on 23 September 1983, thirty-eight PIRA prisoners staged the biggest break-out in British prison history. During the operation, which involved the hi-jacking of a prison food lorry, a prison officer, James Ferris, forty-three, died and six other officers suffered knife and gunshot wounds. (Ferris's death was first believed to be due to stabbing, but a court in 1988 held it could have arisen from natural causes.) Fifteen of the escapees were swiftly recaptured, while another four were picked up within three days. But nineteen got away, including PIRA leader in the H-Block, Brendan McFarlane, who was subsequently extradited from Holland in 1986. 'The Great Escape', as PIRA dubbed it, was a serious embarrassment to NI Ministers, and security was tightened as a result of the Hennessy report on the escape. In April 1988 eighteen of the original escapees were given sentences ranging from five to eight years on firearms and other charges, but sixteen of them were found not guilty of murdering a prison officer. Gerard Kelly, who like McFarlane had been extradited from Holland, was found not guilty of attempted murder. Neither he nor McFarlane could be charged with murder because of the terms of the extradition. Both men got five years for the escape attempt and other offences. Lord Chief Justice Lowry sharply criticised the evidence of prison officers, saying much of it had been unreliable and contradictory. At that time, ten of the escapees were still at large: three were dead, and seven were in custody in the Republic or in England, including Gerard McDonnell, sentenced for his part in the Brighton hotel bombing. In 1988 the remaining ninety-two special category prisoners moved to the H-Blocks but retained their privileges. In the 1990s the NIO and the prison service seem to have been anxious to give the Maze Prison a softer image. At the end of 1990 it was announced that there would be greater freedom of association for inmates. At that time, it was disclosed that in the previous three years 180 prisoners at the Maze had chosen to break their paramilitary links and leave the segregated conditions in the H-Blocks for Maghaberry Prison, with its integrated atmosphere. In 1990, too, there was some Unionist criticism of the H-Blocks regime when the BBC transmitted a TV documentary that showed loyalist prisoners staging a miniature band parade, and a prison officer admitting that the wings were run by the paramilitaries. An NIO discussion document published in 1991 showed that the Maze held 400 prisoners and cost £42 million a year to run. It suggested that a new replacement prison could be built on land available at Maghaberry for £70 million and take four years to complete. The idea was to increase efficiency and achieve more value for money. But it was stressed that progress depended on the attitude of the Treasury. By June 1991, £96,000 had been paid out in compensation to prisoners who complained that they were beaten up by prison officers at the time of the 1983 mass escape. In June 1992 two more of the escapees were detained in California on passport charges and became the subject of extradition proceedings. A further arrest was made in January 1993 and by September it was estimated that seven of the thirty-eight escapees were still at large; two were thought to be in the Republic and five in Europe. In 1991 the controversial special category status was ended. Segregation was also an important issue in Belfast's Crumlin Road Prison. Lord Colville, in a report on violence at the the jail in 1991, came out against formal segregation of the remand prisoners held there – an attitude supported by Secretaries of State Brooke and Mayhew. Two loyalists died in a PIRA explosion at Crumlin Road in 1991, and the UVF fired an RPG7 rocket at the jail in December 1992 in furtherance of the segregation campaign. The rocket, aimed at a dining room being used by Republican prisoners, caused slight damage but no injuries.

HEATH, SIR EDWARD

Conservative PM, 1970–4, and opposition leader, 1965–70 and 1974–5. MP for Bexley Sidcup 1974–83; Old Bexley and Sidcup, 1983–. b. 9 July 1916. There were three decisive points in his policy towards NI as PM and Conservative leader. Firstly, he switched the emphasis of Tory policy away from positive support of the Union. In November 1971 he said: 'Many Catholics in Northern Ireland would like to see Northern Ireland unified with the South. That is understandable. It is legitimate that they should seek to further that aim by democratic and constitutional means. If at some future date the majority of the people in Northern Ireland want unification and express that desire in the appropriate constitutional manner, I do not believe any British Government would stand in the way. But that is not what the majority want today.' Secondly, he moved swiftly to suspend Stormont in March 1972, in the wake of 'Bloody Sunday' in Derry, defying the advice of the NI Premier, Brian Faulkner, and risking a loyalist backlash. Thirdly, he brought all his Prime Ministerial power to bear at the Sunningdale Conference in December 1973 to get the power-sharing administration established. The previous August he made a two-day visit to NI during which he urged politicians to get on with the job of making the Assembly work. On that occasion he made one of his few gestures to unionism when he attended the Belfast memorial service for the former PM, Lord Brookeborough. Earlier visits to NI were in December 1971 (essentially a pre-Christmas visit to the army), and on 16–17 November 1972, when he was pondering the scope of the British political initiative. One of his most surprising comments was made in Dublin in September 1973 after talks with Taoiseach Liam Cosgrave and other Ministers. In a BBC interview he mentioned the possibility of NI being fully integrated with GB. After protests from Harold Wilson, the opposition leader, and many sections of NI and Dublin opinion, he claimed that he was not advocating integration as a solution. In his *Memoirs of a Statesman,* the late Brian (Lord) Faulkner quotes Heath as saying in the critical pre-direct-rule talks at Downing Street that NI should have a county-council- or Greater-London-Council-type administration. Visiting Belfast in January 1983, he described himself as 'the best friend Ulster ever had'. In 1984 he complained that the Wilson Government had not done enough in 1974 to maintain the power-sharing Executive. In November 1989 he criticised the Thatcher Government over the PIRA bombing of Deal barracks. He told the Prime Minister that the use of private security guards at the base was 'just not justifiable' in a terrorist war. On a visit to the Republic in September 1990 he admitted that he was not optimistic about achieving peace in NI. In June 1993 he said in the Commons that Ian Paisley should be excluded from political negotiations – otherwise there could be no agreement. During a visit to the Republic in July he repeated this argument, citing his exclusion of Paisley from Sunningdale, and stating that the UK and Irish Governments should proceed if Unionists refused to talk. He said that the time was not right to talk to PSF.

HELSINKI WATCH

US-based international human rights body, which has criticised both official security policy and the behaviour of paramilitaries in NI. In reports during 1992, it expressed disappointment that the British Government had not responded to its calls for stricter controls over the use of lethal force, and for taping of police interrogations, the banning of the use of plastic bullets, and a better procedure for dealing with complaints against the security forces. It also urged the recruitment of more Catholic prison officers, and alleged harassment of Catholic prisoners by staff in Belfast's Crumlin Road Prison.

HENDRON, JAMES

Alliance Convention member for S. Belfast, 1975–6. b. Belfast, 1931. Solicitor. Founder member and ex-chairman of the Alliance Party; president, 1994–. His brother, Dr Joseph Hendron, was SDLP Convention member for W. Belfast, and became MP for W. Belfast in 1992.

HENDRON, DR JOSEPH (JOE) GERARD

SDLP MP for W. Belfast, April 1992–. Assembly member for W. Belfast, 1982–6. b. Belfast, 1932. MB (QUB); MRCGP, DPH, Dip. Obst., RCOG. General medical practitioner in Falls Road area of Belfast and party's health spokesman. NI Assembly, 1973–4. Convention member for W. Belfast, 1975–6, while his brother James was also in the Convention (All., S. Belfast). Belfast City Council, 1981–93. Chairman of SDLP constituency representatives, 1980–. In the 1983 Westminster election he was runner-up in W. Belfast to Gerry Adams (PSF), who unseated Gerry (now Lord) Fitt, who stood as an Independent Socialist. Fitt had resigned from SDLP, of which he was the first leader, in 1979, and he blamed Hendron for his defeat, claiming that Hendron could not attract the non-Nationalist support that had gone to him. In 1987 Hendron again ran second to Adams, despite a vigorous campaign and the decision of All. to stand aside. In the late 1980s he repeatedly urged a massive development plan for W. Belfast, which he saw as a means of depriving the paramilitaries of the recruits they were getting among the many unemployed young people. The move had some success in that the NIO did announce new projects, notably the Springvale development. In the 1992 general election, he finally gained the seat from Adams, with a majority of 589. Adams virtually held his 1987 vote and Hendron's triumph seemed to be due to two factors – improved organisation and, perhaps more decisively, the decision of hundreds of normally Unionist voters across the Peace Line to vote tactically for him as the candidate most likely to oust Adams. Soon after his election, he joined the N. Belfast UUP MP Cecil Walker on a trip to the US to encourage industrial investment in W. Belfast. His election was challenged by two constituents on the grounds of overspending and failure to lodge the proper declaration. The Election Court, unique in Northern Ireland, ruled that Dr Hendron was personally guilty of failing to verify his election expenses and guilty, through his election agent, of four other illegal practices, including overspending. He was relieved from the penalties on the grounds of 'inadvertence' and because there was 'no sanction or connivance on his part', and the court certified that Hendron was duly returned as MP for W. Belfast. He retired from Belfast City Council in 1993. In the late summer of 1993 his concern at the rise in loyalist paramilitary violence led to a meeting with Sir John Wheeler and a clash with the RUC when he claimed there was not the same level of security presence in loyalist areas. His comment that the Hume–Adams talks had 'undermined' his position as an MP was respected for its honesty even though PSF was critical. He welcomed the decision by the Irish Government in January 1994 to remove the broadcasting restrictions on PSF. His open welcome to the announcement of an NI Select Committee in December 1993 was at variance with SDLP policy.

HENNESSY REPORT *see* H-Blocks

HERMON, SIR JOHN
Chief Constable of the RUC, January 1980–9. b. Larne, Co. Antrim, 1928. He had been in the RUC for twenty-nine years when he was appointed Chief Constable, having risen through the ranks. In 1963, when he became a head constable, he was also the first RUC officer to go to Bramshill police training college in England. In 1966 he was district inspector in charge of the Cookstown area, and in the following year deputy Commandant of the RUC training centre at Enniskillen. He was promoted to Chief

Superintendent in 1970, Assistant Chief Constable, 1974, and in 1975 was awarded the OBE. By 1976 he was deputy Chief Constable (operations) and when he went on attachment to Scotland Yard in 1979, he was widely tipped for the top post. As Chief Constable, he faced a wide variety of challenges. In the early years he had to cope with the revival of street violence during the 1981 hunger strike. In 1982 the Armagh 'shoot to kill' controversy surfaced, which still provokes argument. He has clashed with the local police federation on policy and internal matters, and the EOC over the sacking of women officers. When the Rev. Ian Paisley launched his Third Force at the end of 1981, Sir John gave a strong warning that no private army would be allowed to usurp the authority of the police or army. At private conferences he proved a highly articulate defender of the RUC, and apparently unworried by his detractors. There were periodic 'hiccups' in his relations with the Garda chiefs, but these did not affect the developing cross-border security co-operation, notably after the signing of the AIA. In 1986 he succeeded in dispelling doubts in Dublin that he would be able to handle effectively the loyalist protests against the AIA and new public order legislation. While acknowledging the 'deep-seated' Unionist opposition to the agreement, he insisted that the RUC had acted impartially throughout. In 1992 he said he had a 'quiet determination' that the protests would 'not become a repeat of 1974'. Following the decision not to bring prosecutions against RUC men over an alleged cover-up of evidence related to the 1982 Armagh shootings, the Police Authority in 1988 voted by a majority of one not to pursue disciplinary inquiries against Sir John and two of his senior colleagues. Sir John's subsequent decision to bring disciplinary charges against twenty junior members of the force drew wide criticism. In May 1989 he retired as Chief Constable, and in 1990 he became a consultant to Securicor. In January 1990 he disclosed that he had threatened to resign over the prosecution for murder of four of his officers, who were subsequently acquitted. In a TV interview in 1990, he said, 'It must be recognised that the Provisionals are probably the most proficient terrorist grouping in the world – skilled in surviving within the community which they are attacking.' After his retirement, he successfully pursued a number of libel actions in the courts arising from television programmes on incidents during his period of office. In an interview for Central Television's *The Cook Report,* he claimed that PSF and PIRA were 'inseparable' and that Martin McGuinness was 'very central to all that is going on'.

HERRON, THOMAS (TOMMY)

Vice-chairman and leading spokesman of the UDA, who was found shot dead at Drumbo, near Lisburn, in September 1973. b. 1937. An open verdict was returned at the inquest. UDA leaders dismissed the idea of a serious political motive, ruling out both PIRA and Protestant paramilitary involvement. They suggested that 'cranks', bitterly opposed to Herron, had been responsible. He stood unsuccessfully as a Vanguard Unionist candidate in the Assembly election in 1973.

HESLIP, HERBERT

UUP member for S. Down in the Assembly, 1973–4, and Convention, 1975–6. b. Ballinaskeagh, Co. Down, 1913; d. 1992. Farmer. For many years a leading figure in unionism and local government in S. Down. Member of Down County Council, 1968–73. Banbridge District Council, 1973–85. Vice-president, Down Orange Welfare. Deputy Speaker of NI Assembly, 1973–4.

HILLERY, DR PATRICK JOHN

President of Irish Republic, 1976–90. b. 2 May 1923. B.Sc., MB, B.Ch., BAO (UCD). Dr Hillery made his most dramatic intervention in NI affairs on 6 July 1970, as the Republic's Minister for Foreign Affairs. He drove secretly to Belfast and appeared on the Falls Road. He had not consulted the British Government, and there was an angry protest from Britain's Foreign Secretary Sir Alec Douglas-Home, who said it was a 'serious diplomatic discourtesy' and would add to the difficulties of those working for peace. Taoiseach Jack Lynch defended the visit, saying that there was fear on the Falls and it was vitally important that it should not be exploited by subversive elements. Dr Hillery was Foreign Minister, 1969–73, and earlier ministerial posts were: Education, 1959–65; Industry and Commerce, 1965–6; and Labour, 1966–9. He was EC Commissioner for Social Affairs, 1973–6, and one of his earliest announcements in that office was the setting up of an EC Commission office in Belfast.

HOEY, KATE

Labour MP for Vauxhall, 1989–. b. 21 June 1948 and educated in NI. Represented NI at athletics. Former Senior Lecturer in Physical Education. Founder member of Democracy Now, which campaigns for the Labour Party to organise in NI. She and colleagues Nick Raynsford and Harry Barnes described the 'Oranges and Lemons' publication from Kevin McNamara as 'mischievous and scurrilous' and said it had been issued without the approval of the party leadership.

HOLDEN, SIR DAVID CHARLES BERESFORD

Head of the NI civil service and Permanent Secretary, Department of Finance, 1973–6. b. 26 July 1915. Educated at King's College, Cambridge. Joined the NI civil service in 1937, and after retirement in 1976, served for a year as Director of the Ulster Office in London.

HOLLYWOOD, SEAN

SDLP candidate who lost by 3,567 votes to Enoch Powell (UUP, UUUC) in S. Down in the Westminster election, October 1974. b. 1945. BA (QUB). Teacher. Caught attention as main opponent to Enoch Powell in heavily publicised campaign. His strong showing in a constituency where the Unionist majority had often reached 10,000 to 20,000 clearly owed much to his ability to pull over some votes of Unionists unhappy at Powell's candidature. Newry and Mourne District Council, 1973–7.

Unsuccessful SDLP Convention candidate in N. Down, 1975. In 1978 he was at variance with the party on the power-sharing issue. Left politics to pursue interest in stage and drama.

HOLME, LORD (OF CHELTENHAM)

Liberal Democratic spokesman on NI. b. 27 May 1936. President of Liberal Party, 1980-1. Professor in Business Administration, Middlesex Polytechnic, 1990-. In May 1992 he said he was 'dubious' about decision to give MI5 the lead in anti-PIRA intelligence work in GB.

HOUSE, LIEUTENANT-GENERAL, SIR DAVID

Army GOC, NI, 1975-7. b. 8 August 1922. General House took over in NI when the PIRA ceasefire was petering out. One of his major tasks was to deal with the outbreak of violence in S. Armagh, including the killing of ten Protestant workers in a minibus in January 1976. This led to the introduction of the undercover Special Air Service into S. Armagh, and soon afterwards it was permitted to operate anywhere in NI, mainly to counter sectarian assassinations. In 1977 he left the army to become Black Rod in the House of Lords.

HOWARD, MICHAEL

Home Secretary, 1993-. Conservative MP for Folkestone and Hythe, 1983-. Member of Cabinet Committee on NI, 1993-. b. 7 July 1941. Educated Llanelli Grammar School and Peterhouse, Cambridge. Barrister, 1964; QC, 1982. His first step in Government was as PPS to Sir Patrick Mayhew, 1984-5, when he was Solicitor-General. He was a firm supporter of PM Major's 'back to basics' campaign and in October 1993 he made an exclusion order against Gerry Adams which prevented the PSF president fulfilling an invitation from Tony Benn (Lab.) to speak at Westminster.

HOWE, LORD (OF AVERAVON)

Deputy Prime Minister and Leader of Commons, 1989-90. Foreign and Commonwealth Secretary, 1983-9. b. 20 December 1926. QC. As Chancellor of the Exchequer in December 1980, he was one of Cabinet team who had talks in Dublin with Charles Haughey's Government, which led to the declaration that the Thatcher and Haughey Governments would consider the 'totality of relationships' between the two countries. He backed the radical approach to NI affairs which led to the AIA, and which was at odds with Thatcher's initial insistence that the Irish Government had no right to be consulted on NI matters. In 1988, when relations between London and Dublin were strained, mainly over security issues, he argued that this was exactly the situation the AIA was designed to deal with. And although Haughey, on a US visit in 1988, was critical of British policy, Sir Geoffrey, as he then was, described the Taoiseach as 'an outstanding patriot' and said he did not underestimate the 'hurt' felt by the Irish recently. In November 1988 he visited Dublin for talks with the Government, which was urging greater use of extra-territorial legislation, but he declared that the use of such legislation was no substitute for extradition. In February 1990 he criticised Unionists when he spoke at the opening session of the British-Irish Parliamentary Body. A month later, he stressed that the Irish Supreme Court ruling on the Constitution did not affect NI's position within the UK. Although his criticism of Thatcher's approach to Europe and his resignation from her Government was an important element in the Conservative leadership crisis in 1990, he did not find a place in the Major administration, and in Dublin political circles there was regret that 'a friend of Ireland' was no longer in the Cabinet. Made life peer, 1992.

HOWELL, DAVID

Parliamentary Under-Secretary, NIO, 1972-3. b. 18 January 1936. Energy Minister, 1979-81; Transport Minister, 1981-3. Conservative MP for Guildford, 1966-. After a short period in the economic section of the Treasury, he was leader writer and special correspondent of the London *Daily Telegraph,* 1960-4. As director of the Conservative Political Centre, he had a hand in drafting the party's 1964 election manifesto. At the NIO he had charge of the departments of Finance, Commerce and Agriculture. Chairman of Foreign Affairs Select Committee, 1987–.

HULL, WILLIAM (BILLY)

Chairman of LAW, 1969–73. b. Belfast, 1912. Member, NILP, 1948–73. He became well known as a voice of Protestant workers at the height of the violence. He left the NILP in protest against Harold Wilson's attitude to NI. He had helped organise the Workers' Committee for the Defence of the Constitution, which preceded LAW, and as convenor of shop stewards at the Belfast shipyard engine works, was one of a small group which organised LAW throughout NI to the point when it claimed about 100,000 members. After the murder of three Scottish soldiers in Belfast in early 1971, he led a march of 9,000 engineering workers to Unionist headquarters – a protest which was regarded as one of the main factors which led to the resignation soon afterwards of James Chichester-Clark from the Premiership. He was also involved in planning the forty-eight-hour loyalist strike when direct rule was introduced in 1972. Most of LAW's supporters linked up with the UWC in early 1973, when Hull differed with some of the other leaders on tactics.

HUME, JOHN

SDLP MEP for NI, 1979–. Leader, SDLP, November 1979–. MP for Foyle, 1983–. Assembly member for Londonderry, 1973–4 and 1982–6; Convention member, 1975–6. Head of Commerce Department in power-sharing NI Executive, 1974, and deputy leader, SDLP, 1973–9. b. Derry, 18 January 1937. MA (Maynooth). An ex-teacher, he first came to political prominence in the civil rights movement in Derry in 1968, and was vice-chairman of the Derry Citizens' Action Committee, 1968–9. In the Stormont general election of February 1969, he was returned as MP for Foyle, unseating the Nationalist leader, Eddie McAteer. During the election campaign, he urged the establishment of a social democratic party. He was a founder member of the SDLP in 1970, and soon emerged as the party's chief policy-maker. He was elected to the Assembly, 1973–4, from Londonderry and was heavily engaged in the negotiations with Secretary of State William Whitelaw, and in the Sunningdale Conference, which led to the setting up of the Executive. As head of the Commerce Department, he was deeply involved with the economic problems thrown up by the loyalist strike in 1974. He fought the Londonderry seat unsuccessfully in the Westminster election of October 1974. He was returned to the Convention for Londonderry, and after the failure of the Convention joined his then party colleague, Paddy Devlin, in private but unsuccessful talks with Austin Ardill and the Rev. Martin Smyth, Ulster Unionists, on a possible political settlement. He then became active in liaising with politicians in Europe and the US, and in 1977 he became part-time adviser on consumer affairs to the EC Commissioner, Richard Burke. This entailed considerable travel within the Common Market area. In 1978 the main political parties in the Republic took up in principle his plea that they should seek to spell out in detail their intentions on eventual Irish unity. He suggested at the same time that more thought should be given to a federal solution. In 1978 he was unanimously selected as the SDLP candidate for one of the three NI seats in the 1979 European direct elections. He fought a vigorous campaign, essentially on EC issues, but claimed that the new Parliament would lead to co-operation between MEPs from NI and the Republic, and would form a 'healing process' in Irish affairs. On the first count, he secured 140,622 votes or 24.5 per cent – that is, just short of the quota. He had more votes than the combined total of the two Ulster Unionists, and the poll was a record one for the SDLP. He was elected on the third count, with 146,072, and became a member of the socialist group in the European Assembly, and a member of the Assembly's regional committee. He succeeded Gerry Fitt MP as party leader. Fitt had resigned because of the initial refusal of the SDLP to attend the 1980 Constitutional Conference promoted by Secretary of State Humphrey Atkins, and also because he argued that the SDLP had abandoned a socialist approach and become simply a Nationalist party – a contention hotly denied by Hume. Hume later claimed that at the Atkins conference the SDLP had proposed that power-sharing government should be limited to ten years, and he said it was clear that Unionists were totally opposed to partnership government. He again cited Unionist opposition to power-sharing as one of the reasons for rejecting the 'rolling devolution' scheme put forward by Secretary of State James Prior in 1982. Dubbing the plan 'unworkable', he also complained that the Irish dimension was far too limited. During the passage of the legislation, Hume urged that a parliamentary tier of the Anglo-Irish Intergovernmental Council should have responsibility for security, civil rights and 'identity'. In the event, he led the SDLP into the October 1982 Assembly elections, with a boycott of the Assembly itself, and called for a 'Council for a New Ireland', which would bring together politicians from the Republic and NI to draw up a realistic Irish unity blueprint. The proposal led to the New Ireland Forum. After the polls, he said the Assembly was 'dead as a dodo'. In the European Parliament in 1980 he spearheaded a new economic initiative for NI, which was supported by the other two local MEPs, and which led to a special European Parliament report on ways of strengthening the local economy. He has made frequent visits to the US, making political contacts at many levels and receiving honorary degrees from several universities. In March 1982 he was one of President Reagan's guests at a St Patrick's Day lunch in the White House, at which the Republic's Taoiseach, Charles Haughey, was guest of honour. Hume used the occasion to explain SDLP policy to Congressional leaders. In 1983 he pressed in European Parliament for an inquiry by its political affairs committee into NI's economy and political situation. The idea was adopted, despite opposition from the British Government and

Unionists. In the 1983 Westminster election, he won easily the new Foyle constituency – the first time a non-Unionist had got a Westminster seat in the Derry area since the establishment of NI. In 1984 he saw the NIF report as a pointer to a new era of negotiations aimed at resolving the NI situation, and he had an insider's view of the testing exchanges between London and Dublin which led finally to the AIA in 1985. He sought to blunt the Unionist assault on the AIA by arguing that it was not an end in itself but the beginning of a process in which the two traditions could reach an accommodation. He insisted that devolution had to be judged on whether it was likely to contribute to such a solution, but it was 1988 before he led his party into serious talks with the Secretary of State Tom King on the issue of a local administration. By that time he had also become involved in controversial discussions with PSF president Gerry Adams, aimed, he said, at bringing not a ceasefire but a permanent end to violence. Hume had annoyed the Garret FitzGerald Government with his brief but unsuccessful meeting with PIRA in February 1985, and these exchanges with PSF in 1988 also raised some doubts in Dublin, as well as outright hostility from Unionists, who said they would not have talks with the SDLP while the contacts continued. The SDLP leader apparently saw the talks with PSF as an opportunity to press his claim that the AIA effectively meant that Britain had disclaimed any long-term interest in having a presence in Ireland, and that the 'armed struggle' was, therefore, irrelevant. The talks with PSF ended in September 1988. In his address at the SDLP's 1988 conference, he accused PIRA of 'showing the hallmarks of undiluted fascism'. For Hume and his party, 1989 proved electorally memorable. The SDLP won twenty more council seats than in 1985, and in the European poll, he secured 25.5 per cent of the votes – the best SDLP showing in any election. On a St Patrick's Day visit to Washington in 1990, he had a meeting with President Bush, and later that year he welcomed Peter Brooke's speech claiming that Britain had 'no selfish or strategic interest in NI' as showing that the British Government was now neutral on partition. In the Brooke-Mayhew Talks, he put forward the idea of a six-member Commission to run NI, with the UK, the Republic and the EC each appointing one member, and with a North-South Council of Ministers. But the idea was swiftly rejected by Unionists, and EC President Jacques Delors, on a visit to NI in 1992, seemed unenthusiastic about it. With the ending of the structured talks in 1992, Hume supported the idea of continuing informal inter-party contacts. But he insisted that neither majority rule nor normal power-sharing was the answer in NI. He also had the satisfaction of seeing the party win W. Belfast in the 1992 Westminster election. On the European scene, he criticised PM Major for opposing the Social Charter in the Maastricht Treaty, an approach which, he suggested, could jeopardise NI's case for enhanced EC support. Hume rejected criticism of his renewed talks with Gerry Adams, which were revealed in April 1993. This came from Unionist and Alliance politicians and in Dublin from some opposition spokespersons and from newspapers, much of it centring on a joint statement from Hume and Adams that attacked the idea of an internal settlement in NI and insisted that the Irish people as a whole had the right to 'national self-determination'. Hume claimed that his aim was to end PIRA violence, an end which, he said, could transform the situation. He voiced concern at the Conservative/UUP 'deal' over the vote on the Maastricht Treaty in July and the consequences for inter-party talks. He warned Unionists that 'if you're bought on Thursday you can be sold on Monday'. In August he told BBC Radio Ulster of his duty to work for peace despite Unionist concern at his talks with PSF. He advocated that the two Governments should do a deal, if inter-party talks failed to resume, and then put it to the parties. In September he told Major of his optimism that talks involving PSF could begin in six months. On 25 September he announced agreement on a peace process in a second joint statement

issued with Gerry Adams. However, no document containing the principles was published and no formal report was made to the Irish Government until 7 October, when Hume returned from a ten-day trade mission to the US. In a public relations blunder, the Irish Government, SDLP MPs and party members had been left in the dark, while Adams briefed the PSF executive and became the focus of the media. Hume then insisted on a speedy response from the Government, demanded a meeting with the PM, and told the *Observer* that the PM was sitting on an opportunity for peace. However, Major had not been given a copy of the Hume–Adams document and had only been briefed on its contents by the Irish Government in Brussels on 29 October. Hume was informed by the Taoiseach that the two Governments would follow their own peace path. By 20 November Hume and Adams had met again and issued a third joint statement in which they made the British response crucial for the peace process. When they next met a month later further meetings were suspended until PSF had completed its analysis of the Downing Street Declaration. Hume was very critical of the decision to create an NI Select Committee, which he portrayed as advancing one strand of relationships before others. Early in January 1994 he issued a document on the declaration in which he argued that the PIRA reasons for violence were no longer valid, and he appealed to them to have the 'moral courage' to give up violence and to 'spill our sweat not our blood'. However, as January proceeded without any PIRA cessation of violence, Hume joined those calling for 'clarification' and for the reopening of the informal channels to PSF/PIRA. His political stance was increasingly challenged by other parties, calling for the publication of the Hume–Adams proposals, by the *Irish Press*, claiming it had no separate status but was an early draft of an Irish Government proposal, and by a group of prominent individuals claiming he had a 'blind spot' towards Unionists. In visits to the US – to Boston for the funeral of Tip O'Neill in January and to New York in

February (with Gerry Adams and John Alderdice) – he appealed for a change of attitude all round and asked Irish-Americans to involve themselves in the peace process.

HUME–ADAMS TALKS

In January 1988 John Hume, leader of SDLP, and Gerry Adams, president of PSF, initiated talks at the request of a third party. The talks soon widened to other party members and the exchange of position papers. The SDLP hoped to persuade PSF of British neutrality since the AIA, making violence unnecessary and requiring a more sophisticated policy than 'Brits out'. The talks broke down in September without apparently bridging the differences, though PSF argued that they had helped Nationalist morale. Secret talks were discovered in Derry on 10 April 1993, begun on the initiative of a group of Catholic clergy. These Hume–Adams talks continued, and a statement was issued on 25 April. From late August, as speculation mounted, concern grew in SDLP ranks as loyalist paramilitaries targeted its members. After a meeting with PM Major on 17 September, Hume told reporters about hopeful signs and his estimate of talks within six months. He did not care 'two balls of roasted snow' about the criticism of his talks with Adams. On 25 September, on the eve of his departure on a trade mission to the US, a joint statement reported considerable progress on the creation of a peace process and the suspension of the talks for wider consideration between the two Governments. The appetite of the press discovered that there was no written report at that stage, that the manner of presentation had embarrassed the Irish Government, and appeals made to end speculation left Gerry Adams at the centre of inquiries. There were doubts about how widely within SDLP the contents of agreement were known while the thirty members of the PSF executive had been briefed. On his return from the US on 7 October, Hume handed over a document to Taoiseach Albert Reynolds and Foreign Minister Dick Spring. However, it became clear that the Hume–Adams document would not be forwarded to the British Government, even after a special meeting between Hume and Reynolds on 3 November. A third joint statement, issued on 20 November, stated that the British response was crucial. The next day a rally on the Falls Road in support of Hume–Adams was attended by an estimated 2,000 people. The British and Irish Governments decided to pursue their own path to peace, regarding the Hume–Adams proposals as too unbalanced. Hume and Adams met after the publication of the Downing Street Declaration, and suspended meetings until PSF had completed its analysis of the declaration. Although the Hume–Adams document had not been published by the end of 1993, Seamus Mallon, SDLP deputy leader, said that the difference on self-determination was extremely narrow. A UTV/Ulster Marketing Surveys poll` revealed that over 60 per cent of Catholics were favourably disposed to include paramilitaries in talks, whereas Protestants opposed their inclusion by 60 per cent.

HUNGER STRIKE *see* H-Blocks

HUNT REPORT

The report produced by the committee headed by Lord Hunt which led to far-reaching reforms in the NI security forces in 1969. The report recommended an unarmed RUC and replacement of the controversial USC by a new part-time force under the army GOC (it emerged as the UDR), as well as the setting up of a Police Reserve. The proposal for ending the USC was deeply resented by many Unionists, and led to serious rioting in Protestant areas of Belfast. It was welcomed by those who had supported the civil rights campaign. In 1990 Lord Hunt urged the phasing out of the UDR and its replacement by an enlarged RUC.

HUNTER, ANDREW

Chairman, Conservative backbench NI Committee, 1992–. b. 8 January 1943. Durham and Cambridge Universities. After a period in industry, he was a master at Harrow school before being elected MP for Basingstoke in 1983. PPS to Lord Elton, 1985–6. Vice-chairman, Conservative Agriculture Committee, 1987–91. Secretary of Cons. NI Committee, 1990–2. In January 1994 he expressed sceptical views about the prospects of the Republican movement ceasing violence. His personal security was increased amid fears of attacks on VIPs.

HURD, DOUGLAS RICHARD

NI Secretary of State, September 1984–September 1985. Previously Minister of State at the Home Office, 1983–4, and at the Foreign and Commonwealth Office, 1974–83. MP for Mid Oxon., February 1979–83; MP for Witney, 1983–. b. 8 March 1930. Although he had made political contacts in NI as an opposition spokesman in the 1970s, his appointment was a surprise. In the event his brief stay at Stormont turned out to be a crucial period, since it marked the decisive stage of negotiations preceding the signing of the AIA. But there were ups and downs in London–Dublin relations during his tenure at the NIO. Thatcher had angered the Irish Government and the SDLP with her comment after the November 1984 London summit meeting with Garret FitzGerald that it was 'out, out, out' to the three options of the New Ireland Forum. This had temporarily heartened Unionists, but soon they were using the Assembly as a platform for repeated allegations that the British Government was planning a 'backdoors' deal with Dublin. By March 1985, when Hurd asked junior Minister Chris Patten to mediate between the NI parties, he had already received two reports from the Assembly Devolution Committee. The appointment of a mediator was a signal of Hurd's discontent with their efforts. The feeling seems to have been mutual, for in their one meeting with Hurd the committee found him cold and aloof and their minutes referred to 'a somewhat cavalier attitude to the committee and the Assembly'. The mediation attempt failed as Unionists were in no mood for compromise and the SDLP were still looking for major Irish Government

involvement in NI affairs. Hurd was believed to have been influential in bringing about a change of attitude by Thatcher, and he may have been helped in this by her strong interest in cross-border security. This could only have been heightened by the PIRA assault on Newry police station in February 1985, in which nine RUC officers died. Oddly enough, Hurd's sudden departure from the NIO in 1985 to succeed Leon Brittan as Home Secretary owed something to what was widely seen as Brittan's mishandling of the controversy over the BBC *Real Lives* documentary featuring local politicians: Gregory Campbell (DUP) and Martin McGuinness (PSF). As a thriller writer, Hurd produced in 1975 a novel, *Vote to Kill,* dealing with an IRA plot to kill the PM and which was dedicated to Edward Heath, to whom he had been Political Secretary, 1970–4. His refusal as Secretary of State to have meetings with PSF elected representatives led to references to a meeting which he held privately in 1978 with Gerry Adams and Danny Morrison of PSF in preparation for a BBC programme. In 1987, as Home Secretary, he allowed the six men convicted for the Birmingham pub bombings of 1974 to go to the Court of Appeal, but the appeal failed there and in the Lords. In 1988 Hurd was active in promoting new anti-terrorist measures, and his ban on broadcasts by supporters of terrorism and new official secrets legislation drew particular criticism from the media. In 1990 he was an unsuccessful challenger for the Conservative leadership. A comment by Hurd on NI at a fringe meeting of the Conservative conference in 1991 attracted some interest: 'The discussion now focuses not on the border or the unification of Ireland, but on how NI can run its own affairs within the UK, taking into account the identities and wishes of both the majority and the minority communities.' Irish Ministers subsequently sought assurance that there had been no change in policy. In April 1993 he said Dublin had 'a crucial role' in new talks as a partner in relationships between the two Governments 'and within Ireland in relationships based on trust and mutual respect'. Ian Paisley accused him of really seeking joint authority in NI. In November, after being informed by the Irish Government of the content of the Hume–Adams document, he described it as 'very constructive' but saw no need to underwrite every sentence. Ten days before the Downing Street Declaration was published on 15 December, he told the BBC that the views of the people of NI were what counted. After the three-day PIRA ceasefire at Christmas he said that PIRA must 'take peace or else' because its arguments were now groundless.

HUTCHINSON, DOUGLAS

DUP Assembly, 1973–4, and Convention, 1975–6, member for Armagh. b. Richhill, Co. Armagh, 1918. One of the Rev. Ian Paisley's most active supporters, he was on Armagh Rural Council, 1953–73, and Armagh District Council, 1973–93. Chairman, 1989–90. Former member, USC. In Convention election he said he would share power in government only with those who supported the link with GB. Sentenced to one month's imprisonment after incidents in November 1968 in Armagh, following the civil rights march and loyalist counter-demonstrations there. Expelled from Orange Order for criticism of leadership. Unsuccessfully contested 1982 Assembly election in Armagh.

HUTTON, SIR JAMES BRIAN EDWARD

Lord Chief Justice, NI, 1988–. b. 29 June 1931. Called to NI Bar, 1954. QC (NI), 1970. Called to English Bar, 1972. Senior Crown Counsel, NI, 1973–9. High Court judge, NI, 1979–88. Appointed Lord Chief Justice at a time when the Irish Government pressed unsuccessfully for major changes in court system in NI in the context of the AIA. In 1978 was member of British defence team in European Court of Human Rights when Britain was found guilty of ill-treating internees in 1971.

HUTTON, NORMAN

General secretary of the UUP, 1974–83. b. 1943. A former businessman, he was responsible for planning the party's election campaigns, and was heavily involved in carrying through constituency reorganisation to deal with the five extra Westminster seats.

I

ILLEGAL ORGANISATIONS see

Security System section, p. 454, for list of bodies proscribed under the Emergency Provisons Act

INDEPENDENT ORANGE ORDER

A relatively small organisation which was originally a breakaway from the main Orange Order. It was founded in 1903 after a row following a Belfast by-election in which the official Unionist candidate was defeated by a shipyard worker, T.H. Sloan. When Sloan was expelled from the Orange Order he and his friends set up the Independent Orange Order. It called on its members to 'hold out the right hand of fellowship to those who, while worshipping at other shrines, are yet our countrymen'. It holds its own 12 July demonstrations, some of which have been addressed by the Rev. Ian Paisley, who broke with the main Order in 1962. In 1982 the Rev. Martin Smyth MP, as head of the main Order, said he hoped that the official and independent Orange Orders would eventually reunite. In 1985 the Independent Order criticised Orangemen in Canada for taking part in a 'reconciliation seminar' with Catholics. In July 1990 it was permitted to celebrate the tercentenary of the Battle of the Boyne at the site in the Republic but its larger associate was not.

INDEPENDENT UNIONIST GROUP

see Progressive Unionist Party

INITIATIVE '92

An independent inquiry launched in May 1992, aimed at bringing together the widest possible range of views on NI's political future. Norwegian professor Torkel Opsahl, a noted authority on constitutional and international human rights law and founder member of Amnesty International, was appointed chairman. The other members of the commission were Lady Lucy Faulkner, widow of the former PM of NI; Rev. Eric Gallagher, former president of the Methodist Church; Professor Marianne Elliott of Birkbeck College, London; Eamonn Gallagher, former senior civil servant in the Republic; Professor Ruth Lister of Bradford University; and Padraig O'Malley, who had written and lectured extensively on Irish politics. The main organisers were Professor Simon Lee of Queen's University and two journalists, Robin Wilson (editor of *Fortnight*) and Andy Pollak (*Irish Times*). The main funds for the project came from NI Voluntary Trust, Rowntree Trust and Barrow Cadbury. The Opsahl inquiry opened its hearings in January, and when it closed six weeks later it had received some 500 submissions on behalf of 3,000 people. The report, *A Citizens' Inquiry: The Opsahl Report on Northern Ireland*, published on 9 June, contained twenty-five main findings. The most controversial were the creation of a devolved administration with equal membership from the Unionist and Nationalist communities and a mutual right of veto; the formal legal recognition of the Nationalist aspiration; the inclusion of PSF in talks subject to the renunciation of violence; the opening of informal channels of communication with PIRA through PSF; the introduction of a Bill of Rights and reform of the police, including a decentralised structure. An opinion poll on some of the findings was conducted simultaneously in NI, the Republic and GB between 17 and 28 June and found public support. NI politicians were critical, but the Government welcomed it as a source of ideas and debate while noting the controversy and dissent. The report had become a bestseller by July. In early September two members of the commission called for official talks on the Opsahl findings to end the political deadlock. After the publication of the report Torkel Opsahl returned to chairing the UN war crimes commission on the former Yugoslavia. He died aged sixty-two in Geneva on 16 September 1993, a few days after attending the British Irish Association conference in Cambridge.

INTEGRATION

The idea of complete absorption of NI into the UK without any regional self-government. It has been ruled out by the main parties in GB and was not backed by any group in the Constitutional Convention, 1975–6. After the collapse of the Convention, however, a section of the UUP seemed to be attracted to the possibility, provided that NI was given parity with the rest of the UK in representation at Westminster, and in local government. This presumably inspired the party's suggestions of administrative devolution in the 1982 Assembly. The decision of the Callaghan Government in 1978 to introduce five extra Westminster seats was interpreted by the SDLP as a lurch towards integration. However, British Governments, both Conservative and Labour, have continued to look for devolved government, and have maintained a separate statute book for local legislation during direct rule, and devolution was envisaged in the AIA. Opinion polls have shown around 80 per cent of Protestants in NI prepared to accept integration but, predictably, little support among Nationalists. An Integration Group was set up in NI in 1984 to promote the idea, and the Campaign for Equal Citizenship also attracted integrationists to its ranks. Integration seems to be preferred by most NI Conservatives.

INTERNATIONAL FUND FOR IRELAND

Set up in 1986 to back the AIA with economic measures in NI and, to a lesser extent, in border areas of the Republic. Fund developed from anxiety in US to encourage reconciliation in the wake of the AIA. Washington contributed $120 million over three years up to 1988, and aid was continued under Presidents Bush and Clinton. In 1987 Canada pledged $10 million over ten years, and New Zealand $1 million over the same period. In 1988 the EC Commission proposed £9.75 million per year for three years. The original board was headed by Belfast solicitor Charles Brett, former Housing Executive chairman, who stressed the independence of the board from political control. Its second report, at the end of 1988, stated that grants to 858 projects totalled £26,579,000, and represented 4,500 permanent jobs. The SDLP has been supportive of the initiative, while quarrelling with some of its grants policies. Several Irish-American groups have been critical of the administration of the fund, but the US Senate Appropriations Committee has praised its approach. Unionists have condemned the fund as an attempt to bribe them to accept the AIA. But John B. McGuckian, the Ballymena businessman who was chairman 1989–92, said in 1992 that the fund was breaking down barriers between the communities, particularly in disadvantaged areas of Belfast, Derry, Coalisland and S. Armagh, and in flagship projects like the Ballinamore-Ballyconnell canal. In 1991–2 the fund had provided £46 million for some 500 projects with a potential for 3,300 jobs and hundreds more part-time jobs. In 1991 Tom Foley, Speaker of the US House of Representatives, led a Congressional delegation to NI and the Republic which praised the work of the fund. SDLP leader John Hume said in August 1992 that he regularly briefed members of Congress on the fund, which up to that time had created more than 21,000 jobs. A leading North-West businessman, William McCarter, became chairman in 1993. In March 1993 President Clinton confirmed that the annual $20 million US grant to the fund would continue.

IRELAND FUNDS
Funds established in the US, Canada, France, Australia and GB 'to promote peace, culture and charity in all of Ireland', with priority being given to projects that are innovative, featuring self-help and a high degree of community involvement. The funds derive from the Ireland Fund set up in US in 1976 and which in 1987 merged with the Irish-American Foundation, and up to 1987 total contributions in US were over $8 million. The Canadian fund was set up in 1978; the Australian in 1987; the British in 1988, and the French in 1990. All now operate together under the chairmanship of Dr Tony O'Reilly, who headed the US fund from the outset. The funds have had the endorsement of both the British and Irish Governments, and of US Presidents and the Prime Ministers of Canada and Australia. Fifty per cent of grant aid goes to NI projects. Announcing grants to thirty-nine projects totalling almost £500,000 in June 1992, Dr O'Reilly said: 'From Belfast to Bantry Bay I have seen miracles wrought by people of great heart who are fighting unemployment, homelessness, bigotry, despair and neglect.'

IRISH-AMERICAN UNITY CONFERENCE
Irish-American group which has been critical of British policy in Ireland. In January 1988 its chairman Jim Delaney was also opposed to the Republic's Government's changed attitude to extradition and 'heavy tactics' by its security forces in searching for arms. About the same time, its publicity director Gerry Coleman, on a visit to Belfast, said the group would make an in-depth study of the operation of the International Fund for Ireland because he did not find it helping people in deprived Nationalist areas. The organisation has helped to raise money for some job-creation projects in NI which have been refused Government assistance. Active in lobbying President-elect Clinton in 1992. In the aftermath of the 1993 Downing Street Declaration it supported the PSF demand for 'clarification' and criticised the British Government.

IRISH ASSOCIATION FOR CULTURAL, ECONOMIC AND SOCIAL RELATIONS
Founded on an all-Ireland basis in 1938 to bring together people of differing religious and political views. Idea originated with Maj.-Gen. Hugh Montgomery, of Fivemiletown, Co. Tyrone, and its first president was the liberal-minded Lord Charlemont, a former NI Education Minister. The association was largely inactive during World War II. Since then it has organised regular addresses by leading politicians,

academics and Churchmen. Current
President is Professor Paul Bew of QUB.

IRISH DIMENSION

A term which came into popular usage in
1973, when the Conservative
Government published its Green Paper
on NI. It was used to denote the desire of
the bulk of the Catholic minority for an
eventual united Ireland. It was a counter-
balance to the British Dimension, the
term used to describe the Unionist
attachment to Britain. It was reflected in
the plan for a Council of Ireland, which
emerged in the Sunningdale Agreement,
and which attracted the fierce opposition
of loyalists. The scheme foundered with
the collapse of the power-sharing
Executive in 1974, but found strong
expression in the AIA in 1985. Its future
shape was one of the contentious issues in
the Brooke–Mayhew Talks.

IRISH INDEPENDENCE PARTY

Party launched in 1977 which sought a
British withdrawal from NI to prepare the
way for negotiation of NI's future status in
Ireland. Its main initial tactic was to seek
agreed anti-Unionist candidates in
Westminster elections. The leading
figures in the new group were former
Unity MP for Fermanagh-S. Tyrone,
Frank McManus, and Fergus McAteer,
the Derry Nationalist and son of former
Nationalist leader Eddie McAteer, who
had also expressed support for some move
towards independence. Its main support
was drawn from W. Ulster, N. Antrim,
and S. Down, and it attracted the interest
of several Independent and Nationalist
councillors. In the Westminster election
in May 1979 it ran four candidates, and
secured 3.3 per cent of the total vote,
with the best showing by Pat Fahy in
Mid-Ulster with a vote of 12,055. Soon
afterwards, Fahy was appointed party
leader with McManus deputy leader, and
McAteer chairman. The party improved
its share of the vote to 3.9 per cent in the
1981 council elections, but opted out of
the 1982 Assembly elections because of
its intense opposition to the 'rolling
devolution' scheme. Its showing was
seriously affected by the electoral
participation of PSF from 1982, and in the

1985 council elections it took only 1.1
per cent of the votes and four seats. It did
not contest the 1989 council election.

IRISH NATIONAL CAUCUS

The American umbrella group for the
majority of Irish-American organisations.
It embraces the Gaelic Athletic
Association and the AAOH, Irish county
associations, and scores of local bodies in
New York, Boston, Philadelphia, and
other US cities with strong Irish-
American links. In 1978 it sent a three-
man inquiry team to NI, headed by its
national co-ordinator, Father Sean
McManus (brother of ex-MP Frank
McManus), which urged a 'peace forum'
on NI in Washington and reported to this
effect to the *ad hoc* Congressional
Committee on Irish affairs. The visiting
team had talks with the IRA, UDA, UVF
and some other loyalist organisations, and
said that paramilitary organisations must
be included in any search for a solution.
In 1978 Jack Lynch, as Taoiseach of the
Republic, attacked the Caucus for giving
support to the PIRA, but spokesmen of the
Caucus have insisted that it has no
connection with any organisation outside
the US, and that it has been cleared of any
suspicion of support of violence by FBI
and other inquiries. In the 1980
presidential election, it claimed as a
victory the call for Irish unity in the
Democratic platform. But it failed to get
any commitment from the Republicans,
and was clearly disappointed by the
election of Ronald Reagan. In 1985 the
INC mounted an extensive campaign
against a new US–UK extradition treaty
which could affect the position of
terrorist suspects in America because it
removed the 'political' defence hitherto
available. But the treaty, which had the
support of President Reagan, was cleared
by the Senate in 1986. The INC then
turned its attention to requiring US firms
operating in NI to adopt stringent new
rules known as the 'MacBride Principles'
to force the companies to employ more
Catholics. In 1987 and 1988 it had several
successes in securing legislative backing
for the policy in several states, against
British lobbying in other states. In the
run-up to the 1988 presidential election,

however, the Caucus was able to point to Democratic contender Michael Dukakis, Governor of Massachusetts, as the first Governor to sign 'MacBride' into State law. At the end of 1988 it criticised the new Fair Employment Bill as 'too little too late'. In 1990, Father McManus complained that the FBI was trying to link PIRA to racist crimes. In 1991 he rejected a claim by Peter Brooke that the Caucus failed to condemn PIRA violence. In July 1991 he criticised the UDR merger with the Royal Irish Rangers as 'inadequate' and protested that new US legislation would allow the holding of 'secret courts' to deport Irish-Americans. In 1992 he said the Clinton victory was 'a historic development in the MacBride campaign'.

IRISH NATIONAL LIBERATION ARMY

An illegal Republican paramilitary group set up in 1975 as the military wing of the IRSP and which rapidly gained a reputation for ruthlessness. Its initial strength derived mainly from ex-OIRA members angry at the OIRA ceasefire in 1972, and it is believed to have gained recruits from PIRA during its ceasefire in 1975, when its members were active in the feud between the OIRA and the IRSP. One of its first acts was to kill OIRA commander Billy McMillen in Belfast in April 1975. Its main support has come from the Lower Falls and Markets areas in Belfast, and from parts of Co. Derry, notably S. Derry. Many of its attacks have been on members of the security forces, but it first attracted world attention when it claimed to have placed the car bomb which killed Conservative NI spokesman Airey Neave at Westminster in March 1979. In a statement issued through a Belfast office of IRSP it said that he had been specifically selected for assassination because of his 'rabid militarist calls for more repression against the Irish people'. INLA also said that its primary aim was to secure a British military, political and economic withdrawal from Ireland, and it denied that it was a cover group for PIRA. In fact, PIRA members tended to talk of INLA as 'wild men'. It was declared illegal throughout the UK in July 1979, when NI Secretary of State Humphrey Atkins told

Parliament that it was engaged in violence and contacts with terrorist groups abroad. Government security experts claimed that it was getting arms, including the Russian AK-47 rifle, from the Middle East. In the succeeding years INLA stepped up its activities. It was said to be responsible for nearly thirty deaths in NI in 1982. Seventeen of these were caused by the bombing on 6 December of the Droppin' Well pub at Ballykelly, Co. Derry. Eleven of the victims were off-duty soldiers stationed nearby and most of the others local people. It was the second-highest death toll in any incident during the Troubles, being exceeded only by the Warrenpoint bombing in 1979. In the 1981 H-Block hunger strike, three INLA prisoners died. In the later stages of the protest, Belfast IRSP councillor Sean Flynn said they could not replace hunger-strikers at the same rate as previously, since INLA had only 28 prisoners against PIRA's 380 (see H-Blocks). A period of internal disagreement coincided with the hunger strike, and the injuring of Harry Flynn, press officer of the IRSP, in a machine-gun attack in Dublin was believed to be associated with the feud. The differences were apparently patched up as the operation of informers gave rise to mass arrests of INLA members in 1982. In July 1982 the IRSP publication, *Starry Plough*, denied that there was any split between IRSP and INLA and it also said that the INLA structure had been reformed with a new chief of staff from NI. In September 1982 it brought strong criticism from residents in the Divis Flats in the lower Falls area of Belfast, when it set off a bomb which killed two local boys of eleven and fourteen and a soldier. The flats were regarded as one of INLA's main strongholds. In a statement in September 1982 it said certain Unionist politicians were on a 'hit list' because they had been responsible for inciting the murders of 700 innocent Catholics over the previous ten years. In January 1982 it claimed to have shot dead E. Belfast loyalist John McKeague. In March 1981 it shot and seriously wounded Belfast UDA councillor Sammy Millar at his Shankill Road home. In October 1981 it killed a senior Belfast UDA man, Billy

McCullough, in retaliation, it said, for recent loyalist murders of Catholics. In May 1982 it placed a powerful blast incendiary bomb at the Lisburn home of DUP Assembly member Rev. William Beattie but it was detected before it went off. Soon afterwards, INLA shot and seriously wounded Belfast DUP councillor Billy Dickson (an Assembly candidate) at his home. In January 1983 the Republic's Government proscribed the organisation, which meant that conviction for membership could result in up to seven years' imprisonment. The organisation was said to have committed 'particularly vicious outrages' both north and south of the border and in London. In the Republic INLA was suspected of the murder of a Garda in Co. Dublin in early 1982. In September that year it blew up the radar station at Schull, Co. Cork and it was also thought to have carried out a series of armed robberies in the Republic during 1982. On 25 November 1981 an INLA bomb exploded at a British army camp at Herford, West Germany, but caused no injuries. A similar bomb had failed to explode at the British Consulate in Hamburg the day before. INLA recruited dissident PIRA members from time to time, and one of these was Dominic McGlinchey, who is reputed to have taken over the leadership of the organisation at the point of a gun, and who was to make legal history when he was extradited from the Republic in 1982. (He was later re-extradited when a murder charge failed.) The supergrass system dealt a body blow to INLA – twenty-seven alleged members were convicted on the evidence of supergrass Harry Kirkpatrick. Although all but two had their convictions quashed on appeal in 1986, the authorities acquired a great deal of intelligence in the process. The releases also sparked off new problems since there were sharp differences among the former accused, which were to result in a bloody internal feud. Between December 1986 and March 1987, twelve people died and several were injured as a breakaway group styling itself the Irish People's Liberation Organisation (and also the INLA Army Council) sought to force the dissolution of the organisation. The

succession of murders caused such horror in the Nationalist community that two W. Belfast priests, Father Gerry Reynolds and Father Arthur Reid, became involved in March 1987 as mediators, and eventually secured a truce. IPLO leader Gerard Steenson was among those shot dead by INLA GHQ gunmen. One of the victims of the IPLO was Thomas Power, whose prison writings were claimed to provide a missing political element for INLA. Mary McGlinchey, wife of Dominic, was shot dead during the feud, but apparently for reasons unconnected with it. By late 1987 a reorganised INLA was said to have some fifty activists, and in August 1988 one of its members was shot dead by the security forces in an attack on a border post at Clady, Co. Tyrone. 'Border Fox' Dessie O'Hare, jailed in the Republic on a kidnapping charge, had been prominent in INLA before his expulsion in September 1987. He and another man died as a result of a Garda shoot-out in Co. Kilkenny in November 1987. The ending of the IPLO feud was followed by a period of low-level activity by INLA. In August 1988 it shot dead a Shankill Road shopkeeper who, it alleged, was a top UVF man. And in 1989 it attacked some army checkpoints in the North-West and carried out some punishment beatings in Strabane. But this contrasted sharply with its high profile in earlier years. In 1981, for example, it killed more people than PIRA. In 1990, however, INLA was beginning to reactivate its organisation, and at the same time was warning journalists not to confuse it with IPLO. In November 1990 a Strabane INLA member, Alexander Patterson, was shot dead by the SAS near Victoria Bridge, and it was alleged that he had, in fact, tipped off police about a planned attack on a UDR man's home nearby. His family denied suggestions that he had been working for the Special Branch. In June 1991 INLA said it had shot dead Gerard Anthony Burns in W. Belfast because he had been a Special Branch informer since 1988. In March 1992 it claimed the killing of a Belfast taxi driver, and the following month said it had shot dead an army recruiting sergeant in Derby. In

January 1993 it tried to kill a former leading UVF man in N. Belfast. Former leader Dominic McGlinchey was shot dead in February 1994 in Drogheda. The murder was not claimed by any group but it was attributed by some to a long-standing feud that may have been linked to the murder of his wife Mary in 1987. The funeral oration was given by Bernadette McAliskey. (*See also* Irish People's Liberation Organisation *and* Irish Republican Socialist Party.)

IRISH NORTHERN AID COMMITTEE

The US-based committee, usually known as NORAID, established in 1969 for the declared purpose of providing funds for the relief of families deprived of wage-earners because of the struggle against Britain. The body has been at the centre of angry controversy since its inception. The money raised – probably around $5 million by 1987 – has been handled in Ireland by people associated with PSF, and there have been frequent allegations that some of the money is siphoned off, either in Dublin or in the US, for the purchase of arms for PIRA. NORAID spokesmen have denied this, and PSF has retorted that PIRA has its own means of raising money. British and Irish Government Ministers, on visits to the US, have warned people not to help NORAID. The organisation has about a hundred local groups in centres with substantial Irish-American populations, such as New York, Boston, Philadelphia and Chicago, and it makes no secret of its anti-British stance. In 1977 the organisation was required, as a result of a case brought by the Justice Department, to register as an agent of PIRA under the Foreign Agents' Act. Although this meant that it had to give more detailed information about its activities, it was not a serious obstacle to its operations. NORAID claims that the money it raises is distributed through PSF in Dublin and the Green Cross in Belfast. The organisation got a big fillip from the H-Block hunger strike in 1981, when its income was around $400,000. In 1987 it declared its transfers to Ireland at $200,000. In November 1982 the chairman and founder of NORAID,

Michael Flannery, then aged eighty, was one of five men acquitted in New York of conspiracy to supply arms to PIRA. The accused pleaded successfully before a jury that the CIA were aware of the activities of their supplier, and were involved in monitoring the supply of arms to PIRA. Flannery, an IRA man in the 1920s, said that while he had not been personally involved in gun-running to PIRA, such activity would have his blessing. He also denied that NORAID money had been used for buying arms. He was at the centre of controversy when he was chosen to head the New York St Patrick's Day parade in 1983. But the veteran Republican left the organisation in 1988 in protest at the PSF decision to take Dáil seats if elected. At the same time the organisation has had to cope with the situation created by the AIA, which has proved attractive to many Irish-Americans and added to NORAID's fund-raising problems. In recent years publicity director Martin Galvin has become the best-known NORAID figure, particularly because of his repeated defiance of a Government order banning him from NI. He first defied the ban in 1984, when the RUC made an unsuccessful bid to arrest him at a W. Belfast rally, during which Sean Downes was killed by a plastic baton round fired by an RUC officer at close range. In 1985 he was at the funeral in Derry of a PIRA man, and in 1987 he visited the relatives of eight PIRA men shot dead by the security forces at Loughgall, Co. Armagh. He is on record as condemning the killing of civilians in incidents such as the Harrods bombing in London in 1983, but he has defended PIRA attacks on security forces. In December 1989 Galvin crossed into Fermanagh at Lackey Bridge and joined farmers who were reopening a blocked border road. He failed in an appeal against the NI ban, but it was withdrawn in April 1990, when he claimed Irish citizenship. In June 1991 he attended the funeral of a PIRA member shot dead by the security forces at Coagh. (In October 1990 Peter Brooke commented that NORAID was now 'less significant' in PIRA funding.) In November 1989 a split developed in

NORAID and a rival breakaway group, Friends of Irish Freedom, was set up. Michael Hurley, a former NORAID leader in Boston, said the new body would keep to the original principles of NORAID, including acting as a support group for Republican prisoners and their families. A NORAID spokesman dismissed the new group as 'schismatic' and said it had been formed against the express wishes of the Republican movement. In August 1991 House of Representatives Speaker Tom Foley said during his Irish trip that NORAID was a 'disgusting charade'. In the 1992 Presidential election, NORAID backed Bill Clinton. Its paper, the *Irish People*, said US foreign policy under Clinton 'will no longer be an appendage of British policy'.

IRISH PEOPLE'S LIBERATION ORGANISATION

The INLA faction which tried in 1986-7 to force the disbandment of IRSP–INLA – a move which led to a bitter feud and to the killings of twelve people over a three-month period. When a truce was finally arranged in March 1987, through the mediation of two Belfast priests, IPLO had failed in its aim, and it then continued as a separate organisation and held a convention in Galway in May 1987. In the same year, using the cover-name of Catholic Reaction Force, it claimed the fatal shooting of Belfast loyalist George Seawright. In August 1988 it admitted several explosions in Belfast, and the sending of letter bombs to Rev. William McCrea MP and Ken Maginnis MP which were defused. In October 1988 the organisation was accused by PIRA of unprovoked attacks on people in W. Belfast and warned that PIRA might intervene. IPLO was suspected in the late 1980s of being involved mainly in drug-dealing and in sectarian murders. It denied the drugs allegation, but admitted having a 'hit list' of loyalist paramilitaries. In January 1990 the Republic's Government added it to the list of organisations to which the broadcasting ban applied, and it was proscribed in NI two months later. Around that time, one of its members was arrested in Holland as the security forces investigated reports

that it was seeking to buy arms on the Continent. Another was shot dead by PIRA in Newry as an alleged informer while one of its members was killed by the security forces in N. Armagh. In 1991 it killed five people, none of whom was involved with the security forces. One victim was Belfast businessman John McMaster, who was in the Royal Naval Reserve, which has no operational role in NI. IPLO man Martin O'Prey, who was murdered by the UVF at his Belfast home in August 1991, was said to have been linked to McMaster's murder and also to the killing of loyalist George Seawright. PIRA was clearly unhappy at IPLO tactics, but at the end of 1991 it denied giving a seventy-two-hour warning to IPLO to cease operations, and suggested British Intelligence might be at work. In the summer of 1992, it emerged that a bitter feud had developed within IPLO between members who considered themselves as the 'Army Council' and those in the 'Belfast Brigade'. Jimmy Brown, who had led IPLO since 1987 and also spoke for its political wing, the Republican Socialist Collective, was the first victim of the feud when he was shot dead on the Falls Road in Belfast in August 1992 with the same gun that had killed McMaster. Soon afterwards a Gaelic football player said to be in IPLO was shot dead as he left a playing field at Hannahstown, and in September 1992 a man who was believed to have 'some association' with IPLO was murdered in the Whiterock area. At the end of October 1992 PIRA was believed to have used some hundred members in a bid to disperse IPLO on the grounds that it was heavily involved in drug-dealing. One IPLO member, Samuel Ward, was killed and several others were wounded. Within a week, both factions had announced their disbandment, but in December 1992 PIRA was threatening 'military action' against 'IPLO gangs' which it said were returning to Belfast and dealing again in drugs. IPLO's main strength has been in the Divis area of Belfast. (*See also* Irish National Liberation Army *and* Irish Republican Socialist Party.)

IRISH REPUBLICAN SOCIALIST PARTY

Formed December 1974 and essentially a breakaway group from Official Sinn Féin plus dissidents from PIRA unhappy at their freshly declared ceasefire. By March 1975 they were claiming some 700 members in Belfast. Their best-known personality at that time was former Mid-Ulster MP Bernadette McAliskey, who with other leaders insisted that it did not have a military wing. Its founder was Seamus Costello, who was shot dead in Dublin in 1977. At first it seemed that the group would fight elections, with Bernadette McAliskey a possible candidate for the Convention, but they decided to boycott the election. In early 1975 there was a bitter feud between the OIRA and the IRSP, with claims of assassinations on both sides. When Cathal Goulding, chief of staff of the OIRA, spoke at the funeral of Sean Fox of the OIRA in Belfast's Milltown cemetery in February 1975, he supported the OIRA claim that Fox had been shot by the IRSP. And he described the IRSP as 'a few misguided and confused malcontents'. The feud was a particularly vicious one, and involved shootings both north and south of the border. A leading Official Republican in Belfast, Billy McMillen, shot dead in Belfast in April 1975, was said to be one of the victims. At one point, the IRSP temporarily disbanded its Belfast organisation and Dublin Senator Michael Mullen acted as intermediary in a bid to stop the inter-factional shootings. When it was registered as a political party in the Republic in May 1975, it claimed nearly 400 members in NI. In September 1975 it denied any link with the South Armagh Republican Action Force, which had claimed killings at an Orange Hall in Newtownhamilton. But in 1976, 1977 and 1978 the security authorities alleged that the IRSP's military wing, the Irish National Liberation Army, had been responsible for several murders and attempted murders. In December 1977 there were clear indications that the IRSP was moving closer to PSF, many of whose members attended Seamus Costello's funeral in October. INLA claimed in 1982 that Costello had been shot by a member

of OIRA. Certainly, the 1981 hunger strike brought closer co-operation with PSF, although the IRSP has always regarded itself as being to the left of the Provisionals. In the 1981 council elections, it took two seats in Belfast but, unlike PSF, it opted out of the 1982 Assembly election. There was further convulsion in the IRSP–INLA network between 1983 and 1987 when senior figures were implicated by supergrasses. When twenty-five of those accused on the word of INLA informer Harry Kirkpatrick were freed at the end of 1986, a struggle for power within INLA led to the feud in which twelve people died. A faction calling itself the Irish People's Liberation Organisation tried to force the disbandment of IRSP–INLA but failed in the end and went its own way. In 1987 the reformed IRSP–INLA reportedly began to concentrate on developing a political philosophy with a Marxist-Leninist slant, while building links with revolutionary groups like the French Action Directe. At an IRSP rally in Derry in October 1988 party spokesman Kevin McQuillan said that draconian laws would not demoralise people: 'We would contend that the opposite will be the case.' Several leading party personalities were excluded from GB under the PTA in 1990. (*See also* Irish National Liberation Army *and* Irish People's Liberation Organisation.)

J

JELLICOE REPORT *see* Security System section, p. 454

JOHN, BRYNMORE THOMAS

British Labour Party spokesman on NI, June 1979–80. b. 18 April 1934; d. 1988. LLB (London). Solicitor. Labour MP for Pontypridd, 1970–88. Parliamentary Under-Secretary, Defence, 1974–6; Minister of State, Home Affairs, 1976–9. Defence spokesman, 1980.

JUSTICE WATCH

A US-based human rights group to monitor the NI situation set up in December 1990 by Congressman Joseph

Kennedy and Ray Flynn, the Mayor of Boston, who was appointed Ambassador to the Vatican in 1993.

K

KANE, ALAN JAMES

DUP Assembly member for Mid-Ulster, 1982-6. Youngest member of Assembly; served on Education and Finance and Personnel scrutiny committees. b. 1958. Barrister. Cookstown Council, 1981-93; chairman, 1985-91. Former general Secretary of DUP. In 1987 he urged withdrawal of support from RUC once new public-order laws became effective, declaring that NI was 'beginning to look like a police state'. One of three councillors who resigned from DUP in 1992 in protest at talks with Irish Ministers.

KELLY, LORD JUSTICE SIR (JOHN WILLIAM) BASIL

Judge of NI High Court, 1973-, and NI Attorney-General, 1968-72. b. 10 May 1920. LLB Hons. (TCD). QC, 1958. Unionist MP for Mid-Down at Stormont, 1964-72, and senior Crown Counsel in Tyrone, Fermanagh and Armagh before becoming Attorney-General. He had a key role as law officer of the NI Government in the civil rights period and in the months preceding the imposition of direct rule. In a debate in the NI Commons in 1969, he stated that Westminster had the power to interfere with the powers of the NI Parliament, but that it would be against convention to do so. But he stressed that law was stronger than convention. In May 1971 he was accused by opposition MPs of showing political bias in ordering court prosecutions. But an opposition motion to this effect was rejected by twenty-five votes to nine. In 1983 he presided at a trial of thirty-eight people implicated in PIRA terrorism by supergrass Christopher Black and passed sentences totalling 4,000 years. In 1986 the Court of Appeal quashed the convictions of eighteen of those convicted.

KENNEDY, DENNIS

Head of NI office of the EC Commission, 1985-91. b. Lisburn, 3 August 1936. BA (QUB); Ph.D. (TCD). Previous career mainly journalistic in Ireland, US, and Ethiopia. Chief leader writer, *Belfast Telegraph,* 1964-6. *Irish Times* diplomatic correspondent, 1969, and deputy editor, 1983-5. Wrote mainly on diplomatic, European and Third World affairs, 'with occasional commentaries on NI problem in marked contrast to traditional sentimental nationalism of *Irish Times*'. In 1991, he visited Iraq and Iran to report to EC on the plight of Kurdish refugees. Consultant to NIO on claim for EC aid, 1994-. Author, *The Widening Gulf: Northern Attitudes to the Independent Irish State 1919-49.*

KENNEDY, EDWARD

One of group of Irish-Americans who have been keenly interested in NI situation. b. 22 February 1932. Brother of late President John F. Kennedy. Senator (Teddy) Kennedy's attitude to NI has altered with the growth of PIRA violence. In October 1971 he spoke in Congress in support of a motion calling for the immediate withdrawal of British troops and the calling of a conference of all parties for the purpose of establishing a united Ireland. He argued that this was the only realistic way to bring peace, but his remarks were strongly criticised within NI, especially by Unionists and the Alliance Party. US official spokesmen stressed that Senator Kennedy was not reflecting US Government policy. But he repeated his plea for withdrawal of troops in 1972, saying that they had become a symbol of Protestant supremacy, and he vigorously attacked internment without trial, which he regarded as discriminating against Catholics. When the power-sharing Executive fell in 1974, he described it as a tragedy for the cause of peace in NI, and said Britain could not yield to the tactics of extremists. He has repeatedly advised Irish-Americans not to give moral or financial support to terrorists. In 1977 he joined with other Irish-American leaders to sponsor a call for peace in NI, and he was among those who urged President Carter to promise

US economic aid for NI in the event of a political settlement. The President did this in August 1977. Kennedy took a strong united Ireland line during his unsuccessful campaign for the Democratic presidential nomination in 1980. He was one of the founders in 1981 of the Friends of Ireland group made up of leading Irish-American politicians and in 1983 was one of the sponsors of a Senate motion calling for a united Ireland. He has used his influence to secure support for both the NIF report and the AIA, and has maintained close contacts with Irish Governments. On a visit to Dublin in November 1988 he said the general impression among Irish-Americans was that the AIA had been slow to achieve progress in the areas of fair employment and the administration of justice in NI. In February 1992 he appealed to President Bush to raise with PM Major human rights 'violations' in NI.

KENNEDY, JOHN ANDREW DUNN
Clerk to the NI Assembly, 1982–6. b. Derry, 1934. Barrister. Served on NI Parliamentary staffs, 1962–72, Assembly, 1973–4, and Convention, 1975–6. Head of Office of Law Reform, Stormont, 1976–82. Although the Assembly ceased to function in 1986, he retained the office of Clerk.

KENNEDY, JOSEPH
US Congressman for Massachusetts, son of late Senator Robert Kennedy. b. 24 September 1952. BA (University of Massachusetts). During visit to NI in April 1988 his criticisms of British policy brought unfavourable comments from British press. He accused Britain of not doing enough to counter anti-Catholic discrimination in jobs. He also spoke of the need to encourage non-violent change, but commented that those individuals who had chosen violence as a means to political change 'do so as a direct result of the prejudice and seeming intractability of the British position'. In 1992 he called on White House to intervene more directly in promoting reconciliation in NI and to cease issuing 'well-meaning platitudes'. He urged President Bush to send a special peace

envoy to NI – an idea taken up by President Clinton during his election campaign. In December 1992 he said the PIRA bombing campaign was 'only pulling the people of NI further apart'. He made the point in a letter to PSF president Gerry Adams. At the end of February 1994, he attended, with other members of the Kennedy family, the appeal by Paul Hill, one of the Guildford Four, in Belfast.

KENNEDY, DR LAURENCE
Chairman of NI Area Conservatives, 1989–90, and primarily responsible for success of the campaign to persuade the Conservative Party to organise in NI. b. 24 January 1948. MB, B.Ch., BAO, MD (Belfast), FRCP (London), FRCP (Edinburgh). He sought recognition in 1988 of the N. Down 'model' Conservative Association formed in June, but the idea was rejected by the party conference. In 1989, however, the conference accepted the principle of organising in NI and in November the National Union accepted the affiliation of the association after six Conservative councillors had been elected in N. Down, among them Dr Kennedy, who led the party group on the council. In the 1989 European election, he got 25,789 votes, fewer than Alliance, and which he claimed as a 'very creditable performance' in the then absence of an NI-wide organisation. In the 1992 general election, his showing in N. Down was the best of the eleven Tory candidates in the field. He took 32 per cent of the vote and was runner-up to veteran MP Sir James Kilfedder (UPUP). He voiced doubts about the format of the Brooke–Mayhew Talks and has repeatedly supported integration. He has also contested the idea that a Conservative Secretary of State should be neutral in NI affairs. In 1991 four men held his wife and family hostage at his Holywood home in an attempt on his life. Resigned as a councillor on 27 July 1993 as a result of the Cons./UUP 'understanding'. He accused his party leader of conniving in the 'perpetuation of religiously divisive politics'. At the end of September four men were convicted

of attempting to murder him in November 1991. In January 1994 it was announced that he was to take up a new medical position in Scotland.

KENNEDY, PATRICK

Republican Labour MP for Belfast Central, 1969–72. b. 1943. Became leader of Republican Labour Party when Gerry Fitt MP left in 1970 to head the newly formed SDLP. He had been prominent in opposition protests against the Unionist Government in 1969, and in support of the civil rights campaign. In June 1969 he declared that if extreme Unionists were going to police their side of Belfast, 'we must do something to police our end of the city'. In September 1969 he flew to London in CCDC deputation for a meeting with Home Secretary James Callaghan to discuss the tension over demands for removal of barricades in W. Belfast. In 1970 he refused to join the SDLP, and in July 1971 he withdrew from Stormont, and soon afterwards introduced Joe Cahill as leader of the PIRA at a Belfast news conference. He failed to secure election to the Assembly in 1973 as a candidate in W. Belfast. In a television programme in 1992 he admitted to intimate knowledge about money and arms supplied by Dublin in 1969.

KEOGH, MICHAEL

Nationalist MP for S. Down, 1967–72. When editor of the former Newry weekly newspaper, *Frontier Sentinel*, he retained the seat for the Nationalist Party in a by-election in 1967, with a majority of 5,627 over a Unionist candidate. In the 1969 general election, when no Unionist stood, his majority over a PD candidate was 220. In 1972 he took a strong line against PIRA bombing in Newry, which he said was hitting severely at community relations in the town.

KERNOHAN, (THOMAS) HUGH

Ombudsman and Commissioner of Complaints, NI, 1980–7. b. 11 May 1932. Official (latterly Secretary) of NI Employers' Association, 1953–80. In August 1982 a Westminster select committee praised Kernohan's work and

said he seemed to be 'trusted equally by all sectors of the population'.

KIDD, SIR ROBERT HILL

Head of the NI civil service, 1976–9. b. 3 February 1918. BA, B.Litt. (TCD). Served in army in World War II. Joined NI civil service in 1947; second Secretary in Department of Finance, 1969–76, with rank of Permanent Secretary. In 1980 he carried out a review of NI's industrial incentives. Active in Co-operation North movement.

KILFEDDER, SIR JAMES

MP for N. Down, 1970–. (UUP, 1970–9; UPUP, 1979–.) Speaker, NI Assembly, 1982–6. b. Kinlough, Co. Leitrim, 16 July 1928. BA (TCD). Gave up his London barrister's practice when he entered Parliament. He was MP for W. Belfast, 1964–6, and during that time he was for a period Secretary of the Unionist MPs, and of a number of Conservative committees, including that on NI. He has always pursued a highly individualistic course, and in 1977 he parted from the other Official Unionist MPs at Westminster, complaining that Enoch Powell was dictating policy. In early 1979 he finally broke with the UUP after an exchange of letters with party leader Harry West. In the 1979 election he was opposed by Clifford Smyth for the UUP, but held the seat easily. Apparently, his devotion to constituency work has been the key to his success, since he was able to beat off an earlier challenge in the February 1974 election when Roy Bradford stood against him as a Pro-Assembly Unionist. He topped the poll in N. Down in the Assembly contests of 1973 and 1982, and also in the Convention election. His first-preference vote in 1973 of 20,684 was the largest of the whole election. In the 1979 European election, which he fought as 'Ulster Unionist', he got over 38,000 first-preference votes, and on the sixth count he was runner-up to John Taylor (UUP), last of the three successful candidates. (In the 1984 European election he lost his deposit.) In 1979 he founded the Ulster Progressive Unionist Party, but the party name was changed to Ulster Popular Unionist Party in 1980 because of confusion with the PUP. Although he was critical of the 'rolling devolution' scheme, he accepted nomination as Speaker of the 1982 Assembly. He was elected by DUP and Alliance votes, with the UUP opposing, and his Speaker's salary of £18,000, together with his Westminster salary, made him the the UK's best-paid politician. In the 1983 Westminster election he held off, without the use of posters, a strong challenge from UUP and Alliance in the reduced N. Down constituency. In the 1986 by-election he had a 22,000 majority over Alliance, but this dropped to 3,953 in the 1987 general election, when Robert McCartney QC, standing as a 'Real Unionist', was runner-up, with Alliance in third place. He resented the Conservative decision to oppose him in N. Down at the 1992 general election, since he had frequently backed the Thatcher and Major Governments in key votes, and was the only NI MP to back Poll Tax. His annoyance was shared by eighty Tory backbenchers. In the event, he defeated the challenge of Dr Laurence Kennedy (Cons.) by some 5,000 votes in a five-cornered contest. In the crucial Maastricht Treaty Commons vote in November 1992, he was the only NI MP, apart from the absent Martin Smyth, not to vote against the Government. The longest-serving NI MP, he was knighted in 1992. In March 1994 he was named as one of the thirteen members of the NI Select Committee, and there was speculation that he might chair it.

KINAHAN, CHARLES

Alliance Convention member for S. Antrim, 1975–6. b. Belfast, 1915. Brother of Sir Robin Kinahan, Unionist MP for Clifton at Stormont, 1958–9. Unsuccessfully contested S. Antrim Westminster seat in February and October 1974. Vice-chairman, Alliance Party, 1978. Antrim Borough Council, 1973–85.

KING, GENERAL SIR FRANK DOUGLAS

Army GOC, NI, February 1973–August 1975. b. 9 March 1919. He arrived in NI at a time when sectarian assassinations were running at a high rate. But his most testing time came in 1974, when the loyalist strike, which led to the downfall of the power-sharing Executive, posed new problems for the army. Some Executive Ministers and many opponents of the stoppage accused the army of not moving swiftly in the first few days of the strike to dismantle UDA and other loyalist barricades. There were also complaints that the army was reluctant to take on oil distribution when petrol supplies were halted by the strikers, and disappointment that the army did not have the expertise to run the power stations. There was a widespread belief that General King was not anxious that troops should become involved in strike-breaking activities. After he left NI, he said in an interview that 'if you get a large section of the population which is bent on a particular course, then it is a difficult thing to stop them taking that course'. General King also provoked controversy in April 1975, when he said in a speech in Nottingham that the phased release of internees could help the PIRA. Since the statement came at a moment when the PIRA ceasefire was showing signs of petering out, and politicians were preparing for the Convention elections, the comment was highly unwelcome to the Government. It pleased loyalists, dismayed the SDLP, and brought the remark from PSF that the army wanted to show the British Government who was boss. General King claimed that his words had been taken out of context, since what he meant was that 'in a ceasefire situation it is obviously necessary to take steps to bring about a situation of normality without lowering our guard'.

KING, THOMAS JEREMY (TOM)

NI Secretary of State, September 1985–July 1989 (making him longest-serving NI Secretary of State); Defence Secretary, 1989–92. Successively held three Cabinet offices (Environment, Transport and Employment) before moving to NI. MP for Bridgewater, 1970–. b. 13 June 1933. He had some familiarity with NI as a businessman and shadow Energy Secretary before his

Cabinet appointments and arrival at Stormont in 1985. He inherited the negotiations over the AIA at an advanced stage, and in less than two months he had to face the wrath of Unionists when it was signed at Hillsborough on 15 November 1985. A few days after the signing, he was physically attacked by loyalists outside Belfast City Hall. In an apparent attempt to sell the accord to Unionists, he stressed his own Unionist convictions, and disclosed that he had urged the Irish Government to drop the claim to NI in the Irish Constitution. On 4 December 1985, on a visit to Brussels, he embarrassed Margaret Thatcher when he said that Dr FitzGerald, by signing the AIA, 'has in fact accepted that for all practical purposes and into perpetuity there will never be a united Ireland'. Dr FitzGerald attacked the comment as 'inaccurate', and King apologised in the Commons. Thus, there were some doubts in Nationalist circles about King's level of enthusiasm for the AIA. But his general approach was to defend it strongly and to point to the 473–47 vote by which the agreement was endorsed at Westminster, and to challenge Unionists, whose attitude he described as 'misconceived and negative', to enter into dialogue with him. He shrugged off massive demonstrations against the agreement, as well as the fifteen protest by-elections in January 1986, which showed an increase in the overall Unionist vote. Indeed, King took encouragement from the 10.8 per cent swing in the Nationalist vote against PSF since 1983. Unionist 'withdrawal of consent' from the Government and boycott of Ministers, together with a virtual halt to business in loyalist-controlled councils and abstention of most Unionist MPs from Westminster, did not greatly hamper his administrative task. When the 3 March 1986 Unionist 'day of action' against the AIA produced violence and intimidation, King accused Unionist MPs of making common cause with paramilitaries, despite the clear condemnation of the violence by Unionist leaders. But while steadily denying to Unionists any suspension of the AIA as a basis for renewed talks, he

also faced pressure from the Irish Government for action to meet Nationalist grievances. In particular, Dublin was concerned about delay in reshaping Diplock non-jury courts by having three judges instead of one, but Irish Ministers gradually accepted that the RUC was showing impartiality in the handling of loyalist parades. The Stormont Assembly, launched by James Prior, was wound up in June 1986 by King, who obviously resented the fact that it had become a platform for Unionist attacks on Government policy. In February 1987 the return to office in the Republic of Fianna Fáil, led by Charles Haughey, created a new situation for King. Indeed, Haughey, as opposition leader, had cited King's Brussels speech as vindicating his own criticism of the AIA, and there was uncertainty as to how far the new Irish Government would work the agreement. In the event, Haughey, who led a minority Government, said he would adhere to an international agreement, but he was clearly looking for tangible results from it. King's attitude reflected the desire of Margaret Thatcher that there should be effective extradition of terrorist suspects from the Republic, but Fianna Fáil questioned the quality of justice in Britain and particularly in NI, and when it supported a Dáil vote on extradition it was with the proviso that the Irish Attorney-General should have a flavour of the evidence in advance. Late 1987 and early 1988 produced a variety of other security-related issues which saw King at variance with Irish Ministers in the Ministerial Conference. These included the refusal to prosecute RUC officers allegedly involved in 'shoot to kill' incidents in Co. Armagh in 1982, the rejection of the appeal of the Birmingham Six, and the continuing argument about the courts in NI. But King had the satisfaction of getting strong backing from the Republic for action to prevent arms landed from Libya being used by PIRA. Meanwhile, in 1987 the Unionist leaders had begun tentative 'talks about talks' with King aimed, they said, at finding out whether the British Government was prepared to consider a replacement for the AIA as a preliminary to serious political talks. King was unable to satisfy Unionist wishes, and in mid-1988 opened talks with the SDLP. In July 1988 he retained his post in a Cabinet reshuffle when his length of service would have indicated a move. In the autumn of 1988, although he concentrated very heavily on tightening security measures in response to PIRA attacks – a favourite demand of Unionists – the two Unionist leaders continued to resist any idea of contributing to the review of the working of the Anglo-Irish Intergovernmental Conference and Maryfield secretariat. In this situation he sought a response from the wider community, setting the end of 1988 as the deadline for submissions. At the same time his situation was not made easier by the London–Dublin row on extradition centred on the Republic's refusal to extradite Father Patrick Ryan. In October 1988 two men and a woman from the Republic were convicted of conspiracy to murder King, when they were tried at Winchester Crown Court. Two of them had been arrested close to his Wiltshire home, and they eventually won their appeal against conviction. Lord Beldam, in the Appeal Court, held that remarks by King in January 1989, at the time of the trial, about alleged abuse of the right to silence had prejudiced their case. As they left the court the Winchester Three were served with exclusion orders. Labour spokesman Kevin McNamara MP said King had behaved 'very stupidly', but Thatcher was said to be giving him strong support. Before leaving NI he renewed his efforts to get political talks going, and these were picked up by his successor, Peter Brooke. King's decision as Defence Secretary, in 1991, with the ending of the Soviet threat, to make major cuts in the armed services set the scene for the merger of the UDR and the Royal Irish Rangers in July 1992. The removal of the UDR also served to silence its many critics, although it was officially defended as purely a military decision. Many Anglo-Irish Intergovernmental Conference meetings had been dominated by complaints about the regiment, and British Ministers were clearly impressed by the attack by Cardinal Cahal Daly on its use in Nationalist areas. King supported Douglas Hurd in the Conservative leadership contest, and he was dropped from the Government by PM Major in the reshuffle following the 1992 general election.

KINGSMILLS MASSACRE

Ten Protestant workmen were shot dead in a van at Kingsmills in S. Armagh on 5 January 1976, when they were travelling home from work at Glenanne spinning mill. The shooting was claimed by the S. Armagh Republican Action Force, regarded as a cover name for PIRA. The shootings occurred during a series of tit-for-tat murders, with five Catholic men being killed in two incidents (at Ballydugan and at Whitecross) on 4 January.

KINNOCK, NEIL GORDON

Leader of British Labour Party, 1983–92, MP for Bedwelty, 1970–83; Islwyn, 1983–. b. 28 March 1942. Kinnock pursued a generally low-key line on NI, leaving it to his front-bench spokesmen to make most of the running. But on a visit to NI in December 1984 he described Margaret Thatcher's initial 'out, out, out' reference to the New Ireland Forum report as unhelpful, and said Labour's approach would be 'in, in, in' as a basis for discussion. He said at the same time that Dublin would have to play a part in any solution, although documents produced by the Unionist community would also have to be taken into account. He gave steady backing to the AIA but at a private meeting in December 1986 he was ready to listen to Unionist leaders express their opposition to the AIA and their worries about the security situation. The meeting took place at a time when Unionists were refusing to meet the Secretary of State, but they rejected any suggestion that they were trying to build pre-election bridges with Labour. Within the party, he opposed left-wing moves to remove from party policy the need for consent of the people of NI to a united Ireland. On a visit to NI in January 1987 he defended the action of his party spokesman in meeting PSF councillors, while also saying that he ruled out meetings between himself and PSF as not being 'productive'. He visited NI once a year as leader and on each occasion turned down the idea of Labour organising in NI. He strongly backed the Brooke–Mayhew Talks, but stressed that Labour would not use them to push Irish unity. Rejected post of chairman of European Socialists after 1992 election defeat, and on visit to NI in June 1992 – his last as party leader – he predicted there would be no change in policy on NI.

KIRK, HERBERT VICTOR
Minister of Finance in the old Stormont Parliament, 1965–72, and in the 1974 power-sharing Executive. b. Belfast, 5 June 1912. B.Com.Sc. (QUB). A chartered accountant, he was an influential figure in unionism for many years and also served as Minister of Labour and Minister of Education. In the Parliament he occupied the Belfast Windsor seat, and was returned to the 1973 Assembly from S. Belfast. He was a delegate to the Darlington and Sunningdale conferences as a member of Brian Faulkner's team.

KIRKPATRICK, THOMAS JAMES (JIM)
UUP Assembly member for S. Belfast, 1982–6. Served on Economic Development Committee. b. 1937. Manufacturer (engineering). Ex-UDR officer. Belfast City Council, 1985–. Resigned as secretary of the UUP group on the council when he was barred from a meeting with Unionist leaders because of his opposition to the adjournment policy against the AIA. High Sheriff of Belfast, 1990. Resigned from UUP group on the council in January 1994 and was known to want closer co-operation with DUP.

KOCH, EDWARD (ED)
Mayor (Democrat) of New York, 1978–89. b. 12 December 1924. Lawyer. Congressman, 1969–77. As a long-time critic of British policy in NI, he caused surprise when he rejected the idea of Britain as an 'occupying force', after a peace pilgrimage to NI in July 1988 with Cardinal O'Connor of New York. He also suggested that Britain was playing a constructive role in NI. His remarks on his return to New York were praised by Margaret Thatcher, but infuriated some Irish-Americans who called for a retraction. Koch, with an election approaching, responded by admitting to 'an unfortunate use of language' and called on Britain to fix a date for withdrawal from NI. Conservative MPs accused him of cowardice. In 1989 he was dropped as Democratic candidate for Mayor.

L

LABOUR COMMITTEE ON IRELAND
A left-wing pressure group seeking to persuade the British Labour movement to adopt a policy of British withdrawal from NI, and an end to emergency powers, including the abolition of non-jury courts and use of plastic bullets. Most of its supporters have voiced opposition to the AIA. It has organised fringe meetings at Labour Party conferences, and one of its speakers at a 1986 conference was Armagh PSF councillor Tommy Carroll. In the 1987 general election, the LCI sent a questionnaire to all 633 Labour candidates but only 55 made any reply, and of those who did 40 backed British withdrawal 'within the lifetime of the next Government'.

LABOUR '87
Founded in March 1987, the party brought together the long-standing but declining ULP and NILP, the two-year-old LPNI, and Newtownabbey Labour Party. The party was said to be trade-union based, and its first vice-chairman, Paddy Devlin, said it would have fraternal relations with Labour parties in GB and the Republic, but no direct connection, and its position was that it was impractical in existing circumstances to change NI's constitutional status. A resolution at its initial meeting said that while the AIA had not brought about a significant decrease in violence or sectarian tensions, it had not brought about the 'catastrophic' confrontation many had forecast. In 1989 the party proposed a two-chamber

assembly – the lower, more powerful chamber elected by PR, and the second representing a variety of interests. In the 1989 council elections, it won a seat in Newtownabbey, and in the June 1989 European poll its nominee Dr Brian Caul got 1,274 votes.

LABOUR PARTY, BRITISH

The British Labour movement has been inclined to sympathise with Irish nationalism. This attitude is explained by the long-standing link, formally ended only in 1990, between the UUP and the Conservatives, and the fact that a high proportion of Irish workers in GB tended to back Labour, a fact illustrated by Harold Wilson's comment that he was wont to remind Irish Prime Ministers that he had more Irish people in his constituency than they had in theirs. But it was not until 1981 that the party committed itself to campaign actively for a united Ireland by consent. The NI civil rights campaign attracted considerable support from Labour MPs, notably through the Campaign for Democracy in Ulster. On the left wing of the party there has been some backing for the 'troops out' movement and general disengagement from NI. Thus many Labour people have regarded themselves as having more in common with the SDLP than with the old NILP, despite the latter party's loose association with the British Labour Party. Labour leaders, however, notably since James Callaghan's interventions in NI in 1969, have sought to strike a fairly even balance between the NI parties, in keeping with the broad consensus policy on NI between the major British parties. The Callaghan Government none the less was accused by the SDLP and by some of its own supporters of adopting an uncharacteristic attitude when it backed extra MPs for NI in 1978-9, since this was a long-standing demand of Unionists and many Conservatives. Many critics of the Government saw it as yielding to pressure and seeking to neutralise Unionist votes in the lobbies in the light of the Government's minority position. Both the Government and the Unionists denied any deal as such, but it became

clear just before the fall of the Labour Government in April 1979 that it had been prepared to trade a major inquiry into NI fuel costs for Unionist support. Labour Ministers insisted that they could not oppose extra MPs for NI while retaining Scottish and Welsh representation in their devolution proposals. At its 1979 conference the party rejected a motion passed originally in 1921 calling for withdrawal from Ireland, but in 1981 adopted a new policy of Irish unity by consent. The Labour opposition gave general support to the 1982 NI Assembly plan, while pressing for changes to enlarge the Irish dimension. At its 1982 annual conference the party called for a ban on the use of plastic bullets throughout the UK, despite a warning from its NI spokesman Don Concannon that he could not have his hands tied on the issue. The 1983 election manifesto repeated the commitment to Irish unity by consent, and also called for repeal of the Prevention of Terrorism Act and reform of non-jury courts. Under Neil Kinnock's leadership the party welcomed the NIF report and deplored Margaret Thatcher's 'out, out, out' to the document in 1984, and gave firm backing to the AIA. But he and his friends resisted moves within the party to remove the Unionist veto on constitutional change, and he met the two Unionist leaders at the end of 1986 at a time when they were refusing to meet Ministers. On a visit to NI in January 1987 he defended meetings between his party spokesman and PSF councillors but insisted that it would not be productive if he himself were to hold such meetings. In October 1986 front-bench spokesman Stuart Bell said the party saw the AIA as a move towards a united Ireland, but they would not be 'bounced' into a 'troops out' policy or into setting a date for British withdrawal. The 1986 party conference heavily rejected a call for removal of troops and voted ten to one in a block vote against the termination of British sovereignty in NI. In 1988 a party document warned against precipitate withdrawal from NI, but urged harmonisation of economic policies,

North and South, and a suggestion of interim financial arrangements associated with Irish unity was welcomed by Charles Haughey. On a visit to NI in December 1988 Kinnock said there must be no concession to terrorism by withdrawing army families threatened by PIRA. But the party's criticisms of some of the security measures introduced at that time were strongly articulated by party spokesman Kevin McNamara. Two front-bench spokespersons resigned because of the leadership's decision not to vote against the new Prevention of Terrorism Bill in the main Commons division. One of the rebels was Clare Short, whose family roots are in S. Armagh. In February 1992 Roy Hattersley, as Shadow Home Secretary, opposed the PTA but argued that there should be all-party agreement on anti-terrorist laws. There was united support for the Brooke–Mayhew Talks from Kinnock and PM Major, although McNamara argued that if these were unproductive, there should be a 'deepening and widening' of the AIA. This caused alarm among Unionists, who believed that if Labour had won the election, and the Brooke–Mayhew Talks had then failed, a Labour Government would have given greater power and responsibility to Dublin in NI affairs. In May 1992 Tony Benn revealed that he had tried unsuccessfully to have included in the 1992 Labour election manifesto a pledge of withdrawal from NI. Benn suggested that support for withdrawal would intensify in five years in opposition, but there was no sign that John Smith as leader would adopt a more radical stance than Kinnock. On his first visit as leader to NI in December 1992, Smith supported the Government's refusal to talk to PSF while it espoused violence. The party leadership has continued to urge Labour supporters in NI to support the SDLP as its 'sister party', but some Labour backers in NI insist that the failure of the party to operate in NI is a breach of its constitution, which should be tested in the courts. In July 1992 Kate Hoey, an NI-born Labour MP, claimed that the SDLP was 'not a progressive Socialist party', a claim the SDLP denied.

She was involved in the launch of 'Democracy Now', a group campaigning for NI people to be allowed to join the British Labour Party. In 1993 Labour made an unsuccessful bid to have the PTA amended to end exclusion orders and seven-day detention. During the summer of 1993 the shadow Labour NI team published 'Oranges and Lemons', a document arguing against Labour organisation in NI. In addition, the Institute of Public Policy Research published a study on joint authority. These publications drew criticism from Democracy Now that policy was being created without NEC endorsement. When the motions for conference were published in September, six advocated organising in NI. The eventual composite motion was very long and was interpreted as moving away from bipartisanship. The shadow NI team was displeased when the NEC decided to further investigate the issue of organisation. The party leader, John Smith, welcomed the Downing Street Declaration for the new opportunities it presented. He told BBC radio of his enthusiasm for the 'first step'. Questioned about an NI Assembly, he said it was a subject for the talks but he envisaged a devolved legislature based on power-sharing.

LABOUR PARTY, IRISH

In the November 1992 general election, Irish Labour doubled its representation in the Dáil, with thirty-three TDs against sixteen at the dissolution, and in January 1993 it went into Government with FF. In its campaign it had promised, in a situation of massive unemployment, to concentrate on job creation, and its only miscalculation under the PR system was to run too few candidates (it had seven of the ten poll-topping candidates in the election). By comparison, both FF and FG showed heavy losses. The skilful campaigning of its leader, Dick Spring, who many opinion polls showed to be the popular choice for Taoiseach, was the party's main asset. (His nomination of Mary Robinson, the successful candidate in the 1990 presidential election, was another plus for the party.) But there were prolonged negotiations between

Spring and Taoiseach Albert Reynolds before the first FF–Labour Coalition emerged. Spring was Tánaiste and also Foreign Minister, which gave him a key role in NI policy. In the early 1960s the party was linked to the NILP for a time through a Council of Labour. In 1972 it backed the SDLP policy statement 'Towards a New Ireland'. While it was in Coalition government with Fine Gael, 1973–7, there were some differences of emphasis on NI within the party. One of its Ministers, Dr Conor Cruise O'Brien, was highly critical of the articles in the Constitution claiming all-Ireland jurisdiction. (In the 1992 election, the party said it could be changed in the context of an overall agreement.) At the 1978 party conference, Frank Cluskey, who succeeded Brendan Corish as leader in 1977, criticised Jack Lynch's comments on NI as likely to help the 'godfathers' of the IRA. Michael O'Leary, Cluskey's successor (who joined Fine Gael in 1982), maintained close contact with the NI parties. The party decided, however, not to invite the SDLP to send representatives to its 1982 conference. It was partner with Fine Gael in the 1982–7 Coalition, with Spring as deputy to Taoiseach Garret FitzGerald. The party participated fully in the New Ireland Forum, and Spring was active in the negotiations which led to the AIA. But in January 1987 the party pulled out of the Coalition to pursue its own budgetary policy, and FitzGerald advised its supporters to give their transfers not to Labour but to the Progressive Democrats. In 1988 Spring accused Britain of 'arrogance' in its approach to Anglo-Irish relations, but warned against suspension of the AIA.

LAIRD, JOHN

UUP member for W. Belfast in Assembly, 1973–4, and Convention, 1975–6. b. 1944. Succeeded his father, Dr Norman Laird, as Stormont MP for St Anne's, Belfast, in a by-election in 1970. At twenty-six, he was then the youngest MP at Stormont. Chairman, Young Unionist Council, 1970. Topped the poll in W. Belfast in both the Assembly and Convention elections. In the Assembly he opposed power-sharing and led an

unsuccessful demand for renegotiation of the Sunningdale Agreement. Joint Honorary Secretary of the Ulster Unionist Council, 1976–8. Established his own public relations agency when Convention ended.

LARKIN, AIDAN JOSEPH

SDLP Assembly member for Mid-Ulster, 1973–4. b. Cookstown, 1946. MA (QUB). Barrister; formerly teacher. Magherafelt District Council, 1973–7.

LENIHAN, BRIAN JOSEPH

Leading Fianna Fáil politician who was defeated by Mary Robinson when she became first woman President of the Irish Republic in November 1990. b. Dundalk, 1930. Lenihan, who was Tánaiste (deputy Taoiseach), 1987–90 and was first elected to the Dáil in 1961, has had a lengthy association with NI affairs. He was Foreign Minister in 1974 during the term of the NI power-sharing Executive and again in 1979–81 when the Maze hunger strike and other issues created problems in Anglo-Irish relations. When FF returned to power in March 1987, he became co-chairman of the Anglo-Irish Intergovernmental Conference. He had previously held a variety of Cabinet posts, and in 1973–7 he was FF leader in the Senate and headed the party delegation in the European Assembly. Deputy leader of FF, 1983–90. In November 1988 he assured Unionists that the AIA was not a vehicle designed to destroy them, but also admitted that it had failed to fulfil the expectations and hopes of many Nationalists. In a BBC interview in 1990, he commented that the Republic was 'over-predominantly Catholic'. In the run-up to the presidential election, he became involved in bitter controversy over phone calls he was alleged to have made to the presidential residence ten years before during a political crisis. He was sacked from the Government by Taoiseach Charles Haughey to preserve the FF–PD Coalition. Mary Robinson's victory over such a popular FF figure was a serious blow to the party. In January 1994 he revealed that he had been an official contact with PSF and he was 'cautiously optimistic' over

its attitude to the Downing Street
Declaration.

LENNON, GERALD (GERRY)
Opposition (Nationalist) leader in NI
Senate, 1965–71. b. 1907; d. 1976. He
was the longest-serving Nationalist
Senator, having entered the House in
1944. In 1962 and 1963 he had several
meetings with the grand master of the
Orange Order in Ireland, Sir George
Clark, in an effort to remove what he
termed 'the stigma of religious
discrimination in NI'. The so-called
Orange–Green talks did not produce any
significant result. He was national
president of the AOH for the last year of
his life. A long-established solicitor in
Armagh, he was regarded as a top
authority on smuggling laws.

LIBERAL DEMOCRATS
The successor party to the old Liberal
Party which, with its historical backing
for Irish Home Rule, gave strong support
to the civil rights campaign. Jeremy
Thorpe, as Liberal leader, was highly
critical of successive Unionist
Governments in speeches to the Liberal
conference and to Ulster Liberal Party
gatherings. In 1971 he suggested dual
British-Irish nationality as an approach to
NI problem. On that occasion the Liberal
assembly first voted for the replacement
of British troops by a UN force, but
reversed that decision after an NI delegate
protested that this would be capitulation
to gunmen on both sides. At the start of
the Troubles the party urged that there
should be PR in Stormont elections and
the setting up of a Council of Ireland. It
also came out against internment without
trial. In 1979 it suggested that NI should
have a small advisory committee, elected
by PR, as a first step towards the
restoration of devolved government. In
1982 it gave general support to the
'rolling devolution' initiative. However,
in 1985, against the wishes of party leader
David Steel, the party's annual conference
voted for a commitment to a united
Ireland and the withdrawal of British
troops. But that was effectively set aside
in 1985 when the Liberal-SDP Alliance
accepted the principle of consent along
with power-sharing government and a
British-Irish Security Commission – a
switch in policy which angered some
Dublin politicians. The NI Alliance Party,
under the leadership of John Cushnahan,
developed close links with the party, and
these were strengthened when the
Liberals and the SDP agreed to merge as
the Social and Liberal Democrats in
March 1988. It soon adopted the briefer
title Liberal Democrats. As party leader,
Paddy Ashdown acted for a time as NI
spokesman (the current spokesman is
Lord Holme) and he made regular visits
to NI and maintained close contacts with
Alliance and its present leader, Dr John
Alderdice. On several occasions he has
warned that a devolution initiative is
urgently needed, and in the 1992 general
election campaign he argued that election
deals between the Conservatives and
Unionists would threaten the AIA. Ian
Paisley retorted that he was being 'naïve
and pathetic'. Ashdown opened an
Alliance constituency office in Bangor
during the 1992 election, and canvassed
for Alliance in Belfast. The party
welcomed the Downing Street
Declaration in December 1993. Alan
Beith especially mentioned the possibility
of concurrent referenda North and
South, and the Taoiseach's statement on
human rights.

LIBERAL PARTY see Liberal Democrats

LIBERTY
The London-based human rights body,
formerly known as the National Council
for Civil Liberties, which has targeted
many NI issues over the years. In 1967 it
was represented at the launching of
NICRA, which was modelled on the
London organisation. It has frequently
argued that many NI emergency powers
have been counter-productive in tackling
violence. In particular, it has opposed the
seven-day detention power and exclusion
orders, introduced under the PTA. It was
critical of the supergrass system, and in
1988 was opposed to the ending of the
'right to silence' and the restrictions
imposed on broadcasting.

LIBYAN CONNECTION

Libyan sympathy for PIRA has been one of the most potent elements in the NI Troubles. In 1973 Libya shipped arms and explosives to Ireland, but the gun-running ship *Claudia* with five tons of arms aboard was intercepted by the Republic's Navy in Waterford Bay and five men including Belfast-born Joe Cahill, one of the founders of PIRA, were sentenced in Dublin for their involvement. It is believed that cash aid amounting to several million pounds was also provided by Libyan leader Colonel Moamar al Gaddafi around the same time. But it remains an open question whether other Libyan arms supplies reached PIRA in the 1970s, and the seizure of the *Claudia*'s cargo may well have owed something to British intelligence operations against Libya. But in the 1970s Gaddafi was also in touch with the UDA, who in 1974 had a delegation in Tripoli at the same time as a Republican delegation. The UDA was believed to be seeking oil tanker orders for the Belfast shipyard, but it was also apparently interested in sounding out the possibility of Libyan aid for an independent Ulster. Gaddafi's aim at that time was primarily to embarrass Britain. According to Gaddafi, he renewed his support for PIRA in 1986, when Britain gave facilities for US jets to bomb Libya. In October 1987 French customs intercepted the Panamanian-registered ship *Eksund*, with 150 tons of arms and explosives aboard. These included two tons of Semtex, twenty SAM-7 missiles, 1,000 mortar bombs and rocket-propelled grenades. Security experts believe three other shipments reached PIRA in 1986–7, and were hidden in bunkers in the Republic to fuel its many-sided campaign of the late 1980s and early 1990s. There were also reports of PIRA volunteers being trained in Libya. In 1989 Libyan officials, pushing Gaddafi's attempt to build better relations with the West, claimed their PIRA link was being broken. By 1991 the Libyan ambassador to the UN gave assurances that all assistance to PIRA had been stopped, and Gaddafi himself was offering to give Britain details of arms sent to PIRA. In March 1992 Gaddafi condemned PIRA bombings in London and said the PIRA link had been a 'mistake'. He added: 'I have often said that we consider the actions of the IRA, even though they are in retribution against Britain which tortured the Arabs and colonised the globe, as acts of terrorism.' At a meeting in June 1992 in Geneva, Libyan officials gave British diplomats some details of their contacts with PIRA. These were initially described by Whitehall as 'useful', but comments at the time by Foreign Secretary Douglas Hurd indicated that the information did not go far enough in providing 'chapter and verse' on the Libyan connection. Clearly, Britain wanted names and dates, and it is thought that Libya may not have had the key information on where the arms were hidden. Some movements of arms from the south of the Republic to Donegal in 1992 could point to precautionary action by PIRA. In late 1992 it was thought that enough Semtex remained in PIRA dumps to keep its bombers active for five or more years, and there were hints at the start of 1993 that Libya might not have wholly ceased giving cash aid for the Provisionals.

LIDDLE, LIEUTENANT-COLONEL GEORGE

Imperial grand master of the Orange Order, 1982–5. b. 1901; d. 1988. Colonel Liddle was associated in his youth with the formation of the Ulster Special Constabulary (B Specials) in Co. Fermanagh. He was later in charge of the force in that county, where he was prominent in both unionism and orangeism. He succeeded the Rev. Martin Smyth MP as imperial grand master. At the time of his appointment he was grand master of the order in Fermanagh. He served for many years on the Ulster Unionist Council.

LINDSAY, KENNEDY

VUPP Assembly, 1973–4, and Convention, 1975–6, member for S. Antrim. b. Saskatchewan, Canada, 1924. BA, Ph.D. (TCD, Edinburgh, London). Held university appointments in Canada, US, UK, West Indies and Nigeria, and during an Assembly debate he donned a

Nigerian ceremonial robe to make a point. In the Convention he launched the British Ulster Dominion Party, and stood unsuccessfully in District Council elections in Newtownabbey in 1977. In the 1982 Assembly election, he was an unsuccessful UUUP candidate in S. Antrim. Author, *British Intelligence Services in Action*.

LOGUE, HUGH

SDLP Assembly member for Londonderry, 1982-6. Also represented the constituency in the 1973-4 Assembly and the 1975-6 Convention. b. Derry, 1949. SDLP executive, 1970-3, and chairman, SDLP policy committee, 1971. NICRA executive, 1971-3. Economic affairs spokesman of SDLP, 1975-6. In 1974 he called for disbandment of the UDR because, he said, many of its members had supported the loyalist strike. After the collapse of the Executive in August 1974, he said that a statement of British disengagement would end the uncertainty and desperate political vacuum. After the winding up of the Convention, he was active in political journalism. Unsuccessfully contested Londonderry in February 1974 and 1979 Westminster elections. Member of the Irish Commission for Justice and Peace which had important role in the H-Block hunger-strike controversy in 1981. In 1987 he was appointed to the EC Commission's Science Research and Development Directorate in Brussels.

LONDONDERRY *see* Derry/ Londonderry

LONG, CAPTAIN WILLIAM JOSEPH

Minister of Home Affairs, December 1968-March 1969, a period which included the eventful PD march from Belfast to Derry. b. Stockton-on-Tees, 23 April 1922. Stormont MP, 1962-72, and held a number of junior posts before becoming Minister of Education in 1969. Minister of Development, 1969.

LONG KESH *see* H-Blocks *and* Security System section, p. 458

LOUGHGALL SHOOTINGS

On 8 May 1987 an eight-man PIRA unit was wiped out by the SAS when it attacked Loughgall (Co. Armagh) RUC station. A passing motorist also died in the shooting. The PIRA gang included some of its most experienced gunmen and bombers, apparently drawn from the E. Tyrone-Monaghan ASUs which had been active in attacks on border RUC stations and in the killings of UDR men and Protestant farmers on the Fermanagh border. PIRA sources denied that the ambush had been due to a tip-off from within PIRA; they suggested that police and SAS had been standing by at RUC stations likely to be attacked. The RUC claimed that weapons recovered from the bodies had been used in seven murders and nine attempted murders in the previous two years.

LOWRY, LORD

As Sir Robert Lowry he was chairman of the Constitutional Convention, 1975-6. b. 30 January 1919. QC, 1956. Lord Chief Justice of NI, 1971-88. Sir Robert presided over the Convention's public sittings, and behind the scenes, with the assistance of advisers, he tried to reconcile the conflicting views of the political parties on the type of administration which would prove viable. Notably, he had a scheme prepared for voluntary coalition, as distinct from imposed power-sharing. The circumstances which had given rise to the document proved a major point of controversy, and on the United Unionist side only William Craig and a few of his supporters were attracted to the idea. Despite the failure of the exercise, Sir Robert's efforts were praised on all sides of the Convention. Raised to peerage in 1979. PIRA made an unsuccessful bid to assassinate him at Queen's University Belfast, in March 1982. Four shots were fired, and one injured a QUB professor. After the signing of the AIA in 1985, he was said by Whitehall sources to be against the idea of three-judge Diplock courts – a proposal pressed by the Irish Government and opposed by the then Lord Chancellor, Lord Hailsham.

LOYAL CITIZENS OF ULSTER

A small militant group which first appeared in Derry in October 1968. Its leader, Major Ronald Bunting, threatened that it would hold a meeting on the city walls to coincide with a sit-down in Guildhall Square below by supporters of the Derry Citizens' Action Committee. But the counter-demonstration was banned by William Craig, as Minister of Home Affairs. In January 1969 it announced a counter-demonstration to a PD march in Newry, but it did not proceed with its plan. The LCU appeared at a variety of loyalist demonstrations in 1968 and 1969.

LOYALIST RETALIATION AND DEFENCE GROUP *see* Red Hand Commando

LYELL, LORD

Parliamentary Under-Secretary, NIO, April 1984–9. b. 27 March 1939. He is 3rd Baron (Charles Lyell) and member of Queen's Bodyguard for Scotland. Chartered accountant. At Stormont had responsibility for Agriculture, and NIO spokesman in Lords where he was a Government Whip, 1979–84. Gave strong warnings to local farmers of the challenge they faced in the Single European Market.

LYELL, SIR NICHOLAS

Closely involved with NI legal affairs as Attorney-General, April 1992–, and as Solicitor-General, 1987–92. b. 27 March 1939. MA (Oxon.). Parliamentary Under-Secretary, DHSS, 1986–7. His evidence to the Scott inquiry, into 'arms for Iraq', and the issue of public interest immunity certificates, was widely criticised despite his spirited defence.

LYNCH, JOHN (JACK)

Fianna Fáil Taoiseach of Irish Republic, 1966–73 and 1977–9. b. Cork, 15 August 1917. Hon. LLD (TCD and NUI); Hon. DCL (University College, N. Carolina). Began as civil servant in Department of Justice, 1936, and called to Bar, 1945. TD for Cork constituencies, 1948–81. Junior Minister, 1951–4. Minister for Lands, 1951; Minister for Gaeltacht, 1957;

Minister for Education, 1957–9; Minister for Industry and Commerce, 1959–65; Minister for Finance, 1965–6, when he succeeded Sean Lemass as Taoiseach. As Minister for Industry and Commerce he developed improved economic relations with NI, and had talks with Brian Faulkner, NI Commerce Minister, at the same period as Sean Lemass's historic trip to Stormont in 1965. He brought in special preferential tariffs for some NI goods. As Taoiseach, he had talks at Stormont with PM O'Neill in 1967, and his car was snowballed at Stormont by supporters of the Rev. Ian Paisley. During the early years of the Troubles, his words and actions became a matter of intense controversy in NI. Many Catholics looked to him for moral and sometimes material support. Unionists blamed him for what they termed 'interference in the internal affairs of the United Kingdom'. During the violent clashes in the Bogside area of Derry, he said in a broadcast on 13 August 1969 that it was evident that the Stormont Government was no longer in control of the situation: 'Indeed, the present situation is the inevitable outcome of the policies pursued for decades by successive Stormont Governments. It is clear also that the Irish Government can no longer stand by and see innocent people injured and perhaps worse.' He called for a UN peace-keeping force and said he had asked the British Government to see that 'police attacks on the people of Derry should cease immediately'. Lynch also announced that army field hospitals would be set up at points along the border to treat people who did not wish to go to hospitals in NI. The Scarman report on the Troubles said of Lynch's statement: 'There is no doubt that this broadcast strengthened the will of the Bogsiders to obstruct any attempt by the police to enter their area, and to harass them by missile and petrol bomb attacks, whenever they appeared on the perimeter.' The NI Premier, Major Chichester-Clark, reacted angrily. He said he had heard the broadcast with indignation, and he would hold Lynch personally responsible for any worsening of feeling which his 'inflammatory and ill-considered remarks' might cause. In

1970, during what became known as the 'arms trial crisis', Lynch sacked two Ministers, Charles Haughey and Neil Blaney, who were later acquitted of charges of being involved in illegal arms deals. Lynch also rejected suggestions that Fianna Fáil had been involved in the setting up of the PIRA. He rejected. too, a claim by Blaney that twenty-five Senators and TDs in Dublin had given their guns for use in NI. In 1973 he lost the general election, which he said he had called partly because of the NI situation. In 1975 Fianna Fáil's policy statement, calling on the British Government to declare its commitment to an ordered withdrawal from NI, brought angry protests from many quarters. In Britain and in NI, and to some extent in the Republic, he was accused of adopting PIRA policy. This Lynch hotly denied, and in 1977 he scored a surprise election triumph over the Fine Gael–Labour Coalition, led by Liam Cosgrave. He got an unprecedented twenty-seat majority in the Dáil. Some tension developed in relations between London and Dublin. British Ministers thought he could do more to tighten cross-border security and they argued that the Lynch Government was discouraging a political settlement by stressing Irish unity too strongly. At the end of 1978 he tried unsuccessfully to persuade the British Government to join the new European Monetary System so as to avoid problems in cross-border currency. In September 1979, in the wake of the murder of Lord Mountbatten, he had talks in London with Margaret Thatcher on ways of strengthening cross-border security. Improvements were agreed, but Lynch ruled out in advance two moves sought by the British security forces: the right of the British army to 'hot pursuit' of suspected terrorists across the border, and permission for RUC detectives to interrogate persons held in the Republic. Towards the end of 1979, pressure built up against Lynch in his own party, and in December he gave way to Charles Haughey as party leader and Taoiseach, and in 1981 also gave up his Dáil seat. In 1990 he rejected suggestions that his 1969 attitude to the NI situation had been provocative, and said that if he had sent

army units across the border to secure UN involvement, a quarter of a million people could have been 'exterminated'. In May 1990 he made a surprise call for change in the constitutional claim to NI. After the death in 1991 of former NI Prime Minister Terence O'Neill, he praised the 'vision' of O'Neill at a Dublin memorial service.

LYNCH, SEAMUS

Regional chairman and national vice-president of the Workers' Party (formerly Official Sinn Féin, but Republican Clubs in NI), 1978–92. When the WP split in 1992, he supported the breakaway Democratic Left. b. 1945. Belfast City Council, 1977–81 and 1985–93. (Chairman of community services committee, 1991.) The best-known WP figure in NI, he consistently called for dialogue among the constitutional parties aimed at securing devolved government, and backed the Brooke–Mayhew Talks. He unsuccessfully contested the N. Belfast Westminster seat in all elections since 1979. In the 1992 general election, his vote there as Democratic Left was 1,386 against more than 3,000 in 1987, with a WP candidate taking 419. He also fought N. Belfast in the 1982 Assembly election, and got nearly 6,000 votes in the 1989 European election. He lost his Belfast City Council seat in the 1993 election.

M

MAC GIOLLA, TOMÁS

President of the Workers' Party and its predecessor, Official Sinn Féin, January 1970–88, and earlier president of Sinn Féin, 1962–70. He presided at the Dublin meeting in December 1969 at which the walk-out of the future Provisional members occurred. b. Co. Tipperary, 1924. BA, B. Comm. (UCD); he was a contemporary of FitzGerald and Haughey. TD, 1982–92. Has frequently visited NI, particularly to speak in elections. In 1972 he was cleared of a charge of membership of the OIRA. In that year he was twice deported from Britain, but in 1976 Home Secretary Roy

Jenkins resisted Conservative demands that he should be expelled. On that occasion he addressed a private meeting of MPs at the House of Commons, which had been arranged by Labour MP Joan Maynard. Unsuccessfully contested the 1979 European election in Dublin. In early 1987 he strongly denied reports that WP was associated with OIRA and that violence and robberies had been carried out in NI, the Republic and GB by people linked with the party. On standing down as leader in 1988 (succeeded by Proinsias De Rossa), he urged Protestants in the North to stand 'firm against Provo sectarian terror'. When the WP split in February 1992, he was the only TD among the party's seven Dáil representatives not to join the new Democratic Left. In the November 1992 general election he lost his Dublin seat. In July 1993 he was elected Lord Mayor of Dublin.

MAC STIOFÁIN, SEÁN

Chief of staff of PIRA, 1970-2. b. Leytonstone, London, 17 February 1928. John Edward Drayton Stephenson's adoption of an Irish background and dedication to IRA aims were apparently due to the influence of his mother, who claimed to be a native of Belfast. After National Service with the RAF (he became a corporal), he joined some London-Irish associations and, presumably, the IRA. In 1953 he and two other men - one of them Cathal Goulding, who was later to become chief of staff of the OIRA - were sentenced to eight years' imprisonment for stealing one hundred and eight rifles and eight Bren guns from the cadet armoury of Felstead School in Essex. After his release in 1959, he travelled to Dublin (the first time he had been in Ireland) and became salesman for an Irish-language organisation. By this time he was a fluent Irish speaker. He soon became immersed in IRA intelligence work, and he devoted his organisational skill to the building up of PIRA after the split in the Republican movement. At the height of the PIRA campaign he made many secret trips to NI, but he was believed to be interested in moving over eventually to the political

side of the PIRA. In 1972 he said he was interested in peace, but not peace at any price, and the British must first agree to the basic PIRA aims. In November 1972 he was arrested in Co. Dublin soon after he had recorded a controversial interview with RTE journalist Kevin O'Kelly. Jailed for six months for PIRA membership. PIRA made an unsuccessful bid to free him when he was taken to a Dublin hospital on hunger strike. In January 1973 he ended the fifty-seven-day hunger strike after PIRA leadership stated that it was 'serving no useful purpose'. He then ceased to be PIRA chief of staff. At end of 1981 he resigned from PSF after its Ard Fheis had shown a majority opposed to the 'Éire Nua' federal policy. He has called at intervals for a PIRA ceasefire. A *Sunday Times* report in 1985 that he had been a Garda informer for twenty years was dismissed by PSF as 'British propaganda'.

MCALISKEY, (JOSEPHINE) BERNADETTE

Unity MP for Mid-Ulster, 1969; Independent, 1970-4. b. Cookstown, Co. Tyrone, 23 April 1947. Final-year psychology student at QUB, 1969. As Bernadette Devlin, she first came to prominence in the civil rights campaign as a member of the PD movement. She took part in the student demonstrations in Belfast in the summer of 1968, and in all the major NICRA marches that year in Dungannon, Armagh, and in Duke Street, Derry, on 5 October. She was also in the Belfast-Derry PD march in January 1969, when it was attacked by militant loyalists at Burntollet. She lost her first election when she stood against Major Chichester-Clark (who was soon to become PM) in S. Derry in February 1969. But the next month she won a by-election in Mid-Ulster for Westminster, defeating the Unionist candidate (widow of the former MP) by 4,211 votes in a poll of 92 per cent. She became the youngest woman ever to be elected to Westminster, and the youngest MP for fifty years. She took her seat on her twenty-second birthday. It was, she said, 'the arrival of a peasant in the halls of the great'. Her sponsors were Gerry Fitt MP, and Labour MP Paul Rose, chairman of the Campaign for Democracy in Ulster. Ignoring tradition, she made her maiden speech an hour after taking her seat. In it she attacked the Unionist Government of Captain O'Neill and said an extreme, but possible, solution would be the abolition of Stormont. The Home Secretary. James Callaghan, spoke of her 'brilliance' and said he looked to the day when she might be standing at the Government despatch box. Conservative MP Norman St John Stevas said that not since the days of F.E. Smith had the House listened to such an electrifying maiden speech. Newspapers hailed her triumph as the voice not only of NICRA, but of the student generation. The maiden speech was sandwiched between lunch with the Government Chief Whip and dinner with Lord Longford. But soon Bernadette Devlin was to make very different headlines. In the 'battle of the Bogside' in Derry in August 1969, she became the focus of world attention. The slight, five-foot tall MP was to be seen encouraging the Bogsiders to raise their barricades against the police. The report of the Scarman tribunal described how she was involved in 'inconclusive' telephone conversations from the Bogside to Major Chichester-Clark (then PM) and Lord Stonham (Minister of State, Home Office) at the height of the violence on 13 August 1969. Of that same day, Scarman also noted: 'She was seen in the afternoon to be actively defending the Rossville Street barricades, taking missiles up to its defenders, and shouting encouragement to them. In the morning she led a flag party to the high flats where she unfurled at one end of the roof the "Starry Plough" flag of the Connolly Association.' Bernadette Devlin now became to her admirers 'an Irish Joan of Arc', and to at least one Unionist MP (Stratton Mills) a 'mini-skirted Castro'. In August 1969, on a trip to the US, she raised £50,000 for relief in NI. In December 1969 she was sentenced to six months' imprisonment at Derry Magistrates' Court for incitement to riot and obstruction and disorderly behaviour, arising from the Bogside incidents. She went to Armagh Prison in June 1970,

after she had increased her Mid-Ulster majority to nearly 6,000 in the general election. When she was jailed, there were protest marches and demonstrations in many parts of NI and a protest march in London. In July 1971 she announced that she was going to have a baby. Newspaper opinion was divided. Some papers praised her courage and her insistence that her private life was her own; one critical paper said she seemed to have become a lost leader. In January 1972 she punched the Home Secretary, Reginald Maudling, in the Commons. She accused him of lying about the events of 'Bloody Sunday' in Derry, in which thirteen people had died. The scene was unprecedented in recent history, and she said later that the reaction to it showed a lot about the English. It had created more popular outrage than the Derry shootings. In April 1973 she married Michael McAliskey, a schoolmaster, at a quiet, early morning ceremony. Once again, it was an event on her birthday – her twenty-sixth – and the wedding was at a Catholic church near her home town of Cookstown. In the February 1974 general election she lost her Mid-Ulster seat. The intervention of the SDLP split the anti-Unionist vote, and a Vanguard Unionist, John Dunlop, was returned. The old unity of the civil rights movement had vanished and she helped found the IRSP at the end of 1974. When the 1975 feud developed between the OIRA and the IRSP, she strongly denied that the IRSP had a military wing. On a lecture tour in the US in 1976 she attacked the Peace People as dishonest and said she was not going to tell the PIRA to stop fighting. They were fighting British imperialism in the only way they knew how, she said. In the 1979 European election she championed the Republican prisoners engaged in protests at the Maze Prison to secure political status, but PSF made it clear that it was not supporting her, and it urged voters to boycott the election. She was eliminated on the third count, although she managed to save her deposit. On 16 February 1981 she and her husband were seriously injured when they were shot in their home at Derrylaughan, near Coalisland, Co. Tyrone, by loyalist gunmen. An army patrol arrived quickly and she later acknowledged the value of emergency treatment given by the soldiers. In 1980 and 1981 she was the main spokeswoman of the National H-Block/Armagh Committee. In September 1981 she was expelled from Spain when she arrived to speak at an H-Block meeting in the Basque country. But she managed to slip into Spain again from France, and addressed a meeting without being apprehended. In 1982 she stood unsuccessfully in both the Republic's general elections as PD candidate. She contested Dublin North Central – Charles Haughey's constituency. In 1987 and 1988 she campaigned strongly against extradition from the Republic. In the 1992 general election she supported the PSF candidate in Fermanagh–S. Tyrone. In 1992 she spoke at a founding meeting in Derry of a group to defend Articles 2 and 3 of the Irish Constitution. She said that no one would make 'a Palestinian' out of her. In July 1993 she won a judicial review against the BBC decision, under the direct broadcasting ban, to use sub-titles for her voice in the *Nation* programme of the previous September. She proposed to take legal advice about any appeal to Europe. In October she was a witness for James Smyth, a Maze Prison escapee, who sought to avoid extradition from California. She gave an early lead to the wider Republican movement to reject the Downing Street Declaration. In a *Guardian* article in December she described it as fraudulent for portraying agreement where none existed, for containing nothing new, only reiterating and reaffirming, and she rejected the exclusion of PSF from talks. At the funeral of Dominic McGlinchey in mid-February 1994 she helped to carry his coffin and gave the graveside oration, describing him as 'the finest Republican the struggle has ever produced', and she disavowed any claims linking him to the Droppin' Well bomb in Ballykelly (which killed seventeen people) and the Darkley massacre (in which three men were killed).

MCALLISTER, JAMES (JIM)

PSF Assembly member for Armagh, 1982–6. b. Crossmaglen, Co. Armagh, 1944. Both his parents' families were deeply involved in Republicanism, and his own activity in the movement dates from the early 1960s. After a period in England, he resumed his interest in 1974, and was PRO of the S. Armagh Hunger Strike Action Committee in 1981, and then became chairman of PSF in S. Armagh. Newry and Mourne Council, 1985–. Stood unsuccessfully in Newry and Armagh in 1983, 1987 and 1992 elections, and in 1986 by-election.

MCATEER, EDWARD (EDDIE)

Leader of the Nationalist Party at Stormont, 1964–9. b. Coatbridge, Glasgow, 1914; d. 1986. A civil servant from 1930 until 1944, when he started his own accountancy business. He was returned unopposed as Nationalist MP for Mid-Derry in 1945, and again in 1949. He represented Foyle from 1953 until 1969, when he lost to John Hume. He was on Londonderry Corporation from 1952 until 1958. Early in his career he published a blueprint for civil disobedience entitled 'Irish Action', but in the civil rights campaign he frequently urged moderation. In the wake of the O'Neill–Lemass talks, he accepted the role of official opposition leader at Stormont in 1965, and he argued that much trouble might have been avoided if Unionists had offered concessions at that period; he brought his own brand of wit and sarcasm to parliamentary proceedings. His brother, Hugh McAteer, was at one time chief of staff of the IRA, and staged an escape from Crumlin Road Prison in Belfast. In 1977 Eddie McAteer gave support to the IIP.

MACBRIDE, SEAN

The Nobel Peace Prize winner of 1974 and international jurist and diplomat, who was involved in peace talks in 1977 aimed at securing a paramilitary ceasefire in NI. b. 27 January 1904; d. 1988. MacBride was among the most prominent IRA leaders in the 1920s and 1930s. He was reputedly chief of staff for a time, and was imprisoned three times between 1918 and 1930. He urged a concentration on constitutional action during the 1940s and became leader of the Republican party

Clann na Poblachta, and a member of the Dáil, 1947–58. He was Minister for External Affairs in the inter-party Government, 1948–51. He was Assistant UN Secretary-General and UN Commissioner in Namibia, 1973–4, and returned to Dublin when he left this post. In 1977 he was awarded the Lenin Peace Prize. In that year he tried, without success, to get agreement between loyalist and IRA paramilitaries in NI. These talks also involved Desmond Boal, the NI lawyer and former Unionist MP and first chairman of the DUP. The contacts were made in great secrecy and did not involve face-to-face talks between the two sides. Churchmen were used to some extent as intermediaries. Despite his early involvement with the IRA, he stressed his opposition to the PIRA campaign. He summed up his view by saying that there were injustices in NI, but they were not unbearable and there were probably other ways of remedying the situation. It was disclosed in British Cabinet papers released in January 1980 that MacBride had a meeting at Stormont in 1949 with the then PM Lord Brookeborough. But MacBride said there had been no negotiations as such. Opposed divorce in Republic's 1986 referendum. In 1985 he was associated with the MacBride Principles, which proposed tighter rules against discrimination in jobs than the existing legislation in NI.

MACBRIDE PRINCIPLES

These principles were adopted by the Irish-American lobby to campaign for fair employment in NI. They derived from the Sullivan Principles, applied to S. Africa in 1977 in a campaign of disinvestment, and renamed after Sean MacBride, the former Irish Foreign Minister and winner of the Nobel and Lenin Peace Prizes. The aim was to make US investment in NI conditional on the adoption of the principles. The nine points required increased Catholic representation in workforces, including managerial and administrative posts; security for Catholics at work and travelling to and from work; and training programmes for employees from the minority. The Irish National Caucus campaigned, from their launch in November 1984, for the adoption of the principles into state law and by 1993 some thirteen states had legislated. The UK Government also lobbied against their adoption from 1985 to 1989 on the grounds that they required affirmative action or positive discrimination, which was illegal under the Fair Employment Acts of 1976 and 1989. Stringent new UK legislation in 1989 went beyond MacBride, except in positive discrimination, and the US campaign became more localised with gains in the cities of New York and Boston, but it failed to pass in California. President Clinton had supported the principles during his election campaign and in March 1993 it was reported that Congress had approved them.

MCCANN, EAMONN

Civil rights activist, b. 10 March 1943. Expelled from QUB, 1965, when reading psychology. President of university 'Literific' Society and vice-president of Labour Club. One of the organisers of civil rights march in Derry, 5 October 1968. As chairman of Derry Labour Party, unsuccessfully contested Foyle in Stormont 1969 general election and Londonderry in 1970 Westminster election. Active in 'battle of the Bogside' in Derry and author of *War and an Irish Town*. His Foyle campaign included a demand for take-over of all vacant property suitable for housing accommodation. Later, he took up journalism and became well known as a broadcaster.

MCCARTNEY, ROBERT

UUP Assembly member for N. Down, 1982–6. Served on committees on Economic Development, and Finance and Personnel. b. 1936. A native of the Shankill area of Belfast, he was a QC and one of NI's most successful barristers when he caught the political limelight in 1981 with a sharp attack on the Rev. Ian Paisley, whom he called a 'fascist'. In October 1981 he led a delegation of NI lawyers and businessmen in talks with Taoiseach Dr Garret FitzGerald, on his 'constitutional crusade'. In August 1982, as chairman of the UUP's newly formed Union Group, he visited the US, and in a speech to the Irish Forum in San Francisco described as 'simplistic and dangerous nonsense' the idea that Ireland's problems would be solved if only the British left. When the Assembly collapsed in 1986, he launched an intensive drive as leader of the Campaign for Equal Citizenship urging national parties to organise in NI. In 1987 he was expelled from the UUP when he stood unsuccessfully against Jim Kilfeddder in N. Down in the general election, because there was an agreement among Unionist parties, in their anti-AIA campaign, that sitting Unionists should not be opposed. Standing as a 'Real Unionist', he got within 4,000 votes of Kilfedder. Soon afterwards he stood down as CEC president, but returned to the post in 1988. In 1989 he said that after the Conservative move to organise in NI, Labour must be persuaded to do likewise. In a *Sunday Times* article in March 1992, he described NI as a 'political wasteland'. He was highly critical, in articles in the *Belfast Telegraph*, of the effect on the Unionist position of the Downing Street Declaration of December 1993.

MCCLOSKEY, VINCENT

SDLP Assembly, 1973–4, and Convention, 1975–6, member for S. Antrim. b. Belfast, 1920. Formerly, National Democratic Party. Lisburn Rural District Council, 1968–73.

MCCLURE, WILLIAM JAMES

DUP Assembly member for Londonderry, 1982–6. Deputy chairman, Health and Social Services Committee. Was Convention member for the same constituency, 1975–6. b. 1927. Founder member of DUP; chairman, 1974, of the party's Derry association. Party chairman, 1978–. Prominent in anti-AIA campaign, and in 1987 he became a member of two District Councils – Coleraine and Ballymoney. He had been on the Coleraine Council since 1977, and was then co-opted on to the Ballymoney Council to avoid a by-election arising from the resignation of a DUP member in

protest at the AIA. Past grand master of Independent Orange Order.

MCCONNELL, ROBERT DODD (BERTIE)

All. Assembly, 1973–4, and Convention, 1975–6, member for N. Down. b. Bangor, Co. Down, 1921. Blinded in World War II, during army service; he served on Bangor Borough Council, 1958–73, and N. Down Council, 1973–81. MP for Bangor in NI Parliament, 1969–72; elected as pro-O'Neill Unionist and joined Alliance Party in 1972 as one of first members of Alliance Parliamentary Party. President, Alliance Party, 1976.

MCCREA, RAYMOND STUART

DUP Assembly member for S. Belfast, 1982–6. Served on committees on Environment, and Health and Social Services. b. 1945. Belfast City Council, 1977–85. Leader, DUP group on City Council, 1981. Unsuccessfully contested S. Belfast in 1983 Westminster election.

MCCREA, REVEREND (ROBERT THOMAS) WILLIAM

DUP MP for Mid-Ulster, 1983–. Assembly member for Mid-Ulster, 1982–6. Served on committees on Agriculture, Education, Health and Social Services. b. 6 February 1948. A Free Presbyterian Minister prominent in loyalist politics since 1971, when he was sentenced to six months' imprisonment for riotous behaviour in Dungiven, Co. Derry. Widely known as a gospel singer. Chairman, United Loyalist Front, 1972. Magherafelt Council, 1973–. Chairman, DUP, 1976. Housing Executive Board, 1979–80. Unsuccessfully contested S. Belfast by-election, 1982. His 1983 election majority of 78 in Mid-Ulster was the smallest of the election in NI. But he raised it to over 9,000 in the 1986 by-election and 1987 general election, and had a winning margin of over 6,000 in 1992, as he benefited from the SDLP and PSF splitting the Nationalist vote. In 1990 he opposed power-sharing, and when the political talks involving Irish Ministers were halted in 1991, he said new rules were needed for any restart of the talks. He was reported to be strongly opposed to talks with Irish Ministers in 1992. Because of a visit to the US in July 1993, he was a notable absentee in the tight Maastricht Treaty vote. On 24 November 1993 he was reputed to have documentary evidence of Government–PSF/PIRA contacts in his pocket during a party meeting with PM Major aimed to allay Unionist suspicions. The 'contacts' story broke in the *Observer* four days later.

MCCULLOUGH, RAYMOND

UUP Assembly member for S. Down, 1982–5. Deputy chairman, Agriculture Committee, member, Environment Committee. Banbridge Council, 1973–85; served as chairman and vice-chairman. b. 1919; d. 1985. On executive of UUP; Honorary Secretary, S. Down Unionist Association; and on committee, Grand Orange Lodge of Ireland.

MCCUSKER, JAMES HAROLD

UUP MP for Upper Bann, 1983–90. MP for Armagh, 1974–83. Assembly member for Armagh, 1982–6. Deputy leader, Ulster Unionist Party, 1982–90. b. 7 February 1940; d. 1990. A teacher and later production manager, he was Secretary and Whip of the Unionist Coalition MPs, 1975–6. Active in pressing for tougher security measures in S. Armagh. Voted with the Labour Government in crucial confidence vote which led to the defeat of the Callaghan Government and the 1979 general election. He held off a challenge from the DUP in that election, and in the 1982 Assembly election topped the poll in Armagh. In 1981 he was responsible for setting up a unit based at UUP headquarters which sought to persuade the European Commission on Human Rights that border security was inadequate, and that widows of innocent victims of the violence should be regarded as suffering a deprivation of human rights. In criticism of the AIA in 1986 he said independence might become a viable option, since Unionists were being ignored by Westminster. He said he was not advocating independence, but the Union should be on terms which were mutually acceptable, 'and not those acceptable to Margaret Thatcher and the

Tory party'. In 1987 he served a short sentence in Belfast Prison for withholding a car tax in protest at the AIA. He was a member of the UUP–DUP task force which reported to Unionist leaders on strategy in opposing the AIA in the summer of 1987.

MCDONALD, JAMES

SDLP Assembly member for S. Antrim, 1982–6. b. 1930. Craigavon Council, 1973–85. First SDLP deputy Mayor of Craigavon, 1979. Unsuccessfully contested Convention election in S. Antrim, 1975.

MCFAUL, KENNETH

Founder member of DUP and former member of Protestant Unionist Party. b. 1948. Left DUP in 1984 after the selection of Jim Allister as candidate for the E. Antrim constituency in the 1983 general election. Carrickfergus Borough Council, 1973–85; Mayor, 1981–3. Convention member for N. Antrim, 1975–6. Unsuccessful candidate in N. Antrim in Assembly election, 1982.

MCGIMPSEY CASE

Brothers Christopher and Michael McGimpsey challenged the legality of the AIA before the Dublin High Court in 1988 and subsequently before the Irish Supreme Court. They came from a younger generation of Unionists and had a business and intellectual background. The case, which opened in the Dublin High Court on 14 June 1988, was supported by a legal fund raised by the UUP as part of its multi-strand opposition to the AIA. Their party leader, James Molyneaux, had unsuccessfully challenged the AIA in the UK courts in November 1985 and again early in 1986. Unionists may have believed they had a better chance in Irish courts, working within a written Constitution, whereas in the UK treaty-making was a royal prerogative exercised by the Government of the day. The McGimpseys contended that Article 1 of the AIA conflicted with Articles 2 and 3 of the Irish Constitution; that it fettered the discretion of the Irish Government, for which express constitutional authorisation was required;

and that it discriminated by excluding the interests of Unionists. In his judgement on 29 July Mr Justice Barrington stated that, while there were different views about Articles 2 and 3 of the Constitution, there was no conflict, for Article 1 of the AIA merely expressed 'a political judgement about likely future events', without commitment to a view of the current constitutional status of NI. He rejected the argument about fettered discretion because sovereignty had been preserved in Article 2(c), and the discrimination argument because the AIA respected the rights of the two communities. Despite this defeat Barrington did not make an order for costs and permitted a judicial review. The Supreme Court decision, given on 1 March 1990, upheld the view of Mr Justice Barrington and dismissed the claim that the AIA contravened Articles 2 and 3 of the Constitution. The Supreme Court view of these two articles was that they established a 'claim of legal right' to jurisdiction over the whole national territory. Further, it stated that the Preamble and this interpretation of the two articles meant that the pursuance of reunification was a 'constitutional imperative'. Following Barrington, it argued that Article 1 of the AIA did not deal with the constitutional status of NI but only recognised the current desire for no change, provided for change only by consent and set out a policy if events led to a change of majority view. The judgement also rejected the argument of 'an unconstitutional fetter on executive power' and the claim of discrimination under the 'equal treatment guarantee' of Article 40 of the Constitution. The judgement did not pronounce on the status of NI in Irish constitutional law. The main significance of the decision in McGimpsey and McGimpsey v. Ireland was the declaration that the articles were not merely an aspiration but a claim of legal right and thus a constitutional imperative. This meant that Article 1 of the AIA, regarded as a reassurance to Unionists, did not constitute a recognition of the current status of NI in Irish constitutional law. When talks began with Brooke and then with Mayhew on a new, wider agreement, the articles assumed a central role in the discussions and were the cause of their breakdown in November 1992. The brothers continued their association with Ken Maginnis after the case and during the talks. In 1993 both won seats on Belfast City Council, Christopher McGimpsey in Court and Michael McGimpsey in Laganbank.

MCGLONE, PATRICK (PATSY)

General Secretary of SDLP, 1986–92. b. 8 July 1959. BA Hons. (UU). A former civil servant (Environment), he joined SDLP in 1983, and after holding party posts in Co. Derry, including secretaryship of S. Derry executive, he was elected to executive in 1985, when he also became chairman of University of Ulster branch. Candidate, Magherafelt District Council, 1985; elected Cookstown District Council, 1993. Member, GAA. Information officer in NI of European Socialists, 1992–.

MCGONAGLE, STEPHEN

Parliamentary Commissioner for Administration (Ombudsman) and Commissioner for Complaints, 1974–9. Irish Senator, 1983–7. b. Derry, 1914. Leading local trade unionist before appointment as Ombudsman; district secretary of the ITGWU and president of the NI Committee of ICTU, 1972. He became vice-chairman of Londonderry Development Commission in 1969, but resigned in August 1971, as a protest against the introduction of internment without trial. Chairman of Police Complaints Board set up in 1977 to independently investigate complaints against the RUC, but resigned from this post in 1983, after Unionist protests that it was inconsistent with membership of Irish Senate. In 1982 presided at initial, short-lived inquiry into homosexual scandal at Kincora boys' home in E. Belfast. Irish Labour Party delegate to New Ireland Forum, 1983–4.

MCGRADY, EDWARD KEVIN (EDDIE)

SDLP MP for S. Down, 1987–. SDLP Assembly member for S. Down, 1982–6. Also elected for S. Down to Assembly, 1973–4, and Convention, 1975–6.

b. 3 June 1935. First chairman SDLP, 1971-3. Head of Department of Executive Planning and Co-ordination in NI Executive, 1974. Downpatrick Urban Council, 1961-73 (chairman, 1964-73); Down District Council, 1973-89 (chairman, 1974-5). McGrady was particularly critical of Secretary of State Merlyn Rees after the fall of the Executive. He said that a remark by Rees that he had not expected the Executive to endure showed the 'duplicity and dishonesty' of British policy. Chief Whip, SDLP, 1979-. Unsuccessfully stood against Enoch Powell in S. Down in 1979 and 1983 general elections, and 1986 by-election, and finally won the seat in 1987, when the rise in the Nationalist electorate defeated a strong Powell campaign. Has been prominent in highlighting health dangers from Sellafield nuclear plant, and opposing effect of expenditure cuts on local hospitals. Unenthusiastic about 1988 talks between SDLP and PSF. In 1991 he visited Chicago in a bid to attract investment to S. Down. In the run-up to the 1992 general election, UUP were said to be strengthening their challenge, but the outcome showed that UUP suffered by the intervention of the Conservative candidate, while the drop in the PSF vote also helped McGrady. Thus his 700-plus majority which unseated Enoch Powell in 1987 went up to over 6,000 in 1992. Associate member, BIPB, 1989-. Party spokesman on local government. Took part in Brooke-Mayhew Talks. The Maastricht Treaty vote, in July 1993, when three out of four Conservatives failed to honour pairing arrangements with SDLP and it appeared that a 'deal' had been done with UUP, provoked some angry comments. When Molyneaux later predicted a new Assembly in two years' time, McGrady appeared to veto it when he argued that it did not address the three strands and required the acceptance of both Governments and both communities in NI. Early in January 1994 he said the Downing Street Declaration of December 1993 favoured Unionists.

MCGUINNESS, (JAMES) MARTIN
PSF Assembly member for Londonderry, 1982-6. Vice-president, PSF, 1983-.

b. Bogside area of Derry, 1950. An active Republican since 1969, he was a member of the top-level PIRA delegation which met NI Secretary of State William Whitelaw in London, July 1972. The previous year he had become leader of PIRA in Derry, and he has been imprisoned on several occasions both in NI and the Republic. In 1981 he gave the oration at funeral of PIRA hunger-striker Francis Hughes in Bellaghy, Co. Derry, and has been prominent at many PIRA funerals. With PSF's entry into the NI electoral scene, he became a major figure in the movement. In 1984 he indicated that PIRA would be dropping punishment shootings, but the practice continued. In 1985 he denied that he was PIRA chief of staff, and claimed that the allegation was part of a British plan to have him assassinated. This was during the angry controversy which erupted over the BBC *Real Lives* TV programme in which he was featured, and which was eventually transmitted with minor changes despite opposition from the Government. Stood unsuccessfully in Foyle against John Hume in the 1983, 1987 and 1992 Westminster elections. In 1990 an Order excluding him from GB was renewed. In 1991 and 1992 he made several calls for the Government to enter into talks with PSF, and in May 1992, after Peter Brooke's remark that he would have liked to meet Gerry Adams, he said Brooke and Edward Heath should meet PSF. In February 1992 he said the British Government was 'sadly mistaken' if it thought PSF was going to turn its back on PIRA and condemn it. In 1992 he joined Derry PSF councillor Mitchel McLaughlin in talks with Bishop Edward Daly of Derry. In August 1992 *Esquire* magazine named him Britain's second most powerful man after Rupert Murdoch. In August 1993 Central Television's *The Cook Report* named him 'Britain's number one terrorist'. After an update the following week he described the programme as 'a cowardly and dishonest piece of television masquerading as journalism'. A month later he stated that the Hume-Adams talks were at an important stage with the prospect of a new agreement respecting diversity and earning the allegiance of Unionists. In October, after the Hume–Adams agreement on a peace process, he and others accused PM Major of blocking the 'Irish peace initiative'. He changed tactics in November when it became clear that neither Major nor Taoiseach Reynolds would adopt the Hume–Adams proposals. McGuinness (and Adams) claimed 'protracted contact and dialogue' with the British Government and when the *Observer* broke the story on 28 November they sought to further embarrass the Government with claims of a special 'inner Cabinet' meeting on a May ceasefire proposal and by alleging that PSF had been briefed on the 1992 confidential inter-party talks. In the aftermath of the December Downing Street Declaration he was forthright in his views. He told the *Derry Journal* that unless there was a different 'private' position the declaration was not enough: he wanted unconditional talks and an amnesty for prisoners. At the beginning of January 1994 he told the *Sunday Business Post* that the declaration was 'totally unacceptable': he required British withdrawal to a timetable of six or seven years, Irish national self-determination with the British Government acting as a 'persuader' of Unionists, and the release of prisoners.

MCGURRAN, MALACHY

Chairman of the six-county executive of Republican Clubs and vice-president of Official Sinn Féin from 1970 until his death from bone cancer in July 1978. b. Lurgan, 1938. Active in the 1956 IRA campaign and interned for a time. Candidate for Armagh in October 1974 general election and 1975 Convention election. Craigavon District Council, 1977–8.

MCIVOR, (FRANCES) JILL

Ombudsman and Commissioner for Complaints, 1991–. b. 10 August 1930. LLB (Hons.), QUB. Barrister, and first woman Ombudsman. Has served on great variety of bodies, including Independent Broadcasting Authority, Radio Authority, Fair Employment Commission, and Board of Co-operation North. In her first annual report, she said 550 complaints had been lodged, against 495 and 393 in the previous two years. Most had been against the Housing Executive, an increase of 8 per cent, with others directed mainly at jobs, planning permission and social security benefits. Chairperson, Ulster-New Zealand Trust, 1987–.

MCIVOR, (WILLIAM) BASIL

Education Minister in Executive, 1974. b. 17 June 1928. LLB (QUB). Barrister, 1950. Unionist MP for Larkfield, 1969–72. Minister of Community Relations, 1971. After direct rule, he dissociated himself from Unionist attacks on Secretary of State William Whitelaw. One of the Unionist team at the Sunningdale Conference, December 1973. As head of the Education Department in the power-sharing Executive, he announced the scheme for shared schools for Protestant and Catholic pupils, but the scheme was never implemented owing to the short life of the Executive. In 1981 he became first chairman of Lagan College – NI's first integrated school. Resident Magistrate, 1976–. In 1987 four Unionist MPs tabled a Commons motion calling for his removal from the Bench on the grounds that he had shown bias against Unionists and Orangemen in a case at Ballymoney.

MCKAY, JOHN ALEXANDER

UUP member of Convention, 1975–6, for Fermanagh-S. Tyrone. b. 1945.

MCKEAGUE, JOHN DUNLOP

A leading Belfast loyalist who was shot dead by an INLA gunman in his E. Belfast shop in January 1982. b. 1930. First came to prominence as chairman of the Shankill Defence Association, 1969–70. He stood unsuccessfully as Protestant Unionist candidate for Belfast Corporation by-election in Victoria in 1969, and as an Independent in N. Belfast at the 1970 Westminster election. He was often described as a founder of the loyalist paramilitary group the Red Hand Commando, but always denied that he was involved with the organisation. He was cleared in 1969 of charges of conspiracy to cause explosions. In October 1969 he was sentenced to three months' imprisonment for unlawful assembly. In 1971 his elderly mother was burned to death when his shop and flat in E. Belfast were set on fire by petrol bombs. *Loyalist News,* the paper run by McKeague, said she had been 'murdered by the enemies of Ulster'. In the same year he and two others were the first persons to be accused under the Incitement to Hatred Act, after they published a *Loyalist Song Book.* The jury disagreed at the first trial and they were acquitted at the retrial. In 1976, as a member of the ULCCC, he was prominent in advocating independence for NI.

MCKEE, JOHN (JACK)

DUP Assembly member for N. Antrim, 1982-6. Served on committees on Environment, and Health and Social Services. b. 1944. Larne Council, 1973-. Leader of DUP on Larne Council, 1981-; Mayor, 1984-5.

MCKEOWN, CIARAN

One of the three founders of the Peace People in 1976. b. Derry, 24 December 1943. Graduated in philosophy at QUB, 1966, and in that year president of the Students' Union. President of Union of Students of Ireland, 1967. On Belfast staff of *Irish Press* (Dublin), before joining Peace People full time in 1976. In 1977 awarded scholarship worth £4,000 a year by Norwegian Government to help with peace work and the writing of articles for the Norwegian Institute for Peace Research. Director and editor of *Fortnight,* NI current affairs magazine, for a period during 1977. Editor, Peace People newspaper, 1978-9. Stood down as chairman of Peace People executive in 1978 and resigned in 1980. He later returned to journalism.

MCLACHLAN, PETER

UPNI Assembly member for S. Antrim, 1973-4. b. 1937. In 1977 he became a full-time official of the Peace People and was elected chairman when the original leaders stood down from the executive in 1978. He resigned from this post in February 1980, and became Secretary of the Belfast Voluntary Welfare Society. Worked in a great variety of posts – teacher, civil servant at Stormont and Westminster, secretary to the Youth

Orchestra of Great Britain, personal assistant to Fleet Street newspaper chief Cecil King – before taking charge of NI desk at Conservative Central Office in 1970. Parliamentary lobbyist at Westminster, 1972-3. In the Assembly he was one of Brian Faulkner's closest advisers, particularly during the Sunningdale Conference. But he declined a post in the Executive, arguing that he would be better employed as a backbencher and in building up UPNI. Stood unsuccessfully in Westminster election in E. Belfast in 1974 and in Convention election in S. Antrim in 1975. Specially interested in penal reform and community groups and chairman of NI Federation of Housing Associations, 1977. Active in Campaign for Devolved Parliament group launched in 1988.

MCMANUS, FRANCIS JOSEPH (FRANK)

Unity MP for Fermanagh-S. Tyrone, 1970-4. b. Enniskillen, 16 August 1942. BA, Dip.Ed. (QUB). Chairman of Fermanagh Civil Rights Association, 1968-71, and leading speaker at civil rights demonstrations throughout NI. Chairman, Northern Resistance Movement, 1972. Chairman, Comhairle Uladh (Republican-oriented, nine-county forum), 1972. Leading figure in Unity Movement which contested a variety of elections, and in 1977 one of founders of IIP, of which he became deputy leader in 1981. In 1971 he was sentenced to six months' imprisonment for defying a parade ban in Enniskillen. In same year he was cleared of charge relating to PIRA documents. Injured by one of four shots fired at him in September 1973. Irish representative of US-based Irish National Caucus, 1976-.

MCMASTER, STANLEY EDWARD

Unionist MP for E. Belfast, 1959-74. b. 23 September 1926; d. 1992. Barrister in practice in London. Lecturer in company law, Regent Street Polytechnic.

MCNAMARA, (JOSEPH) KEVIN

Labour front-bench spokesman on NI, 1987-. Chairman of party's NI committee, 1974-9. b. 5 September

1934. Labour MP for Kingston-upon-Hull North/Central since 1966. Lecturer in law. Co. Down family background. Has maintained interest in NI since he was prominent in Campaign for Democracy in Ulster. In 1987 he said Neil Kinnock had appointed him front-bench spokesman not in spite of, but because of, his record for campaigning for Irish unity. He claimed that bipartisanship with the Conservatives on NI had ended in 1981 when Labour became committed to a united Ireland by consent. Reviewing the AIA in 1988, he voiced disappointment that it had not achieved more in internal reforms in NI, but said there were signs of flexibility among Unionists which was essential to any resolution of the conflict. Expressed hope in 1988 that he would become last NI Secretary of State. In 1989 he attacked calls at the party conference for withdrawal of troops from NI and criticised a request by Cardinal Ó Fiaich for a statement on British withdrawal which, he said, could lead to preparations for civil war. In 1990 he suggested a special European court to deal with extradition, and questioned some new security powers, arguing that 'quick fix' security policies could heighten terrorism. In 1991 he urged the video recording of RUC interrogations. In 1991–2 he voiced strong support for the Brooke–Mayhew Talks, but Unionist leaders made it clear in advance of the 1992 election that if Labour won, they would ask Neil Kinnock not to appoint him Secretary of State. In the event, he remained NI spokesman under John Smith and in the autumn of 1992 he suggested that if political talks failed, the AIA should be 'deepened and widened'. In July 1993 he denied that his defence of joint rule of NI, contained in a leaked publication from the Institute of Public Policy Research, had affected his party's chances of gaining Unionist support on Maastricht. Later in the month his shadow NI team published 'Oranges and Lemons', a document that argued against organising in NI and attacked the views of Democracy Now. He told a conference in Cork in October that the Irish Government should not unilaterally abandon its constitutional claim to NI. He welcomed the December Downing Street Declaration as a 'first step' and discouraged the speculation about internment when PIRA did not extend its three-day Christmas ceasefire. Early in January 1994 he argued that PSF be given 'clarification'. Towards the end of the month he advised Adams to accept the declaration, which he regarded as anti-status quo, and thereby call the Unionist bluff. He stated that the British Government's primary interest was 'not the Union' and in the circumstances it was wrong to continue killing.

MCQUADE, JOHN

DUP MP for N. Belfast, 1979–83. b. 1912; d. 1984. Ex-docker, ex-soldier, ex-boxer, he was one of the best-known personalities on the Protestant Shankill Road in Belfast. Unionist MP for Woodvale at Stormont, 1965–72, he broke with the Unionist Parliamentary Party in 1971, and resigned as MP when Stormont was suspended in 1972. He then joined the DUP, and was returned as a DUP Assembly member for N. Belfast, 1973–4. When the Assembly was prorogued in May 1974, he refused to take his salary and donated it to a holiday fund for old people. In February 1974 he unsuccessfully contested W. Belfast as UUUC candidate. He then broke with the DUP but rejoined in 1979, and with a split in the Unionist vote gained N. Belfast from the Ulster Unionists by a majority of 995 in a seven-candidate contest in which he obtained 27.6 per cent of the vote.

MACRORY, SIR PATRICK

Chairman of the review body which produced the plan for local government reform in NI, 1970. b. 21 March 1911; d. 1993. A barrister, Sir Patrick was a director of a variety of top companies and a member of the NI Development Council, 1956–64. The Macrory proposals produced a great deal of controversy. They were strongly attacked by existing councillors, and supported by the NICRA. They were accepted by the Chichester-Clark Government, and the twenty-six District Councils which replaced the former complex structure were first elected in 1973. Apart from the councils, the scheme provided for area boards for education, library and health services, which were strongly attacked by Unionists on the grounds that the majority of members of the boards were nominated by the Government rather than elected representatives. The disappearance of the Assembly removed what was intended to be the top tier of local government, and this has been dubbed the 'Macrory gap'. Its absence was frequently criticised by Sir Patrick. In 1984 Sir Patrick was chairman of a 'think tank' under the auspices of the Institute for European Defence and Strategic Studies which urged the setting up of a joint British-Irish Security Commission to fight terrorism.

MCSORLEY, MARY KATHERINE
SDLP Assembly member for Mid-Ulster, 1982-6. Magherafelt Council, 1978-93. Party spokeswoman on tourism. Member, local government Staff Commission, 1985-. In 1989 became first SDLP-elected representative to accept a royal honour (MBE); the party, angered at her action, said she could not run as SDLP candidate in May 1989 District Council elections. But she held her seat as an Independent. Retired at May 1993 election.

MAGINNIS, JOHN EDWARD
Unionist MP for Armagh, 1959-February 1974. b. Tandragee, Co. Armagh, 7 March 1919. Served in RUC, 1939-45. Group Secretary, Ulster Farmers' Union, 1956-9. Stood unsuccessfully as UPNI candidate in Armagh at the Convention election, 1975.

MAGINNIS, KENNETH (KEN)
UUP MP for Fermanagh-S. Tyrone, 1983-. Assembly member for same constituency, 1982-6. b. 1938. Teacher. Formerly served in Ulster Special Constabulary (B Specials), and was later part-time Major and Company commander, UDR, for eleven years. UUP security spokesman, 1982-. Chairman of Assembly's Security committee, 1983-6. Deputy chairman, finance and personnel committee. Dungannon Council, 1981-93. Unsuccessfully contested Fermanagh-S. Tyrone by-election,

August 1981, but had 7,000-plus majority in 1983 election when SDLP competed for Nationalist vote, and he raised majority to over 12,000 in 1986 by-election and 1987 general election, and to 14,000 in 1992. As UUP security spokesman he has repeatedly called for stronger action against PIRA in border areas (there have been some 220 murders in his constituency, most of them unsolved), and he has also urged selective internment. Has supported power-sharing in government, which he has termed 'responsibility sharing'. In 1987 he served a brief prison sentence for refusal to pay car tax in protest at the AIA. In 1990 he expressed disappointment when the Irish Supreme Court ruled that the Republic's claim to NI was a 'Constitutional imperative', and sought a meeting with Taoiseach Haughey on the issue. But Haughey said the court had stated what he had always thought to be the position, and no meeting took place. In November 1990 there was praise from Catholics and criticism from the DUP for his attendance at the inauguration of President Robinson and the installation of Catholic Primate Archbishop Cahal Daly. He had a key role in the 1991-2 Brooke-Mayhew Talks, but he again angered the DUP with what they regarded as too close social contacts with Irish Ministers. Said to be as unworried by the censure as by the various attempts on his life. In 1991 he was chairman for a period of Dungannon Council under a local power-sharing arrangement. In 1993 he lost his council seat – a result of party tactical voting that misfired. Early in September 1993 he criticised the ECHR decision to investigate the case brought by the relatives of the PIRA volunteers killed in Gibraltar and the rejection of two earlier pleas by a UDR widow and the McGimpsey brothers. He also stated that the Republic's border security bill, usually expressed as £1 million per day, was grossly exaggerated and was closer to £2.1 million per annum. He told the *Belfast Telegraph* about the extent of UUP preparation for the talks in 1992, the tangible proposals presented and the absence of reciprocation by Dublin and the SDLP – 'they had nothing for us'. He wanted devolution now and urged Mayhew to publish his promised 'direction and focus' paper. He rejected joint authority and a ceasefire, unless accompanied by the surrender of weapons, which were rumoured when Hume and Adams presented their joint communiqué on 25 September. At the end of the month he claimed Hume had lost his way and had 'endorsed the armalite and ballot box philosophy'. In the short debate on the Downing Street Declaration on 15 December he sought assurance from PM Major that the cessation of violence by PIRA would have a verification process involving the surrender of arms and explosives and a new manifesto tested by the electors. Early in January 1994 he argued that, since PIRA had rejected the declaration, internment should be introduced. He was critical of President Clinton's decision to issue a visa to Gerry Adams for a visit to New York because it would add to Adams's credibility. The *Spectator* magazine named him 'Parliamentarian of the Year' in 1988.

MAGUIRE, FRANCIS (FRANK)
Independent MP for Fermanagh–S. Tyrone, October 1974–81. b. 1929; d. 5 March 1981. A publican, he was active in the Republican movement and was interned for nearly two years in the late 1950s. As an MP he took a special interest in the welfare of Irish prisoners in English jails. He came close to practising the abstentionist policy so often favoured by Republicans, and rarely attended at Westminster and still had not made a maiden speech at the time of his death. But he did support the Callaghan Government in some key divisions, and his absence from the final vote of confidence contributed to its defeat. In the 1979 election he increased his majority and his death gave rise to the by-election in which hunger-striker Bobby Sands was elected.

MAGUIRE, PAUL
All. Assembly member for N. Belfast, 1982–6, Health and Social Services Committee. Barrister and lecturer in law, QUB, and party spokesman on legal affairs.

Party adviser at Stormont Constitutional Conference, 1980.

MAITLAND, LADY OLGA
Secretary, Conservative backbench NI Committee, 1992–. b 23 May 1944. MP for Sutton and Cheam, 1992–. *Sunday Express* columnist, 1967–91; now freelance journalist (NUJ). Patron of Parents of Murdered Children, and serves on wide variety of bodies, including European Union of Women. Author of *Margaret Thatcher: the First Ten Years*. Has shown special interest in defence issues affecting NI and in response of emergency and other services dealing with major bombing incidents.

MAJOR, JOHN
British PM and Conservative Party leader, November 1990–. b. 29 March 1943. When he succeeded Margaret Thatcher, he had some previous acquaintance with NI issues. As a junior Government Whip he had been responsible for NI business and had atteneded some meetings of the NI Committee of backbench Conservative MPs, and his contacts were enlarged as Chancellor of the Exchequer and as Foreign Secretary. Essentially, he seemed to stick to well-established policy on NI. He supported the AIA and declared there should be 'no hiding place' for PIRA and he would be 'hard as nails' in tackling terrorism. He reappointed Peter Brooke as NI Secretary and showed greater readiness than Thatcher to deal directly with the NI party leaders in discussing possible political progress. His meeting with the four leaders on security matters in February 1992 – the first such meeting at 10 Downing Street for sixteen years – helped restart the talks process in March 1992. The growth of sectarian killings in NI, along with increased PIRA activity in GB, including a mortar attack on Downing Street during a Gulf War Ministerial meeting in February 1991, had increased the security profile and reminded him that PIRA chiefs were still as anxious to strike at the Cabinet as in 1984 in Brighton. With his April 1992 general election victory, he named Sir Patrick Mayhew as NI Secretary of State in place of Peter Brooke, who was

dropped from the Government, temporarily as it turned out. Sir Patrick had once had John Major as his PPS, and it was well known that he had coveted the Stormont post for some years. Sir Patrick, as Attorney-General, had not endeared himself to NI Nationalists with his decision to prevent, on grounds of 'national security', the prosecution of RUC officers over shootings in Co. Armagh in 1982. He had also clashed with the Dublin Government over the Republic's extradition policies. And when he was joined at Stormont by former army officer Michael Mates as Security Minister, many NI politicians forecast a tougher law-and-order approach with less emphasis on political dialogue. Major, however, sought to give fresh impetus to the inter-party talks, and he quickly established a rapport with the Republic's new Taoiseach, Albert Reynolds, whom he had known from EC Finance Ministers' meetings. He re-established regular Anglo-Irish summit meetings, which Thatcher had dropped after the signing of the AIA. In July 1991 David Blatherwick, a former NIO official, was appointed Ambassador in Dublin, an obvious attempt to improve London–Belfast–Dublin liaison. At the same time, Unionists took some comfort from Major's repeated assertions, in resisting Scottish devolution, of the unity of the UK. But he held to Thatcher's privatisation line in NI, with electricity, water and the international airport on the immediate agenda. His campaign of more open government included the unsurprising disclosure that he personally chaired the Cabinet committee on NI. A version of his Citizen's Charter was introduced in NI. The election of Democrat Bill Clinton as US President, with his campaign commitment to an NI peace envoy and his criticism of some security and fair employment issues in NI, led to some diplomatic exchanges. And while Clinton reaffirmed the 'special relationship', it looked as if Stormont would show some extra sensitivity on questions where an unfavourable reaction in the US could damage NI effort to attract goodwill and investment across the Atlantic. Under Major's presidency of EC

in 1992, NI retained its Objective One priority in EC funding. On a two-day visit to NI in April 1993, he offered strong encouragement to local Conservatives and promised Government proposals to put before new inter-party talks. His itinerary included Derry, Strabane and Coleraine. But within weeks, the NI Conservatives had been sharply rebuffed in council elections. He told Michael Brunson of ITN that it would have been 'an act of gross injustice' to have sacked NIO Minister, Michael Mates, and he cited Sir Robin Butler's view that the Minister had done nothing wrong in helping a constituent, Asil Nadir. He was pleased to have the security of UUP votes in the Maastricht Treaty vote but he quickly asserted that 'nothing was asked for, nothing was offered and nothing was given' against claims of a 'deal'. After the Anglo-Irish Intergovernmental Conference meeting early in September he tried to revive the inter-party talks by seeing the main party leaders, starting with Hume and Paisley. In his keynote speech to the Conservative conference in October he said he wanted only one message from PIRA – namely, that it was finished with violence for good. His insistence that he 'knew nothing' of the Hume–Adams proposals, to the annoyance of Hume, was pushed further when he accused Adams of blackmail in offering peace in exchange for acceptance. At the Brussels summit at the end of the month he joined Reynolds in praising Hume's 'courageous and imaginative efforts' but neither endorsed the document, preferring to follow their own path despite Hume's protestations that they were ignoring 'peace in a week'. Major proposed to intensify the inter-party talks by meeting the four main party leaders. In his Guildhall speech on 15 November he said there was a 'better opportunity for peace in NI than for many years'. He said no deadlines would be set but he would 'never talk to organisations which did not renounce violence'. In the debate on the Queen's Speech he presented a balanced approach in which he was ready to respond to 'a cessation of violence', gave a cast-iron guarantee that the people of NI would determine its constitutional future, while stressing that no party could veto progress. This message – cessation of violence and a constitutional pledge to Unionists – was regularly repeated while the British and Irish Governments met on their own peace process. In his Commons statement on the December Downing Street Declaration he seemed anxious to maintain balance. He stressed that it was the product of contact with Taoiseach Reynolds over two years, and, after setting out its contents, he went on to emphasise what was *not* in it as a reassurance to Unionists. The decision on the NI Select Committee the day after the declaration was also seen as reassurance. His visit to NI on 22 December could be seen as an anxiety to reassure NI opinion. Early in January 1994 he accused PSF of running away from a decision on the declaration. He reiterated his intention to renew inter-party talks 'to restore properly based democracy in NI', which would be locally accountable and command support in all sections of the community. He repeated the offer of talks with PSF in three months if violence ceased. He told *Frost on Sunday* that he was still open to a response to the declaration but he would not be drawn into negotiation by the back door, that violence must stop before negotiations. He replied to a letter from Adams, saying that the declaration was the only text available, and not the Irish draft paper of June or the PIRA paper of October. At the end of January his opposition to a visa for Gerry Adams's visit to the US was rejected by Clinton.

MALLON, SEAMUS

SDLP MP for Newry and Armagh, 1986–. Deputy leader of SDLP, 1979–. b. Markethill, Co. Armagh, 1936. Elected Assembly member for Armagh in 1982, but disqualified on grounds that he was a member of the Republic's Senate. Former Co. Armagh Gaelic footballer and head teacher. Prominent in civil rights campaign and chairman, Mid-Armagh Anti-Discrimination Committee, 1963–8. Armagh Council, 1973–89. Represented Armagh in both the 1973–4 Assembly and the 1975–6 Convention.

Unsuccessfully contested Armagh in Westminster elections, October 1974, 1979 and the new constituency of Newry and Armagh in 1983. But in the January 1986 by-election forced by Unionists in protest at the AIA, his persistence was rewarded, and he unseated Jim Nicholson of the UUP by some 2,500 votes, and doubled that majority in 1987. Before becoming deputy leader to John Hume, he had been chairman of the SDLP in the 1973 Assembly and chairman of constituency representatives, 1977–9. His appointment to the Republic's Senate by Taoiseach Charles Haughey in May 1982 was a major surprise. When it led to his exclusion from the Assembly, Mallon protested that the situation highlighted the 'incongruity' of British political involvement in Irish affairs. Despite the SDLP decision not to attend the Assembly, he was unseated in an Election Court on a petition brought by Armagh MP Harold McCusker. From 1979 to 1982 he was party spokesman on relations with Westminster, and in 1982 took over as law-and-order spokesman. In that capacity he was particularly critical of the NIO's handling of controversial RUC shootings in Co. Armagh in 1982, and in the wake of the AIA urged a speed-up in reform of the judiciary. In 1988 he called for a rethink of the Republic's neutrality policy. He was critical of several of the anti-terrorist measures introduced in late 1988, including intensive house searches in Nationalist areas. He has also consistently criticised the Prevention of Terrorism Act and said 'idiotic changes' were made in the Emergency Provisions Act of 1991. As more permanent checkpoints were erected on the border in 1992, he attacked the idea of static checkpoints and the presence of a security base for every 500 people in his constituency. In particular, he voiced concern about the behaviour of the Parachute Regiment in E. Tyrone. At the same time, he has vigorously condemned PIRA shootings and bombings, some of them close to his own home in Markethill, and has backed efforts to improve the image of S. Armagh. He took part throughout in the Brooke–Mayhew Talks. As the talks ended, he declared that the Republic's Government must have an executive role in any settlement. In February 1993 he suggested reshaping police services to include more localised forces for ordinary civil policing and an all-Ireland anti-terrorist force. He said that, as things stood, there was not a single policeman living in S. Armagh, Derry's west bank, or in Nationalist W. Belfast. He was the most supportive of his party leader during the Hume–Adams talks. At the Labour Party conference in Brighton he asked PIRA for a declaration of intent, remarking that the SDLP's patience was not infinite. In the short debate on the Downing Street Declaration on 15 December, he urged that further efforts be made to persuade the men of violence through the 'channels' and sought reassurance for the Nationalist section of the community. In a strong speech interpreted as redefining constitutional nationalism in the NI debate in the Commons on 21 January 1994, he declared that there was 'not a whisker' between the Hume–Adams proposals and the declaration. Early in February he went further when he quoted from Hume–Adams, paragraph five (on self-determination), to support his point.

MANSFIELD AND MANSFIELD, LORD

Minister of State, NIO, 1983–4. b. 7 July 1930. (Heir, Viscount Stormont.) Minister of State, Scottish Office, 1979–83. Member of British delegation to European Parliament, 1973–5. Opposition spokesman in House of Lords, 1975–9. Apart from being departmental spokesman in the Lords, he took responsibility for Agriculture in NIO. Resigned for health reasons. First Crown Estates Commissioner, 1985–.

MARKETS

A district close to the centre of Belfast, where there were many bombing and shooting incidents in 1969–70. At the start of the Troubles, OIRA had a strong presence in the area, and after 1972 it was largely displaced by INLA, which continued to be active in the area in the early 1980s. The area has been transformed by new housing developments.

MARSHALL, JAMES

Labour front-bench spokesman on NI, 1987–. MP for Leicester South, October 1974–83; 1987–. b. 13 March 1941. Assistant Government Whip, 1977–9. Strongly against privatisation of Short Brothers plc in 1988. BIPB, 1989–.

MARTIN, (THOMAS) GEOFFREY

Head of EC office in Belfast, 1979–85. b 26 July 1940. B.Sc. Hons. (QUB). President of the National Union of Students, 1966–8. Diplomatic staff, Commonwealth Secretariat, 1974–9. After the Dublin summit of December 1980, he suggested that the EC could provide 'a useful institutional relationship' in the future strategy of Anglo-Irish relations, and that the European dimension could have a growing importance in NI affairs. Moved to EC post in Bangkok. Currently Head of External Relations, London EC office.

MASON, LORD (OF BARNSLEY)

As Roy Mason, NI Secretary of State, September 1976–May 1979. b. 18 April 1924. As a boy of fourteen he went down the mines in his native Barnsley, Yorkshire, and remained in the coal industry until 1953, when he became Labour MP for Barnsley. Labour Party spokesman on Defence, Home Affairs and Post Office, 1960–4. Minister of State, Board of Trade, 1964–7. Minister of Defence, Equipment, 1967–8. Minister of Power, 1968–9. President of the Board of Trade, 1969–70. Secretary for Defence, 1974–6. His appointment to Stormont was unexpected, and regarded by many non-Unionists as indicating a tougher direct-rule regime than that of his predecessor, Merlyn Rees. Some SDLP members suggested that he was concerned only with a military solution. He was also handicapped in some quarters by a statement which he had made as Defence Secretary in April 1974: 'Pressure is mounting on the mainland to pull out the troops. Equally, demands are being made to set a date for withdrawal, thereby forcing the warring factions to

230

get together and hammer out a solution.' The comment caused alarm in the three-party NI Executive, and deputy Chief Executive Gerry Fitt flew to London to seek clarification from the PM Harold Wilson. In a statement after a Cabinet meeting, the PM said the troops would stay in the front line against terrorism, and a statement from the Defence Ministry said Mason did not intend to suggest any change of policy. At the same time, he was responsible for a military initiative in NI: the introductiion of units of the controversial SAS in S. Armagh in 1976. As Defence Secretary, he called an early-morning meeting of his top advisers and presented the plan to Wilson, who accepted it immediately as an answer to some horrific murders in the area. At Stormont Mason was helped by three factors: his experience of the army role during his previous two years at the Defence Ministry; a more friendly attitude towards him by the Conservative opposition than Rees had enjoyed; and the tendency for violence to decline, notably from the loyalist side. In his early months in NI he ran into criticism from the media because of an attempt to introduce voluntary censorship of news of 'sensitive terrorist incidents'. He wanted to bring in the equivalent of the Whitehall 'D' notice system which is designed to discourage the dissemination of information likely to be damaging to national security. He was also opposed to the BBC and ITV broadcasting interviews in support of allegations of ill-treatment directed against the RUC. This was clearly part of a psychological approach. At his initial news conference in September 1976 he spoke of the IRA 'reeling'; at the end of the year the 'net was tightening on the terrorist'; and by the end of 1977 the 'corner is being turned in the war against the terrorists'. Certainly, the security forces achieved major successes in terms of arrests during 1977, and there was a distinct drop in the level of killings and bombings. But at the end of 1977, with a fireman's strike, the PIRA mounted a new incendiary bomb campaign, which caused heavy damage. And the PIRA said Mason was being a 'fool' to predict their defeat. One of the important changes which he

made in security policy during 1977 was to increase the use of covert tactics of the army, and the SAS was allowed to operate throughout NI. Other features of his security approach were to enlarge the role of the RUC and UDR (more 'Ulsterisation' of security was the local phrase). At the start of 1978 he also aimed to switch a larger section of the army locally from men on four-month tours to units which would remain on a long-stay basis, that is, for two years. In 1977 he had a substantial political success in defeating the efforts of the UUAC to repeat the triumph of the 1974 UWC strike. During that year, he also made two attempts to get some movement towards a political settlement. After talks with the various parties in February and March, he reported to Parliament that there was little sign that the divide could be bridged. Towards the end of the year he had more talks on the possibility of 'interim devolution', but these rapidly petered out. Mason also put emphasis on bringing forward controversial legislation during direct rule – a regime which he claimed was 'positive, compassionate and caring'. Legislation was brought forward to bring the laws on divorce and homosexuality into line with those in GB, and the Government committed itself to comprehensive education. The courts system in NI was substantially reformed. As Secretary of State, he forcefully projected his dominant personality on the local scene. In 1987 Lord Mason claimed that PIRA 'high command' had admitted, after he left NI, that if his policies had continued for another six months, they would have been defeated. In January 1992 his name was found on a PIRA 'hit list' and later that year the Government turned down his plea for identity cards as an anti-terrorist measure.

MATES, MICHAEL JOHN
Minister of State at NIO and deputy Secretary of State, April 1992-3. b. 9 June 1934. Cons. MP for Petersfield, 1974-. Served with army in NI as Lieutenant-Colonel. Secretary of Cons. backbench NI Committee, 1974-9; vice-chairman, 1979-81. Chairman of Anglo-Irish all-party committee at

Westminster, 1979–92. Supported James Prior's 'rolling devolution' scheme in 1982, despite opposition to it by right-wing MPs in Cons. NI Committee. Strongly backed the successful campaign for a parliamentary tier of the AIA. In 1988 he spearheaded the backbench revolt against the Poll Tax. Was in charge of Michael Heseltine's bid for party leadership in 1990. Chairman of Select Committee on Defence, 1987–92, and frequent media commentator on defence and NI matters before his appointment to NIO as deputy to Sir Patrick Mayhew. His arrival at Stormont drew some criticism from Nationalists, who felt he was too ready to dismiss allegations of army misbehaviour and to play down the threat of loyalist paramilitaries. But some of these doubts were silenced by the banning of the UDA in August 1992 and disciplinary and other action against members of the Parachute Regiment in E. Tyrone in 1992. Defended siting of strengthened army border checkpoints and the general principle of such static installations against local opposition in several areas. The revelation, at the end of May 1993, of his efforts on behalf of a constituent, the fugitive businessman Asil Nadir, brought additional pressure to his job. He decided to resign on 24 June amid general allegations about overseas funding of the Conservatives. In an extensive interview with the *Belfast Telegraph* he claimed to have evidence of dirty tricks in the Asil Nadir case. He supported a devolved Assembly for NI but annoyed some when he suggested the use of the annual financial subvention from the Treasury as an incentive for political change. He supported the December 1993 Downing Street Declaration but underlined that if the opportunity for peace was not taken then a concerted effort should be made with the Republic to end terrorism. Early in January 1994 he was among those who did not see the need to keep the door open any longer for the men of violence and he did not distinguish between PSF and PIRA.

MAUDLING, REGINALD

As Home Secretary, responsible for NI affairs at Westminster, 1970–2. b. 7 March 1917; d. February 1979. Conservative MP for Barnet, 1950–79. When he took over from James Callaghan when the Conservatives returned to power in 1970, he made it clear that he would continue to support reform moves in NI. But with the PM, Edward Heath, concerning himself closely with NI matters, Maudling's influence was secondary. His relaxed approach also brought criticism within NI when he stated in March 1971 that the London and Stormont Governments were in agreement on security, and shortly afterwards NI Premier James Chichester-Clark resigned, leaving little doubt that he was dissatisfied with Westminster's approach to law and order. Best remembered in NI for having coined the phrase 'acceptable level of violence'. The remark drew a strong protest from the NI Government despite his denial that he was in any way complacent. In January 1972, when he made his statement on 'Bloody Sunday' in the Commons, he was struck by the Mid-Ulster MP Bernadette Devlin (later McAliskey). He is believed to have only reluctantly backed internment without trial in 1971.

MAWHINNEY, BRIAN STANLEY

Minister of State, NIO, 1990–2; Under-Secretary, NIO, 1986–90. b. 26 July 1940. B.Sc. (QUB); M.Sc. (Michigan); Ph.D. (London). First NI-born Minister at NIO under direct rule, and one of longest-serving Ministers there. His early responsibilities were education and information, and as Minister of State, successively finance and security. He had been PPS for Secretary of State Tom King at Employment for five months before arriving at Stormont. Some Unionists regarded his appointment as an attempt to damp down loyalist protest against the AIA, and in speeches he sought to counter the Unionist claim that the agreement was a threat to the UK link. As Cons. MP for Peterborough (1979–) he had been active in the party's backbench NI Committee and in 1980 suggested an NI Assembly scheme that was the inspiration for the 'rolling devolution' plan of James Prior. As Education Minister, he incurred the displeasure of the Catholic Church with his policy of giving special encouragement to integrated schools. In 1988 he visited the US to explain the Government's case on fair employment. In 1989 Tom King asked him to sound out the political parties on the possibility of inter-party dialogue, and when structured talks began in 1991, he accompanied the then NI Secretary of State, Peter Brooke, in the exchanges involving the NI parties. But in the 1992 post-election reshuffle, he became Minister of State in the Whitehall Health Department. Privy Council, 1994–. Author of *Conflict and Christianity in Northern Ireland*.

MAWHINNEY, GORDON

All. deputy leader, 1987–91 and Assembly member for S. Antrim, 1982–6. b. 1943. Served on Assembly committees on Economic Development, Environment and Security. All. Chief Whip, 1984–6. Newtownabbey Council, 1981–. Specialist in valuation and rating. Took part in Duisburg Talks, 1988.

MAYHEW, SIR PATRICK

Secretary of State for NI, April 1992–. b. 11 September 1929. QC, 1972. Cons. MP for Tunbridge Wells, 1974–. Unlike his predecessors at Stormont, the tenth Secretary of State had been attracted to the post for some years. He also had considerable experience of legal issues affecting NI as Attorney-General, 1987–92, and Solicitor-General, 1983–7. Sir Patrick, like his immediate predecessor Peter Brooke, has an Anglo-Irish background (his mother was a Roche, family name of the Lords Fermoy), but after John Major's election victory there were claims that the Irish Government was not reacting well to suggestions that he would go to Stormont. Members recalled that as Attorney-General he had objected to the extradition procedure in the Republic which required Britain to produce an outline of the evidence in every case. Sir Patrick had been angered by the refusal of the Irish Attorney-General, John Murray, to authorise the hand-over of Father Patrick Ryan on terrorist charges in 1988. The Dublin Government also saw Sir

Patrick as helping to block its idea of three judges in non-jury courts in NI. And both in Dublin and among Northern Nationalists, there had been resentment that in 1988 he had ruled against the prosecution of eleven RUC officers in connection with the shootings of six unarmed Catholic men (five of them with alleged terrorist links) in Co. Armagh in 1982. Sir Patrick had held that while there was *prima facie* evidence of attempts to pervert the course of justice, there would be no prosecutions on the grounds of 'national security'. But John Major, who had been PPS to Sir Patrick when he was Minister of State at the Home Office (1981–3), was not swayed by such matters, and Sir Patrick moved quickly to pick up the political talks which had started the previous year. His determination to press ahead with the dialogue got a welcome from the constitutional parties in NI and from the Reynolds Government which had recently taken office in the Republic. UUP leader James Molyneaux thought he would persevere with the discussions without making them into a 'media circus'. SDLP deputy leader Seamus Mallon said the Stalker affair had not been Sir Patrick's 'finest hour', adding, 'He must rise above that and so must we.' DUP spokesman Sammy Wilson promised 'a short honeymoon'. Sir Patrick was soon on good terms with Irish Foreign Minister David Andrews, with whom he shared a legal background, and who was equally anxious to facilitate the talks. And on 10 August 1992, four months after his appointment, Sir Patrick earned high marks from Nationalists with his unexpected decision to ban the UDA. In the inter-party talks, he displayed the skills he had often deployed in the Commons in handling complex legislation, and he relished the historic bits – the arrival at Stormont of Irish Ministers to meet Unionists, the visit of UUP delegates to Dublin Castle, and the return of British Ministers, as visitors, to its state rooms. Initially, he was dismayed by leaks of key documents from supposedly private talks. In a newspaper interview in July 1992, he disclosed that he himself would like to see devolved powers 'at least' equal to those of the old Stormont, but there remained a large gap between the committee system of government favoured by Unionists and Alliance and the radical SDLP approach of bringing both the Irish Government and the EC into the Stormont Executive. He echoed Peter Brooke's line that the Republic's claim to jurisdiction in NI was 'unhelpful'. But Irish Ministers, who spent 200 hours in the talks between July and November 1992, were not willing to commit themselves to a referendum on the claim except in the context of a comprehensive settlement. Unionists insisted that there must be a prior commitment on a referendum. When the talks were wound up in November 1992, Sir Patrick looked to continuing informal exchanges between the parties and talked of things never being the same again. But Ian Paisley took exception to his claim that progress had been made in the last week of the talks through contacts in bars and corridors. The DUP leader demanded an apology for such remarks and called the Secretary of State 'wicked and vile'. In 1992 Sir Patrick had to face an upsurge of PIRA attacks across NI, accompanied by PIRA bombing assaults in London and Manchester that gave force to PIRA's threat of an 'economic war'. But loyalist terrorists of the UFF and UVF were also maintaining the high level of activity they had established in 1991. In July 1992 he used some harsh words about the behaviour of Orangemen parading on the Ormeau Road in Belfast past a bookmaker's shop where five Catholics had been murdered by the UFF. They had behaved like 'cannibals', he said. In a speech in December 1992 at the Institute for the Study of Conflict at the University of Ulster, Sir Patrick announced the ending of the legal ban on Irish street names – a ban that had not been enforced. He also reviewed Government policy at length, seemingly anxious to set the scene for renewed political exchanges. There was a restatement of the constitutional guarantee, a reminder that the British Government would present 'no obstacle' to a united Ireland if Unionists could be persuaded to go along with it, and a hint

that PSF could be brought into political dialogue if its renunciation of violence was shown to be 'for real'. He also made it clear that the British Government had no 'pre-selected constitutional outcome' in talks and added that with the ending of violence the army would be withdrawn to barracks. The speech provoked much controversy. It was seen by many loyalists as pitched to appeal to Nationalists, particularly some sections of PSF. Some UUP people saw it as spurring loyalist violence. The DUP was scathing about it. Alliance regarded it as showing that there was no difference between Conservative and Labour policy. Some local Conservatives argued that it could not be squared with the Secretary of State's comment that he looked to the day when an NI Conservative MP would be doing his job. (One S. Belfast Conservative said the speech made 'poor bloody suckers' of those who had campaigned that 'the Union would be safe' with the Conservatives.) If it was intended to reinforce any 'doves' in the PIRA camp, it brought forth only an assurance from that quarter that nothing had changed. With the new FF-Labour Coalition in the Republic taking office in January 1993, he quickly began testing the possibility of an 'open and flexible approach' in fresh political talks on NI, as promised by the Labour leader and new Foreign Minister, Dick Spring. In April 1993 he revealed a switch in policy – the NIO would now put forward its own proposals in an attempt to restart inter-party discussions. But Dublin Ministers indicated they would have a voice in shaping proposals, and some Unionists suspected that an intensification of the Anglo-Irish process was under way, despite the Secretary of State's denial that British–Irish joint authority over NI was envisaged. Eventually, he said the Government's ideas to focus new inter-party talks would not be disclosed until the parties came together, and this seemed a distant prospect in the summer of 1993. In July 1993 Sir Patrick had to react to some unwelcome events. In Newtownards, a town he said he knew, a crowd jeered him after a PIRA bomb destroyed one of the main shopping streets. Then, on the morning of the Anglo-Irish Inter-governmental Conference meeting, he had to respond to a new agenda set by Dick Spring in a *Guardian* article which advocated joint authority. He expressed surprise that the article went beyond 'the position of the Irish Government hitherto' and stated that 'these talks are not going to end in joint administration'. The issue was still alive when he met Unionists before the Maastricht vote. In Downpatrick early in August he restated his wish to return power to NI elected representatives and promised a 'focus and direction' paper. Early in September there were hints of a secret document but there was a denial that it was a blueprint. The British Irish Association meeting in Cambridge was an opportunity to relaunch talks before an interested audience. Mayhew called for urgency, patience and flexibility and a product after new talks. He was slow to comment when the Hume–Adams joint statement was issued on 25 September, but when the BBC revealed that Irish self-determination was the key element, he set out his principles in a wide-ranging interview with the *Belfast Telegraph*. He stated that he was not prepared to contemplate 'any change to the status of NI that does not represent the self-determination of the people living in NI'. He said that cessation of violence must precede discussion and 'enough time must elapse to show it is for real' before PSF was admitted to talks. He also outlined his stance on a number of specific reforms including an NI Select Committee, legislation by Orders in Council and local government reform. When he reported to the Commons in October, it was still clear that his objective was inter-party talks. He argued that it was not yet the time for round-table talks and asserted that he would not accept 'peace at any price'. As the feeling grew that Hume's efforts for a peace process were being ignored, he praised his courage but refused to bargain with those using force to back up argument, despite the bloodiest month since 1976 with the Shankill bomb and the Greysteel massacre. He denied Adams's claim of protracted Government negotiations with

PSF, and he also denied there was any conflict with the Irish Government over his policy of 'peace and talks' agenda. Mayhew was at the centre of controversy when the *Observer* broke the story of extensive Government contact with the Republican movement on 28 November. The origins, duration and level of contact were all controversial but even when the Government decided to release its selected documents to limit the damage, Sir Patrick had to admit to twenty-two errors, conceding credibility to PSF, and later admitting an offer to resign. While PSF issued its own papers, the Government refused to do so and steadfastly stuck to its story. His was a supportive role to PM Major during the period immediately after the Downing Street Declaration and the temporary Christmas ceasefire. In the NI debate in the Commons on 21 January 1994 he challenged PSF to 'see an end to terrorism' and the next day said they could stay out or join in but they could not stop the process to which there was no guaranteed outcome. Having resisted demands to follow Dublin's 'clarification' policy during January, he changed stance after the Anglo-Irish Intergovernmental Conference meeting to clarify some aspects, which were published in the *Irish Times* in mid-February. In an interview with the *Financial Times* he promised a 'focus and direction' paper in a couple of weeks that would include plans for an NI Assembly.

MAZE PRISON *see* H-Blocks *and* Security System section, p. 458

MELCHETT, LORD
Minister of State at NIO, 1976–9; House of Lords spokesman on NI. b. 24 February 1948. BA (Cantab.); MA (Keele). Government Whip, 1974–5. Parliamentary Under-Secretary, Trade, 1975–6. Chairman, Government working party on pop festivals, 1975–6, and described himself as a punk rock fan. Responsibilities at NIO: departments of Education, and Health and Social Services; also probation court services; youth matters. His strong support of comprehensive education proved

controversial in NI. Executive director of Greenpeace.

MI5 *see* Security System section pp. 461–5, and Rimington, Stella

MI6 *see* Security System section, pp. 461–4

MILLAR, FRANCIS (FRANK)
Ind. U. Assembly member for N. Belfast, 1982–6. Served on committees on Economic Development and Environment. Was Ind. Loyalist member of the 1973–4 Assembly and UUUC member of the Convention, 1975–6. b. Belfast, 1925. Founder member, Belfast Protestant Action, 1956–64. Belfast City Council, 1972–93; deputy Lord Mayor, 1992–3. As a former shipyard worker and shop steward he was active in 1988 in opposing privatisation of Harland and Wolff plc. In January 1993 he was in City Council delegation lunching in Dublin with its Lord Mayor, Gay Mitchell (FG). He retired from the council in 1993.

MILLAR, FRANCIS (FRANK)
Elected unopposed to Assembly for S. Belfast at by-election, March 1984. General Secretary, UUP, 1983–7. b. Belfast, 1954; son of Ind. U. councillor Frank Millar. Press officer, Young Unionist Council, 1972–3. Research officer for UUP MPs at Westminster, 1977–81. Press officer at party HQ, 1981–3, before becoming youngest-ever general secretary of the party. One of three members of Unionist inter-party task force set up by Unionist leaders to advise on tactics in opposing the AIA. His resignation as general secretary in September 1987, to become a TV researcher in London, was believed to be due to disappointment that the task-force report had not been more fully implemented. In the 1987 general election he was the party's candidate in W. Belfast, polling some 7,000 votes. He rejected suggestions that the UUP should have stood aside to maximise vote against sitting PSF MP Gerry Adams. He said that for the party to have called for support for the SDLP would have incurred the

contempt of Unionists across NI. London editor of *Irish Times,* 1991–.

MILLS, SIR PETER
Parliamentary Under-Secretary, NIO, 1972–4, with special responsibility for Agriculture. Previously, Parliamentary Secretary, MAFF. b. 1921. Conservative MP for Torrington, 1964–70; Devon West, 1974–9; Devon West and Torridge, 1983–7. Retired in 1987.

MILLS, WILLIAM STRATTON
MP for N. Belfast, 1959–74. b. 1 July 1922. One of a group of Unionist MPs – styled a 'truth squad' by the party – who visited the US and Canada in August 1969 to counter statements by Bernadette Devlin MP. He had served on several Conservative Party committees, including the executive of the 1922 (backbenchers') Committee, and as vice-chairman of the NI Committee. But in February 1971 he voted against the Heath Government as a protest against its 'inadequate security policy' in NI. After the introduction of direct rule, he expressed the view that any future Stormont Assembly should not be dominated by one party and should not have control of security. This was unwelcome to many Unionists, and when he failed to persuade the party's Standing Committee in 1972 that members of Vanguard should be expelled, he resigned from the party. He continued to sit at Westminster, initially as an Ind. Unionist and then as an Alliance MP from 1973 until the February 1974 general election.

MINFORD, NATHANIEL (NAT)
Speaker of the NI Assembly, 1973–4. b. 1913; d. 1975. Unionist MP for Antrim, 1960–72. Leader of the Commons, 1971–2. Elected to Assembly for S. Antrim, 1973.

MITCHELL, SIR DAVID BOWER
Parliamentary Under-Secretary, NIO, January 1981–3. b. 20 June 1928. Conservative MP for Basingstoke, 1964–83; Hampshire North West, 1983–. He took charge of the Environment Department at Stormont – the department which has the most wide-ranging responsibilities, taking in much of

local government, housing and planning, the 'enterprise zones' in Belfast and Derry and the Belfast integrated operation, for which EC aid was provided. Under-Secretary of State at Transport 1983–6; Minister of State, 1986–8. Left Government, 1988. BIPB, 1989–.

MITCHELL, CAPTAIN ROBERT

Unionist MP for N. Armagh 1969–72. b. 1912. Lurgan Borough Council, 1957–73; Coleraine Council, 1977–93. Captain Mitchell, as secretary of the Unionist Backbenchers' Committee, 1971–2, was often critical of the Government's law-and-order policies. He questioned the value of the Unionist anti-AIA council boycott campaign. Vice-chairman, E. Londonderry Conservative Association, 1989–.

MOLYNEAUX, JAMES HENRY

Leader of the Ulster Unionist Party, 1979–. MP for S. Antrim, 1970–83; MP for Lagan Valley, 1983–. Assembly member for S. Antrim, 1982–6. Privy Councillor, 1983. Antrim Co. Council, 1964–73. b. 27 August 1920. He was Whip and Secretary of the Unionist Coalition MPs from March to October 1974. He had been defeated by Harry West in a contest for the party leadership in January 1974, but he succeeded West as leader of the coalition MPs when West lost his seat in October 1974. Molyneaux held this post until the break-up of the coalition in 1977, and he continued as leader of the Ulster Unionist MPs. Vice-president of the Ulster Unionist Council, Imperial grand master of the Orange Order, and Sovereign Commonwealth grand master of the Royal Black Institution. His leadership has been marked by the adoption of a neutral stance at Westminster, in contrast to the party's former close association with the Conservative Party. He had a leading role in persuading the Callaghan Government to give NI more MPs. In early 1977 he advocated some form of interim devolution, but his critics within unionism accused him of seeking integration rather than full devolution. When he took over the party leadership in 1979, the party was somewhat

demoralised by the triumph of the Rev. Ian Paisley in the European election. But he vigorously defended the UUP decision to stand aside from the Atkins constitutional conference at Stormont in 1980, and seemed to be determined to build a more broadly based leadership and to tighten party organisation at the grass roots. At the same time, he tried to project himself to a greater extent through the media. Despite this, the DUP achieved a small lead in votes over the UUP in the 1981 council elections, and this was followed by some rumblings against his leadership. In the run-up to the 1982 Assembly elections, he was active in Parliament and outside, warning that the Prior plan was a serious threat to unionism. He pressed one argument repeatedly – that the 'rolling devolution' Assembly could not produce majority-rule government since it basically sought to re-establish the Sunningdale formula, both in terms of power-sharing government and a new cross-border institution. At the end of 1981 he announced the setting up of a Council for the Union 'to defeat the drift towards a united Ireland, as indicated by the Anglo-Irish talks'. In his speech at the Royal Black Preceptory demonstration at Scarva, Co. Armagh, in 1982 he commented that 'certain not-so-loyal Crown servants' had not been surprised by the murder of the Rev. Robert Bradford. James Prior described it as an 'appalling charge' and referred it to the Chief Constable. In the 1982 Assembly election he led his party to a modest victory – the UUP took five more seats than the DUP, and achieved a 3 per cent swing in votes from the DUP as compared with the 1981 council elections. His own first-preference vote of 19,978 in S. Antrim was the largest of the whole election. In the 1983 Westminster election he tried to establish an electoral pact with DUP in marginal seats, but largely failed. His majority in the 1983 Westminster election in the new seat, Lagan Valley, was more than 17,000 and the UUP achievement in taking eleven NI seats in that election, putting it ahead of the SDP in Parliament, strengthened his position as leader. Margaret Thatcher appointed him a Privy Councillor in 1983, but his efforts, in partnership with the Rev. Ian Paisley, to persuade the PM to drop plans to give the Republic a direct say in NI affairs failed. The AIA was clearly a major blow to the UUP leader, who had taken comfort from Thatcher's rejection in 1984 of the main options of the NIF report. An immediate consequence of the AIA was a cementing of the Molyneaux–Paisley joint leadership of unionism, which had been evident earlier in action against PSF membership of councils. They lead the 'Ulster Says No' campaign with considerable vigour, and Molyneaux's majority in Lagan Valley in the 1986 protest by-election rose to nearly 30,000. With his attachment to Westminster, the Unionist ploy of staying away from Parliament cannot have been easy for him, and he had the painful experience of seeing UUP representation reduced in the by-elections with the defeat of Jim Nicholson in Newry and Armagh, and again in the 1987 general election with Enoch Powell unseated in S. Down. The drop in the overall Unionist vote in 1987 was apparently taken by Molyneaux as a signal that a more sophisticated campaign was called for, and one result was the start in 1987 of 'talks about talks' with Secretary of State Tom King. No great optimism surrounded the discussions, however, for while Unionists were prepared to offer a role in Government to the SDLP, it was nothing like full-blooded power-sharing, which, indeed, the UUP leader described as a 'dead duck' in July 1988. And direct talks with Dublin were envisaged by Unionists only after a devolved administration had been established in NI. In the spring of 1988, with Irish Premier Charles Haughey offering talks to Unionist leaders without conditions, Molyneaux made several intriguing comments about the possibility of North–South contacts short of a summit. One upshot was nervousness in the DUP, but by late 1988 the Molyneaux–Paisley axis remained intact. The Molyneaux affability was shown to have concealed some unexpected toughness, for the anti-AIA campaign called for the expulsion of the N. Down

association of the party in the run-up to the 1987 election. It also entailed the expulsion of some councillors opposed to the boycott of local government. He made his own personal protest at the AIA by resigning as a JP in 1987. During the prolonged 'talks about talks' with Secretaries of State between 1988 and 1991, which were to lead to the Brooke–Mayhew Talks, he maintained a fairly close liaison with Ian Paisley but, as the substantive talks revealed, their tactical approach differed on occasion. He left no doubt, however, about his attitude to power-sharing. In March 1989 he said NI's age-old divisions could not be ignored by 'forcing a shotgun marriage between those who are British and those who with varying degrees of enthusiasm are attracted to the ideals of Irishness'. At the same time, he sought without success to tempt Charles Haughey into conceding a replacement of the AIA in the shape of a 'much wider British–Irish agreement', but rejected Haughey's call for cross-border economic talks. Throughout the run-up to the Major talks he argued against 'high wire' devolution, and maintained his view that devolution was best organised in the context of greater powers for Scotland and Wales. He deplored Peter Brooke's comment in 1991 that Britain had 'no selfish or strategic interest' in staying in NI. In the crucial stages of the Brooke–Mayhew negotiations in 1992, his delegation lined up with DUP and Alliance in 'broad agreement' on a committee-based system of government at Stormont, but he supported the DUP in saying that no agreement was possible unless the Republic was prepared to drop its claim to NI. But, unlike Paisley, he was prepared to travel to Dublin for talks with Irish Ministers and to put forward ideas for North–South consultation in the absence of any assurance from Dublin that its claim would be put to a referendum. His general approach to the exchanges, and his plea for inter-party contacts to be continued when the process was wound up without agreement in November 1992, served to fuel Dublin opposition attacks on Taoiseach Albert Reynolds. With John

Major having a smaller Commons majority than Margaret Thatcher, he continued to pursue an independent course in Parliament and UUP MPs united against the Government on the Maastricht Treaty vote in 1992, cutting the Government lead to three. In August 1992 he told Orangemen in New York that NI people were 'victims of ethnic cleansing'. As the British and Irish Governments tried to restart talks in early 1993, he urged a 'two-strand' approach. He wanted talks between local parties and major interest groups, such as the Churches, business and farming, in order to create stability, whilst the British and Irish Governments would tackle issues such as the Republic's constitutional claim to NI. He said repeated political initiatives had only created instability, and the North–South talks in 1992 had been a 'charade' and had widened the gulf between the communities. On 12 July 1993 he claimed that a peace plan with up to fifty-five points had been put to PIRA the previous Christmas in a 'very significant exercise'. While he and others returned that night to the Commons to vote against VAT on domestic fuel, the UUP support for the Government on the Maastricht Treaty vote led to claims of a 'deal'. He told the *Independent* that '[Major and I] do understand each other'. He also made it clear that Major's Scottish campaign in 1992 and McNamara's view of 'consent' had influenced his support for the Conservatives. On 2 August he appeared to launch a flier when he predicted an eighty-five-member Assembly by 1995. He said it had been part of his 'Blueprint for Stability' presented to Major in April. The Assembly would have administrative power, exercised by a committee structure, and would have functional links with the Republic. He told his party conference in Craigavon in October that the Hume–Adams contacts had wrecked any chance of inter-party talks by seeking a future for NI outside the UK, and he also proposed a lengthy quarantine period before PSF could enter talks. He conveyed these views to PM Major. He described Dick Spring's six principles as 'a great improvement' whereas the

Hume–Adams proposals were 'a recipe for bloodshed'. In November he warned that diplomats were creating instability unseen since the 1970s and that there was a hardening of middle-class attitudes. He urged the dropping of the search for a comprehensive constitutional settlement in favour of a new Assembly. In a cryptic message on 26 November he warned that significant developments would break over the weekend about the terrorist campaign and on 28 November the *Observer* broke the story of contacts with the Provisionals over twenty years and in detail over the past three years. His reaction to the December Downing Street Declaration was in marked contrast to the outright rejection by Rev. Ian Paisley and the DUP. In a short speech he said that in a previous Downing Street Declaration in 1969 PM Harold Wilson had described NI as an 'internal matter for the Parliament of UK' and he hoped the drift from that position had now stopped. He said the declaration had brought the destabilising to an end and he wanted the form of government wished by 85 per cent of the population. He sought a series of assurances about the non-Irish character of the agreement, which Major confirmed. In December he said his aim was an NI Assembly in 1994 with eighty-five members and with formal contacts with Dublin but not of an executive character; PSF could enter talks when it had clearly rejected violence. When the Provisional movement had not formally responded to the declaration by early January 1994 he told a Lisburn party meeting that there should be a crackdown on PIRA and a restoration of accountable democracy. With Paisley arguing 'sellout', Molyneaux argued the reverse in the *Belfast Telegraph*. As the Irish Government began to offer clarification, and brought the broadcasting ban to an end before any cessation of violence, his tone became sharper. He argued that PIRA had rejected the declaration and by early February argued that the declaration was dead.

MONDAY CLUB

The Ulster Monday Club was established in 1975 and is linked to the National

Monday Club, which has frequently featured Unionists at its Conservative conference gatherings. National Monday Club chairman David Storey told the local club at its tenth anniversary luncheon in 1985 that if terrorism in NI were to triumph, Ireland could become Britain's Cuba.

MORGAN, WILLIAM JAMES

UUP Assembly, 1973–4, and Convention, 1975–6, member for N. Belfast. b. 1914. MP for Oldpark (Belfast) at Stormont, 1949–58. MP for Clifton (Belfast) at Stormont, 1959–69. Minister of Health and Local Government, 1961–4. Minister of Labour, 1964–5; Minister of Health and Social Services, 1965–9; NI Senate 1970–2. Took strong line against the Council of Ireland proposal during Assembly debate on Sunningdale proposals, and on this issue transferred support from Brian Faulkner to Harry West in May 1974.

MORRELL, LESLIE JAMES

Head of the Department of Agriculture in NI Executive, 1974. b. Enniskillen, 1931. B.Agr. (QUB). Farms near Coleraine and active in Royal Ulster Agricultural Society. Assembly member for Londonderry, 1973–4, but failed there in Convention election, 1975. Deputy Leader of UPNI, 1974–8. Londonderry County Council, 1969–73. Coleraine District Council, 1973–7.

MORRICE, JANE ELIZABETH

Head of EC Commission office in NI, March 1992–. b. Belfast, 11 May 1954. BA (Hons.), UU. Trainee, EC Agriculture Division, Brussels, 1980. Brussels-based journalist with French press agency European Report, also contributing to BBC World Service, 1980–6. Made films on Africa for production company C91, 1986–7. Journalist with BBC NI (labour relations and business correspondent), 1988–92. Author of *The Lomé Convention: from Politics to Practice* and *The North–South Dialogue* (on Third World issues).

MORRISON, DANIEL GERARD (DANNY)

PSF Assembly member for Mid-Ulster, 1982–6. b. 1953. A former internee; a charge of PIRA membership was dropped in 1979. Became well known through TV appearances during the 1981 Maze Prison hunger strike, because he was nominated by Bobby Sands MP as external spokesman for the fasting prisoners. PSF director of publicity, 1981–90. (Also editor for a time of *An Phoblacht/Republican News*.) His remark at the PSF Ard Fheis in 1981 about Republicans, 'with an Armalite in one hand and a ballot paper in the other, we will take power in Ireland', became a familiar phrase to illustrate the stance of the movement. In January 1982 he was arrested when trying to enter the US from Canada with Owen Carron MP. In December 1982 he was banned from entering GB when invited by GLC leader Ken Livingstone to speak to Labour MPs and councillors in London. In the 1983 general election he was only 78 votes behind the DUP winner in Mid-Ulster, but in the 1986 by-election the DUP margin had increased to nearly 10,000, and he was just a little ahead of SDLP. In 1987 he did not contest the seat. In the 1984 European election he secured 13.3 per cent of the first-preference votes (91,476) to emerge as runner-up. In the 1989 European election he was again runner-up, but his vote was almost halved compared with 1984. Seven months later, in January 1990, he was arrested on a charge of conspiracy to murder and PIRA membership. At his trial it was claimed that he had been in a house in W. Belfast where an RUC informer was being unlawfully imprisoned. In court, he claimed PIRA had the right to kill RUC informers. He was sentenced to eight year's imprisonment on the unlawful imprisonment charge. His novel *West Belfast* was published in 1989.

MORRISON, GEORGE

VUPP (and later UUUM) Convention member for S. Antrim, 1975–6. b. 1924. A founder member of the Vanguard Unionist Party, he is a former chairman of the Lisburn branch. In the row over William Craig's plan in the Convention for a voluntary coalition between Unionists and the SDLP he opposed Craig and became a member of UUUM, later the

UUUP led by Ernest Baird. Lisburn Borough Council, 1973–93. Joined UUP, 1983. Grand master, Co. Antrim, in Orange Order, 1985–. Eastern Health Board, 1989–.

MORROW, ADAM JAMES (ADDIE)

All. Assembly member for E. Belfast, 1982–6. Served on Agriculture and Education scrutiny committees. All. deputy leader, 1984–7. Castlereagh Council, 1973–89 (deputy Mayor, 1981). b. 1929. He was a founder member of Alliance Party and, as he had a large dairy farm in Castlereagh, was a natural for party spokesman on agriculture. Unsuccessfully contested Strangford in 1983 and 1987 general elections, and N. Down in 1992. Stood down as party chairman in March 1993, disillusioned by continued 'tribal voting'. Founder member of Corrymeela Community.

MOWLAM, MARJORIE

A Labour Party front-bench spokeswoman on NI, 1988–90. b. 18 September 1949. MA, Ph.D. (University of Iowa). MP for Redcar, 1987–. In 1988 she was critical of new education proposals in NI. Spokeswoman on Citizen's Charter and women, 1992–3; National Heritage, 1993–.

MOYLE, ROLAND DUNSTAN

Minister of State, NIO, 1974–6. Labour MP for Lewisham North, 1966–74; Lewisham East, 1974–83. Defeated 1983. b. 12 March 1928. Son of late Baron Moyle, a Labour peer. MA, LLB (Cantab.). Barrister. In the NIO he took charge of the departments of Education and Environment after the collapse of the NI Executive. Joint deputy chairman, Police Complaints Authority, 1985–91.

MOYNIHAN, DANIEL PATRICK

US Senator (New York State), 1977–. b. 16 March 1927. Associated with Senator Edward Kennedy and other Irish-American Democratic politicians in urging peace in NI and in setting up the Friends of Ireland Group in 1981. In June 1979 he said he hoped to see Ireland united, and that American interest in NI was consistent. 'I hope it will not be

supposed that we will be everlastingly patient,' he said. He also attacked the PIRA as a 'band of sadistic murderers'. Strong advocate in Senate of International Fund for Ireland. In 1992 US Catholic Church leaders protested at the award to Moynihan of the prestigious Laetare Medal by the Notre Dame University of Indiana, their objection being his support for abortion rights.

MOYOLA, LORD

Formerly Major James Chichester-Clark, PM of NI, May 1969–March 1971. b. 12 February 1923. Returned unopposed as Unionist MP for S. Londonderry in 1960; again unopposed in 1965, but had to fight off a challenge from Bernadette Devlin (PD) in 1969. Unionist Chief Whip in 1963, leader of the Commons, 1966, and succeeded Harry West as Minister of Agriculture in 1967. On 23 April 1969 he resigned from the O'Neill Government, following speculation that he might become Premier if Captain O'Neill resigned. He gave as his reason for resignation the timing of the 'one man, one vote' reform, although he said he was not against the principle of the reform. Five days later O'Neill stood down and on 1 May 1969 Chichester-Clark was elected PM by seventeen votes to sixteen over Brian Faulkner. One of his first acts was to order an amnesty for those convicted of, or charged with, political offences since the previous October. The Rev. Ian Paisley was among those released from prison. But neither this gesture, nor an appeal to opposition MPs to join in a declaration that NI was at peace and would remain so, brought any response. The demands for reform were intensified and the violence grew to a climax in August 1969 when the serious rioting in the Bogside area of Derry and in Belfast forced the Chichester-Clark Government to ask for troops to be sent to help maintain order. The situation led to angry exchanges between Chichester-Clark and the Republic's Taoiseach Jack Lynch. Lynch had called for UN intervention, moved army field hospitals to the border, and arranged special camps in the Republic to accommodate people who had fled their homes in NI. Chichester-

Clark attacked Lynch for 'inflammatory and ill-considered' comments. The entry of British troops subtly changed the position of Chichester-Clark and his Government. At Downing Street talks with PM Harold Wilson, the NI Premier agreed that the army GOC should be director of security operations. At Downing Street, Wilson gave a TV interview in which he indicated that the USC (B Specials) would be phased out. This was denied by Chichester-Clark and his Ministers, but by October the USC was on the way out, the RUC was being disarmed, and the Inspector-General of the RUC, Anthony Peacocke, had been succeeded by Sir Arthur Young. It was all extremely embarrassing for Chichester-Clark, who argued, however, that the new UDR would essentially fill the role of the USC. (In a BBC interview in 1989, he claimed that the NI Government had been told by James Callaghan that if it did not agree to disband the B Specials, they would be abolished by the British Government and it would not get the UDR.) Home Secretary Callaghan, who had ministerial responsibility for NI, had, in the meantime, twice visited the region to encourage reforms such as anti-discrimination measures, action to ensure fair housing allocations, and to improve community relations. The NI Premier now had to face a double threat – a loyalist backlash, reflected in widespread violence, including shooting and the erection of barricades in loyalist areas, and, on the other side, the obvious growth of the IRA, with rioting in Republican areas, which produced a threat from the GOC, General Freeland, that troops might shoot to kill. Besides, he had to face the loss of two Stormont seats to the Rev. Ian Paisley and his deputy, the Rev. William Beattie, and in June 1970 the election which brought the Conservatives back to power also returned Paisley to Westminster. Early July brought a fierce gun battle between the army and IRA snipers after soldiers had begun to search houses in the area. A three-day curfew was clamped on the Falls area, and more than 100 firearms and some 20,000 rounds of ammunition were found by soldiers. But the continued existence of Republican no-go areas made many Unionists furious with Chichester-Clark. Groups of paramilitaries mushroomed in loyalist areas of Belfast. At the same time the PIRA emerged, and the murder of three young Scottish soldiers in Belfast in March 1971 was the signal for a new loyalist campaign demanding Chichester-Clark's resignation. On 18 March the Premier flew to London for talks with Heath and other Ministers. He pressed for some dramatic security initiative, but Heath would only authorise an extra 1,300 troops, and many Unionists regarded this as derisory. Chichester-Clark was believed to have pressed for, among other things, saturation by the security forces of areas which he considered were dominated by the PIRA. Some of his colleagues wanted internment without trial. Two days later he resigned from the Premiership, after the Defence Secretary, Lord Carrington, had flown to Belfast for special talks with the NI Cabinet. In a statement he repeated his view that some further security initiative was needed. He also said: 'I have decided to resign because I see no other way of bringing home to all concerned the realities of the present constitutional, political and security situation.' In 1985 he was critical of lack of consultation with Unionists over AIA. Trustee, Friends of the Union Group, 1986–. In 1989 he admitted his Government had made a mistake in interning thirty men in August 1969.

MURNAGHAN, SHEELAGH MARY
Only Liberal MP to sit in NI Parliament. b. Dublin, 26 May 1924; d. 14 September 1993. LLB (QUB). Irish hockey international. A barrister, she was MP for QUB, 1961–9, and prominent in pressing for reforms, notably the introduction of PR voting in NI. Member of NI Advisory Commission and Community Relations Commission, 1972–3. Served as chairwoman of Industrial and National Insurance Tribunals. Associated with a great variety of bodies, including United Nations Association, Protestant and Catholic Encounter, and a committee

devoted to finding sites for the settlement of itinerants.

MURRAY, HAROLD (HARRY)

Chairman of the Ulster Workers' Council during the loyalist strike in May 1974. b. 1921. A Belfast shipyard shop steward, he announced the decision of the UWC to mount the stoppage which brought about the collapse of the power-sharing Executive. He was a leading spokesman of the strikers throughout the stoppage. But after the fall of the Executive, he split with the loyalist paramilitaries. At an Oxford conference on NI in July 1974 he ran into criticism from loyalists when he said that he would talk to the PIRA on condition that they put down their guns and bombs. He said his own methods had proved the best in the end since he had brought a country to a standstill in five days while PIRA had not been able to do it in five years. In July 1974 he resigned from the UWC and said that both communities would have to be brought together, and he proposed to devote himself to promoting peace. In 1975 he stood unsuccessfully as an Alliance candidate in a N. Down Borough Council by-election in Bangor, but he said later that he had not actually joined the Alliance Party. In 1982 he was involved in an effort to re-form the UWC as an organisation campaigning for jobs and worker unity, and free of paramilitary links.

N

NAPIER, SIR OLIVER

All. Assembly member for E. Belfast, 1982-6. Served on committees on Economic Development, and Finance and Personnel. Leader of Alliance, 1972-84, of which he was one of the founders, and earlier prominent in the New Ulster Movement. b. 11 July 1935. LLB (QUB). Belfast solicitor. Elected in E. Belfast to both the Assembly, 1973-4, and Convention, 1975-6. Took a prominent role in the Sunningdale Conference in 1973, and became Head of the Office of Law Reform in the power-sharing Executive. Belfast City Council,

1977-89. In the 1979 Westminster election, he stood unsuccessfully in E. Belfast, where the Alliance Party had high hopes of gaining the seat. But although he polled strongly, the seat went to DUP and he was in third place. He had another disappointment in the 1979 European election, in which he secured 39,026 (6.8 per cent) first-preference votes. He headed his party delegation in the Atkins conference at Stormont in 1980, pressing the case for partnership government, and gave strong support to the 1982 Assembly. In the 1983 Westminster election in E. Belfast he again ran third despite party hopes that he might capture the seat, and his vote further declined in the 1986 by-election. When he stepped down from the party leadership in 1984, Secretary of State Douglas Hurd said that all who had sought a political solution in NI owed him a deep debt of gratitude. Knighted in 1985. Chairman of the Standing Advisory Commission on Human Rights, 1988-92.

NATIONAL COUNCIL FOR CIVIL LIBERTIES see Liberty

NATIONAL DEMOCRATIC PARTY

A political party formed in 1965 which operated mainly in the Greater Belfast area until 1970. It developed from the National Unity movement established in 1959 to press for reform of the Nationalist Party. National Unity organised a conference in April 1964, which gave rise to a 'National Political Front'. This included Nationalist MPs and 'new frontier Nationalists' who sought a more democratically organised party. But the NPF collapsed after only five months, since there was disagreement about party organisation, and the provisional council of the NPF complained that the Nationalist MPs had not consulted them before deciding not to contest the Fermanagh-S. Tyrone seat. The 'new frontier' Nationalists then set up Nat. Dem., which had a high proportion of teachers in its ranks. It produced a variety of discussion papers but had little electoral success. When it was wound up, its members had a strong influence within the newly established SDLP.

NATIONAL H-BLOCK/ARMAGH COMMITTEE

The committee which publicised throughout the world the case for political status for Republican prisoners in the Maze and Armagh prisons during the 1980–1 hunger strikes. The committee, which covered a wide spectrum of nationalism, operated with such skill that it created serious problems for the British information services in the US, Canada, Europe, and many other areas. Its chairman was Father Piaras Ó Duill, and its main spokeswoman Bernadette McAliskey. The committee supplanted the Relatives Action Committee which operated in the initial phase of the campaign. (*See also* H-Blocks.)

NATIONALIST PARTY

Deriving from the old Irish Parliamentary Party, it was the main vehicle of anti-partition politics until the civil rights campaign developed in 1968–9. For much of its existence it was very locally based, and there was a good deal of clerical influence within it. In the 1960s, under the leadership of Eddie McAteer, there was an attempt to give it a more radical image and a constituency-based organisation, but the more dynamic approach of the civil rights movement proved to have greater popular appeal. Much of its support went over to the SDLP, and one of its MPs, Austin Currie, was a founder of the SDLP.

NATURAL LAW PARTY

Launched in March 1992, the party ran nine candidates in NI in the 1992 Westminster election, but secured only 2,147 votes and all its candidates lost their deposits. Urged merits of transcendental meditation in fighting fear and hatred. Also pledged to cut unemployment and end VAT.

NEAVE, AIREY (MIDDLETON SHEFFIELD)

Conservative MP for Abingdon, 1953–79; spokesman on NI, 1975–9. b. 23 January 1916; killed by car bomb as he drove out of House of Commons car park, 30 March 1979, an event which cast a shadow over the start of general election campaign. BA Hons. (Oxon.). Barrister. Notable army record in World War II. Wounded and taken prisoner by Germans in France, 1940, and first British officer to escape from Colditz POW camp, 1942. Attached after the war to British War Crimes Executive and served indictments on Göring and other leading war criminals tried at Nuremberg. Masterminded campaign for election of Margaret Thatcher as Conservative leader, and headed her private office from 1975 until his death. Between 1975 and September 1976 he was extremely critical of Government security policy in NI and also critical of RUC interrogation techniques, but took a more friendly attitude when Roy Mason finally succeeded Merlyn Rees as Secretary of State in 1976. He claimed that increased army covert operations and other measures to tighten security were due to Conservative prompting. Often critical of British media which, he argued, over-publicised the PIRA and magnified faults of security forces. In early 1978 his speeches and notably his reference to power-sharing as being 'no longer practical politics' caused Unionists to look on him with a more friendly eye, and the SDLP to see his policy as a retreat from that of Edward Heath and William Whitelaw. In particular, he urged the setting up of regional councils in NI. Responsibility for his murder was claimed by the INLA, and it led to strict new rules restricting the movements of visitors to Westminster. In 1986 Enoch Powell claimed he had been killed not by the INLA but by 'high contracting parties' for political purposes.

NEEDHAM, RICHARD FRANCIS

As Parliamentary Under-Secretary, NIO, September 1985–April 1992, he became longest-serving Minister under direct rule. b. 29 January 1942. Cons. MP for Chippenham, 1979–83, and N. Wiltshire, 1983–. As Sixth Earl of Kilmorey – an Irish title which he does not use – he has family links with S. Down, and his first job was a junior managerial post with Murray's tobacco factory in Belfast. He was PPS to James Prior as NI Secretary of State, so he had considerable familiarity with local issues when he took responsibility for Environment and Health and Social Services, and later the Department of Economic Development. He faced unexpected problems in the disruptive tactics employed by loyalist councillors in their campaign against the AIA and in protests at the presence of PSF councillors. In 1986 there was some opposition to his plan for the Sunday opening of pubs. But his enthusiasm for measures to strengthen the local economy was widely praised. In 1987 he launched the Laganbank and Castle Court developments in Belfast and was associated with a variety of projects in Belfast, Derry and across NI. His abrasive manner was particularly evident in his condemnation of PIRA bombing of Belfast city centre. In 1990 he suffered temporary embarrassment when loyalists monitored a telephone conversation he was having with his wife, in which he referred to PM Margaret Thatcher as 'that cow'. He dismissed it as 'a term of endearment'. He completed several engagements despite PIRA knowledge of his destination. Although he repeatedly made it clear that he wished to stay at Stormont, PM John Major switched him to the Department of Trade and Industry as Minister of State after the 1992 general election. In that election, he canvassed for NI Conservative candidates. His book, *Honourable Member*, describes the work of an MP.

NEESON, SEAN

All. Assembly member for N. Antrim, 1982–6; served on Economic Development and Education committees. b. 1946. Chairman, Alliance Party, 1982–3. Carrickfergus Council, 1977– (first Catholic Mayor, 1993–)'. Neeson, who was deputy Speaker in the Assembly and economic spokesman of his party, announced in 1988 that he was standing down from active politics, but changed his mind and was re-elected in 1989. He was a member of the party delegation in the Brooke–Mayhew Talks, 1991–2.

NEILL, MAJOR SIR IVAN

Last Speaker of NI House of Commons, 1969–72. b. Belfast, 1 July 1906. B.Sc.

(Econ.) (QUB). MP for Ballynafeigh (Belfast), 1949–72. Minister of Labour and National Insurance, 1950–61; additionally, Minister of Home Affairs, August–October 1952. Minister of Education, 1962. Minister of Finance and leader of Commons, 1964–5. (Resigned from Government, 1965.) Minister of Development, 1968. Alderman and councillor, Belfast City Council, 1964–70.

NEW CONSENSUS GROUP

A group formed in the Republic in early 1989, urging democratic devolved government in NI, integrated education and a Bill of Rights. Two Senators – John A. Murphy and David Norris – were among a widely representative delegation which travelled to NI in 1989 for talks with political parties and other groups. It claims members from FG, Prog. D. and Irish Labour, and has staged pickets at PSF conferences. Its first chairman, Michael Nugent, said its strength lay in the inclusion of people of differing ideological backgrounds. Its supporters have included Westminster MPs Peter Bottomley (Cons.) and Harry Barnes (Lab.).

NEWE, GERARD BENEDICT

Minister of State in PM's office, NI Government, 1971–2. b. Cushendall, Co. Antrim, 5 February 1907; d. November 1982. MA (QUB), D. Litt. (NUU). Newe was the only Catholic to serve in an NI Government during the fifty-one years' operation of the Government of Ireland Act, 1920. He was invited by PM Brian Faulkner to join the Government to help promote better community relations, and his acceptance of the appointment caused misgivings among some of his co-religionists. He made it clear that he was not, and never had been, a member of the Unionist Party. He believed that people must have the right to work peacefully for a united Ireland, if they wished, but he recognised the social and economic benefits for NI of the link with Britain. He was regional organiser and secretary to the NI Council of Social Service, 1948–72. Founder member of Protestant and Catholic Encounter.

NEW IRELAND FORUM

The conference of the four main Nationalist parties – Fianna Fáil, Fine Gael, Irish Labour Party and SDLP – which had its initial meeting in Dublin in May 1983, with the aim of working out an agreed approach to an NI settlement. The body owed its existence primarily to SDLP leader John Hume, who had pressed strongly for an agreed Nationalist strategy. The NIF produced its report on 3 May 1984, which comprised a detailed historical analysis from the Nationalist standpoint, together with options for a new all-Ireland constitution. The parties made it clear that their first preference was for a unitary thirty-two county state, but they also put forward the options of a federal arrangement and joint authority in NI exercised by the London and Dublin Governments equally. The report also stated: 'The parties in the Forum also remain open to discuss other views which may contribute to political development.' It was clear, however, that Fianna Fáil was laying much greater stress on the unitary-state idea than Fine Gael or Labour, and the Coalition Government led by Garret FitzGerald put strong emphasis on the offer to discuss other views 'with all others involved in the problem of NI who oppose the use of violence'. Secretary of State James Prior said the British Government could not accept the 'Nationalist interpretation' of past events or the dismissal of the strenuous efforts of successive UK Governments to deal with 'the intractable problems of NI'. Although the Government welcomed 'positive elements' in the report, it found the Forum's account of the British position to be 'one-sided and unacceptable'. The UK Government, said Prior, stood by its undertaking that NI should not cease to be part of the UK without the consent of a majority of its people 'and remains willing to give effect to any majority wish which might be expressed in favour of unity' – a clear pointer to the constitutional formula of the AIA. The Secretary of State said Unionist opposition to Irish unity was to the principle rather than the form, and there was no reason to expect consent to

change in sovereignty in NI in any of the three forms suggested. But he said it remained necessary to face the problems of division and violence in NI 'including the feelings of alienation among the Nationalist community'. In NI only the SDLP wholeheartedly backed the report. To Unionists it was another example of outside interference. To PSF it was 'a major dilution of national aspirations'. But British Labour spokesman Peter Archer described it as 'a unique initiative in recent Irish history'. The report attracted considerable international interest and support and although Thatcher dismayed the Irish Government with a comment in November 1984 that it was 'out, out, out' to the three options of the NIF report, diplomatic pressure, notably from the US and Europe, was seen as a key element in the British–Irish negotiating process which led eventually to the AIA in November 1985.

NEW IRELAND GROUP/
MOVEMENT *see* Robb, John

NEW LODGE

District adjoining Antrim Road in N. Belfast, which was regarded as a stronghold of PIRA at the height of the Troubles. When sectarian tension was high, demonstrations and car hi-jackings were frequent. In recent years, there have been some disputed killings in the area and incursions by loyalist gunmen, but also local efforts to improve its image. The *Irish News* claimed in January 1993 that twenty-five people had been killed in the New Lodge Road in twenty-three years.

NEWMAN, SIR KENNETH LESLIE

Chief Constable of the RUC, 1976–9. b. 1926. Served with Palestine Police, 1946–8, and with London Metropolitan Police, 1948–73. Became Commander at New Scotland Yard, 1972, in charge of the community relations branch. Senior deputy Chief Constable, RUC, 1973–6. As Chief Constable of the RUC, he was responsible for setting up regional crime squads to deal with terrorism and for closer intelligence liaison with the army. His period as Chief Constable was also marked by the introduction of the policy known as 'primacy of the police' which gave the RUC a more dominant role in security relative to the army. But there was also continuing criticism of RUC interrogation practices, criticism which Sir Kenneth attacked as 'less than fair'. But a number of reforms were made in interrogation procedures (*see* Bennett Report). On leaving the RUC, he became Commandant of the Police Staff College at Bramshill and was Metropolitan Police Commissioner, 1982–7. Professor of law at Bristol University, 1987–8.

NEWRY

The border town in S. Down with a mainly Catholic population, which demonstrated strong support for the civil rights movement in 1968 and 1969. There was a riot in the town on 11 January 1969 when some police vehicles were set on fire and others pushed into the canal. Ten members of the RUC and twenty-eight civilians were injured and there was much damage to shops. Spokesmen for NICRA and PD deplored the violence and said it would not help the civil rights movement. In August 1969 there was prolonged rioting and severe damage to public buildings and private property. The Scarman tribunal found that an action committee had planned the takeover of the town, but that it had been foiled by skilled police work and lack of public support. The introduction of internment in 1971 brought further violent scenes. In October 1971 the shooting dead by the army of three youths who had failed to halt was followed by burning and looting on a large scale. The town suffered several bomb attacks, notably during 1971. The biggest protest march was held on 6 February 1972, after 'Bloody Sunday'. In August 1972 the Newry branch of NICRA made a strong appeal to PIRA to call off its bombing campaign. But PIRA remained active in the area, and there was some evidence that local units of OIRA were slow to observe the ceasefire called by their leaders in 1972. There have been considerable efforts in the 1980s to counter the heavy local unemployment and to encourage tourism, but PIRA has been active in the town and adjoining border areas. In the autumn of 1984 there were ten bomb attacks in eight weeks in the town centre, and on 28 February 1985 nine RUC officers, including two women constables, died in a mortar attack on the RUC station. It was the highest RUC death toll in a single incident since the force was formed. Three RUC men also died in a PIRA attack in the summer of 1986. Violence was less serious in the late 1980s and early 1990s, but PIRA mounted several attacks in this period on the major security checkpoint on the Newry–Dundalk road. The reconstruction of the checkpoint in the summer of 1992 led to the decision of the nearby Cloghogue School authorities to move the pupils to a new site in the town. Local MP Seamus Mallon (SDLP) took up the issue with the Irish Government. Security Minister Michael Mates strongly defended the retention of the checkpoint on its existing site, but engaged in talks with local representatives on the problems raised. In 1992 there was increased Government interest in development of the town which, with the ending of border customs controls in 1993, experienced a surge in shopping traffic from the Republic.

NEWS, HUGH

SDLP Assembly member for Armagh, 1982–6. Also represented the constituency in the 1973–4 Assembly and the 1975–6 Convention. b. Lurgan, 1931. Publican and pharmaceutical chemist. Lurgan Borough Council (Independent Citizens' Association member), 1964–7. Craigavon District Council, 1973–89. National vice-president, AOH, 1974.

NEW ULSTER MOVEMENT

A movement which developed in early 1969 to urge moderation and non-sectarianism in politics and to press for reforms. It was among the first groups to call for a community relations commission, a central housing executive and the abolition of the USC. In a pamphlet in 1971, *The Reform of Stormont*, it put forward proposals for power-sharing in government and later that year urged the suspension of the Stormont

Parliament. Many of its early members (it claimed a membership of 7,000 in 1969) became active in the Alliance Party. Its first chairman, Brian W. Walker, became director of Oxfam in 1974, and he was succeeded by Dr Stanley Worrall, former headmaster of Methodist College Belfast.

NEW ULSTER POLITICAL RESEARCH GROUP *see* Ulster Defence Association

NICHOLSON, JAMES (JIM)
UUP MEP for NI, 1989–. UUP MP for Newry and Armagh, 1983–6. Assembly member for Armagh, 1982–6 (served on Agriculture Committee). b. 1945. Armagh Council, 1975–. Secretary–organiser, Mid. S. Armagh Unionist Association, 1973–83. He took the new Newry and Armagh seat in 1983 against the odds, when the overall Nationalist majority was split between SDLP and PSF and the DUP backed him. But he lost to SDLP deputy leader Seamus Mallon in the 1986 by-election called in protest at the AIA and so could be said to be the only parliamentary casualty of the Unionist tactic. He lost out again to the SDLP in 1987, but was returned as the UUP MEP in 1989, slightly improving on the UUP's 1984 share of the vote. As a Westminster MP, he was on the Commons Select Committee on Agriculture. He was chairman of UUP in 1991, when he became a leading figure in the delegation at the Brooke–Mayhew Talks. In January 1994 sought a 'new NI', arguing that direct rule had caused more 'suffering and strife' than Stormont had previously. Chairman, European Parliament Shipping/Shipbuilding Committee. Early in February 1994 he complained that £170 million of EC money for NI was being held up by red tape.

NO-GO AREAS
The term coined for the districts behind the barricades between the summer of 1969 and July 1972, where paramilitary groups, rather than the forces of law and order, tended to hold sway. The most notable were the Bogside in Derry – Free • Derry – and parts of W. Belfast, although similar enclaves existed in other places. The term persisted for some time after the barriers had come down, and even after 'Operation Motorman', undertaken by the security forces on 31 July 1972, which sought to re-establish official control in such areas. Although most of the no-go areas were PIRA-dominated, loyalists on occasions set up their own no-go areas, particularly in the Shankill–Woodvale district of Belfast, through the agency of the UDA. Some of these moves were designed to pressurise the Government to act against the Republican no-go areas. Some loyalists continued to see a no-go element in the refusal of the Government to allow the deployment of the UDR in some Republican districts.

NORAID *see* Irish Northern Aid Committee

NORTHERN CONSENSUS GROUP
A group of professional people, Protestant and Catholic, who have been calling since 1982 for a political solution within NI, involving both traditions in government. It gave evidence to NIF and to the Assembly committee on the AIA, and has had talks with British and Irish Ministers. Leading members include Professor Desmond Rea, Professor Robert W. Stout, John G. Neill, and Terence Donaghy, a Belfast solicitor.

NORTHERN IRELAND CIVIL RIGHTS ASSOCIATION
The body established in January 1967, which spearheaded the civil rights campaign. Its constitution was similar to that of the London-based National Council for Civil Liberties, whose secretary, Tony Smythe, attended the inaugural meeting in Belfast. Its initial committee comprised Noel Harris (chairman), of the Draughtsmen and Allied Trades' Association; Dr Conn McCluskey (vice-chairman), of the Campaign for Social Justice; Fred Heatley (treasurer), of the Wolfe Tone Society; Jack Bennett (information officer), of the Wolfe Tone Society; Michael Dolley (QUB); Ken Banks (trade union); Kevin Agnew (Republican Labour Party); John

Quinn (Ulster Liberal Party); Paddy Devlin (NILP); Terence O'Brien (unattached); and Robin Cole (chairman of Young Unionist Group at QUB), co-opted. The basic aims of NICRA were: one man, one vote in council elections; ending of 'gerrymandered' electoral boundaries; machinery to prevent discrimination by public authorities and to deal with complaints; fair allocation of public housing; repeal of Special Powers Act; and disbanding of B Specials. NICRA's initial impact was in organising protest marches. The first was held at Dungannon, Co. Tyrone, on 24 August 1968, on the suggestion of Nationalist MP Austin Currie, who had already staged a sit-in at a house in nearby Caledon over a housing allocation. Some 4,000 people singing 'We shall overcome' marked this first NICRA event, but it was the next march in Derry, on 5 October 1968, which put the civil rights campaign in the world headlines and on TV. Several leading opposition figures, including Gerry Fitt MP and Nationalist leader Eddie McAteer MP, were injured in a clash with the RUC. Lord Cameron, in his report, found that they had been batoned without justification or excuse, although Fitt's conduct was described as 'reckless and wholly irresponsible'. The Duke Street affair, in which eleven policemen and seventy-seven civilians were hurt, made a big impression internationally and particularly on Labour opinion in Britain. It brought strong pressure from the Wilson Government on Stormont to introduce reforms. The NICRA campaign was attacked by Unionists as a front for the IRA. The Cameron Commission held that while there had been evidence that IRA members were active in the association, there was no sign that they were dominant or in a position to control or direct the policy of NICRA. With the arrival of internment, it was engaged in promoting a civil disobedience campaign, which led to widespread withholding of rent and rates. The setting up of the power-sharing Executive led to some alienation from the SDLP. During the Convention, it was active in pressing for a Bill of Rights. It also became a point of contact for outside bodies interested in civil rights. Old controversies within the movement were revived in 1988, when events were organised to mark the twentieth anniversary of the initial demonstration.

NORTHERN IRELAND LABOUR PARTY

A socialist party drawing its support mainly from Greater Belfast, founded in 1924. The party, which had only limited electoral success, was essentially neutral on the border issue until 1949. In that year its annual conference supported the link with Britain, and this gained it more Protestant support but added to its difficulties in attracting Catholic votes. The peak of its success was from 1958 to 1965, when it had four MPs at Stormont, all from Belfast constituencies. Indeed, in 1962 it was only 8,000 votes short of the Unionist total in the city. One of its weaknesses was its failure to secure full trade-union backing, and the British Labour Party was only fitfully interested in its fate, occasionally providing money for Westminster elections and the endorsement of candidates by the national leader. It never won a Westminster seat, despite amassing nearly 100,000 votes in the 1970 election, but it often polled strongly in E. Belfast. Its main personalities in its heyday were secretary Sam Napier, Billy (now Lord) Blease, Charles Brett (chairman, later Sir Charles), Brian Garrett (chairman) and Stormont MPs Tom Boyd, Billy Boyd, Vivian Simpson, David Bleakley and Paddy Devlin. Devlin, MP for Falls, was one of the founders of the SDLP, and the creation of that party made the task of the NILP even more uphill. In the 1973-4 Assembly and 1975-6 Convention it held only one seat (David Bleakley), and in the 1977 and 1981 council elections took only one seat (in Ards). In the 1973 Assembly election it supported power-sharing, but when the Executive collapsed it came out against both a Council of Ireland and formal power-sharing. When all three Belfast candidates lost their deposits in the 1979 Westminster election, and the party opted out of the 1982 Assembly contest, few people saw any future for it, and it was absorbed in Labour '87, set up in 1987.

O

Ó BRÁDAIGH, RUAIRÍ

President of PSF, 1970–83. b. 1932. An ex-technical school teacher, he was a TD for a period in the 1950s, being elected for Sinn Féin on an abstentionist ticket in Longford–Westmeath. He is also believed to have been chief of staff of the IRA for two periods before the organisation split at the end of 1969. In 1973 he was sentenced in Dublin to six months' imprisonment for PIRA membership. He was the first person to be prosecuted under the provision of the Republic's Offences Against the State Act, which allows a court to convict on the evidence of a senior Garda officer that a person is a member of a proscribed organisation. He took part in the Feakle Talks with Protestant Churchmen in 1974. He brought a certain organisational flair to the central direction of PSF, and energetically promoted the federal 'Éire Nua' policy. He opposed the dropping of this policy in 1981, telling the Ard Fheis: 'Don't swop a policy for a slogan.' He was active in building up contacts with revolutionary groups abroad, and in opposing the EC. In 1983 he was succeeded as president of PSF by Gerry Adams, and at the 1986 Ard Fheis also lost out to Adams on the issue of the ending of the traditional policy of abstention from the Dáil. Ó Brádaigh led the resistance to change, but Adams and his supporters won the day easily. Ó Brádaigh was among a group which then set up Republican Sinn Féin. In 1991 he attacked the Brooke Talks as based on the premiss that NI remained under British rule.

Ó CONAILL, DÁITHÍ

A leading strategist of the Provisional Republican movement, 1972–86. b. Cork, 1937; d. 1991. He is believed to have joined the IRA at the age of eighteen, and he was wounded in the 1956 IRA campaign. In 1958 he escaped from the Curragh camp in the Republic,

where he had been interned. He worked for a time as a teacher of building and woodwork at Ballyshannon, Co. Donegal, vocational school. In 1960 he was sentenced to eight years' imprisonment for carrying a gun and ammunition with intent to endanger life, but he served only three years. In 1971 he narrowly avoided capture when Interpol set up a big search operation after a consignment of Czechoslovakian arms had been found at Amsterdam airport. He had been travelling with a companion, Maria McGuire, who later fled to England and described her IRA experiences in a book: *To Take Arms*. He was said to have invented the car bomb, and by April 1973, when he slipped through a police-and-army security net to give an oration in Milltown cemetery, Belfast, he was believed to have become chief of staff of the PIRA. In a TV interview in 1974 he stated – as he did on many other occasions – that there would be no end to the PIRA campaign until the British made a declaration of intent to withdraw from NI. By 1974 he was a vice-president of PSF, and he was among the PIRA leaders who talked to Protestant Churchmen at the secret meeting in Feakle, Co. Clare – the meeting which led to the 1975 PIRA ceasefire. His arrest in Dublin during the ceasefire was presented by the PIRA as a bid by Dublin to end what the PIRA called a 'truce'. He was sentenced to twelve months' imprisonment for PIRA membership, and was again arrested in July 1976, coincidentally on the same day as the British Ambassador in Dublin, Christopher Ewart-Biggs, was killed in a landmine explosion. After his release in 1977, he appeared to be absorbed by political work, but there were strong Unionist protests when he slipped into Derry at Easter 1978 to address a Republican ceremony, just as he had done four years earlier. In the 1981 general election in the Republic he was active in supporting the H-Block candidates. But his influence waned in the 1980s. He had encouraged some contacts with Protestant paramilitaries, and had seen the 'Éire Nua' federal policy as a concession of sorts to loyalists. But his arguments were swept aside by NI delegates at the 1981 Ard Fheis who brought about the defeat of the federal idea. Soon after the PIRA bombings in London in July 1982, he threatened more bombs in Britain when he spoke at a rally in Monaghan. But in 1986 he walked out of the PSF Ard Fheis, when it voted to end abstention from the Dáil, and he became one of the founders of Republican Sinn Féin. His funeral was attended by both sections of the movement.

O'BRIEN, CONOR CRUISE

Irish politician and journalist. b. 3 November 1917. BA, Ph.D. (TCD). In his many-sided career, he has often spoken out on NI, and took a strongly individualist viewpoint as Irish Labour Party spokesman when he was elected to the Dáil in 1969, and later as Minister for Posts and Telegraphs in the Coalition Government of 1973-7. He was defeated in the Dáil general election in 1977, but was then elected to the Senate from TCD. He resigned from the Senate in 1979. In his earlier career he had been in the Irish diplomatic service and in 1961 represented the UN Secretary-General in Katanga. He was vice-chancellor of the University of Ghana, 1962-5, and Professor of Humanities at New York University, 1965-9. His general theme on NI has been that repeated calls from the Republic for a united Ireland are counter-productive, and may even encourage violence. In opposition after the defeat of the Coalition Government in 1977, he resigned from the Irish Labour Parliamentary Party so that he could be free to speak on NI. At a conference on NI at Oxford University in September 1977 he argued forcibly that opinion surveys showed that there was not a majority in the whole of Ireland in favour of Irish unity - a claim which was hotly contested inside the Republic. As Minister for Posts and Telegraphs, he banned broadcasts by illegal paramilitary organisations and PSF. In his book, *States of Ireland* (1972), he suggested that the NI civil rights campaign had failed to make use of its victories and allowed itself to be used as a springboard for the re-emergence of the IRA. From 1978 to 1980 he was editor-in-chief, the *Observer*, London. He was critical of the AIA and in 1988 he suggested that the AIA would fade away gradually; he hoped it would be followed by talks, not about moving towards a united Ireland, but about how to live and work together, while agreeing to differ on political allegiance. In 1990 he publicly embraced unionism. In the run-up to the inter-party talks in 1991, he was mentioned by some Unionists as a possible independent chairman for the North-South strand of the talks. But he did not think the talks would succeed. In the 1992 general election, he supported Cons. candidates in N. Down and S. Belfast.

O'BRIEN, WILLIAM

Labour MP for Normanton, 1983-. b. 25 January 1929. Leeds University. Opposition spokesman on NI, 1992-; Environment, 1988-92. Wakefield Council, 1973-. Former coalminer and member NUM since 1945.

O'DONOGHUE, PATRICK

SDLP Assembly member for S. Down, 1982-6. Also represented S. Down in the 1973-4 Assembly and the 1975-6 Convention. b. Castlewellan, Co. Down, 1930; d. 1989. Deputy Speaker in the 1973 Assembly. SDLP spokesman on Education. Down District Council, 1973-85. Active in ALJ and GAA.

OFFICIAL IRISH REPUBLICAN ARMY

The term 'Official IRA' dates from the beginning of 1970, when the split in the Republican movement meant that there were now two branches, the Officials and the Provisionals, each comprising an IRA, or military, wing, and a political counterpart, Sinn Féin. In NI the 'Officials' were often dubbed the 'Stickies', because of their practice of sticking Easter lilies on their coat lapels during the annual commemorations of the 1916 Easter Rising in Dublin. OIRA appears to have been largely inactive since the summer of 1972 when it declared a ceasefire. It represented those militant Republicans who remained loyal to

Cathal Goulding as chief of staff, when the movement divided on the issue of parliamentary action during the December 1969–January 1970 period. There was majority support in the IRA at the end of 1969 for switching to political action – that is, seeking to have candidates elected to the Parliaments in Dublin, Belfast and London on a leftist, broadly Marxist policy. Clearly, Goulding and many of his associates felt that the lack of public support for the IRA border campaign in 1956–62 suggested that Republicans generally wanted more emphasis on strictly political action. But those who sought this new approach failed to secure a two-thirds majority at the Dublin Ard Fheis of Sinn Féin in January 1970. At that point the Provisionals walked out of the meeting and because they went off to hold a meeting in Kevin Street, Dublin, and established their HQ there, they were initially known as Kevin Street Sinn Féin to distinguish them from the Officials, who for similar reasons were frequently described as Gardiner Place Sinn Féin. Each side claimed to be the true inheritor of 1916, and the OIRA said later that it had been able to hold 70 per cent of the total of IRA volunteers when the PIRA broke away. In NI the IRA strength in 1970 was probably about 600, and mainly in Belfast. All the indications, however, were that PIRA rapidly outstripped the Officials in number. Notably in the Belfast Republican areas, the Provisionals built on the strength of local defence committees and were widely accepted as the defenders of the people against loyalist attacks. The OIRA also had to face the taunts of the new 'Provos' that it was totally unprepared in the Belfast violence of 1969. The OIRA insisted that the split in the movement had been engineered by Fianna Fáil agents so that a separate IRA would develop and operate only in the North. Certainly, the tension between Officials and Provisionals was intense in 1970–1, and in March 1971 there was a fierce gun battle between the two groups in the Lower Falls area of Belfast. One man was shot dead and several wounded, with the British army standing carefully aside. A ceasefire was quickly negotiated

in this inter-IRA struggle, but there were to be many more clashes between the two groups. In Belfast and many other centres the annual Easter parades to cemeteries where Republicans are buried were split into separate Official and Provisional efforts. The OIRA was still involved in violence in early 1971. It bombed a Shankill Road public house in Belfast in April. But Cathal Goulding's warning that PIRA tactics were likely to bring internment without trial in NI proved to be justified. And although OIRA, like PIRA, had been keeping many of its members away from their usual haunts, a good many key OIRA members were rounded up in the dawn swoop on 9 August 1971. PIRA claimed that only thirty of its members had been arrested, but this was probably a serious under-estimation. OIRA suffered, though, from the handicap that many of its activists were people who had a record in the IRA earlier and thus figured in Special Branch lists. Internment, however, created extra problems for OIRA because it stirred up hostility towards the British authorities and the NI Government on a massive scale. It was an emotion more geared to PIRA strategy than to the politically oriented approach of Cathal Goulding and his friends. Violence became much more the order of the day for OIRA. In December 1971 it killed Unionist Senator Jack Barnhill in Strabane, and burned the Rostrevor home of the Stormont Speaker, Ivan Neill. In February 1972 – that is, immediately after 'Bloody Sunday' in Derry – it claimed responsibility for an explosion at the Aldershot (Hampshire) HQ of the Parachute Regiment. Seven people were killed, including five women canteen workers. Also in February it mounted an assassination attempt on Unionist Government Minister John Taylor in Armagh. He was hit by six bullets and his jaw shattered. In March 1972 Cathal Goulding and three other men were charged in Dublin with membership of an illegal organisation, but they were freed after the prosecution had applied for the charges to be struck out. When direct rule of NI from Westminster was announced at the end of March, OIRA announced that it would continue the struggle. In April 1972 OIRA was responsible for a spate of violence in Belfast, including many attacks on RUC stations. These were in response to the shooting dead by soldiers of Joe McCann, one of OIRA's most revered leaders. Even members of the Provisionals turned out in a separate parade among the 5,000 people at McCann's funeral. In May 1972 OIRA admitted that it had shot dead Ranger William Best, of the Royal Irish Rangers, home on leave in Derry. They said it was a reprisal for crimes by the British army, but it brought angry protests from many Bogside women and calls for OIRA to leave the Bogside and Creggan areas. On Monday 29 May 1972 OIRA announced a ceasefire. It said it was doing so in accordance with the wishes of the people it represented in NI, although it reserved the right to act in self-defence and to defend areas attacked by British troops or 'sectarian forces'. This ceasefire followed an anxious meeting of the OIRA leadership from all thirty-two counties of Ireland, including some women who were said to be local OIRA commanders. It was stated that the decision had been taken by an overwhelming majority. Goulding seems to have argued that the PIRA bombing campaign could only increase sectarianism. He also claimed the PIRA would soon be forced to call a ceasefire as well, but this prediction was only partially borne out, for the PIRA ceasefire, which came soon afterwards, was short-lived. The Goulding policy was to seek to develop class politics, and to secure more joint action with Protestants on issues such as housing. This concentration by OIRA on community politics meant that it tended to coalesce completely in most areas with the Republican Clubs – that is, the NI equivalent of Sinn Féin (the Workers' Party) in the Republic. In 1973 there was trouble between PIRA and OIRA prisoners in Crumlin Road Prison in Belfast, and in 1974, after clashes at the Maze Prison, twenty-one OIRA men there were moved to Crumlin Road Prison for ten days. But PIRA and OIRA made common cause on occasional anti-internment protests and worked together to some extent in the Catholic areas of Belfast to reduce

hardship during the loyalist strike in 1974. OIRA guns were brought out again in the spring of 1975, when it was involved in a bitter struggle with the newly formed IRSP. There were deaths and injuries on both sides in Belfast, and a suspicion among the security forces that the IRSP had drawn some recruits from PIRA members who were doubtful about their ceasefire. In April 1982 the Dublin magazine *Magill* claimed that OIRA was still active, well-armed and engaged in recent years in murders, robberies and intimidation. It also alleged that Seamus Costello, leader of IRSP, had been killed by a senior member of OIRA in 1977. The magazine added that £2 million had been taken in armed robberies since 1972, and that one major bank robbery had been carried out in NI immediately before the Republic's general election in June 1981. It also asserted that almost all the hundred or so members of OIRA, including several of its leaders, were members of the Workers' Party. A spokesman for the WP dismissed the allegations as 'muck' and the WP president Tomás Mac Giolla (elected a TD in the November 1982 election), said he had no knowledge of the continued existence of OIRA, and certainly they had no association with any military organisation. In July 1982 INLA claimed that OIRA had provided information for 'loyalist death squads' which had resulted in the deaths of three Republican activists in Belfast – Miriam Daly, Ronnie Bunting and Noel Little. INLA also said it had murdered Jim Flynn in Dublin after they had been informed by former OIRA members that he had murdered Seamus Costello. In May 1983 the Republic's Justice Minister, Michael Noonan, said he could confirm that OIRA was still in existence. Its continued activity in NI was also reported by the RUC at that time. In December 1985 the WP denied allegations by the Republic's Labour Minister, Ruairí Quinn, that OIRA still existed and had links with the WP. The party described it as a 'smear tactic'. But claims by Government Ministers North and South that OIRA survived into the 1990s added strength to a variety of police and other reports that the organisation was still in being. In October

1991 Taoiseach Charles Haughey and Justice Minister Ray Burke insisted that the WP was still associating with OIRA. A year earlier, NI Minister Brian Mawhinney said OIRA was still active. In 1991 and 1992 there were reports that the organisation was engaged in the distribution of forged 100-dollar bills. OIRA was mentioned in January 1992 when three men were convicted in Belfast of a liquor lorry robbery, and in May 1992 a man killed in Co. Armagh was said to have been intimidated by OIRA. In Belfast there were rumours in early 1992 that OIRA then had some hundred volunteers and substantial arms, and had some sort of agreement with PIRA to avoid clashes. But this hardly squared with suggestions that the British security services used OIRA against PIRA. In any event, the controversy over the organisation was a major element in the split in the WP in early 1992, which led to the setting up of the Democratic Left. The happenings in NI were cited during the crucial debates, and one allegation, which was denied, was that a WP official had been recruiting for OIRA in 1991. It seems clear that OIRA remains on the agenda of the security forces.

OFFICIAL SINN FÉIN see Workers' Party

OFFICIAL UNIONIST PARTY see Ulster Unionist Party

O'HANLON, PATRICK MICHAEL
SDLP Assembly member for Armagh, 1973–4. b. Drogheda, 8 May 1944. B.Comm. (UCD). Independent MP for S. Armagh, 1969–72. Active in civil rights campaign. Founder member of SDLP. Party Chief Whip in the Assembly, 1974. Member of several party delegations in talks with Republic's Government, 1973–4. Unsuccessful candidate in Convention election, 1975, and Assembly election, 1982. Called to the NI Bar in 1986.

O'HARE, PASCHAL JOSEPH
SDLP Assembly member for N. Belfast, 1982–6. b. 1932. Belfast City Council, 1973–85. Solicitor. A founder member and former executive member of the

SDLP, he stood unsuccessfully in the 1975 Convention election for W. Belfast and the 1979 Westminster election in N. Belfast. Resigned from SDLP in 1985 because of the party's involvement in the AIA, which he regarded as an acceptance by the Republic's Government of 'a settlement in a six-county context'. In 1986 he called for talks with men of violence, both Republican and loyalist.

O'KENNEDY, MICHAEL
Minister of Agriculture in Republic, 1987–92. Foreign Minister, 1977–9. EC Commissioner, 1981–2. b. 21 February 1936. MA (NUI). Barrister and classical scholar. Fianna Fáil Senator, 1965–9; TD, 1969–81. Minister of Transport and Power, 1973; Minister of Finance, 1979–81. As Foreign Minister, he was the member of Lynch's Government most closely involved with NI affairs, and he was an early advocate of the idea of an all-Ireland court to deal with terrorism. As Foreign Minister, he was closely involved with the EC-backed Derry–Donegal schemes. In August 1979, while president of the EC Council of Ministers, he urged early efforts to break the NI 'political log-jam' through informal talks between the British and Irish Governments and the NI parties. In October 1979 he reached agreement in London with NI Secretary of State Humphrey Atkins on secret anti-terrorist measures. In 1985 he came out strongly against any internal settlement in NI. Dropped from Government by Taoiseach Albert Reynolds in February 1992 and lost his Dáil seat in 1992 election.

OLDFIELD, SIR MAURICE
Chief Security Co-ordinator, NI, from 1979 until his death in 1980. b. 16 November 1915. Sir Maurice, who retired from the Foreign Office in 1977, held a great variety of diplomatic posts, including counsellor in Washington, but his real fame rested on his post as head of the Secret Intelligence Service (MI6) between 1965 and 1977. The NI appointment was said to be aimed at increasing pressure on terrorists and bringing them to justice. It followed reports that the army was anxious to see

more co-ordination of the security effort and that there were differences between the intelligence services, army and RUC. Sir Maurice (dubbed 'Maurice the Mole' by PIRA) kept a very low profile in NI, and in 1986 Thatcher told the Commons that he had been a homosexual and had admitted such activities although there was no reason to suggest that security had ever been compromised. But several of his former associates in MI6 rejected this suggestion of homosexuality. In 1975 PIRA planted a bomb outside his London flat; he escaped injury.

OLIVER, JOHN ANDREW

Chief adviser to chairman of Constitutional Convention, 1975–6. b. Belfast, 1913. BA, Ph.D. (QUB). Entered NI civil service in 1936 and rose to be Permanent Secretary in Development Ministry in 1970, and Housing Department, 1974. Retired from civil service in 1976, and books include an analysis of NI's constitutional options, *Ulster Today and Tomorrow* (1978).

O'MALLEY, DESMOND

Leader (and founder) of the Republic's Progressive Democrats, 1985–93. He was Parliamentary Secretary to Taoiseach Jack Lynch, Minister for Defence, and Government Chief Whip at the start of the NI Troubles in 1969 and held various Cabinet posts, including Trade and Commerce, in Fianna Fáil Governments until 1982, when he resigned after refusing to support a vote of confidence in Haughey's leadership. In 1984 he was expelled from Fianna Fáil for challenging the line of the then Taoiseach, Charles Haughey, that the unitary state was the only acceptable form of Irish unity. The following year he launched Prog. D. with the object of 'breaking the mould of Irish politics'. In the 1987 election he emerged at the head of a fourteen-strong Dáil party. In 1989 Charles Haughey, still lacking an overall FF majority, negotiated a Coalition Government with O'Malley which involved two Prog. D. seats in the Cabinet with O'Malley as Minister for Industry and Commerce. But the repeated calls by Prog. D. for 'integrity' and 'standards' in government led to severe tensions within the Coalition under the leadership both of Haughey and of his successor, Albert Reynolds. Under Prog. D. pressure, Brian Lenihan was dropped as Tánaiste in 1990, and lost out to Mary Robinson in the presidential election. O'Malley and his colleagues were again crucial in Haughey's resignation in 1992. And soon after, a severe clash developed between O'Malley and Reynolds over the beef tribunal set up to inquire into alleged irregularities in that industry. In July 1992 O'Malley told the tribunal that decisions by Reynolds as Industry Minister in 1987 had been 'grossly unwise, reckless and foolish'. Two months later, Reynolds told the tribunal that O'Malley's allegations were 'reckless, irresponsible and dishonest'. Prog. D. left the Government when Reynolds refused to withdraw, and in the November 1992 general election FF fared even worse than under Haughey. It lost nine seats. Prog. D. returned with ten seats, but its hopes of forming a 'rainbow coalition' with FG and Labour soon vanished, as Reynolds worked successfully for a coalition with Labour, which had more than doubled its representation, with thirty-three seats. O'Malley, who strongly supported NI devolution and close relations with the Alliance Party, attended the North–South strand of the Brooke–Mayhew Talks. In September 1993 he blamed Reynolds for the breakdown of talks in 1992, and he also called for the appointment of a full-time NI minister.

OMBUDSMAN

Popular title for Parliamentary Commissioner for Administration, who deals with complaints of maladministration against Stormont departments. The office was established in 1969, and later linked with that of Commissioner of Complaints.

O'NEILL, LORD (OF THE MAINE)

PM of NI, 1963–9. b. 10 September 1914; d. June 1990. Captain Terence O'Neill had an Anglo-Irish background – among his ancestors were the ancient Ulster O'Neill family, and the English Chichesters. When, in 1963, Lord

Brookeborough resigned after twenty years as PM, O'Neill had been Finance Minister for seven years and seemed the natural successor. He quickly made it clear that he was set on a reformist course: firstly in terms of stronger cross-border economic links; and secondly, in trying to accommodate the political ambitions of an increasingly educated Catholic community. In January 1965 he sprang a surprise with an unannounced visit to Stormont of the Republic's Taoiseach Sean Lemass. Even the majority of his Cabinet colleagues were not told of the meeting in advance, and the trip angered right-wing Unionists, always suspicious of Southern motives. The Rev. Ian Paisley attacked the visit in what can be seen as the start of his 'O'Neill must go' campaign. The extremist UVF emerged on the loyalist side, and the civil rights campaign built up to the torrent of protest reached in 1968. The violent scenes at the civil rights march on 5 October 1968 went round the world on TV and made a tremendous impression on the PM. He saw that reforms must be pressed forward, and in this he clashed with those who shared the view of Home Affairs Minister William Craig that the civil rights agitation was an expression of republicanism, encouraged by the IRA. In December 1968 O'Neill sacked Craig, and made it evident that he regarded him as an advocate of UDI. He warned against the growth of a 'Protestant Sinn Féin' and appealed to the protest marchers to get off the streets. At the end of 1968 he announced a five-point programme of reforms – a points system for housing allocations, an Ombudsman, the ending of the company vote in council elections, a review of the Special Powers Act, and the setting up of the Londonderry Development Commission. In London the British PM Harold Wilson spoke of Captain O'Neill being 'blackmailed by thugs' and he warned that there would be a reappraisal of NI's position if he was overthrown. In the event, Captain O'Neill decided to challenge his Unionist critics in a general election in February 1969. But this 'crossroads election', as he termed it, was extremely confused. He

took the gamble of endorsing pro-O'Neill candidates who, in many cases, were opposing the official nominees of the local Unionist associations. Although his leadership was confirmed by the Unionist Parliamentary Party after the election, with twenty-three MPs voting for, Brian Faulkner against, and William Craig abstaining, the election left a legacy of bitterness throughout unionism. Also, the pressure for change from the civil rights movement was intensified. On 28 April 1969 O'Neill resigned as PM and was succeeded by James Chichester-Clark, who had resigned from the O'Neill Government five days before. In the House of Lords O'Neill spoke frequently on NI issues. In comments on the 1968–9 period, he said that the Troubles in NI had to happen, and that Westminster only acted when there was trouble. But for trouble, he said in a 1978 radio interview, Britain would probably still be in India. He supported the 1974 power-sharing project, but he insisted that there had been two mistakes – an over-elaborate cross-border Council of Ireland, and the withdrawal from Stormont of Secretary of State William Whitelaw before the new administration got under way. Memorial services to him were held in Belfast and Dublin, where ex-Taoiseach Jack Lynch praised his vision.

O'NEILL, PHELIM *see* Rathcavan, Lord

O'NEILL, THOMAS P. ('TIP')
Speaker of the US House of Representatives, 1977–86. b. 9 December 1912; d. 6 January 1994. Inherited the Massachusetts Congressional district of John F. Kennedy (later President) in 1952 and when he retired in 1986 passed it on to Joseph Kennedy (Bobby Kennedy's son). One of a group of Irish-American politicians, including Senator Edward Kennedy, who have maintained interest in Washington DC in NI issues and warned Americans against giving aid to funds that could help finance violence in Ireland. These politicians set up the Friends of Ireland Group in 1981. President Carter praised his efforts to promote reconciliation in Ireland, and

Jack Lynch, former Taoiseach of the Republic, called him 'a true friend of Ireland'. In April 1979 he paid a brief visit to NI with other Congressmen and urged the new Conservative Government to launch a political initiative in NI. In a speech in Dublin he complained that NI had been made a 'political football' at Westminster – a comment criticised by Thatcher and Labour spokesmen. O'Neill's influence was crucial in getting Congressional and White House opinion behind the NIF report after Thatcher had curtly dismissed its options towards the end of 1984. He was also insistent on economic aid for NI to back the AIA. He was a long-standing political opponent of President Ronald Reagan, whom he accused of losing touch with his Irish roots. In 1989, for personal reasons, he declined President Bush's offer of the post of ambassador to Ireland.

'OPERATION MOTORMAN'

Code name of the security forces operation in the early hours of 31 July 1972 to clear barricades in no-go areas in Derry and Belfast. Some 21,000 troops, together with 9,000 mobilised UDR men and 6,000 members of the RUC, were involved. In Derry, 1,500 troops with armoured cars and other vehicles swept into the Bogside and Creggan areas. The operation had clearly been signalled in advance and resistance was confined to minor sniping and two people were killed by the army. There had been talk previously of at least 100 deaths if the areas were reoccupied. There was little resistance in Belfast Republican areas, and loyalists helped to dismantle their own barricades which they claimed were simply a response to the existence of Republican no-go areas. The Secretary of State William Whitelaw told a news conference that the operation had been designed to 'remove the capacity of the IRA to create violence and terror'. Shortly before he spoke, six people were killed in the Derry village of Claudy when three car bombs exploded. It was immediately assumed to be PIRA's reply to 'Motorman', although it denied responsibility.

ORANGE ORDER

The largest Protestant organisation in NI, where it probably has between 80,000 and 100,000 active members, with some 4,000 members in the Republic. The Loyal Orange Institution owes its character to the victories of King William III (William of Orange) in the religious wars of the late seventeenth century. Its annual twelfth of July demonstrations at more than twenty centres in NI celebrate King William's victory over King James at the Battle of the Boyne in 1690. It was formed in September 1795, in Co. Armagh, after a clash between Protestants and Catholics at the 'Battle of the Diamond'. Its lodges were based on those of the Masonic Order. Although one of its main objectives is the defence of the Protestant succession to the British throne, its relations with London have often been strained. The Order fiercely resented the ban on Orange processions in the 1860s, and it was widely defied. The Order took on a distinctly Unionist flavour when Home Rule threatened. The effective beginning of the Unionist Party was a meeting of seven Orangemen, elected as MPs, at Westminster in January 1886. The Unionist–Conservative link was forged in the opposition to Liberal plans for Irish Home Rule. A leading Conservative, Lord Randolph Churchill, 'played the Orange card' when he told an anti-Home Rule rally in Belfast's Ulster Hall: 'Ulster will fight and Ulster will be right.' Orangemen did not want the devolution accorded to NI in 1921, but once the state had been established, they defended it energetically and attacked any idea of a link-up with the South. Most Ministers in Unionist governments were Orangemen, and the controversial B Specials, the auxiliary police force which many Unionists regarded as Ulster's army, were almost exclusively Orangemen. While the defence of civil and religious liberty is a prime Orange aim, it attacked the civil rights movement as Republican- or Communist-inspired. The imposition of direct rule and the scheme for power-sharing between Protestants and Catholics in government got little support from Orangemen. The Order remains close to the UUP, although the ties have been loosened a little by the fragmentation of unionism. And throughout the violence the Order has been calling for tougher security policies, particularly against the IRA, and its leaders have claimed that it has exercised a restaining influence on loyalists. When the Order's World Council met in Belfast in 1976, there were representatives present from ten countries – NI, the Republic, England, Scotland, US, Canada, New Zealand, Australia, Ghana and Togoland. There were also plans to set up lodges in South Africa and Sweden. There is a lodge at the House of Commons founded originally by James Craig, NI's first PM, and in the past military lodges existed in places like Hong Kong, Singapore and Egypt. It was reported in 1982 that there had been a 48 per cent increase in membership in Africa in the previous three years. One lodge established in Ghana in 1985 was said to comprise 300 men and women, all former Catholics. The World Council met in Belfast in 1985 to make plans for celebrations in 1990 of the three-hundredth anniversary of the Battle of the Boyne. It also appointed an Australian, John Gowans, as Imperial grand master. He was succeeded by James Molyneaux MP. S. Belfast UUP MP, Rev. Martin Smyth, who was formerly Imperial grand master, has been grand master in Ireland since 1972. In 1986 Belfast grand master John McCrea became grand secretary of the Order in Ireland in succession to Walter Williams, who had held office for thirty years. But the secretaryship was then made an honorary post, and George Patton was named full-time executive officer. The Order has been active in opposition to the AIA, and was also highly critical of new public order laws introduced in 1987. In 1988 Orangemen had their own celebrations of the tercentenary of King William's arrival in England, but they had no part in the official celebrations (confined to GB) of the 'glorious revolution'. They were refused permission to hold a special service in Exeter cathedral. Tens of thousands of Orangemen marched through Belfast on 29 September 1990 to mark the Boyne

tercentenary, 'bloodied, but unbowed', according to Martin Smyth. Heads of the Order had abandoned a plan for a July ceremony at the site of the battle because, they said, of the 'outright hostility' to the ideals of Orangeism among people in authority in the Republic. In January 1991 the Government made a £75,000 grant towards a heritage centre to be established in the Loughgall, Co. Armagh, house in which the Order began. In a statement on the Brooke–Mayhew Talks, the Irish Grand Lodge warned against any involvement of the Republic in the government of NI, which would be regarded as 'unwarranted interference'. In 1991–2 there were many attacks on rural Orange halls, particularly in counties Armagh and Down. NI Secretary of State Sir Patrick Mayhew said some Orange supporters had behaved like 'cannibals' when a 1 July parade passed the bookmaker's shop on the lower Ormeau Road, Belfast, where the UFF had killed five Catholics earlier in the year. In 1992 the NI High Court overturned the expulsion from his lodge of a Larne Conservative councillor who had attended an AOH function. In 1993 there was renewed pressure to reroute some Orange parades. After the events of 1992 the Ballynafeigh district accepted a rerouting away from the lower Ormeau Road for the mini-Twelfth. There was an unsuccessful legal challenge over the use of the main Ormeau Road on the Twelfth. There were legal challenges in Dungannon and Pomeroy. The main trouble occurred over the annual Whiterock parade on 26 June. The rerouting, the third in twenty years, was accepted by the Orange Order but not the accompanying crowd, and disorder ensued over several nights after Brian McCallum was killed by a grenade he had been carrying. In the rural areas, where halls were also social centres, there had been a series of fire-bomb attacks. The outcome had been the payment of over £1 million in compensation. The senior branch of the Order is known as the Royal Black Institution – it is headed by UUP leader James Molyneaux MP – and it is also closely associated with the Apprentice Boys of Derry, with membership often overlapping. There are also women's and junior branches.

ORANGE VOLUNTEERS
A loyalist paramilitary group started in 1972 with about 500 members and closely linked with the Vanguard movement. Its membership was restricted to Orangemen and ex-servicemen, and it frequently provided stewards at rallies addressed by William Craig. In 1974, when it was thought to have grown to about 3,000 members, it was involved in setting up road blocks and in communications during the loyalist strike. It also supported the more limited loyalist strike in May 1977.

O'REILLY, JAMES
Nationalist MP for Mourne, 1958–72. He was Whip for his party in the later days of the Stormont Parliament, and frequently spoke on farming issues. In 1964 he unsuccessfully promoted a bill to establish an Ombudsman in NI. In the 1971 census he refused to complete his return, and went to prison rather than pay a fine. He said he was protesting against the 'biased administration of justice'.

ORME, STANLEY
Minister of State, NIO, 1974–6. b. 5 April 1923. Soon after he was elected Labour MP for Salford W. in 1964, Orme visited NI at the invitation of Gerry Fitt, the W. Belfast MP, to study the local situation in company with several other Labour MPs. Soon afterwards, when the Campaign for Democracy in Ulster was formed at Westminster, Orme became associated with it, and was a strong critic of Unionist administrations. He opposed internment without trial, and in 1973 told an audience in Dublin that he believed in the eventual reunification of Ireland. He was at that time a front-bench Labour spokesman, and prominently associated with the left-wing Tribune group of MPs. When he was appointed to the NIO in 1974, the move was immediately criticised by Unionists. The UUP, in a statement, questioned whether he could deal with NI matters impartially in view of the 'somewhat partisan' opinions which he had aired

previously. Friction with the Unionists was increased when he took up a highly critical attitude towards the UWC strike in May 1974. As the Minister responsible for Economic Affairs, he had charge of the departments of Commerce and Manpower Services, and made several overseas trips in a bid to find new industrial investment. He was Minister of Social Security, 1976–9. Since 1983, MP for Salford E. Chairman, Parliamentary Labour Party, 1987–. BIPB, 1989–.

ORR, CAPTAIN LAWRENCE PERCY STORY (WILLIE)
Leader of the Unionist MPs at Westminster, 1954–74, and MP for S. Down, 1950–74. b. Belfast, 16 September 1918; d. 1990. Son of a former Dean of Dromore, he was Unionist organiser in S. Down before becoming the first MP for the newly created constituency. Former Imperial grand master of the Orange Order, he revived the Orange Lodge (LOL 1688) in House of Commons in 1955. He was an officer of many Conservative committees during his long career in Parliament. In August 1974 he announced he would not be standing again, and supported Enoch Powell as his successor.

OVEREND, ROBERT
Initially VUPP and later UUUM Convention member for Mid-Ulster, 1975–6. b. 1931. Magherafelt District Council, 1977–85. A farmer and pedigree-livestock dealer, prominent in the Orange Order and Apprentice Boys of Derry. Unsuccessful UUUP candidate in Mid-Ulster in 1982 Assembly election.

OWEN, LORD
As David Owen, leader of SDP, 1983–90. b. 2 July 1938. MP for Plymouth Devonport (Labour, 1966–81, and SDP, 1981–92). As Foreign Secretary, 1976–7, he became familiar with Anglo-Irish affairs, but later had doubts about the AIA. In 1990 he urged renegotiation of the agreement and in his memoirs (1991) he suggested PM Margaret Thatcher had conceded too much to Taoiseach Garret FitzGerald. In 1988 he supported Thatcher in her criticisms of the Republic

over extradition. He said Gerry Adams should have been deprived of his MP status because of his abstention from Parliament. One of the 'gang of four' who founded SDP, which in its day claimed to be 'the only national party operating in NI', Owen spoke for an SDP candidate in the Upper Bann by-election in May 1990, but the party got only 154 votes. He was joint leader of the Liberal–SDP Alliance, but opposed the merger between the two parties, which became the Liberal Democrats, and wound up the SDP in 1990. Made life peer, 1992. International peace negotiator in former Yugoslavia, 1992–.

P

PAISLEY, EILEEN

Wife of the Rev. Ian Paisley. DUP Assembly, 1973–4, and Convention, 1975–6, member for E. Belfast. b. Belfast, 1934. Belfast City Council, 1967–75. In 1982 she was a member of a joint UUP–DUP publicity team visiting the US. She stood in for her husband, who had been refused a US visa.

PAISLEY, REVEREND IAN RICHARD KYLE

Democratic Unionist MEP for NI, June 1979–. MP for N. Antrim, 1970–. Assembly member for N. Antrim, 1982–6. Chairman of Agriculture Committee; member, Security Committee. Leader of DUP, 1971–. b. Armagh, 6 April 1926. Son of a Baptist minister, he preached his first sermon at the age of sixteen. In 1951 he started a Free Presbyterian Church in the Ravenhill Road area of Belfast, where he later erected his large Martyrs' Memorial Church. It was in 1963 that his interest in political action developed. He organised a march to protest against the lowering of the Union flag on Belfast City Hall to mark the death of Pope John XXIII. And when it was the first loyalist march to be banned under the Special Powers Act, he persisted with his plan. He was fined £10, and said he would go to prison rather than pay the fine. But the fine was paid anonymously, and Paisley alleged

that it had been paid by the Government. In 1964, during the Westminster general election campaign in W. Belfast, he made a big issue of the display of a tricolour flag in the window of the Republican HQ in Divis Street, adjoining the Catholic Falls Road. The RUC broke into the premises and removed the flag. The flag was later replaced, and when the police returned, serious rioting broke out. These incidents established a pattern of protest which he was to employ in many different circumstances. The visit of the Republic's Taoiseach, Sean Lemass, to Stormont in January 1965 gave him a new and potent campaign issue. He insisted, with his booming oratory, that the threat of a united Ireland had been opened up by the 'treachery' of PM Captain O'Neill. The 'O'Neill must go' drive was pursued at rallies and meetings. In June 1966 he infuriated O'Neill by having a march to the General Assembly of the Presbyterian Church in Belfast to protest against its 'Romeward trend'. The Governor, Lord Erskine, and Church dignitaries, had abuse shouted at them outside the hall, and in Parliament the PM deplored what he called 'tendencies towards Nazism and fascism'. O'Neill also accused Paisley of having associations with the UVF, something which Paisley firmly denied. But Paisley had now set up two organisations – the Ulster Constitution Defence Committee and Ulster Protestant Volunteers – which were to figure frequently in counter-demonstrations during the civil rights campaign. One of the largest demonstrations which Paisley and his supporters mounted against a civil rights march was in Armagh on 30 November 1968. He and Major Ronald Bunting arrived in Armagh early in the morning and, with their supporters, blocked the town centre, forcing the civil rights demonstrators to cut short their parade. Paisley and Bunting had to serve six weeks' imprisonment for unlawful assembly. The resignation of O'Neill in April 1969 brought the comment from Paisley that he had 'brought down a Captain and could bring down a Major as well'. The Major, of course, was Major Chichester-Clark, who succeeded

O'Neill. Paisley's chance to challenge the new Government came in April 1970, when by-elections were held in two Co. Antrim seats – Bannside (former seat of Captain O'Neill) and S. Antrim. Paisley won the Bannside constituency and his colleague, the Rev. William Beattie, the S. Antrim seat. It was a double blow to the Government and two months later Paisley achieved another parliamentary success – he gained the N. Antrim seat in the Westminster election. In 1971 he set up the Democratic Unionist Party to replace the Protestant Unionist Party. Towards the end of 1971 he angered many Unionists by predicting direct rule from Westminster, despite denials from London and by NI PM Brian Faulkner. At that period he seemed to be keen on integration of NI with GB, with a Greater Ulster Council at Stormont. And his concentration on attacks on the 'theocratic' nature of the Republic's Constitution gave rise to suggestions that Paisley was softening a little in his attitude towards the South – an impression which he moved quickly to dispel. The Sunningdale Conference, aimed at setting up the power-sharing Executive, was his next major target. He claimed that by excluding his party from full participation in Sunningdale the Government had gone back on its White Paper promise. And he and his supporters now adopted a wrecking approach towards the Assembly. On 22 January 1974 he and several of his loyalist colleagues were removed bodily from the Chamber after they had refused to give up the front-bench seats to the new Executive members and had mounted a noisy protest. Paisley himself was carried out by eight uniformed policemen. In February 1974 he increased his N. Antrim majority in the general election from under 3,000 in 1970 to some 27,000. Although he was abroad when the loyalist strike started in May 1974, he soon became deeply involved, with the message, 'This is one we can't afford to lose.' He, together with Harry West and William Craig, represented the UUUC leadership in the strike committee, and his oratory was employed frequently at the anti-Executive rallies at Stormont and

elsewhere. With the fall of the Executive, he was active in calling for new elections. These were granted in terms of the Constitutional Convention, and in the Convention, Paisley served on UUUC deputations which met the Alliance Party. There were conflicting assessments of his position in the Convention. Some Ulster Unionists said he had been more conciliatory in private than in public towards some form of partnership government. His public stance was certainly one of full support for the majority Convention report. After the Convention was wound up, it was clear however that his relations with many Ulster Unionists were strained. Paisley and Ernest Baird backed a United Unionist Action Council, designed to take a more militant line towards direct rule and in favour of tougher security. But the Ulster Unionists opted out, and refused to back a loyalist strike called in May 1977 with the support of the loyalist paramilitaries. The strike was only a shadow of the 1974 affair, and Paisley's prestige undoubtedly suffered, not least because of an unredeemed pledge to quit politics if it failed. It also meant a break with the UUP MPs. The Scarman report dealt with the suggestion that Paisley had been largely responsible for the disturbances of 1969. It said: 'Those who live in a free country must accept as legitimate the powerful expression of views opposed to their own, even if, as often happens, it is accompanied by exaggeration, scurrility and abuse. Dr Paisley's spoken words were always powerful and must have frequently appeared to some as provocative: his newspaper [*Protestant Telegraph*] was such that its style and substance were likely to rouse the enthusiasm of his supporters and the fury of his opponents. We are satisfied that Dr Paisley's role in the events under review was fundamentally similar to that of the political leaders on the other side of the sectarian divide. While his speeches and writings must have been one of the many factors increasing tension in 1969, he neither plotted nor organised the disorders under review and there is no evidence that he was a party to any of the acts of violence investigated by us.' The European election in June 1979 was seized by Paisley as an opportunity to demonstrate that he had more popular support than the Ulster Unionists. And since his party had gained two seats from the UUP in the May general election, he was well placed to stage a successful campaign. He travelled throughout NI, attacking the EC both as disastrous in economic terms and as a threat to Protestantism. In the event, he headed the poll easily, with more than 170,000 votes, or just under 30 per cent of first preferences, and 8 per cent ahead of the total UUP vote for two candidates. He claimed that the election gave him a mandate to speak for the NI majority in any political negotiations, and to answer criticisms at Strasbourg by MEPs from the Republic. At the first session in Strasbourg in July 1979 he intervened twice. On the opening day he was the first MEP to speak, apart from the acting president, when he protested that the Union flag was flying the wrong way up outside the Parliament Buildings. Later, he interrupted Jack Lynch (president in office of the European Council), saying that he was protesting against the Republic's refusal to sign the European Convention on Terrorism. In the European Parliament he was appointed member of the Energy Committee and later of the Political Affairs Committee. In July 1979 he strongly attacked any suggestion that Pope John Paul II should enter NI during the Irish Papal visit in September. Paisley's campaigning in the early 1980s was directed at some familiar targets. In 1980 he castigated the UUP for failing to take part in the Atkins conference, in which the DUP stood out against power-sharing. His other main assaults were on Anglo-Irish contacts and Government security policy. The Thatcher–Haughey meeting in Dublin in December 1980, with its launch of joint studies by the British and Irish Governments, was presented by him as a threat comparable to that faced by Edward Carson and Ulster loyalists in 1912. He accused Thatcher, when he met her privately, of 'undermining' NI's constitutional guarantee, a contention which she angrily repudiated. In February

1981 he organised a demonstration involving 500 men who paraded late at night on a Co. Antrim hillside, brandishing gun licences. This dramatic gesture was followed by a new 'Ulster declaration' on the lines of the original Covenant, to be signed by loyalists as a protest against the Thatcher–Haughey 'conspiracy'. It was linked to eleven 'Carson trail' rallies, culminating in a march to Stormont on 28 March, attended by some 30,000 people. Meantime, he was suspended from the Commons for five days for calling Secretary of State Humphrey Atkins a 'liar' when MPs discussed the murder of Sir Norman Stronge and his son. In the May 1981 council elections, the DUP put itself marginally ahead of the UUP in total votes. After the assassination of S. Belfast MP the Rev. Robert Bradford, in November 1981, he was involved in another scene in Parliament. He and his two party colleagues, Peter Robinson and John McQuade, were ordered out of the Commons by the Speaker when they noisily interrupted Secretary of State James Prior as he was giving the Government's reaction to the killing. At that point Paisley was promoting a Third Force to protect loyalists, and it was claimed that 5,000 members of the force paraded at a rally in Newtownards on 23 November which he addressed. That was the day designated by Unionists as a 'Day of Action' to demand a tougher security policy. Many Protestants stopped work and UUP and DUP leaders spoke at separate rallies. In early December 1981 he claimed that the Third Force had 15,000–20,000 members, and was organised on a county basis. Soon afterwards, some Irish-American Congressmen, headed by Senator Edward Kennedy, urged the State Department to withdraw his US visa in the light of his recent activities. Just before Christmas the visa was withdrawn, on the grounds of the 'divisiveness' of his recent statements and actions so that he was unable to visit the US in January 1982, on a joint DUP–UUP publicity operation. He made the best of it, however, since he travelled to Canada, and got on to the US national TV networks from Toronto, while his wife read his speeches in the US. James Prior's 'rolling devolution' initiative in 1982 was a further occasion for friction between the DUP and UUP. Paisley shared with the UUP a dislike of the 'cross-community support' condition attached to devolved government. But he argued that it was the last chance in his lifetime to secure devolved government at Stormont, and that the initial scrutiny powers could be a powerful check on direct rule. He was disappointed, however, by the election results, since the UUP took twenty-six Assembly seats to the DUP's twenty-one. He took over the chairmanship of the Assembly's Agriculture Committee, and to those who marvelled at his spread of commitments, taking in Strasbourg and Westminster, he explained that he would give up his Westminster seat if devolved government was achieved. He also found time to protest on the ground during Pope John Paul II's visit to Britain. In 1983 his N. Antrim seat was cut in half by redistribution, but he held it by a 13,000-plus majority. The 1984 European election was a further personal triumph, when he took more than one-third of all the votes (230,251 first preferences). But when the AIA was signed, he threw in his lot with UUP leader James Molyneaux to mount the 'Ulster Says No' campaign with a massive rally in Belfast and a variety of other protest actions – virtual withdrawal from Parliament, the forcing of by-elections in all Unionist-held seats, a boycott of Ministers, adjournment of Unionist-controlled councils, and protests against new public order laws in 1987, which were presented as deriving from Dublin pressure. When the fifteen protest by-elections were held in January 1986, the device of a 'dummy candidate' had to be resorted to in N. Antrim to enable Paisley to chalk up a 33,000-plus majority. Given the long-standing rivalry with the UUP, he braved some opposition from within the DUP to keep in harness with the Glengall Street HQ. In particular, he stamped on plans to oppose the UUP in E. Antrim in the 1987 election. But in that election he sensed the need for something more imaginative than the anti-AIA campaign to date. The

commitment of no talks until the AIA was at least suspended was interpreted as allowing the two Unionist leaders to engage in probing 'talks about talks' with NI Secretary of State Tom King which, surprisingly, reached into the summer of 1988. Publicly, the exchanges were aimed at securing a British Goverment assurance that it would consider an alternative to the AIA more acceptable to Unionists, with the hint of generosity towards the SDLP in new arrangements for internal government if the AIA could be set aside. In early 1988 it seemed that a rift might be developing between Paisley and Molyneaux, when the latter seemed to be responding with some warmth to the public statements of Taoiseach Charles Haughey. But in mid-1988 both were saying that there could be no talks with the Dublin Government before an agreed internal NI settlement, and both were rejecting power-sharing. The upsurge in PIRA violence in July–August 1988 found Paisley demanding capital punishment and detention of Republican terrorist suspects. In October 1988 Paisley was ejected from the European Parliament when he interrupted an address by Pope John Paul II. In the 1989 European election, he maintained his poll-topping position, although he had 4 per cent fewer votes than in 1984. In the detailed 'talks about talks' that continued until 1991 with Secretaries of State King and Brooke, he worked for the most part in close co-operation with Jim Molyneaux, despite occasional friction between the two parties. In the formal Brooke–Mayhew Talks, however, there were distinct differences in tactics, even if both agreed that abandonment by the Republic of its constitutional claim to NI was essential to any settlement. Paisley had looked forward to an 'eyeball to eyeball' confrontation with Haughey, but by the time the North–South talks began in 1992, Haughey was out of office. Paisley and his negotiating team eventually curtailed their exchanges with Dublin Ministers, notably by refusing to join the UUP in talks at Dublin Castle. The DUP leader was particularly angered by the UUP's action in putting forward a scheme for North–South relations on the final day of the talks. In early 1993 he spoke of a 'sellout' by some UUP negotiators, and said firmly that there could not be further talks without removal by Dublin of the constitutional claim. In September 1993 he advocated the return of capital punishment to counter the upsurge in loyalist paramilitary violence. In the run-up to the September Anglo-Irish Intergovernmental Conference meeting he told PM Major to stand up to Taoiseach Reynolds who, he said, was holding the threat of a US peace envoy over him. In the aftermath, when the PM was meeting party leaders, Paisley presented his ideas in the document 'Breaking the Log-Jam'. After the meeting he told the press the situation in NI was 'so desperate'. He shrugged off the remarks from Reynolds that talks might proceed without him and accused the Taoiseach of seeking the annexation of NI. After the Hume–Adams joint statement on 25 September he accused Mayhew and Major of conniving at 'Mark 2 of the sellout of Ulster' by being prepared to consider a document originating with PSF/PIRA. He accused the Government and John Hume of not caring 'two balls of roasted snow about the Unionist people of NI'. In October, in the wake of the Shankill bomb, he accused Mayhew of betraying the people of NI and at a meeting with the PM in early November, he expressed his concerns. At a further meeting later in the month he was reassured by Major's 'kicked it over the house tops' comment on the leaked Irish Foreign Affairs draft paper. However, at his party conference he warned of 'the greatest threat to the Union since the Home Rule crisis'. The *Observer* story of protracted Government contacts with PIRA/PSF over three years broke on 28 November and when Sir Patrick tried to limit the damage in the Commons the following day, Paisley was suspended for calling him a 'liar'. He travelled to Dublin Castle, where Reynolds and Major were working on their draft document, and handed in a protest letter. The speed and directness of his negative reaction to the Downing Street Declaration – 'you have sold Ulster

to buy off the fiendish Republican scum' – was put down by the PM to Paisley not having read it, but he said he obtained its substance from Dublin the day before. In the short debate in the House he protested at the linking of NI self-determination to that of Ireland as a whole, to the absence of mentions of the UK, to Articles 2 and 3 of the Irish Constitution, and the offensiveness of a brief three-month delay after a cessation of violence before PSF could enter negotiations. In the aftermath of the declaration he organised a series of Save Ulster campaign meetings. A regular demand was for a border poll in NI and by January 1994 this was extended to a referendum in the UK on the Union. He also demanded a firmer place in the Union, the removal of 'Dublin rule', the removal of the territorial claim and the creation of a new Stormont Assembly. He opposed any 'clarification' of the declaration and any change in the broadcasting ban. When the Irish Government began to do both, it fed his belief that Reynolds and Adams were 'the Siamese twins of the Republican movement'. However, a further target for his wrath was the UUP, which he accused of supporting a sellout and, while some called for closer Unionist co-operation, he refused until their 'repentance'. At the beginning of February 1994 the issue by the US of a visa for Gerry Adams to attend a New York conference produced a protest visit to Ambassador Seitz in London.

PARKER COMMITTEE

The committee, headed by Lord Parker, which reported in 1972 on the methods used in interrogating detainees in NI. The committee was particularly concerned with the 'five techniques' which were held by the European Court of Human Rights in January 1978 to amount to inhuman and degrading treatment, but not to torture. Lord Parker and John Boyd-Carpenter held that the methods could be justified in exceptional circumstances, subject to certain further safeguards. But the third member, Lord Gardiner, said he did not believe such measures were morally justifiable, whether in peacetime or even in war against a ruthless enemy. The PM, Edward Heath, told MPs that the five techniques – hooding, wall-standing, subjection to noise and deprivation of food and sleep – would not be used again.

PASCOE, LIEUTENANT-GENERAL SIR ROBERT

Army GOC, NI 1985–8. b. 1932. Was army commander at a time when the Government was pressing for greater cross-border security co-operation in face of a PIRA build-up, and when the Irish Government through the AIA was calling for more sensitivity towards the Catholic minority in day-to-day operations. Had previously served in NI with Royal Greenjackets between 1971 and 1974, and at HQ in Lisburn in 1980. ADC to the Queen, 1989–.

PASSMORE, THOMAS

UUP Assembly member for W. Belfast, 1982–6. Served on committees on Education, Health and Social Services, and Security. b. 1931; d. 1989. A prominent Orangeman, he was grand master in Belfast, 1974–84, and Irish deputy grand master for twenty years prior to his death. He stood unsuccessfully in W. Belfast in the 1979 and 1983 elections, and was chairman for some years of Woodvale Unionist Association. In the Assembly he was frequently critical of Government security policy. When his father was shot dead by PIRA at their W. Belfast home in 1976, he said that he thought he himself had been the intended target.

PATTEN, CHRISTOPHER FRANCIS

Parliamentary Under-Secretary, NIO, 1983–5. b. 12 May 1944. Balliol College, Oxford. Director, Conservative Research Department, 1974–9. MP for Bath, 1979–92. During his period in NI, he was regarded as one of the most able junior Ministers under direct rule. But he was somewhat more popular with the SDLP than with Unionists, who were intensely angry at his decision as Environment Minister in 1984 to adopt Derry City Council as the official title, thus dropping the name 'Londonderry'. He was called

'Lundy' by some Unionists in the Assembly, and there were references to his Catholicism. In 1985 Secretary of State James Prior got him to investigate the chances of breaking the political deadlock, but the inquiry was short-lived, and in September 1985 he returned to Whitehall as Minister of State at Education, 1985–6. Minister for Overseas Development, 1986–9. Became Environment Secretary in 1989, when he was first Cabinet Minister to talk to NI Conservatives and only Catholic in Cabinet. In 1990 he backed Douglas Hurd for Conservative leadership, and was appointed party chairman by PM John Major. In Belfast in July 1991, he predicted a restart of the political talks, and praised local Tories who, incidentally, were critical of the talks. He masterminded Conservative victory in 1992, but lost his own seat in Bath. Soon afterwards he was appointed last Governor of Hong Kong. Had an Irish great-great-grandfather.

PATTEN, JOHN HAGGIT CHARLES

Parliamentary Under-Secretary, NIO, 1981–3. b. 17 July 1945. Cambridge University. Fellow of Hertford College, Oxford, 1981–. Conservative MP for Oxford, 1979–83; Oxford W. and Abingdon, 1983–. Oxford City Council, 1973–6. Took charge of Department of Health and Social Services at Stormont. Parliamentary Under-Secretary, Department of Health in London, 1983–5; Minister of State, Home Office, 1987–92; Education Secretary, 1992–.

PEACE LINE

The barrier put up by British troops between the Catholic Falls area and the Protestant Shankill area in Belfast in September 1969. Sometimes known as the Orange–Green line, it was erected because of the violent disturbances in the summer of 1969. Since 1982 it has been converted into a brick wall and similar barriers have been erected in other confrontation areas of the city.

PEACE '93

A peace initiative launched in Dublin in the wake of the PIRA bombing of a shopping area of Warrington, Cheshire, on 20 March 1993, which led to the deaths of two boys aged three and twelve years. The organiser was a Dublin housewife and mother, Susan McHugh, and there was a huge emotional response in the Southern capital, marked by a large rally in O'Connell Street, the signing by thousands of people of books of condolence, and the sending of planeloads of flowers to the Warrington funerals. The initiative did, however, provoke questions as to why the deaths of so many young people in NI had not brought forth a comparable demonstration in the Republic, and McHugh sought to make amends by travelling to Belfast to speak to relatives of children killed by plastic bullets, and to hold a peace festival at QUB Students' Union along with representatives of the Peace People. Peace '93 organised a rally in London's Hyde Park in April 1993. Rallies were held in Dublin, Limerick and Galway at the end of October.

PEACE PEOPLE
The peace movement established in August 1976, and inspired by the deaths of the three Maguire children, who had been struck by a gunman's getaway car in the Andersonstown area of Belfast. It was founded by Betty Williams, Mairead Corrigan and Ciaran McKeown. Betty Williams and Mairead Corrigan were awarded the 1976 Nobel Peace Prize. The movement was initially marked by large rallies in Belfast and other centres in NI, and rallies of supporters in London, Dublin, and various places abroad. The movement has had strong financial support from Norway, and substantial aid from Germany, the US and several other countries. It has defined its aim as a 'non-violent movement towards a just and peaceful society'. In 1977 it began to switch its effort from large meetings to small groups, particularly in areas of confrontation, and to encourage increased community effort, better recreational facilities and, in some cases, the establishment of local industry. It created a good deal of controversy because its leaders were critical of established politicians. It set up its own forum for

discussion – the Peace Assembly – which brought together annually delegates from groups throughout NI to debate current social and political issues. In February 1980 there was serious internal dissension, although not apparently on policy. Betty Williams resigned for family reasons, and she settled in the US in 1982. Peter McLachlan, who had become chairman of the movement in 1978, also left in 1980. Ciaran McKeown eventually resumed his journalistic career and has written extensively on peace issues. Mairead Corrigan was chairwoman, 1980–1, when she married Jackie Maguire, whose wife Anne (Mairead's sister) had committed suicide the previous year. She was said to have been heartbroken at the loss of her children and the continuing violence. Mairead Corrigan-Maguire has continued with the organisation, working on the ground through local groups, raising money for it abroad, and with her Nobel prizewinner status is a regular speaker at international peace gatherings. She was particularly active in opposing the Gulf War in 1991. She has claimed that the split in the movement arose because the German organisation wanted to attach the condition that its financial aid to the PP should be on the basis that it avoided controversy, and the PP could not accept that. For much of the 1980s the movement maintained a low media profile, but in 1989 it came out against the broadcasting ban and the ending of the 'right to silence' for accused persons. The organisation continues to run holiday camps for young people in Norway and holidays in GB and Europe for religiously mixed groups and a five-a-side football league which brings together Catholics and Protestants. It also helps families of paramilitary prisoners, and provides buses to prisons for relatives. In 1993 the organisation backed the Dublin-based Peace '93 movement. In January 1994 it ran a conference on 'Changing Attitudes', in which Mairead Corrigan-Maguire spoke of an 'identity crisis in NI'.

PEACE TRAIN ORGANISATION
A group that developed in the late 1980s to counter the PIRA effort to disrupt train

services, mainly between Belfast and Dublin, by bombs on the line or threats of attacks. Members travelled on special trains North and South, and also visited London to push their case. In October 1992 hundreds of teenagers travelled from Belfast to Derry. The organisation, which claims the support of many politicians from parties in NI and the Republic and the backing of several local authorities North and South, launched an all-Ireland peace petition in 1992. Chairman is writer and broadcaster Sam McAughtry, and Eileen Bell of the Alliance Party is administrator.

PEACOCKE, JOSEPH ANTHONY

The last head of the RUC to hold the title of Inspector-General. He was criticised by the Scarman tribunal for his handling of the situation in the riots of August 1969. b. 1908; d. November 1975. He joined the RUC as a cadet in 1932, and became Inspector-General in February 1969. But he held the post only until October 1969, when he was succeeded by Sir Arthur Young with the rank of Chief Constable. The direction of the RUC had been one of the controversial aspects of 1969, and he was widely blamed for not having called for army assistance before 14 August. The Scarman report said Peacocke had acted in August as though RUC strength were sufficient to maintain the public peace. 'It was not until he was confronted with the physical exhaustion of the police in Derry on the 14th and in Belfast on the 15th that he was brought to the decision to call in the aid of the army. Had he correctly appreciated the situation before the outbreak of the mid-August disturbances, it is likely that the Apprentice Boys' parade [in Derry] would not have taken place, and the police would have been sufficiently reinforced to prevent disorder arising in the city. Had he correctly appreciated the threat to Belfast that emerged on 13 August he would have saved the city the tragedy of the 15th. We have no doubt that he was well aware of the existence of political pressures against calling in the army, but their existence constituted no excuse, as he himself recognised when in evidence

he stoutly and honourably asserted that they did not influence his decision.' This reference to 'political pressure' related to the point that entry of the army to the streets would involve the British Government in a reappraisal of the whole position of the Stormont administration.

PENDRY, THOMAS (TOM)

Parliamentary Under-Secretary, NIO, October 1978–May 1979. b. 10 June 1934. Labour MP for Stalybridge and Hyde, 1970–. Opposition Whip, 1971–4. Government Whip, 1974–7. Appointed to NIO to look after Finance and Agriculture owing to illness of James Dunn MP. Chairman, All-Party Football Committee.

PENTLAND, JOHN WESLEY

DUP Assembly member for N. Down, 1982–6. Served on committees on Economic Development, Health and Social Services, Finance and Personnel. Member of former Lurgan Borough Council and deputy Mayor in early 1960s. Institute of Travel and Tourism; British Travel Association.

PEOPLE'S DEMOCRACY

A radical leftist group, which had its beginnings at QUB on 9 October 1968. After a student march to Belfast city centre to demand an impartial inquiry into police brutality in Derry and the repeal of the Special Powers Act and the Public Order Act, among other things, a committee of ten was established at the inaugural meeting. Apart from the repeal of what it regarded as repressive legislation, it also urged one man, one vote, with the redrawing of electoral boundaries, and action to outlaw discrimination in jobs and housing allocations. Its best-known original members were Bernadette Devlin, Kevin Boyle and Michael Farrell. Its most dramatic move was a four-day march from Belfast to Derry, starting on 1 January 1969, with between forty and seventy people taking part. The project was attacked as provocative by loyalists, and it was harassed by extreme elements at various points. The most serious incident was near Burntollet Bridge in

Co. Derry, when the marchers were ambushed by some 200 loyalists. Stones and sticks were used in the assault and thirteen marchers had to have hospital treatment. The affair gave rise to angry recriminations, and criticism of the RUC by civil rights spokesmen. In the February 1969 Stormont general election, PD tried its appeal at the polls. None of its eight candidates was successful, but it got a total of 23,645 votes and the PD nominee was only 220 behind the Nationalist in S. Down. In 1972 it put out a detailed policy statement, proposing a secular, all-Ireland republic, with the dissolution of both the existing states. It said there was no point in submerging the North in the 'gombeen state' in the South. It also called for the disbanding of the RUC and UDR. PD has frequently campaigned in close association with PIRA but in 1974 the PIRA called PD 'weak and pseudo-revolutionary'. PD secured two council seats in Belfast in the 1981 local government contests. It expressed total opposition to the 1982 'rolling devolution' initiative but put up its two councillors – Fergus O'Hare and John McAnulty – in W. and N. Belfast in the Assembly election. They got fewer than 500 votes between them. Bernadette McAliskey (née Devlin) stood unsuccessfully as PD candidate in the 1982 general elections in the Republic.

POLITICAL COLLECTION (LINEN HALL LIBRARY)

Unique documentation of the Troubles is provided by the Political Collection at the independent Linen Hall Library (founded 1788) in Belfast city centre. Its aim has been to collect any printed item produced since 1 January 1966 pertaining to NI politics. It now houses over 75,000 items, including over 6,000 books, pamphlets and reports; more than 1,500 periodical titles; 400 volumes of political fiction (novels, poetry and drama); and 35,000 other ephemeral items ranging from posters and badges to postcards and Christmas cards. Robert Bell, who supervises the collection (with the assistance of Yvonne Murphy), says the existence, throughout the Troubles, of a neutral archive makes NI unique among the conflict centres of the world. 'The open availability of the publications of all sides to each other, and to outsiders, cannot but have affected the nature of the conflict itself.'

PLASTIC BULLET *see* Security System section, pp. 449–50

POOTS, CHARLES BOUCHER

DUP Assembly, 1973–4, and Convention, 1974–5, member for N. Down. b. 1929. Member, Lisburn District Council, 1973–. Deputy Mayor, 1991–2. Unsuccessful candidate for Stormont Iveagh seat, 1969. Treasurer, Hillsborough Free Presbyterian Church. In the Assembly in January 1974 he was suspended for a day for calling Chief Executive Brian Faulkner 'a lying tramp'. Stood unsuccessfully in 1982 Assembly election.

POPULATION

The April 1991 census showed NI's population as 1,577,836, an increase of 89,759 over the 1981 count. But the fact that the 1981 census was hit by a Republican boycott arising from the Maze hunger strike and by the shooting dead of a census-taker in Derry left a question mark over any precise comparison (non-returns in 1981 were estimated at around 19,000). The 1991 returns showed the continuing trend for the population within the city of Belfast to decline, with a corresponding rise in adjoining council areas. The population in the City Council area had dropped to 279,237, but the Belfast urban area – the city plus adjoining wards in Castlereagh, Lisburn, Newtownabbey, Carrickfergus and N. Down – contained 475,967 people. The 1991 count showed NI with a youthful population – 26 per cent of the population under sixteen (against 27.9 per cent in 1981). Fifteen per cent were of pensionable age compared with 14.5 per cent in 1981. The Registrar-General's return for 1989 showed NI still had the highest birth rate in UK (16.5 per 1,000), but there were 1,600 fewer births than in 1988. According to a report by the charity Child Care (NI) published in July 1992, NI had the largest average family size in Europe (2.94 children per family).

The census religion volume provoked interest in whether the Protestant/Catholic gap was closing. Some 7.3 per cent refused to answer the question but 38.4 per cent of Catholics and 50.3 per cent of Protestants did so, with 4 per cent stated as non-Christian.

PORTER, SIR ROBERT WILSON

Minister of Home Affairs, 1969-70. b. Derry, 23 December 1923. LLB (QUB). QC, 1965. Unionist MP for QUB, 1966-9; Lagan Valley, 1969-72. Minister of Health and Social Services, 1969. One of the strongest supporters of Terence O'Neill as PM. In the Chichester-Clark Government he took part in the crucial Downing Street talks in August 1969. He often argued that unionism could no longer operate on the 'no surrender' approach, or 'stand still while the rest of the world is changing'. In June 1972 he resigned from the Unionist Party because Faulkner, as PM, had associated himself with the Vanguard movement in attacking direct rule. He joined the Alliance Party soon afterwards and resumed his Bar practice, occasionally acting as deputy Recorder of Belfast and frequently as a prosecuting counsel in terrorist cases. County Court judge, 1978-.

POUNDER, RAFTON JOHN

Unionist MP for S. Belfast, 1963-74. b. Belfast, 13 May 1933; d. 1991. Chartered accountant; internal auditor, QUB, 1962-3. Parliamentary Private Secretary to Conservative Industry Minister, 1970-1. Member, UK delegation, European Parliament, 1973-4. Staff of EC Commission, 1974-6, working on scheme for Court of Auditors to check Common Market spending and counter abuses. Defeated by UUUC candidate in S. Belfast, February 1974. Secretary, NI Bankers' Association, 1977-91.

POWELL, (JOHN) ENOCH

UUP MP for S. Down, October 1974-87. b. 16 June 1912. MA (Cantab.). Enoch Powell had been Conservative MP for Wolverhampton S.W., 1950-74, Minister of Health, 1960-3, and an internationally known personality before he became interested in NI affairs. He displayed his Unionist sympathies intermittently for some years, notably by addressing party meetings in NI before his break with the Conservatives left him without a seat in Parliament. So his entry into active NI politics in 1974 was seen as being of mutual benefit to the Unionists and to Powell. He had been out of the Commons for some six months when he was selected as Unionist candidate in S. Down, and the Unionists saw him as a controversialist with the ability to project their case in GB. They were disappointed, however, to find that his majority in October 1974 over the SDLP candidate in S. Down was only 3,500 in a seat which normally yielded Unionist majorities of 10,000 or more. But in the circumstances of direct rule, his mastery of parliamentary and Whitehall procedure was a real asset to the UUUC, particularly since several of their MPs were new to Westminster and lacked even Stormont experience. Powell's support for Labour in the election was an embarrassment to many Unionists, who believed that despite Edward Heath's suspension of Stormont, every effort should be made to restore the former Conservative-Unionist partnership – a belief which was strengthened when Margaret Thatcher took over as Conservative leader. Powell's tactics were, however, to extract as much advantage as possible from the narrowly balanced Parliament, and he pointed to the Labour Government's acceptance of the case for more NI seats at Westminster as one of the key gains. He was regarded on all sides in NI as basically an integrationist who had no time for the revival of a strong devolved government at Stormont, but he answered this point by saying that he always stuck to the letter of his election manifesto. On the Common Market issue, his unwavering opposition reflected the majority view in unionism. As S. Down MP, he displayed little friendliness towards the Republic, which he has always described as a foreign state. He questioned, among other things, the right of the Republic's citizens to enjoy equal voting rights in Britain. By having a house in S. Down and by intensive canvassing, he sought to dispel the 'carpetbagger' image, and when he came to fight his second election in S. Down in 1979, he substantially increased his majority. He was also helped by the fact that the Bill to give NI five extra MPs had been put on the statute book, and it was accepted that he had played a major part in the campaign to achieve increased representation. In 1982 he mounted a major attack on the Prior 'rolling devolution' initiative. He saw it as closely tied up with the Anglo-Irish talks, which he regarded as an 'Anglo-American plot' to secure a united Ireland within NATO. Undeterred by Government denials, he spoke vigorously against the devolution Bill both inside and outside Parliament, and reinforced the efforts of Conservative right-wing critics by some skilful filibustering. But Powell proved to be one of the most forceful parliamentary supporters of Thatcher during the Falklands operation. He was among leading politicians to whom she accorded a personal briefing on the crisis, and there were Conservative MPs who thought he should be back in Government. In 1982, at age seventy, he was reselected as candidate by S. Down Unionists. In the 1983 election he survived in S. Down despite the handicaps of boundary changes favouring the SDLP, and opposition from the DUP. A PSF vote of more than 4,000 blunted the SDLP challenge and gave him a majority of 548. In 1985 he regarded the signing of the AIA as treachery by the Thatcher Government, and as confirming his warning of US pressure on Britain. He joined, some thought hesitantly, his Unionist colleagues in forcing protest by-elections, and his majority in S. Down, with the DUP giving support, rose to 1,842. But he stood aside from many Unionist demonstrations against the AIA; he did not boycott Parliament, join illegal parades, or stop paying rates. The rise in the Nationalist vote in S. Down, together with a weakening of support for PSF, however, proved too much for him in the 1987 general election. He lost by some 700 votes to his long-time opponent Eddie McGrady (SDLP). He has retained his links with S. Down

Unionists, latterly as patron of the local UUP Association. In line with his anti-devolution stance he warned that the Brooke–Mayhew Talks were a step to Irish unity, and said in June 1991 that the British Government wanted to 'ditch' NI.

PREVENTION OF TERRORISM ACT *see* Security System section, pp. 453–5

PRIOR, LORD
As James Prior, NI Secretary of State, September 1981–Sepember 1984. b. 11 October 1927. Educated Charterhouse and Pembroke College, Cambridge. Conservative MP for Lowestoft, 1959–83. MP for Waveney, 1983–7. Employment Secretary, 1979–81. His appoinment to NI came after repeated rumours that he was favourite to succeed Humphrey Atkins but that he had told Margaret Thatcher he would prefer to resign rather than leave Employment. At the time he was known to have qualms about Government economic policy, and to be high on the PM's list of Cabinet 'Wets'. He was also reckoned to be a possible future challenger for the Conservative leadership. In the end, he deferred to the PM's wishes. It was his duty, he said, to put the nation first, and he seems to have been concerned with the 'international dimension' of the NI job. Thatcher also allowed him to remain on the influential Cabinet Economic Committee, and to take three of his close political friends to NI with him – Lord Gowrie, Nicholas Scott and John Patten. In his first Stormont statement, he said he was prepared to lay his political reputation 'on the line' in a bid to secure a political settlement. His immediate challenge was the H-Block hunger strike, which had already led to the deaths of ten Republican prisoners. It was, however, petering out as next-of-kin of those close to death sought medical intervention, and within a month PIRA and INLA bowed to the inevitable. Prior announced only one substantial concession when the protest ended – the right of all prisoners to wear their own clothes at all times. But the easing of tension was followed by a new upsurge of violence and the murder of

the Rev. Robert Bradford, MP for S. Belfast. He was now brought face to face with loyalist wrath – notably at Bradford's funeral – and calls from the UUP and Democratic Unionists for a tougher security policy. The DUP-sponsored Third Force appeared at several rallies, and Rev. Ian Paisley mounted night-time demonstrations on lonely hillsides to dramatise his campaign. But Prior continued to pursue the possibilities of political advance, despite the obvious lack of agreement on how devolution could be achieved. His first thoughts were directed to the setting up of a local administration to which he would appoint Ministers – rather like a US President. But he abandoned this quickly for what became known as 'rolling devolution' (see Systems of Government section, p. 418) He got little encouragement for his gradualist approach. Both main Unionist parties were obsessed by fears of new pressure for power-sharing and the shadow of the new Anglo-Irish Intergovernmental Council. The DUP, though, was more enthusiastic than the UUP about the Assembly's scrutiny powers. The SDLP were sharply critical of what they saw as the absence of any firm assurances on power-sharing and an Irish dimension. The major Dublin parties were equally unfriendly to the proposals, and Prior had to face strong criticism from the Conservative far right during the passage of the legislation in the spring of 1982. At the same time, Charles Haughey's refusal to back sanctions against Argentina during the Falklands crisis brought Anglo-Irish relations to a new low. But despite this unhappy context, Prior pressed on with the initiative, and the 20 October 1982 poll found the SDLP fighting the election, but committed to boycott the Assembly. This was clearly disappointing for Prior, who was also unable to take any comfort from the achievement of PSF in getting five seats and 10 per cent of the vote in contesting a Stormont election for the first time. He saw the Assembly start with fifty-nine members present: twenty-six UUP; twenty-one DUP; ten All.; one UPUP; and one Independent Unionist. The fourteen SDLP and five PSF members

stayed away. He sought to boost the Assembly's prestige by addressing it on security policy within three weeks of its first meeting, but it was evident that a host of questions hung over this latest British initiative. Prior had the satisfaction, however, of having the Assembly plan supported in the 1983 Conservative manifesto. By the time he left NI in 1984, it was clear that the Assembly would not produce a political solution. Shortly before his departure to become chairman of GEC, he ran into criticism for saying that mistakes had been made in banning Martin Galvin of NORAID from the UK. In 1985 he referred to his differences with Thatcher and admitted that they sometimes shouted at each other. 'It is hell being a rebel if you are a Tory,' he said. In 1987 he left the Commons and was appointed a life peer. In his memoirs he disclosed that because of a tip-off of an assassination attempt, he was secretly flown home nightly to England for a period while he was NI Secretary of State. In January 1992 he was said to be on a PIRA 'hit list', and nine months later PIRA placed a bomb at the block of London flats where he lived. He was away at the time, but PIRA indicated in a statement that he was the target.

PRIVY COUNCIL
The Privy Council in NI has been suspended since direct rule. In the old Stormont Parliament all Cabinet Ministers were appointed to the Privy Council for life. Some senior judges were also admitted to the Council, which met at the Governor's residence at Hillsborough. Ex-Cabinet Ministers have been permitted to retain the title. Ministers in the power-sharing Executive of 1974 had no Privy Council membership. After the signing of the AIA, some NI Privy Councillors met to consider whether they could make any useful move, but no action resulted.

PRO-ASSEMBLY UNIONISTS
The name given to Unionists who supported the approach to partnership government in the Government's 1973 White Paper. When the NI Executive

collapsed in 1974, many of them moved to UPNI or the Alliance Party.

PROGRESSIVE DEMOCRATS

The Progressive Democrats were the Republic's newest political party (founded December 1985) when they secured fourteen seats in the 1987 general election and became the third-largest party, a position formerly held by Irish Labour, which got twelve seats. The party was founded by Desmond O'Malley, a former Fianna Fáil Minister, who had become disillusioned with that party and who now urged changes in the Constitution. These included a call for the dropping of the territorial claim to NI and its replacement by a statement of 'aspiration'. The party's ideas were projected as being in keeping with the AIA and a separation of Church and state. The party quickly developed close relations with the Alliance Party in NI. In the 1989 general election it slipped back to six seats, but yet made history by becoming the first party with which FF was prepared to enter a coalition – Taoiseach Charles Haughey chose to abandon FF's traditional 'no coalition' stance rather than go into opposition when he again failed to secure an overall majority. With O'Malley in the Government along with Prog. D. colleagues Bobby Molloy and Mary Harney, the party obviously had a considerable influence on policy on NI, the economy and security, and in January 1992 it forced the resignation of Haughey over claims that he had knowledge of the tapping of reporters' telephones some years earlier. When Albert Reynolds succeeded Haughey, friction developed over the proceedings of a tribunal inquiring into alleged irregularities in the beef industry. The Prog. D. Ministers withdrew from the Government and Taoiseach Reynolds called an election in November 1992, in which he fared even worse than Haughey. Prog. D. got ten TDs, but the real winners this time were Labour, with thirty-three seats. For a time it looked as if the Progressive Democrats could find themselves in a 'rainbow coalition' with Labour and FG, but it soon emerged that FF and Labour,

commanding a huge majority, were prepared to set up a coalition committed to an interventionist economic programme. O'Malley attended most of the 1992 sessions of the Brooke–Mayhew Talks involving Irish Ministers. Michael McDowell TD became party spokesman on NI in 1993. When O'Malley resigned as leader, Mary Harney was elected ahead of Pat Cox MEP in October 1993.

PROGRESSIVE UNIONIST PARTY

Started in the Shankill Road area of Belfast in 1978 as the Independent Unionist Group, becoming PUP in 1979. Alderman Hugh Smyth, an Ind. Unionist member of the Convention, 1975–6, was among the founders; he stood unsuccessfully in W. Belfast in the 1982 Assembly election. It urged in a statement in June 1978 that there should be a devolved administration based on a 153-seat parliament, with departments run by committees elected by the parliament, which would have power to co-opt non-voting members from outside. The party tried unsuccessfully to take part in the Stormont Constitutional Conference in 1980.

PROTESTANT ACTION FORCE *see* Ulster Volunteer Force

PROTESTANT ACTION GROUP *see* Ulster Protestant Action Group

PROTESTANT AND CATHOLIC ENCOUNTER

An organisation established in 1968 to bring together people of differing religious and political affiliations so as to promote harmony and goodwill. It aimed at the creation of a 'social order based upon justice and charity, and enlivened by mutual respect and understanding'. In 1991 it was fostering better community relations through the arts.

PROTESTANT TASK FORCE

Believed to be a small group involved in assassinations of people it claimed were associated with the PIRA. In press interview in November 1974, an unofficial spokesman of the organisation in mid-Ulster stated that it had murdered twenty-eight people in two months. He also said that the PTF had no scruples in dealing with Republicans, was restricted to ex-servicemen, and unconnected with any leading loyalist paramilitary group.

PROTESTANT UNIONIST PARTY

The party led by the Rev. Ian Paisley that gave way to the DUP in 1971. The term 'Protestant Unionist' was used by four candidates in the Belfast Corporation elections in 1964 . Prot. U. nominees stood unsuccessfully in the 1969 Stormont election, and its first successes were achieved in April 1970, when Paisley and the Rev. William Beattie won the Bannside and S. Antrim by-elections. In June 1970 Paisley won N. Antrim in the Westminster election as a Protestant Unionist.

PROVISIONAL IRISH REPUBLICAN ARMY

The PIRA, the dominant element in the NI violence, dates effectively from December 1969. In that month the IRA army council voted by three to one to give at least token recognition to the three Parliaments – Westminster, Dublin and Stormont. This switch in policy ran directly against the traditional abstentionism and physical-force policy of the IRA. It was too much for the more militant members, who split off to create the PIRA. The break was mirrored in Sinn Féin, the political counterpart of the IRA. When the Sinn Féin Ard Fheis (annual convention) met in Dublin in January 1970, there was a majority for a change in policy, but not the necessary two-thirds majority. So the new Provisionals walked out of the meeting in the Intercontinental Hotel to set up their organisation in Kevin Street, Dublin. There were now two IRAs – Provisional and Official – and the same applied to Sinn Féin. Events in NI, and particularly in Belfast, meant that PIRA was better placed than the Officials to attract public support in the Northern ghettos. For the IRA, so far as it existed in Belfast in the violent summer of 1969, had little credibility. Falls Road Catholics complained that it was unable to prevent the burning of Catholic homes. 'IRA – I Ran Away' was scrawled on some walls in W. Belfast. The Scarman tribunal, which investigated the early Troubles, said that the main difference between the Derry Citizens' Defence Association, which had some IRA members, and the IRA in Belfast was that the DCDA was ready while the IRA in Belfast was not. Scarman also found that while there was IRA influence in the 1969 riots in Belfast, Derry and Newry, the IRA did not start or plan the riots, and that the evidence was that they were taken by surprise and did less than many of their supporters felt they should have done. But Stormont was convinced that there was a strong IRA influence in the civil rights campaign. The point was made many times by William Craig, as Minister of Home Affairs. Scarman published a letter from the head of the RUC Special Branch to the Minister of Home Affairs, dated 18 August 1969. This claimed that at the end of May 1969 members of Republican Clubs controlled two-thirds of the executives of all local civil rights associations in NI, while six of the fourteen members of the NICRA executive were from the Republican movement. The head of the Special Branch also stated that the citizens' defence committees which had developed in Belfast, Derry, Newry, Lurgan, and other towns were all IRA-dominated, and that IRA units in these areas had been making hundreds of petrol bombs and some grenades. They were also instructing people in the use of petrol bombs through the citizens' defence committees. Thus, the situation in NI was highly favourable to the Provisionals, who attracted not only many young recruits but a high proportion of veterans of former IRA campaigns, and one survivor of the 1916 Easter Rising in Dublin – the late Joe Clarke. The Provisionals were short of both arms and ammunition at the start of 1970, but friendly sources in Dublin provided some, others were shipped in secretly from Britain and the Continent. The guns which they got from the Republic were, of course, sometimes intended for the local defence committees. And the charging in the Republic in 1970 of two Cabinet Ministers (Charles Haughey and Neil Blaney) with illegal import of arms was seen by PIRA chiefs as having a valuable publicity spin-off, even if both Ministers were later cleared. The Provisionals duplicated the military organisation of the former IRA. In Belfast, for example, there was a commander and brigade staff, and three battalions. By mid-1970 PIRA strength overall was believed to be around 1,500, including 800 in NI divided roughly as follows: Belfast, 600; Derry, 100; other areas, 100. The growing Provisonal strength was reflected in the big increase in violence in 1970 compared with 1969. Twenty-three civilians and two RUC men died during the year. There were 153 explosions compared with 9 in 1969. Street violence also remained at a high level in 1970, and the security forces held that much of it could be traced to inspiration by PIRA. PIRA further stepped up attacks in 1971. It was held responsible for most of the 304 explosions between January and July. In February 1971 General Farrar-Hockley, Commander of Land Forces, named five men as leaders of the PIRA in Belfast, and blamed them for recent rioting. They were Francis Card, William McKee, Liam Hannaway and his son, Kevin, and Patrick Leo Martin. About the same time, the army blamed the Provisionals for organising attacks by children, and claimed that the PIRA were using petrol bombs, grenades and rifles against the troops. In the early part of 1971 a bitter feud went on between the PIRA and OIRA and there was much of what the authorities termed inter-factional shooting. The murder in Belfast of three young Scottish soldiers in March 1971 brought strident loyalist demands for the use of internment without trial against PIRA. The army and police began to lean heavily on PIRA suspects. Billy McKee, the Belfast commander, was arrested in March. His successor, Joe Cahill, held a news conference in Belfast in the summer of 1971, much to the discomfiture of the Government and security chiefs. At that period the leading figures in the top PIRA leadership were Seán Mac Stiofáin, English-born chief of staff, and Dáithí Ó Conaill. In July 1971 there was a big round-up of people believed to be connected with both wings of the IRA. It

was designed to secure information for the coming internment operation. Government intelligence was satisfied that most of the thirty people killed up to 9 August 1971 – the date of the start of internment – had been victims of PIRA. They comprised eleven soldiers, two policemen and seventeen civilians. The European Court of Human Rights report on the ill-treatment of some of the IRA suspects interned in August 1971 stated: 'Prior to August 1971, the intelligence obtained by the police had failed to provide anything but a very general picture of the IRA organisation.' The internment move was designed to sweep up activists and sympathisers of the IRA. Of the 452 names on the army's list, 342 were taken into custody and 104 were released within 48 hours, and it was evidently the Government's belief that the operation would deprive the Provisionals of their more experienced people and damp down the violence. But the reality was otherwise: the use of internment alienated a huge section of the Catholic population, increased support for PIRA, and violence was intensified. From the date of internment (9 August) to the end of 1971, the count of violence was: 143 people killed (including 46 members of security forces); 729 explosions; 1,437 shooting incidents. Security forces put the great bulk down to PIRA, and loyalists were accused of only one killing. At this point, PIRA had assembled a great diversity of weapons, despite the uncovering of a Czechoslovakian arms deal in Amsterdam in October 1971. Apart from the old standby of the IRA, the Thompson sub-machine-gun (the 'Chicago piano'), it had also some US-made M1 carbines and Garard rifles, and a variety of .303 rifles and German and American pistols. It was using the car bomb, the nail bomb (usually a beer can containing nails wrapped in explosive), and the hold-all bag bomb, often left outside business premises. It had also displayed ingenuity in producing small incendiary devices which could easily be hidden in shops. Two popular types were the cigarette-packet incendiary, and the device in which a contraceptive acted as a fuse, with the detonation achieved by acid burning through the rubber. The existence of internment made it easier for the Provisionals to get funds from abroad, particularly from Irish-Americans. The Provisionals were also helped by the non-acceptability of the RUC in many Catholic areas, and they got a new boost at the start of 1972, when thirteen people were shot dead by the army in Derry on what became known as 'Bloody Sunday'. In March 1972 Provisional Sinn Féin launched its 'Éire Nua' policy – a scheme for four provincial parliaments in Ireland – which was also linked with demands for the abolition of Stormont, a declaration of intent of British withdrawal, and a full amnesty for all political prisoners. PIRA ordered a three-day ceasefire in association with this policy, but they called it off because they had not got a British response, and arrests had been continued by the security forces. In fact, there were 900 internees at the end of March 1972, when direct rule was imposed from London, and they were all held because of alleged IRA involvement. But the closing down of the Stormont Parliament was not enough to induce PIRA to drop its campaign. Its determination to fight on was announced after a Dublin meeting in April which was said to have been attended by representatives of every active service unit. On 29 May 1972 the OIRA declared a ceasefire, which soon took on permanence. Exactly four weeks later, PIRA began a truce of its own, but it lasted only thirteen days. The collapse occurred after a row about housing in Belfast. Two days before the ceasefire ended, a party of PIRA leaders was flown secretly to London for talks with Secretary of State William Whitelaw. The Government was believed to have received intelligence suggesting that PIRA was ready to make major concessions, but the talks proved unproductive. The restart of the PIRA campaign produced a massive upsurge in violence. For July 1972 alone there was an unprecedented tally of violence: 74 civilians and 21 members of the security forces killed, nearly 200 explosions and 2,800 shooting incidents. Throughout 1972 there had

also been a mounting toll of sectarian assassinations carried out, for the most part, by loyalists. Faced with this two-pronged campaign, the Government decided to move against the no-go areas. But few PIRA men remained in the W. Belfast Republican areas or in the Bogside area of Derry, since the Government's intentions had been signalled well in advance. The second half of 1972 was a period of strong pressure on the Provisionals both in NI and in the Republic, and there were sporadic incidents involving members of PIRA and OIRA. A leading Belfast PIRA man, Martin Meehan, was recaptured in Belfast in August – he had escaped from Belfast Prison at the end of 1971. Documents seized by the security forces in Belfast were claimed to reveal a good deal about the PIRA structure in the city and especially its measures to prevent 'leaks'. It was also stated about the same time in *An Phoblacht*, the Provisional newspaper, that of the forty-four PIRA members killed since 1969, eighteen had been executed for mistakes or for giving information to the security forces. In November 1972 the PIRA chief of staff, Séan Mac Stiofáin, was arrested after he had given an interview to RTE. He was charged with IRA membership and then went on hunger strike, and an unsuccessful attempt was made to rescue him from a Dublin hospital. With Ruairí Ó Brádaigh, president of PSF, held in December 1972 for alleged IRA membership, there were rumours that Mac Stiofáin was seeking a larger political role. The British Government was claiming that it was getting truce 'feelers' from PIRA, despite denials by the organisation. There was a leadership crisis in PIRA when Mac Stiofáin abandoned his hunger strike. He was thought to have been succeeded by a three-man council made up Dáithí Ó Conaill, Joe Cahill, and Gerry Adams, a Belfast Provisional who was one of the deputation flown secretly to London in July 1972 to meet Whitelaw. At the end of 1972 Whitelaw said in London that 1,000 IRA men had been arrested and convicted during 1972 and the organisation's command structure greatly weakened. There were also signs that PIRA was finding difficulty in getting conventional explosives because of the clamp-down in the South. The weedkiller chemical sodium chlorate was figuring increasingly in PIRA weapons. At this period, PIRA continued its attacks alongside loyalist violence on a substantial scale. Official estimates suggested that between 1 April 1972 and 31 January 1973, PIRA was responsible for about 300 deaths, including those of some 120 members of the security forces. In the case of 'factional' or 'sectarian' assassinations, PIRA was blamed for thirty-four and the loyalists for seventy. Throughout 1973, when the total of deaths was 250 – 171 civilians and 79 security forces – the pattern of PIRA bombing and shooting of soldiers and policemen was continued, while the loyalists concentrated on the shooting of Catholics. In February PIRA warned the UDA that it would take 'ruthless action' against it to halt sectarian killings. PIRA called for the rejection of the British Government White Paper which led to the Assembly system, and it also called for a boycott of the 1973 council elections. In May 1973 Joe Cahill was sentenced to five years' imprisonment arising from gun-running charges associated with the vessel *Claudia*, seized off Waterford with a cargo of arms and ammunition from Libya – a precursor of future supplies along the same route. In May 1973 the Government published figures of IRA casualties going back to 1969. It claimed that 123 IRA men had been killed. PIRA admitted that it had lost ninety-nine men, and said the British claim was 'outlandish'. In 1974 there was some falling off in PIRA violence. In part, this was believed to be due to a desire to encourage the loyalists to make the running against the Government in their opposition to the Sunningdale Agreement and power-sharing. But PIRA had its own troubles at this time. A coup for the authorities was the uncovering in the select Malone Road area of Belfast of the brigade HQ of PIRA. In a flat, and posing as a businessman, was Brendan Hughes, the brigade commander, and one of his aides. About the same time several other key figures in PIRA in the city were also

picked up. In the Commons, PM Harold Wilson referred to documents seized at the Provisionals' HQ which, he said, were a 'specific and calculated' plan to take over certain areas of Belfast by creating inter-sectarian hatred, chaos, violence and hardship. The areas to be taken over were said to include loyalist districts like Woodvale and Sandy Row, together with key buildings, such as Telephone House, the gas works, BBC and UTV. PIRA admitted that the plans had been drawn up some time before as a doomsday contingency. The end of 1974 was a period of mixed fortunes for the Provisionals. On the one hand, they came under greater pressure after the passing at Westminster of new and tougher anti-terrorist legislation in the wake of the Birmingham bombings. On the other, their leaders became involved in secret talks with Protestant Churchmen in Feakle, Co. Clare. PIRA immediately came under suspicion for the bombings which resulted in the deaths in November of nineteen people in two Birmingham pubs. The Provisionals denied that they had been responsible but there were later PIRA statements promising an inquiry into the bombings, although no result of such an investigation was ever issued. Meantime, six men had been jailed for life for the Birmingham bombings. An intensive campaign to prove their innocence only succeeded in 1991, when they were freed by the Court of Appeal (*see* Birmingham Six). The immediate effect of the Birmingham tragedy was to unite Parliament in support of the Prevention of Terrorism Act, which declared the IRA illegal in GB, allowed suspects to be held without charge for up to seven days, and permitted the expulsion of people to either NI or the Republic. The upshot of the Feakle Talks with Churchmen was that there was a flurry of talks in mid-December. The Secretary of State Merlyn Rees met some of the Churchmen to hear the Provisionals' demands, which included a call for a declaration of intent of British withdrawal. (Six months later, one of the Churchmen, the Rev. William Arlow, claimed that the Government had told the Provisionals that the army would be withdrawn if the Convention broke down – a claim denied by Rees.) There was also a lengthy secret meeting of the PIRA army council, and its then chief of staff, Dáithí Ó Conaill, met Arlow in Dublin. The only public response from the British Government was a comment by Rees that it would naturally respond to any genuine cessation of violence. PIRA then announced a ceasefire from 22 December to 2 January 1975, to give the Government time, they said, to consider their proposals. In an atmosphere in which many policiticans, and particularly the loyalists, were highly suspicious of what was going on, the Government insisted that there was no question of negotiations with PIRA. But there were meetings between Government officials and members of PSF. So the ceasefire was extended first to 16 January and then to 10 February when an open-ended ceasefire was announced. It emerged that a plan to monitor the ceasefire involved the setting up of 'incident centres' manned by PSF in Catholic areas of Belfast and Derry and other major towns. These would be in instant contact with Government officials with the object of avoiding a breakdown of the ceasefire through misunderstanding about individual incidents. There was a great deal of scepticism about the operation. Loyalists feared 'Provo policing', the SDLP were worried that the Provisionals were being given new credibility through ready access to Government; and Official Republicans saw signs of co-operation with the RUC through 'Royal Ulster Provisionals', a charge which PIRA was quick to deny. Not all the PIRA activists put away their guns; some joined the IRSP which was engaged in a feud with OIRA. In March 1975 the Belfast sisters Dolours and Marion Price, sentenced for the London car bombings, were moved from Durham Prison to Armagh Women's Prison – a decision which was seen as a definite gesture by the Government towards the PIRA ceasefire. The ceasefire became more fragile, and more controversial, as time went on. At the beginning of July four soldiers were killed in an ambush in S. Armagh, and the Secretary of State told Parliament that

one of the key questions was whether the Provisionals could control their followers. By mid-August the number of soldiers killed still stood at four during the ceasefire period, compared with nineteen in the same period of 1974. But the total of civilian deaths had risen by 26 to 119, and since the increase was entirely accounted for by a rise in the number of Protestants murdered (57), the security forces suspected that some of the PIRA effort had been switched to revenge killings of loyalists in view of the continued assassinations of Catholics. There were also murmurings from loyalist politicians at what they saw as a deliberate policy by the security forces of turning a blind eye to Provisionals who had returned to their old haunts in W. Belfast. Notably, there was confusion as to whether Seamus Twomey, a former PIRA commander in the city, was still on the wanted list. The implication seemed to be that, with the suspension of the detention process at the start of the ceasefire in February, Provisionals were only being arrested where specific charges could be brought against them. One of the imponderables of the situation was the extent to which PIRA had been preparing during the ceasefire for a new onslaught. Certainly, it had gone to the length of establishing a new, fourth battalion in Belfast. In September six men were killed during a raid on an Orange Hall at Tullyvallen in S. Armagh. Although the raid was claimed by the 'South Armagh Republican Action Force', this was treated by the authorities as a cover name for PIRA. Indeed, S. Armagh, which Secretary of State Merlyn Rees had described as 'bandit country', was never effectively covered by the ceasefire. How far this was due to lack of control by the PIRA army council was never very clear. In November 1976 it was claimed that PIRA had carried out twenty-one killings in the area during the nine months of the ceasefire. In that month three soldiers were killed in a S. Armagh border dug-out by PIRA and two soldiers were killed by an explosion. Outside S. Armagh, September had brought eighteen PIRA explosions in one day throughout NI. In November the

Government closed the incident centres, but PSF claimed that contacts continued with the Government and that there was still a 'truce situation'. On 5 December the Secretary of State ordered the release of the last seventy-five detainees, among them fifty-seven members of the PIRA. The 1975 security figures reflected the ceasefire in several respects. The 31 deaths of members of the security forces compared with 50 in 1974; the number of shooting incidents was down from 3,206 to 1,803; and the total of explosions from 685 to 399. Then, 1976 opened with the shooting dead of ten Protestant workers, when their bus was ambushed in Kingsmills, S. Armagh, on 5 January. This incident was not claimed by PIRA, but British security forces insisted that it had been carried out by a PIRA unit based in the Republic. The killings were, apparently, a reprisal for the murder of five Catholics in two separate incidents the previous day. With many Catholics in S. Armagh voicing their fears of loyalist vengeance, the British Government announced that men of the Special Air Services (SAS) would be sent into the area. Although there had been many reports of SAS units operating earlier, these had always been denied by the British authorities. In February the ceasefire finally came to an end, with the death in prison in England of IRA hunger-striker Frank Stagg. His death provoked widespread violence in NI. In April the arrival of James Callaghan as PM was the signal for more PIRA attacks on troops. During the month, five part-time UDR men died. In May there was a further round of bombing, which was repeated in August at the time of the internment anniversary. Two events then occurred which created problems for PIRA chiefs. The Peace People movement got off the ground in Belfast, and probably accounted in part for an increased flow of information to the security forces. And in September Roy Mason, who had been Defence Secretary, succeeded Merlyn Rees as NI Secretary of State. He had a reputation for toughness, and while his immediate claim that PIRA was 'reeling' caused problems for him, he was

obviously intent on stepping up army undercover activity. He also permitted the SAS to operate anywhere in NI. By late autumn he claimed in Parliament that 690 members of PIRA had been charged since the start of the year, that is, more than twice the total (320) in 1975. The weight of police and army intelligence was directed to cataloguing the movements of suspected terrorists and their life-style, contacts, 'safe-houses', and general tactics. But the Mason approach did not prevent a sharp rise in the level of violence in 1976, mostly by PIRA. The number killed was 297, an increase of 50. Twenty-nine soldiers died, as against twenty in 1975; and twenty-three RUC members against eleven in 1975. The total of 766 explosions was roughly double the 1975 figure. In 1977 there were signs that the pressure by the security forces on PIRA was beginning to tell. It was also apparently short of explosives, and the car bomb had all but vanished. In February, however, PIRA activated an earlier threat when it killed three businessmen and injured four others. At Easter the feud between PIRA and OIRA also flared up again. The response of PIRA to growing undercover police and army activity was to mount a large-scale reorganisation. The effect of this was to substitute very small active service units – possibly with only two or three members – for its larger companies. It is also likely that the new tactics were based on the 'need to know' principle – that is, probably only one member of a bombing unit would be informed in advance of the actual target. The organisation had also come to rely largely on the small incendiary device, with only a very limited explosive content. Increased 'knee-cappings' – shooting through the knees as a punishment – reflected a growing effort by PIRA to punish members who were careless and to increase 'policing' in Republican areas by dealing with those whom they termed 'petty criminals'. The end of 1977 brought a serious loss for PIRA – the recapture in Dublin of Seamus Twomey, its chief of staff. The total of soldiers killed by PIRA in 1977 was 29 – the same figure as in 1976 – but violence generally had dropped sharply, and the total death toll was down to 112. PIRA began 1978 with an atrocity which horrified even its own sympathisers, and which it rapidly acknowledged to have been a mistake. On 17 February fire bombs were used to attack the La Mon House Hotel, near Comber, Co. Down, while it was crowded with about five hundred people attending two social functions. Twelve people died instantly in the blaze, and twenty-three were badly burned. Following the attack, the security forces clamped down heavily on PSF and mounted a big effort to prove that it was working closely with PIRA. Meantime, PIRA prisoners in the Maze Prison staged a protest against the withdrawal of special category status. They refused to leave their cells to wash or go to the toilet. In August 1978 PIRA was blamed by the security forces for a series of bomb attacks on British army barracks in West Germany. On 21 September PIRA bomb attacks destroyed the terminal building at Eglinton airfield, and caused other extensive damage. In November the organisation murdered the deputy governor of Belfast Prison, Albert Miles, and bombed the centres of many towns and villages; on 30 November explosives and fire bombs were set off in fourteen centres. At the same time PIRA warned that it was 'preparing for a long war'. In November the Intelligence Staff of the Defence Ministry concluded that PIRA was still a force to be reckoned with. The Ministry's report, which was regarded as top secret, apparently fell into PIRA hands in May 1979. The leak of the report was obviously an embarrassment to Ministers. It predicted that PIRA would have the manpower to sustain violence during the next five years and that it would show 'more precise targeting and greater expertise'. And it said that the calibre of members of ASUs did not support the view that they were merely 'mindless hooligans'. It suggested that the Provisional leadership was committed to a long campaign of attrition, and events in the first half of 1979 indicated that it had settled on striking at a variety of targets – shops, offices, hotels, security installations – and keeping up its assault on members

of the security forces and prison officers at about the same level as in 1978. PIRA's activities in the early 1980s became more diffuse, since some members were diverted to promoting the hunger-strike campaign and the efforts of H-Block and PSF candidates in Dáil elections in 1981 and 1982, and the 1982 NI Assembly election. This increased political involvement seems to have had full PIRA backing, and its muscle was obviously an element in strengthening anti-H-Block demonstrations, particularly the closing of business premises in Republican areas. The organisation had also to cope with the appearance of informers on a large scale, so that 1982 became known as 'the year of the supergrass'. PIRA let it be known in early 1982 that there would be an amnesty for informers who made themselves and the extent of their disclosures known. This contrasted with the established PIRA practice of killing informers. But there were signs that the 1981 hunger strike brought extra recruits and resources and an increase in Republican solidarity. Army intelligence sources had reported in 1980 that PIRA strength could be 'measured in tens' but later the same year ex-GOC Sir Timothy Creasey talked of 500 hard-core terrorists overall in NI. But the deaths of ten hunger-strikers, seven of them PIRA and including Bobby Sands MP, undoubtedly spurred support from US Irish Republican sympathisers and others in Europe and elsewhere. And PIRA chiefs were obviously impressed by the arguments of people like Gerry Adams (later to become PSF president and MP for W. Belfast), that the Republican movement must have an increasing political content, with no prospect of 'Brits out' being achieved in the foreseeable future. Two PIRA prisoners in the Maze won Dáil seats in the June 1981 election. They were hunger-striker Kieran Doherty (Cavan–Monaghan), who later died from his fast, and Paddy Agnew (Louth) (*see* H-Blocks). In the early 1980s PIRA's NI campaign became extremely varied. Russian RPG rockets (handled with varying confidence), the M-60 machine gun, car and beer-keg bombs and landmines with plastic gelignite and other inferior explosives, homemade mortars, and more sophisticated incendiaries incorporating silicon chips – all these figured in assaults. Much of PIRA's effort in this period was directed against the security forces, but there were also attacks on property and two coal boats, the *Nellie M* and *St Bedan*, were sunk in Lough Foyle. Some forty-two deaths were believed to have resulted from PIRA attacks in 1982. But the assassination which attracted most attention in this period was that of the S. Belfast Ulster Unionist MP, the Rev. Robert Bradford, shot in November 1981 at a community centre in Finaghy. He was the first Westminster MP for an NI seat to be killed in the Troubles. PIRA accused him of being 'one of the key people responsible for winding up the loyalist paramilitary sectarian machine'. In March 1982 it made an unsuccessful bid to assassinate Lord Chief Justice Lord Lowry at QUB. Immediately before that there was a lull in PIRA activity, and a PIRA spokesman admitted in March 1982 that they had supply and other problems. These no doubt included difficulties in getting explosives across the border, with the stepped-up operations of anti-terrorist units in the Republic. In mid-November 1982 three PIRA members were shot dead by the RUC near Lurgan when they were alleged to have driven through a checkpoint. The incident provoked much controversy and allegations that the RUC was operating a new 'shoot to kill' policy. This was denied by the authorities, although they admitted to the existence of specialised RUC anti-terrorist units. Controversy continued over whether RUC officers involved could be compelled to give evidence at the inquest, which the House of Lords decided in 1993 in favour of the officers. The Lurgan shootings came two weeks after three RUC men had been killed by a PIRA landmine in the area. The extent to which PIRA should mount attacks in GB has always been a matter of debate within the organisation. The result has been intermittent action there which has probably added greatly to the detection problems of the anti-terrorist squads. But PIRA chiefs are obviously attracted by the

greater publicity attached to such incidents. In October 1981 it placed a bomb in the car of Maj.-Gen. Sir Stuart Pringle, Commandant General of the Royal Marines, at his London home, as a result of which he lost a leg. The next month and on the eve of its assassination of Robert Bradford, it seriously damaged with a bomb the London home of Sir Michael Havers, the Attorney-General, although no one was injured. On 10 October 1981 it set off a nail bomb outside Chelsea barracks in London which killed a woman and injured twenty-three soldiers and seventeen civilians. But PIRA bombings in London on 20 July 1982 were much more spectacular, and clearly intended to dispel suggestions by the security forces that they were a waning force. Attacks by nail bombs on the Household Cavalry at Hyde Park left ten soldiers dead and some fifty people injured, both soldiers and civilians, while seven army horses also died in the Hyde Park bombing. Margaret Thatcher denounced the attacks as 'callous and cowardly'. In the mid-1980s, in the course of the supergrass trials, some of the mystique of PIRA was dispelled by detailed disclosures on the life-style and *modus operandi* of ASUs. Scores of alleged PIRA members found themselves charged on the word of informers like Christopher Black, Robert Quigley, Kevin McGrady and Raymond Gilmour. The supergrass system was bitterly criticised by Nationalists and by the Irish Government, as well as a section of loyalism. Cardinal Ó Fiaich described it as 'internment under another name'. It eventually collapsed as many convictions were overturned on appeal, and some informers retracted their stories. But the widespread arrests disrupted many PIRA units, and in face of the challenge of the 'converted terrorist' – the RUC term – the PIRA army council set about reorganisation and the diversifying of tactics. One dramatic move was the mass break-out of thirty-eight prisoners from the Maze Prison in September 1983, with nineteen getting away. In early 1984 PIRA also shot dead the assistant governor of the prison because, according to prison officers, he threatened the PIRA command structure at the Maze. With PIRA apparently gearing up for fresh attacks in Britain, British, Irish and US intelligence units had a major success in September 1984, when the trawler *Marita Ann* was intercepted off the Kerry coast with a huge cargo of arms and ammunition which it had transported across the Atlantic for PIRA. Thatcher remained a prime target of PIRA and in October 1984 it came close to killing her with its bombing of the Grand Hotel in Brighton. Among the aims of PIRA chiefs were the countering of Government attempts to promote an image of normality within NI, and to 'sicken' British opinion. (Interestingly, a 1984 MORI poll in GB showed 50 per cent of people believing that any attempt to solve the NI problem must have the co-operation of PIRA.) The Brighton bombing led to a major increase in anti-terrorist measures in GB, which killed PIRA's 1985 plan to bomb major seaside resorts. It was not until the summer of 1988 that PIRA struck again in London, with a bomb at the Inglis army barracks at Mill Hill, in which one soldier died. In the interim, its grand plan seemed to be to switch targets in a random way. In 1985, however, it mounted a sustained assault on RUC stations, mainly in border areas, to which it linked murder threats against contractors and their employees who became involved in repair of the stations. In the course of this campaign it killed nine RUC officers in a mortar attack on Newry station. But at the same time, PIRA was quietly building up substantial supplies of new weapons and explosives from Libya. Two such shipments are believed to have reached Ireland in 1985 and two more in 1986. But this reinforcement of the PIRA effort seems not to have been suspected until the Irish-crewed vessel *Eksund* was intercepted by French customs in October 1987, with a massive cargo of weaponry and explosives, including ground-to-air missiles, heavy machine guns and plastic explosive. Libya denied involvement but French intelligence was satisfied that the *Eksund* had been loaded at Tripoli, and that its cargo was intended to be shared between PIRA and a

European terrorist group, possibly the Basque ETA which has always had strong links with PIRA. Libya's Colonel Gaddafi has repeatedly expressed sympathy with Irish republicanism, and his anger at British support for US air raids on Libya gave him an extra reason for wanting to hit British interests. As the extent of Libyan arms in PIRA hands became apparent, there was alarm in both British and Irish security establishments. They were forced to conclude that the PIRA arsenal was larger than ever before, and there were extensive searches on both sides of the border. Part of the Libyan haul was uncovered on a beach near Malin Head in Co. Donegal and there was a variety of smaller seizures. Many new PIRA bunkers were revealed on farms and in remote areas, ready to receive arms and to provide a choice of 'hides'. The AIA was a new spur to North–South security co-operation, and put severe pressure on PIRA lines of communication, where occasional carelessness proved costly to the organisation in terms of arms seizures. None the less, the widespread perception of PIRA as almost a spent force after the Enniskillen Remembrance Sunday atrocity in 1987, when it felt obliged to express 'deep regret' for the bombing in which eleven civilians died, was soon dispelled. Following Enniskillen, there was a series of similar blunders by PIRA which led to deaths of innocent civilians, but PIRA shrugged off such embarrassments, even if some PSF members found 'contradictions' arising from the armed struggle where PSF was seeking to maximise its vote. PIRA also has its own political role. No major Republican departure in policy (for example, the 1986 decision to end abstention from the Dáil) is taken without PIRA endorsement. PIRA has also hit at British Ministers' description of it as 'Marxist' and has also apparently ruled out any idea of a further ceasefire. But in the late 1980s it does seem to have suffered from lack of experienced terrorists to match the new sophistication of its weaponry. Some of its losses were obvious, including fourteen members shot dead by the SAS: eight as they attacked Loughgall RUC station (May

1987); three in Gibraltar (March 1988); and three more in Tyrone (August 1988). Indeed, PIRA suffered twenty-two casualties within NI between 1 January 1987 and 31 August 1988. But it also inflicted appreciable losses on the security forces during the same period: the twenty-four regular soldiers killed included eight in a landmine attack on their bus near Ballygawley (August 1988); six bombed in Lisburn after taking part in a 'fun run' (June 1988); and two shot dead after being attacked by mourners at a PIRA funeral in Belfast (March 1988). During the same twenty months, nineteen RUC members and eighteen UDR soldiers died. PIRA also mounted attacks on members of the security forces in Europe, forcing a change of car number plates by BAOR. In 1988 three off-duty RAF men died in the Netherlands, and a soldier in Belgium. The inclusion of the Czechoslovakian explosive Semtex in Libyan supplies also gave its campaign a new edge. Smaller and more powerful bombs resulted, and were evident in landmines in rural areas and a renewal of the assault on Belfast city centre in the summer of 1988. It used one of its new heavy machine guns to bring down an army helicopter in S. Armagh in 1988, and kept the security forces guessing as to how it might deploy ground-to-air missiles. In 1987 it killed Lord Justice Gibson and his wife Cecily and also UDA leader John McMichael, and in 1988 threatened civil servants and bombed the home of Stormont civil service chief Sir Kenneth Bloomfield, who escaped injury. At the end of 1988 PIRA attacked several housing estates occupied by army families. As the twentieth anniversary approached of the entry of the army in August 1969, it also mentioned politicians and members of the royal family as likely targets. It came under pressure from PSF to avoid the civilian casualties which were a strong feature of PIRA violence in 1987–8, and in response it was announced that a Donegal-based unit active on the Fermanagh border had been disbanded in January 1989. The PIRA strategy of avoiding any set pattern of attack was well illustrated in the period 1989–92. One security source remarked

that 'a man with a grasshopper mind could be at the centre of its operations web'. Twenty years on from its foundation, its overall manpower probably consisted of a hard core of 50 to 70 people, 400 or so other activists, and pockets of sympathisers who could be employed in a minor way as required. The ASU remained the key to minimising leaks of information, along with a ruthless attitude to the informer – three alleged informers were shot dead in a single operation in July 1992. It is likely that more members have had to be employed in countering informers. PIRA is also believed to have given more latitude to individual units in selecting operations in order to reduce communications. It may also have been forced to duplicate its bomb-making efforts by arrests of key people with technical expertise. Although its horizontally fired 'Mark 12' mortar and an improved 'Mark 15' ('barrack buster'), introduced in 1992, have proved deadly, other types of mortar have been unreliable. The coffee-jar Semtex bomb, launched in 1991, has been widely used with varying effects. PIRA failed to explode its biggest-ever, 8,000-lb bomb at the Annaghmartin border checkpoint in Co. Fermanagh in September 1991. But it still seems to have ample supplies of arms and explosives. In May 1992 there were reports that 60 per cent of its Libyan arms had been recovered by the security forces in the Republic as a result of Operation Silo, but some independent experts believed that 45 per cent might be a more realistic figure (see Libyan Connection). But the Gardaí have apparently succeeded in disrupting movements of detonators from the Republic to England, and seizures of PIRA arms in Co. Donegal in 1991–2 may be attributable to detection of vehicles used in transporting them North. And in the US, FBI operations have undoubtedly scotched PIRA efforts to restore its old transatlantic supply route of the early 1970s. But the organisation is believed to be still receiving cash aid from Irish-American supporters. In July 1992 Security Minister Michael Mates said in the Commons that it might be getting $1 million a year from the US. There are suspicions that it benefited from a large bank robbery in Waterford in 1992, and also from the pirate video racket and sale of the growth promoter 'angel dust', or clenbuterol, to farmers. In January 1992 the *Financial Times* suggested it was raising £6 million a year. An appreciable slice of spending is going into promoting the 'spectacular' in GB, since it will generate far more publicity than a similar attack in NI. Thus, the April 1992 general election was followed by a massive PIRA explosion in the City of London which killed three people and caused £800 million damage – a compensation bill more costly than that for twenty-three years of bombings in NI. On 11 February 1992 serious disruption was caused by a bomb in a phone kiosk in Whitehall when PM Major was due to meet the leaders of the four main NI parties. In October 1992, the month MI5 took over responsibility for anti-PIRA intelligence in GB, PIRA set off fifteen bombs in London, killing one man. One bomb was at a block of flats one of whose residents was Lord Prior, former NI Secretary of State, and another was close to Downing Street, which PIRA had attacked the previous year with a rocket device which came close to killing PM Major and several of his colleagues (*see* Downing Street Bombings). PIRA has also struck at individuals who have been seen as particular enemies. In July 1990 it murdered Conservative MP Ian Gow at his home in Sussex with a car bomb, and two months later shot and wounded Sir Peter Terry, Governor of Gibraltar at the time of the shooting there of three PIRA members. The GB campaign is thought to have involved twenty to twenty-five people at a time in recent years, many of them people with no terrorist record. In September 1989 PIRA killed eleven Royal Marine bandsmen at a barracks in Deal, Kent, setting off an almost permanent alert at service establishments. But most attacks have been on civilian targets. The killing of two young boys by litter-bin bombs in Warrington, Cheshire, on 20 March 1993 caused a wave of revulsion on both sides of the Irish Sea which reportedly stung PIRA chiefs into warning their bombers against attacks that could be politically costly. There have been

bombs at London railway stations, fire bombs in shops in London, Manchester, Blackpool and other centres, and bomb hoaxes to cause disruption. An embarrassment for the authorities was the leaking of minutes of a Scotland Yard conference which showed that in December 1991 the police had 'little intelligence' on PIRA fire bombings at that time. But PIRA has suffered some notable failures in GB. In November 1992 it succeeded in placing a van bomb close to London's tallest building, at Canary Wharf, but it was spotted and defused, while a bomb on a lorry was seen by a policeman in N. London, who was shot and injured. 'Sheer bad luck,' said PIRA. Some long-time PIRA operators in GB have been jailed in the 1990s, and important caches of arms and explosives uncovered. In November 1991 two PIRA terrorists blew themselves up in St Albans while handling a bomb close to the civic centre in which a military band was performing. Within NI, there has been equal diversity. Great outrage was engendered by the PIRA killing in January 1992 of eight Protestant workmen, who had been engaged in work for the security forces, at Teebane in Co. Tyrone. In 1990 there were several 'proxy' bombings – that is, attacks in which the family of the person forced to drive the vehicle carrying the bomb was held hostage. In Derry, five soldiers and a civilian died at a border base in October 1990 in a 'proxy' operation. In 1991–2 the PIRA car bomb reappeared to blast business premises in Belfast, Lurgan, Bangor and Coleraine. In Belfast in 1992, the city centre suffered severe bomb damage and a massive bomb wrecked the forensic science laboratory in S. Belfast and caused extensive damage in the Belvoir Park area. In response, the RUC ringed the city with permanent checkpoints, lifted only for the seventy-two-hour Christmas ceasefire. A similar ceasefire applied in 1991 and 1992. But PIRA, notably during 1991, replied to the upsurge in loyalist attacks on PSF people and random Catholics by murders in loyalist areas. SAS-type operations led to the deaths of several PIRA members. Four were shot dead near Coalisland in

February 1992, and in October 1990 Dessie Grew (ex-INLA and believed to be a senior PIRA figure) and Martin McCaughey (an ex-councillor) were killed near Loughgall. At Coagh, Co. Tyrone, in June 1991 three PIRA members 'on active service' were shot dead in a stolen car, an operation that PSF president Gerry Adams said was in revenge for the deaths of three UDR men in the PIRA bombing of the Glennane, Co. Armagh, security base the previous month. Peter Ryan, thirty-seven, who died at Coagh, was believed to be one of PIRA's top gunmen. The drop in the death toll of security force members in the 1990s suggested that more effort was going into softer targets. Twenty-seven members of the security forces died in NI in 1990, nineteen in 1991, nine in 1992 and fourteen in 1993. On the Continent, PIRA was still co-operating with groups like the Basque ETA and the French Action Directe, but its killing in Holland in May 1990 of two Australian lawyers, who were mistaken for British soldiers, and two incidents in Germany in 1989 – the shooting dead of the German wife of a British soldier and of an RAF corporal and his six-year-old daughter – were obviously counter-productive. Gerry Adams called the killings of the Australians 'inexcusable'. But there was no evidence that PIRA was preparing to abandon its campaign, despite the urgings of politicians, peace campaigners and Church leaders. In January 1993 the PIRA army council ruled 'no change' after NI Secretary of State Sir Patrick Mayhew spoke of 'profound consequences' if violence were ended, and even called in aid the philosophy of Wolfe Tone, in his Coleraine speech of December 1992. As a variety of peace efforts developed on both sides of the Irish Sea, PIRA made several statements around Easter 1993 reaffirming its commitment to the 'armed struggle'. Its most specific comment was in a corporate video: 'As we face into our twenty-fifth year of unbound and unbroken resistance, we proclaim our determination not to desist from our efforts until our national sovereign right to self-determination is finally recognised. We call on our enemy to pursue the

pathway to peace or resign yourselves to the inevitability of war.' Senator Gordon Wilson, of Enniskillen, who met PIRA representatives a few days earlier in what he later called a 'pointless' meeting, was told by them that the 'pathway to peace' meant the British Government talking unconditionally to PIRA and making a commitment to end partition. In April 1993 PIRA returned to the City of London to cause £400 million bomb damage in Bishopsgate, and in four days after the May 1993 council elections it set off huge bombs in Belfast, Portadown and Magherafelt, causing more than £20 million damage. PIRA continued its bombing campaign in provincial towns with attacks in Strabane and Newtownards early in July. There were two bombs in Belfast in August and another destroyed a restaurant on the city's outskirts. In September bombs were placed at a supermarket at Derriaghy and at the Stormont Hotel in east Belfast. At the end of August there was a formal reply to Sir John Wheeler's comment that PIRA had been 'defeated' which said: 'We are equipped and utterly determined to meet head on any British persistence in the failed policies of the past.' PIRA endorsed the Hume–Adams peace process in September but a ceasefire was not envisaged as a prerequisite. It was followed by the killing of the manager of a building supplies firm and the issuing of warnings to others. The Shankill bomb, with ten people dead and fifty-eight injured, and bombs in England at Reading and Basingstoke stations, meant it was business as usual. The Greysteel atrocity produced a PIRA offer to stop targeting loyalists if the UFF ended its campaign against Catholics. From the correspondence released later in the year, the 'contact' with the British Government ended in early November, but contact with the Irish Government continued through 'channels', while the Downing Street Declaration was worked on. The declaration posed a choice and an opportunity for the Republican movement. In its New Year's message PIRA spoke of twenty-six years of unbroken struggle, of having brought a viable framework for peace to London and Dublin, and it asserted that lasting peace was inextricably linked to the 'right of the Irish people to national self-determination'. During January 1994, as the movement debated the situation and sought clarification, there were persistent rumours that the army council was split four to three against the declaration.

PROVISIONAL SINN FÉIN

The political counterpart of PIRA, which dates from January 1970, when the split occurred in the Republican movement. At the Ard Fheis (annual conference) in Dublin, the dispute centred on whether Sinn Féin should drop its long-standing policy of non-recognition of the Parliaments in Belfast and Dublin. Those against recognition called themselves the Provisionals – an echo of the 'Provisional Government' of 1916 – and they walked out to set up their own organisation with HQ in Kevin Street, Dublin. There was another important point of difference between the two groups. Those who remained in what became known as Official Sinn Féin (later the Workers' Party) inclined to a Marxist approach. PSF policy was rooted in the demand for British withdrawal from NI, usually expressed in the slogan 'Brits out'. Originally, it favoured a phased withdrawal and Ruairí Ó Brádaigh, who became its president in 1970, defended this approach on the grounds that it did not want a sudden British pull-out which could create a Congo situation. But its 1980 Ard Fheis committed the party to calling for immediate British withdrawal. At the 1981 Ard Fheis it effectively abandoned its initial policy of a federal Ireland, with parliaments for each of the four provinces, which it called 'Éire Nua'. This issue produced bitter debate, with the change spearheaded by the NI leaders, headed by the then vice-president Gerry Adams, while leading Southern figures such as Ó Brádaigh and Dáithí Ó Conaill argued for the status quo. The federal idea was seen by its supporters as a gesture to NI loyalists, but the new NI leaders of PSF were in no mood for compromise and the change was sealed at the 1982 Ard Fheis. In 1981

PSF also decided to take up any seats won in council elections in NI. This removed an anomaly because the party was already contesting local elections in the Republic and it held thirty seats on twenty-six councils in fourteen counties. (During the 1956 IRA campaign, the former Sinn Féin took four Dáil seats on an abstentionist basis, one being held by Ó Brádaigh.) Increasingly, there was pressure from within PSF to seek elected status since one of the party's obvious aims was to supplant the SDLP as the main voice of NI Nationalists. In the early 1980s PSF's total membership is believed to have been around 5,000 with 400 branches (or cumainn) throughout Ireland. Although a registered political party in the Republic, its spokesmen have been denied access to TV and radio there. This ban was first imposed by the Coalition Government of 1973–7, and the then Minister for Posts and Telegraphs, Dr Conor Cruise O'Brien, defended it on the grounds that PSF was essentially a front for PIRA. This ban was continued by successive governments, including those of Fianna Fáil, and it survived a PSF challenge to its constitutionality in the Courts in 1982. In NI a long-standing ban on Sinn Féin was raised by the British Government in 1974 in the hope that it would contest the 1975 Convention elections. But it decided to ignore these contests, although Albert Price, father of the Price sisters (who had been convicted of the London bombings in 1973), supported PSF policies when he stood unsuccessfully as an Independent in W. Belfast in the February 1974 Westminster election. At this period Maire Drumm was the leading PSF personality in Belfast, as a vice-president. She was murdered by loyalists in the city's Mater Hospital in 1976. Senior Belfast members of PSF were involved in talks with British officials in 1975, and party members manned the seven incident centres set up to monitor the PIRA ceasefire and maintain contact with the NIO. Although the British Government insisted that the officials were doing no more than explaining British policy and were not engaged in negotiations, the exercise brought sharp criticism from Unionist and other politicians in NI, who claimed that it tended to give credibility to PSF. There is no bar to dual membership of PSF and PIRA, and many leading people in Sinn Féin have had a background associated with PIRA or the earlier IRA. Normally, at least one member of the PSF executive, or *ard comhairle*, is on PIRA's army council. At the 1982 Ard Fheis it was decided that all future PSF candidates must give their 'unambivalent' support to the 'armed struggle'. At the 1981 Ard Fheis PSF's director of publicity, Danny Morrison, articulated the policy in these words: 'Who here really believes that we can win the war through the ballot-box? But will anyone here object if, with a ballot paper in this hand and an Armalite in this hand, we take power in Ireland?' Morrison was speaking at a point where two PIRA prisoners in the Maze had secured election in the Republic's general election of June 1981 – hunger-striker Kieran Doherty (who fasted to death) in Cavan–Monaghan; and Paddy Agnew in Louth. PSF joined other anti-H-Block elements in that campaign, but PSF alone was unable to repeat these successes in the February 1982 election and it had under 2 per cent of the vote in the 1987 Dáil election. In NI the hunger strike brought Sinn Féin more substantial benefits. In Fermanagh–S. Tyrone it had backed PIRA hunger-striker Bobby Sands in his successful campaign in the April 1981 by-election for Westminster. And a rank-and-file member of PSF, Owen Carron, was elected as an abstentionist to fill the vacancy created by Sands's death. The October 1982 Assembly election found PSF urging initially a boycott of the new institution and the election, but it also committed itself to fighting the election on an abstentionist ticket if a general Nationalist boycott could not be achieved. In the event SDLP's decision to run candidates, but not to attend the Assembly, seems to have benefited PSF, which ran twelve candidates. Many Nationalists apparently saw PSF as representing a more dynamic boycott policy at a time when there was intense polarisation in the community. The outcome for PSF was highly gratifying in terms of its overall 10 per cent vote, but

it might have expected to get more than the five seats which it actually won, since Alliance, with fewer votes, had got ten seats. None the less, it was a breakthrough, and encouraged PSF to talk of fighting as many as possible of the seventeen new Westminster seats. The first major controversy sparked off by the election came in December 1982 when two of the successful PSF Assembly candidates, Gerry Adams (W. Belfast) and Danny Morrison (Mid-Ulster), were invited to London by GLC leader Ken Livingstone to explain their policies. Both were banned from GB by Home Secretary William Whitelaw under the Prevention of Terrorism Act. The ban also applied to Derry Assembly member Martin McGuinness. Thatcher claimed that the ban had been imposed for security and not political reasons. The 1983 Westminster election was broadly successful for PSF. It did not make a net advance in terms of seats, since it gained only W. Belfast and lost Fermanagh–S. Tyrone, but it achieved its target of 100,000 votes and had a percentage poll of 13.4 – 3 per cent more than in the 1982 Assembly election. It also failed by only 78 votes to win Mid-Ulster. Gerry Adams's victory in W. Belfast attracted attention for two reasons – it led to the unseating of colourful MP Gerry Fitt, who had held the seat for seventeen years, and it was secured in face of strong warnings from the Catholic Church against supporting a group committed to backing PIRA violence. Adams's triumph also reinforced his growing authority in PSF, and it was no surprise that he was elected president later that year. The balance of power in PSF had now shifted decisively to the North. The 1984 European election saw Danny Morrison (then PSF publicity director) virtually maintain the PSF 1983 vote in percentage terms, although he was 10 per cent behind John Hume. In 1984 the organisation developed its advice–centre network and strongly pushed community issues in readiness for its foray into council politics in NI in 1985. Unionists, outraged at Gerry Adams's description of the 1984 Brighton bombing as 'an inevitable result of Britain's interference in Irish affairs' and 'a democratic act', made repeated calls for proscription of PSF. In the event, PSF was well satisfied with the outcome of the 1985 elections – it ended up with fifty-nine council seats and 11.8 per cent of the votes. Indeed, the PSF showing set alarm bells ringing in London and Dublin and undoubtedly helped along the Anglo-Irish process, which was to produce the AIA later that year. British and Irish Ministers looked to the AIA to strengthen the appeal of the SDLP, and Thatcher also looked for easier extradition from the South and stronger cross-border security co-operation – both prospects unwelcome to the Provisionals. Certainly, PSF found the going hard in the January 1986 by-elections forced by the Unionists in protest at the AIA. In four constituencies where there was a PSF–SDLP clash, there was a 6 per cent swing from PSF to SDLP as compared with 1983, a trend which helped SDLP to gain Newry and Armagh. PSF in the council chambers infuriated Unionists, and Ministers refused to talk to PSF councillors, although they recognised the few PSF council chairmen. In 1986 Adams and his supporters forced another major change on the party – a decision to occupy any Dáil seats won in elections. The question gave rise to angry debate, and Southern traditionalists like Ó Brádaigh and Ó Conaill walked out of PSF to establish Republican Sinn Féin. But the general loss in membership to RSF was minimal. In the 1987 Westminster election PSF also felt the effect of the AIA. The PSF vote dropped 2 per cent compared with 1983, while the SDLP put on 3 per cent. The party took comfort, however, from its retention of W. Belfast, where SDLP mounted a determined challenge and got Alliance votes. Shortly before the 1987 election, PSF put out a policy document, 'Scenario for Peace', which suggested an all-Ireland convention to work out a new Irish constitution, British financial support for a time towards a united Ireland, and written guarantees for loyalists. In 1988 the party seemed to be in a mood of reassessment and to be looking for a pan-Nationalist front. And in the first nine months of 1988 it had talks with the

SDLP. These apparently left both parties as far apart as ever, although PSF argued that they had helped morale in the Nationalist community. The PSF analysis of the situation was firmly rejected by John Hume, who failed to persuade Gerry Adams that the AIA had made simple 'Brits out' politics redundant. For PSF, the test of the 1989 council elections loomed ahead, with the party allowing its nominees to sign a statutory anti-violence declaration, despite the possibility of civil actions in the courts when it was breached. Its leaders were also active in seeking ways round the direct broadcasting ban imposed in late 1988 on supporters outside election periods. In January 1989 the Ard Fheis featured a strong appeal to PIRA to try to avoid accidental civilian deaths likely to frighten off electoral support. In the event, the 1989 council elections showed PSF with 11.2 per cent of first-preference votes, slightly down on 1985, but it lost sixteen seats. In Belfast it was 2.6 per cent ahead of the SDLP but got the same number of seats – eight. In the European election that followed, Danny Morrison held his runner-up position, but his total of votes was almost halved compared with 1984. (In 1990 Morrison was sentenced to eight years' imprisonment for unlawfully imprisoning an RUC informer.) In October 1989 Gerry Adams claimed that talks between PSF and the British Government were 'inevitable' despite repeated British statements that this could not happen while violence continued. Adams also said killing of non-combatants by PIRA was 'not legitimate' and he suggested the UN and the EC could have a role in a settlement. He described the 1990 PIRA killing of two Australians in Holland by mistake as 'inexcusable'. He also rejected the Brooke–Mayhew Talks as a 'non-starter'. The British and Irish Governments were united in denying a role to PSF in the talks, and in Dublin the City Council voted 38–7 to refuse the use of the Mansion House for the PSF Ard Fheis. A court bid to have the broadcasting ban lifted also failed. In 1991, too, Archbishop Cahal Daly turned down a PSF request for talks. In August 1991 the PSF executive's vice-chairman,

Joe Austin, gained a seat in a by-election to make it the second largest party in Belfast City Council. In the run-up to the 1992 Westminster election, Adams made some interesting comments in press interviews: 'Sinn Féin and the IRA are not as one' (*Belfast Newsletter*) and 'I do not agree with everything they [PIRA] do' (*Irish News*). He argued during the campaign that the slogan 'with a ballot paper in this hand an Armalite in the other' was outdated. Martin McGuinness revised it as 'with a ballot paper in one hand and a solution in the other'. But the outcome in W. Belfast was a serious setback. Adams lost his seat to long-time SDLP contender Dr Joe Hendron, largely because of Protestant tactical voting for Hendron. At the same time the overall PSF vote dropped to 10 per cent. In the wake of the election, Adams and chairman Tom Hartley had talks with two former Presbyterian Moderators, Dr Jack Weir and Dr Godfrey Brown, whilst in Derry Martin McGuiness and councillor Mitchel McLaughlin had meetings with Bishop Edward Daly, a frequent critic of PIRA violence. These developments, taken with some PSF speeches, notably that of executive member Jim Gibney referring to 'a sustained period of peace' being necessary before a British withdrawal, led to speculation that PSF might be moving to distance itself decisively from PIRA. But there was no real evidence of this, although in late 1992 there were clearly internal differences on tactics. But some speeches by British Ministers, notably that of Sir Patrick Mayhew in December 1992, were partly designed to increase the pressure on PSF to take a purely constitutional course. The party was also anxious about the security of its members, particularly councillors. For some time, the UFF and UVF had been targeting leading PSF figures – a tactic that PIRA held to justify its murders of individual loyalists. In May 1991 the UFF crossed the border to kill PSF councillor Eddie Fullerton in Buncrana, Co. Donegal, and in October 1992 the UVF shot dead Sheena Campbell, a mature QUB law student, who had stood as PSF candidate in the Upper Bann by-election

in 1990. Adams claimed in November 1992 that seventeen PSF members had been shot dead in recent years. In February 1992 three men were shot dead in the PSF advice centre on the Falls Road by an off-duty RUC constable who took his own life hours later. In December 1992 the NI High Court ruled that the Unionist policy in Belfast City Council of excluding PSF from subcommittees was unlawful. In the 1992 general election in the Republic, PSF slightly improved on its 1989 vote, but it stayed under 2 per cent and most candidates lost their deposits. In April 1993 a new round of talks between Gerry Adams and John Hume was discovered. The exchanges in Derry were arranged by Catholic clergy. Adams stressed that a ceasefire was not being discussed since he was not representing PIRA. The SDLP rejected some Unionist claims that the exchanges enhanced PSF's credibility. The PSF vote in the 1993 council polls went up to 12.4 per cent, or 1.3 per cent above its 1989 showing, and it gained nine extra seats. Indeed, it had the highest vote of any party in Belfast, and in W. Belfast took seven seats to the SDLP's three. The attack on the home of a PSF councillor in Lisburn in July was a prelude to a court case in which PSF sought personal protection weapons. The evidence revealed that five councillors had licensed weapons, that each application was judged on its merits and there was no automatic bar against PSF councillors. The Hume–Adams agreement on a peace process, announced on 25 September, provided a major boost, because PIRA endorsement meant that PSF could deliver 'peace'. However, the Shankill bomb and the image of Gerry Adams carrying the bomber's coffin damaged the position. The ending of the long-established British contact in early November and its public revelation produced a flurry of documents and a battle for veracity, but in the end the contact was broken. The publication of the Downing Street Declaration on 15 December posed the organisation with a choice of direction. Its reaction – going into consultation with the Republican movement and then seeking 'clarification' – put off a decision until the Ard Fheis at the end of February 1994 and beyond. There was still no formal answer by April but it was clear that the movement would not accept unless it could guarantee unity within its own ranks.

PYM, LORD

As Francis Pym, NI Secretary of State, November 1973–February 1974. b.13 February 1922. MP for Cambridgeshire S.E., 1983–7. Defence Secretary, 1979–82. Foreign Secretary, 1982–3. On taking office at Stormont, he was immediately plunged into the Sunningdale Conference; he was better informed on NI issues than outside observers supposed since he had insisted as Chief Whip on attending Cabinet committees dealing with NI. His predecessor, William Whitelaw, had already carried through the delicate negotiations leading to the power-sharing Executive, and one of Pym's first major duties was the swearing-in of the new Ministers. Soon afterwards, there was a PIRA threat to kill him because he had interned a Derry man. The Heath Government was defeated in February 1974, so he had little opportunity to make his presence felt in NI, although he was later to become involved in NI security issues as Defence Secretary and in Anglo-Irish relations as Foreign Secretary.

Q

QUANGOS see Systems of Government section, p. 428

R

RATHCAVAN, LORD

As Phelim O'Neill, first leader of the Alliance Parliamentary Party, 1972–3. b. 2 November 1909. One of NI's most individualistic politicians, he switched from the Unionist Party to the Alliance Party shortly before direct rule was declared in 1972, and with two other MPs formed the first Alliance group at Stormont. A cousin of Terence O'Neill (PM, 1963–9) and son of first Lord Rathcavan (first Speaker at Stormont and for many years MP for N. Antrim at Westminster), Phelim O'Neill rarely toed the party line, and often treated Ministers scornfully in the former Stormont House of Commons. He described his politics as 'left-wing Conservative'. He was Unionist MP for N. Antrim at Westminster from 1952 to 1959, and Stormont MP for N. Antrim, 1969–72. He was Minister of Education in NI Government in 1969 and Minister of Agriculture, 1969–71. He led the Alliance delegation at the Darlington conference in 1972. He was expelled from the Orange Order in 1958 after attending a Catholic service during a community week in Ballymoney. When he switched to Alliance he said that whether they liked it or not, both the Unionists and the SDLP were sectarian parties. He succeeded to the title in 1982, when his father died aged ninety-nine.

REAGAN, RONALD

US President, 1981–9. b. 6 February 1911. One of the many US Presidents who can claim Irish ancestry. His great-grandfather, Michael O'Regan, left Ballyporeen, on the Tipperary–Cork border, during the Irish potato famine in the 1840s. The family went first to the Peckham area of London, and later to Illinois. Although his parents were married in a Catholic church in Fulton, Illinois, his Protestant mother brought him up in her faith. In the early period of his presidency, he avoided any deep entanglement with the Irish issue. Although Taoiseach Charles Haughey was among St Patrick's Day guests at the White House in 1981, the President did not endorse Haughey's bid to make Irish unity a stated objective of US foreign policy. In his 1981 St Patrick's Day statement he 'took note' of the violence and suffering in NI and the importance to the US of a 'peaceful, just and swift solution'. He also urged Americans on this and other occasions not to give money which might be used for violence. While welcoming the Anglo-Irish initiative, the President made it clear in a letter to Taoiseach Garret FitzGerald in December 1981 that his administration had no position on the question of Irish unity. He said it was not for the US to chart a course which others must follow, and that if solutions in NI were to endure, they must come from the people who lived there. He also appears not to have responded to a plea by the Irish Government in 1981 to intervene with Britain over the Maze hunger strike. But the following year, the President did see the Republic having some role in a settlement, while Thatcher was insisting that Britain had no obligation to consult the Republic on NI affairs. Certainly, Reagan praised the New Ireland Forum initiative on his visit to the Republic in 1984. Speaker 'Tip' O'Neill was a strong influence on the President in securing a positive White House approach to a strong Anglo-Irish initiative, and the idea of US financial aid to back it. It appears that within a month of Thatcher's 'out, out, out' comments on the Forum options, she was being told by the President in Washington (December 1984) of his deep interest in progress on NI at a meeting arranged to discuss the Star Wars project. When the AIA was signed, he stressed strong US support for it. The President has clearly enjoyed his St Patrick's Day parties in Washington. At a 1987 gathering he recalled that St Patrick had died in AD 461, adding: 'Leave it to the Irish to be carrying on a wake for 1,500 years.'

RED BRANCH KNIGHTS

After incendiary devices were defused at a supermarket and a blast bomb was dealt with at a Dublin-based bank in Newtownabbey in September 1992, statements were sent to the media purporting to be from a loyalist group, the Red Branch Knights, which threatened action against anyone with political or economic links with the Republic. Other communications to individuals and companies contained live bullets, and some sugar produced in the Republic was removed from shelves for checking. The existence of the group had not previously been reported.

RED HAND COMMANDO

A loyalist paramilitary group launched in 1972, and declared illegal in 1973 at the same time as the UFF. It was believed to be involved in sectarian assassinations. In 1974 the RHC in Fermanagh and S. Tyrone wrote to a local newspaper threatening to shoot five Catholics for every Protestant killed in border areas. When Secretary of State Merlyn Rees met loyalist paramilitaries on 7 August 1974, it was claimed that the UVF delegate also spoke for the RHC. It announced a ceasefire a few days later, but said it reserved the right to defend loyalist lives and property. In 1978 there was further evidence of its association with the UVF – a statement from a prisoners' council representing both organisations in the Maze Prison. There was a claim that it had murdered E. Belfast loyalist John McKeague in 1982, but the INLA claim was generally accepted. McKeague always denied reports that he had been one of the founders of RHC. In 1985 it claimed to have placed a bomb in Castlewellan after the banning of an Orange parade in the town, but nothing was found. In October 1992 in E. Belfast it shot dead a man claimed to be an informer, and in November 1982 it shot and critically wounded a security guard at the Mater Hospital in Belfast. In January 1993 it shot and seriously wounded two Catholic men in N. Belfast in retaliation for the PIRA killing of a RIR soldier. Earlier, it was said to be included in the Combined Loyalist Military Command that called a ceasefire during the early stages of the Brooke–Mayhew Talks. The Loyalist Retaliation and Defence Group, which carried on a campaign in 1991 against shops selling *Republican News,* murdering two Catholic newsagents in W. Belfast, was believed to be linked to RHC. In September 1992 the LRDG threatened to renew its murder campaign if PIRA killed or wounded any more Protestant workers.

REES, LORD

As Merlyn Rees, Secretary of State for NI, March 1974–September 1976. b. 18 December 1920. When he arrived at Stormont, he had been Labour Party spokesman on NI for two years. He had been at the Home Office with James

Callaghan in 1969, and as a teacher he was familiar with Irish history. He was immediately faced with a crisis. The general election which had brought Labour to office and Rees to Stormont had also given the UUUC eleven of the twelve NI seats at Westminster. And the loyalists were not slow to claim the result as a landslide against the whole existence of the power-sharing Executive at Stormont which had taken office on 1 January. The UUUC was pledged to fight the Sunningdale Agreement, on which the Executive was based. Its main slogan was 'Dublin is just a Sunningdale away', indicating its opposition not only to Unionists joining the SDLP in government, but to any cross-border Council of Ireland. With nearly 60 per cent of all votes secured by anti-White Paper candidates, 51 per cent by loyalists alone, the UUUC presented the outcome as a vote of no confidence in the Executive and demanded fresh Assembly elections. At the same time, PIRA stepped up its bombing campaign, and made it more difficult for Rees to accelerate the phasing out of internment. Then, on 13 May 1974, he faced his biggest test. Loyalists, led by the Ulster Workers' Council, which brought together politicians and paramilitary leaders, as well as some key shop stewards, mounted what they called a 'constitutional stoppage'. With loyalist paramilitary groups backing the strike, together with power workers, much of industry came to a standstill. And with many accusations of intimidation directed against the strikers, Rees was under intense pressure to use troops to keep power stations going and to maintain essential supplies. The Executive, whose morale was already shaken by the election result, was urging Rees to adopt a much tougher line against the strikers. But while he refused to negotiate with the strike organisers, Rees and the British Government were obviously cautious about using the army directly to help break the strike. And this attitude clearly reflected the senior army view that 'the game isn't worth the candle'. Rees also appears to have been doubtful about the capacity of the Executive to survive in any event. With

vital services threatened, particularly sewerage, the Unionist members resigned on the fifteenth day of the strike, and the Secretary of State decided to end the Executive and resume direct rule. Rees told MPs that NI now needed a breathing space. He also called the loyalists 'Ulster Protestant Nationalists'. On 4 July 1974 Rees announced a new initiative – an elected Constitutional Convention to work out a political settlement. And during the summer he resisted strong pressure from Unionists for a new Home Guard or Third Force to supplement the efforts of the RUC and UDR. In mid-September he had talks with the Dublin Government aimed at improving cross-border security and co-operation. But the SDLP was clearly unhappy with Rees: the party's then deputy leader, John Hume, said in October that he had lost all credibility. In November 1974 came the horrific Birmingham bombings and Rees was immediately involved in bringing in the new Prevention of Terrorism legislation so far as it affected NI. The effect was to allow people to be deported from Britain to both the Republic and NI, and after protests that this would turn NI into a 'Devil's Island', Rees took power to expel people from NI to the Republic. Oddly enough, the tightening of security laws coincided with a meeting in early December 1974 between Churchmen and Provisionals (both IRA and Sinn Féin) at Feakle, Co. Clare – a meeting which was kept secret until it had ended and which was widely criticised by loyalists. But it offered Rees a pause in PIRA violence. After a brief stop over Christmas, the Provisionals declared a ceasefire on 10 February 1975. The Feakle Talks had produced a document which the Churchmen involved conveyed to Rees. But he insisted that the PIRA demands (including a call for a declaration of intent of British withdrawal) would not be considered by the Government, although 'a genuine and sustained cessation of violence over a period would create a new situation'. None the less, the ceasefire got a degree of official co-operation. Rees authorised the setting up of seven 'incident centres' manned by Provisionals so that they could make contact easily with Government officials. The purpose was to prevent a small incident developing into a threat to the ceasefire. But the exercise was regarded with great suspicion by loyalists, and the army, apparently, were also unhappy about it. The Secretary of State was evidently activated by the hope that the Provisionals might become 'politicised' as a result of the facility, which he had also granted them, of direct talks, if not negotiations, with Government officials. But the Provisionals showed no interest in the Convention elections in 1975 and, more importantly, these elections gave the UUUC a decisive overall majority. This ruled out any prospect of a repeat of the power-sharing experiment. By the summer of 1975, the PIRA ceasefire was no more than a technicality. The overall total of deaths in 1975 was 247. This included an estimated 144 deaths arising from inter-factional or sectarian assassinations, many of them carried out by loyalists. However, at the end of 1975 Rees set free the last of those detained without trial. And in 1976 he witnessed the final collapse of the Constitutional Convention, and the death toll increased yet again. In September Rees moved to the post of Home Secretary, and was succeeded by the Defence Secretary, Roy Mason. As Shadow Home Secretary in August 1979, he declared that PIRA could not be defeated militarily, and that any attempt to reintroduce internment would be a 'a grave error of judgement'. In his memoirs, published in 1985, he said: 'The hope of finding a successful solution lies with the Northern Irish people, not with outsiders in Dublin and London talking by proxy.' In November 1987 he urged a top-level reassessment of the AIA and revealed in the Commons that he was 'extremely worried' about allegations of army undercover activities in NI during his period of office. In 1989 he became one of the first members of the British-Irish Parliamentary Body, and in 1991 was mentioned by some Unionists as a possible independent chairman for the Brooke–Mayhew Talks. Stood down as an MP in 1992 and was made a life peer.

REFORMS

The changes which have taken place outside the security field include: the closing down of the Stormont Parliament in March 1972, and the introduction of direct rule from Westminster (interrupted only by the five-month tenure of the NI Executive in 1974); the acceptance of the principle of one man, one vote (1969) and the use of PR for all elections except those for Westminster (1972); the dismantling of the system of local government and its replacement by area boards to cover health, education, libraries and so on, with twenty-six District Councils with very limited powers (1972); the setting up of a central Housing Executive to look after all public housing (1970); the establishment of a Community Relations Department and Community Relations Commission (both subsequently dropped, but a Community Relations Council was established in 1990); the appointment of a Standing Advisory Commission on Human Rights (1973), and the creation of an Ombudsman and Commissioner of Complaints to inquire into charges of maladministration by Government departments and other public bodies (1969 – the posts have been merged); the setting up of a Fair Employment Agency to counter discrimination in employment on political or religious grounds (1976; under a 1989 Act, this body was replaced by a Fair Employment Commission backed by stronger powers); establishment of an Equal Opportunities Commission to guard against sex discrimination in employment (1976). In 1980 divorce laws were brought into line with those in GB, and in 1982 the laws on homosexuality were treated similarly after they had been condemned by the European Court of Human Rights. Catholic schools have been granted 100 per cent capital funding (1992). The controversial 'trust hospitals' plan has been extended to NI (1992). Trade union laws have followed the GB pattern set by Conservative Governments; likewise, the ending of Wages Councils (1992). In March 1994 Parliament created an NI Affairs Committee.

REID, RICHARD

DUP Convention member for Mid-Ulster, 1975-6. b. 1922. Cookstown District Council, 1971-81. Refused to stand again after a party disagreement. Founder member of the DUP.

RELATIVES FOR JUSTICE

A group comprising relatives of people killed by the security forces in disputed circumstances, launched in N. Belfast in April 1991. At its 1992 annual meeting, plans were disclosed for specialist teams to make immediate investigations at the scene of such shootings and to produce a report. Armagh priest, Father Raymond Murray, who suggested the move, said it should be seen as co-operation with the state rather than opposition to it. It was proposed that the inquiry team would have pathologists, forensic scientists, lawyers and photographers, and that there should be co-operation with the Committee on the Administration of Justice.

RELIGION

The 1991 census showed that the religious make-up of the NI population remained as complex as ever. The count found the proportion of Catholics in the NI population to be 38.4 per cent, with a rise of nearly 200,000 in the number declaring themselves Catholic, but some uncertainty remained because 114,827 people refused to declare their religion (7.3 per cent against 18.5 per cent in 1981). There were also 59,234 who said they had no religion, a new category. Some analysts suggested that the tally could mean that the actual Catholic percentage in the NI population could have reached 40 per cent or more. The figures for the main denominations were: Catholic, 605,639; Presbyterian, 336,891; Church of Ireland, 279,280; Methodist, 59,517; Baptist, 19,484; Brethren, 12,446; Free Presbyterians (led by Rev. Ian Paisley), 12,363; Congregational, 8,176. Some 12,386 described themselves as 'Protestant' and 10,556 simply as 'Christian'. The 1991 census was more accurate than that conducted ten years earlier when there was a Republican boycott in support of the Maze hunger strikers and a census-taker was shot dead in Derry. At that time, there were doubts in Government circles about the value of the religious question, but the drop in non-respondents in 1991 has assured its inclusion in the 2001 count. Nearly eighty denominations were listed in the 1991 census. These ranged from the very localised Cooneyites, with 26 members (unchanged since 1981) to Zoroastrians (10), and there were 410 Jews, 972 Muslims, 270 Buddhists, and 157 Sikhs. Two new denominations were listed: the Church of the First Born (21) and Church on the Way (19). Atheists numbered 740 and agnostics 742. Within the Belfast urban area – the Belfast City Council area plus adjoining areas of Castlereagh, Lisburn, Newtownabbey, Carrickfergus and N. Down – 46.4 per cent of the population belonged to the three main Protestant denominations, 31.2 per cent were Catholics, while 8.3 per cent refused to disclose their religion and 5.6 per cent said they had none.

REPUBLICAN CLUBS see Workers' Party

REPUBLICAN LABOUR PARTY

Founded in Belfast in 1960, when two MPs for Stormont seats of Dock and Falls, Gerry Fitt (Dock Labour Party) and Harry Diamond (Socialist Republican), decided to unite under one label. It supported a non-violent republicanism, linked to socialist objectives, and when Fitt was elected to Westminster for W. Belfast in 1966, he supported the British Labour Party in the lobbies. Harry Diamond, who had represented the Falls constituency under various labels, including Éire Labour and Socialist Republican, lost the seat in the 1969 general election to Paddy Devlin of the NILP. But Paddy Kennedy gained the Belfast Central seat. In the 1969 election, Rep. Lab. ran five candidates, and got 2.4 per cent of the total vote. The party was active in the civil rights campaign, but it split in 1970 when Fitt assumed the leadership of the newly formed SDLP. When Kennedy withdrew from Stormont in 1971, the party also withdrew its six councillors from Belfast

Corporation, and it was heavily engaged in the civil disobedience campaign directed against internment without trial. Kennedy's failure to win a seat in the 1973 Assembly election marked the disappearance of Rep. Lab. as an electoral force.

REPUBLICAN SINN FÉIN

The breakaway group which emerged after the PSF Ard Fheis in 1986 voted to end abstention from the Dáil. It opposed the change, and included the two main PSF figures in the Republic – Ruairí Ó Brádaigh, former president, and Dáithí Ó Conaill, ex-PIRA chief of staff. Ó Brádaigh became first president and Ó Conaill first vice-president. According to a spokesman, RSF would remain in support of the armed struggle and Republican prisoners. At its 1988 Ard Fheis it reaffirmed support for 'an armed struggle to re-establish the democratic socialist republic'. In August 1990 RSF accused the army of 'calculated harassment' in NI and in April 1991 it said the inter-party talks were 'doomed'. It rejected the 1993 Downing Street Declaration, describing it as a trick to get Nationalist participation in a Unionist-dominated Assembly. In contrast to PSF, it stated that no clarification was necessary and promised to work for its failure.

RESISTANCE

A loyalist paramilitary group, said to be part of the Combined Loyalist Military Command that in 1991 organised a loyalist ceasefire during the first stage of the Brooke–Mayhew Talks. It is believed to contain some former members of Ulster Resistance and, while it had no apparent record of paramilitary activity up to the end of 1992, security sources suggest that it has had access to arms imported for loyalist groups in 1988 that did not fall into the hands of the security forces when they made a large seizure at Portadown. In early 1993 there was speculation that Resistance could have supplied weapons to UVF and UFF units. In 1991 the SDLP said it should be banned.

REYNOLDS, ALBERT

Taoiseach of Irish Republic and leader of FF, February 1992–. b. November 1932. Reputedly now a millionaire, he started out as a clerk in the state transport organisation, CIE, and went on to own a chain of dance halls, a Dublin nightclub, and a bacon-processing factory before being elected to Longford County Council in 1974. Three years later he became a TD, and in 1979 Taoiseach Charles Haughey appointed him Minister for Posts and Telegraphs and Industry. He was Minister for Industry and Energy in the second Haughey Government in the early 1980s, and on the party's return to power in 1987 took over Industry and Commerce until 1988 when he succeeded Ray MacSharry, who became EC Commissioner, as Minister for Finance. In November 1991 he backed a challenge to Haughey's leadership, and indeed made clear his ambition to succeed him. Haughey promptly sacked him, but three months later Reynolds had his wish, and in an initial display of ruthlessness sacked eight of the twelve serving FF Cabinet Ministers in the FF-Prog. D. Coalition. The NI inter-party talks resumed as Reynolds took office, and he joined PM John Major in welcoming the development. The two leaders had already established a strong rapport at meetings of EC Finance Ministers, and the only immediate change in the Anglo-Irish agenda was that Reynolds insisted that the Government of Ireland Act, 1920, should be on the table as a counterbalance in the Stormont talks to Unionist objections to the Republic's constitutional claim to NI. This brought some sharp criticism from Unionists, which was intensified when Reynolds commented in September 1992 that the Articles of the Constitution expressing the claim, numbers 2 and 3, were 'not for sale'. When Sir Patrick Mayhew became NI Secretary of State in April 1992, Reynolds readily accepted gaps in Anglo-Irish Intergovernmental Conference meetings to allow the talks to proceed. But he and John Major agreed that a meeting of the conference had to proceed in mid-November 1992, and Unionists said this must bring talks to a halt. At the same time the three Prog. D. members of his Government resigned because he questioned the honesty of the evidence given by Prog. D. leader Des O'Malley to a tribunal investigating alleged irregularities in the beef industry. In consequence, he was forced into a general election (25 November) aimed at securing an overall majority. In the event, he dropped nine seats, to sixty-eight, and the FF vote was under 30 per cent, the lowest since 1927. But the failure of the opposition parties to combine successfully against him led him into negotiations with Labour, which had doubled its representation in the election to thirty-three. By January 1993, Reynolds and Labour leader Dick Spring had hammered out a deal which produced the first FF–Labour Government, with a record thirty-six majority in the Dáil. Reynolds stayed as Taoiseach, and Spring became his deputy (Tánaiste) and also Foreign Minister. Reynolds had conceded much of the Labour programme of job creation and changes in social policies and benefits and agreed to Labour holding six of the fifteen Cabinet posts. While promising 'a new approach' and 'flexibility' in any renewed talks with NI parties, the new administration seemed unlikely to yield to Unionist demands for a firm commitment to drop the constitutional claim to NI in advance of any fresh talks. In April 1993 Reynolds made a strong defence of the constitutional claim to NI, saying that any attempt to walk away from it in a political vacuum would 'most certainly provide a new recruiting platform for terrorism'. The speech angered Unionists, and was widely seen in the Republic as a bid to reassure elements of FF who claimed that Foreign Minister Dick Spring was not speaking for them on NI policy. On his first visit to NI as Taoiseach, in April 1993, he opened an office in Derry symbolising the cross-border co-operation of councils in the North-West in EC matters, and warned against seeking an 'internal or part-solution' in NI of the sort which, he said, had not worked in the past. He shared the concerns of Nationalists at the Conservative/UUP link on the Maastricht

Treaty vote but he accepted the assurances offered 'until the facts established the contrary'. After the September Anglo-Irish Inter-governmental Conference meeting, which aimed to restart talks, he said that talks could proceed without the Democratic Unionists. He now said that Articles 2 and 3 'would' be put to the electorate in the context of an overall agreement. Despite the confusion over the existence of a report to his Government from the Hume–Adams talks he remained supportive as he awaited a personal report on Hume's return from the US. After a briefing by Hume in early October, the document was discussed at the next Cabinet meeting, but he refused , as 'too delicate', an opposition request for a Dáil debate on NI. At Bodenstown he ruled out secret agreements with organisations supporting violence. He told his party Ard Fheis at the start of November that peace could begin at the end of the year. He later stated his objective as the complementary pursuit of peace and political talks without deadlines. On a visit to Derry he disowned a leaked Irish Foreign Affairs draft paper that anticipated UK recognition of the 'full legitimacy and value of the goal of Irish unity by agreement'. Thereafter he seemed anxious to reassure Unionist opinion, and early in December told RTE he was willing to give a written pledge of a referendum on the territorial claim to NI. He was with PM Major for the press conference to launch the Downing Street Declaration. In comments, he stressed the work they had put into it over twenty-two months and he told the Irish Senate that it was a 'statement of principles not a basis for negotiation'. However, he was very critical of the decision, the following day, to set up an NI Affairs Committee in Parliament. In his New Year's message he expressed the hope that the declaration 'can be the first step to restore intimacy and trust between Irish traditions'. He told an Irish Association meeting in Dublin Castle that the document was a 'framework of democratic principles for peace and potential progress' and the 'potentially most important statement of principle for seventy years'. He was the first to offer 'clarification', and the decision to remove the 'Section 31' broadcasting ban in January 1994 was seen as a further move to encourage the Republican movement to accept the declaration. At the end of the month he provided an unpublished detailed letter of 'clarification'. His high personal standing in the opinion polls was taken as popular acceptance of his actions. However, the stalling of Mayhew's proposed paper for NI institutions was criticised by Unionists for giving precedence to PSF/PIRA rather than new structures for NI.

RICHARDS, SIR BROOKS

Security Co-ordinator, NIO, 1980–1. b. 18 July 1918. Succeeded late Sir Maurice Oldfield in Stormont post after a long career in the diplomatic service and a period at the Cabinet Office as Intelligence Co-ordinator.

RICHARDSON, SIR ROBERT FRANCIS

Army GOC, NI 1982–5. b. 2 March 1929. Commanded 39th Infantry Brigade in NI, 1974–5. Army's director of manning, 1980–1. In March 1983 he said it was important to reduce the role of the army to the point where it was seen by everyone as supporting the civil power, and not as the visible embodiment of that power.

RIFKIND, MALCOLM

Conservative MP for Edinburgh, Pentlands, 1974–; Secretary of State for Defence, 1992–; Transport Secretary, 1990–2; Secretary of State for Scotland, 1986–90. Privy Councillor, 1986. b. 21 June 1946. Edinburgh University. In July 1993 he rejected suggestions of army budget savings in NI made by a former Minister of State, Archie Hamilton, describing the NI commitment as a 'first call'. In the middle of the month he visited the army HQ in Lisburn and attracted criticism from local politicians when he said that 99 per cent of people had a 'normal life'. On a visit to NI in January 1994 he announced noise insulation grants for those living near heliports in S. Armagh.

RIMINGTON, STELLA

First woman Director-General of MI5, the security service, February 1992–. b. London 1935. MA (Edinburgh) and trained archivist. When appointed, she was senior deputy director and had served in MI5 for twenty-three years. In May 1992 MI5 was given the lead role in directing the intelligence effort against PIRA in GB, and she is said to have made a special study of PIRA and to be inclined 'not to underestimate that organisation or its determination to hit major British targets'. In the 1980s, she headed the counter-terrorism section of MI5. Her appointment coincided with PM John Major's decision to name publicly the heads of the intelligence services, but a proposal that she would be questioned by the Home Office Select Committee in late 1992 was dropped, although she lunched with officers of the committee. In March 1992 she was reported to have visited Belfast during discussion of the allocation of PIRA intelligence responsibilities. Soon after becoming Director-General, she was expected to move to MI5's new HQ, close to the Palace of Westminster. She has been described as 'the Provisionals' number one target, replacing Mrs Thatcher'. Early in 1993, the *Sunday Times* sent her details of its own investigation of her personal security measures. (*See* Security System section, pp. 461–5.)

RITCHIE, BRIGADIER CHARLES

Commander, UDR, 1988–90. b. 1942. After Sandhurst, commissioned in Royal Scots Regiment, 1961; served two brief tours in NI, 1971–2, with another Scottish regiment. He returned to Sandhurst as an instructor until 1978 when he became a staff officer with the British Commanders in Chief (Soviet Mission) in West Germany. After attending the National Defence College in 1981, he returned to NI to command 3rd (Co. Down) Battalion UDR until 1983. His two most recent appointments were at the Joint Staff Defence College at Greenwich until 1985 and as Assistant Director Military Assistance Overseas (Army). In the 1960s he served a year in Libya and from 1965 to 1967 he was ADC to the Governor of Victoria in Australia.

ROBB, JOHN
Founder of the New Ireland Group in 1982, and earlier the New Ireland Movement. Irish Senator, 1982–9. b. 1932. As a Protestant Ulsterman and a surgeon at the Royal Victoria Hospital in Belfast in the early 1970s, he was so moved by the results of the bombing that he began campaigning for a new approach to local problems. His proposals have included the idea of Britain and the Republic foregoing all claims to sovereignty over NI so that they could jointly sponsor a new constitutional convention in NI and jointly guarantee its outcome. He says he was greatly influenced by the philosophy of Gandhi during a visit to India and by seeing Mother Teresa of Calcutta visiting a Belfast woman blinded by the violence and who was the mother of eight children. His appointment by Charles Haughey to the Irish Senate in 1982 caused some surprise, and one of his first acts there was to call for cross-border extradition arrangements. His group made several appeals to PIRA to abandon its campaign of violence, and the group picketed the PSF Ard Fheis in Dublin in 1991. In December 1991 he called on both Britain and the Republic to withdraw their claims to sovereignty over NI. In 1992, when he left his post of consultant surgeon in Ballymoney hospital, he had successfully campaigned for a new Coleraine hospital and argued for an 'open public forum' on NI. After Opsahl, he sought a new forum or constitutional convention and urged the need for a Unionist 'deal-maker'. Member, RTE Authority, 1973–7. QUB Senate, 1991–.

ROBINSON, MARY
First woman President of Irish Republic, December 1990–. b. 21 May 1944. BA (TCD); LLM (Harvard Law School). Barrister. Irish Senator, 1969–89. Her surprise defeat of the Fianna Fáil candidate, Brian Lenihan, by a large margin on the second count after the elimination of Fine Gael candidate Austin Currie TD owed much to the sacking of Lenihan from the Haughey Government during the campaign over allegations that Lenihan had sought to bring pressure on President Hillery in 1982 to refuse dissolution of the Dáil. But it was also widely seen as a desire by Irish women to end male dominance at the top of the Irish establishment and to recognise Robinson's devotion to women's causes, as well as support for a more liberal spirit in Irish affairs. Although her candidature was sponsored by the Irish Labour Party, Unionists in NI had noted her resignation from that party in protest at the AIA, and prominent Unionists voiced a cautious welcome for her victory. But as guardian of the Constitution, she could no longer pursue controversy on that front or repeat her doubts about the nature of the constitutional claim to NI. None the less, she was emphatic about 'extending friendship and love' across the border, and entertained many groups and individuals from NI. When in February 1992 she visited NI, she was, however, denied a reception at Belfast City Hall, and Unionist councillors stayed away from functions linked with her first official visit to Derry in May 1992. She appointed Quintin Oliver, chairman of NICVA, to her Council of State. In April 1993, she attended a memorial service in Warrington, Cheshire, for two young boys killed in the town by PIRA bombs. In May 1993 she met President Clinton in Washington and paid a courtesy call on the Queen at Buckingham Palace – the first such meeting between the British and Irish heads of state. In June 1993 she provoked controversy when she shook hands with Gerry Adams at a W. Belfast reception. The British Government and Unionists were particularly hostile, but she argued that the encounter had no significance. In October she launched a new peace project in Warrington.

ROBINSON, PETER DAVID
Deputy leader of the DUP; MP for E. Belfast, 1979–. Assembly member for E. Belfast, 1982–6. b. 1948. His career has epitomised the rise of the DUP. In 1975 he became full-time general secretary, and was an unsuccessful candidate that year in the Convention election in E. Belfast. But two years later he was on Castlereagh Council, and in 1979 gained

a surprise victory in E. Belfast, when he unseated William Craig, UUP, by sixty-four votes in a five-way contest. As deputy leader of the DUP, he has been at Rev. Ian Paisley's side in the various DUP campaigns, notably in opposition to the Anglo-Irish talks in early 1981 and the AIA since 1985. In 1981 he was associated with the Third Force and demands for tougher security, and with the Ulster Resistance organisation which developed in the early days of the anti-AIA campaign. With his two party colleagues, he was suspended from the Commons in 1981 in the row arising from the assassination of the Rev. Robert Bradford MP. In the 1982 Assembly elections he headed the poll in E. Belfast, and he was chairman of the Assembly's Environment Committee and deputy chairman of the Devolution Committee. In August 1986 he accompanied some hundreds of loyalists on a late-night incursion into the Co. Monaghan village of Clontibret to prove, he claimed, that there was a 'gaping hole' in border security. Two members of the Garda Síochána were injured by loyalists and this led to Secretary of State Tom King expressing his regret to Dublin for the incident. Robinson was eventually fined IR£15,000 for unlawful assembly. In 1987 he was active in protests against the new public order laws, and was a member of a three-man task force set up by the two Unionist leaders to consider anti-AIA strategy. In October 1987 he resigned as DUP deputy leader, apparently because he disagreed with tactics in the anti-AIA campaign, but took up the post again three months later without making any detailed explanation. He served several brief prison sentences for refusal to pay fines arising from protests against the AIA and the public order laws. At one point in 1988 both he and his wife, Iris, were in prison at the same time. Mayor of Castlereagh, 1986. Participant in Duisburg Talks, October 1988. His attitude to the Brooke-Mayhew Talks seemed to have been dictated by a strong desire to secure devolution, and in May 1990 he warned against attaching further conditions to talks. In June 1991, as the serious dialogue began, he said he did not trust either Labour or the Conservatives to negotiate NI's future, and suggested the Union was in 'mortal danger'. But he said the talks would not fail because of the DUP, and when they finally ended without agreement in 1992, he said the SDLP had put forward proposals that Unionists could never agree and the electorate would never endorse. He also argued that there could be no settlement while the Republic maintained its constitutional claim. In August 1993 he alleged that the reduction in numbers of part-time members of the RIR was due to a conspiracy to remove part-timers completely. After the publication in September of the DUP's paper, 'Breaking the Log-Jam', events were judged in the light of its fundamental position. When Rev. Martin Smyth (UUP) set out conditions under which PSF might enter talks, Robinson described this as 'monumental folly'. He dismissed sixteen peace rallies in mid-November as a 'phoney peace fracas'. On 15 December he accompanied his party leader, Rev. Ian Paisley, to Downing Street, where a protest letter was handed in before the official press conference and launch of the Downing Street Declaration. He described the document as 'a watershed in political direction, 'shifting NI from its UK axis into an all-Ireland plane'. He was strongly critical of the US decision, at the end of January 1994, to issue a visa to Gerry Adams. The Secretary of State received more criticism when his long-promised paper on future NI institutions was sent to Dublin without its contents being revealed to any of the local parties. Robinson described this as 'an outrage and indicative of the joint authority they are operating over NI'. The high level of loyalist paramilitary attacks produced the comment that it was no longer reactive to PIRA violence but to perceived constitutional changes.

RODGERS, BRID

General Secretary of SDLP, 1981–3. Irish Senator, 1983–7. Party chairwoman, 1978–80. Advisory Commission on Human Rights, 1977–80. Craigavon Council, 1985–93. b. 1937.

Unsuccessfully contested Upper Bann in 1987 and 1992 general elections. Delegate to the Brooke–Mayhew Talks, 1991–2. In 1991 she was appointed to a new Government water and sewage company as speculation began about the shape of water privatisation in NI. Formerly on Southern Education and Library Board.

ROLLING DEVOLUTION see Systems of Government section, p. 418

ROSE, PAUL
Labour MP for Blackley, Manchester, 1964–79, and chairman of the Campaign for Democracy in Ulster, 1965–73. b. 26 December 1935. LLB Hons. (Manchester). He led many deputations of MPs to see Ministers in the early days of the civil rights campaign, and frequently visited NI on fact-finding trips. Resigned as chairman in 1973 on the publication of the White Paper on the future government of NI and from Parliament in 1979 in frustration at the role of backbenchers.

ROSS, LORD (OF NEWPORT)
As Stephen Ross, Liberal Party spokesman on NI, June 1979–83. b. 1926. Liberal MP for Isle of Wight, February 1974–87. LLB, MA (Edinburgh).

ROSS, WILLIAM
UUP MP for E. Londonderry, 1983–. MP for Londonderry, 1974–83. b. 4 February 1936. Farms at Dungiven, Co. Derry, and Chief Whip and Treasury spokesman of the UUP Parliamentary Party, 1992–. Secretary of the local Unionist Association before entering Parliament. In April 1982 he resigned from the National Union of Conservative and Unionist Associations and three of its committees as a protest against James Prior's 'rolling devolution' initiative. In 1987 and again in 1992 he urged a return to the Airey Neave formula of 1979 for local government. Member of the Monday Club. In 1988 he opposed power-sharing because it would have an in-built Nationalist veto, and in October 1991 he said the Republic could never have a say in the government of NI. He was highly critical of SDLP submission to

Brooke–Mayhew Talks. He was among the most sceptical about the Downing Street Declaration in December 1993. In later comments he expressed doubts about whether Reynolds really accepted the 'consent' principle or if he saw the declaration as a means of circumventing the right of Unionists to say no.

ROSSI, SIR HUGH
Minister of State, NIO, 1979–81. b. 21 June 1927. LLB (London). Solicitor. Knight of Holy Sepulchre, 1966. Conservative MP for Hornsey, 1966–83; Hornsey and Wood Green, 1983–. Government Whip, 1970–2. Council of Europe Whip, 1971–3. Lord Commissioner of Treasury, 1972–4. Parliamentary Under-Secretary, Department of Environment, 1974. Deputy leader, UK delegation to Council of Europe, 1972–3. Responsible at NIO for Finance and Manpower Services. On leaving NIO, he became Social Security Minister. He was dropped from the Government after the 1983 election but given knighthood. In 1990, as chairman of the Commons Select Committee on Environment, he was critical of some NIO environment policies.

ROWNTREE TRUST
The Joseph Rowntree Social Service Trust has contributed substantially to help political parties and pressure groups in NI. Its total grants in 1974 amounted to £70,000. Some £11,000 of this went to the SDLP, including a contribution to the party's election expenses in October 1974. The Alliance Party, NILP and the New Ulster Movement have also been helped, and the trust assisted the loyalist paramilitaries to finance a conference in Belfast in 1975, and contributed to the expenses of paramilitary delegates attending an Oxford conference on NI in 1974. It partially funded the political inquiry project Initiative '92.

ROYAL BLACK INSTITUTION
Effectively the senior branch of the Orange Order. Its full title is the Imperial Grand Black Chapter of the British Commonwealth. Like the Orange Order, it has a substantial membership outside

NI, including lodges in GB, US, Canada, Australia, New Zealand and various African countries. Its HQ is at Lurgan, Co. Armagh, and its sovereign grand master is UUP leader James Molyneaux MP, who has travelled extensively to meet overseas members. Its main demonstrations are staged on the last Saturday of August each year, when some 30,000 members parade with bands and banners. The 'Blackmen', as they are commonly termed, also sponsor an event on 13 July each year – the 'sham fight' at Scarva, Co. Down – when a colourful mock battle is staged between 'King William' and 'King James'. Although there are few political speeches at its demonstrations, it is just as committed as the Orange Order generally to unionism and defence of Protestantism.

ROYAL IRISH REGIMENT *see* Security System section, pp. 451–3

ROYAL ULSTER CONSTABULARY *see* Security System section, pp. 437–40

RUBBER BULLET *see* Security System section, pp. 449–50

S

SANDELSON, NEVILLE DEVONSHIRE
SDP spokesman on NI, 1981–3. b. 27 November 1923. MP for Hayes and Harlington, 1971–83. (Labour, 1971–81; SDP, 1981–3.)

SANDS, ROBERT (BOBBY)
Anti-H-Block MP for Fermanagh–S. Tyrone, April–May 1981. b. Rathcoole, Belfast, 1954; d. 5 May 1981 on hunger strike in Maze Prison, on sixty-sixth day of his fast in support of the demand for political status or the 'five demands' (*see* H-Blocks). He was the first of ten Republican prisoners to die during the protest. In 1972 Sands's family moved from Rathcoole to Twinbrook, on the fringe of W. Belfast, and are said to have been forced by loyalists to move home. He was sentenced in 1973 to five years' imprisonment on an arms charge, and had

special category status in the Maze Prison until his release in April 1976. Soon afterwards, he and three others were found in a car with weapons. In 1977 he was sentenced to fourteen years' imprisonment, and alleged that he had been subjected to ill-treatment while being interrogated at Castlereagh. He immediately joined PIRA prisoners protesting against the denial of special category status, and during the 1980 hunger strike became leader of the PIRA prisoners in the H-Blocks. On 1 March 1981 he began his fast 'unto death' in support of political status, and the readiness of some 30,000 voters in Fermanagh–S. Tyrone to give him a majority in the April by-election (*see* Election Results section, p. 388) gave a new spur to republicanism. Many politicians and Churchmen sought to persuade him to end his fast, among them Monsignor John Magee, Newry-born emissary of Pope John Paul II, who gave Sands a crucifix sent by the Pope. Westminster moved quickly to prevent another hunger-striker being nominated for the by-election following his death. Teheran named one of its thoroughfares Bobby Sands Street.

SANDY ROW
Ultra-loyalist area close to central Belfast, usually linked with the Shankill Road as denoting militant Protestantism. During the 1969 violence, local people put up barricades at the Boyne Bridge to prevent, they said, Republicans entering from the nearby Grosvenor Road area. Some bomb damage was caused to pubs and other premises in the main thoroughfare. Housing in the area has been radically improved.

SAOR ÉIRE
This name appeared originally in Dublin in 1931 as the title of a strongly left-wing Republican group, which was declared illegal for a time in Southern Ireland. It had some support from the IRA at the time. The name emerged again in the early 1960s as the Saor Éire Action Group, and it was blamed for many bank raids in the Republic in 1966 and 1967. In 1971 a Marxist journal, *Red Mole*,

carried what purported to be a statement from Saor Éire strongly criticising the Official Republican movement. In 1973 there were claims of a threat by its Derry unit to avenge sectarian murders by loyalists. In the same year there were reports of misappropriation of funds by some of its leaders. In 1975 it was credited with a threat to take action against either the IRSP or the OIRA if those two groups did not cease their feud in Belfast. The group has been regarded by the security forces in NI as a minor element in the violence, and little credence is attached to a claim that it was responsible for killing some members of the security forces in 1972.

SCARMAN TRIBUNAL

The inquiry body that investigated the riots and shootings in the summer of 1969. Mr Justice (now Lord) Scarman presided, and he was assisted by two NI businessmen – William Marshall, Protestant, and George Lavery, Catholic. It heard 400 witnesses at 170 sittings. It reported in April 1972 that there was no plot to overthrow the NI Government or to mount an armed insurrection. The riots were described as communal disturbances arising from a complex political, social and economic situation. It also said that while there was no conspiracy, it would be the height of naïveté to deny that the teenage hooligans, who almost invariably threw the first stones, were manipulated and encouraged by those seeking to discredit the Government. The tribunal found that the RUC was seriously at fault on six occasions. It said there was lack of firm direction in handling the disturbances in Derry during the early evening of 12 August; in the decision to put the USC (B Specials) on riot control in Dungannon and Armagh without disarming them; and in the use of Browning machine guns in Belfast on 14 and 15 August. It described as 'wholly unjustifiable' the firing of a Browning gun into Divis Flats on the Falls Road, killing Patrick Rooney, aged nine. The RUC were also blamed for failing to prevent Protestant mobs from burning the homes of Catholics in Belfast, and for failure to take any

effective action to disperse crowds or protect lives and property in the riot areas on 15 August before the army came in. The tribunal said the RUC did, however, struggle manfully to do their duty in a situation they could not control, and their courage had been beyond praise. The report added: 'Once large-scale communal disturbances occur, they are not susceptible to control by police. Either they must be suppressed by overwhelming force which, save in the last resort, is not acceptable in our society – and it was not within the control of the NI Government – or a political solution must be devised.' The tribunal cleared the RUC of the charge that it was a partisan force co-operating with Protestant mobs to attack Catholics. But it added that the incidents in W. Belfast on 14 August had resulted in a complete loss of confidence by the Catholic community in the police force as it was then constituted. The USC was said to have neither the training nor the equipment for riot duty, and outside Belfast it had shown on several occasions a lack of discipline with firearms. The tribunal found that politicians opposed to the Government, and specifically the Rev. Ian Paisley, had not been implicated in the violence, although their speeches had helped to build up tension. It found that the Protestant and Catholic communities had exhibited the same fears, the same sort of self-help, and the same distrust of lawful authority. (*See also* Security Systems section, p. 436–8.)

SCOTT, NICHOLAS PAUL

Deputy Secretary of State, NIO, 1986–7; Under-Secretary, NIO, 1981–6. b. 1933. Conservative MP for Chelsea, 1974–, and Paddington S., 1966–74. Under-Secretary, Employment, 1974. He faced a great variety of problems during a Stormont career longer than that of any previous Minister under direct rule. As Under-Secretary, he dealt with education and, later, security, and rode out the storm over the mass escape from the Maze Prison in 1983. In education he encountered criticism over school closures and the future of the Catholic training colleges, and merged the New

University of Ulster and the Ulster Polytechnic to create the University of Ulster. He campaigned for greater co-operation between Catholic and State schools. But it was his role as a strong defender of the AIA which attracted most attention. This earned him esteem in Dublin Government and SDLP circles, but Unionists showed him only hostility, and some of them dubbed him 'Minister of Discord', and welcomed his departure in the June 1987 reshuffle. Despite his left-of-centre stance in the Conservative Party, his work was clearly valued by Margaret Thatcher, who apparently saw the need to keep him at Stormont in 1985, when she was forced to move Secretary of State Douglas Hurd to the Home Office. His safe Chelsea seat was probably another factor. His vigorous response to loyalist protests over the AIA in 1986 earned him promotion to Minister of State and deputy Secretary of State and he emerged as a strong personality in the Anglo-Irish Intergovernmental Conference of the AIA, where he pushed security reforms and maintained close contacts with Dublin. Social Security Minister, 1987–. In 1990 he was critical of the Conservative decision to organise in NI, since it made the Secretary of State a player rather than a referee in NI affairs.

SCOTTISH UNIONIST PARTY

Set up in April 1986 to support the Unionist campaign against the AIA. Backed by Orange Order in Scotland. Initially, its chairman, Bill McMurdo, said it would be fighting nine seats in the 1987 general election, including that of Scottish Secretary Malcolm Rifkind, but later the party decided simply to work actively against the Conservatives.

SEAWRIGHT, GEORGE

Militant loyalist politician, fatally wounded in IPLO shooting in November 1987, and who died the following month. Born in Glasgow, his power base was in the Shankill area of Belfast, and he was elected to Belfast City Council in 1981, and to the Assembly in 1982 on the slogan 'A Protestant candidate for a Protestant people'. In the Assembly he served on committees on Health and Social Services, Finance and Personnel, and Security. He was expelled from the DUP for failing to clarify a comment at a Belfast Education and Library Board meeting in 1984 that Catholics and their priests should be burned, following objections by Catholic parents to the playing of the British national anthem at joint school concerts. The incident also led to a three-month suspended sentence and £100 fine. In 1986 he was active in protests directed at Secretary of State Tom King over the AIA; the first led to a three-month suspended sentence and the second to a nine-month sentence. His other activities included support for loyalist prisoners' campaigns and denunciation of the rerouting of Orange parades. But he bowed out of politics when he failed to take N. Belfast in the 1987 election. A massive funeral on the Shankill was attended by representatives of all the main sections of unionism. His wife, Elizabeth, won his council seat.

SHANKILL DEFENCE ASSOCIATION

A loyalist vigilante group formed in the Shankill Road area of Belfast in the violent summer of 1969. It was under the chairmanship of John McKeague, and soon claimed a membership of 1,000. Its members, armed on occasion, were involved in clashes in areas adjoining the Falls Road, and according to the Scarman report, it was 'active in assisting Protestant families to move out of Hooker Street, and there is evidence, which we accept, that it encouraged Catholic families to move out of Protestant streets south of the Ardoyne'. On 2 August 1969 it was claimed by the security forces that SDA members had set up a cordon round the Unity Flats complex, occupied by Catholics, and had tried to force their way into the flats after reports that Junior Orangemen had been attacked in the area. Petrol bombs were used in the rioting which followed, and the SDA was particularly critical of the use by the RUC of water cannon. They gave a warning that the people of the Shankill would not have any further confidence in the RUC. The UCDC, headed by the Rev.

Ian Paisley, denied that either the UCDC or the UPV had any connection with the SDA. Many members of the SDA were believed to be members of the USC. When the Hunt report in 1969 recommended the replacement of the USC by a new part-time force under the army GOC, the SDA called for the resignation of the Chichester-Clark Government, and said the time was fast approaching when responsible leaders of the SDA would not be able to restrain the 'backlash of outraged loyalist opinion'. In October 1969 there was serious rioting on the Shankill Road, and the RUC suffered its first fatality of the Troubles when Constable Victor Arbuckle was shot dead. In November 1969 SDA chairman John McKeague was cleared of a charge of conspiracy to cause explosions.

SHANKILL ROAD

A Befast area which is a major loyalist stronghold. Organisations like the UVF and the UDA have drawn much of their support from the Shankill. In 1969 there were serious riots in the area, and the Peace Line was erected between the Shankill Road and adjoining (Catholic) Falls Road to prevent confrontations between hostile crowds. By a strange irony, the first RUC man to be shot dead in the Troubles (Constable Victor Arbuckle) was killed during a riot on the Shankill Road in October 1969. The character of the area has been greatly affected by large-scale demolition and redevelopment. In 1978 the UVF was threatening to prevent further demolition. In 1988 the Shankill Community Council was calling for revitalisation of the area if it was not to sink into deprivation. In the 1990s, substantial plans have emerged for Government aid for W. and N. Belfast, which have been welcomed by local politicians. Some of these plans involve cross-community co-operation with the Falls area. In 1992 local Unionist MP Cecil Walker teamed up with W. Belfast SDLP MP Joe Hendron on a job-seeking tour in the US. A local poll in 1991 showed majority support in the area for the Brooke–Mayhew Talks. Growing

loyalist paramilitary violence in 1992–3 led to local activity by undercover police and soldiers, which produced several violent incidents. Homes of some leading loyalists in the area were targeted by Republicans. A no-warning bomb in Frizell's fish shop killed nine (ultimately ten) people and injured fifty-eight others on the afternoon of Saturday 23 October 1993. At first, PIRA claimed that its target was the UFF leadership, which it incorrectly said was meeting above the shop. It later claimed that there was to have been a warning but the bomb exploded prematurely and admitted that one of those killed, Thomas Begley, and one of the people injured were its volunteers. The public revulsion was palpable and drew many comments of hypocrisy when PSF pressure in favour of the Hume–Adams peace process was high. The Anglo-Irish Intergovernmental Conference meeting of 27 October was postponed as a mark of respect, the UFF 'fully mobilised' its members, and, when pressed by journalists, Gerry Adams said the bombing could not be excused.

SHAW, SIR GILES

As Giles Shaw, Parliamentary Under-Secretary, NIO, 1979–81. b. 1931. MA (Cantab.) and president of the Union, 1954. Marketing director, Rowntree Mackintosh Limited, 1970–4. Conservative MP for Pudsey, February 1974–. Responsible at NIO for the departments of Commerce and Agriculture. After serving in several departments, including Minister of State at Home Office, and Trade and Industry, he left Government in 1987. Treasurer, Conservative 1922 Committee. In charge of Douglas Hurd's bid for Conservative leadership in 1990. BIPB, 1989–.

SHILLINGTON, SIR GRAHAM

Chief Constable of the RUC, 1970–3. b. Portadown, Co. Armagh, 1911. When he took charge of the RUC, he had been deputy Chief Constable for nearly two years, and had been concerned with the reorganisation of the force as a consequence of the Hunt report. Earlier, he had been RUC City Commissioner in Belfast. His appointment as Chief

Constable was welcomed by Unionists, but questioned by civil rights supporters. His tenure of office as Chief Constable covered the introduction of internment and the violence that followed direct rule. He also had to cope with a high level of sectarian assassinations.

SHORT, CLARE

Labour MP for Birmingham Ladywood, 1983–. b. 15 February 1946. BA Politics (Hons.), Leeds University. Former Home Office civil servant, 1970–5, and director of Youthaid and the Unemployment Unit. Chair, All-Party Group on Race Relations, 1985–6. Home Affairs Select Committee, 1983–5; front-bench spokeswoman on employment, 1985–8, and on social security, 1989–91. Labour NEC, 1988–. She has identified with a number of social, ethnic and women's issues. She is a strong supporter of Labour Party policy of a united Ireland by consent and, with relatives in Crossmaglen, Co. Armagh, takes a keen interest in NI issues. She opposed Labour policy on the Gulf War and resigned her social security brief on 14 February 1991, when disciplined by party leader Neil Kinnock. She remained popular with the wider Labour movement and continued to be elected to the NEC. She returned as a front-bench spokeswoman on Women in the autumn of 1993.

SHORT STRAND

A mainly Catholic enclave in predominantly Protestant E. Belfast. In the early days of the Troubles, notably in 1972, there were clashes between Protestants and Catholics, and occasionally serious riots on the fringes of the district. In the 1990s efforts have been made to create jobs locally, and its environment will benefit from the Laganside project and other riverfront developments.

SILENT TOO LONG

An organisation established in 1981 by relatives of innocent Catholic victims of violence. It claimed at that time that the deaths of 600 such victims had been virtually ignored by the authorities. In 1986 a publicity trip to the US by

representatives of the organisation was sponsored by NORAID.

SIMPSON, FREDERICK VIVIAN

NILP MP for Oldpark, 1958–72. b. Dublin, 23 August 1903; d. 1977. Draper and footwear merchant in Carrickfergus, where he served on local council, 1947–58. Methodist lay preacher.

SIMPSON, MARY

UUP Assembly member for Armagh, 1982–6. Served on Environment Committee, and vice-chair, Education. Craigavon Borough Council, 1977–89; first Lady Mayor 1981–2. Honorary Secretary, Central Armagh Unionist Association, 1974–83. Founding member, Craigavon and District Housing Association, 1980–; chair 1990–.

SIMPSON, DR ROBERT

First Minister of Community Relations, 1969–71, the appointment being part of the reform package arising from the visit of James Callaghan as Home Secretary. On taking office, Dr Simpson resigned from the Masonic and Orange Orders. b. Ballymena, 3 July 1923. MB (QUB). Unionist MP for Mid-Antrim, 1952–72.

SIX COUNTIES

A term sometimes used to designate NI, particularly in Nationalist circles.

SKELMERSDALE, LORD

Parliamentary Under-Secretary, NIO, July 1989–December 1990. b. 2 April 1945. Trained horticulturist. He had been a Government Whip and had held junior posts at DOE and DHSS before coming to NI, where he initially had responsibility for health and social services, and later took over agriculture. Criticised for implementing privatisation of some services associated with health. In 1991 he voiced support for internment without trial in NI.

SMITH, SIR HOWARD

Last UK Government representative, NI, 1971–2. b. 15 October 1919. He was the last holder of an office that extended from 1969 until the introduction of direct rule in March 1972. His main activity was in the crucial period leading up to direct rule, including 'Bloody Sunday' in Derry. He became ambassador to Moscow in 1976 and later that year was appointed by Home Secretary Merlyn Rees as head of MI5.

SMITH, JEAN KENNEDY

US Ambassador to Dublin, 1993-. b. 1928. Sister of late President John F. Kennedy and Senator Edward Kennedy. Her appointment was announced by President Clinton on St Patrick's Day 1993, during the visit of Taoiseach Albert Reynolds. It was clearly intended as a gesture to Irish-Americans and as a means of signalling the President's interest in an NI settlement, despite his decision to think again about the appointment of a presidential envoy to NI, which he had promised during his election campaign. Smith was seen in diplomatic circles as providing Clinton's 'eyes and ears' in the Irish scene, of which she had a close knowledge, as well as paving the way for an Irish presidential trip, possibly including NI. Both the UUP and DUP were suspicious of the appointment, which was widely regarded as a triumph for Senator Kennedy. The *Boston Globe* suggested that the appointment would complement the election of Mary Robinson to the Irish presidency. On an unofficial two-day visit to IFI projects in Fermanagh and Derry in mid-August 1993 she spoke about the positive change in Derry since 1974. She repeated President Clinton's concern but said the envoy idea would only happen if the UK and the Republic agreed and if it would help with a solution. A month later she made a private visit to IFI projects in Belfast and was briefed by the NIO.

SMITH, JOHN

Leader of British Labour Party, 1992-4. b. 13 September 1938; d. 12 May 1994. MA, LLB (Glasgow). QC (1986). MP for Lanarkshire N., 1970-83; Monklands E., 1983-94. After holding a number of junior Government posts, he was Secretary for Trade, 1978-9. On taking up leadership, he retained Kevin McNamara MP as main opposition spokesman on NI. On his first visit to NI

as leader in December 1992, he supported the Government in its refusal to talk to PSF while PIRA violence continued. He said Labour policies were needed to boost employment in NI, and shortly afterwards, in attacking the Government record on jobs, he said manufacturing in NI had accounted for 146,000 jobs in NI in 1979 against 97,000 in June 1992. He was under some pressure from a new Labour group at Westminster, Democracy Now, and some trade unionists and Labour supporters in NI to drop the party line of refusing to organise in NI, but there was no hint of a change of policy. On a visit to Derry early in December 1993 he said PSF could be admitted to talks if PIRA violence ended. He strongly supported the Downing Street Declaration and spoke of power-sharing devolution as the next stage, though this was not Labour Party policy.

SMITH, TIMOTHY J.

Parliamentary Under-Secretary, NIO, January 1994-. Replaced Robert Atkins, who moved to Environment after the resignation of Tim Yeo. Responsible for Economic Development and the Environment. Conservative MP for Beaconsfield, 1982-; MP for Ashfield, 1977-9. b. 5 October 1947. Educated at Harrow and St Peter's College, Oxford, he was a chartered accountant, with a special interest in finance and investment. Treasurer, Conservative Party, 1992-. At his first press conference in NI he said that comments made by him about the Irish vote in Britain before the 1992 general election, and criticised by Kevin McNamara, had been misunderstood. He explained that his comments had been about itinerants and not the Irish in general, whose historic rights and contribution to Britain he respected.

SMYTH, A. CLIFFORD

DUP Assembly, 1974, Convention, 1975-6, member for N. Antrim. b. Derry, 1944. BA, Ph.D. (QUB). Chairman, QUB Conservative and Unionist Association, 1971. He was elected to the Assembly in June 1974, after it had already been prorogued, heading the poll in the by-election. In the Convention, he was secretary of the UUUC. In 1977 he returned to the UUP (as a student he had been secretary of the Young Unionist Council) and unsuccessfully contested N. Down in 1979 Westminster election. Chairman, CEC, 1986–7.

SMYTH, HUGH

Independent Unionist Assembly, 1973–4, and Convention, 1975–6, member for W. Belfast. b. Shankill, Belfast, 1941. Belfast City Council, 1972–. Deputy Lord Mayor, 1983 and 1993. Heavily involved in political and welfare work in the Shankill area, he was one of the founders of the Loyalist Front, which was active in 1974, and which had the support of the UVF. After the 1974 loyalist strike, he claimed that loyalist leaders had only shown their hand when they were sure that the strike was going to succeed, and that in future the decisions must be taken by the workers. He helped to found the short-lived Volunteer Political Party – political arm of the UVF – and in 1978 he was appointed leader of the Belfast-based Independent Unionist Group which became the Progressive Unionist Party in 1979. Unsuccessful candidate in W. Belfast for 1982 Assembly. In March 1991 he was instrumental in having the Belfast City Council ban on Ministers visiting the City Hall lifted. It had been imposed in 1985 in protest at the AIA.

SMYTH, REVEREND (WILLIAM) MARTIN

UUP MP for S. Belfast, 1982–. Grand master of the Orange Order in Ireland, 1972–. b. Belfast 15 June 1931. BA, BD (TCD). Originally joined junior Orange lodge in Sandy Row area of Belfast, and for ten years (1972–82) combined his career as a Presbyterian Minister (Alexandra Church in N. Belfast) with leadership of the Orange Order and the post of vice-president of the council of the UUP. During that period, he was Imperial grand master of the Orange Order as well as head of the Order in Ireland. On his election as MP for S. Belfast in the February 1982 by-election (created by the assassination of the Rev. Robert Bradford), he resigned his church

ministry and the post of Imperial grand master of the Orange Order. He also suggested that he should give up the post of Irish grand master, but was persuaded by Orange colleagues to remain. He made his first election bid in the Convention election of 1975, and headed the poll in S. Belfast. When the Convention broke up, he incurred some criticism for taking part in secret, but unsuccessful, talks with the SDLP, represented by John Hume and Paddy Devlin, in an attempt to break the political deadlock. His win in the 1982 by-election in S. Belfast was psychologically important for his party since it seemed to mark a halt to the loss of electoral ground to the DUP. He has been strongly critical of the AIA, but in 1987 urged the development of a federal system of government covering the whole UK, with a provincial parliament in Belfast, and a place for the return of the Republic to the UK. NI, he said, had not been the success it should have been because British Governments had not the will to make it work. Chairman of the 1982 Assembly's Health and Social Services, and Finance and Personnel committees. Member of Devolution Committee. When he led the Orange Order in its Belfast celebrations of the Battle of the Boyne in 1990, he described the Order as 'bloodied, but unbowed'. In the Brooke–Mayhew Talks, he co-ordinated the presentation of the UUP case. Party spokesman on health and foreign affairs, 1992–. In September 1993 he called for the reintroduction of internment after four murders by loyalists and several PIRA bombs within four days. When he was criticised for using the phrase 'pan-Nationalist', he pointed out that it had first been used by PSF in January 1985. He attracted DUP criticism when he told the BBC in early October 1993 that PSF could be included in talks, on certain conditions. When those conditions turned out to be strict and the statement proved to be party policy, the criticism declined, as did the attempt to challenge his re-election as Orange grand master. Amid the hype of Gerry Adams's visit to New York at the beginning of February 1994, Smyth had a 'prayer breakfast' meeting with President Clinton in Washington.

SOCIAL AND LIBERAL DEMOCRATS *see* Liberal Democrats

SOCIAL DEMOCRATIC AND LABOUR PARTY

The party that speaks for most Catholics in NI. Founded on 21 August 1970, it absorbed most supporters of the old Nationalist Party, National Democratic Party and Republican Labour Party. It joined the Confederation of Socialist Parties of the European Community. The party was launched by seven Stormont politicians: Gerry Fitt MP, then Republican Labour, who became party leader; three Independent MPs, who had been prominent in the civil rights campaign – John Hume, Ivan Cooper and Paddy O'Hanlon; Austin Currie, a Nationalist MP; Paddy Devlin, NILP MP; and Paddy Wilson, Republican Labour Senator, who was to become a murder victim. It presented itself as a radical, left-of-centre party, which would seek civil rights for all and just distribution of wealth. It would work to promote friendship and understanding between North and South, with a view to the eventual unity of Ireland, through the consent of the majority of the people, North and South. The SDLP's first major move was to withdraw from Stormont in July 1971. It stated that it was withdrawing its consent from the institutions of government. With the introduction of internment without trial in August 1971, it sponsored a civil disobedience campaign, involving the withholding of rents and rates. In the autumn of 1971 it was involved in the Assembly of the Northern Irish People – the unofficial 'Dungiven Parliament'. With the imposition of direct rule in 1972, it proposed a form of condominium, with Britain and the Republic exercising joint sovereignty over NI. There would be an Assembly elected by PR, but legislation would have to be approved by commissioners appointed by the British and Irish Governments. The Executive would be elected by the Assembly, also by PR. The

party also called for a declaration by Britain in favour of Irish unity, and the setting up of a 'National Senate' by the Assembly and the Dáil to plan progress towards Irish unity. The SDLP opted out of the Darlington conference, organised in September 1972 by Secretary of State William Whitelaw, despite an appeal by Edward Heath. But it took comfort from the Government's Green Paper, which urged power-sharing between the communities and an Irish dimension, and it supported the White Paper which followed. Its Assembly election manifesto stressed partnership government and a cross-border Council of Ireland. In the election the SDLP got nineteen of the seventy-eight seats, and 22.1 per cent of first-preference votes. It had four seats in the 1974 power-sharing Executive including that of deputy Chief Executive, held by Gerry Fitt. The collapse of the Executive as a result of the loyalist strike was a serious blow to the party. It angrily blamed the British Government for failing to tackle the paramilitary groups backing the stoppage. In its Convention manifesto, *Speak with Strength*, it stuck to the main points of its policy, with perhaps a shade less emphasis on the Irish dimension. It secured 23.7 per cent of first-preference votes but got only seventeen seats, two fewer than in the Assembly. The loyalist majority in the Convention showed no disposition to accept power-sharing other than in the framework of departmental committees. And since the UUUC rejected William Craig's plan for an emergency voluntary coalition, the SDLP was never called upon to declare its attitude to a scheme that fell short of full power-sharing and excluded a Council of Ireland. After the Convention was wound up, the party's deputy leader, John Hume, and Paddy Devlin had private exploratory talks with the Rev. Martin Smyth and Austin Ardill of the Ulster Unionists, but the exchanges were unproductive. With renewed direct rule, the SDLP became unhappy at what it saw as lack of effort by the British Government to deal with 'loyalist intransigence'. It also saw evidence of a trend towards integration, with Westminster support for five extra

NI MPs. In a policy statement, *Facing Reality,* endorsed at its 1977 conference, it urged an 'agreed Ireland – the essential unity of whose people would have evolved in agreement over the years, whose institutions of government would reflect both its unity and diversity, and whose people would live in a harmonious relationship with Britain'. Many Unionists regarded the statement as more angled towards a united Ireland than previous statements, but this was denied by party spokesmen. They also rejected the claim of Paddy Devlin that there was a move away from socialism, and Devlin was expelled in the autumn of 1977. In 1978 the three major Dublin parties indicated that they would respond to a plea by John Hume that they should spell out precisely their ideas for Irish unity. In local government elections the party has established a firm base. In the 1977 District Council elections, it won 113 seats (20.6 per cent of first-preference votes), compared with 83 seats in 1973. At its 1978 conference the party renewed its call for the British and Irish Governments and both sides of the NI community to get together to work out a settlement, but its motion also referred to eventual British withdrawal as 'desirable and inevitable' and this point was seized on by Unionist critics. In the 1979 Westminster election the party retained W. Belfast, but did not come close to winning any other seat. Its Chief Whip, Austin Currie, resigned to fight, unsuccessfully, Fermanagh–S. Tyrone as Independent SDLP. In the 1979 European election the party's deputy leader, John Hume, achieved a record vote for the party – nearly 25 per cent – in taking one of the three NI seats in the European Parliament. The announcement of a Constitutional Conference by Secretary of State Humphrey Atkins in November 1979 created a crisis for the party. The SDLP regarded the agenda as far too limited to produce a political settlement. Gerry Fitt immediately denounced its attitude and resigned from the party, claiming that it was losing its socialism and becoming 'green Nationalist'. John Hume rejected the charge and succeeded Fitt as party leader. In the end the SDLP

did join the Stormont conference, after persuading the Secretary of State to set up a parallel meeting in which cross-border relations, security and the economy could be discussed. In the main conference the party proposed a power-sharing administration in which places would be allocated in proportion to party strength. In the parallel conference it attacked Government policy, and when the main conference failed to produce agreement, it turned down a further Government idea of a fifty-member advisory council. During the H–Block hunger strike, it called for concessions short of political status, but its proposals were rejected by the Government. Throughout the hunger strike it suffered some internal strains as a result of its decision to stay out of the Fermanagh–S. Tyrone by-elections, and the Maze protest also hit its expectations in the 1981 council elections. Although it lost only a few council seats, its share of the poll dropped 3 per cent to 17.5 per cent. In 1982 the party came out strongly against the 'rolling devolution' plan, which it attacked as 'unworkable', and it was firmly supported in this view by the Republic's Taoiseach, Charles Haughey, while the Fine Gael leader, Dr Garret FitzGerald, also expressed reservations. The SDLP went into the election urging a 'Council for a New Ireland' to enable politicians from NI and the Republic to get together to discuss the implications of Irish unity. It also decided not to attend the Assembly. It had to face widespread competition from PSF candidates in strongly Nationalist areas, and in consequence its total of fourteen Assembly seats was down on both the 1973 Assembly and the 1975 Convention. With just under 19 per cent of first-preference votes, its share of the vote was also down on previous Stormont elections, although an improvement on the 1981 council contests. It lost one of its Assembly seats in Armagh when its deputy leader, Seamus Mallon, was unseated because of his membership of the Republic's Senate. At its 1983 conference, the party reaffirmed its opposition to the Assembly, and backed Hume's call for it to meet the PSF challenge 'head on' and contest all seventeen seats at the Westminster election. It did so and fought on the platform of support for the New Ireland Forum. It maintained its vote numerically, but because of the larger poll and PSF competition, its share of the poll dropped to 18 per cent and it secured only the Foyle seat, taken by John Hume. For the party, 1984 was a period of great uncertainty. Margaret Thatcher was thought to be planning some new Anglo-Irish initiative in the light of the Assembly's failure to produce an acceptable scheme for devolution. But the party was unprepared for the PM's sharp rebuff to the main Forum options in November 1984. Her 'out, out, out' remarks seemed to preclude any major move by London. But the SDLP, like the Irish Government, built on the international diplomatic support for the Forum. The US Congress had unanimously backed the NIF report in May 1984, and it also had a favourable response in Europe, while the British Labour Party was inclined to say 'in, in, in'. The SDLP benefited, strangely enough, from PSF's strong showing in its first council elections contest in 1985. A total of fifty-nine PSF councillors left the SDLP position virtually unchanged, but it was a new spur to London and Dublin to seek some way of strengthening constitutional politics. The outcome was the AIA of 1985, but SDLP hopes that it might lead to inter-party talks were swiftly disappointed. John Hume who pressed the AIA as the beginning of a process of reconciliation, made no headway in face of the fierce opposition of Unionists, who presented the AIA as the brainchild of the SDLP and Dublin, accepted by Thatcher against her better judgement. But immediate SDLP disappointments were out-weighed by its electoral gains. First, Seamus Mallon took Newry and Armagh in the 1986 by-elections, and then Eddie McGrady unseated veteran MP Enoch Powell in S. Down in the 1987 election. The decline in the PSF vote was a factor in both victories. By 1988 public opinion polls in NI were showing Catholics not greatly impressed by the fruits of the AIA. John Hume (joined later by some of his

colleagues) had talks over nine months with PSF president Gerry Adams, aimed, apparently, at persuading PSF that the AIA had shown the British Government to be essentially neutral in its attitude to a British presence in Ireland and that violence was unnecessary. The talks, unsurprisingly, did not lead to agreement. The party enjoyed electoral good fortune in 1989. Not only did it secure an extra twenty seats in the council elections, but John Hume's vote of 25.5 per cent in the European election was the highest-ever SDLP share of the vote in any election. These advances were largely at the expense of PSF and enabled the party to bring a note of self-congratulation to its twentieth anniversary celebrations in 1990. In the 1990s party spokesmen made many appeals to PIRA to call off its campaign, and Hume urged Church leaders to talk to the paramilitaries – 'the sinners in your flocks'. In 1990 Hume had a meeting with President Bush, and welcomed Peter Brooke's comment that Britain now had 'no selfish or strategic interest' in NI. As 'talks about talks' developed between the Government and the constitutional parties, the party developed its key proposal for a local settlement – government by a panel of six commissioners, three elected locally by PR, with the British and Irish Governments and the EC Commission each nominating one commissioner. There would also be a North–South body of Ministers. But this radical approach was rejected in the Brooke–Mayhew Talks by both Unionist parties, who concentrated their fire on the Republic's constitutional claim to NI. Denis Haughey said, however, that Articles 2 and 3 of the Constitution must stay. As the talks ended, Hume stressed that neither majority rule nor power-sharing would work in NI, and Seamus Mallon said the Republic must have an executive role in NI. But although the formal exchanges ended in November 1992, the party seemed set to continue bilateral talks with the other parties on matters of common concern. In the 1992 election, the SDLP's Joe Hendron finally wrested the W. Belfast seat from Gerry Adams, with the help of some normally Unionist voters across the Peace Line. On the security front, 1992 also brought some gains for the party. The UDR, a frequent target of SDLP criticism, was merged with the Royal Irish Rangers and the UDA was outlawed. The party was critical of the British Government's continuing privatisation in NI, and the idea of trust status for hospitals. In the 1993 council elections, the party's 21.9 per cent vote represented a 1 per cent gain and its 127 seats marked a 4-seat gain on 1989. But in W. Belfast (where it had gained the Westminster seat from PSF in 1992) it took only three seats to PSF's seven. The party did not vote on the Maastricht Treaty Bill in July but were involved in controversy when it appeared that pairing arrangements with three Conservatives had been broken. The support by UUP for the Conservatives resulted in claims of a 'deal' and allegations about the future position of the Government in the talks process. From late August the party regularly voiced its concern at the rising level of loyalist paramilitary violence. In September Joe Hendron MP and four SDLP councillors had explosive devices planted at their homes. Doubts within the party about the risks and value of the Hume–Adams talks increased until a meeting of MPs on 21 September and a report from the party leader on his meeting with PM Major restored unity behind the aims of 'lasting peace' and a 'complete cessation of violence'. Unity was further strained when the party was apparently left uninformed of the details of the Hume–Adams agreement, while Hume accompanied a trade mission to the US. On his return there was disappointment that there was no unilateral ceasefire by PIRA and that publication of the agreement had to await PSF consent. The party conference at Cookstown in November was informed by Hume of the opportunity for peace and that PM Major held the key. The party welcomed the Downing Street Declaration and encouraged individuals to read it and make up their own minds. Its MPs stated that too much reassurance was being given to Unionists at the expense of Nationalists. The party criticised the decision to set up an NI

Affairs Committee at Westminster for addressing one strand of the problem in isolation. The publication of the Parliamentary Boundary Commission's provisional recommendations which, while removing one Unionist seat from Belfast appeared to threaten the S. Down seat of Eddie McGrady, produced an angry response. The issue was on the agenda of a meeting with Michael Ancram in January 1994 and by the end of the month the party chairman, Mark Durkan, was calling for PR in Westminster elections. Further pressure fell on the party after the PIRA three-day ceasefire at Christmas came to an end. While Hume supported 'clarification' and deputy leader Mallon quoted Hume–Adams to argue 'no difference', the party was stymied while awaiting a PSF response. Other differences within the party began to appear, for example in Banbridge, when two councillors left the party over local power-sharing.

SOCIAL DEMOCRATIC PARTY

In 1982 the SDP claimed to be the only major national party recruiting members in NI. This may have been partly due to the influence of one of its founders, Shirley Williams, who had taken a special interest in NI affairs as a member of Labour's NEC and as a Home Office Minister at the start of the Troubles. In the 1987 general election the SDP, then in partnership with the Liberals, co-operated closely with the Alliance Party in NI, and there was much common ground in their manifestos. SDP leader Dr David Owen was a little less enthusiastic about the AIA than most Westminster politicians. He did not think enough had been done to grapple with the problems of the community within NI. He hoped profoundly that it would work, 'but I am a bit dubious', he said. In 1988, when the bulk of the SDP had teamed up with the Liberals in the SLD, the NI branch of SDP was pressing party chiefs to run candidates in NI. In the Upper Bann by-election in 1990 a candidate took only 154 votes. In June 1990 the party was wound up.

SOLEY, CLIVE
Labour front-bench spokesman on NI,

1981–5. b. 7 May 1939. BA Hons. (Strathclyde); DASS (Southampton). MP for Hammersmith W., 1979–83; Hammersmith, 1983–. In January 1983 he suggested an all-Ireland economic council and an all-Ireland court and police force to strengthen cross-border security. Party housing spokesman, 1990–2.

SOUTH ARMAGH REPUBLICAN ACTION FORCE

An organisation which claimed many murders in S. Armagh, particularly in 1975. Regarded by the security forces as a 'flag of convenience' for some local PIRA units.

SPEAKER'S CONFERENCE

Conference headed by Speaker of the Commons, George Thomas MP, which reported in February 1978 that NI should have seventeen MPs at Westminster instead of twelve. It also suggested that the NI Boundary Commission should be free to vary this figure by one either way to facilitate drawing of boundaries and the Commission settled on seventeen seats, which took effect in 1983. The conference represented all the parties, and included three NI MPs – Enoch Powell, James Molyneaux (both UUP), and Gerry Fitt (SDLP), who was alone in standing out against any increased representation.

SPECIAL AIR SERVICE see Security System section, pp. 446–7

SPECIAL CATEGORY

The special status accorded to prisoners who were members of paramilitary organisations, as a result of a decision by William Whitelaw, Secretary of State, in June 1972, after a prolonged hunger strike by prisoners in Belfast Prison. The privileges applied to prisoners sentenced to more than nine months' imprisonment for offences related to the civil disturbances. Because of the lack of cell accommodation they were housed in compounds. They were not required to work, could wear their own clothes, and were allowed extra visits and food parcels. By 31 December 1974, the number of prisoners enjoying special category, or

political, status had risen to 1,116, including 51 women. At that time there were 545 male special category prisoners at the Maze Prison; 502 at Magilligan, Co. Derry, and 18 in Belfast. The women were in Armagh Prison. The prisoners were from both wings of the IRA and the various loyalist paramilitary groups, and the paramilitary organisations ran a prisoner-of-war-type regime in the compounds, some of which had ninety prisoners each. The Gardiner committee, in 1975, came out against special category status. It said it meant virtually the loss of disciplinary control by the prison authorities. Merlyn Rees, as Secretary of State, announced the phasing out of special category status as from 1 March 1976. No one convicted of an offence committed after that date was admitted to special category status, and in 1980 Secretary of State Humphrey Atkins stopped all new admissions to special category status. At the end of 1976 the total of special category prisoners was more than 1,500; by mid-1978 it had dropped to about 800. Prisoners who would normally have been placed in compounds were now put in cells, and 8 new blocks, each with 100 cells, were built at the Maze Prison. They became known as H-Blocks because of the layout, and were linked to recreational facilities, as well as special workshops and vocational training accommodation. But Republican prisoners immediately made it clear they would refuse to co-operate with the removal of special status. They refused to wear prison clothing, and simply covered themselves with a blanket; hence the description of protestors as 'on the blanket'. With the British Government refusing to make any concessions to the protesters, the prisoners involved – they now numbered more than 300 – began to intensify their protest in March 1978. They refused to wash or use the toilets, and smashed up the furniture in their cells. This 'dirty protest' continued, with one interruption, until March 1981, when it was dropped so as to focus attention on Bobby Sands's hunger strike. At the beginning of 1983, 230 prisoners at the Maze were still enjoying special category status, and living in compounds.

There were 105 in the PIRA–INLA compound, 12 OIRA, 67 UVF, and 46 UDA. But by 1988, when the remaining occupants of the compounds moved into H-Block cells, without giving up their privileges, they totalled about ninety. The last two special category prisoners moved from the Maze to Maghaberry Prison as conforming prisoners in September 1991, bringing the system to an end. (*See also* H-Blocks.)

SPECIAL POWERS ACT *see* Security System section, pp. 453–5

SPEERS, JAMES ALEXANDER (JIM) UUP Assembly member for Armagh, April 1983–6. Served on committees on Agriculture, Environment, and deputy chairman, Health and Social Services. b. 1946. Local official of Ulster Farmers' Union. Armagh Council, 1977–. Secretary, Mid- and S. Armagh Unionist Association, 1970–. Stood unsuccessfully in 1982 Assembly election in Armagh, but returned in April 1983 by-election following disqualification of Seamus Mallon (SDLP). In the 1992 Westminster election, he unsuccessfully contested Newry and Armagh.

SPENCE, AUGUSTUS (GUSTY) Best-known figure in the revived UVF, the illegal loyalist paramilitary group. b. Belfast, 1933. Like many UVF men, he had served in the army – with the Royal Ulster Rifles in West Germany and later in Cyprus during the EOKA campaign. He was sentenced to twenty years' imprisonment in 1966 for shooting a young Catholic barman at a public house in Malvern Street in the Shankill Road area of Belfast. Soon afterwards, the UVF was proscribed. He and his friends always insisted that he was innocent of the crime. On several occasions he went on hunger strike to support his claim, and in 1972, when he was given parole to attend his daughter's wedding, UVF members 'kidnapped' him to draw attention to his case. Four months later, he was recaptured, but his friends said he had given himself up because of his heart condition. Among militant loyalists on the Shankill Road, he remained a local hero. Tea towels were produced with his portrait, and facsimile five-pound notes were printed on which the Queen's head was replaced by Spence's. 'His only crime was loyalty' was the slogan used by those who campaigned for his release. In 1977, as UVF commander inside the Maze Prison, he issued a message supporting reconciliation and attacking violence, which, he said, could now be counter-productive. He believed that the loyalists had achieved their aim of self-determination. He was also reported to be learning Irish, and his general attitude was not welcomed by all UVF prisoners. In March 1978 he resigned as UVF commander in the prison. Spence was finally released in December 1983, when he was said to be in very poor health. In an interview for the *Shankill Bulletin* in June 1985 he criticised the two main Unionist parties for failing to outflank PSF by talking to the SDLP. He said his future would be in community politics, and in 1989 his work was praised by SDLP councillor Dr Alisdair McDonnell, who said Spence had been 'most co-operative' regarding projects involving the Phoenix Trust on both the Falls and the Shankill.

SPRING, DICK Tánaiste (deputy Taoiseach) and Foreign Minister of Irish Republic, 1993–. Leader of Irish Labour Party, 1982–. b. 1950. TCD. Barrister. TD since 1981, when he became junior Justice Minister, and held successively the portfolios of Environment and Energy as Tánaiste (1982–7) in the FG–Lab. Coalition headed by Garret FitzGerald. At that period he was closely involved along with FitzGerald in the negotiations that led to the AIA. A key success in opposition was the triumph of the party's candidate, Mary Robinson, in the 1990 presidential election against all the odds. In November 1990 he called for a review of the constitutional claim to NI in the pending inter-party talks on NI. In November 1992 this attitude was reflected in his party's policy at the general election. In the poll, Labour was the real winner, doubling its representation to thirty-three seats. At first, it looked as if the main opposition parties, FG, Labour and Prog. D., would unite to produce a 'rainbow coalition' to defeat the FF caretaker government headed by Albert Reynolds. But strains rapidly developed between Spring, the FG leader John Bruton and the Prog. D. leader Des O'Malley. Spring then opened talks with Reynolds, who showed that he was ready to accept many of the radical economic ideas of the Labour Party, although it was not until mid-January 1993 that a programme for a FF–Lab. Coalition emerged. Thus, for the first time since 1932, the two parties co-operated; they had a majority of nearly forty, the largest any government in the history of the state. Spring insisted on being Foreign Minister, mainly because it was the department dealing with NI, and he promised flexibility in any new talks on its future. His first speech on NI was widely welcomed for a 'change of tone', but most observers saw it as conceding nothing of substance to Unionists. He had a very high profile early in July 1993. In bargaining for £8,000 million from the EC Structural Fund, he was reported as blocking the £2,250 million for the UK. His *Guardian* interview on the day of the Anglo-Irish Intergovernmental Conference meeting, with its advocacy of joint rule and the two Governments acting together if talks did not restart, surprised many. Mayhew said it went beyond 'the position of the Irish Government hitherto'. The Alliance Party described it as 'dangerous, highly irresponsible and unhelpful'. Later in the month he was 'very much concerned' at the Conservative/UUP 'deal' lest it jeopardise talks. In August he continued to assert that the Governments would go it alone if Unionists boycotted talks. John Hume left him in some embarrassment over the announcement of the Hume-Adams agreement on 25 September, which failed to arrive at Leinster House. The Shankill bomb in October saw him declare the postponement, as a mark of respect, of the Anglo-Irish Intergovernmental Conference meeting, and he demanded the immediate cessation of PIRA violence accompanied by a condemnation of the atrocity from Gerry Adams. Two days

later he outlined to the Dáil six democratic principles for a sustainable peace, including the right to withhold consent – which marked a considerable change – and these were the basis for the Major–Reynolds statement in Brussels at the end of the month. During a visit to the US in mid-November he met President Clinton in Washington and told the Johns Hopkins University that there could be no 'internal solution'. With speculation running high early in December, he told reporters that the Republic had to 'preserve and protect the rights of Unionists as British subjects'. He played a full supporting role to Taoiseach Reynolds during the publication of the Downing Street Declaration in December. Early in 1994 he said Government patience was wearing thin when, despite some clarification and the ending of the Republic's broadcasting ban, PSF only issued a thirteen-page document and failed to accept a cessation of violence. At the end of January he welcomed the US decision to grant Adams a visa. Early in February he was reported to have rejected moves towards devolution in NI and the further isolation of PSF.

STALKER AFFAIR

The shooting dead by the RUC in Co. Armagh in 1982 of six unarmed Catholic men, five of them with alleged terrorist links, proved a traumatic affair for the force. The RUC consistently denied suggestions of an official shoot-to-kill policy but Dublin politicians and the SDLP complained that there was an official cover-up of some aspects of the killings. The deaths were investigated initially by Manchester's former deputy Chief Constable John Stalker, who claimed that he had been hampered in his inquiries. He was taken off the case when he faced disciplinary charges, which were later dropped, and the investigation was continued by W. Yorkshire Chief Constable Colin Sampson. Reports of the inquiries were not published, but in 1988 Attorney-General Sir Patrick Mayhew said that while there was evidence of attempts to pervert the course of justice, there would be no prosecution of police officers, on the grounds of national security. The NI Police Authority also decided, by one vote, that there would be no disciplinary charges against the three top officers of the RUC. But a report to the RUC Chief Constable Sir John Hermon by Staffordshire Chief Constable Charles Kelly led to disciplinary charges against twenty junior officers. Interest in the affair remained high in the context of MI5 taking responsibility for anti-PIRA intelligence in GB, since the decision of Sir Patrick Mayhew, who was now NI Secretary of State, to rule out prosecutions of RUC officers was believed to be directed at protecting MI5 agents within the Republic. In his own book, Stalker claims he was removed from the inquiry as a result of a Government decision since he had 'in short, become an embarrassment'. In 1991 the British Labour Party called for a judicial inquiry into all the circumstances of the killings. At the start of 1994 adjourned inquests into the Armagh killings had still to be completed.

STANBROOK, IVOR

Chairman, Conservative backbench NI Committee, 1990–2. b. 13 January 1924. Barrister. MP for Orpington, 1970–92. In August 1991 he said internment without trial in NI would be 'highly undesirable'. A strong critic of the AIA, he retired from Commons at 1992 general election.

STANDING ADVISORY COMMISSION ON HUMAN RIGHTS

An official body set up under the Constitution Act of 1973 to monitor the effectiveness of laws against discrimination on the grounds of religion or politics. The Commission has taken a highly independent line. In May 1979 it recommended to the Secretary of State the dropping of the power to intern without trial. Soon after it was established, it urged that the laws on divorce and homosexuality should be brought into line with those in GB. The divorce reform took effect in 1980 but the homosexuality laws were only changed in 1982 after a ruling by the European Court of Human Rights. In 1981 the Commission was strongly critical of the change in electoral law passed in the wake of the election of hunger-striker Bobby Sands as an MP, which prevented a convicted prisoner being nominated. The Commission said it was an infringement of the citizen's right to choose. In the wake of the AIA it supported the case for three-judge courts to deal with terrorist-type offences. In 1988 it also urged the ending of PTA exclusion orders banning UK citizens from GB or NI, and an easing of port-control procedures. It called for review of the law on the use of reasonable force by the security forces, which it said was 'vague and unsatisfactory'. It suggested 'clear and comprehensive' measures on fair employment, and questioned whether the new police complaints procedure was sufficiently impartial. In January 1989 the Commission accused the Government of failing to consult more widely before introducing anti-terrorist measures. It considered that the anti-violence declaration for councillors would be counter-productive; that a new broadcasting restriction affecting supporters of violence was too wide; and described as disappointing the Government's decision to derogate from the European Convention on Human Rights to maintain the seven-day detention power. It also protested that ending of the 'right to silence' had been rushed. In the 1990s the Commission has tackled a variety of issues, including fair employment, a Bill of Rights, and the varied problems of disability, on which a three-year project was launched in 1992. It also had the satisfaction of seeing the Government explore its proposal of race relations laws tailored to NI needs, and including reference to the 'travelling people'. In 1993 a Bill of Rights was one of its main priorities, although it first pressed the idea in its 1980–1 report. It suggested to the Brooke–Mayhew Talks that such a local measure should incorporate the European Convention on Human Rights. The Commission said: 'The proposal would ensure a framework for the effective, inexpensive and expeditious enforcement of minimum standards of human rights and would not be disruptive of the present legal system.'

The Commission has also called for enlargement of its powers to include enforcement and promotion of human rights issues in line with those of the FEC and EOC. In June 1993 it was highly critical of Order-in-Council legislation at Westminster. Charles Hill QC was appointed chairman in 1992 in succession to Sir Oliver Napier. Joan Harbinson is deputy chair and Denis Carson secretary.

STANLEY, SIR JOHN PAUL

NI Minister of State and deputy Secretary of State, 15 June 1987–26 July 1988. Conservative MP for Tonbridge and Malling, 1983–. b. 19 January 1942. Parliamentary Private Secretary to Margaret Thatcher, 1976–9; Housing Minister, 1979–83; Minister for Armed Forces, 1983–7. His Defence Ministry job had given him some familiarity with local security problems, and with his close contacts with the PM, his move to Stormont was variously interpreted as heralding a tougher security policy, as a gesture to Unionists still furious at the AIA, and as providing an 'eyes and ears' for Thatcher in the Stormont scene. In the event, he stayed only thirteen months. In the July 1988 reshuffle he resigned for 'personal reasons' and returned to the back benches. Secretary of State Tom King praised his work and the PM awarded him a knighthood. At Stormont he inherited his predecessor's portfolios – law and order and finance – but not Nicholas Scott's flair for public relations.

STEPHEN, SIR NINIAN

Independent chairman in 1992 of the North–South strand of the Brooke–Mayhew Talks on the political future of NI. b. 15 June 1923. LLB (Melbourne). Barrister and solicitor. Australian High Court judge, 1972–82. Governor-General of Australia, 1982–9. Sir Ninian emerged as acceptable to both the British and Irish Governments and the four NI constitutional parties after several prominent personalities, including Lord Carrington, former British Cabinet Minister and international mediator in the former Yugoslavia, failed to secure all-round endorsement. Sir Ninian was involved in sessions at Stormont and in London and Dublin over a period of six months. When the talks ended without agreement in November 1992, Sir Ninian said he was prepared to act in a similar role in future.

STEVENS INQUIRY

The inquiry headed by Cambridgeshire deputy Chief Constable John Stevens into the circumstances in which security forces files, including photographs, of Republican terrorist suspects came to be in the possession of loyalist paramilitaries. Complaints about the practice were widespread during 1989, when evidence accumulated that Catholic victims of loyalist gunmen were being increasingly selected on the basis of the files. There were rumours that the investigation received less than full co-operation from some elements of the security forces, but Stevens denied suggestions that he had conducted a 'lame duck' inquiry. In the event, the RUC was cleared of any complicity in the leaks, but charges were brought against ten UDR members in 1990, and prominent UDA man Tommy Lyttle was sentenced in 1991 to seven years' imprisonment for possession of documents likely to be of use to terrorists. The inquiry had a considerable spin-off in police activity against the UDA, which was held to have a 'central role' in the handling of Loyalist paramilitary intelligence, and which was banned in August 1992. It also uncovered Brian Nelson, army spy within the UDA, who in 1992 was sentenced to ten years' imprisonment for conspiracy to murder five Catholics – a case that provoked intense controversy about the control of informers. The inquiry cost £500,000. In August 1993, at the request of Alasdair Fraser, DPP for NI, and the Chief Constable, Sir Hugh Annesley, Stevens reopened his inquiry into new information revealed by the Nelson trial. The new files were sent to the DPP in February 1994.

STEWART, SIR IAN

Minister of State and deputy to Secretary of State, NI, July 1988–July 1989.

Conservative MP for Hitchin, October 1974–83; Hertfordshire N., 1983–92. b. 10 August 1935. MA, D. Litt. (Cantab.). Merchant banker before entering Government in January 1983 as Under-Secretary at Defence (Procurement); Economic Secretary to Treasury, November 1983. Promoted Minister of State at Treasury, 1984. Became Minister for Armed Forces, 15 June 1987, in succession to John Stanley and again succeeded him in the NIO. Soon after his arrival at Stormont he annoyed the Irish Government by revealing an agreement on over-flying of the border for bomb disposal. Retired from Commons, 1992.

'STICKIES' *see* Official Irish Republican Army

STORMONT
The seat of Government in NI, on a commanding site about eight kilometres from Belfast city centre. Comprises Parliament Buildings, Stormont Castle (Secretary of State's office), and Stormont House (originally residence of Speaker of NI Commons, but has provided accommodation for British Ministers under direct rule). Parliament Buildings were designed by Sir Arnold Thornley in Greek classical style, and with exterior faced in Portland stone above a plinth of unpolished granite from the Mountains of Mourne. The building is 110 metres long, 49 metres wide, and rises to 28 metres.

STOTT, ROGER
British Labour spokesman on NI, 1989–. Lab. MP for Westhoughton, 1973–83, Wigan 1983–. b. 7 August 1943. PPS to James Callaghan as opposition leader and PM, 1976–9. Previously spokesman on trade and industry, and transport. He expressed annoyance at the NEC decision, early in September 1993, to investigate further the support for Labour organising in NI, despite Labour policy and the publication of 'Oranges and Lemons'.

STOWE, SIR KENNETH RONALD
Permanent Secretary, NIO, October 1979–81. b. 17 July 1927. MA (Oxon.). Principal private secretary to the Prime Minister, 1973–9. During his earlier civil service career, he was seconded to the UN Secretariat in 1958.

STRABANE
The Co. Tyrone border town that usually tops the NI jobless table and is one of the major unemployment black spots of the EC. It began the 1990s with close to 30 per cent unemployment and has sometimes recorded 80 per cent male unemployment. Reflecting the hope that it would benefit from the Single European Market in 1993, a commission was established in December 1991, representing the town and its cross-border neighbour, Lifford, to encourage joint economic regeneration; it got a £200,000 grant from IFI in 1992. In the late 1960s and early 1970s several civil rights rallies were held in the town, some of them attended by British Labour MPs. The town has suffered heavily from PIRA violence, and INLA has also carried out bombings. There have been suggestions that both organisations have relied on caches of arms and explosives in Donegal. In February 1985 three PIRA members were shot dead, apparently by the SAS, close to the town. The shooting dead of Unionist Senator Jack Barnhill by OIRA there in 1971 was one of the earliest political assassinations. In the summer of 1992 PIRA warned eight local men to leave the town because of 'anti-social activities'. The action was condemned by priests at local Masses. In the council chamber, the election of Ivan Barr (PSF) as council chairman in 1988 led to lively exchanges. A 1989 Act making the council franchise uniform with that for Parliament, enabling non-NI-born Irish citizens to vote in NI council elections, had more effect in Strabane than elsewhere – the local register increased by almost 5 per cent. The council elections in 1989 saw a solitary Alliance councillor hold the balance betwen Unionists and Nationalists on the council. Visiting Strabane in April 1993 to open a new RUC station, PM John Major strongly urged the restart of political talks.

STRONGE, JAMES
UUP MP for Mid-Armagh in Stormont

Parliament, 1969–72. b. 1933. Shot dead along with his father, Sir Norman Stronge, aged eighty-six, ex-Speaker of the Stormont Commons, by PIRA in January 1981. They were killed at their home, Tynan Abbey, close to the border, and the house was destroyed by explosives which set it on fire. The PIRA admission described them as 'symbols of hated unionism' and said the killings were a reprisal for loyalist assassinations of Nationalist people. In the 1969 general election, James Stronge succeeded his father in the seat which Sir Norman had held for thirty-one years, and where he had been opposed only once (1965). Stronge was firmly against the Sunningdale Agreement, which he described as 'a great act of political appeasement'.

SUNNINGDALE CONFERENCE
The conference between the British and Irish Governments and the three parties involved in the NI Executive held at the Sunningdale (Berkshire) Civil Service College, 6–9 December 1973. Agreement to set up the power-sharing Executive made up of the Unionists led by Brian Faulkner, the SDLP and the Alliance Party, and the distribution of offices had been reached at talks at Stormont on 21 November 1973. The Sunningdale Conference was intended to establish the 'Irish dimension' and the political framework in which the new government would operate. But the proposed formal conference to sign the declaration on the status of NI was never held and in May 1974 the Executive collapsed in face of the UWC loyalist strike. Main points of the Sunningdale Agreement were:

1   The Government of the Republic and the SDLP upheld their aspiration for a united Ireland, but only by consent. The Unionist and Alliance parties voiced the desire of the majority in NI to remain part of the UK.
2   The Irish Government fully accepted and solemnly declared that there could be no change in the status of NI until a majority of the people of NI desired a change in that status.

3   The British Government solemnly declared that it was, and it would remain, its policy to support the wishes of the majority of the people of NI. The present status of NI was that it is part of the UK. If in the future the majority of the people of NI should indicate a wish to become part of a united Ireland, the British Government would support that wish.
4   Declarations to this effect by both Governments would be registered at the UN.
5   A Council of Ireland would be set up, limited to representatives from both parts of Ireland, but with 'appropriate safeguards' for the British Government's financial and other interests. The Council of Ministers, which must make decisions by unanimous vote, would have seven Ministers from either side, and there would also be a Consultative Assembly with an advisory role. The Assembly would have sixty members – thirty from the Dáil and thirty from the NI Assembly. They would be elected by the members of each Parliament on PR.
6   The Council of Ireland was to have a wide range of functions, including the study of the impact of EC membership, development of resources, co-operative ventures in trade and industry, electricity generation, tourism, roads and transport, public health advisory services, sport, culture and the arts.
7   It was agreed that persons committing crimes of violence, however motivated, in any part of Ireland should be brought to trial, irrespective of the part of Ireland in which they were located. The conference discussed various approaches, including extradition, the creation of a common law enforcement area in which an all-Ireland court would have jurisdiction, and the extension of the jurisdiction of domestic courts so as to enable them to try offences committed outside the jurisdiction. Because of the legal complexity of these problems, it was agreed that the British and Irish Governments should set up a Joint Law Commission to examine the various proposals. (In the event, this was the only point in the Sunningdale Agreement which was jointly implemented. The Joint Law Commission's report led to

reciprocal legislation, which permits a person accused of a terrorist offence to be brought to trial on whichever side of the border he is arrested.)

8   In the field of human rights the Council of Ireland would consider what further legislation was needed.

9   On law and order and policing, it was accepted that the two parts of Ireland were to a considerable extent interdependent, and that the problems of political violence and identification with the police service could not be solved without taking account of that fact.

10   Accordingly, the British Government stated that, as soon as the security problems were resolved and the new institutions were seen to be working effectively, it would wish to discuss the devolution of responsibility for normal policing, and how this might be achieved, with the NI Executive and the police. The Irish Government agreed to set up a police authority (it did not do so) and together with the NI police authority would consult with the Council of Ministers on appointments. The Secretary of State undertook to set up an all-party Assembly committee to examine how best to introduce effective policing.

11   The conference took note of the reaffirmation by the British Government of its intention to bring detention without trial to an end as soon as the security situation permitted.

The PM, Edward Heath, presided at the conference, travelling back and forth by helicopter to Chequers, his country home. The Council of Ireland and policing were the crunch issues, and there is much evidence that Brian Faulkner's team was divided on the Council, and that strong pressure was brought to bear by Heath to get quick agreement. The NI Secretary of State, Francis Pym, also attended, having only recently taken over at Stormont. The Irish team was headed by Taoiseach Liam Cosgrave, the SDLP delegates were led by Gerry Fitt and the Alliance Party members by Oliver Napier. The loyalists opposed to the Sunningdale exercise – that is, the Unionists led by Harry West, the Rev. Ian Paisley and William Craig – were not

invited to the talks. After Paisley and Craig protested at this, they were invited to one session, but rejected this as inadequate. When the communiqué appeared they sharply attacked it, and in early January 1974, Faulkner lost his battle to 'sell' Sunningdale to the Unionist Council and the power-sharing Executive lasted only five months (January–May 1974).

SUPERGRASS SYSTEM
Betwen 1981 and 1986 the supergrass system proved to be one of the most controversial features of the administration of justice in NI. The British Government and the RUC strongly defended the use of accomplice evidence as being well-established in English law. RUC Chief Constable Sir John Hermon saw the use of 'converted terrorists' as a fully justified means of bringing paramilitary gunmen and bombers to book. But the charging of large numbers of defendants on the word of a supergrass emerging from the ranks of a terrorist group was a practice with little support in the Nationalist community, and it was also widely attacked by Irish Governments and British Labour politicians. It also attracted considerable criticism among lawyers, particularly when the prosecution used the novel device of a Bill of Indictment, which avoided witnesses having to give evidence at a preliminary hearing as well as at the trial. Critics accused the RUC of using blackmail, intimidation and the offers of large sums of money to produce informers willing to speak in court against alleged fellow terrorists. Some supergrasses were given immunity from prosecution, police protection, and the means to start a new life outside NI. The informers came from PIRA (including Christopher Black and Raymond Gilmour), INLA (Harry Kirkpatrick and Jackie Grimley, among others), and the UVF (William 'Budgie' Allen and Joseph Bennett were the best-known). In the period 1981 to 1983 evidence from nearly thirty supergrasses led to charges against some three hundred people, but thirteen of these retracted their evidence before the trials began. In his report on

emergency legislation in 1984 Sir George Baker agreed with the use of supergrasses, but recommended that there should be no more than twenty defendants in any trial and that fewer charges should be brought. In the event, the proportion of convictions dropped, and many appeals were successful. In 1986, when the Court of Appeal quashed the convictions of eighteen men jailed on the word of PIRA supergrass Christopher Black, Labour spokesman Peter Archer said it was the 'last nail in the coffin' of a discredited system. Irish Ministers claimed that it had been ended as a result of the AIA – something which GB denied. The RUC consoled itself with the thought that evidence presented in the various trials had cast a revealing light on the *modus operandi* of paramilitaries. A high proportion of those cleared in supergrass cases have been targeted by paramilitaries. Up to January 1993, four of those involved in the Bennett case had been assassinated, and others had been injured.

T

TARA

A secret loyalist organisation which began as an anti-Catholic, anti-Communist pressure group in the mid-1960s, but which took on a paramilitary character with the outbreak of violence in 1969. It described itself as 'the hard core of Protestant resistance', and in a statement issued in August 1971 it urged loyalists to organise themselves into platoons of twenty under the command of someone capable of acting as a sergeant. It said that every effort must be made to arm these platoons with 'whatever weapons are available'. Its membership was drawn mainly from Orange ranks, and it disclaimed any connection with any other political or paramilitary group. It also said that the Catholic Church should be declared illegal, and all its schools closed. In September 1986 the group said the Republic was a haven for PIRA and it threatened attacks on Dublin and towns in the South, and action against those involved in cross-border trade.

TARTAN GANGS

Gangs of Protestant youths who often wore tartan scarves in memory of the three young soldiers of the Royal Highland Fusiliers who were shot dead in Belfast on 10 March 1971. (Both the OIRA and PIRA denied responsibility for the murders.) The tartan gangs were largely based in Protestant estates in the Belfast area. The slogan 'Tartan Rule OK' became common in 1971 and 1972, and they were active during the loyalist strike in 1974, when they were frequently accused of intimidation of shopkeepers and workers who wanted to stay at work.

TAYLOR, JOHN DAVID

UUP MEP for NI, June 1979–89. MP for Strangford 1983–. Castlereagh Council, 1989–. Assembly member for N. Down, 1982–6. Served on the Agriculture Committee. Minister of State, Home Affairs, 1970–2. b. Armagh, 24 December 1937. B.Sc. (QUB). Joined Young Unionist movement at QUB and was youngest Stormont Unionist MP when returned for S. Tyrone in 1965. He was Parliamentary Secretary at Home Affairs, 1969–70. He was one of twelve Unionist MPs who, in February 1969, signed a statement saying that only a change of leadership from Terence O'Neill could unite the party. At Home Affairs he was sometimes critical of the British Government's approach to security and he was boycotted for a period by the SDLP when he was appointed to the Cabinet in August 1970. In 1972 OIRA tried to assassinate him in Armagh city. In a hail of machine-gun bullets his jawbone was shattered and he had to have extensive plastic surgery. As Assembly member for Fermanagh–S. Tyrone, 1973–4, he was a strong opponent of the Sunningdale Agreement. At the meeting of the Ulster Unionist Council in January 1974 he moved the motion criticising the deal. The motion was carried and Brian Faulkner resigned as Unionist Party leader. On several occasions between 1972 and 1974 he mentioned the possibility of negotiated independence for NI, stressing that this was very different from UDI. In April 1974 he said that, apart from integration, this might be the only option open to loyalists. A prominent Orangeman, he told the 12 July demonstration in Belfast in 1974 that a new Home Guard should be set up 'with or without London Government legislation'. He was returned to the Convention in 1975 from N. Down, and after its collapse in 1976, he became UUP spokesman on the EC. In the European election in 1979 he was returned as one of the three MEPs from NI, but he had to wait until the sixth count, when he benefited from the lower preferences of UUP leader Harry West, who had been eliminated. He campaigned on the line that local issues should not be pursued in the European Assembly, and that there must be extensive renegotiation of the EC to help areas like NI. In the European Parliament he joined British Conservatives in the European Democratic Group, and as a member of the Parliament's regional committee urged greater EC aid for NI. He also opposed discussion in the Parliament of constitutional and security issues affecting NI. In 1981 he urged his party to be 'more positive' about devolution, and when the UUP boycotted economic talks with Secretary of State James Prior, he insisted on attending. In January 1982 he took part in 'Operation USA', a joint UUP–DUP mission to the US to present the Unionist viewpoint. When the 1982 Stormont Assembly held its initial sitting, he was described as 'father of the House', since he was the longest-serving member of Stormont institutions actually attending. He was elected to represent the new parliamentary constituency of Strangford in June 1983. His re-election to the European Parliament in 1984 meant that he joined Rev. Ian Paisley and John Hume in having a 'dual mandate' – a position he argued against in 1979. In his opposition to the AIA he was critical of the boycott of councils, and in 1987 he also urged the return of MPs to Westminster to put the Unionist case. He also wanted a bigger anti-AIA effort in mainland constituencies and more support for the newly founded Scottish Unionist Party. In 1987 he broke with the European Democratic Group (which then included British Tory MEPs) because

of the EDG's support for the AIA, and joined the European Right Group. He rejected suggestions that the ERG was 'fascist' in character, and he was elected to the Parliament's Agriculture Committee on the nomination of the ERG. In 1988 he ruled out power-sharing with John Hume in view of the latter's talks with PSF, and confirmed that he would not be standing in the 1989 European election. Whilst he was not in the UUP team at the Brooke–Mayhew Talks, he had a good deal to say about their implications. He ran into Unionist criticism over his suggestion in 1989 that there should be talks with Dublin Ministers during the Irish presidency of the EC and over his remark in early 1990 that 'only Haughey can deliver'. As the talks approached, however, he warned against meeting SDLP and Dublin preconditions on the timing of talks. When the formal exchanges began in 1991, he described the talks as 'flawed' – first, because Unionists had abandoned the position that the internal affairs of NI were strictly reserved to parties within NI, and, second, because as at Sunningdale Unionists were outnumbered by the SDLP, Alliance, London and Dublin. During the break in the talks at the end of 1991, he suggested direct UUP–SDLP meetings. But when the SDLP plan for six commissioners in NI was revealed in May 1992, he said Unionists should not give it 'the light of day'. He interpreted the 1991 census figures as showing Catholics would remain a minority in NI. In September 1993 he condemned the upsurge in killings but his remark that in a perverse way Catholic fears 'may be helpful', for they now could appreciate Protestant fears over twenty years, was condemned by Nationalists as 'dancing on the graves of the dead'. He told a Young Unionist conference on 18 September that the IRA was winning and the SDLP was riding on their backs. He claimed there was a pan-Nationalist front to remove NI from the UK. He regarded the report from the Hume–Adams talks to the Irish Government as evidence of the 'front' and warned RTE that loyalist violence would eventually reach Dublin unless halted quickly. His comments were condemned by Denis Haughey and Austin Currie as 'dangerous and irresponsible'. Early in October he told loyalist paramilitaries to end their murder campaign. In December he repeated the message to all paramilitaries amid the increased tension in the run-up to the Downing Street Declaration. He also warned that in the event of a united Ireland he anticipated an exodus of Protestants. In the short debate in the Commons on the declaration he was reassured by the PM that it in no way weakened the guarantee in the NI Constitution Act, 1973, and that it did not give the Republic any additional say in the affairs of NI. At the end of December he warned that giving PSF the 'clarification' it sought could endanger UUP support for the Government. He was critical of President Clinton's decision to issue a visa to Gerry Adams, which he attributed to political necessity and 'the political scoundrels of Boston'. Party spokesman on agriculture/EC/regional affairs, 1992–.

TEEBANE BOMBING

Eight Protestant workmen who had been working at the Omagh security base died in a PIRA explosion near Teebane crossroads on the Omagh–Cookstown road in Co. Tyrone on 17 January 1992. The 1,500-lb device blasted their van apart and brought to twenty-six the number of people killed by PIRA because of their involvement in security contracts. On the first anniversary of the attack, a granite memorial was unveiled at the scene.

TEMPLE-MORRIS, PETER

Co-chairman of the working party that led to setting up of the British–Irish Parliamentary Body, and first British co-chairman of BIPB, 1990–. b 12 February 1938. MA (Cantab.). Cons. MP for Leominster, 1974–. Vice-chairman of the Cons. backbench NI Committee, 1989–92.

THATCHER, BARONESS

As Margaret Hilda Thatcher, British PM, 1979–90. Leader of Conservative Party, 1975–90. MP for Finchley, 1959–92. b. 13 October 1925. Lady Thatcher has confirmed that her great-great-grandmother on her father's side was Irish. She says she does not have further details, but there have been suggestions that the ancestor to which she refers was Mary Selewin, born in Co. Kerry. As Conservative leader, she seemed initially to be anxious to rebuild the links between her party and the Ulster Unionists, shatttered by the Heath Government's abolition of the Stormont Parliament in 1972. On one occasion she spoke of NI being 'as British as Finchley', and Hugo Young in his biography, *One of Us,* calls her 'the most Orange leader' ever to have been PM. On her third visit to NI as opposition leader, in June 1978, she voiced strong support for the link with Britain. She said it was fashionable to talk of a federal Ireland, but it was a fashion her party did not intend to follow. She also expressed support for the restoration of a top tier of local government – one of the demands of the UUP. Her attitude was criticised by the SDLP and the Liberals. The promise of a regional council or councils was contained in the Conservative manifesto in 1979, but it was conditional on a failure to achieve devolved government. Thatcher acknowledged in her first Commons speech as PM that political progress in NI would not be easy, and she indicated a tough security policy in NI and ruled out any amnesty for convicted terrorists. The UUP MPs, or the majority of them, helped Thatcher bring down the Labour Government but they made it clear during the election that they would maintain their neutral stance. After the killing of eighteen soldiers and the murder of Lord Mountbatten in August 1979, she made a one-day trip to NI to see the security situation for herself. She became the first PM to visit S. Armagh and Crossmaglen during a rapid border tour. Soon afterwards, she met Taoiseach Jack Lynch in London to urge closer cross-border security co-operation. In Anglo-Irish relations, her December 1980 meeting in Dublin with Charles Haughey, the Fianna Fáil Taoiseach, was regarded as a landmark, since it promised a review 'of the totality of relations between the two countries'. It was also the most powerful British Government delegation ever to have visited Dublin, for she was accompanied by Foreign Secretary Lord Carrington, Chancellor of the Exchequer Sir Geoffrey Howe, and NI Secretary of State Humphrey Atkins. Predictably, it drew fierce opposition from Unionists and heartened Nationalists, despite her claim that the summit held no constitutional threat to NI. At a private meeting at Westminster the Rev. Ian Paisley accused her of 'undermining the NI constitutional guarantee', but she denied that she was doing anything of the sort and said she was 'dismayed' by the accusation. She rejected suggestions from Unionists that the setting up in 1981 of the Anglo-Irish Intergovernmental Council was in any sense a 'sell-out', and stressed the importance of friendship with the Republic, as well as security and economic co-operation. She agreed with Taoiseach Dr Garret FitzGerald in November 1981 that the two Governments should pursue the idea of an Advisory Council and parliamentary tier of the Anglo-Irish Intergovernmental Council. She had a deteriorating relationship, however, with Haughey, and was particularly angered by his opposition during the Falklands crisis to anti-Argentina sanctions. And she included Enoch Powell MP in Privy Council briefings on the Falklands, although he had several times alleged that the Foreign Office was intriguing against NI's position. She also kept lines open to UUP leader James Molyneaux (appointed PC, 1983). Her basic unionism was underlined by her declaration in July 1982 that 'no commitment exists for HM Government to consult the Irish Government on matters affecting Northern Ireland'. She said that had always been her Government's position, but in Dublin the Fianna Fáil Government said it was difficult to find any justification for Thatcher's claim. In the H-Block hunger strike she stood out against any major concessions, and was accused by those sympathetic to the protest of being the real obstacle to a settlement. She certainly reflected

Unionist attitudes during the crisis and angered the SDLP, whose leader, John Hume, had a tense meeting with her at the height of the dispute. Her relationship with NI Secretary of State James Prior was uneasy at the time of his appointment in September 1981. He was among the Cabinet 'Wets' in his doubts about Government economic policy, and she insisted on moving him from Employment to the NIO – a move which it had seemed initially he might oppose to the point of resignation. When Prior brought forward his 'rolling devolution' initiative, Whitehall sources suggested that she was distancing herself a little from the plan. The PIRA attack on the Conservative conference in Brighton in October 1984 (see Brighton Hotel Bombing) probably swung her thoughts away from Irish political to mainly security issues. Thus, in November 1984 Garret FitzGerald's initial efforts to sell her the approach of the NIF report clearly failed. She publicly dismissed the main Forum options with the words 'out, out, out', to the delight of Unionists and the dismay of Dublin and the SDLP. But the communiqué issued after that London summit committed London and Dublin to reflect the identities of both communities 'in the structures and process of Northern Ireland'. The patient diplomacy of FitzGerald concentrated on this point and also the Forum's readiness to accept other ideas outside the main options. Pressure for a new departure in British–Irish relations was also evident in the Cabinet Office and Foreign Office, as well as in Europe and in the US. By February Thatcher in Washington was speaking of her 'excellent relations' with FitzGerald and she told Congress that they would 'continue to consult together in the quest for peace'. (The Irish Government's move in pushing through a special Bill to seize £1.7 million held in an Irish bank, allegedly for PIRA, particularly appealed to the PM.) That quest led to the AIA in November 1985, and the Republic's strong consultative role in NI. FitzGerald disclosed in his memoirs that she had been willing to consider a redrawing of the border, but he made it clear that he was not seeking that. She was clearly disappointed by the fierce resistance of Unionists to the agreement, but while repeatedly voicing her own support for the Union, she made no move to appease them. She was also apparently unimpressed by the Republic's anti-terrorist efforts in the wake of the agreement. In particular, she was angered by the Fianna Fáil Government's decision to attach to the new extradition arrangements the proviso that the Irish Attorney-General must have a preview of the evidence supporting each application. Her close relationship with US President Reagan was partly reflected in their common anxiety to defeat terrorism, and both saw PIRA in an international context especially after Libya's role in directly supplying arms to PIRA had been disclosed. There was little surprise that Thatcher went personally to the memorial service for the victims of the Enniskillen bombing in 1987, or that she chose to make her next visit to NI in September 1988, after PIRA had stepped up its assaults, notably against the army. She returned to Brighton for the Conservative conference four years after the PIRA attempt there on her life to tell the party that 'this Government will never surrender to the IRA – never'. She was obviously greatly affected by the PIRA murder of her close friend, Ian Gow MP, in 1990. She recognised that she herself was a 'prime target' of PIRA and she already had had tall gates installed at the entrance to Downing Street as an anti-terrorist precaution, a barrier circumvented by PIRA in its attack on Number Ten in 1991. Within a week of her resignation in November 1990, she paid her last visit as PM to NI. As always, she praised the UDR and the security forces generally. Out of office, she found support in Unionist ranks for her demand for a referendum on European union. But according to an NI social attitudes survey in June 1991, eleven years of the Thatcherite philosophy had made little impact in NI. In her memoirs, *Margaret Thatcher: The Downing Street Years*, published in 1993, she revealed disappointment at the AIA and expressed the need for an alternative approach.

THIRD FORCE

A DUP-sponsored vigilante organisation set up towards the end of 1981. It made an appearance at several rallies addressed by the Rev. Ian Paisley, and it was claimed that its existence had reduced the number of murders of Protestants in border areas. It was organised on a county basis, and a strength of 15,000 to 20,000 was mentioned. It occasionally set up road checks, but around March 1982 adopted a lower profile, although it was claimed that it was still active in offering protection to loyalists living in isolated areas. The launching of the organisation was accompanied by warnings from the authorities that private armies would not be tolerated, and sharp criticism from Nationalists.

THOMPSON, (FRANCIS HENRY) ESMOND

UUP Convention member for Mid-Ulster, 1975-6. b. Maghera, Co. Derry, 1929. UUP executive, 1971-. Ex-Royal Navy, ex-UDR.

THOMPSON, ROY

DUP Assembly member for S. Antrim, 1982-6. Served on committees on Agriculture, Economic Development, and Security. Dairy farmer. b. 1946. Founder member, DUP, and serves on party executive. Antrim Council, 1981-. In 1987 he was potential candidate in S. Antrim when the DUP decided not to oppose the sitting UUP member. He resigned from the DUP in August 1992, while deputy mayor of Antrim, but stressed he was not criticising party leadership. Re-elected in May 1993 as an Ind. Unionist, but later joined UUP.

THOMPSON, WILLIAM JOHN

UUP Assembly member for Mid-Ulster, 1982-6. Chairman, Finance and Personnel Committee; served on committees on Education, Health and Social Services, and Security. Also represented the constituency in 1973-4 Assembly and 1975-6 Convention. b. 1939. Returned in 1973 as anti-White Paper Unionist. Member of UUP committee that drew up party's Convention manifesto. Resigned in

January 1983 from UUP's Assembly party as a protest against its refusal to join Assembly committees, but remained party member. Omagh District Council, 1981–93. Secretary, Mid- and W. Tyrone Unionist Association, 1972–. Methodist lay preacher.

TIGER BAY

A militant Protestant area adjoining North Queen Street in N. Belfast which has tended to erupt violently when Unionist interests are thought to be threatened.

TIME TO GO

A group launched in July 1988 to promote debate on the withdrawal of troops from NI. Diverse supporters included historian A.J.P. Taylor, the then *Mirror* group political editor Joe Haines (he was Press Secretary to Harold Wilson in Downing Street), actress Julie Christie, and Labour MP Clare Short, whose parents came from Crossmaglen, Co. Armagh.

TRIMBLE, (WILLIAM) DAVID

UUP MP for Upper Bann, 1990–. VUPP Convention member for S. Belfast, 1975–6. b. 15 October 1944. LLB (QUB). Barrister. Lecturer in Law Faculty, QUB, 1968–77, Senior Lecturer, 1977–90, and was assistant dean of the faculty when returned to Convention, where he had key role in drafting UUUC proposals. When the Vanguard Party split over William Craig's plan for voluntary coalition, including the SDLP, he backed Craig and became deputy leader of VUPP. When VUPP abandoned its political role in 1978, he joined UUP and continued to press case for devolved government. He was associated for a time with Ulster Clubs movement before being elected to UUP executive, of which he became honorary secretary. He tried unsuccessfully for his party's nomination in 1989 European election, but won Upper Bann by-election in 1990 to succeed late Harold McCusker. This was the first NI election contested by the Conservatives, whose candidate lost her deposit. In November 1991 he suggested that local Conservatives might be part of an NIO conspiracy to weaken Unionists. During the Gulf War he compared the Republic's claim to NI to Saddam Hussein's claim to Kuwait. In November 1992 he said that in the Brooke–Mayhew Talks, in which he took part, the furthest Dublin Ministers would go was to say that if there was a fair and honourable agreement, and it had constitutional implications for the Republic, then it 'could' support changes. Efforts to get them to change that 'could' to 'would' had failed. At the end of August 1993 he said the Hume–Adams talks had the 'understanding, if not the blessing, of the Irish Government'. He told Young Unionists in his constituency that Hume's strategy was 'misconceived and bound to fail'. He argued that the unpublished Hume–Adams document was the basis on which Taoiseach Reynolds was negotiating with PM Major. This he graphically expressed in *The Walden Interview* on 12 December, when he accused Reynolds of negotiating on behalf of PIRA and offering Unionists 'surrender by stages'. He maintained his focus on the Irish premier in January 1994, criticising him for parroting PSF language in speeches and for ending the broadcasting ban before the Downing Street Declaration had been accepted. He also argued for a change of strategy 'from the carrot to the stick'; the Government had followed Hume–Adams – 'it was wrong and bad advice' to be 'publicly negotiating with terrorists'. Party spokesman on legal affairs/home office, 1992–.

TROOPS OUT MOVEMENT

A group that operates from a London office and campaigns for the immediate withdrawal of British troops from NI. It has been active since the end of 1969. It organises conferences on the issue, and occasionally sends deputations to NI, which include leading leftist figures in trade unions and trade councils. It has had the support of a small number of Labour MPs, and has been particularly critical of strong anti-terrorist measures. In 1988, when it claimed to be drawing increased support in GB, it condemned the move to ban TV and radio interviews with PSF.

TURNLY, JOHN

IIP councillor, who was shot dead by the
UFF in June 1980. He had been SDLP
Convention member for N. Antrim,
1975-6, and joined the newly established
IIP in 1977, after a policy disagreement
with SDLP. b. Ballycastle, Co. Antrim,
1935. A company director who had spent
some years in Japan, and a Protestant, he
was sitting in his car with his Japanese
wife and their two children when he was
killed. One of the three men convicted
of the murder claimed that he had been
working for the SAS. Larne Council,
1973-80. Unsuccessfully contested N.
Antrim in 1974 Assembly by-election and
1979 Westminster election.

TUZO, GENERAL SIR HARRY CRAUFURD

Army GOC, NI, 1971-3. b. 1917. Oxford-
educated, with a flair for diplomacy, he
had a larger political role than any other
GOC during the period of violence. He
arrived in February 1971, and
immediately became involved in the
arguments between Stormont and
Whitehall that preceded the resignation
of Major Chichester-Clark as PM. In a
BBC TV interview in June 1971, he said
he did not think a permanent solution
could be achieved by military means. He
thought that about half the Catholic
population in NI had Republican
aspirations, and of these 25 per cent were
prepared to lend passive or active support
to the IRA or similar organisations. He
was reputed to have agreed to internment
without trial only with great reluctance.
He once described it as 'distasteful'. But
he said the alternatives were to kill IRA
men or to bring them before courts
where juries could be fixed or witnesses
intimidated. He had to cope with the
upsurge of violence after the introduction
of internment, and following direct rule.
With the escalating PIRA bombing
campaign, he developed undercover army
activity against the paramilitaries. These
included the Military Reconnaissance
Force, which went to the length of
setting up a fake laundry service, which
was eventually uncovered by the PIRA.
He was also responsible for the direction
of 'Operation Motorman', mounted in

the summer of 1972 for the reoccupation
of no-go areas.

TWOMEY, SEAMUS

Became a leading figure in PIRA in 1971,
when he succeeded Joe Cahill as head of
the organisation in Belfast. b. Belfast,
1919; d. 1989. Believed to have joined
the IRA originally in the 1940s, but was
not active in the 1956 campaign. In
August 1969 he rejoined the IRA and was
one of the IRA leaders active during
loyalist attacks in the Falls Road area. At
that time he was manager of a Falls Road
bookmaker's. In 1972, as brigade
commander in Belfast, he negotiated a
brief truce with the British army. Soon
afterwards, he was flown to London for
the secret talks with Secretary of State
William Whitelaw. Became chief of staff
of PIRA in March 1973, but after three
months as leader he was arrested in the
Republic and sentenced to three years'
imprisonment for PIRA membership. But
in October 1973 he made a dramatic
helicopter escape from Dublin's
Mountjoy Prison, together with two
other leading Republicans, Kevin Mallon
and Joe O'Hagan. In 1974 he acted again
as chief of staff when Dáithí Ó Conaill
was arrested, and he attended the
Feakle meeting with Protestant
Churchmen in December 1974. During
the ceasefire in 1975, at an Easter
ceremony at Milltown cemetery in
Belfast, he warned that the PIRA would go
back to war if its demands were not met
in full. In an interview published in the
autumn of 1977 Twomey described
himself as chief of staff. In December
1977 he was recaptured by the Gardaí in
Dublin. He was released in January 1982,
and was active in the PSF election
campaign in the Republic in February
1982. In 1988 some Conservative MPs
protested that the US authorities were
continuing to permit Twomey to address
NORAID meetings.

TYRIE, ANDREW (ANDY)

Commander of the UDA, 1973-88. b.
Belfast, 1940. He was in the UVF before
becoming a UDA officer on the Shankill
Road in Belfast, and then head of the
paramilitary organisation. He was

prominently associated with the loyalist strike in 1974, and the unsuccessful loyalist stoppage in 1977. A tough man of few words, he was credited initially with taking action to 'clean up' the organisation and restrain its violent fringes, and he said on several occasions that the UDA must not get into confrontation with with the Catholic community. In July 1974 he led a UDA deputation in talks with the SDLP – a discussion which showed agreement only on opposition to internment. In 1976 he took the UDA out of the ULCCC after claiming that some ULCCC members had been talking to Republicans about independence. But in 1979 the UDA, under his leadership, sponsored the New Ulster Political Research Group, which produced a plan for negotiated independence for NI, and he visited the US with UDA deputation for talks with politicians to promote the policy. Independence was also a central point of policy for the political party, the ULDP, which the UDA launched in 1981. All the indications were that Tyrie had faced a serious problem in reconciling conflicting views within the UDA on what its role should be. In early 1981 he said the UDA might have to cross the border to 'terrorise terrorists', a threat that precipitated fresh demands for the proscription of the organisation. In 1984 terrorist charges against him were dropped, and in 1986 a charge of possessing documents likely to be of use to terrorists was dismissed. Coincidentally, there was growing emphasis on military action within the organisation which was reflected in increased violent activity by the UFF. The UDA, while giving muscle to the anti-AIA protest, was critical of its direction and leadership and put forward a new 'Common Sense' plan for devolved power-sharing. But while this political initiative was attracting praise in unexpected quarters, there was also publicity on protection rackets associated with the UDA. The leadership of the UDA had indeed become a hot seat, and Tyrie faced particular hostility from sections of the organisation in late 1987 and early 1988, and was finally ousted in March 1988 shortly after a mystery booby-trap bomb had been found attached to his car. Earlier, he had rejected suggestions that the killing by PIRA in December 1987 of his deputy, John McMichael, had any links with the investigation of racketeering. In 1984 he was co-author of a play, *This is It!*, with the theme of an Ulster identity. (*See also* Ulster Defence Association.)

U

ULSTER

A term frequently applied to NI. It is strictly the name of one of the four ancient provinces in Ireland. Historically nine counties, it varied in size and when NI was formed, three counties – Cavan, Monaghan and Donegal – were separated from the other six and placed in what is now the Republic of Ireland.

ULSTER ARMY COUNCIL

A grouping of loyalist paramilitary organisations which had a vital role in building support for the 1974 loyalist strike. The body was formed in December 1973 and included the UDA, UVF, Ulster Special Constabulary Association, Loyalist Defence Volunteers, Orange Volunteers, and Red Hand Commando. It said it would work closely with the newly formed UUUC. When the UUUC politicians held a conference in Portrush, Co. Antrim, in April 1974, it joined the UWC in urging the politicians to call for an end to the power-sharing Executive, a return to direct rule without any power of veto for the Secretary of State, new elections by PR in smaller constituencies, and an end even to discussion of a Council of Ireland. The UAC warned on the eve of the 1974 loyalist strike that 'if Westminster is not prepared to restore democracy, that is, the will of the people made clear in an election, then the only way it can be restored is by a *coup d'état*'. After the strike, it was replaced by the Ulster Loyalist Central Co-ordinating Committee in 1974.

ULSTER CITIZEN ARMY

The name cropped up several times in 1974, apparently being the title of a group of dissidents from the UDA and UVF. In February 1974 it put out a statement saying that it would assassinate business executives and army officers if the Government succeeded in throwing NI into 'vicious sectarian warfare'. Then in October 1974 it was issuing handbills which alleged that 'power-crazed animals have taken over control of the loyalist paramilitary organisations and have embarked on a programme of wanton slaughter, intimidation, robbery and extortion'. It said that during the previous month a dozen people had been butchered by psychopaths, acting on the orders of loyalist leaders. It promised to supply the addresses of those involved to the security forces. The UCA was also believed to have operated under the name 'The Covenanters'.

ULSTER CLUBS

The organisation was formed in the autumn of 1985 to oppose the rerouting of traditional loyalist parades. After November 1985, it pledged to destroy the AIA. It regarded itself as an umbrella organisation to which all Unionists could belong but denied that it was a paramilitary body. By January 1986 it claimed to have 8,000 members in 48 branches. It had four main aims: to assert the right to self-determination of the Northern Irish people; to maintain the Union so long as it was in NI's interest; to combat the encroachment of Irish nationalism; and to unify the talents, abilities and resources of Unionists. It professed to stick by the constitutional process but was sceptical about its value and the attitude was to 'hope for the best but to prepare for the worse'. The leader of the Ulster Clubs, Alan Wright, said that he had no faith in the political system after Nationalists had got every concession going for sixteen years through violence. After the January 1986 by-elections, Ulster Clubs said it was instigating a campaign of withdrawal of consent and civil disobedience and awaited a call to action by Unionist political leaders. Alan Wright had lost his

father, a policeman, killed by INLA. In 1988 a number of its members were fined for breaches of the new public order legislation. In October 1988 Alan Wright was jailed for failure to pay fines for car tax offences as a protest at the AIA and non-payment of fines for taking part in parades illegal under the public order laws. In October 1988 the membership of Ulster Clubs was said to be about 12,000. Wright stood down as leader in February 1989, because he was considering entering Bible college. The Ulster Clubs now supports total integration of NI within the UK. Philip Black, general secretary since 1985, said a declaration of intent to pursue integration as a common aim of all Unionists would be a blow to the PIRA and make the constitutional position 'clear and unambiguous'.

ULSTER CONSTITUTION DEFENCE COMMITTEE

Set up in 1966 under the chairmanship of Rev. Ian Paisley, and active initially in mounting counter-demonstrations to Republican Easter parades and later to coincide with civil rights marches. Closely linked with UPV. In June 1966 Paisley said in a speech in Holywood, Co. Down, that the UCDC had absolutely no connection with the UVF, which had just been proscribed. The UCDC was prominent in Paisley's 'O'Neill must go' campaign.

ULSTER DEFENCE ASSOCIATION/ ULSTER FREEDOM FIGHTERS

The UDA has remained throughout the Troubles the largest Protestant paramilitary organisation, and it was legal until 10 August 1992, when NI Secretary of State Sir Patrick Mayhew proscribed it. A component part, the Ulster Freedom Fighters, often regarded simply as a cover name for murder operations and first mentioned in 1973, was already illegal. The UDA was launched in September 1971 as the umbrella body for loyalist vigilante groups, many of which called themselves 'defence associations'. In the growing violence, they sprang up in Protestant areas of Belfast and in estates in adjoining areas including Lisburn, Newtownabbey and Dundonald. The new body adopted the motto 'Law before violence', and soon became a formidable force on the ground in loyalist districts, in many of which it was considered a replacement for the disbanded B Specials. It took on a distinctly working-class image, excluding MPs and clergymen from membership. It was organised on military lines and at its peak in 1972 it probably had about 40,000 members. By 1978 this had dropped to between 10,000 and 12,000 – a reduction brought about, according to its spokesmen, not by lack of support, but because of a deliberate policy of limiting membership to a readily controllable size. In the 1980s that total dropped further, although the organisation mounted occasional recruiting campaigns. In 1986 one of its recruiting posters showed a member holding an automatic weapon. Indeed, its varied history has been marked by sectarian violence, by strong-arm tactics in support of loyalist protests, by forays into political thinking via the NUPRG and ULDP and even some acceptance of Gaelic culture as an element in the Ulster identity. This confused image dates from its earliest days. Its first leader, Charles Harding Smith, was acquitted, together with five other men, of being concerned in dealing in £350,000 worth of arms, including a large number of rifles, in early 1972. Smith claimed that meetings set up in London at the time, and which came to the attention of the Special Branch, were really intended to trap PIRA arms dealers. He also said that he had assisted the security forces in NI, and at the trial a letter was read from the Assistant Chief Constable of the RUC, stating that on many occasions Smith had been a pacifier in quarrels between Protestants and Catholics in Belfast. According to police evidence, an official document listing names and ranks of junior PIRA officers, and mentioning Seamus Twomey, Belfast commander of the PIRA, had been found at Smith's Belfast home. In the anti-direct-rule protests of 1972 the UDA was closely involved with the Vanguard movement and LAW, and intermittently with the more violent UVF. Its largest demonstrations took the form of massive parades in Belfast in the summer of 1972.

Thousands of UDA men, sometimes masked and wearing combat jackets with military-style caps or bush hats, marched through the city centre. In July and August 1972 local units set up their own no-go areas in some loyalist districts of Belfast as a protest against the existence of no-go areas in the Bogside and Creggan areas of Derry. The erection of barricades often entailed the use of concrete mixers, cement blocks and metal spikes. One dispute, on 3 July 1972, over a plan for loyalist barricades between the Springfield (Catholic) and Shankill (Protestant) areas led to about 8,000 uniformed UDA men, many of them carrying iron bars, confronting some 250 troops for an hour and a half while anxious negotiations went on between UDA chiefs and senior officials and army officers. The situation, the ugliest involving Protestants and the security forces since the Shankill Road riots of 1969, was regarded by the UDA as an impressive demonstration of the speed with which it could rally a large force of its supporters. But this incident, and the massive parades, were regarded by Catholic interests as evidence that the security forces were adopting too soft a line towards loyalist militants. Privately, however, the army was talking toughly to the UDA. In the no-go areas row the UDA held its hand over the 12 July period of 1972 and then its thirteen-man council had talks with Secretary of State William Whitelaw. They got the impression that Government action was pending against the Derry barricades, and in the event the Bogside and Creggan were opened up in 'Operation Motorman' at the end of July. But in the autumn of 1972, when the UDA mounted street protests against the Government's security policy, it was involved in disputes with the army about the circumstances in which some Protestants had been killed. In mid-October, after a meeting between UDA leaders and the army, there was a statement that both sides would try to take the heat out of the situation, and an assurance that all complaints against the army would be investigated by the RUC. In September 1973 Tommy Herron, who had been the UDA's deputy leader until he unsuccessfully fought the Assembly election in E. Belfast, was murdered in mysterious circumstances. His body was found near Lisburn; he had been shot in the head. There were many rumours that he had been killed by loyalist extremists but this was rejected by the UDA, who said it was satisfied that no Protestant organisation had been involved. The biggest operation of the UDA was in the loyalist strike of May 1974, which led to the break-up of the power-sharing administration. The UDA was first involved in the Ulster Army Council, a small grouping of Protestant paramilitaries, and then in the larger Ulster Workers' Council, which organised the strike effort. The UDA commander, Andy Tyrie, was on the UWC Co-ordinating Committee, and the organisation provided much of the muscle in mounting road blocks. It was widely accused of intimidation of people who wanted to stay at work. In June, after the fall of the Executive, the UDA said that while it ruled out talks with PIRA, it was prepared to meet elected representatives, including PSF. In the same month the UDA issued a statement 'on behalf of the UFF', saying that it wanted an end to violence. It now became clear that the UFF was indeed the violent arm of the UDA. When it first became active in mid-1973, it was thought to be a breakaway group from the UDA. PIRA made contradictory allegations about its make-up, saying in January 1974 that it was a British army killer squad, and then six months later that it was composed of 'criminals from the Catholic and Protestant communities'. From 1974 on there were numerous UFF telephone claims of murders of Catholics (often alleging that their victims had PIRA associations), and bomb attacks on Catholic churches, schools and public houses. The phone calls were often said to be from 'Captain White' or 'Captain Black'. Among such claims were the murder of Fine Gael Senator Billy Fox in Co. Monaghan in March 1974, and of SDLP Senator Paddy Wilson in Belfast in June 1973. The claim in respect of Senator Fox was not, however, taken seriously in the Republic. The UDA's June 1974 statement, saying that the UFF had

seen enough of violence, added that it would be happy if, after the Assembly elections, it was discovered that all shades of opinion could work together. But the UFF reserved the 'right' to retaliate if attacks were made on loyalist areas. In July 1977 the UFF in Derry claimed to have bombed a Catholic church at Greysteel, Co. Derry, in reprisal, they said, for the burning of Bellaghy Orange Hall. In June 1979 eleven Scottish UDA men were given heavy prison sentences for furthering the aims of the organisation by unlawfully acquiring arms and ammunition. One group of seven were given 164 years between them, and the supreme commander of the UDA in Scotland, James Hamilton, aged forty-four, was sentenced to 15 years – the heaviest sentence. Four others were sentenced to between 7 and 12 years for furthering the aims of the UDA in Paisley and the west of Scotland. The judge, Lord Wylie, spoke of a 'reign of terror' by the UDA commander in Paisley, William Currie, who was sentenced to 12 years' imprisonment. (The Scottish connection was stressed again in February 1981, when a Scottish member claimed on TV that there were 2,000 UDA members in Scotland. He also said there were Scottish stockpiles of arms and 'safe houses' for loyalist fugitives, and that arms and ammunition had been smuggled to NI through Larne.) A clandestine news conference in Belfast in 1979, following the PIRA murder of Lord Mountbatten, was told that the UDA had been reorganised and re-equipped and was now the most powerful loyalist paramilitary organisation. It also claimed to have drawn up a 'death list' of known Republicans in NI, GB and the Republic. Almost immediately afterwards, it claimed the murder of a twenty-seven-year-old married man in N. Belfast. Two men jailed for the murder of IIP councillor John Turnly in Carnlough, Co. Antrim, in June 1980 were said by the prosecution to be members of the UFF. It was active during the H-Block hunger strike, and is believed to have carried out at least five sectarian murders during 1981. In September 1981 it referred to another 'death list', this time related to alleged PIRA and INLA informers. In 1981 INLA shot dead a leading UDA man, Billy McCullough, on the Shankill Road in Belfast, in retaliation, it said, for loyalist murders of Catholics. In the same year it shot and seriously injured UDA councillor Sammy Millar at his home in the Shankill area. In the early 1980s the UDA seemed to be beset by uncertainties, with an internal clash between those who argued for more political action and those who regarded it as essentially a Protestant counter-terror organisation. Although it had backed the patchy UUAC stoppage in 1977, it refused to support the Rev. Ian Paisley's 'Day of Action' and Third Force in 1981, and seemed to ridicule the idea of protest marches. But in April and May 1981 it mounted some local shows of strength, putting some 2,500 men on the Shankill Road in what was termed 'purely defensive mobilisation' and several hundred men on parade in the Fountain area of Derry. In February 1981 Tyrie threatened that UDA men might cross the border to 'terrorise the terrorists'. This statement revived demands from Nationalists for the outlawing of the organisation, but proscription was once more rejected by the NIO. But the security forces kept up pressure on the UDA, and in April 1982 terrorist charges were brought against several leading members, though they were later dropped. The court was told during a preliminary hearing that files on judges, police and IRA suspects had been found during the police raids. In the mid- and late 1980s it was frequently involved in sectarian murders, and the seizures in 1988 of large quantities of weapons and ammunition intended for the UDA raised fears of major confrontations between loyalists and PIRA. In early January 1988 the UDA's Belfast HQ was raided by the RUC, who took away documents. The UDA seemed to be intent on avenging the murder, in December 1987, by PIRA of the UDA's deputy leader, John McMichael, who died when a bomb went off under his car outside his Lisburn home. In October 1988 the UFF claimed the murder of prominent UDA man James Craig, who was shot dead in a bar in E.

Belfast. They accused him of 'treason' and linked his actions to the killing of McMichael. When McMichael died, there were suggestions that he might have been set up for PIRA by people within the UDA who resented his investigation of UDA racketeering, although Andy Tyrie rejected the idea of any such connection. The killing of Craig came shortly after another leading UDA man, Billy Quee, was shot dead in N. Belfast by IPLO. In 1985 charges against both Craig and Quee of extorting money from building contractors had failed. (In 1988 security sources were suggesting that the UDA might be raising as much as £3 million a year from a variety of protection rackets.) But alongside strictly paramilitary activities, the UDA has often sought to project a political dimension, something which its Nationalist critics have tended to regard as a smokescreen for violence. In August 1974, after the UDA had resigned from the UWC and the ULCCC, it had a meeting with SDLP representatives. The SDLP spokesmen were Gerry Fitt, John Hume, Paddy Devlin, Ivan Cooper and Hugh Logue. The UDA was represented by Andy Tyrie, Bill Snoddy, Tommy Lyttle, and Ronnie Reid. But while there was united opposition to internment, there was no agreement about the political future. The UDA said the SDLP had been hypocritical, and insisted that it should drop its united Ireland aspiration. Fitt felt that the meeting had shown an intense power struggle within the UDA. In November 1974 a UDA delegation visited Libya, headed by its political adviser, Glenn Barr, a Vanguard Assembly member. The meeting created controversy, since a PSF deputation was in Libya at the same time. Both sides denied that there had been any negotiations between them, and a Dublin banker who had arranged the UDA visit said it had been concerned with the development of offshore oil and other resources. But in a personal comment Barr admitted that the deputation had been seeking possible economic aid for an independent NI. (See Libyan Connection.) During the Constitutional Convention, Barr's support for Vanguard leader William Craig's idea of a voluntary coalition, including the SDLP, seems to have influenced UDA thinking. Andy Tyrie expressed support for Craig's scheme, and blamed the Rev. Ian Paisley and Harry West for the failure of the Convention, and suggested that they would be responsible for further deaths. It warned in July 1978 that it would 'no longer be the willing tool of any aspiring or ready-made politician'. In February 1979 a deputation visited the US for talks with leading politicians. In March 1979 a plan for an independent NI was proposed by the New Ulster Political Research Group, which the UDA had set up in January 1978, after discussions between Andy Tyrie and Glenn Barr. It claimed that negotiated independence was the only settlement acceptable to both sides of the community. The proposal envisaged that an Assembly would be elected for four years, but Ministers would be appointed – as in the US – and neither they, nor the PM, would sit in the Assembly. The Ministers would be chosen by the elected president, his deputy, and the PM, although they would have to be endorsed by the Assembly, which would deal with legislation. In the May 1981 council elections, one NUPRG candidate out of three was returned in Belfast (Sammy Millar, who had been seriously injured in an assassination attempt). Soon afterwards, and coincidental with the withdrawal of NUPRG chairman Glenn Barr from active politics, the Ulster Loyalist Democratic Party was launched in June 1981 to replace it. Its line seemed to be independence within the Commonwealth and the EC, which its first chairman, John McMichael, suggested would be acceptable to many Catholics. The party seemed to take a good deal of encouragement from the support for independence from the *Sunday Times* and ex-PM James Callaghan. But it found the electoral going hard. It failed in its first bid – a Belfast council by-election in E. Belfast in August 1981, where the candidate received 3.2 per cent of the vote. John McMichael got fewer than 600 votes in the S. Belfast by-election in February 1982. Its two candidates in the 1982 Assembly election

(both in N. Belfast) polled only 1,086 votes (0.2 per cent). The party did not contest the 1983 general election or the 1984 election for the European Parliament. It contested the 1985 District Council elections with only two candidates, but neither succeeded and they gained only 782 votes (0.1 per cent). In the protest actions against the AIA the UDA voiced its opposition but seemed content that mainstream Unionist political leaders took the lead. In particular, it ruled out any repetition of the 1974 stoppage but favoured civil disobedience, and its members were active in protests against the AIA and in the March 1986 'Day of Action'. ULDP did not contest the January 1986 by-elections and in February John McMichael caused some surprise by urging that PSF be included in any constitutional conference. What the conference should discuss emerged at the end of January 1987 when the UDA published 'Common Sense'. The document showed sensitivity to the Ulster-identity issue and to minorities; it envisaged an Assembly and Executive, elected by PR and resulting in an all-party coalition, a Bill of Rights and a written constitution. The proposals received a very favourable response in Britain and in Ireland, and SDLP leader John Hume termed it 'constructive' and said his party was prepared to treat it as a basis for discussion despite its 'surprising source'. The NIO broadly welcomed it. But the UDA supported the Unionist demand that the AIA must be set aside, at least temporarily, for negotiations to go ahead, and with the continuing political impasse, UDA activity tended to switch towards the military. Its involvement in the importation in 1988 of large quantities of sophisticated weaponry, and growing fragmentation at the top, together with UFF sectarian murders, created a dangerous mixture. The murder by PIRA of McMichael in December 1987 was followed three months later by the ousting of Tyrie as leader, soon after a bomb was found under his car. Tyrie's leadership was replaced by collective control by the six members of the inner council. They claimed that, together with the UFF, they would direct a military campaign against PIRA, and build on the political front created by their devolution document. No 'innocent Catholic' had anything to fear from them, they said. But in March 1988 three men – two of them ex-UDR – were sentenced for their part in an armed raid of a massive haul of weapons for the UDA from a UDR camp in Coleraine. In October 1988 four members of a UDA killer squad from N. Belfast were jailed for life, with Mr Justice Nicholson commenting that the UDA was 'comparable in many ways' to PIRA and INLA. In November 1988 Judge Nicholson urged the Protestant community to stop the UDA 'living off them', when he sentenced Davy Payne, a one-time prominent UDA man, to nineteen years' imprisonment for possession of the biggest haul of loyalist arms uncovered during the Troubles, at Portadown in January 1987; two accomplices were sentenced to fourteen years. The following month four UDA men were sentenced to a total of thirty years on blackmail charges after two of the accused had been filmed by TV investigator Roger Cook, who posed as an English financier planning a major development in Co. Armagh. The two principals were sentenced to ten years each and two others to seven and three years respectively. Both the UDA and UFF were named in the 'direct broadcasting' ban of October 1988 applied to paramilitary and other organisations supporting the use of violence. In 1988 the ULDP declared itself a political party wholly separate from the UDA and in 1989 it changed its name to Ulster Democratic Party (see separate entry). At this period the UDA was seen as being increasingly involved in assassinations of Catholics listed in intelligence files leaked from the security forces – a situation that led to the setting up of the Stevens inquiry. The inquiry had enormous consequences for the UDA. At the 1991 trial of leading UDA personality Tommy Lyttle, who was sentenced to seven years' imprisonment for the possession of documents likely to be of use to terrorists, and for threats to witnesses, a vast range of seized UDA files were among the exhibits. These covered

the 1979–90 period and included 'restricted' documents that had originated in RUC HQ, details on PSF leaders including Gerry Adams and 150 pages of 'country suspects', in particular listing PSF councillors, photomontages of alleged PIRA and INLA members in Belfast and S. Down, and the pinpointing of possible bombing targets in the Republic. Several other UDA men were also convicted as a result of the inquiry. The Stevens investigation also led to the arrest of double agent Brian Nelson, who was simultaneously operating as a UDA intelligence officer and as an agent of army Intelligence. The charging of Nelson, who was jailed for ten years in 1992 for conspiracy to murder five Catholics, forced a major shake-up of the organisation, since the security forces were now better informed than ever before about its workings. (Some of the arms then available to the UDA were said to have been supplied by arms dealers contacted by Nelson during a trip to South Africa before his cover was blown.) Younger men took over in the Inner Council – average age around thirty – and they seemed motivated largely by the desire to demonstrate their military prowess. In consequence forty people died at the hands of loyalist gunmen in 1991, the majority murdered by the UFF. They killed several PSF members, including councillor Eddie Fullerton in Buncrana, Co. Donegal. Some victims were described as PIRA members, although usually this was denied by their families and friends. They shot and wounded South-African-born QUB politics lecturer Adrian Guelke, probably through mistaken identity. And they set off fire bombs in Dublin. Their activities in 1991 were punctuated during the inter-party talks at Stormont by a brief summer ceasefire, which was organised by the Combined Loyalist Military Command, which also covered the UVF and RHC. In September 1991, NI Secretary of State Peter Brooke specifically denied allegations that UFF killings were being directed by British Intelligence. In October 1991 the RUC Chief Constable, Sir Hugh Annesley, estimated that the UFF and UVF together had seventy to ninety gunmen on the streets. In January 1992 the UFF promised to step up its campaign, and on 5 February shot dead five Catholics, one of them a fifteen-year-old boy, in a bookmaker's shop on the lower Ormeau Road in Belfast, in response to the PIRA killing of eight Protestant workers in Co. Tyrone three weeks earlier. Nine months later, on 14 November 1992, the UFF claimed the killing of three Catholic men in a bookmaker's on Belfast's Oldpark Road in retaliation for the PIRA bombing of Coleraine town centre. Of the estimated thirty-eight loyalist killings in 1992 , the UFF probably accounted for at least twenty-one, but several loyalist murders were unclaimed. In banning the UDA in 1992, Sir Patrick Mayhew held that it was 'actively and primarily' engaged in terrorism. Proscription had been a long-standing demand of Nationalists, but up to 1992 Ministers apparently accepted the arguments against a ban put forward by Sir George Baker in his review of the EPA in 1984. He said proscription would revive interest in the UDA and hinder rather than help the police since it would drive underground the small section concerned in organising military activity. The ban was not followed by an early swoop on suspected members and in the five months after it was imposed only one person was charged with membership – and he also faced a murder charge. In 1992 the organisation carried out more punishment shootings than PIRA, and it was also, according to security force sources, operating profitable rackets. At the start of 1993 the UFF struck a sinister note with a threat to the 'pan-Nationalist front of the SDLP, Sinn Féin, the Irish Government and the IRA'. Fourteen murders by loyalists in the first three months of 1993 were largely carried out by the UFF; during March it killed six Catholic men in less than forty-eight hours, four of them building workers who died at Castlerock, Co. Derry, and one of whom was a PIRA member. By the end of the year they had claimed thirty-one killings. During July, in their campaign against a pan-Nationalist front, they attacked the homes of Joe Hendron,

MP for W. Belfast, and seven councillors or former councillors. In many instances the devices were 'pipe bombs' but speculation continued about loyalist technology to make larger fertiliser bombs. In pursuit of their prison campaign there was a series of attacks on prison officers and their homes at the end of August. The murder of prison officer Peacock coupled with demands by Unionist politicians for capital punishment resulted in the ending of death threats to prison officers on 11 September. There were reports that Young Militant had obtained a considerable influx of new members. The UDA called for a Unionist boycott of government after the Hume-Adams joint statement but this was rejected by UUP and DUP. Members were mobilised after the Shankill bombing in October and attacks in the following week killed four Catholics before the assault on the Rising Sun bar in Greysteel, Co. Derry, killed seven (one Protestant) and injured thirteen. As tension rose during November, there were rumours of recruitment to the youth wings of the organisation. In the aftermath of the December Downing Street Declaration they marked their differences from loyalist politicians by warning that they would not automatically support Paisley's Save Ulster campaign. They refused a cessation of violence until PIRA had started the process. The publication by the *Sunday Life* in January 1994 of a Doomsday plan, appropriated from academic work that had been conducted on the 1981 census, envisaged a reduced NI, and many people feared an even more intensive loyalist campaign of violence. Their first killing in 1994 took place at the end of January and in mid-February attacks on SDLP personnel were renewed.

ULSTER DEFENCE REGIMENT *see* Security System section, pp. 451–3

ULSTER DEMOCRATIC PARTY
The party dates from December 1989 and was formerly known as the Ulster Loyalist Democratic Party. The ULDP was set up by the UDA in June 1981 in succession to the New Ulster Political Research Group,

but in 1988 it claimed that it was now an independent political party with no paramilitary links. The ULDP failed to make any real impact in elections (*see* entry on UDA) and its first chairman, John McMichael, was murdered by PIRA at his Lisburn home in 1987. In the 1989 council elections, UDP's leader, Ken Kerr, was returned as ULDP to Derry City Council. He denied suggestions that Republicans had had an input into the 'Common Sense' policy it had inherited from ULDP, and which had been widely praised. In November 1989 the party attacked the leaders of the main Unionist parties as 'self-centred and gutless'. Its nominee, Gary McMichael (son of John McMichael), took some six hundred votes in the Upper Bann parliamentary by-election in 1990. In June 1991 the party chairman, Cecil McKnight (also UDA), was murdered by PIRA at his home in Derry. The UDP rejected PIRA claims that he had been involved in the murder of PSF councillor Eddie Fullerton from Buncrana. In August 1991 Gary Lynch, a UDP election worker, was killed by PIRA at his workplace in Derry. PIRA claimed he was in the UFF, but this was denied by his family. In the run-up to the 1992 general election, Kerr was criticised by some Unionists for urging loyalists in W. Belfast to vote SDLP. Kerr lost his Derry City Council seat in 1993, but Gary McMichael compensated with a surprise win in Lisburn.

ULSTER DOMINION GROUP *see* British Ulster Dominion Party

ULSTER FREEDOM FIGHTERS *see* Ulster Defence Association

ULSTER INDEPENDENCE ASSOCIATION
A group campaigning for an independent, sovereign NI. Urges an assembly of up to 100 members elected by PR list system, with a consensus government and non-political president. The transfer of responsibility from Westminster would be achieved by negotiation, particularly on interim financial arrangements. It would seek a declaration from the Republic that it respects the sovereignty of an independent, peaceful NI. Claims some Catholic support. The association was active in 1979 in seeking to arrange a Washington peace forum, and it handled invitations on behalf of Congressman Mario Biaggi, chairman of the *ad hoc* Congressional Committee on Irish affairs in Washington. Its chairman, George Allport, a businessman, visited the US in 1977 and 1979 for talks with politicians. One of its deputy leaders was E. Belfast loyalist John McKeague, shot dead in 1982 by INLA.

ULSTER INDEPENDENCE COMMITTEE
The committee was formed early in 1988 under the leadership of the Rev. Hugh Ross, a Presbyterian minister from Newmills, Dungannon, Co. Tyrone. It seeks an end to sectarian politics through unity on a common Ulster identity. It advocates a written Constitution, a Bill of Rights and the existence of a sovereign, independent NI as an alternative to the 'tyrannical and arbitrary rule of the London/Dublin coalition' leading to a united Ireland. In 1989 it unveiled a suggested flag for an independent NI and a replacement for the British national anthem, while also saying that the Queen could be head of state of an independent NI. In 1990, when it polled 1,534 votes (4.3 per cent) in the Upper Bann by-election, Rev. Ross accused Unionist leaders of betraying NI by conceding Dublin a role in its affairs, and on 12 July 1993 he claimed that the head of state in NI was now shared by the Queen and President Mary Robinson, and that the Irish Government shared in the running of the province.

ULSTER INDEPENDENCE PARTY
Launched on a small scale in October 1977 with the object of securing 'by democratic means, a sovereign, free and independent Ulster'. Government would be based on proportional power-sharing at all levels, and the party said Protestants and Catholics should join hands in a spirit of friendship. An initial statement said that in May 1976 the Ulster Independence movement had issued an economic survey and feasibility study.

This was published in the US in July 1976 by the Ulster Heritage Society, under the title *Towards an Independent Ulster*. These documents claimed that NI could be economically viable on its own. In January 1978 the UIP said it could not accept the idea of 'interim independence' mentioned as a possibility by the then Catholic Primate, Cardinal Ó Fiaich, since this would be a contradiction in terms.

ULSTER LIBERAL PARTY

The party, linked with the British Liberal Party, never achieved a high profile. Sheelagh Murnaghan sat in the old Stormont Parliament for QUB. She and the former chairman, Rev. Albert McElroy, were prominent in the demand for reforms. Two candidates who stood in the Assembly elections in 1973 forfeited their deposits and the party was not represented in the Convention election in 1975. In 1977 and 1978 it organised 'fringe' meetings on NI at the British Liberal assemblies. The party put up a candidate, Jim Murray, a teacher, in the 1979 European election, but he received only 932 first-preference votes (0.1 per cent). In the next few years its activities seemed to be minimal, although it did sponsor a candidate in S. Belfast in the 1982 Assembly election, who secured sixty-five votes. In 1985 the party had one candidate, Michael Colin J. McGuigan, for Ards Council, and he polled only thirty-five votes.

ULSTER LOYALIST ASSOCIATION

A body prominent between 1969 and 1972 in opposing any interference with the NI Constitution, and urging stronger security policies, notably against the PIRA. Its leading figures were William Craig, the Rev. Martin Smyth and Captain Austin Ardill, and many of its members were also Orangemen. The ULA organised a series of rallies throughout NI, and Captain Ardill, speaking as chairman in 1971, called for the severing of diplomatic relations with the Republic and for the sealing of the border.

ULSTER LOYALIST CENTRAL CO-ORDINATING COMMITTEE

The organisation set up after the 1974 loyalist strike to act as a forum for loyalist paramilitary organisations. It replaced the Ulster Army Council set up in 1973. The ULCCC originally included the UDA, UVF, RHC, LAW, VSC, Orange Volunteers, and Down Orange Welfare. In 1976 the UDA and Down Orange Welfare withdrew after suggestions that some members of the ULCCC were meeting members of the PIRA and talking to a wide range of Catholics about the possibility of an independent NI. Its co-chairman, loyalist John McKeague, was shot dead in his E. Belfast shop in January 1982. A claim by INLA that it was responsible was generally accepted, although there had been a telephone claim of responsibility, allegedly from the RHC. A reformed ULCCC was active in 1991 in the run-up to the inter-party talks. In April 1991 it sent an open letter to TDs saying that the Irish Government could have no role in the internal affairs of NI. Its spokesman, Ray Smallwoods, urged the establishment of a pan-Unionist Convention to lead 'the fight for democracy in NI'. The committee welcomed the loyalist ceasefire in April 1991 that marked the first stage of the Brooke–Mayhew Talks.

ULSTER LOYALIST DEMOCRATIC PARTY *see* Ulster Defence Association *and* Ulster Democratic Party

ULSTER POPULAR UNIONIST PARTY

Founded by Sir James Kilfedder MP in January 1980 as the Ulster Progressive Unionist Party but the name was changed in March to Popular Unionist to avoid confusion with the Progressive Unionist Party of Hugh Smyth. Kilfedder's break with UUP resulted from disagreements on party policy and leadership after 1976 when the leader at Westminster was James Molyneaux. The formal break came in 1979 when Kilfedder took offence at a personal letter written to him by party leader Harry West. Encouraged by a 23,625 majority over UUP opposition in the 1979 general election, and runner-up in the election to the European

Parliament in May 1979, the UPUP was launched in 1980. Its first electoral test was the District Council elections of 1981 when twenty candidates (including seven women) were promoted, and a temporary electoral pact was concluded with nine UPNI candidates. Five UPUP candidates were elected, two in Ards and three in N. Down. The appearance of being more than a personality party took a knock in the Assembly election of 1982 when two candidates polled 2.5 quotas, but only Kilfedder was elected as his surplus transferred more to other parties than to his running mate George Green. In 1983 Kilfedder was the sole flag-bearer for his party in the new constituency of N. Down, which he held against UUP, Alliance Party and SDLP competition, with 22,861 votes, and a majority of 13,846. He also contested the 1984 election for the European Parliament, receiving 20,092 votes (2.9 per cent), but he did not stand under his party label but as Speaker of the NI Assembly. By the 1985 District Council elections some of his members had drifted back to the main parties and the five UPUP candidates polled 3,139 votes (0.5 per cent), and three were elected, two in N. Down and Kilfedder's sister Gladys McIntyre in Ards. In the aftermath of the AIA in 1985, by which he felt strongly betrayed by the Conservatives, he resigned his seat with the other Unionist MPs and fought the January by-elections without opposition from UUP or DUP. At the general election of June 1987 he remained unopposed by UUP and DUP but his majority was reduced to 3,953 by Robert McCartney QC, an expelled UUP member standing as a 'Real Unionist' candidate. In 1992, when he received a knighthood, many Conservative backbenchers were angry at the decision of NI Tories to stand against him in the general election. But although the DUP also contested the seat, he had a majority of nearly 5,000 over Dr Laurence Kennedy, Conservative. In the 1989 council elections, UPUP had two seats in N. Down and one in Castlereagh; they held the three seats in 1993.

ULSTER PROTESTANT ACTION GROUP

A paramilitary group active mainly in 1974 which was responsible for the assassination of many Catholics. The security forces believed that it was comprised of dissident members of the UDA. In a statement in October 1974 it said that the assassinations would continue 'until the Provisional IRA are exterminated'. The group apparently adopted the name of an organisation active before the Troubles in encouraging the employment of Protestants in industry. The name 'Protestant Action' reappeared in 1981 when there were claims at a clandestine news conference that it would kill 'active Republicans'. In 1982 it claimed the murders of several people, including a PSF election worker in Armagh. At that time there were suggestions that it had some link with the illegal RHC.

ULSTER PROTESTANT VOLUNTEERS

A loyalist paramilitary group associated with the UCDC. It was involved in many counter-demonstrations to civil rights meetings in the period 1968–9. Organised in local divisions, it styled itself a united Society of Protestant patriots, pledged by all lawful methods to uphold and maintain the constitution of NI as an integral part of the UK so long as the UK maintains a Protestant monarchy and the terms of the revolution settlement'. The UPV accompanied most of the Rev. Ian Paisley's parades during the early civil rights period.

ULSTER RESISTANCE

The organisation was launched at an invitation-only rally in the Ulster Hall, Belfast, in November 1986. It was attended by the Rev. Ian Paisley MP, Peter Robinson MP, and the Rev. Ivan Foster. Rallies were then held in other towns such as Portadown, Kilkeel, Larne, and Derry and the organisation became identified with a red beret. At one time it was said to have comprised nine battalions. It was rumoured that relations with the DUP and politicians began to cool when the politicians opted for talks rather than a more hostile campaign against the AIA and the British Government. However, a major arms find in Co. Armagh in November 1988 – with weapons similar to those seized earlier from the UDA at Portadown and the UVF in Belfast – the discovery of five red berets and the arrest of a former DUP District Council candidate brought Ulster Resistance and the links with DUP under close scrutiny. A statement by DUP said that it had been informed that the organisation was being put on ice in the summer of 1987, and party association and contacts ended, though individuals might have continued membership. Experts accepted that Ulster Resistance then had no record of paramilitary involvement. The organisation was in the news, however, in April 1989, when Noel Little, one of its founders, and two other men were arrested in Paris with a South African diplomat, Daniel Storm, and pieces of a demonstration missile from Shorts were found in their possession. When freed on bail, Little denied that he and his co-defendants, James King and Sammy Quinn, were seeking to obtain guns from South Africa for Ulster Resistance in return for missile technology. A campaign was mounted in loyalist circles in NI calling for the release of the 'Paris Three'. When they appeared in Paris on arms charges in October 1991, they were released after being fined and given suspended sentences. All three denied being in any paramilitary group. In November 1989 Ulster Resistance claimed two of its members, a Lurgan businessman and a Kilrea building worker, had been murdered by PIRA after they had been 'set up' by MI5. In 1991 'Resistance' (see separate entry) was mentioned as one of the organisations in the Combined Loyalist Military Command.

ULSTER SERVICE CORPS

A loyalist vigilante group established in 1977, with the support of the United Unionist Action Council. In the spring of 1977 it mounted road blocks from time to time in parts of S. Derry, Armagh and Tyrone, and claimed to have some liaison with members of the RUC and UDR,

although this was denied by the authorities. Its activities included observation of alleged PIRA 'safe houses'. It claimed to have a membership of about 500 throughout NI. Some of its members were summoned for obstruction, and a spokesman for the Government accused it of wasting the time of the security forces who had to be diverted to deal with it. The SDLP protested strongly that there was evidence of collusion with the UDR to the extent that joint patrols were operated in some areas of mid-Ulster. Most of its original members are believed to have served with the former Ulster Special Constabulary (B Specials).

ULSTER SPECIAL CONSTABULARY
see Security System section, pp. 437, 451

ULSTER SPECIAL CONSTABULARY ASSOCIATION

An association bringing together former B Specials, who were disbanded officially in 1970 following the adoption by the Government of the Hunt report. The USCA has operated as a pressure group, calling for tougher anti-IRA measures and more local control of security. It has been associated with loyalist paramilitary groups, notably in support of the loyalist strike in 1974. Exact strength uncertain, but probably had backing of 10,000 ex-B Specials in 1970.

ULSTER UNIONIST PARTY

Popularly styled the Official Unionist Party for many years, it is the largest political entity in NI. It provided the Government of NI at Stormont from 1921 to March 1972, when direct rule from London was imposed. Up to the late 1960s, when pro- and anti-Premier O'Neill factions became sharply differentiated, the party was essentially a coalition embracing a left-to-right spectrum of opinion committed to the maintenance of the link with Britain and the defence of the NI Parliament. In the face of demands for reform from the civil rights movement, and tensions caused by the violence, it was weakened by a series of breakaway movements: supporters of O'Neill who moved to the Alliance Party or out of active politics; anti-O'Neill people who moved to Vanguard or the DUP; pro-Faulkner members who moved to UPNI. In most of the Parliaments from 1921 until 1972, the Unionists held up to forty of the fifty-two seats in the NI House of Commons, and they usually held at least ten of the twelve Westminster seats. It was unquestionably a party of government, and some Unionist MPs had never had to fight an election. So the closing down of the old Stormont Parliament in 1972 was a severe shock, and one that eventually forced the hard core of the party into combination with smaller Unionist parties. Under the pressure of events, the working-class element in the party became more powerful, and the influence of the 'county families' was visibly reduced. Key meetings of the party ceased to be held midweek when few workers were able to attend. An enlarged executive took charge of policy, instead of the former 1,000-strong Unionist Council and 300-member Standing Committee which had held frequent meetings during the O'Neill crisis. And although the party was a branch of the British Conservative Party, entitled to send full voting representatives to party conferences, the action of the Heath Government in suspending Stormont strained to breaking point an inter-party link that had existed from the days of the earliest Home Rule controversy in the late nineteenth century. In the 1973 election to the new Assembly, the party was split between those who followed Faulkner's lead and backed the power-sharing policy of Westminster and those who opposed the British Government's White Paper. The election resulted in the return of twenty-four candidates supporting the White Paper (one, Anne Dickson in S. Antrim, was not recognised as 'official' by party headquarters), and ten who were against. A major crisis for the party developed in January 1974, after Faulkner and his colleagues had joined a power-sharing Executive which included the SDLP and the Alliance Party. The United Ulster Unionist Council, or Coalition (UUUC), rejected by 427 to 374 the Sunningdale Agreement, which provided the basis for the Executive. This brought about the

resignation of Faulkner as party leader, and he was succeeded by Harry West. Soon afterwards, the February 1974 Westminster election gave the anti-Sunningdale Unionists the opportunity to test their support. They chose to join with the DUP and Vanguard in the UUUC. The Unionist Coalition secured eleven out of the twelve seats, and West was returned in Fermanagh–S.Tyrone. He led the Coalition at Westminster into a neutral stance at a time when their votes, if they had been sought, could have kept the Heath Government in office. The fact that the Unionist coalition had got more than 50 per cent of the votes in NI was a severe blow to the three-party Executive. But the new Labour Government was just as committed to power-sharing as the Conservatives, and by rejecting the demand for fresh Assembly elections, the Executive survived until the loyalist strike, organised by the UWC and backed by the UUP and its partners, effectively brought life to a standstill in May 1974. The Coalition continued into the elections for the Constitutional Convention in 1975, but the fragmentation of unionism had its effects. The Ulster Unionists now obtained 25.8 per cent of the vote and nineteen seats; they were no longer the predominant party, and if they were still against any partnership with the SDLP, they had to face the fact that they must co-operate with some other parties to achieve anything. The Ulster Unionists together with the DUP and Vanguard backed the majority Convention report which provided for majority Cabinet rule, and argued that opposition influence should be achieved through a system of committees linked to the various Stormont departments. But that did not meet Westminster's criteria for devolved government. In the later stage of the Convention the UUP stood out against the move by William Craig to try to get agreement for a voluntary coalition which would include the SDLP for the period of the emergency. And it now formed part of the UUUC which included the DUP and those members (the majority) of Vanguard who disagreed with Craig, and who now made up the

UUUM under Ernest Baird, who had been Craig's deputy in Vanguard. After the break-up of the Convention in 1976, two Ulster Unionists (the Rev. Martin Smyth and Captain Austin Ardill) became involved in private, but unsuccessful, talks with John Hume and Paddy Devlin of the SDLP. The secrecy surrounding these talks gave rise to friction between the Party and the Rev. Ian Paisley and Ernest Baird. This gap was widened in 1977 when the Ulster Unionists stood aside from the Action Council or UUAC, which organised the loyalist strike – a largely abortive stoppage – in May 1977 against direct rule and in support of tougher security policy. The Ulster Unionists also refused to support a parallel operation – an unofficial vigilante group known as the Ulster Service Corps, which appeared briefly in some areas during 1977. Again, Ulster Unionists declined to have any UUUC endorsement of their candidates in the May 1977 District Council elections. In that election Ulster Unionists had 29.6 per cent of the first-preference votes and 33.8 per cent of the seats (178). In June 1977 the UUP accepted 'the *de facto* collapse of the UUUC'. The party was now set upon a more independent course, and the Parliamentary Unionist Coalition at Westminster also ended. Six Ulster Unionist MPs, under the leadership of James Molyneaux, became a separate group, and William Craig joined them in 1978. Since October 1974, Enoch Powell in S. Down had been an UUP MP, and his aversion to the Conservatives, plus tactical awareness, were obviously factors in securing from a Labour Government, lacking an overall majority after April 1976, support for a Speaker's conference to examine the long-standing demand of Unionists for extra seats for NI at Westminster. This all-party conference reported in 1978 in favour of five extra NI seats, with discretion to the Boundary Commission to have one more or one less. But the Conservatives, also with an eye to Unionist votes at Westminster, strongly backed the UUP call for the introduction of regional councils in NI as a way of filling the administrative gap created by the absence of any Stormont Assembly. In 1978 the UUP turned down

a plea by the DUP for some sort of agreement on the allocation of candidates in the coming Westminster elections. Party leader Harry West pointed out to the Rev. Ian Paisley that the party's constitution prevented it giving any directions to local associations on the choice of candidates. Although the UUP retains its long-standing association with the Orange Order, its importance has declined in recent years with the divisions in unionism. In the 1979 European election, one of its two candidates, John Taylor, was successful on the sixth count, but party leader Harry West was eliminated. The party's overall performance was not impressive. The combined total of first-preference votes for the party was 21.8 per cent compared with 29.8 per cent for DUP leader the Rev. Ian Paisley, and 24.5 per cent for SDLP candidate John Hume. West conceded that perhaps 100,000 party supporters had refused to back the party line of calling for extensive renegotiation of the EC as distinct from the outright opposition of Paisley. The result led directly to the resignation of Harry West as party leader in July 1979. The Parliamentary leader, James Molyneaux, succeeded him. But the hopes of the UUP that the Thatcher Government would prove helpful to their aims were soon disappointed. The party's annual report regretted that the PM 'has followed, not her own instincts, but those of Lord Carrington and the Foreign Office'. There was some surprise, however, that the UUP decided to boycott the Stormont Constitutional Conference announced by Secretary of State Humphrey Atkins in November 1979. Molyneaux called it 'a time-wasting exercise and window-dressing'. But although the party stayed away from the discussions, it sent proposals for majority government to the PM. When the failure of the Constitutional Conference was followed by a plan for a fifty-member Advisory Council, this too was turned down by the party. The UUP was also highly suspicious of the London–Dublin contacts, and especially the December 1980 summit in Dublin at which Margaret Thatcher and Charles Haughey initiated a review of 'the totality of relations between the two countries'. Although the PM repeated on every possible occasion the constitutional pledge on NI, many UUP people, and notably Enoch Powell, saw a Foreign Office conspiratorial approach in every Anglo-Irish gesture. UUP–DUP rivalry was renewed in the 1981 council elections, and again the UUP fell behind the DUP, if only marginally, in terms of votes, although it maintained its superiority in seats. The UUP also became quickly antagonistic towards Atkins's successor, James Prior. After the murder of the party's S. Belfast MP, the Rev. Robert Bradford, in November 1981, its anger was directed at the Government's security policy. It joined in the loyalist 'Day of Action' on 23 November, when rallies and meetings were sponsored by both the UUP and DUP to demand a more aggressive approach to security by the authorities. It also co-operated for a time with the DUP in the adjournment of loyalist-controlled councils as part of the security protest. The UUP tended, however, to distance itself from the DUP, and rejected the DUP suggestion that a united Unionist candidate should be run in the S. Belfast by-election in February 1982, and it had the satisfaction of seeing its candidate, the Rev. Martin Smyth, win easily, with the DUP in third place. Prior's 'rolling devolution' initiative in 1982 found the UUP slightly divided, but most opinion went along with the leadership in regarding the Assembly as a revival of power-sharing and Sunningdale and as an institution which could fit in with Government plans for a parliamentary tier of the Anglo-Irish Intergovernmental Council. Since the DUP was welcoming the scrutiny powers of the proposed Assembly, many UUP members saw the possibility of outflanking the Rev. Ian Paisley in the Assembly elections. UUP MPs, for the most part, were active in opposing the legislation for the Assembly and they co-operated to some extent with right-wing Conservatives who mounted a filibuster on the committee stage. They also propagated the view that Thatcher was by no means wholeheartedly behind the Prior plan. When the Falklands crisis broke, the UUP MPs threw themselves enthusiastically behind the PM's strong response, and even drew parallels with the Irish Republic's claims over NI. They were aided in this by the Republic's opposition to sanctions against Argentina, and Thatcher pointedly included Enoch Powell in her Privy Council briefings on the situation. Prior warned against making comparisons between the Falklands and the NI situation. In the end the UUP had to face the fact that Prior had got his Assembly measure through virtually unscathed, but they did recover their lead in the popular vote in the Assembly elections, with 29.7 per cent to 23 per cent, and got twenty-six seats to the DUP's twenty-one. In the 1983 Westminster election the party went a small way with the Rev. Ian Paisley's bid to secure an electoral pact. It reached an arrangement on three seats whereas the DUP leader wanted to cover six. The 1983 Westminster election represented the party's best showing since before direct rule. It took 34 per cent of the vote and eleven of the seventeen seats. It thus pulled 14 per cent ahead of DUP which got three seats and 20 per cent of the vote. There was, however, a 'limited understanding' between the two parties. This meant that DUP did not contest Newry and Armagh, and Fermanagh–S. Tyrone, while UUP stood down in Foyle. However, in the personality contest of the second election to the European Parliament in 1984 the Rev. Ian Paisley and DUP pulled ahead with 33.6 per cent to 20 per cent for John Taylor (UUP). The results of the 1985 District Council elections showed that UUP had reversed the 1981 position and confirmed its position ahead of DUP in 1982 and 1983. UUP polled 29.5 per cent of the votes compared to 24.3 per cent for DUP and won 180 seats to 142. The signing of the AIA six months later forced the two party leaders to co-operate over their tactics of constitutional opposition. The by-election tactic, when fifteen Unionist MPs resigned their seats and forced by-elections as a test of opinion on the AIA, saw them poll 418,230 votes in what was the fourth-best poll since 1920. But they lost one seat, Newry and Armagh, to

Seamus Mallon (SDLP), and because of restricted competition as in 1983, there was no guide as to whether public opinion was behind the more radical young bloods of the DUP or the more restrained UUP. After the March 'Day of Action' and some minor violence, the differences became more apparent. Despite the clear frustration of some DUP members the two parties contested the 1987 general election in the same constituencies as in 1983. While another seat was lost, S. Down, and the vote fell to below 400,000, UUP was seen to be clearly ahead with 37.8 per cent to 11.7 per cent. The vote fell because of limited competition in the hope of electing a block of fourteen MPs; but it also fell because of Alliance Party criticism of the Unionist negative stance and boycott of Parliament, and because of competition from Campaign for Equal Citizenship arguments by Robert McCartney QC in N. Down. The return of the Conservative Government with a majority of 101 and a commitment to the AIA forced a rethink of Unionist strategy. MPs returned to Westminster, Unionist leaders began a series of 'talks about talks' on whether the Government was willing to consider an alternative to the AIA. Early in 1988 the nature of the talks changed and a set of proposals was submitted. The boycott of District Council business gradually petered out. When no reply was received to the outline proposals after eight months, they were sent to the PM and her reply commented that they were 'interesting and progressive'. Within UUP, criticism of the links with DUP became muted just as the association became a restraint on DUP. Further, despite some pressure, especially from Fermanagh Unionists Ken Maginnis and Raymond Ferguson, and the Charter Group, for progress on devolution, the position of the leadership was secure at the November 1988 conference. With devolution available only under the AIA and much opinion in favour of integration, the conference acclaimed Molyneaux's assertion that 'this is no time for turning' and his appeal to 'stand fast'. In the 1989 council elections, UUP strengthened its position slightly, gaining three extra seats – total 193 – and took control of three councils, while it was the largest party in ten others. In the European election that followed soon after, Jim Nicholson, who had lost his Newry and Armagh seat to Seamus Mallon in 1986, was returned in succession to John Taylor, with a slightly enhanced share of the vote compared with 1984. In 1990 David Trimble had no difficulty in retaining the Upper Bann seat formerly held by the late Harold McCusker, and a Conservative lost deposit there was obviously very satisfying to the UUP, several of whose spokesmen had questioned Conservative motives in organising in NI. In the UUP-initiated case in the Dublin Supreme Court, 1990 also brought the ruling that Articles 2 and 3 of the Republic's Constitution represented a 'constitutional imperative' (*see* McGimpsey Case). Molyneaux told the Ulster Unionist Council in March 1990 that this sounded the 'death knell' for Unionist–Nationalist meetings. The party seemingly took some encouragement from comments by PM Major on the unity of the UK, made in the context of his opposition to Scottish devolution, although Major was also firmly committed to the AIA. UUP involvement in the 1991 inter-party talks was on the basis that the AIA might be negotiated away and Irish Ministers persuaded to mount a referendum with a recommendation that the constitutional claim be rescinded. In the event, the party found 'broad agreement' with the DUP and All. on a committee-based scheme for devolution, but the SDLP wanted a much more radical approach, with NI run by a panel of six commissioners and a strong role for Dublin in a North–South ministerial council. But whilst both the UUP and DUP rejected the SDLP propositions, the two Unionist parties no longer pursued a wholly united approach. In the 1992 general election, the UUP easily fought off DUP challenges in E. Antrim and Strangford. In the resumed Brooke–Mayhew Talks in 1992, the DUP refused to travel to Dublin for talks on North–South relations. By contrast,

Molyneaux led his team to Dublin Castle, and earned warm praise from Southern politicians. And when the Brooke–Mayhew Talks broke up without agreement in 1992, it was revealed that in the final stage of the negotiations the UUP had tabled a plan for a settlement entailing a Bill of Rights, a 'meaningful role' for the SDLP in a new Assembly, and an 'inter-Irish relations committee'. When the DUP said the UUP had departed from 'the agreed joint Unionist position' in the talks, the UUP retorted that the DUP had shown 'gross hypocrisy' in unilaterally leaving the talks. The UUP seemed set at that point on pursuing its Westminster agenda of an NI select committee and an improved format for local legislation, while the impact of the new FF–Labour Coalition in Dublin, pledged to a more flexible approach to NI, remained uncertain. In January 1993 Molyneaux wanted more emphasis on talks between NI party leaders than on a new 'political circus'. The party had mixed fortunes in the 1993 council elections, taking 2 per cent fewer votes than in 1989 and giving way to PSF as the biggest vote-getter in Belfast, while increasing its tally of seats overall. In 1993 too, the party began a review of its Constitution, which has always involved very considerable autonomy for the seventeen constituency associations. The party now has a European office. In July 1993 the party's 'understanding' with the Conservatives enabled the Maastricht Treaty Bill to pass but it brought general claims of a 'deal'. UUP MPs stressed that their support was only to ensure against the premature end of the Government, that they had opposed VAT on domestic fuel and they hinted that the understanding may have begun with the coal-mine closures of 1992. Early in September the party met the Morrison delegation from the US while DUP declined the offer. The party was concerned that the Hume–Adams agreement on a peace process might become the basis of Government policy. It also warned against diverting away from the party talks towards a less clearly defined peace initiative. While the Government began to focus on the peace

process, consultation took place and there was reassurance from the Irish Government's new definition of consent, elaborated by Dick Spring. The party did not oppose the December Downing Street Declaration and PM Major seemed anxious to keep UUP on board by saying what was *not* contained in it. The announcement of an NI Affairs Committee on 16 December may have helped steady the leadership. In the immediate speculation, it was clear that any talk of amnesty for prisoners could alter the UUP position. A party delegation met Michael Ancram in January 1994, presented him with a copy of its document, 'Blueprint for Stability', and urged him to 'get a move on' with his talks. As it became clear that there would be no acceptance of the declaration, formal or otherwise, by the Republican movement, UUP began to urge a change of policy – new security measures and a return to seeking agreement based on internal structures. Despite DUP criticism of its stance on the declaration, UUP was still able to retain a Belfast City Council seat in a by-election in February, which DUP turned into a referendum on the issue. There were some signs of intra-party dissent at the party council meeting in March but it produced only two changes in elected offices and the leadership policy was confirmed.

ULSTER VANGUARD

A pressure group within unionism, led by William Craig, and launched at the beginning of 1972, when the possibility of direct rule from Westminster began to be discussed seriously. Its purpose was to provide an umbrella organisation for loyalists in a bid to overcome the weaknesses of their party divisions. It had strong support from loyalist paramilitary groups. The deputy leaders, at the start, were the Rev. Martin Smyth and Captain Austin Ardill. Vanguard organised rallies, to which Craig travelled frequently in an open car with a motor cycle escort provided by the Vanguard Service Corps, a paramilitary group directly linked with the organisation. A rally in Ormeau Park, Belfast, in March 1972 attracted about 60,000 people, and it mounted a

342

forty-eight-hour strike by its supporters against direct rule. William Craig's remark at the Ormeau Park rally that 'if the politicians fail, it will be our duty to liquidate the enemy', brought angry protests from his critics that Vanguard was a fascist movement. Craig denied that it was neo-Nazi. He said that any paramilitary appearance was due simply to the symbolic gesture of men of different political affiliations standing together shoulder to shoulder. Vanguard turned out in strength for a demonstration at Parliament Buildings on 28 March 1972 to protest against the introduction of direct rule. It was the last sitting day of the old Stormont Parliament, and Craig appeared on the balcony of Parliament Buildings and was joined by PM Brian Faulkner and several Cabinet Ministers. But the unity was more apparent than real on that occasion, and Faulkner made it clear later that he was embarrassed by the link-up with Vanguard. In May 1972 Vanguard shed some support among Ulster Unionists with a policy statement entitled 'Ulster – a Nation'. It said that NI might, if reluctantly, have to go it alone. More immediately, it called for renegotiation of the relationship with Westminster to ensure local control of security in view of the unilateral application of direct rule. In 1973 the setting up of the VUPP meant the disappearance of Vanguard as an umbrella group. But Ulster Vanguard re-emerged in February 1978, when VUPP was wound up as a political party. Craig, who had now rejoined the UUP, remained at its head, and David Trimble, the deputy leader of VUPP, was appointed his deputy. (*See also* Vanguard Unionist Progressive Party.)

ULSTER VOLUNTEER FORCE
Illegal Protestant paramilitary force, sometimes described as the 'secret Protestant army'. Also uses the cover name Protestant Action Force. In 1966 it revived the title applied to the Unionist-Protestant force established in 1912 to fight Irish Home Rule. Known sometimes as 'Carson's Army', after Lord Carson, the original UVF organised the training of volunteers as well as gun-

running to Ulster. When war broke out in 1914, and Home Rule was set aside for the moment, its members very largely became the 36th (Ulster) Division in the British army, which suffered severe losses at the Battle of the Somme in July 1916. The new UVF of the 1960s was completely opposed to the liberal Unionist regime of Terence O'Neill. It first attracted attention in May 1966, when a statement over the name 'Capt. Wm. Johnston' threatened war against the IRA, and said that it was the UVF's intention to kill IRA men mercilessly. Six days later, a man named John Scullion was fatally stabbed on the Falls Road in Belfast. On 26 June an eighteen-year-old Catholic barman, Peter Ward, was shot dead as he left a bar in the Protestant Shankill Road area of the city. Augustus (Gusty) Spence, the best-known UVF leader, was sentenced to life imprisonment for this murder. PM O'Neill announced in Parliament that the UVF was to be declared illegal. He said that 'this evil thing in our midst' had misappropriated the name UVF and would now take its proper place alongside the IRA in the schedule of illegal bodies. He also branded it as 'a dangerous conspiracy'. The PM claimed that the Rev. Ian Paisley had links with the UVF and that he had voiced support for it in speeches, but Paisley and his newspaper angrily denied that he had been associated with the organisation or had advocated violence. The UVF, organising underground on military lines, and apparently attracting many ex-soldiers, is thought to have attained a strength of about 1,500 by 1972. In that year – the year in which direct rule from Westminster was imposed – it was heavily involved in the assassination of Catholics. It also claimed to be well armed with a variety of weapons, including Browning, Bren, Sterling and Thompson guns. In October 1972 it admitted to a raid on a military arsenal in Lurgan, Co. Armagh. Its main centres of strength at that time were the Shankill area of Belfast, E. Antrim and Co. Armagh. In July 1972 Gusty Spence, then described as second-in-command, vanished while on two days' parole from Belfast Prison. He was said to have been held by his UVF comrades in a bid to force a new trial for Spence, but a few months later he was recaptured and went to the Maze Prison to preside over the compound where UVF prisoners who had special category status were held. In April 1974 Secretary of State Merlyn Rees removed the proscription on the UVF to encourage it to turn to political activity and in the October 1974 election the Volunteer Political Party chairman, Ken Gibson, was a candidate in W. Belfast. (*See also* Volunteer Political Party.) But on 3 October 1975 the UVF admitted that it had been responsible for violence of the previous day in which twelve people died and about forty were injured, most of them Catholics. In declaring the organisation illegal again, Rees said that the UVF had shown that it was still wedded to violence, including the murder of innocent citizens. In reply, the UVF threatened further 'anti-IRA action' and expressed its 'utter disgust' at what it said was the failure of the military and civil authorities to act effectively against the PIRA. Shortly before it was banned, leading members of the UVF met Government officials and put a series of demands to the Government. These were, apparently, that the IRSP should be declared illegal and that the incident centres set up to monitor the PIRA ceasefire should be closed. However, these talks were unproductive. In fact, the security forces were already poised to swoop on the homes of UVF suspects in Belfast and E. Antrim. On 5 October 1,000 troops and police were involved in the operation, which had been planned since a day in the previous August when a 27-year-old UVF officer ran to a police station in Carrickfergus to report that a UVF court-martial was under way in the Royal British Legion Hall in the town. He feared that he was going to be tried and shot by the UVF, and his information on the organisation proved to be the link the security forces needed to break up a strong UVF unit in that area. In March 1977 after a £2 million trial, the most costly in NI's criminal history, twenty-six UVF men were given a total of 700 years' imprisonment, including eight life

sentences. There were fifty-five charges against the men, including four murders. One was the murder of a UVF man, and two others were the murders of UDA men Hugh McVeigh and David Douglas, whose bodies were found in a shallow grave in Co. Antrim five months after they disappeared. About the same time, ten men from the Ballyclare, Co. Antrim, unit were sentenced for a variety of terrorist offences, and it is known that units in Bangor, Co. Down, and Coleraine, Co. Derry, also found difficulty in surviving arrests in early 1977. In June 1977 there were confused reports about a ceasefire, which seemed to confirm the belief that the UVF was somewhat divided in its leadership. In June 1979 nine Scottish UVF members were sentenced to between twelve and eighteen years' imprisonment for plotting to further the aims of the UVF. Four of the men were also convicted of bombing two Glasgow pubs and the judge, Lord Ross, described the gang as 'wicked, brutal and senseless'. He also urged that the organisation should be declared illegal in Scotland. The convictions were believed to have broken up a sixty-strong UVF unit in Glasgow which had been engaged in supplying explosives to the UVF in NI. In the early 1980s the UVF suffered from informers both in Belfast and in Co. Armagh. Eighteen of twenty men arrested in Co. Armagh in 1982, on the evidence of ex-UVF informer Clifford McKeown, pleaded guilty to a variety of terrorist offences, some of which indicated that the organisation was then involved in sectarian murder attempts. In the Shankill area in the same year, police raids broke up a UVF group and uncovered firearms, including a homemade machine gun, and ammunition, and seven UVF men from Larne got a total of eighty-nine years' imprisonment on charges such as armed robbery and having guns and bombs. There were reports about the same time of internal differences in the organisation, notably in Belfast. In 1982 the UVF reacted angrily to a comment by the Chief Constable that weapons favoured by PIRA had been found in the possession of loyalists. In a statment the UVF asked:

'Is he not aware that the black market on which these weapons are purchased is not interested in the politics of Northern Ireland, but only in the cash and business which our conflict brings?' The same statement described the UVF as 'political soldiers with the spirit of 1912'. The organisation suffered a severe blow in April 1983, when one of its battalion commanders, Joseph Bennett, turned supergrass and gave evidence that resulted in the conviction of fourteen leading members, two of whom were sentenced to life imprisonment. Those convicted included John Graham, described as 'brigadier-general'. He was among those freed on appeal. Bennett was given immunity in respect of two murders and other offences. In the summer of 1983 there were more arrests arising from the activities of informers. In fact, the evidence since then was of more and more UVF members being made amenable for crimes. In June 1985 six UVF men were sentenced for eighty crimes, including four murders; another received seventeen years for the attempted murder of *Sunday World* journalist Jim Campbell. The only 'good news' for the organisation in 1985 was the collapse of the trial of supergrass William 'Budgie' Allen when Judge Higgins said his evidence was 'seriously flawed and unworthy of belief'. As a result twenty persons named by him were released, but five others, who had confessed, were sentenced. There was evidence of PIRA and INLA using those named in such trials as targets for assassination, and by 1993 four of those named by Bennett had been murdered. In addition to the loss of personnel due to court cases and assassinations, sources of arms for the organisation were also drying up. In 1988 a plot to smuggle arms from Toronto to NI via Liverpool was broken up. A Canadian citizen and a man from Liverpool were jailed for four years each for their involvement, and another Canadian was jailed in Canada. A fourth man was fighting efforts to return him for trial in GB. Early in 1988 the UVF share of a consignment of arms was discovered at Ligoniel in Belfast. In January 1988 a court was told of drugs stolen from the Royal Victoria Hospital being supplied to the UVF. In the early 1990s the UVF was active mainly in Belfast, counties Armagh and Tyrone, and to a lesser extent in E. Antrim and N. Down. Its most determined killers have been based, apparently, in the Portadown area and in N. Belfast. The Portadown unit is thought to have killed around twelve people in the area around Lough Neagh in 1990 and early 1991. Four Catholic men were gunned down at a pub in the Nationalist area of Cappagh, Co. Tyrone, in early March 1991. The rifles used had been employed in seven murders of Catholics in Lurgan, Cookstown and Stewartstown during the previous two years. Also in March 1991, in Craigavon, it shot dead two Catholic teenage girls and a man at a mobile shop, whose owner had received threats to his life. After two Catholics and a Protestant had been killed by the UVF at Portadown in November 1991, a local UVF commander told a Dublin newspaper that if PIRA laid down its arms, the UVF would do likewise. He said that he was regarded as 'a devil' by Catholics, but he was 'teetotal, non-smoking and deeply religious' and that 80 per cent of the thirty or so people killed by the UVF in mid-Ulster were Republicans. He also said the UVF shooting of a Lurgan Catholic as he sat in a car park with his girlfriend was a replica of the PIRA killing of a UDR man as he sat with his girlfriend in the same spot a fortnight earlier. In October 1991 the RUC Chief Constable said that the UVF and the UFF together had seventy to ninety gunmen on the streets. He did not give a breakdown of the figures, but the UVF is thought to be a much smaller organisation than the UFF. Security experts believe, however, that they have always co-operated to some extent, and probably much more closely since the Combined Loyalist Military Command emerged in 1991 and called a nine-week ceasefire at the start of the Brooke–Mayhew Talks. In 1992 the UVF was believed to have accounted for at least eleven murders; one of those who died was Sheena Campbell, a QUB student, who stood as PSF candidate in the Upper Bann by-election in 1990. The

UVF began 1993 by killing a Catholic father and son in the Dungannon area and a Catholic woman in N. Belfast, and before the end of 1993 it had claimed twelve lives. After the death of a volunteer, when a grenade exploded during the re-routed Whiterock Orange parade at the end of June, there was rioting on the Shankill for several nights. In November a large arms and explosives shipment from Poland, believed to be destined for the UVF, was intercepted at Teesport.

ULSTER WORKERS' COUNCIL

The body that organised and ran the loyalist strike in May 1974, which led to the collapse of the power-sharing administration. By the cutting of power supplies and extensive backing from Protestant paramilitary groups, it halted industrial and other activity, and the chaotic situation which had developed after fourteen days caused Unionist members to resign from the Executive and so render it ineffective. The UWC operated through a co-ordinating committee, headed by Vanguard Assembly member Glenn Barr. It included three leading politicians – Harry West (UUP); Rev. Ian Paisley (DUP); and William Craig (Vanguard). Among the paramilitary representatives were Andy Tyrie (UDA), Colonel Brush (Down Orange Welfare), Ken Gibson and Bill Hannigan (UVF political spokesmen), George Green (USC Association) and Bob Marno (Orange Volunteers). Its best-known spokesmen during the stoppage were Jim Smyth and Harry Murray, and other members were Billy Kelly (power workers), Hugh Petrie and Tom Beattie. The UWC was again active in the 1977 loyalist strike – a more limited affair – which had been backed by the United Unionist Action Council. But failure to halt electricity supplies in 1977 reduced its effectiveness. And in 1977 the UUP and Vanguard were opposed to the strike, although it was supported by the Rev. Ian Paisley and Ernest Baird, then leading the UUUP. In February 1981 its former chairman Harry Murray announced that the UWC was being reformed to campaign for jobs and to promote the

unity of workers. He said it would not have paramilitary links.

UNIONIST COALITION *see* United Ulster Unionist Council

UNIONIST PARTY OF NORTHERN IRELAND

Formed by those ex-members of the UUP who continued to support Brian Faulkner after the Sunningdale proposals had been rejected by the UUP, and Faulkner had resigned as party leader. Initially those who had rallied round Faulkner simply adopted the description 'Unionist Pro-Assembly', and six candidates employing this label unsuccessfully contested the February 1974 Westminster election. UPNI was formally launched in September 1974, four months after the collapse of the Executive, and Faulkner boldly expressed the view that it could become the 'mainstream' Unionist Party. But two of its nominees failed to get elected in the October 1974 Westminster election. In the Constitutional Convention, UPNI continued its support for power-sharing, and stressed the need for a strong regional government, with a maintenance of the UK link. But it dropped the idea of a Council of Ireland, which it held to be counterproductive in developing social and economic co-operation between NI and the Irish Republic. Its total of first-preference votes in the election was 50,891 (7.7 per cent of the total) and it got five seats out of the seventy-eight. In 1976, after the failure of the Convention, Faulkner (later Lord Faulkner) withdrew from the leadership of the party, and from active politics, and he died in a hunting accident in 1977. He was succeeded by Anne Dickson. In the 1977 District Council elections, the party fought on a narrow front, with only twenty-four candidates, and secured 13,691 first-preference votes (2.4 per cent of the total) and took 6 seats out of the 526. The party's viewpoint was represented in the House of Lords by Lord Brookeborough and Lord Moyola, and it continued to enjoy the support of several other former members of Unionist governments, including Sir John Andrews. In 1978 there were some rumours of a possible link-up with the UUP, but the party continued to differ with the UUP on the power-sharing issue, and seemed to be determined to maintain its independent stance. In the 1979 Westminster election it ran three candidates in Belfast, but its total vote was only 8,021 (1.2 per cent of the total vote) and all three candidates lost their deposits. In the 1979 European election it fared even worse. Its candidate, consultant engineer Eddie Cummings, had 0.6 per cent of first-preference votes and lost his deposit. Because of its poor showing in the 1981 council elections, when it shared seven seats and 1.9 per cent of the votes in a temporary coalition with UPUP, the party decided to wind up its organisation.

UNITED LABOUR PARTY
A party launched in 1978, with the declared aim of trying to establish a government in NI based on democratic socialism. Paddy Devlin, formerly of the SDLP, was one of the founders. Its draft constitution urged co-operation with other Labour movements throughout the British Isles. It also stated that the constitutional position of NI should only be changed if that would further political accommodation and have majority support from the electors. Devlin got just over 6,000 first-preference votes when he ran unsuccessfully as ULP candidate in the 1979 European election, and its nominee in the S. Belfast by-election for Westminster in 1982 secured 303 votes. It was absorbed in Labour '87, set up in 1987.

UNITED ULSTER UNIONIST COUNCIL
Sometimes called the Unionist Coalition, it was set up in January 1974 to fight the Sunningdale Agreement which it saw as a step to a united Ireland. It followed on the split in the Ulster Unionist Party, which elected Harry West as leader in succession to Brian Faulkner, who had become Chief Minister in the power-sharing Executive. The UUUC comprised the UUP, headed by West, the DUP, led by the Rev. Ian Paisley, and the Vanguard Unionists, headed by William Craig. The

group won eleven of the twelve NI seats in the February 1974 Westminster election. After the election a UUUC conference in April 1974 at Portrush, Co. Antrim, set out its immediate programme. It included the ending of the power-sharing Executive, fresh elections using PR but in smaller constituencies, the removal of the Secretary of State's veto power and an end to the Council of Ireland or even discussion of it. In Parliament these MPs formed a Unionist Parliamentary Coalition led by West, and later James Molyneaux MP succeeded West when the latter lost his Fermanagh–S. Tyrone seat in October 1974. The support of the UUUC for the UWC strike in May 1974 was an important element in the success of the stoppage. It continued to operate in the Convention election in 1975, and in the Convention it carried through the majority report which failed, however, to get backing from other parties. Craig's support for the idea of a voluntary coalition, embracing the SDLP for the period of the political emergency, led to a split in Vanguard, the majority of whose Convention members remained loyal to the UUUC when Craig was expelled from the Unionist Coalition. In early 1977 the UUUC , now made up of the UUP, DUP and the UUUM, headed by Ernest Baird (the UUUM included the majority section of Vanguard which had refused to follow Craig), began to show signs of serious internal strain. This was aggravated by the formation by the UUUC steering committee of United Unionist Action Council, which eventually took in paramilitary groups and mounted the abortive 'loyalist strike' in May 1977. The UUP condemned this venture, and the UUUC effectively collapsed. The Parliamentary Coalition at Westminster also broke up at the time of the 1977 stoppage, since two of its MPs , the Rev. Ian Paisley and John Dunlop, supported the stoppage. But the UUUC experiment at Westminster had important political implications. It marked the real break between the Conservative Party and Ulster Unionists in Parliament, and the end of Labour's overall majority in the Commons in 1976 gave the Unionist MPs the influence in 1977 to secure Labour Government support for a Speaker's conference to consider extra NI seats at Westminster – a long-standing demand of all shades of unionism and a move hitherto opposed by Labour – and the NI Boundary Commission recommended seventeen seats. The change took effect in the 1983 election and immediately benefited the UUP and SDLP.

UNITED ULSTER UNIONIST MOVEMENT *see* United Ulster Unionist Party *and* Vanguard Unionist Progressive Party

UNITED ULSTER UNIONIST PARTY

The party led by Ernest Baird which emerged to fight the District Council elections in May 1977. It was based on the UUUM – the breakaway movement from the Vanguard Party during the Constitutional Convention. UUUM was made up of the former Vanguard Convention members who were opposed to William Craig's idea of a voluntary coalition. Initially, UUUM campaigned for the creation of a single united Unionist party. When this appeared unattainable, Baird announced that the UUUM would become a political party as UUUP. In the 1977 council elections, it got 3.2 per cent of first-preference votes and twelve seats. In the 1979 Westminster election it retained Mid-Ulster, where the sitting MP, John Dunlop, was not opposed by the UUP. Ernest Baird was unsuccessful in Fermanagh–S. Tyrone. The party share of the vote in the election was 5.6 per cent (two seats contested). The party contested only seven District Councils in 1981 and won five seats with 4,653 votes (0.7 per cent). Although it was evident that the DUP had now captured the more fundamentalist Unionist vote, UUUP made a final effort in the 1982 Assembly election. It ran twelve candidates, but none was returned, and its share of the total vote was 1.8 per cent. The candidates included party leader Ernest Baird, deputy leader Reg Empey, and John Dunlop MP. The party did not contest the 1983 Westminster election or any subsequent election and ceased to exist.

UNITED UNIONIST ACTION COUNCIL

The body that organised vigilante patrols, known as the Ulster Service Corps, in the spring of 1977. It also promoted the loyalist strike in May 1977 against direct rule and in favour of tougher security measures – a stoppage which drew much less support than the UWC strike of 1974. The UUAC included the Rev. Ian Paisley and Ernest Baird, and its chairman was former Unionist MP Joseph Burns. It included representatives of the UWC, UDA, Orange Volunteers and Down Orange Welfare. The UUAC was technically a sub-committee of the steering committee of the UUUC. It was not, however, supported by the UUP or the VUPP and, unlike the organisers of the 1974 stoppage, failed to get the backing of the power workers.

UNITY MOVEMENT

An anti-Unionist group launched in April 1973. Its main personality was Frank McManus, then MP for Fermanagh–S. Tyrone. In May 1973 it issued a manifesto calling for an amnesty for all political prisoners, disbandment of the RUC, the setting up of a new police force, and repeal of all 'offensive and repressive' legislation. In the February 1974 Westminster election, McManus lost his seat and another Unity candidate in Armagh polled very few votes. In 1977 McManus was one of the founders of the Irish Independence Party.

V

VANGUARD SERVICE CORPS

The paramilitary organisation linked with Ulster Vanguard in its early years. When Ulster Vanguard became the Vanguard Unionist Progressive Party in 1973, the VSC took the title 'Ulster Volunteer Service Corps'. Its main purpose was to provide an escort for Vanguard speakers.

VANGUARD UNIONIST PROGRESSIVE PARTY

A political party which developed out of the Ulster Vanguard movement, led by William Craig. It was established as a party in March 1973, and mainly comprised ex-members of the UUP disenchanted with the policies of recent leaders – Terence O'Neill, James Chichester-Clark and Brian Faulkner. In the Assembly election of 1973 it secured seven seats and 10.5 per cent of the total vote, and in the Convention election of 1975 (as part of the UUUC) it doubled its representation to fourteen seats, although its share of the total vote had increased only to 12.7 per cent. This indicated the shrewdness with which the UUUC had distributed its candidates. VUPP reflected the strong opposition to direct rule of the Vanguard movement from which it sprang. It also opposed the British Government's White Paper on which the Assembly was based, and it pressed for tough measures against the PIRA. In the Convention, it was seriously split over Craig's support for the idea of voluntary coalition with the SDLP. Apart from Craig himself and two other members, David Trimble and Glenn Barr, the rest of the party broke away under the leadership of Ernest Baird, deputy leader, to form the UUUM, which in 1977 became the UUUP. The VUPP did not contest the 1977 District Council elections as an entity and in February 1978 it ceased to be a political party and reverted to its former status as Ulster Vanguard. Craig, then MP for E. Belfast moved to the UUP. The VUPP's other MP elected in 1977, John Dunlop in Mid-Ulster, had already joined the UUUP. In 1982 Craig, clearly disillusioned with the UUP, stood as Vanguard Unionist in the Assembly election in E. Belfast, but got only 2,000 first-preference votes. (*See also* Ulster Vanguard.)

VAN STRAUBENZEE, SIR WILLIAM
Minister of State, NIO, 1972–4. b. 27 January 1924. Conservative MP for Wokingham, 1959–87. Church (of England) Commissioner, 1967–. Known as 'the Bishop' in Westminster circles, he presided as NI Minister of State over a committee which drew up proposals to counter religious and political discrimination in jobs, and which led eventually to the setting up of the Fair Employment Agency.

VIGGERS, PETER
Parliamentary Under-Secretary, NIO, 1986–9. b. 13 March 1938. Conservative MP for Gosport since February 1974. Parliamentary Private Secretary to Solicitor-General, 1979–83; Paliamentary Private Secretary to first Secretary at Treasury, 1983–6. His appointment to Stormont as Industry Minister was his first Government job, but he had some previous business contacts with NI. He arrived at a difficult moment, with Unionist hostility to Ministers at its height in the wake of the AIA. Also his predecessor at the Department of Economic Affairs, Dr Rhodes Boyson, had run into criticism for suggesting that there should be a Government-supported system of emigration and that he would be raising the matter with US and Canadian immigration officials. Viggers did not pursue this idea, and although he was active in pushing small-firm developments locally and seeking to find outside industrial investment, he was able to record only modest gains in jobs, and trade unionists argued that changes in the official statistics tended to under-state real unemployment. In 1988 he found all the local political parties united against him when he proposed privatisation of the Belfast shipyard, Harland and Wolff plc, Short Brothers' aerospace factories, and the NIE.

VITTY, DENNY
DUP Assembly member for E. Belfast, 1982–6. Served on committee on Economic Development. b. 1950. Castlereagh Council, 1977–89. Mayor, 1987–8. North Down Council, 1989–93. Resigned council seat in January 1993. Fought North Down parliamentary constituency, 1992.

VOLUNTEER POLITICAL PARTY
Political wing of Protestant paramilitary organisation the UVF, it emerged briefly in September 1974. Its chairman, Ken Gibson, contested the October 1974 Westminster election in W. Belfast. He had some support from the UDA in the area but polled only 2,690 votes. The VPP supported the link with Britain, and said either a united Ireland or UDI would

mean higher taxes and a cut in social security benefits. (*See also* Ulster Volunteer Force.)

W

WALKER, (ALFRED) CECIL

UUP MP for N. Belfast, 1983–. b. 17 December 1924. Manager of timber firm before entering Parliament. He has repeatedly expressed concern about sectarian killings in his constituency, where more than 600 deaths had occurred up to the start of 1993 and where both Republican and loyalist paramilitaries were extremely active in the early 1990s. In 1988 became first MP to go to prison for refusing to pay a fine for contravening new public order laws, which, he claimed, were 'shackling traditional freedoms'. With the SDLP standing aside and a united Unionist vote, he had a majority of some 16,000 in the 1986 by-election held to protest against the AIA, but his winning margin was halved to some 8,000 in 1987 when he was opposed by George Seawright, standing as a Protestant Unionist. In 1992 he had a 9,600 winning margin in an eight-cornered contest. In April 1992 he urged that the terms of the broadcasting ban should be extended to newspapers. In October 1992 he joined the recently elected SDLP MP for W. Belfast Dr Joe Hendron on a US tour seeking investment in their constituencies. In June 1993, in the aftermath of the rioting that followed the re-routing of a Whiterock Orange parade, he asked the RUC to 'arrest known members of the UDA and its ringleaders'. Party spokesman on housing/environment, 1992–.

WARRENPOINT

South Co. Down port and seaside resort, near which eighteen soldiers died on 27 August 1979 in two PIRA explosions. It was the largest death toll in any incident up to that date. The ambush came only a few hours after Lord Mountbatten had been killed when his boat was blown up by PIRA off the Co. Sligo coast in the Republic.

WATERS, LIEUTENANT-GENERAL SIR JOHN

Army GOC, NI, June 1988–90. b. 2 September 1935. Sandhurst. Commissioned Gloucestershire Regiment, 1955. Served in NI early in the Troubles; after a second tour, promoted to command regiment in 1975. Commanded 3rd Infantry Brigade (based at Portadown), 1979–81. Deputy Commander Land Forces in Falklands campaign, 1982. Commander, 4th Armoured Division, BAOR, 1983–5. Commandant, Staff College, Camberley, 1986–8. His experience of service in other trouble spots – Aden, Persian Gulf, Cyprus, Belize – has resulted in the description 'one of the most experienced anti-terrorist experts in the army'. His arrival in NI as GOC in June 1988 coincided with an upsurge in PIRA attacks on regular soldiers and the establishment of a new brigade based at Armagh.

WELLS, JAMES HENRY (JIM)

DUP Assembly member for S. Down, 1982–6. Served on committees on Environment, and Health and Social Services. b. 1957. BA Hons. Diploma in Town and Country Planning (QUB). Lisburn Borough Council, 1981–5; Banbridge District Council, 1985–8. Announced decision to leave active politics in September 1988.

WEST, HENRY WILLIAM (HARRY)

Leader of the UUP, 1974–9. b. Enniskillen, 27 March 1917. High Sheriff, Fermanagh, 1954. President, Ulster Farmers' Union, 1955–6. Unionist MP for Enniskillen, 1954–72. Parliamentary Secretary, Ministry of Agriculture, 1958. Minister of Agriculture, 1960–6 and 1971–2. MP for Fermanagh–S. Tyrone, 1974, and leader of United Unionist Parliamentary Coalition at Westminster, 1974. Elected from Fermanagh–S. Tyrone to Assembly, 1973–4, and Constitutional Convention, 1975–6. During the 1968–71 period, he led the West Ulster Unionist Council and strongly criticised reforms which he saw as weakening unionism and the position of the NI Government. In particular, he opposed local government changes and the setting up of a central housing authority. He also resisted the idea of an unarmed police force, and the abolition of the USC. But he resigned from the West Ulster Unionist Council in June 1971, and accepted Brian Faulkner's invitation to return as Minister of Agriculture. He was not, however, prepared to follow Faulkner on the issue of power-sharing government and the Sunningdale Agreement, and in January 1974 he was elected to succeed Faulkner as UUP leader, when the Ulster Unionist Council rejected the Sunningdale package. He aligned the UUP with the DUP and Vanguard in the UUUC and he gained the Fermanagh-S. Tyrone seat as official UUUC candidate in the February 1974 election. He lost it again in October 1974 when the anti-Unionists combined to support Frank Maguire, Independent. In the Assembly he led his party in opposition to the three-party Executive, although he dissociated his supporters from rowdy scenes in and around the Assembly chamber. He backed the UWC strike in May 1974 which led to the fall of the Executive. In the Constitutional Convention, he continued to resist the idea of power-sharing at Cabinet level, although he always insisted that his attitude was not anti-Catholic, but only directed to refusing co-operation in government with those who sought a united Ireland. In early 1977 he gradually drifted apart from the Rev. Ian Paisley and Ernest Baird, the other two leaders of the UUUC. The differences centred on a Unionist Action Council which mounted a strike in May 1977 against direct rule and in favour of a much tougher security policy. West and his party refused to back the strike, which got only limited support from loyalists, and the result was to confirm the break-up of the UUUC. Between 1977 and 1979 he was engaged in many discussions with Secretary of State Roy Mason on the possibility of some form of interim devolution, but the talks were unproductive. In the European Parliament election in June 1979, he secured just under 57,000 first-preference votes, which inevitably led to comparisons with the Rev. Ian Paisley's 170,000, and he was eliminated on the fourth count. He claimed that some 100,000 UUP voters had refused to turn out because of their doubts about the Common Market. But he immediately tendered his resignation as party leader, and on 2 July – within four weeks of the election – he confirmed this and was succeeded by James Molyneaux MP. He lost to hunger-striker Bobby Sands, with a united anti-Unionist vote behind him, in the April 1981 Westminster by-election in Fermanagh-S. Tyrone. He has been the leading figure in the Charter Group, which challenged UUP leadership and called for devolution.

WEST ULSTER UNIONIST COUNCIL

A large pressure group within the UUP, active between 1969 and 1971 in defending traditional unionism. It opposed reforms such as the reduction of the powers of local authorities and the setting up of a central housing authority. It also demanded tougher security policies. It was spearheaded by Fermanagh Unionist Association, and although the bulk of its membership was made up of Unionist associations in W. Ulster, it also had the support of several constituency associations in Belfast and E. Ulster. It was frequently attacked by liberal Unionists as a divisive force, but Harry West MP, who led it for most of the time, insisted that it spoke for the majority of grass-roots Unionists. He resigned from the council in 1971, when he became Minister of Agriculture in the Faulkner Government.

WHEELER, SIR JOHN (DANIEL)

Minister of State at NIO from June 1993, when he replaced Michael Mates and acquired his responsibilities for law and order, including policing and prisons, and the Department of Finance and Personnel. Privy Council, 1993–. Conservative MP for Westminster North, 1983–; previously represented City of Westminster, Paddington, 1979–83. b. 1 May 1940. Assistant prison governor until 1974 at Wandsworth Prison and then Brixton, where his interest in the causes of crime developed. He continued his career in the private security industry and its inspectorate, while the Home Office made use of his expertise on its Crime Prevention Committee, 1976–92. On his election to Parliament in 1979 he became a member of the Home Affairs Select Committee and served as chairman from 1987 to 1992; he also chaired its sub-committee on Race Relations and Immigration, 1980–7. Although knighted in 1990, ministerial preferment had passed him by for fourteen years, when the opportunity at the NIO arrived. During the summer of 1993 he pointed to the success of the security forces in arms and explosives finds and the numbers arrested and charged with terrorist offences. He also indicated a willingness to consider, for Belfast, the London experience of a video camera surveillance system. In August he told the *Belfast Telegraph* that the defeat of terrorism would come not from armies or police but 'principally from the people themselves' and that it would be within the rule of law. He defended the spending of £373,000 on anti-terrorism television adverts and stated that security co-operation with the Republic had never been better. He dismissed as 'personal thoughts' which 'sprang from no policy considerations of any kind' comments made by his predecessor, Michael Mates, that cuts in financial subvention from the Treasury to NI could change attitudes. He attracted criticism at the end of August with his Mason-like comment to the BBC that the 'IRA is already defeated', because its aims were unobtainable. Early in September he condemned loyalists for the murder of prison officer Jim Peacock and their 'bloody trail'. Towards the end of the month he restated his priority of a complete and final end to terrorism and claimed that the PSF attempt to 'combine the bullet and the ballot box [was] doomed'. After the December Budget he warned of 700 job losses in the civil service but by the spring of 1994 the Next Steps initiative in the public sector threatened 3,000 jobs with privatisation.

WHEELER, MAJOR-GENERAL ROGER

Army GOC, NI, January 1993–. b. 1941. Served with the Royal Ulster Rifles in Borneo and later commanded the Royal Irish Rangers in Belize and Berlin, 1979–82. He was Chief of Staff of the forces involved in the Falklands war and Chief of Staff at the Ministry of Defence before taking up his NI appointment.

WHITELAW, LORD

As William Whitelaw, first Secretary of State of NI, March 1972–November 1973. b. 28 June 1918. Golfing blue, Cambridge University, 1936–9. Took up farming on Cumberland estate after resigning army commission, 1947. Conservative MP for Penrith and the Border, 1955–83. Chief Conservative Whip, 1964–70. Lord President of the Council and leader of the Commons, 1970–2. Employment Secretary, 1973–4. Chairman, Conservative Party, 1974–5. Deputy leader of Conservative Party, 1975–9, and spokesman on Home Affairs, 1975–9. Deputy PM, 1979–88 (also Home Secretary, 1979–83, Lord President of the Council and leader of Lords, 1983–88). On taking over at Stormont in 1972, the genial Whitelaw had to face a double threat – the wrath of loyalists deprived of a local Parliament and Government and a big effort by the PIRA, so that the overall result was a year with 467 violent deaths. In a bid to keep a brief PIRA ceasefire going, he tried a controversial initiative in early July 1972. He met PIRA leaders secretly in London, but the Provisionals' terms were too sweeping to be acceptable to the British Government. The Secretary of State reported to MPs that the PIRA wanted:

1 A public declaration that the Irish people as a whole should decide the future of Ireland.
2 The withdrawal of all British troops from Irish soil by 1 January 1975.
3 Pending the withdrawal, all troops should be withdrawn immediately from 'sensitive areas'.
4 A general amnesty for all political prisoners, internees and persons on the wanted list.

Whitelaw also said the Provisionals had expressed regret that internment had not been halted in response to their ceasefire, which had been ended after a fortnight, following a single dispute about housing in W. Belfast which, Whitelaw claimed, could easily have been resolved peacefully. The thinking behind the meeting with PIRA, according to the Minister of State at the time, David Howell, (*The Times*, 10 February 1975) was that the Government wanted to show that everything had been tried, including truce and meeting, so that PIRA would be seen to be concerned only with violence. But it is also thought that the Government had intelligence that PIRA planned concessions which never materialised. (That meeting – the only one between a NI Secretary of State in office and PIRA – was recorded by the BBC. This was disclosed in October 1989, in the BBC house journal *Ariel,* by the then Controller of Editorial Policy, John Wilson. Commenting on the broadcasting ban on paramilitaries, he said there were 'overwhelming arguments against it'. He added: 'Just one example: when the IRA went to meet Mr [now Lord] Whitelaw, we recorded the meeting. We have the tapes but they cannot now be used.') About the same time, Whitelaw made what he later admitted to Parliament was a mistake – he agreed to special privileges for convicted terrorists who belonged to the political paramilitary groups. This 'special category' system began following a hunger strike in Belfast Prison during which PIRA leader Billy McKee was close to death. After 'Bloody Friday' in Belfast – 21 July 1972 – when ten civilians and three soldiers died in the city, Whitelaw ordered the takeover of the no-go areas. These were the areas, mainly in W. Belfast and in Derry's Bogside, where there was little control by the security forces. On 31 July 1972 the army moved into the areas in strength in 'Operation Motorman', and while two people were killed by troops in Derry, there was little resistance generally. But despite the continuance of violence, both from PIRA and loyalist groups, he tried to move the emphasis to political progress, and organised a conference of local political parties at Darlington in September 1972. Too few parties

accepted to make the exercise worth while. None the less, at the end of October 1972 he produced a discussion paper (a Green Paper in British parliamentary terms, but the phrase was officially avoided) which pointed to the need to recognise both the British and Irish dimensions in the NI situation. In March 1973 this was translated into a White Paper which set out the Government's plans for new-style devolved government. It proposed a seventy-eight-member Assembly elected by PR, and power-sharing between the parties as an alternative to majority government. Unionists were sharply divided on the document, but SDLP and Alliance gave it a general welcome. Whitelaw began the most severe test of his diplomacy on 5 October 1973 (that is, precisely five years after the violent scenes in Derry's Duke Street) when he met the delegations from three parties at Stormont Castle. The Unionists were led by Brian Faulkner, the SDLP by Gerry Fitt, and Alliance by Oliver Napier. The talks were patiently piloted by Whitelaw over seven weeks, and often they came close to breakdown. But finally, on 21 November 1973, a formula was agreed for a three-party Executive (in effect, a coalition). But the final seal on strategy and details of the Council of Ireland had to be left to a conference at Sunningdale in Berkshire, in early December, attended by PM Edward Heath and by Irish Ministers, headed by the Taoiseach Liam Cosgrave. Immediately before the conference Whitelaw moved to the Department of Employment, and he was succeeded by Francis Pym as NI Secretary of State. As Conservative deputy leader, he resisted pressures from within the party to depart from the broadly bipartisan approach to NI that had been established in 1969. As Home Secretary and deputy Premier in the Thatcher Government, he caused some surprise when he hinted at the 1982 Conservative conference that citizens of the Irish Republic living in GB might lose their voting rights. In December 1982 he banned two PSF Assembly members, Gerry Adams and Danny Morrison, from entering GB because of their alleged links with terrorism. One of his last acts as Home Secretary in June 1983 was to remove the ban on Adams, once he had been elected in W. Belfast. Although on Cabinet committee which planned the AIA, he declared in 1987 that the political log jam could only be broken by NI politicians themselves. He suggested that if they were to sink their differences and work together, they would have a very strong hand to play with any British Government. On loyalist protests against the AIA, he said the Government would not bow to any kind of undemocratic pressure. When he retired from the Government for health reasons in 1988, he said the collapse of power-sharing in 1974 had been 'one of the great sadnesses of my life'. In 1992 he described the NI post as the most 'challenging' of his career and the setting up of the power-sharing Executive as his 'single most successful action'. His worst moment had been the PIRA bombs in Hyde Park and Regent's Park in London in July 1982.

WHITTEN, HERBERT

UUP member of NI Assembly, 1973–4, and Convention, 1975–6, elected from Armagh. b. Portadown, Co. Armagh, 1909; d. 1981. He was one of three UUP members of the Assembly who voted against a vote of confidence in the power-sharing Executive in February 1974. Prominent in Orange Order in Co. Armagh. Stormont MP for Central Armagh, 1969–72. Portadown Borough Council, 1968–72, Mayor, 1968–9; Craigavon District Council, 1973–81.

WIDGERY REPORT see 'Bloody Sunday'

WILLIAMS, BETTY

One of the three founders of the Peace People in 1976. She was joint recipient, with Mairead Corrigan, of the Nobel Peace Prize, 1976. b. Belfast 1943. A housewife from Andersonstown, one of Belfast's Republican strongholds, she witnessed the tragedy (that is, the accident in which the three Maguire children were killed) which inspired her, together with Mairead Corrigan and Ciaran McKeown, to launch the Peace

People movement. She travelled abroad extensively to talk about the movement. In 1980 she stepped down from the PP executive, although continuing to campaign for it. Before leaving NI to live in the US in 1982, she said she had had 200 job refusals in eighteen months. In December 1982 she married an American businessman, Jim Perkins, in Florida. In 1986, when she returned for a TV programme to mark the tenth anniversary of the PP, her two co-founders declined to meet her. She said her crime had been to accept the £38,000 Nobel Prize. 'I took it; I needed the money; I am guilty as charged,' she said.

WILSEY, LIEUTENANT-GENERAL SIR JOHN

Army GOC, NI, 1990–3. b. 18 February 1939. Had extensive previous experience in NI when he arrived at Lisburn HQ. Served in Belfast, Derry and other centres as a company commander with his regiment (Devonshire and Dorset) in 1970s, and at later periods was Chief of Staff and commander of the 3rd Infantry Brigade based at Portadown. He had been deputy commander in the Falklands and also served in Libya, British Guiana, Cyprus, Malta and Germany. Other senior posts included Chief of Staff, UK Land Forces, and when he left NI he was appointed Commander-in-Chief, UK Land Forces. He was in NI at a time when PIRA directed much of its effort at security bases, particularly on the border. He briefed PM John Major on his first visit to NI, and handled merger of Royal Irish Rangers and UDR. He also brought about alignment of RUC and army areas so as to achieve closer co-ordination. In 1991 he had talks with Bishop (now Cardinal) Daly. In the autumn of 1992 he was said to be the source for press speculation concerning internment. Before leaving NI in January 1993, he was criticised by the SDLP and PSF for saying he was 'not ashamed' of the situation in which an army spy, Brian Nelson, had been convicted of conspiracy to murder five Catholics. In August the *Sunday Times* claimed that he had sought approval for a sixty-point peace plan put to PIRA at Christmas 1992.

WILSON, LORD (OF RIEVAULX)
As Harold Wilson, Labour PM, 1964–70
and 1974–6. b. 11 March 1916. Harold
Wilson's career touched NI at many
points. As a young civil servant, he toyed
with the idea of seeking the post of
economic adviser to the NI Government.
As Labour Party leader (1963–76), he was
highly conscious of the importance of the
Irish vote in Britain. He often remarked
that he had reminded successive Irish
leaders that he had more Irish people in
his Huyton (Liverpool) constituency than
they had in theirs. As PM at the start of
the civil rights campaign in 1968, he,
with Home Secretary James Callaghan,
had to deal with the crisis produced by
the demands for reform and later, in
1969, with the serious violence in Belfast,
Derry and other towns. Harold Wilson
had, apparently, already made up his
mind to send troops to NI when the
appeal for them came from Stormont in
August 1969. And he personally handled
the critical talks with NI Ministers that set
the stage for reforms – social, political and
in the reorganisation of the RUC and
disbandment of the B Specials. His most
comprehensive statement of his personal
views was in a speech as opposition leader
in the Commons in November 1971. He
urged more attention to the aspiration of
a united Ireland, while stressing that it
could come only with the agreement of
people in NI. But he said the dream must
be there. 'If men of moderation have
nothing to hope for, men of violence will
have something to shoot for.' So he
suggested talks between the Westminster,
Dublin and Stormont Parliaments which
could lead to a Constitutional
Commission which would work out
arrangements for a united Ireland, which
could become effective fifteen years after
agreement had been reached, provided
that political violence had ceased. He also
urged the participation of Catholics at all
levels of Government, and the removal of
all security powers from Stormont and
their transfer to London. His approach
was condemned by Unionists and by
some members of the NILP, but given a
cautious welcome by Catholic politicians.
Wilson had never been enthusiastic about
direct rule, but he backed the decision of

the Heath Government to impose it in
1972. In 1974 he returned to power to
face the challenge of the loyalist strike,
and was attacked both by loyalists and by
the SDLP. The Unionists resented fiercely
his speech on 25 May 1974, in which he
condemned the strike organisers as people
'purporting to act as though they were an
elected government, spending their lives
sponging on Westminster'. The SDLP said
he had failed to act toughly enough to
smash the strike. In 1975 he travelled to
Stormont to announce the Convention
election, and he saw the Convention fail
before he left office in 1976. Life peer,
1983.

**WILSON, GERARD PATRICK
(PADDY)**
SDLP Senator who was stabbed to death at
a lonely quarry on the Upper Hightown
Road in N. Belfast on 26 June 1973. b.
1933. A woman friend, to whom he had
given a lift in his car, was murdered at the
same time. The murders were claimed by
the UFF as part of a campaign to secure
the release of their members from
detention. He had been elected to Senate
in 1968 as Rep. Lab. but left that party in
1970 when he was one of the founders of
the SDLP. He was also a Belfast City
Councillor. At the time of his death he
had been acting as election agent to
Gerry Fitt MP for the Assembly elections.

WILSON, GORDON
Independent member of the Republic's
Senate, February 1993–. b. 1927. Retired
draper. Appointed Senator on
nomination of Taoiseach Albert
Reynolds. His account of the death of his
twenty-year-old daughter, Marie, in the
Enniskillen Remembrance Sunday
bombing in 1987 attracted interest
around the world, and he has become
widely known as a peace campaigner. He
hoped his acceptance of the Senate seat
would 'help to build bridges'. In April
1993 he met two representatives of PIRA
at a secret venue in NI in a bid to dissuade
the organisation from its 'armed struggle',
but admitted afterwards that it had been
'a pointless meeting' and he now believed
internment of Republican and loyalist
suspects should be considered. In

November he told BBC Radio Ulster that he and two others had met three loyalist paramilitary leaders and a further meeting was planned. He attended a PSF peace commission meeting in Dublin in February 1994 and made a plea for an end to violence.

WILSON, HUGH

Alliance Asssembly, 1973–4, and Convention, 1975–6, member for N. Antrim. b. Ballyclare, Co. Antrim, 1905. MB, B.Ch., BAO (QUB). Consultant surgeon (FRCS). Narrowly defeated in Larne by William Craig in the 1969 Stormont election. Unsuccessfully contested N. Antrim seat (held by the Rev. Ian Paisley) in Westminster election, October 1974. Member of Larne Borough Council, 1977–85.

WILSON, JAMES (JIM)

Secretary and chief executive, Ulster Unionist Party, November 1987–. b. 15 December 1941. Chairman, Ballyclare Unionist Association, 1982–. Newtownabbey Council, 1975–89. North Eastern Education and Library Board, 1981–5. Prominent in Orange and Black institutions. In 1987 general election he was seconded by party to help Jim Kilfedder (UPUP) in his N. Down campaign. Accompanied party delegation at Brooke–Mayhew Talks, 1991–2.

WILSON, JOHN

As Tánaiste (deputy Taoiseach) in the FF–Prog. D. Coalition headed by Albert Reynolds, in 1992 he led the Republic's delegation in the Brooke–Mayhew Talks on NI's future. b. Kilcogy, Co. Cavan, 1923, son of a schoolmaster who taught in Belfast for some years. MA, H.Dip.Ed. A former schoolteacher and university lecturer, he became a TD in 1973 and held many ministerial posts, including Posts and Telegraphs, Transport and Education. He was Tánaiste 1989–92, and his decision not to stand again for the Dáil was announced immediately the NI talks ended in November 1992, and caused surprise in Dublin. He had been a noted Gaelic footballer.

WILSON, SAMUEL (SAMMY)

First DUP Lord Mayor of Belfast, 1986–7. Press Officer, DUP, 1982–. b. 4 April 1953. Belfast City Council, 1981–. Teacher of economics. Was Lord Mayor at height of Unionist local government campaign against AIA, and refused to meet Dublin's Lord Mayor because of it. Strong supporter of devolution, with 'left-of-centre approach in national politics'. He was vocal in the DUP publicity effort in 1993 to re-establish its separate identity and recover ground lost to UUP in the 1992 talks. The UUP's rebuff to a sudden change in DUP tactics – offering a united front when its District Council election campaign did not turn the tide – was met by an allegation of 'treachery'. He was responsible for the Belfast City Council motion banning the Irish President, Mary Robinson, from council property because of her handshake with Gerry Adams earlier in the year. Believing that the 1992 talks had broken down because of 'pan-Nationalist intransigence', he dismissed the threat by Taoiseach Reynolds to proceed without the DUP when it refused to take part in the Ancram bilateral talks in September. From the publication of the party document, 'Breaking the Log-Jam', until the Downing Street Declaration in mid-December, his was a less visible presence than that of Nigel Dodds. His description of the UDA Doomsday document in January 1994 as a 'very valuable return to reality' appeared strident.

WINDLESHAM, LORD

Minister of State, NIO, 1972–3. b 28 January 1932. Lord Windlesham, a Catholic, was deputy to William Whitelaw when he took over as Secretary of State, NI, in March 1972. Has strong Irish links – his ancestor, Richard Hennessy (1720–1800), b. Co. Cork, went to Cognac, France, in 1765, and founded the firm of Hennessy. At the NIO Lord Windlesham was spokesman in the House of Lords, and his responsibilities included community relations, Home Affairs and Development. In 1973 he became Government leader in the Lords, and Conservative leader there when Labour came to power in 1974. Headed inquiry into *Death on the Rock* programme made by Thames Television in 1988. Principal, Brasenose College, Oxford, 1989-.

WOMEN TOGETHER

A peace movement launched in November 1970, which has brought together women from Protestant and Catholic areas to campaign against violence. The group was strongly criticised by PSF, some of whose supporters disrupted WT meetings. Monica Patterson, who was chairwoman of the movement from 1970 to 1973, said that it quickly achieved the position where it was listened to by the army chiefs, the Secretary of State and even PM Harold Wilson. She said that if it vouched for the innocence of youths who had been 'lifted', they were released. 'We were out on the streets,' she wrote in 1978, 'stopping rowdyism between gangs of youths . . . stopping armed youths engaged in vandalism of property, sweeping the streets and having burned-out vehicles removed . . . supporting the victims of intimidation.' In the 1990s it has been particularly involved in supporting families bereaved by sectarian killings.

WOOD, ANDREW

Director, NI Information Service, February 1987-. b. 1943. Head of Information in NIO (London), 1983-7; Chief Press Officer, Home Office, 1980-3; and Press Officer, Downing Street, 1976-80. Before joining civil service, worked for newspapers on Teeside, BBC radio news, BBC TV features, and *Visnews*.

WOODFIELD, SIR PHILIP

Permanent Secretary, NIO, 1981-3. b. 30 August 1923. His arrival as head of the official side of the NIO almost coincided with James Prior's appointment as Secretary of State, and he brought to the post very diverse political experience, including a spell in the early 1970s as deputy Secretary at Stormont. He joined the Home Office in 1950 and served there for three different periods, and from 1961 to 1965 he was at 10 Downing

Street, as private secretary to three PMs – Macmillan, Douglas-Home, and Wilson. He was also with the Federal Government of Nigeria from 1955 to 1957, and in 1966 was secretary to Lord Mountbatten's committee of inquiry into prison conditions. In 1987 he was named as first Ombudsman for the security services, MI5 and MI6. On Royal Commission on Criminal Justice set up after a series of miscarriages of justice, including the Birmingham Six case.

WORKERS' PARTY

A Republican party with a strong socialist content operating in both NI and the Republic. In 1992 it suffered a serious split when six of its seven TDs left the party to set up a new organisation, initially called New Agenda, and from 28 March, Democratic Left. In 1982 its three Dáil TDs supported Charles Haughey as Taoiseach and enabled him to form a minority government. Its change of name was clearly designed to dissociate itself from paramilitarism, since with the split in the Republican movement in 1970, Official Sinn Féin and the Republican Clubs were the political counterpart of the OIRA. As Republican Clubs, the organisation was declared illegal in NI in March 1967 by William Craig as Minister of Home Affairs. In April 1973 – that is, a year after the OIRA had begun its ceasefire – the proscription was removed. It was a move by the British Government to try to bring more militant elements into the political process. By that time the Republican Clubs had become more Marxist, in line with the general trend in Official Sinn Féin. In the Assembly election in 1973 it opposed the Government's White Paper and urged an all-Ireland socialist republic. It put up ten candidates, but none of its nominees was returned, and the party's total first-preference vote was 13,064 (1.8 per cent of the total). In the Convention election it again failed to secure a seat with 2.2 per cent of the vote. In the District Council elections in May 1977 it got six seats out of the 526, with 14,277 first-preference votes (2.6 per cent of the total). By the end of the decade they were firmly committed to the political path and experimented with various names from Republican Clubs The Workers' Party to Sinn Féin The Workers' Party before settling on The Workers' Party in 1982. However, in the 1981 council elections it lost three of its six seats, and had only 1.8 per cent of first-preferences, while in the 1985 council contests, its vote dropped slightly to 1.6 per cent but gained one seat. In the 1982 Assembly election the party improved its showing in terms of the overall vote, with 2.7 per cent of first-preferences, but failed to secure any representation. Its vote in the European election in 1984 was 1.3 per cent. It also contests Westminster elections, but has not so far achieved a significant vote. The WP refused to take part in the NIF, and its attitude to the AIA was 'reluctantly in favour', although its TDs backed the agreement in the Dáil. In NI the party stressed its demand for devolution worked out by local parties. Seamus Lynch, Northern chairman, dismissed as 'laughable' press allegations in 1987 that the party was linked with the OIRA and serious crime. But the OIRA controversy would not go away, and it was a major factor in the 1992 split in the party. The break was fully reflected in NI, although there were some claims that the numbers joining the new group were smaller in NI than in the Republic. Seamus Lynch was among those who joined Dem. L. and when he fought N. Belfast in the 1992 Westminster election, he got 1,386 votes to 419 for Margaret Smith of WP. Fighting eight seats in the election, WP got only 0.6 per cent of the votes against 2.6 per cent in the 1987 Westminster election and 2.1 per cent in the 1989 council elections. Best showing of the WP in 1992 was in Upper Bann where its new Northern leader, Tom French, got 1,120 votes, well down on 1987. In the November 1992 election in the Republic, the WP had only 0.7 per cent of the votes againt 4.3 per cent in 1989, and the only TD who had stayed with WP, Tomás Mac Giolla, lost his seat in Dublin. In 1992 Marian Donnelly of Maghera, Co. Derry, became national chairwoman of the party. The party emerged from the 1993 council poll with just one seat. Its NI chairman, Tom French, lost his seat in

Craigavon. In September French accused Hume of giving 'a cloak of respectability' to PSF through his talks with Adams. He called for inter-party talks or devolution and the introduction of a Bill of Rights.

WRIGHT, JAMES CLAUDE

Speaker, US House of Representatives, 1987–9. b. 22 December 1922. Congressman, 1954–. Majority leader (Democrat) in House, 1976–87. His family forebears were from Castlecaulfield, Co. Tyrone, and he demonstrated the same close interest in Irish affairs as his predecessor, 'Tip' O'Neill. In 1989 he was involved in a scandal that forced his resignation. Former Presbyterian lay minister.

WRIGHT, SIR OLIVER

First UK Government representative in NI, August 1969–March 1970. b. 6 March 1921. A senior diplomat, he was sent to NI in a 'watch-dog' role for PM Harold Wilson. He was engaged in the delicate negotiations about the removal of barricades in Belfast's Falls Road in 1969, and in monitoring the NI Government's reform programme. On leaving, he said that Britain had tended to neglect NI in the past, and NI had tended willingly to run its own affairs, and this had been wrong for both sides of the equation. British Ambassador to West Germany, 1975–81. With increased Irish-American activity and with US opinion playing an increasing role in Anglo-Irish exchanges, his appointment as ambassador to Washington DC in 1982 was seen by NIO as timely. He stayed there until 1986. Co-chairman, Anglo-Irish Encounter, 1986–.

Y

YOUNG, SIR ARTHUR

Chief Constable, RUC, 1969–70. b. 1908; d. January 1979. Sir Arthur interrupted his career as City of London Police Commissioner to take over control of the RUC during the crucial period of reorganisation of the RUC arising from the Hunt report. He did so at the personal request of PM Harold Wilson, who saw

Sir Arthur's experience in terrorism in Malaya and elsewhere as valuable in restoring the morale of the force, which had been shaken by the violence of the summer of 1969. In reorganising the RUC he angered many Unionists, some of whom dubbed him 'Mr Softly, Softly'.

YOUNG CITIZENS VOLUNTEER FORCE

A Protestant extremist youth group active mainly in 1974 and 1975. An RUC detective told a court in February 1975 that it had been formed for the sole purpose of killing Catholics. In the summer of 1974 there were reports that it was involved in the petrol-bombing of Catholic homes.

ELECTION RESULTS

1968–93

1968 STORMONT BY-ELECTIONS

Lisnaskea, 22 March 1968

Elec. 10,600	% Poll 83.0
Brooke, J. (U.)	4,428
Patterson, F. (Ind. U.)	3,270
Wynne, J. (U. Lib.)	1,102
U. maj.	1,158
No change	

Londonderry City, 16 May 1968

Elec. 19,688	% Poll 68.8
Anderson, A.W. (U.)	9,122
Wilcox, Mrs J. (NILP)	3,944
U. maj.	5,178
No change	

South Antrim, 6 November 1968

Elec. 38,672	% Poll 49.6
Ferguson, R. (U.)	16,288
Coulthard, J. (NILP)	2,848
U. maj.	13,440
No change	

1969 STORMONT GENERAL ELECTION

The Stormont general election on 24 February 1969 was dubbed by PM Captain Terence O'Neill the 'crossroads election'. He insisted that it was the last chance for Northern Irish people to vote for sensible, reformist policies that would enable NI to have the respect of Westminster, and that would assure its continued membership of the UK. At the same time civil rights supporters were suspicious of the will, or the ability, of the Premier to deliver reforms. And within unionism he was assailed by many who suggested he was selling out to those who wanted a united Ireland. So the election battle took on a wholly new character – there were Unofficial Unionists who supported O'Neill against Official Unionists who opposed him. There were Independents who represented the broad civil rights platform, and People's Democracy candidates who spoke for the more revolutionary wing. The PM had been strongly criticised for attacking Official Unionists who did not share his view. But the Premier replied that he could not support those who equivocated or hedged, and who did not back vital parts of the Unionist manifesto. He was under fire from the former PM Lord Brookeborough, and from his ex-ministerial colleague, Brian Faulkner, who had resigned from the Government the previous month. The overall result of the election posed no problem for Unionists, who improved their position slightly. Of the thirty-nine Unionist MPs, twenty-four were Official (pro-O'Neill) and three Unofficial (pro-O'Neill), while ten were Official (anti-O'Neill) and two were Official but unclear in their attitude to the Premier. The NILP retained two seats, and while Rep. Lab. lost Falls, it won Central and held Dock. But the Nationalist Party lost three of its nine seats to Independents identified with the civil rights movement and, most notably, the Foyle seat of party leader Eddie McAteer to John Hume. But the divisions at the grass roots of unionism were serious, and tensions were steadily building up with civil rights marches and loyalist counter-demonstrations. And although Captain O'Neill declared after the election that he would stay on and fight, he resigned two months later. The turnout was 71.9 per cent.

Overall figures,
1969 Stormont general election

Party	Votes	% Valid poll
Off. U. (pro-O'Neill)	173,805	31.1
Off. U. (anti-O'Neill)	95,696	17.1
Unoff. U. (pro-O'Neill)	72,120	12.9
Ind. U.	13,932	2.5
Prot. U.	20,991	3.8
NILP	45,113	8.1
Rep. Lab.	13,155	2.4
Nat.	42,315	7.6
Nat. Dem.	26,009	4.6
PD	23,645	4.2
PPP	2,992	0.5
U. Lib.	7,337	1.3
Independents	21,977	3.9
Total valid votes	559,087	100.0
Spoiled votes	4,783	
Total votes polled	563,870	

*INDICATES OUTGOING MP

Belfast – Ballynafeigh

Elec. 14,572	% Poll 64.0
*Neill, I. (U.)	6,523
Holmes, E. (NILP)	2,675
U. maj.	3,848
No change	

Belfast – Bloomfield

Elec. 21,142	% Poll 70.4
*Scott, W. (U.)	9,084
Spence, W. (Prot. U.)	3,568
Caldwell, W. (NILP)	2,196
U. maj.	5,516
No change	

Belfast – Central

Elec. 6,384	% Poll 58.3
Kennedy, P. (Rep. Lab.)	2,032
*Brennan, J. (Nat. Dem.)	1,538
Rep. Lab. maj.	494
Rep. Lab. gain	

Belfast – Clifton

Elec. 16,196	% Poll 74.5
Hall-Thompson, L. (Unoff. U.)	6,066
*Morgan, W. (U.)	3,215
Thompson, N. (NILP)	1,681
McKeown, M. (Nat. Dem.)	1,079
Unoff. U. maj.	2,851
Unoff. U. gain	

Belfast – Cromac

Elec. 13,541	% Poll 61.5
*Kennedy, W. (U.)	6,320
Barkley, J. (NILP)	1,134
Wiegleb, E. (PD)	752
U. maj.	5,186
No change	

Belfast – Dock

Elec. 7,212	% Poll 73.0
*Fitt, G. (Rep. Lab.)	3,274
Smith, H. (U.)	1,936
Rep. Lab. maj.	1,338
No change	

Belfast – Duncairn

Elec. 18,415	% Poll 66.0
*Fitzsimmons, W. (U.)	7,435
Porter, N. (Unoff. U.)	4,321
U. maj.	3,114
No change	

Belfast – Falls

Elec. 19,802	% Poll 60.5
Devlin, P. (NILP)	6,275
*Diamond, H. (Rep. Lab.)	5,549
NILP maj.	726
NILP gain	

Belfast – Oldpark

Elec. 17,817	% Poll 69.0
*Simpson, V. (NILP)	6,779
Cairns, J. (U.)	5,224
NILP maj.	1,555
No change	

Belfast – Pottinger

Elec. 8,328	% Poll 68.5
Cardwell, J. (U.)	2,902
McBirney, M. (NILP)	2,744
U. maj.	158
U. gain	

Belfast – St Anne's

Elec. 19,041	% Poll 71.0
*Laird, Dr N. (U.)	7,126
McKee, Sir C. (Unoff. U.)	4,183
Murphy, J. (Nat. Dem.)	2,136
U. maj.	2,943
No change	

Belfast – Shankill

Elec. 18,186	% Poll 72.0
*Boal, D. (U.)	6,384
Walsh, H. (Unoff. U.)	4,545
Overend, D. (NILP)	1,997
U. maj.	1,839
No change	

Belfast – Victoria

Elec. 19,504	% Poll 76.0
*Bradford, R. (U.)	9,249
Coulthard, J. (NILP)	2,972
Bunting, R. (Prot. U.)	2,489
U. maj.	6,277
No change	

Belfast – Willowfield

Elec. 12,427	% Poll 68.9
*Caldwell, T. (Unoff. U.)	4,613
Hinds, W. (U.)	2,134
Boyd, B. (NILP)	1,747
Unoff. U. maj.	2,479
Unoff. U. gain	

Belfast – Windsor

*Kirk, H.V. (U.)	unopposed

Belfast – Woodvale

Elec. 19,984	% Poll 72.2
*McQuade, J. (U.)	7,209
Boyd, W.R. (NILP)	3,878
Bell, L. (Unoff. U.)	3,231
U. maj.	3,331
No change	

Bannside

Elec. 20,635	% Poll 78.7
*O'Neill, Capt. T. (U.)	7,745
Paisley, Rev. I. (Prot. U.)	6,331
Farrell, M. (PD)	2,310
U. maj.	1,414
No change	

Carrick

Elec. 22,905	% Poll 64.3
Dickson, Mrs A. (U.)	9,529
Craig, J. (Unoff. U.)	5,246
U. maj.	4,283
No change	

Larkfield

Elec. 20,774	% Poll 68.3
McIvor, B. (U.)	8,501
Sherry, T. (Nat. Dem.)	2,386
Magee, T. (NILP)	1,714
O'Hare, G. (Rep. Lab.)	1,591
U. maj.	6,115
New seat	

Larne

Elec. 20,728	% Poll 79.5
★Craig, W. (U.)	8,550
Wilson, H. (Unoff. U.)	7,897
U. maj.	653
No change	

Antrim

★Minford, N. (U.)	unopposed

Mid-Antrim

Elec. 21,992	% Poll 58.8
★Simpson, Dr R. (U.)	10,249
Galbraith, R.H. (NILP)	2,124
U. maj.	8,125
No change	

Newtownabbey

Elec. 22,151	% Poll 59.9
Bailie, R. (U.)	9,852
McDowell, J. W. (NILP)	3,410
U. maj.	6,442
New seat	

North Antrim

Elec. 19,611	% Poll 63.0
★O'Neill, P. (U.)	9,142
Wylie, Rev. J.W. (Prot. U.)	3,241
U. maj.	5,901
No change	

South Antrim

Elec. 24,693	% Poll 64.7
★Ferguson, R. (U.)	10,761
Beattie, Rev. W. (Prot. U.)	5,362
U. maj.	5,399
No change	

Ards

★Long, Capt. W. (U.)	unopposed

Bangor

Elec. 20,886	% Poll 61.8
McConnell, R.D. (Unoff. U.)	7,714
Campbell, R. (U.)	5,190
Unoff. U. maj.	2,524
New seat	

East Down

Elec. 18,230	% Poll 86.0
*Faulkner, B. (U.)	8,136
McGrady, E. (Nat. Dem.)	6,427
Rowan-Hamilton, Lt.-Col. D. (Unoff. U.)	1,248
U. maj.	1,709
No change	

Iveagh

Elec. 16,172	% Poll 70.0
*McGowan, S. (U.)	6,869
Poots, C. (Prot. U.)	4,365
U. maj.	2,504
No change	

Lagan Valley

*Porter, R., QC (U.)	unopposed

Mid-Down

Kelly, B., QC (U.)	unopposed

Mourne

Elec. 16,272	% Poll 81.0
*Reilly, J. (Nat.)	7,335
Newell, C. (U.)	5,960
Nat. maj.	1,375
No change	

North Down

Elec. 18,408	% Poll 57.0
*Babington, R. (U.)	9,013
Murnaghan, Miss S. (U. Lib.)	1,567
U. maj.	7,446
No change	

South Down

Elec. 17,486	% Poll 56.0
*Keogh, M. (Nat.)	4,830
Woods, P. (PD)	4,610
Nat. maj.	220
No change	

West Down

Elec. 16,584	% Poll 77.7
*Dobson, J. (U.)	7,608
Buller, A.W. (Unoff. U.)	5,219
U. maj.	2,389
No change	

Central Armagh

*Whitten, H. (U.)	unopposed

Mid-Armagh

Elec. 15,901	% Poll 80.8
Stronge, J. (U.)	6,932
Toman, C. (PD)	3,551
Magowan, I. (Unoff. U.)	2,321
U. maj.	3,381
No change	

North Armagh

Elec. 20,652	% Poll 72.0
Mitchell, R.J. (U.)	9,087
Kennedy, A. (Nat. Dem.)	5,847
U. maj.	3,240
No change	

South Armagh

Elec. 18,140	% Poll 71.0
O'Hanlon, P. (Ind.)	6,442
*Richardson, E. (Nat.)	4,332
Byrne, P. (NILP)	1,794
Ind. maj.	2,110
Ind. gain	

Londonderry City

Elec. 19,344	% Poll 81.5
*Anderson, A. (U.)	6,480
Wilton, C. (U. Lib.)	5,770
Campbell, P. (Unoff. U.)	4,181
U. maj.	710
No change	

Foyle

Elec. 19,875	% Poll 84.0
Hume, J. (Ind.)	8,920
*McAteer, E. (Nat.)	5,267
McCann, E. (NILP)	1,993
Ind. maj.	3,653
Ind. gain	

Mid-Londonderry

Elec. 16,411	% Poll 82.0
Cooper, I. (Ind.)	6,056
Shields, R. (U.)	4,438
*Gormley, P. (Nat.)	2,229
O'Kane, J. (Rep. Lab.)	709
Ind. maj.	1,618
Ind. gain	

North Londonderry

Elec. 24,457	% Poll 76.6
*Burns, J. (U.)	9,364
Barr, J. (Unoff. U.)	9,249
U. maj.	115
No change	

South Londonderry

Elec. 18,393	% Poll 83.5
*Chichester-Clark, Maj. J. (U.)	9,195
Devlin, Miss B. (PD)	5,812
U. maj.	3,383
No change	

East Tyrone

Elec. 17,358	· % Poll 89.9
*Currie, A. (Nat.)	9,065
Curran, E. (U.)	6,501
Nat. maj.	2,564
No change	

Mid-Tyrone

Elec. 11,779	% Poll 69.4
*Gormley, T. (Nat.)	5,149
McDonald, P. (PPP)	2,992
Nat. maj.	2,157
No change	

North Tyrone

Elec. 18,024	% Poll 85.5
Fyffe, W. (U.)	8,290
McLaughlin, D. (Nat. Dem.)	6,596
O'Kane, L. (Ind.)	559
U. maj.	1,694
No change	

South Tyrone

Elec. 17,132	% Poll 83.6
*Taylor, J. (U.)	7,683
Eakins, Rev. G. (Unoff. U.)	6,533
U. maj.	1,150
No change	

West Tyrone

*O'Connor, R. (Nat.)	unopposed

Enniskillen

Elec. 11,695	% Poll 87.0

★West, H. (U.)	4,891
Bowes-Egan, M. (PD)	2,784
Archdale, D. (Unoff. U.)	2,418

U. maj.	2,107
No change	

Lisnaskea

Elec. 10,506	% Poll 88.0

★Brooke, Capt. J. (U.)	4,794
Henderson, Maj. J. (Unoff. U.)	2,702
Carey, M. (PD)	1,726

U. maj.	2,092
No change	

South Fermanagh

Elec. 8,322	% Poll 74.9

★Carron, J. (Nat.)	4,108
Cosgrove, P. (OD)	2,100

Nat. maj.	2,008
No change	

1969 WESTMINSTER BY-ELECTION

In the by-election caused by the death of George Forrest, the Unionist MP for Mid-Ulster, his wife, Anna, the Unionist candidate, was defeated by Bernadette Devlin, Unity, in a hard-fought contest.

Mid-Ulster, 17 April 1969

Elec. 68,973	% Poll 91.5

Devlin, Miss B. (Unity)	33,648
Forrest, Mrs A. (U.)	29,437

Unity maj.	4,211
Unity gain	

1970 STORMONT BY-ELECTIONS

The two by-elections which took place in 1970 were probably the most vital in the history of the Stormont House of Commons. They were at Bannside, vacated by the former PM, Captain Terence O'Neill, and at S. Antrim, left vacant by the resignation of one of his leading supporters, Richard Ferguson, a young barrister. First, the by-elections were a test of Unionist feeling on the reforms carried through by the Chichester-Clark Government. Second, they were a measure of the support for the Rev. Ian Paisley, since he was standing in Bannside, and the deputy leader of his Protestant Unionist Party, the Rev. William Beattie, in S. Antrim. In the event, the Government suffered a shattering defeat, losing both seats.

Bannside, 16 April 1970

Elec. 22,954	% Poll 79.6

Paisley, Rev. I. (Prot. U.)	7,981
Minford, Dr B. (U.)	6,778
McHugh, P. (NILP)	3,514

Prot. U. maj.	1,203
Prot. U. gain	

South Antrim, 16 April 1970

Elec. 28,633	% Poll 70.9

Beattie, Rev. W. (Prot. U.)	7,137
Morgan, W. (U.)	6,179
Corkey, D. (Ind.)	5,212
Whitby, A. (NILP)	1,773

Prot. U. maj.	958
Prot. U. gain	

1970 WESTMINSTER GENERAL ELECTION

The main local feature of the 18 June 1970 Westminster general election was that, for the first time, Unionists secured only eight of the twelve seats. The Rev. Ian Paisley gained N. Antrim and Frank McManus, Unity, Fermanagh–S. Tyrone, while Gerry Fitt held W. Belfast, and Bernadette Devlin held Mid-Ulster. In UK terms, the big change was that James Callaghan was no longer masterminding the reforms from London, since the Conservatives returned to power and Reginald Maudling replaced Callaghan at the Home Office. The turnout was 76.8 per cent.

Overall figures, 1970 Westminster general election

Party	Votes	% Valid poll
Unionists	422,041	54.3
NILP	98,194	12.6
Unity	76,185	9.8
Independent (B. Devlin)	37,739	4.8
Prot. U.	35,303	4.5
Rep. Lab.	30,649	3.9
Nat.	27,006	3.5
U. Lib.	12,005	1.5
Nat. Dem.	10,349	1.3
Others	29,642	3.8
Total valid votes	779,113	100.0
Spoiled votes	2,176	
Total votes polled	781,289	

*INDICATES OUTGOING MP

East Belfast

Elec. 59,524	% Poll 75.7
*McMaster, S.R. (U.)	26,778
Bleakley, D.W. (NILP)	18,259
U. maj.	8,519
No change	

North Belfast

Elec. 75,740	% Poll 78.1
*Mills, S. (U.)	28,668
Sharkey, J. (NILP)	18,894
Beattie, Rev. W. (Prot. U.)	11,173
McKeague, J.D. (Ind.)	441
U. maj.	9,774
No change	

South Belfast

Elec. 57,112	% Poll 68.4
*Pounder, R. (U.)	27,523
Coulthard, J. (NILP)	11,567
U. maj.	15,956
No change	

West Belfast

Elec. 68,665	% Poll 84.6
*Fitt, G. (Rep. Lab.)	30,649
McRoberts, B. (U.)	27,451
Rep. Lab. maj.	3,198
No change	

North Antrim

Elec. 79,930	% Poll 73.4
Paisley, Rev. I. (Prot. U.)	24,130
*Clark, H.M. (U.)	21,451
McHugh, P. (NILP)	6,476
McDonnell, A. (Nat. Dem.)	4,312
Moore, G. (U. Lib.)	2,269
Prot. U. maj.	2,679
Prot. U. gain	

South Antrim

Elec. 143,274	% Poll 68.0
Molyneaux, J. (U.)	59,589
Johnston, R. (NILP)	19,971
Caldwell, H. (Ind. U.)	10,938
MacAllister, J. (Nat. Dem.)	6,037
Smith, A.M. (U. Lib.)	913
U. maj.	39,618
No change	

Armagh

Elec. 86,847	% Poll 78.5
*Maginnis, J. (U.)	37,667
Lewis, H. (Unity)	21,696
Holmes, E. (NILP)	8,781
U. maj.	15,971
No change	

North Down

Elec. 121,196	% Poll 66.6
Kilfedder, J. (U.)	55,679
Young, K. (NILP)	14,246
Nixon, R. (Ind. U.)	6,408
McGladdery, J.R. (Ind.)	3,321
Simonds-Gooding, H. (U. Lib.)	1,076
U. maj. (largest in UK)	41,433
No change	

South Down

Elec. 87,079	% Poll 73.9
*Orr, L.P.S. (U.)	34,894
Golding, H. (Unity)	21,676
Quinn, J.G. (U. Lib.)	7,747
U. maj.	13,218
No change	

Fermanagh–South Tyrone

Elec. 70,381	% Poll 91.2
McManus, F. (Unity)	32,813
*Hamilton, Lord (U.)	31,390
Unity maj.	1,423
Unity gain	

Londonderry

Elec. 90,302	% Poll 81.6
*Chichester-Clark, R. (U.)	39,141
McAteer, E. (Nat.)	27,006
McCann, E. (Ind. Lab.)	7,565
U. maj.	12,135
No change	

Mid-Ulster

Elec. 77,143	% Poll 91.4
*Devlin, Miss B. (Ind.)	37,739
Thornton, W.N.J. (U.)	31,810
Cunningham, M. (Ind. Unity)	771
O'Neill, P. (Nat. Soc.)	198
Ind. maj.	5,929
Ind. gain	

1973 DISTRICT COUNCIL ELECTIONS

In the first election for the twenty-six new District Councils, held on 30 May 1973, PR (STV) was used in NI for the first time since the 1920s. Parties tended to regard the contest as a trial run for the coming Assembly election. Unionist and loyalist candidates secured more than 300 of the 526 seats. Official Unionists and Unionists, adopted almost exclusively by UUP associations, got control of twelve councils, with 233 seats, and Loyalist Coalition candidates controlled Larne. The DUP won twenty-one seats and a variety of other loyalists had about sixty in all. The SDLP took eighty-three seats, and was the largest party in three councils, while Alliance took sixty-three seats and Republican Clubs seven. The turnout was 68.1 per cent.

Party composition of councils, 1973

Council	DUP	VULC	Loy. Coal.	Off. U.	Ind. U.	All.	NILP	SDLP	Rep. C.	Nat./ Unity	Others
Antrim	1	1	0	9	0	2	0	0	0	0	2
Ards	0	1	0	11	0	2	1	1	0	0	1
Armagh	2	0	0	11	0	1	0	5	0	0	1
Ballymena	5	1	0	9	0	1	0	0	0	0	5
Ballymoney	1	0	0	9	0	1	0	2	0	0	3
Banbridge	0	0	0	11	0	0	0	1	0	0	3
Belfast	2	1	2	25	2	8	2	7	2	0	0
Carrickfergus	0	0	6	6	0	3	0	0	0	0	0
Castlereagh	0	0	3	10	0	5	0	0	0	0	1
Coleraine	0	0	0	13	1	3	0	1	0	0	2
Cookstown	0	0	1	8	0	0	0	3	1	0	2
Craigavon	3	2	3	10	0	4	0	2	0	0	1
Down	0	1	0	8	0	2	0	8	0	0	1
Dungannon	0	0	0	11	0	0	0	5	0	4	0
Fermanagh	0	0	0	9	1	0	0	4	0	4	2
Larne	0	0	8	1	0	3	0	0	0	0	3
Limavady	0	0	0	8	0	2	0	4	0	0	1
Lisburn	4	1	0	14	0	3	0	1	0	0	0
Londonderry	0	0	9	0	0	4	0	10	1	3	0
Magherafelt	0	1	1	5	0	0	0	6	1	0	1
Moyle	0	0	0	7	0	0	0	2	0	0	7
Newry and Mourne	0	0	0	3	0	4	0	13	2	0	8
Newtownabbey	3	0	2	12	0	3	1	0	0	0	0
North Down	0	0	4	9	0	7	0	0	0	0	0
Omagh	0	0	0	8	0	3	0	4	0	2	3
Strabane	0	0	1	6	0	2	0	4	0	0	2
Total	21	9	40	233	4	63	4	83	7	13	49

Overall figures,
1973 District Council elections

Party	1st-preference votes	% votes
DUP	29,610	4.3
VULC	14,467	2.1
Loy. Coal.	52,875	7.7
Off. U.	286,112	41.4
Ind. U.	7,818	1.1
All.	94,474	13.7
NILP	17,422	2.5
SDLP	92,600	13.4
Rep.C.	20,680	3.0
Rep. Lab.	2,594	0.4
Nat./Unity	16,737	2.4
Ind./Non Party	51,197	7.4
Others	4,393	0.6
Total	690,979	100.0

1973 NI ASSEMBLY ELECTION

The Assembly of 78 members was elected by PR (STV) on 28 June 1973, contested by 219 candidates. Because of the divisions in unionism, the party labels were not always an accurate guide to the attitude of candidates to the British Government's White Paper, which envisaged a partnership government. For example, several Official Unionists, that is, candidates who had been endorsed by Unionist associations, were against the scheme and the policy of the UUP leader, Brian Faulkner. So the anti-White Paper Unionists were split between ten Official candidates, here described as 'Unionists', the Vanguard Unionist Loyalist Coalition (led by William Craig), the Democratic Unionist Loyalist Coalition (led by Rev. Ian Paisley) and three members of the West Belfast Loyalist Coalition. The Alliance Party and Northern Ireland Labour Party did less well than they expected, and for the first time in the history of NI no Nationalist was elected. The SDLP, with nineteen seats, established itself as the second party. The electorate stood at 1,022,820 and the turnout was 72.3 per cent.

Seats and votes, 1973 NI Assembly election

Party	Seats	1st-preference votes	% Valid poll
Official Unionists	24	211,362	29.3
Unionists	8	61,183	8.5
DULC	8	78,228	10.8
VULC	7	75,759	10.5
WBLC	3	16,869	2.3
Other Loyalist	0	3,734	0.5
SDLP	19	159,773	22.1
Alliance	8	66,541	9.2
NILP	1	18,675	2.6
Rep. C.	0	13,064	1.8
Nat.	0	8,270	1.2
Rep. Lab.	0	1,750	0.2
U. Lib.	0	811	0.1
Communist	0	123	0.0
Independents	0	6,099	0.9
Total	78	722,241	100.0

East Belfast	Elec. 80,421	% Poll 71.7
6 elected	Quota 8,113	1st-preference votes
Count 1	Bradford, R.H. (Off. U.)	13,187
Count 13	Cardwell, J. (Off. U.)	5,001
Count 16	Paisley, Mrs E. (DULC)	5,518
Count 18	Napier, O.J. (All.)	4,941
Count 18	Bleakley, D.W. (NILP)	4,425
Count 18	Agnew, N. (Off. U.)	3,615

North Belfast	Elec. 75,768	% Poll 68.7
6 elected	Quota 7,255	1st-preference votes
Count 1	Fitt, G. (SDLP)	8,264
Count 11	McQuade, J. (DULC)	5,148
Count 14	Hall-Thompson, L. (Off. U.)	5,694
Count 15	Morgan, W.J. (Off. U.)	5,190
Count 15	Millar, F. (U.)	4,187
Count 15	Ferguson, J. (All.)	1,958

South Belfast	Elec. 75,990	% Poll 70.6
6 elected	Quota 7,532	1st-preference votes
Count 11	McIvor, W.B. (Off. U.)	6,930
Count 12	Glass, J.B.C. (All.)	5,148
Count 14	Burns, T.E. (DULC)	4,640
Count 15	Elder, N. (Off. U.)	4,807
Count 15	Kirk, H.V. (Off. U.)	5,426
Count 16	Magee, R.A.E. (Off. U.)	3,656

West Belfast	Elec. 70,791	% Poll 62.5
6 elected	Quota 5,911	1st-preference votes
Count 1	Laird, J.D. (U.[WBLC])	11,479
Count 1	Devlin, P.J. (SDLP)	7,743
Count 3	Smyth, H. (Ind. U.[WBLC])	3,625
Count 9	Coulter, R.J. (U.[WBLC])	1,765
Count 12	Cooper, R.G. (All.)	3,160
Count 12	Gillespie, D.E. (SDLP)	1,940

North Antrim	Elec. 99,635	% Poll 72.5
7 elected	Quota 8,907	1st-preference votes
Count 1	Paisley, Rev. I.R.K. (DULC)	14,533
Count 1	Baxter, J.L. (Off. U.)	9,009
Count 2	Craig, W. (VULC)	8,538
Count 12	O'Hagan, J.J. (SDLP)	6,204
Count 15	McCarthy, D. (Off. U.)	5,125
Count 15	Wilson, J. (All.)	2,876
Count 15	Craig, J. (DULC)	3,871

South Antrim	Elec. 114,240	% Poll 66.9
8 elected	Quota 8,338	1st-preference votes
Count 1	Beattie, Rev. W.J. (DULC)	10,126
Count 1	Dickson, Mrs A.L. (Off. U.)	9,033
Count 9	McCloskey, E.V. (SDLP)	7,899
Count 13	Crothers, D.S.F. (All.)	5,975
Count 17	Minford, N.O. (Off. U.)	5,289
Count 18	Ardill, R.A. (Off. U.)	5,234
Count 18	Lindsay, K. (VULC)	3,055
Count 18	McLachlan, P. (Off. U.)	3,983

Armagh	Elec. 89,056	% Poll 71.1
7 elected	Quota 7,676	1st-preference votes
Count 1	O'Hanlon, P.M. (SDLP)	8,219
Count 1	Mallon, S.F. (SDLP)	7,995
Count 7	Whitten, H. (Off. U.)	6,891
Count 8	Carson, T.D. (VULC)	6,866
Count 10	Stronge, J.M. (Off. U.)	4,355
Count 12	News, H. (SDLP)	4,731
Count 12	Hutchinson, D. (DULC)	4,552

North Down	Elec. 89,682	% Poll 69.4
7 elected	Quota 7,682	1st-preference votes
Count 1	Kilfedder, J.A. (Off. U.)	20,684
Count 2	Brooke, J. (Off. U.)	6,160
Count 12	Poots, C.B. (DULC)	4,364
Count 13	Dunleath, Lord (All.)	4,482
Count 13	Campbell, R.W. (Off. U.)	3,760
Count 13	Brownlow, W.S. (Off. U.)	2,620
Count 13	McConnell, R.D. (All.)	3,271

South Down   Elec. 89,324   % Poll 73.2

7 elected	Quota 8,005	1st-preference votes
Count 1	Faulkner, A.B.D. (Off. U.)	16,287
Count 7	McGrady, E.R. (SDLP)	7,870
Count 12	Broadhurst, R.J.C. (Off. U.)	1,515
Count 14	Feely, F. (SDLP)	6,857
Count 15	O'Donoghue, P. (SDLP)	4,322
Count 17	Harvey, C. (VULC)	5,006
Count 17	Heslip, H.J. (U.)	3,838

Fermanagh–South Tyrone   Elec. 68,733   % Poll 84.6

5 elected	Quota 9,488	1st-preference votes
Count 1	Currie, J.A. (SDLP)	11,016
Count 4	Baird, E.A. (VULC)	8,456
Count 7	Taylor, J.D. (U.)	8,410
Count 7	Daly, T.A. (SDLP)	7,511
Count 7	West, H.W. (U.)	8,198

Londonderry   Elec. 89,849   % Poll 75.9

7 elected	Quota 8,308	1st-preference votes
Count 1	Hume, J. (SDLP)	12,596
Count 1	Morrell, L.J. (U.)	9,685
Count 2	Logue, H.A. (SDLP)	7,230
Count 3	Douglas, W.A.B. (U.)	8,245
Count 9	Barr, G. (VULC)	6,511
Count 11	Canavan, M.W.E. (SDLP)	3,647
Count 11	Conn, Mrs S.E. (U.)	6,550

Mid-Ulster   Elec. 79,331   % Poll 82.4

6 elected	Quota 9,145	1st-preference votes
Count 1	Cooper, I.A. (SDLP)	12,614
Count 1	Pollock, T.D. (Off. U.)	9,557
Count 10	Duffy, P.A. (SDSLP)	4,437
Count 11	Dunlop, J. (VULC)	7,082
Count 11	Thompson, W.J. (U.)	5,352
Count 13	Larkin, A.J. (SDLP)	4,045

FEBRUARY 1974 WESTMINSTER GENERAL ELECTION

This election, held on 28 February, proved to have enormous political repercussions. It was fought in constituencies revised by the Boundary Commission. Changes were made in seven constituencies – E. Belfast, N. Belfast, S. Belfast, W. Belfast, N. Antrim, S. Antrim and N. Down. The NI power-sharing Executive had been in office only since the start of the year and the UUUC campaign was directed both against the principle of partnership with the SDLP and the idea of a Council of Ireland as envisaged in the Sunningdale

Agreement. The three Executive parties – Brian Faulkner's Unionists, the SDLP and the Alliance Party – were seriously embarrassed at having to defend a system that had barely got off the ground while competing against one another in the elections. To maximise its effort, the UUUC had a single candidate in each constituency, and it adopted what proved to be a telling slogan, 'Dublin is just a Sunningdale away.' The UUUC got eleven of the twelve seats, with Gerry Fitt, deputy Chief Executive, retaining his W. Belfast seat for the SDLP. The UUUC, having secured more than half the total votes cast, claimed that the result was a vote of no confidence in the new administration. The turnout was 70.4 per cent.

Overall figures, February 1974 Westminster general election

Party	Votes	% Valid poll
UUUC:		
UUP	232,103	32.3
VUPP	75,944	10.6
DUP	58,656	8.2
U. Pro-A.	94,301	13.1
All.	22,660	3.2
NILP	17,284	2.4
SDLP	160,437	22.4
Rep. C.	15,152	2.1
Unity	17,593	2.4
Independents	23,496	3.3
Total valid votes	717,626	100.0
Spoiled votes	4,676	
Total votes polled	722,302	

*INDICATES OUTGOING MP

East Belfast

Elec. 78,821	% Poll 73.1
Craig, W. (VUPP-UUUC)	27,817
*McMaster, S.R. (U. Pro-A.)	20,077
Bleakley, D.W. (NILP)	8,122
Gillespie, D.E. (SDLP)	1,502
UUUC maj.	7,740

North Belfast

Elec. 71,081	% Poll 69.9
Carson , J. (UUP-UUUC)	21,531
Smyth, D.W. (U. Pro-A.)	12,755
Donnelly, T. (SDLP)	12,003
Scott, A. (NILP)	2,917
UUUC maj.	8,776

South Belfast

Elec. 74,534	% Poll 69.8
Bradford, Rev. R.J. (VUPP-UUUC)	22,083
*Pounder, R.J. (U. Pro-A.)	18,085
Cook, D.S. (All.)	5,118
Caraher, J.B. (SDLP)	4,149
Holmes, J.E. (NILP)	2,455
UUUC maj.	3,998

West Belfast

Elec. 65,651	% Poll 73.0
*Fitt, G. (SDLP)	19,554
McQuade, J. (DUP-UUUC)	17,374
Price, A. (Ind.)	5,662
Brady, J. (Rep. C.)	3,088
Boyd, W.R. (NILP)	1,989
SDLP maj.	2,180

North Antrim

Elec. 102,983	% Poll 63.4
*Paisley, Rev. I.R.K. (DUP-UUUC)	41,282
Utley, T.E. (U. Pro-A.)	13,651
McAlister, Miss M. (SDLP)	10,056
UUUC maj.	27,631

South Antrim

Elec. 116,710	% Poll 61.5
*Molyneaux, J.H. (UUP-UUUC)	48,203
Kinahan, C.H.G. (All.)	12,559
Rowan, P.J. (SDLP)	8,769
Kidd, R.J. (Ind.)	1,801
UUUC maj.	35,644

Armagh

Elec. 90,262	% Poll 67.7
McCusker, J.H. (UUP-UUUC)	33,194
O'Hanlon, P.M. (SDLP)	18,090
Glendinning, R.J. (All.)	4,983
Moore, T.O. (Rep. C.)	4,129
Lewis, H. (Unity)	1,364
UUUC maj.	15,104
No change	

North Down

Elec. 92,800	% Poll 67.6
*Kilfedder, J.A. (UUP-UUUC)	38,169
Bradford, R.H. (U. Pro-A.)	21,943
Curran, D. (SDLP)	2,376
UUUC maj.	16,226

South Down

Elec. 90,613	% Poll 66.6
*Orr, L.P.S. (UUP-UUUC)	31,088
Hollywood, S. (SDLP)	25,486
Golding, H. (Rep. C.)	3,046
UUUC maj.	5,602
No change	

Fermanagh–South Tyrone

Elec. 70,615	% Poll 87.6
West, H.W. (UUP-UUUC)	26,858
*McManus, F.J. (Unity)	16,229
Haughey, P.D. (SDLP)	15,410
Brown, H.I. (U. Pro-A.)	3,157
UUUC maj.	10,629
UUUC gain	

Londonderry

Elec. 92,192	% Poll 68.1
Ross, W. (UUP-UUUC)	33,060
Logue, H.A. (SDLP)	23,670
Montgomery, M.J. (Rep. C.)	4,889
Foster, R.J. (Lab. and TU)	1,162
UUUC maj.	9,390
No change	

Mid–Ulster

Elec. 80,982	% Poll 82.7
Dunlop, J. (VUPP-UUUC)	26,044
Cooper, I.A. (SDLP)	19,372
*McAliskey, Mrs. B. (Ind. Soc.)	16,672
Thornton, W.N.J. (U. Pro-A.)	4,633
UUUC maj.	6,672
UUUC gain	

1974 NI ASSEMBLY BY-ELECTION

The by-election was caused by the death of David McCarthy (Off. U.) in a car accident on 15 July 1973. The UWC strike in May 1974 forced the postponement of polling for four weeks until 20 June. By that time the whole political landscape had changed: the Executive had fallen on 28 May and the NI Assembly Prorogation Order had prorogued the Assembly for four months from 29 May. Hence, while the Assembly remained in existence it could not perform any of its functions. Despite this, 46.7 per cent of the electorate voted on 20 June and Clifford Smyth was elected on the first count, with the prospect of performing only constituency duties.

North Antrim, 20 June 1974

Elec. 104,168	% Poll 46.7
Quota 24,069	

Party candidates	1st-preference votes
Smyth, A.C. (DUP-UUUC)	29,739
Turnly, J. (SDLP)	10,421
Agnew, Dr Iris (U. Pro-A.)	5,546
Fawcett, J. (All.)	2,430

Smyth elected on the first count.

OCTOBER 1974 WESTMINSTER GENERAL ELECTION

The Westminster election of 10 October brought only one change of party strength. The UUP leader, Harry West, lost his Fermanagh–South Tyrone seat to Independent Frank Maguire, who had stood as an agreed anti-Unionist nominee. In a sense, the contest was a test of the standing of the UUUC after its successful campaign against the power-sharing Executive, and also of the more independent line adopted by Unionists at Westminster. After the election, West was succeeded as UUUC Parliamentary leader by James Molyneaux, and Enoch Powell's election in South Down provided valuable Parliamentary expertise for the UUUC. Gerry Fitt, for the SDLP, stressed partnership in government, and Brian Faulkner's newly established UPNI

made its first election bid, and one which proved disappointing for it. Alliance ran five candidates but found that its call for an end to violence as the first priority did not make sufficient impact. The turnout was 68.5 per cent.

Overall figures, October 1974 Westminster general election

Party	Votes	% Valid poll
UUUC:		
UUP	256,065	36.5
VUPP	92,262	13.1
DUP	59,451	8.5
UPNI	20,454	2.9
Ind. U.	7,942	1.1
All.	44,644	6.3
NILP	11,539	1.6
SDLP	154,193	22.0
Rep. C.	21,633	3.1
Ind. N.	32,795	4.7
Others	1,386	0.2
Total valid votes	702,364	100.0
Spoiled votes	7,805	
Total votes polled	710,169	

*INDICATES OUTGOING MP

East Belfast

Elec. 79,629	% Poll 67.4
*Craig, W. (VUPP-UUUC)	31,594
McLachlan, P. (UPNI)	14,417
Bleakley, D. (NILP)	7,415
UUUC maj.	17,177
No change	

North Belfast

Elec. 71,774	% Poll 66.6
*Carson, J. (UUP-UUUC)	29,622
Donnelly, T. (SDLP)	11,400
Ferguson, J. (All.)	3,807
Boyd, W. (NILP)	2,481
UUUC maj.	18,222
No change	

South Belfast

Elec. 75,147	% Poll 67.9
*Bradford, Rev. R.J. (VUPP-UUUC)	30,116
Glass, B. (All.)	11,715
McMaster, S. (Ind. U.)	4,982
Caraher, B. (SDLP)	2,390
Holmes, E. (NILP)	1,643
UUUC maj.	18,401
No change	

West Belfast

Elec. 66,278	% Poll 67.2
*Fitt, G. (SDLP)	21,821
McQuade, J. (DUP-UUUC)	16,265
O'Kane, Mrs K. (Rep. C.)	3,547
Gibson, S. McK. (VPP)	2,690
Kerins, P. (CPI)	203
SDLP maj.	5,556
No change	

North Antrim

Elec. 103,763	% Poll 57.7
*Paisley, Rev. I.R.K. (DUP-UUUC)	43,186
Wilson, H. (All.)	8,689
McAlister, Miss M. (SDLP)	7,616
UUUC maj.	34,497
No change	

South Antrim

Elec. 118,483	% Poll 58.0
*Molyneaux. J. (UUP-UUUC)	48,892
Kinahan, C. (All.)	10,460
Rowan, P. (SDLP)	9,061
UUUC maj.	38,432
No change	

Armagh

Elec. 91,085	% Poll 69.5
*McCusker, H. (UUP-UUUC)	37,518
Mallon, S. (SDLP)	19,855
McGurran, M. (Rep. C.)	5,138
UUUC maj.	17,663
No change	

North Down

Elec. 93,641	% Poll 61.2
*Kilfedder, J.A. (UUP-UUUC)	40,996
Jones, K. (All.)	9,973
Brownlow, W. (UPNI)	6,037
UUUC maj.	31,023
No change	

South Down

Elec. 91,792	% Poll 70.0
Powell, E. (UUP-UUUC)	33,614
Hollywood, S. (SDLP)	30,047
O'Hanlon, G. (Rep. C.)	2,327
Vipond, D. (CPI)	152
UUUC maj.	3,567
No change	

Fermanagh–South Tyrone

Elec. 71,343	% Poll 88.7
Maguire, F. (Ind.)	32,795
*West, H.W. (UUP-UUUC)	30,285
Evans, A.J. (CPI)	185
Ind. maj.	2,510
Ind. gain	

Londonderry

Elec. 93,207	% Poll 71.3
⋆Ross, W. (UUP-UUUC)	35,138
Hume, J. (SDLP)	26,118
Montgomery, M.J. (Rep. C.)	2,530
Foster, R. (Lab. and TU)	846
UUUC maj.	9,020
No change	

Mid–Ulster

Elec. 82,718	% Poll 79.2
⋆Dunlop, J. (VUPP-UUUC)	30,552
Cooper, I. (SDLP)	25,885
Donnelly, F. (Rep. C.)	8,091
UUUC maj.	4,667
No change	

1975 CONVENTION ELECTION

The election for the Constitutional Convention, like the Assembly contest, was conducted on PR (STV) for seventy-eight seats based on the twelve Westminster constituencies. It was held on 1 May 1975. Because it was not a parliamentary election, but simply the return of delegates to an elected conference, the clash was purely on the basis of what type of constitution would have the widest acceptance in the NI community and would be approved by Westminster. The UUUC, embracing the UUP, DUP and VUPP, was firmly committed to having 'British Parliamentary standards' – that is, majority rule on the Westminster model – whereas the parties representing the former power-sharing Executive – that is, SDLP, Alliance and UPNI – urged partnership government of the type that they felt had not had a fair trial in the Assembly. The UUUC, with a special steering committee, worked with great skill to deploy its candidates in order to secure the maximum advantage from PR. In the event a total of 165 candidates contested the 78 seats – 54 fewer than in the Assembly election. The electorate stood at 1,026,987 and the total turnout was 65.8 per cent as compared with 72.3 per cent in the Assembly election, indicating perhaps a little election weariness, since this was the seventh poll in NI in little more than two years.

Seats and votes, 1975 Convention election

Party	Seats	1st-preference votes	% Valid poll
UUUC:			
UUP	19	169,797	25.8
DUP	12	97,073	14.8
VUPP	14	83,507	12.7
Ind. U.	1	5,687	0.9
Other Loyalists	1	4,453	0.6
SDLP	17	156,049	23.7
All.	8	64,657	9.8
UPNI	5	50,891	7.7
Rep. C.	0	14,515	2.2
NILP	1	9,102	1.4
Communist	0	378	0.1
Independents	0	2,052	0.3
Total	78	658,161	100.0

East Belfast   Elec. 78,340   % Poll 65.3

6 elected	Quota 7,166	1st-preference votes
Count 1	Craig, W. (VUPP-UUUC)	11,958
Count 6	Napier, O. (All.)	6,341
Count 8	Empey, R. (VUPP-UUUC)	4,657
Count 11	Cardwell, J. (UPNI)	3,039
Count 11	Paisley, Mrs E. (DUP-UUUC)	3,606
Count 11	Bleakley, D. (NILP)	3,998

North Belfast   Elec. 70,673   % Poll 63.3

6 elected	Quota 6,230	1st-preference votes
Count 1	Fitt, G. (SDLP)	6,454
Count 1	Bell, W. (UUP-UUUC)	6,268
Count 7	Millar, F. (Ind. U.-UUUC)	5,687
Count 8	Morgan, W. (UUP-UUUC)	5,558
Count 10	Hall–Thompson, L. (UPNI)	3,577
Count 10	Annon, W.T. (DUP-UUUC)	4,132

South Belfast   Elec. 73,324   % Poll 66.3

6 elected	Quota 6,831	1st-preference votes
Count 1	Smyth, Rev. M. (UUP-UUUC)	15,061
Count 1	Glass, B. (All.)	7,961
Count 2	Burchill, J. (UUP-UUUC)	4,230
Count 8	Hendron, J. (All.)	2,499
Count 9	Trimble, D. (VUPP-UUUC)	2,429
Count 11	Burns, T. (DUP-UUUC)	2,529

West Belfast   Elec. 63,869   % Poll 58.7

6 elected	Quota 5,103	1st-preference votes
Count 1	Laird, J. (UUP-UUUC)	8,433
Count 1	Devlin, P. (SDLP)	6,267
Count 6	Coulter, Miss J. (UUP-UUUC)	2,325
Count 8	Cooper, R. (All.)	3,293
Count 8	Hendron, Dr J.G. (SDLP)	2,840
Count 8	Smyth, H. (Ind. Loy.)	2,644

North Antrim   Elec. 103,469   % Poll 61.0

7 elected	Quota 7,778	1st-preference votes
Count 1	Paisley, Rev. I. (DUP-UUUC)	19,335
Count 2	McFaul, K. (DUP-UUUC)	7,658
Count 2	Smyth, C. (DUP-UUUC)	5,806
Count 9	Wilson, H. (All.)	4,601
Count 10	Turnly, J. (SDLP)	4,888
Count 12	Wright, W. (VUPP-UUUC)	2,761
Count 12	Allen, D. (VUPP-UUUC)	2,268

South Antrim   Elec. 119,723   % Poll 58.6

8 elected	Quota 7,646	1st-preference votes
Count 1	Beattie, Rev. W. (DUP-UUUC)	11,834
Count 1	Ardill, A. (UUP-UUUC)	10,895
Count 4	McCloskey, V. (SDLP)	6,756
Count 8	Kinahan, C. (All.)	5,294
Count 9	Dickson, Mrs A. (UPNI)	5,723
Count 11	Dunlop, S. (DUP-UUUC)	2,461
Count 11	Lindsay, K. (VUPP-UUUC)	4,529
Count 12	Morrison, G. (VUPP-UUUC)	2,943

Armagh   Elec. 90,640   % Poll 67.7

7 elected	Quota 7,424	1st-preference votes
Count 1	Mallon, S. (SDLP)	8,999
Count 1	Armstrong, M. (UUP-UUUC)	8,802
Count 1	Hutchinson, D. (DUP-UUUC)	7,746
Count 9	Whitten, H. (UUP-UUUC)	4,843
Count 9	Carson, T.D. (VUPP-UUUC)	5,974
Count 9	Black, A. (VUPP-UUUC)	5,435
Count 9	News, H. (SDLP)	3,303

North Down   Elec. 93,884   % Poll 62.6

7 elected	Quota 7,223	1st-preference votes
Count 1	Kilfedder, J. (UUP-UUUC)	21,693
Count 1	Taylor, J. (UUP-UUUC)	7,238
Count 3	Green, G. (VUPP-UUUC)	4,408
Count 6	Poots, C. (DUP-UUUC)	2,962
Count 7	Dunleath, Lord (All.)	4,616
Count 8	McConnell, R. (All.)	3,099
Count 8	Brookeborough, Lord (UPNI)	3,555

South Down	Elec. 89,912	% Poll 68.9
7 elected	Quota 7,594	1st-preference votes
Count 1	Feely, F. (SDLP)	9,730
Count 1	Harvey, C. (VUPP-UUUC)	8,843
Count 2	McGrady, E. (SDLP)	7,257
Count 4	O'Donoghue, P. (SDLP)	6,657
Count 9	Faulkner, B. (UPNI)	6,035
Count 9	Brush, E. (UUP-UUUC)	6,293
Count 9	Heslip, H. (UUP-UUUC)	6,380

Fermanagh–South Tyrone	Elec. 70,344	% Poll 78.4
5 elected	Quota 8,843	1st-preference votes
Count 1	West, H. (UUP-UUUC)	12,922
Count 1	Currie, A. (SDLP)	9,984
Count 3	Baird, E. (VUPP-UUUC)	8,067
Count 7	Daly, T. (SDLP)	7,145
Count 9	McKay, J. (UUP-UUUC)	3,194

Londonderry	Elec. 92,003	% Poll 69.8
7 elected	Quota 7,801	1st-preference votes
Count 1	Hume, J. (SDLP)	11,941
Count 1	Conn, Mrs S. (UUP-UUUC)	8,789
Count 1	Barr, G. (VUPP-UUUC)	7,883
Count 4	Logue, H. (SDLP)	6,661
Count 5	Douglas, W. (UUP-UUUC)	4,939
Count 6	Canavan, M. (SDLP)	4,600
Count 12	McClure, J. (DUP-UUUC)	3,436

Mid-Ulster	Elec. 80,806	% Poll 72.5
6 elected	Quota 8,068	1st-preference votes
Count 1	Thompson, W. (UUP-UUUC)	9,342
Count 1	Cooper, I. (SDLP)	9,073
Count 1	Reid, R. (DUP-UUUC)	8,250
Count 10	Duffy, P. (SDLP)	4,130
Count 11	Thompson, E. (UUP-UUUC)	4,292
Count 11	Overend, R. (VUPP-UUUC)	5,573

1977 DISTRICT COUNCIL ELECTIONS

The second election for the twenty-six District Councils was held on 18 May 1977, in the immediate aftermath of the abortive UUAC strike against the security policy pursued by the direct-rule regime. The refusal of the UUP to join with Paisley (DUP) and Baird (UUUP) in the strike produced a terminal rift in the UUUC and, for the first time since 1974, candidates from the main Unionist parties stood without the endorsement of the UUUC. Two main features emerged from the elections: first, despite a party system that was still fragmenting, political support concentrated on four main parties – UUP, SDLP, Alliance and DUP – who together won 77.3 per cent of the vote and 82.7 per cent of the seats; second, there was a radical change away from council control by a single party with an absolute majority of seats. Only three councils – Antrim and Banbridge (UUP) and Ballymena (DUP) – were controlled by a single party, in contrast to 1973 when twelve were dominated by the UUP and one by loyalists. In 1977 the UUP was the largest party on ten councils and the SDLP on six, but both depended on support from other parties to win control. These features and the break-up of the UUUC opened the way to bargaining for position on some councils. The turnout was 57.9 per cent, 10.2 per cent lower than 1973.

Overall figures, 1977 District Council elections

Party	1st-preference votes	% votes
DUP	70,850	12.7
UUUP	17,901	3.2
Loy.	13,218	2.4
UUP	164,900	29.6
VUPP	8,135	1.5
UPNI	13,691	2.4
All.	80,011	14.4
NILP	4,732	0.8
SDLP	114,776	20.6
Rep. C.	14,277	2.6
Nat./Unity	8,161	1.5
Others	46,055	8.3
Total	556,707	100.0

Party composition of councils, 1977

Council	DUP	UUUP	Loy.	VUPP	UUP	UPNI	All.	SDLP	Rep. C.	Nat./ Unity	Others
Antrim	3	0	0	0	8	0	2	0	0	0	2
Ards	3	0	0	0	6	0	5	1	0	0	2
Armagh	2	1	0	0	9	0	0	7	0	0	1
Ballymena	11	0	2	0	4	0	1	0	0	0	3
Ballymoney	3	0	1	0	5	0	1	3	0	0	3
Banbridge	3	0	1	0	8	0	0	2	0	0	1
Belfast	7	0	2	0	15	2	13	8	3	0	1
Carrickfergus	3	0	1	0	5	1	5	0	0	0	0
Castlereagh	4	0	0	0	7	0	7	0	0	0	1
Coleraine	2	0	1	0	10	0	2	2	0	0	3
Cookstown	1	3	0	0	4	0	0	5	0	0	2
Craigavon	4	1	0	0	10	0	3	6	1	0	0
Down	0	0	0	0	7	0	3	10	0	0	0
Dungannon	2	0	0	0	8	0	0	6	0	0	4
Fermanagh	0	3	0	0	6	0	0	7	0	2	2
Larne	3	0	1	3	1	0	4	1	0	0	2
Limavady	2	0	0	0	6	0	0	6	0	0	1
Lisburn	6	2	0	0	9	1	3	2	0	0	0
Londonderry	2	0	0	0	6	0	2	13	0	4	0
Magherafelt	3	1	0	0	4	0	0	5	1	0	1
Moyle	2	0	0	0	5	0	0	3	0	0	6
Newry and Mourne	1	0	0	0	7	0	3	15	0	0	4
Newtownabbey	4	0	1	0	8	1	6	0	0	0	1
North Down	1	1	1	2	7	1	7	0	0	0	0
Omagh	0	0	0	0	8	0	3	6	1	0	2
Strabane	2	0	0	0	5	0	0	5	0	0	3
Total	74	12	11	5	178	6	70	113	6	6	45

382

1979 WESTMINSTER GENERAL ELECTION

The 3 May 1979 Westminster general election found Unionists, anti-Unionists and centre parties all split, and three seats, E. Belfast, N. Belfast and N. Down, changed hands. The first two were gained from the UUP by the DUP, each by a narrow majority. In N. Down, although there was no change of MP, James Kilfedder's victory in face of opposition from the UUP, from which he had just resigned, was in effect an Ind. Unionist gain. The turnout was 68.4 per cent.

Overall figures, 1979 Westminster general election

Party	Votes	% Valid poll
UUP	254,578	36.6
SDLP	126,325	18.2
All.	82,892	11.9
DUP	70,975	10.2
UUUP	39,856	5.7
Ind. U.	36,989	5.3
IIP	23,086	3.3
Ind. N.	22,398	3.2
Rep. C.	12,098	1.7
Ind. SDLP	10,785	1.6
UPNI	8,021	1.2
NILP	4,411	0.6
Others	3,573	0.5
Total valid votes	695,987	100.0
Spoiled votes	7,512	
Total votes polled	703,499	

*INDICATES OUTGOING MP

East Belfast

Elec. 75,496	% Poll 67.6
Robinson, P. (DUP)	15,994
*Craig, W. (UUP)	15,930
Napier, O. (All.)	15,066
Agnew, N. (UPNI)	2,017
Chambers, G. (NILP)	1,982
DUP maj.	64
DUP gain	

North Belfast

Elec. 65,099	% Poll 66.0
McQuade, J. (DUP)	11,690
Walker, C. (UUP)	10,695
O'Hare, P. (SDLP)	7,823
Dickson, Mrs A. (UPNI)	4,220
Cushnahan, J. (All.)	4,120
Lynch, S. (Rep. C.)	1,907
Carr, A. (NILP)	1,889
DUP maj.	995
DUP gain	

South Belfast

Elec. 68,946	% Poll 68.0
*Bradford, Rev. R. (UUP)	28,875
Glass, B. (All.)	11,745
McDonnell, A. (SDLP)	3,694
Brennan, V. (UPNI)	1,784
Dudgeon, J. (Lab. Integrationist)	692
UUP maj.	17,130
No change	

West Belfast

Elec. 58,915	% Poll 60.4
*Fitt, G. (SDLP)	16,480
Passmore, T. (UUP)	8,245
Dickson, W. (DUP)	3,716
Brennan, B. (Rep. C.)	2,282
Cousins, J. (All.)	2,024
Peters, D. (NILP)	540

SDLP maj.	8,235
No change	

North Antrim

Elec. 102,224	% Poll 62.6
*Paisley, Rev. I. (DUP)	33,941
Burchill, J. (UUP)	15,398
Wilson, H. (All.)	7,797
Farren, S. (SDLP)	4,867
Turnly, J. (IIP)	3,689

DUP maj.	18,543
No change	

South Antrim

Elec. 126,493	% Poll 58.8
*Molyneaux, J. (UUP)	50,782
Kinahan, C. (All.)	11,914
Rowan, P. (SDLP)	7,432
Kidd, R. (ULP)	1,895
Smyth, K. (Rep. C.)	1,615

UUP maj.	38,868
No change	

Armagh

Elec. 93,097	% Poll 70.9
*McCusker, H. (UUP)	31,668
Mallon, S. (SDLP)	23,545
Calvert, D. (DUP)	5,634
Moore, T. (Rep. C.)	2,310
Ramsay, W. (All.)	2,074

UUP maj.	8,123
No change	

North Down

Elec. 99,889	% Poll 62.4
*Kilfedder, J. (Ind. U.)	36,989
Jones, K. (All.)	13,364
Smyth, C. (UUP)	11,728

Ind. U. maj.	23,625
Ind. U. gain	

South Down

Elec. 89,597	% Poll 72.0
*Powell, E. (UUP)	32,254
McGrady, E. (SDLP)	24,033
Forde, P. (All.)	4,407
Markey, J. (IIP)	1,853
O'Hagan, D. (Rep. C.)	1,682
Rice, S. (Ind.)	216
Courtney, P. (Reform)	31

UUP maj.	8,221
No change	

Fermanagh–South Tyrone

Elec. 71,541	% Poll 88.9
*Maguire, F. (Ind.)	22,398
Ferguson, R. (UUP)	17,411
Currie, A. (Ind. SDLP)	10,785
Baird, E. (UUUP)	10,607
Acheson, P. (All.)	1,070

Ind. maj.	4,987
No change	

Londonderry

Elec. 94,800	% Poll 67.6
*Ross, W. (UUP)	31,592
Logue, H. (SDLP)	19,185
Barr, A. (All.)	5,830
McAteer, F. (IIP)	5,489
Melaugh, E. (Rep. C.)	888
Webster, B. (Derry Lab.)	639

UUP maj.	12,407
No change	

384

Mid–Ulster

Elec. 81,499	% Poll 80.9
*Dunlop, J. (UUUP)	29,249
Duffy, P. (SDLP)	19,266
Fahy, P. (IIP)	12,055
Lagan, A. (All.)	3,481
Donnelly, F. (Rep. C.)	1,414
UUUP maj.	9,983
No change	

1979 EUROPEAN PARLIAMENT ELECTION

The election for the European Parliament on 7 June 1979 resulted in the three NI seats being filled by: the Rev. Ian Paisley MP, leader of the DUP, John Hume, deputy leader of the SDLP, and John Taylor, UUP EC spokesman. Paisley's easy victory on the first count, and Hume's record SDLP poll, with the two UUP candidates – party leader Harry West and John Taylor – well behind in first preferences, was regarded as something of a watershed in local politics. The Alliance Party also lost ground seriously by comparison with the 1979 Westminster election. The DUP campaign was characterised by Paisley's condemnation of the EC, and his repeated declarations that he would seek to counter Catholic influence at Strasbourg. And he insisted that his vote meant that he must be regarded as speaking for the NI majority. The UUP, while accepting the UK's commitment to EC membership, called for major changes to meet NI conditions. It claimed that the result showed that many of its supporters, being opposed to the Common Market, had deserted to Paisley. Both the SDLP and Alliance took a strong pro-European line, but urged more effort to meet regional needs. Hume, as a candidate of the European Socialist group, accepted the Socialist manifesto, with its commitment to deal energetically with unemployment. He also argued that the new European Parliament would have a healing effect locally, because MEPs from both NI and the Republic would be likely to find themselves on the same side in European politics. The election took place in the single NI constituency with voting by PR (STV) and the outcome was in accordance with the intention of the European summit meeting which had allocated a third seat to NI in the hope that this would ensure representation of both communities. The turnout of nearly 57 per cent reflected a higher level of interest than in GB.

Note The method of determining the number of votes transferred from one candidate to another under this PR system can vary, according to usage in different countries. In NI the method employed in this election allowed for the calculation of transfers to be determined to two decimal places. This differs from the system which obtains in the Republic, where only whole numbers of votes are transferred.

1979 European Parliament election

Details of the count

3 seats

Electorate 1,029,490	Percentage poll 56.92
Valid votes 572,239	Quota 143,060
Spoiled votes 13,773	Votes unaccounted for 47

First count

Party candidates	1st-preference votes	% valid poll
Paisley, Rev. I. (DUP)	170,688	29.8
Hume, J. (SDLP)	140,622	24.6
Taylor, J. (UUP)	68,185	11.9
West, H. (UUP)	56,984	10.0
Napier, O. (All.)	39,026	6.8
Kilfedder, J. (Ulster Unionist)	38,198	6.7
McAliskey, Mrs B. (Ind)	33,969	5.9
Bleakley, D. (Utd. Community)	9,383	1.6
Devlin, P. (ULP)	6,122	1.1
Cummings, E. (UPNI)	3,712	0.6
Brennan, B. (Rep. C.)	3,258	0.6
Donnelly, F. (Rep. C.)	1,160	0.2
Murray, J. (U. Lib.)	932	0.2

Paisley elected; his surplus votes were distributed.

Second count

Party candidates	Distribution of surplus votes	Total votes
Hume	+54.56	140,676.56
Taylor	+9,043.68	77,228.68
West	+4,179.04	61,163.04
Kilfedder	+12,424.32	50,622.32
Napier	+378.08	39,404.08
McAliskey	+6.72	33,975.72
Bleakley	+217.76	9,600.76
Devlin	+24.80	6,146.80
Cummings	+124.96	3,836.96
Brennan	+5.44	3,263.44
Donnelly	+4.00	1,164.00
Murray	+16.00	948.00

Non-transferable votes, 1,148.64. Bleakley, Brennan, Cummings, Devlin, Donnelly and Murray eliminated, all with lost deposits. Their votes were distributed.

Third count

Party candidates	Distribution of votes	Total votes
Hume	+5,396.00	146,072.56
Taylor	+2,979.28	80,207.96
West	+789.12	61,952.16
Kilfedder	+3,363.84	53,986.16
Napier	+6,298.88	45,702.96
McAliskey	+2,129.72	36,105.44

Accumulative non-transferable votes, 5,151.76. Hume elected. McAliskey eliminated; her votes were distributed.

Fourth count

Party candidates	Distribution of votes	Total votes
Taylor	+197.96	80,405.92
West	+187.96	62,140.12
Kilfedder	+637.72	54,623.88
Napier	+5,560.80	51,263.76

Accumulative non-transferable votes, 34,672.76. Napier eliminated; his votes were distributed.

Fifth count

Party candidates	Distribution of votes	Total votes
Taylor	+16,001.44	96,407.36
Kilfedder	+14,760.08	69,383.96
West	+3,775.52	65,915.64

Accumulative non-transferable votes, 51,399.48. West eliminated; his votes were distributed.

Sixth count

Party candidates	Distribution of votes	Total votes
Taylor	+57,059.00	153,466.36
Kilfedder	+3,174.00	72,557.96

Accumulative non-transferable votes 57,082.12. Taylor elected.

1981 DISTRICT COUNCIL ELECTIONS

The District Council elections on 20 May 1981 were marked by a highly polarised atmosphere, largely due to the H-Block hunger strike, and the results showed a decline in support for centre parties. The DUP took most satisfaction from the outcome because it succeeded in replacing the UUP as the party with the largest popular vote, but its lead was so slender (0.1 per cent) that it left the UUP the strongest party in terms of seats. But the DUP more than doubled its share of the first-preference votes as compared with 1977 – 26.6 per cent against 12.7 per cent – and its total of seats increased by 68 to 142. The UUP, however, got 152 seats compared with 178 in the 1977 election; that is, it lost 5 per cent of the total seats although its share of the vote dropped by only 3 per cent. The UUP first-preference votes reached 26.5 per

Overall figures, 1981 District Council elections

Party	1st-preference votes	% votes
DUP	176,816	26.6
Loy.	21,699	3.3
UUP	176,342	26.5
UPUP/UPNI	12,491	1.9
All.	59,219	8.9
Lab.	9,854	1.5
WPRC	12,237	1.8
SDLP	116,487	17.5
IIP	25,859	3.9
Ind. Nat.	9,487	1.4
Others	45,011	6.7
Total	665,502	100.0

cent against 29.6 per cent four years earlier. The Alliance Party fared worst – its vote dropped from 14.4 per cent to

8.9 per cent, and it now held thirty-eight seats instead of seventy. The SDLP also lost ground, although much less dramatically. Its percentage poll was 17.5 as compared with 20.6 in 1977, although, because of the larger turnout, it dropped fewer than 2,000 votes overall. Its tally of seats fell from 113 to 103 in face of increased competition from a variety of Republicans and Nationalists, but most notably from the Irish Independence Party. The IIP, which came into being soon after the 1977 elections, took 3.9 per cent of the votes and picked up twenty-one seats. The smaller parties found the going hard. A combination of UPUP and UPNI got seven seats and 1.9 per cent of votes. WPRC halved its representation with three seats and 1.8 per cent of votes; IRSP and PD got two seats each, and the NILP held its single seat. The turnout was 66.2 per cent.

Party composition of councils, 1981

Council	DUP	Loy.	UUP	UPUP/ UPNI	All.	Lab.	WPRC	SDLP	IIP	Ind. Nat.	Others
Antrim	4	0	7	0	1	0	0	2	1	0	0
Ards	7	0	3	2	3	1	0	1	0	0	0
Armagh	3	1	8	0	0	0	0	7	0	0	1
Ballymena	13	0	5	0	0	0	0	0	0	0	3
Ballymoney	7	0	3	0	1	0	0	2	0	0	3
Banbridge	4	0	8	0	0	0	0	2	0	0	1
Belfast	15	3	13	1	7	1	0	6	0	4	1
Carrickfergus	7	2	3	0	3	0	0	0	0	0	0
Castlereagh	9	0	5	0	4	0	0	2	0	0	3
Coleraine	6	0	8	0	1	0	0	2	0	0	3
Cookstown	3	1	4	0	0	0	0	5	0	0	2
Craigavon	7	1	9	0	1	0	2	5	0	0	0
Down	3	0	6	0	1	1	1	8	0	0	0
Dungannon	3	0	8	0	0	0	0	3	1	0	5
Fermanagh	2	0	8	0	0	0	0	4	4	0	2
Larne	6	1	4	0	3	0	0	0	0	0	1
Limavady	2	0	6	0	0	0	0	5	1	0	1
Lisburn	10	1	8	0	2	0	0	2	0	0	0
Londonderry	5	0	4	0	0	0	0	14	4	0	0
Magherafelt	4	1	2	0	0	0	0	5	1	0	2
Moyle	2	1	4	0	0	0	0	5	0	0	4
Newry and Mourne	2	0	6	0	0	0	0	16	4	0	2
Newtownabbey	5	2	9	0	3	1	0	0	0	0	1
North Down	5	1	4	4	6	0	0	0	0	0	0
Omagh	4	0	4	0	2	0	0	5	5	0	0
Strabane	4	0	3	0	0	0	0	4	0	0	4
Total	142	15	152	7	38	4	3	103	21	4	37

APRIL 1981 WESTMINSTER BY-ELECTION

The by-election, created by the death of Frank Maguire, Ind. MP for Fermanagh–S. Tyrone, aroused world-wide interest, because it resolved itself into a straight fight between Bobby Sands, leader of the H-Block hunger-strikers, and Harry West (UUP), who had held the seat briefly in 1974. Sands had been on hunger strike since 1 March and was said to have lost about 13 kilograms in weight by polling day. His campaign from his Maze Prison cell stimulated widespread media attention, and in the end provoked an astonishing unity among all shades of Nationalists. Failure to fight the seat created angry dissension within the SDLP. The British authorities made it clear that Sands's narrow victory would not weaken their opposition to the H-Block prisoners' demands, but the result was a powerful boost to the hunger-strike campaign.

Fermanagh–South Tyrone,
9 April 1981

Elec. 72,283	% Poll 86.9
Sands, R.G.(Anti-H-Block/ Armagh Political Prisoner)	30,492
West, H.W. (UUP)	29,046
Anti-H-Block/Armagh Political Prisoner maj.	1,446
Spoiled votes	3,280

AUGUST 1981 WESTMINSTER BY-ELECTION

In this second by-election in Fermanagh–S. Tyrone in five months, to fill the vacancy created by the death of hunger-striker Bobby Sands, his election agent, Owen Carron, was successful in a six-cornered contest. With the hunger strike still going on, and the previous by-election result having failed to move the British Government, there was some surprise that Carron, an ordinary member of PSF, got 786 votes more than Sands, despite the split in the anti-Unionist vote. The UUP vote, with a new candidate in Ken Maginnis, a Dungannon councillor, was virtually the same as in the April contest.

Fermanagh–South Tyrone,
20 August 1981

Elec. 72,834	% Poll 88.6
Carron, O. (Anti-H-Block Proxy Political Prisoner)	31,278
Maginnis, K. (UUP)	29,048
Close, S. (All.)	1,930
Moore, T. (WPRC)	1,132
Green, M. (General Amnesty)	249
Hall-Raleigh, S. (Peace)	90
Anti-H-Block Proxy Political Prisoner maj.	2,230
Spoiled votes	804

1982 WESTMINSTER BY-ELECTION

The by-election on 4 March 1982, to fill the vacancy arising from the murder of the Rev. Robert Bradford, UUP MP for S. Belfast, developed into a bitter struggle between the UUP and the DUP, who were particularly angry at the refusal of the 'Officials' to consider the idea of a United Unionist candidate. The DUP selected a strong contender in the Rev. William McCrea, of Magherafelt, a well-known gospel singer. But in an eight-cornered contest, the UUP nominee, the Rev. Martin Smyth, head of the Orange Order, had a 5,397 majority over Alliance candidate David Cook, and the DUP candidate was in third place.

South Belfast, 4 March 1982

Elec. 66,219	% Poll 66.2
Smyth, Rev. M. (UUP)	17,123
Cook, D. (All.)	11,726
McCrea, Rev. W. (DUP)	9,818
McDonnell, Dr A. (SDLP)	3,839
McMichael, J. (ULDP)	576
Caul, B. (ULP)	303
Narain, J. (One Human Family)	137
Hall-Raleigh, S. (Peace State)	12
UUP maj.	5,397
No change	

1982 NI ASSEMBLY ELECTION

The 'rolling devolution' election on 20 October 1982 was notable for two things – the achievement of PSF, in its first Stormont election, of taking five of the seventy-eight seats with more than 10 per cent of the first-preference votes, and the re-emergence of the UUP as the largest group, with twenty-six seats. The PSF showed an advance of 2.4 per cent over the aggregate pro-hunger-strikers vote in the 1981 District Council elections, and it contested only seven of the twelve constituencies. It was unlucky in that it might have expected to get two more seats on the basis of its voting strength. The PSF gains led to SDLP losses, and the total of SDLP seats, at fourteen, was five down on the 1973 Assembly and three down on the 1975 Convention, although it made a small recovery in terms of first-preference votes as against the 1981 District Council elections. Both SDLP and PSF fought on an abstentionist policy. PSF simply called for British withdrawal, and the SDLP argued that the Assembly was 'unworkable' since Unionists continued to reject power-sharing and the Government had failed to promise a strong enough Irish dimension. On the Unionist side, the DUP had hoped to repeat its 1981 District Council performance of a slight lead in votes over the UUP, but in the event the UUP had a 7 per cent margin over the DUP in first-preference votes. Both the UUP and the DUP pledged themselves to seek to persuade the Government to concede majority rule, but the DUP was more enthusiastic than the UUP about the interim scrutiny powers given to the Assembly. With almost the same percentage of first-preference votes as in the 1973 Assembly election, Alliance profited from late transfers to give it ten seats – two more than it held in 1973 and in the 1975 Convention. For the most part, the smaller parties and Independents fared badly. The electorate stood at 1,048,807 and the turnout was 63.5 per cent.

Seats and votes, 1982 NI Assembly election

Party	Seats	1st-preference votes	% Valid poll
UUP	26	188,277	29.7
DUP	21	145,528	23.0
SDLP	14	118,891	18.8
PSF	5	64,191	10.1
Alliance	10	58,851	9.3
WP	0	17,216	2.7
UPUP	1	14,916	2.3
UUUP	0	11,550	1.8
Other Unionists	1	9,502	1.6
Others	0	4,198	0.7
Total	78	633,120	100.0

East Belfast	Elec. 74,273	% Poll 54.8
6 elected	Quota 5,632	1st-preference votes
Count 1	Robinson, P. (DUP)	15,319
Count 1	Burchill, J. (UUP)	7,345
Count 1	Napier, O. (All.)	6,037
Count 2	Vitty, D. (DUP)	235
Count 10	Dunlop, Mrs D. (UUP)	1,696
Count 10	Morrow, A. (All.)	2,966

North Belfast	Elec. 62,391	% Poll 59.2
5 elected	Quota 5,957	1st-preference votes
Count 1	Carson, J. (UUP)	7,798
Count 11	Seawright, G. (DUP)	4,929
Count 13	Millar, F. (Ind. U.)	2,047
Count 14	O'Hare, P. (SDLP)	3,190
Count 14	Maguire, P. (All.)	2,527

South Belfast	Elec. 66,683	% Poll 58.1
5 elected	Quota 6,245	1st-preference votes
Count 1	Smyth, Rev. M. (UUP)	13,337
Count 1	Cook, D. (All.)	6,514
Count 4	McCrea, S. (DUP)	4,091
Count 6	Graham, E. (UUP)	2,875
Count 6	Kirkpatrick, J. (UUP)	1,126

West Belfast	Elec. 57,726	% Poll 62.5
4 elected	Quota 6,852	1st-preference votes
Count 1	Adams, G. (PSF)	9,740
Count 5	Hendron, Dr J. (SDLP)	5,207
Count 8	Passmore, T. (UUP)	4,505
Count 8	Glendinning, W. (All.)	2,733

North Antrim	Elec. 104,683	% Poll 57.5
8 elected	Quota 6,512	1st-preference votes
Count 1	Paisley, Rev. I. (DUP)	9,231
Count 2	Allister, J. (DUP)	5,835
Count 6	Gaston, J. (UUP)	5,856
Count 8	Farren, S. (SDLP)	5,006
Count 9	Neeson, S. (All.)	3,258
Count 10	McKee, J. (DUP)	4,515
Count 10	Beggs, R. (UUP)	4,885
Count 11	Cousley, C. (DUP)	4,133

South Antrim	Elec. 131,734	% Poll 52.0
10 elected	Quota 6,041	1st-preference votes
Count 1	Molyneaux, J. (UUP)	19,978
Count 1	Beattie, Rev. W. (DUP)	7,489
Count 2	Agnew, F. (UUP)	3,302
Count 2	Davis, I. (DUP)	5,394
Count 18	Forsythe, C. (UUP)	1,612
Count 19	Thompson, R. (DUP)	2,646
Count 22	McDonald, J. (SDLP)	2,071
Count 23	Close, S. (All.)	2,916
Count 23	Mawhinney, G. (All.)	2,660
Count 23	Bell, W. (UUP)	979

This count, involving twenty-six candidates, is believed to have established a record for the UK and the Republic. It extended over more than thirty hours.

Armagh	Elec. 95,610	% Poll 66.9
7 elected	Quota 7,739	1st-preference votes
Count 1	McCusker, H. (UUP)	19,547
Count 1	Mallon, S. (SDLP)	8,528
Count 7	Nicholson, J. (UUP)	2,590
Count 9	McAllister, J. (PSF)	5,182
Count 11	Simpson, Mrs M. (UUP)	721
Count 13	Calvert, D. (DUP)	2,661
Count 14	News, H. (SDLP)	2,871

North Down	Elec. 103,619	% Poll 53.8
8 elected	Quota 6,069	1st-preference votes
Count 1	Kilfedder, J. (UPUP)	13,958
Count 2	Taylor, J. (UUP)	5,852
Count 6	Gibson, S. (DUP)	4,500
Count 8	Cushnahan, J. (All.)	4,416
Count 9	Dunleath, Lord (All.)	3,841
Count 10	Pentland, W. (DUP)	3,340
Count 11	McCartney, R. (UUP)	3,782
Count 13	Bleakes, W. (UUP)	2,692

South Down	Elec. 93,261	% Poll 65.6
7 elected	Quota 7,382	1st-preference votes
Count 1	Feely, F. (SDLP)	7,391
Count 2	McGrady, E. (SDLP)	7,313
Count 6	Brown, W. (UUP)	5,220
Count 7	O'Donoghue, P. (SDLP)	5,916
Count 10	McCullough, R. (UUP)	5,802
Count 11	Graham, G. (DUP)	4,075
Count 11	Wells, J. (DUP)	3,779

Fermanagh–South Tyrone	Elec. 73,930	% Poll 82.9
5 elected	Quota 9,864	1st-preference votes
Count 1	Carron, O. (PSF)	14,025
Count 1	Maginnis, K. (UUP)	10,117
Count 8	Ferguson, R. (UUP)	5,877
Count 9	Currie, A. (SDLP)	6,800
Count 10	Foster, Rev. I. (DUP)	4,324

Londonderry	Elec. 100,198	% Poll 66.0
7 elected	Quota 8,058	1st-preference votes
Count 1	Hume, J. (SDLP)	12,282
Count 1	McGuinness, M. (PSF)	8,207
Count 10	McClure, J. (DUP)	6,857
Count 10	Allen, J. (UUP)	6,107
Count 11	Douglas, W. (UUP)	5,031
Count 13	Logue, H. (SDLP)	4,828
Count 13	Campbell, G. (DUP)	5,305

Mid-Ulster	Elec. 84,699	% Poll 75.5
6 elected	Quota 8,853	1st-preference votes
Count 1	McCrea, Rev. W. (DUP)	10,445
Count 6	Haughey, D. (SDLP)	8,413
Count 10	Thompson, W. (UUP)	5,546
Count 11	Kane, A. (DUP)	3,981
Count 12	McSorley, Mrs M. (SDLP)	4,169
Count 12	Morrison, D. (PSF)	6,927

1983 NI ASSEMBLY BY-ELECTION

The by-election on 20 April 1983 was created by the unseating, by an Election Court, of Seamus Mallon (SDLP, Armagh) on the grounds that he was disqualified from Assembly membership because he was also an Irish Senator at the time of the Assembly election in October 1982. The SDLP called on voters to ignore the by-election. There were 571 spoiled votes.

Armagh, 20 April 1983

Elec. 95,100	% Poll 34.07
Quota 15,914	

Party candidates	1st-preference votes
Speers, J. (UUP)	26,907
French, T. (WP)	4,920

Speers elected on the first count.

1983 WESTMINSTER GENERAL ELECTION

The 9 June 1983 Westminster election was fought in seventeen seats – five extra as compared with the 1979 election. The Boundary Commission gave additional representation to five of the previous constituencies: Londonderry – Foyle; Armagh – Newry and Armagh; N. Antrim – E. Antrim; S. Antrim – Lagan Valley; and N. Down – Strangford. The other constituencies were adjusted accordingly and renamed as necessary. The main feature of the results was the dominance of the UUP, which took eleven seats and 34 per cent of the poll and went strongly ahead of the DUP, with three seats and a 20 per cent vote. UPUP had one seat. Thus, Unionists had fifteen of the seats, with the other two going to PSF (W. Belfast) and SDLP (Foyle). The campaign had been marked by a bitter struggle on both sides of the community, although a very limited accommodation between UUP and DUP meant that there was only one Unionist in three constituencies – Foyle, Newry and Armagh and Fermanagh–S. Tyrone. The SDLP rejected any idea of a pact with PSF, and fought all seventeen seats – the only party to do so. None the less, the SDLP's share of the vote was down slightly as compared with the 1982 Assembly election – to 17.9 per cent – while PSF passed its target vote of 100,000 and achieved a 13.4 per cent poll, about 3 per cent up on the Assembly election. Main interest was centred in W. Belfast where Gerry Adams of PSF repeated his 1982 Assembly election success and unseated veteran MP Gerry Fitt. Owen Carron of PSF, who won the August 1981 by-election in Fermanagh–S. Tyrone, was defeated by Ken Maginnis (UUP). There was a high turnout of 73.3 per cent of the 1,048,766 electors.

Overall figures, 1983 Westminster general election

Party	Votes	% Valid poll
UUP	259,952	34.0
DUP	152,749	20.0
SDLP	137,012	17.9
PSF	102,701	13.4
All.	61,275	8.0
UPUP	22,861	3.0
WP	14,650	1.9
Ind.	10,326	1.3
Others	3,399	0.3
Total valid votes	764,925	100.0
Spoiled votes	4,353	
Total votes polled	769,278	

*INDICATES OUTGOING MP

East Belfast

Elec. 55,581	% Poll 70.0
*Robinson, P. (DUP)	17,631
Burchill, J. (UUP)	9,642
Napier, O. (All.)	9,373
Donaldson, D. (PSF)	682
Tang, Mrs M. (Lab. and TU)	584
Prendiville, P. (SDLP)	519
Cullen, F. (WP)	421
Boyd, H. (Anti-Noise)	59
DUP maj.	7,989

North Belfast

Elec. 61,128	% Poll 69.4
Walker, A.C. (UUP)	15,339
Seawright, G. (DUP)	8,260
Feeny, B. (SDLP)	5,944
Austin, J. (PSF)	5,451
Maguire, P. (All.)	3,879
Lynch, S. (WP)	2,412
Gault, W. (Ind. DUP)	1,134
UUP maj.	7,079

South Belfast

Elec. 53,694	% Poll 69.6
*Smyth, Rev. M. (UUP)	18,669
Cook, D. (All.)	8,945
McCrea, R.S. (DUP)	4,565
McDonnell, A. (SDLP)	3,216
McKnight, S. (PSF)	1,107
Carr, G. (WP)	856
UUP maj.	9,724

West Belfast

Elec. 59,750	% Poll 74.3
Adams, G. (PSF)	16,379
Hendron, Dr J. (SDLP)	10,934
*Fitt, G. (Ind.)	10,326
Passmore, T. (UUP)	2,435
Haffey, G.A. (DUP)	2,399
McMahon, Ms M. (WP)	1,893
PSF maj.	5,445

North Antrim

Elec. 63,254	% Poll 69.9
*Paisley, Rev. I. (DUP)	23,922
Coulter, Rev. R.(UUP)	10,749
Farren, S. (SDLP)	6,193
McMahon, P. (PSF)	2,860
Samuel, M.H. (Ecol.)	451
DUP maj.	13,173

South Antrim

Elec. 59,300	% Poll 65.5
Forsythe, C. (UUP)	17,727
Thompson, R. (DUP)	10,935
Mawhinney, G. (All.)	4,612
Maginness, A. (SDLP)	3,377
Laverty, S. (PSF)	1,629
Smyth, K. (WP)	549
UUP maj.	6,792

East Antrim

Elec. 58,780	% Poll 65.0
Beggs, R. (UUP)	14,293
Allister, J. (DUP)	13,926
Neeson, S. (All.)	7,620
O'Cleary, M. (SDLP)	1,047
Cunning, W. (Ind.)	741
Kelly, A. (WP)	581
UUP maj.	367

North Down

Elec. 61,574	% Poll 66.2
*Kilfedder, J. (UPUP)	22,861
Cushnahan, J. (All.)	9,015
McCartney, R. (UUP)	8,261
Ó Baoill, C. (SDLP)	645
UPUP maj.	13,846

South Down

Elec. 66,987	% Poll 76.6
*Powell, E. (UUP)'	20,693
McGrady, E. (SDLP)	20,145
Fitzsimmons, P. (PSF)	4,074
Harvey, C. (DUP)	3,743
Forde, P.M.D. (All.)	1,823
Magee, Ms M. (WP)	851
UUP maj.	548

Strangford

Elec. 60,232	% Poll 64.9
Taylor, J. (UUP)	19,086
Gibson, S. (DUP)	11,716
Morrow, A. (All.)	6,171
Curry, J. (SDLP)	1,713
Heath, R. (Ind. Lab.)	430
UUP maj.	7,370

Lagan Valley

Elec. 60,099	% Poll 67.5
*Molyneaux, J. (UUP)	24,017
Beattie, Rev. W. (DUP)	6,801
Close, S. (All.)	4,593
Boomer, C. (SDLP)	2,603
McAuley, R. (PSF)	1,751
Loughlin, G. (WP)	809
UUP maj.	17,216

Upper Bann

Elec. 60,797	% Poll 72.0
*McCusker, H. (UUP)	24,888
McDonald, J. (SDLP)	7,807
Wells, J. (DUP)	4,547
Curran, B. (PSF)	4,110
French, T. (WP)	2,392
UUP maj.	17,081

Newry and Armagh

Elec. 62,387	% Poll 76.0
Nicholson, J. (UUP)	18,988
Mallon, S. (SDLP)	17,434
McAllister, J. (PSF)	9,928
Moore, T. (WP)	1,070
UUP maj.	1,554

Fermanagh–South Tyrone

Elec. 67,880	% Poll 88.6
Maginnis, K. (UUP)	28,630
*Carron, O. (PSF)	20,954
Flanagan, Mrs R. (SDLP)	9,923
Kettyles, D. (WP)	649
UUP maj.	7,676

Mid–Ulster

Elec. 63,899	% Poll 84.3
McCrea, Rev. W. (DUP)	16,174
Morrison, D.G. (PSF)	16,096
Haughey, P.D. (SDLP)	12,044
Thompson, W.J. (UUP)	7,066
Lagan, Dr J.A. (All.)	1,735
Owens, T.A. (WP)	766
DUP maj.	78

East Londonderry

Elec. 67,365	% Poll 76.3
*Ross, W. (UUP)	19,469
McClure, J. (DUP)	12,207
Doherty, A. (SDLP)	9,397
Davey, J. (PSF)	7,073
McGrath, Mrs M. (All.)	2,401
Donnelly, F. (WP)	819
UUP maj.	7,262

Foyle

Elec. 67,431	% Poll 77.6
Hume, J. (SDLP)	24,071
Campbell, G. (DUP)	15,923
McGuinness, M. (PSF)	10,607
O'Grady, G. (All.)	1,108
Mclaugh, E. (WP)	582
SDLP maj.	8,148

1984 NI ASSEMBLY BY-ELECTION

In the 1 March 1984 by-election, caused by the murder of Edgar Graham (UUP, S. Belfast) by PIRA in December 1983, Frank Millar (UUP) was returned unopposed.

South Belfast, 1 March 1984

Millar, Frank (UUP)	unopposed

1984 EUROPEAN PARLIAMENT ELECTION

NI representation at Strasbourg was unchanged as a result of the election on 14 June 1984, with the three seats being taken by the Rev. Ian Paisley (DUP), John Hume (SDLP) and John Taylor (UUP). But there were some notable polling features. The overall vote showed an increase of 7.4 per cent (about 120,000 votes) and Paisley demonstrated even more convincingly than in 1979 his dominance as a Unionist standard-bearer. He took almost exactly one third of all the votes cast – a rise of about 4 per cent. For the UUP John Taylor maintained his party's 1979 share of the vote at 21.4 per cent. The UUP had run two candidates in 1979, but on this occasion Taylor was his party's sole representative. John Hume put on about 11,000 extra votes as compared with 1979, but his share of the poll dropped by 1.7 per cent, no doubt due partly to the substantial PSF challenge mounted by Danny Morrison, who took over 13 per cent of first-preference votes. Alliance lost some ground. As in 1979, the contest was essentially a counting of party heads rather than any real test of EC policies.

1984 European Parliament election

Details of the count	
3 seats	

Electorate 1,065,363	Percentage poll 65.4
Valid votes 685,317	Quota 171,330
Spoiled votes 11,654	Votes unaccounted for 23

First count

Party candidates	1st-preference votes	% valid poll
Paisley, Rev. I. (DUP)	230,251	33.6
Hume, J. (SDLP)	151,399	22.1
Taylor, J. (UUP)	147,169	21.5
Morrison, D. (PSF)	91,476	13.3
Cook, D. (All.)	34,046	5.0
Kilfedder, J. (UPUP)	20,092	2.9
Lynch, S. (WP)	8,712	1.3
McGuigan, C. (Ecol.)	2,172	0.3

Paisley elected; his surplus votes were distributed.

Second count

Party candidates	Distribution of surplus votes	Total votes
Taylor	+38,545.52	185,714.52
Hume	+265.20	151,664.20
Morrison	+49.40	91,525.40
Kilfedder	+18,201.82	38,293.82
Cook	+846.04	34,892.04
Lynch	+101.14	8,813.14
McGuigan	+64.74	2,236.74

Non-transferable votes, 847.14. Taylor elected. Lynch and McGuigan eliminated, with lost deposits; their votes were distributed.

Third count

Party candidates	Distribution of votes	Total votes
Hume	+4,646.12	156,310.32
Morrison	+1,119.12	92,644.52
Kilfedder	+561.78	38,854.60
Cook	+2,509.24	37,401.28

Accumulative non-transferable votes, 3,061.76. Cook and Kilfedder eliminated, with lost deposits; their votes were distributed.

Fourth count

Party candidates	Distribution of votes	Total votes
Hume	+26,946.00	183,256.32
Morrison	+435.00	93,079.52

Accumulative non-transferable votes 51,936.64. Hume elected.

1985 DISTRICT COUNCIL ELECTIONS

Before these elections the boundaries of the twenty-six District Councils and the 526 wards were reviewed by an independent Boundary Commission. The result was no sigificant change in council boundaries but an increase in the number of wards to 566. The UUP and PSF had most reason to be happy with the outcome of the 15 May 1985 council elections. The UUP recovered well from its marginal defeat by the DUP in the 1981 elections in terms of first-preference votes. With 29.5 per cent of first-preference votes, it was a full 5 per cent ahead of the DUP's 24.3 per cent and took 190 seats against the DUP's 142. This underlined the DUP's problem of matching, in elections, the massive personal vote achieved by the Rev. Ian Paisley in the European elections. PSF was fighting District Council elections for the first time, and with 11.8 per cent of the vote and fifty-nine seats, it improved on its own understated predictions by more than twenty seats. The SDLP was not much affected by the PSF intervention – its 17.8 per cent showing was slightly up on 1981 (17.5 per cent), although its total of seats dropped by 2 to 101. Alliance recorded 7.1 per cent of the vote, which

Overall figures, 1985 District Council election

Party	1st-preference votes	% votes
DUP	155,297	24.3
Loy./U.	19,712	3.1
UUP	188,497	29.5
All.	45,394	7.1
Lab.	3,692	0.6
WP	10,276	1.6
SDLP	113,967	17.8
PSF	75,686	11.8
IIP	7,459	1.1
Ind. Nat.	8,191	1.3
Others	11,451	1.8
Total	639,622	100.0

was a drop on its poll of 8.9 per cent in 1981 when its support was squeezed in a highly polarised contest. The Alliance total of thirty-four seats was four down on 1981. WP gained one seat as compared with 1981 (a total of four), but its poll of 1.6 per cent was very slightly down on 1981 (1.8 per cent). IIP evidently suffered most from the PSF challenge – it took only four seats against twenty-one in 1981 and saw its poll decline from 3.9 per

398

cent to 1.1 per cent. A feature of the
elections was that single-party control was
achieved in only two councils –
Banbridge (UUP) and Ballymena (DUP).

The overall valid poll was 60.1 per cent
(4 per cent down on 1981) but it varied
from 83 per cent in Cookstown and
Fermanagh to 45.7 per cent in N. Down.

Party composition of councils, 1985

Council	DUP	Loy./ U.	UUP	All.	Lab.	WP	SDLP	PSF	IIP	Ind. Nat.	Others
Antrim	5	0	9	1	0	0	3	1	0	0	0
Ards	8	1	6	3	1	0	0	0	0	0	1
Armagh	3	0	11	0	0	0	7	1	0	0	0
Ballymena	15	0	6	0	0	0	1	0	0	0	1
Ballymoney	6	0	6	0	0	0	2	1	0	0	1
Banbridge	3	0	8	0	0	0	3	0	0	0	1
Belfast	11	4	14	8	0	1	6	7	0	0	0
Carrickfergus	3	1	7	3	0	0	0	0	0	0	1
Castlereagh	10	0	8	3	0	0	0	0	0	0	0
Coleraine	6	0	10	2	0	0	2	0	0	0	1
Cookstown	5	1	3	0	0	0	3	4	0	0	0
Craigavon	6	0	11	0	0	2	5	2	0	0	0
Derry	5	0	5	0	0	0	14	5	1	0	0
Down	3	0	7	0	0	1	10	2	0	0	0
Dungannon	3	0	8	0	0	0	5	4	0	2	0
Fermanagh	2	0	8	0	0	0	4	8	1	0	0
Larne	6	0	6	2	0	0	0	0	0	1	0
Limavady	2	0	7	0	0	0	4	2	0	0	0
Lisburn	8	0	13	3	0	0	2	2	0	0	0
Magherafelt	4	0	3	0	0	0	4	4	0	0	0
Moyle	3	2	2	0	0	0	4	2	0	0	2
Newry and Mourne	2	0	7	0	0	0	14	5	1	1	0
Newtownabbey	9	2	10	2	1	0	0	0	0	0	1
North Down	6	3	8	7	0	0	0	0	0	0	0
Omagh	4	0	4	0	0	0	5	6	1	0	1
Strabane	4	0	3	0	0	0	3	3	0	2	0
Total	142	14	190	34	2	4	101	59	4	6	10

1985 NI ASSEMBLY BY-ELECTION
The by-election in S. Down on 17
October 1985 was caused by the death of
Raymond McCullough (UUP) in June
1985. The turnout of 21.3 per cent was
one of the lowest ever recorded in an
election in NI. Elected on the first count,
the successful candidate, Jeffrey
Donaldson (UUP), was twenty-two years
old and became the youngest member of
the NI Assembly.

South Down, 17 October 1985

Elec. 98,126	% Poll 21.3
Quota 10,184	

Party candidates	1st-preference votes
Donaldson, J. (UUP)	17,528
Smyth, Mrs E. (Utd. Ulster Loyalist)	2,838

Donaldson elected on the first count.

1986 WESTMINSTER BY-ELECTIONS

Fifteen by-elections on 23 January 1986 were forced by all the sitting Unionist MPs – eleven UUP, three DUP and one UPUP – to allow Unionists to express their opposition to the AIA. When the British Government rejected a call for a local referendum on the issue, the MPs resigned simultaneously on the understanding that they would be the sole Unionist nominees in their seats. The SDLP members, as supporters of the AIA, were not anxious to help the Unionist manoeuvre, and therefore limited their interest to the four seats which they regarded as marginal – Mid-Ulster, Fermanagh–S. Tyrone, S. Down, and Newry and Armagh. Unionists were forced to run a 'token' candidate, using the name of Irish Foreign Minister 'Peter Barry', in four other constituencies to avoid any 'unopposed' return. (Unionist supporter Wesley Robert Williamson changed his name by deed poll to 'Peter Barry' in order to provide 'opposition in constituencies where other pro-AIA parties refused to contest.) Although the Unionists failed to reach a reputed half-million-vote target, they recorded 418,230 votes against the AIA, but at the expense of losing Newry and Armagh to the SDLP's deputy leader, Seamus Mallon. The Unionist vote represented 71.5 per cent of the total valid poll, which compared with 62.3 per cent in the 1983 election. This was just under 44 per cent of the total electorate. The SDLP also had the satisfaction of seeing the PSF vote drop by 5.4 per cent in the four 'marginals', and their own vote rise by 6 per cent, which was seized on by the British and Irish Governments as one of the fruits of the AIA. Alliance and WP benefited in votes, particularly in seats where they were the sole opponents of Unionists, but still suffered defeat by large majorities. Overall turnout was 62.2 per cent compared with 72.4 per cent in the same seats in 1983.

Overall figures, 1986 Westminster by-elections

Party	Votes	% Valid poll
UUP	302,198	51.7
DUP	85,239	14.6
SDLP	70,917	12.1
PSF	38,821	6.6
All.	32,095	5.5
UPUP	30,793	5.2
WP	18,148	3.1
'P. Barry'	6,777	1.2
Total valid votes	584,988	100.00
Spoiled votes	7,888	
Total votes polled	592,876	

*INDICATES OUTGOING MP

East Belfast

Elec. 55,319	% Poll 61.9
*Robinson, P. (DUP)	27,607
Napier, Sir O. (All.)	5,917
Cullen, F. (WP)	578
DUP maj.	21,690
No change	

North Belfast

Elec. 59,820	% Poll 51.5
*Walker, A.C. (UUP)	21,649
Maguire, P. (All.)	5,072
Lynch, S. (WP)	3,563
UUP maj.	16,577
No change	

South Belfast

Elec. 53,971	% Poll 56.9
*Smyth, Rev. M. (UUP)	21,771
Cook, D. (All.)	7,635
Carr, G. (WP)	1,109
UUP maj.	14,136
No change	

North Antrim

Elec. 65,334	% Poll 54.7
*Paisley, Rev. I. (DUP)	33,937
'Barry, P.' (AIA)	913
DUP maj.	33,024
No change	

South Antrim

Elec. 61,296	% Poll 53.5
*Forsythe, C. (UUP)	30,087
'Barry, P.' (AIA)	1,870
UUP maj.	28,217
No change	

East Antrim

Elec. 60,851	% Poll 59.1
*Beggs, R. (UUP)	30,386
Neeson, S. (All.)	5,405
UUP maj.	24,981
No change	

North Down

Elec. 64,278	% Poll 60.6
*Kilfedder, J. (UPUP)	30,793
Cushnahan, J. (All.)	8,066
UPUP maj.	22,727
No change	

South Down

Elec. 70,108	% Poll 74.0
*Powell, E. (UUP)	24,963
McGrady, E. (SDLP)	23,121
McDowell, H.F. (PSF)	2,936
Magee, S.D. (WP)	522
UUP maj.	1,842
No change	

Strangford

Elec. 62,896	% Poll 56.1
*Taylor, J.D. (UUP)	32,627
'Barry, P.' (AIA)	1,993
UUP maj.	30,634
No change	

Lagan Valley

Elec. 63,369	% Poll 57.8
*Molyneaux, J.H. (UUP)	32,514
Lowry, J.T. (WP)	3,328
UUP maj.	29,186
No change	

Upper Bann

Elec. 63,663	% Poll 57.9
*McCusker, H. (UUP)	29,311
French, T. (WP)	6,978
UUP maj.	22,333
No change	

Newry and Armagh

Elec. 65,482	% Poll 76.9
Mallon, S. (SDLP)	22,694
*Nicholson, J. (UUP)	20,111
McAllister, J. (PSF)	6,609
McCusker, P. (WP)	515
SDLP maj.	2,583
SDLP gain	

Fermanagh–South Tyrone

Elec. 69,919	% Poll 80.9
*Maginnis, K. (UUP)	27,857
Carron, O. (PSF)	15,278
Currie, J.A. (SDLP)	12,081
Kettyles, D. (WP)	864
UUP maj.	12,579
No change	

Mid-Ulster

Elec. 66,830	% Poll 77.6
*McCrea, Rev. W. (DUP)	23,695
Morrison, D.G. (PSF)	13,998
Colton, A. (SDLP)	13,021
Owens, T.A. (WP)	691
DUP maj.	9,697
No change	

East Londonderry

Elec. 70,375	% Poll 48.4
*Ross, W. (UUP)	30,922
'Barry, P.' (AIA)	2,001
UUP maj.	28,921
No change	

1987 WESTMINSTER GENERAL ELECTION

The 11 June 1987 general election showed an unexpected drop in the total Unionist poll, including independents, as compared with the 1983 general election, given the continuing strong campaign by Unionists against the AIA. Indeed, hostility to the agreement was the main feature of the common manifesto on which the UUP, DUP, and Jim Kilfedder (UPUP) fought the election. The drop of 2.3 per cent to 54.8 per cent in their share of the poll, as against 1983, seemed to reflect misgivings by some Unionist voters about the virtue of the boycott of Parliament's proceedings by their MPs as part of the anti-AIA protest. Unionist representation also dropped to thirteen, with the UUP suffering a severe loss in the defeat of veteran parliamentarian Enoch

Powell in S. Down, where an increase in his personal vote was not enough to hold off the challenge of Eddie McGrady (SDLP). Although disappointed by its failure to dislodge PSF president Gerry Adams in W. Belfast, the SDLP apparently profited in most seats from the existence of the AIA. Its share of the poll was up by 3.2 per cent as compared with 1983. This was largely at the expense of PSF, which dropped by 2 per cent but remained at 35 per cent of the Nationalist vote. Alliance was 2 per cent up on 1983 at 10 per cent and the WP also did better than in the last election. The turnout fell by 5.9 per cent to 67.4 per cent, as compared with 1983.

Overall figures, 1987 Westminster general election

Party	Votes	% Valid poll
UUP	276,230	37.8
SDLP	154,087	21.1
DUP	85,642	11.7
PSF	83,389	11.4
All.	72,671	10.0
WP	19,294	2.6
UPUP	18,420	2.5
RU	14,467	2.0
PUP	5,671	0.9
Ecol.	281	0.0
Total valid votes	730,152	100.0
Spoiled votes	4,851	
Total votes polled	735,003	

*INDICATES OUTGOING MP

East Belfast

Elec. 54,666	% Poll 60.6
*Robinson, P. (DUP)	20,372
Alderdice, Dr J. (All.)	10,574
Cullen, F. (WP)	1,314
O'Donnell, J. (PSF)	649
DUP maj.	9,798
No change	

North Belfast

Elec. 59,159	% Poll 62.7
*Walker, A.C. (UUP)	14,355
Maginness, A. (SDLP)	5,795
Scawright, G. (Prot. U.)	5,671
McManus, P. (PSF)	5,062
Lynch, S. (WP)	3,062
Campbell, T. (All.)	2,871

UUP maj.	8,560
No change	

South Belfast

Elec. 54,284	% Poll 60.6
*Smyth, Rev. M. (UUP)	18,917
Cook, D. (All.)	6,963
McDonnell, Dr A. (SDLP)	4,268
Carr, G. (WP)	1,528
McKnight, S. (PSF)	1,030

UUP maj.	11,954
No change	

West Belfast

Elec. 59,400	% Poll 69.6
*Adams, G. (PSF)	16,862
Hendron, Dr J. (SDLP)	14,641
Millar, F. (UUP)	7,646
McMahon, Ms M.(WP)	1,819

PSF maj.	2,221
No change	

North Antrim

Elec. 65,774	% Poll 63.3
*Paisley, Rev. I (DUP)	28,383
Farren, S (SDLP)	5,149
Williams, G. (All.)	5,140
Regan, S. (PSF)	2,633

DUP maj.	23,234
No change	

South Antrim

Elec. 61,706	% Poll 59.4
*Forsythe, C. (UUP)	25,395
Mawhinney, G. (All.)	5,808
McClelland, D. (SDLP)	3,611
Cushinan, H. (PSF)	1,592

UUP maj.	19,587
No change	

East Antrim

Elec. 60,600	% Poll 55.5
*Beggs, R. (UUP)	23,942
Neeson, S. (All.)	8,582
Kelly, A. (WP)	936

UUP maj.	15,360
No change	

North Down

Elec. 65,044	% Poll 63.0
*Kilfedder, J. (UPUP)	18,420
McCartney, R. (RU)	14,467
Cushnahan, J. (All.)	7,932

UPUP maj.	3,953
No change	

South Down

Elec. 71,443	% Poll 79.6
McGrady, E. (SDLP)	26,579
*Powell, E. (UUP)	25,848
Ritchie, Ms G. (PSF)	2,363
Laird, Miss S.E. (All.)	1,069
O'Hagan, D. (WP)	675

SDLP maj.	731
SDLP gain	

Strangford

Elec. 64,475	% Poll 57.9
*Taylor, J. (UUP)	28,199
Morrow, A. (All.)	7,553
Hynds, Miss I. (WP)	1,385
UUP maj.	20,646
No change	

Lagan Valley

Elec. 64,937	% Poll 64.4
*Molyneaux, J. (UUP)	29,101
Close, A. (All.)	5,728
McDonnell, B. (SDLP)	2,888
Rice, P.J. (PSF)	2,656
Lowry, J.T. (WP)	1,215
UUP maj.	23,373
No change	

Upper Bann

Elec. 64,596	% Poll 66.0
*McCusker, H. (UUP)	26,037
Rodgers, Mrs B. (SDLP)	8,676
Curran, B. (PSF)	3,126
Cook, Mrs F. (All.)	2,487
French, T. (WP)	2,004
UUP maj.	17,361
No change	

Newry and Armagh

Elec. 66,151	% Poll 79.4
*Mallon, S. (SDLP)	25,137
Nicholson, J. (UUP)	19,812
McAllister, J. (PSF)	6,173
Jeffrey, W.H. (All.)	664
O'Hanlon, G. (WP)	482
SDLP maj.	5,325
No change	

Fermanagh–South Tyrone

Elec. 69,131	% Poll 80.8
*Maginnis, K. (UUP)	27,446
Corrigan, P. (PSF)	14,623
Flanagan, Mrs R. (SDLP)	10,581
Kettyles, D. (WP)	1,784
Haslett, J. (All.)	941
UUP maj.	12,823
No change	

Mid-Ulster

Elec. 67,343	% Poll 77.9
*McCrea, Rev. W. (DUP)	23,004
Haughey, P.D. (SDLP)	13,644
Begley, S. (PSF)	12,449
Bogan, P. (All.)	1,846
McClean, P.J. (WP)	1,133
DUP maj.	9,360
No change	

East Londonderry

Elec. 71,097	% Poll 69.1
*Ross, W. (UUP)	29,532
Doherty, A. (SDLP)	9,375
Davey, J. (PSF)	5,464
McGowan, J. (All.)	3,237
Donnelly, F. (WP)	935
Samuel, M.H. (Ecol.)	281
UUP maj.	20,157
No change	

Foyle

Elec. 70,583	% Poll 69.5
*Hume, J. (SDLP)	23,743
Campbell, G. (DUP)	13,883
McGuinness, M. (PSF)	8,707
Zammitt, Mrs E. (All.)	1,276
Melaugh, E. (WP)	1,022
SDLP maj.	9,860
No change	

1989 DISTRICT COUNCIL ELECTIONS

District councils had been contentious bodies since 1985. At first the issue was the PSF presence on fourteen councils but later that controversy was overlaid by the Unionists' using councils as part of their protest campaign against the AIA. The Elected Authorities (NI) Act, 1989, had imposed a declaration against violence on all candidates and equalised the local and parliamentary franchise so that almost 11,000 Irish citizens could vote. The elections, held on 17 May, were low-key, attracting fewer candidates than those of 1985. In Ballymoney Town, five candidates were elected unopposed. Turnout fell 4 per cent to 56.1 per cent and was markedly lower in the east than in the west. The highest turnout was in Fermanagh (80 per cent), North Down had only 40.5 per cent. The vote for the two main Unionist parties fell to 49 per cent from 54 per cent due mainly to a fall in DUP support by 6.5 per cent to 17.8 per cent, while the UUP share of the vote rose to 31.2 per cent. The SDLP gained a further 3.2 per cent to win 21 per cent, while PSF fell 0.6 per cent to 11.2 per cent. The change was even more marked in terms of seats, with PSF losing sixteen and declining to 43, whilst the SDLP rose to its best ever total, 121. The Alliance share of the vote declined below 7 per cent but it increased its tally of seats by achieving a total of 38. More independents were elected than in 1985, and in North Down the Model Conservatives were the largest single party with six seats.

Overall figures, 1989 District Council election

Party	1st-preference votes	% votes
DUP	109,332	17.7
Loy./U.	28,359	4.6
UUP	193,028	31.3
All.	42,659	6.9
Cons.	5,956	1.0
Lab.	1,726	0.3
WP	13,078	2.1
SDLP	129,557	21.0
PSF	69,032	11.2
Ind. Nat.	804	0.1
Others	23,678	3.8
Total	617,209	100.0

Party composition of councils, 1989

Council	DUP	Loy./U.	UUP	All.	Cons.	Lab.	WP	SDLP	PSF	Ind. Nat.	Others
Antrim	4	0	10	1	0	0	0	4	0	0	0
Ards	7	0	8	4	0	0	0	0	0	0	1
Armagh	2	0	11	0	0	0	0	8	1	0	0
Ballymena	12	0	7	1	0	0	0	1	0	0	2
Ballymoney	6	0	6	0	0	0	0	3	0	0	1
Banbridge	2	0	9	0	0	0	0	3	0	0	1
Belfast	8	6	14	6	0	0	1	8	8	0	0
Carrickfergus	3	3	4	4	0	0	0	0	0	0	1
Castlereagh	9	2	6	4	0	0	0	0	0	0	0
Coleraine	5	1	10	2	0	0	0	2	0	0	1
Cookstown	5	1	3	0	0	0	0	5	2	0	0
Craigavon	4	0	12	2	0	0	1	6	1	0	0
Derry	4	3	3	0	0	0	0	15	5	0	0
Down	2	0	8	1	0	0	0	12	0	0	0
Dungannon	3	0	8	0	0	0	1	5	3	0	2
Fermanagh	2	0	10	0	0	0	1	5	4	0	1
Larne	4	0	7	2	0	0	0	0	0	0	2
Limavady	1	0	7	0	0	0	0	6	1	0	0
Lisburn	5	0	15	2	1*	0	0	3	2	0	0
Magherafelt	3	0	4	0	0	0	0	4	3	0	1
Moyle	3	2	2	0	0	0	0	4	1	0	3
Newry and Mourne	0	1	6	0	0	0	0	17	4	0	2
Newtownabbey	6	2	11	4	0	1	0	1	0	0	0
North Down	4	3	5	4	6	0	0	0	0	0	2
Omagh	3	0	5	0	0	0	0	6	6	0	1
Strabane	3	1	3	1	0	0	0	3	2	0	2
Total	110	25	194	38	7	1	4	121	43	0	23

* Stood as an Independent Conservative.

1989 EUROPEAN PARLIAMENT ELECTION

There was bound to be at least one change of personnel, as a result of the decision of John Taylor (UUP) to retire after ten years in the European Parliament. Ten candidates, two more than in 1984, contested the election on 15 June 1989 and they included candidates arguing for the organisation of the British Conservative and Labour parties in Northern Ireland as well as the local parties. Turnout fell to a record low, 48.3 per cent, some 16 per cent lower than in 1984 and 8 per cent lower than in the District Council elections in May. The Rev. Ian Paisley (DUP) again topped the poll, but his 29.9 per cent vote was

3.7 per cent lower than in 1984. John Hume was also elected on the first count, and his personal vote of 25.5 per cent was higher than his party had ever achieved before. The second stage, the distribution of Paisley's surplus, resulted in the election of Jim Nicholson (UUP) after improving on his predecessor's vote to win 22.2 per cent of first preferences. Danny Morrison (PSF) was runner-up, but his party vote had slipped to 9.1 per cent from 13.3 per cent. The other six candidates lost their deposits but their order of first preferences had two small surprises. First, Laurence Kennedy, without any official Conservative Party endorsement, polled 4.8 per cent and was only 0.4 per cent behind the Alliance

Party. Second, the Green Party candidate Malcolm Samuel, experienced a modest rise to 1.2 per cent, far short of the 15 per cent gained by the party in Britain, but locally ahead of the Workers' Party and the two Labour candidates.

1989 European Parliament election

Details of the count

3 seats

Electorate 1,106,852	Percentage poll 48.3
Valid votes 534,811	Quota 133,703
Spoiled votes 5,356	

First count

Party candidates	1st-preference votes	% valid poll
Paisley, Rev. I. (DUP)	160,110	29.9
Hume, J. (SDLP)	136,335	25.5
Nicholson, J.F. (UUP)	118,785	22.2
Morrison, D. (PSF)	48,914	9.1
Alderdice, Dr J. (All.)	27,905	5.2
Kennedy, Dr A.L. (Cons.)	25,789	4.8
Samuel, M.H. (Green)	6,569	1.2
Lynch, S. (WP)	5,590	1.0
Langhammer, M.F. (LRG)	3,540	0.7
Caul, Dr B.P. (Lab. '87)	1,274	0.2

Paisley and Hume elected; Paisley's surplus votes were distributed.

Second count

Party candidates	Distribution of surplus votes	Total votes
Nicholson	+22,798	141,583
Morrison	+73	48,987
Alderdice	+728	28,633
Kennedy	+1,083	26,872
Samuel	+307	6,876
Lynch	+78	5,668
Langhammer	+121	3,661
Caul	+30	1,304

Nicholson elected. Non-transferable votes, 1,190. Alderdice, Kennedy, Samuel, Lynch, Langhammer and Caul lost their deposits.

1990 WESTMINSTER BY-ELECTION

The by-election on 17 May 1990, caused by the death of Harold McCusker MP in February 1990, attracted an extraordinary number and range of candidates. Eleven candidates were nominated, five from the traditional parties and five from new groups hoping to replace them, including the Model Conservatives, SDP, and Green Party, plus a 'Right to Vote Labour' candidate. The Ulster Independence Committee tested its support and the UDP promoted Gary McMichael, son of the former UDA leader. The turnout of 53.4 per cent was 12.2 per cent lower than that in the general election but the traditional parties broadly retained their share of the vote – except Alliance, whose vote halved. The Conservative, Labour, SDP and Green parties together polled only 2,003 votes, 5.6 per cent. The Conservative candidate, Mrs Colette Jones, had the biggest disappointment, for despite a visit by the party chairman, Kenneth Baker, several Ministers and a letter from the PM, Margaret Thatcher, she received only 2.9 per cent of the vote. Eight of the eleven candidates lost deposits.

Upper Bann, 17 May 1990

Elec. 66,377	% Poll 53.4
Trimble, D. (UUP)	20,547
Rodgers, Mrs B. (SDLP)	6,698
Campbell, Ms S. (PSF)	2,033
Ross, Rev. H. (UIC)	1,534
French, T. (WP)	1,083
Jones, Mrs C. (Cons.)	1,038
Ramsay, Dr W. (All.)	948
McMichael, G. (UDP)	600
Doran, P. (Green)	576
Holmes, E. (Lab.)	235
Dunn, A. (SDP)	154
UUP maj.	13,849
Spoiled votes	174

1992 WESTMINSTER GENERAL ELECTION

The general election on 9 April 1992 was notable for the number of candidates seeking election and for the W. Belfast seat changing hands from PSF to the SDLP.

The total number of candidates, 100, for the seventeen constituencies was a record, and they represented fourteen different party labels. The minimum choice was from four labels, and three constituencies had to choose from eight. The new parties to the contest were the NI Conservatives, the Natural Law Party and New Agenda, a result of the split in the Workers' Party. Choice was increased, too, because the Unionist parties permitted more freedom of nomination in safe seats. Interest in the election helped raise turnout to 69.7 per cent compared with 67.4 per cent in 1987. The victory of Joe Hendron (SDLP), at his third attempt, over Gerry Adams (PSF) was the only seat change. The slender majority of 589 was attributed to tactical voting by some Unionists but the SDLP had also targeted previous non-voters. The SDLP improved its overall share of the vote to 23.5 per cent (up 2.4 per cent) and its three sitting MPs, in Foyle, S. Down and Newry and Armagh, each improved his position. Although the PSF vote had declined slowly to 10 per cent from 11.4 per cent in 1987, the loss of the W. Belfast seat, held since 1983, was a blow for the electoral strategy and international standing of the party. The decline was evident in the rural areas, especially Fermanagh–South Tyrone, where the SDLP surpassed PSF and Mid-Ulster, where the SDLP extended its lead. The increased competition between the two main Unionist parties in E. Antrim, Strangford and N. Antrim resulted in the DUP improving its percentage to 13.1 from 11.7 and the UUP falling to 34.5 per cent from 37.8 per cent. The two parties' combined share had declined to 47.6 per cent from 49.5 per cent in 1987. The primary cause was probably the presence of eleven Conservative candidates, who polled 5.7 per cent. The best Conservative performance was in N. Down, where Laurence Kennedy was defeated by Jim Kilfedder (UPUP) by 4,934 votes but only after the leader of the UUP, Jim Molyneaux, had intervened to commit supporters to the sitting member and away from the DUP candidate, Denny Vitty. The Alliance vote was also affected by the

408

Conservatives, and fell to 8.7 per cent from 10 per cent but the Alliance lead over that party was maintained everywhere except N. Down. The recent split in the WP seriously affected its electoral performance. Its share of the vote fell to 0.6 per cent from 2.6 per cent, and all its candidates lost their deposits and were only saved from coming bottom of the poll by the presence of Natural Law Party candidates. Their former colleagues in New Agenda (now the Democratic Left), fared no better.

Overall figures, 1992 Westminster general election

Party	Votes	% Valid poll
UUP	271,049	34.5
SDLP	184,445	23.5
DUP	103,039	13.1
PSF	78,291	10.0
All.	68,695	8.7
Cons.	44,608	5.7
UPUP	19,305	2.5
Ind. U.	2,256	0.2
WP	4,359	0.6
NLP	2,147	0.3
NA	2,133	0.3
Ind.	4,766	0.6
Total valid votes	785,093	100.0
Spoiled votes	4,737	
Total votes polled	789,830	

East Belfast

Elec. 52,869	% Poll 67.7
*Robinson, P. (DUP)	18,437
Alderdice, Dr J. (All.)	10,650
Greene, D. (Cons.)	3,314
Dunlop, Mrs D. (Ind. U.)	2,256
O'Donnell, J. (PSF)	679
Bell, J. (WP)	327
Redden, G. (NLP)	128
DUP maj.	7,787
No change	

North Belfast

Elec. 55,068	% Poll 65.2
*Walker, C. (UUP)	17,240
Maginness, A. (SDLP)	7,615
McManus, P. (PSF)	4,693
Campbell, T. (All.)	2,246
Redpath, Mrs M. (Cons.)	2,107
Lynch, S. (Dem. L.)	1,386
Smith, Ms M. (WP)	419
O'Leary, D. (NLP)	208
UUP maj.	9,625
No change	

South Belfast

Elec. 52,050	% Poll 64.5
*Smyth, Rev. M. (UUP)	16,336
McDonnell, A. (SDLP)	6,266
Montgomery, J. (All.)	5,054
Fee, L. (Cons.)	3,356
Hayes, S. (PSF)	1,123
Hadden, P. (LTU)	875
Lynn, P. (WP)	362
Mullen, Ms T. (NLP)	212
UUP maj.	10,070
No change	

West Belfast

Elec. 54,644	% Poll 73.1
Hendron, J. (SDLP)	17,415
*Adams, G. (PSF)	16,826
Cobain, F. (UUP)	4,766
Lowry, J. (WP)	750
Kennedy, M. (NLP)	213

SDLP maj.	589
SDLP gain	

East Antrim

Elec. 62,864	% Poll 62.4
*Beggs, R. (UUP)	16,966
Dodds, N. (DUP)	9,544
Neeson, S. (All.)	9,132
Boal, Ms M. (Cons.)	3,359
Palmer, Mrs A. (NLP)	250

UUP maj.	7,422
No change	

North Antrim

Elec. 69,114	% Poll 65.8
*Paisley, Rev. I. (DUP)	23,152
Gaston, J. (UUP)	8,216
Farren, S. (SDLP)	6,512
Williams, G. (All.)	3,442
Sowler, R. (Cons.)	2,263
McGarry, J. (PSF)	1,916

UUP maj.	14,936
No change	

South Antrim

Elec. 67,192	% Poll 62.9
*Forsythe, C. (UUP)	29,956
McClelland, D. (SDLP)	5,397
Blair, J. (All.)	5,224
Cushinan, H. (PSF)	1,220
Martin, D.D. (IRLOFP)	442

UUP maj.	24,559
No change	

North Down

Elec. 68,662	% Poll 65.5
*Kilfedder, J. (UPUP)	19,305
Kennedy, L. (Cons.)	14,371
Morrow, A. (All.)	6,611
Vitty, D. (DUP)	4,414
Wilmot, A. (NLP)	255

UPUP maj.	4,934
No change	

South Down

Elec. 76,186	% Poll 80.8
*McGrady, E. (SDLP)	31,523
Nelson, D. (UUP)	25,181
Fitzpatrick, S. (PSF)	1,843
Healy, M. (All.)	1,542
McKenzie-Hill, Mrs S. (Cons.)	1,488

SDLP maj.	6,342
No change	

Fermanagh–South Tyrone

Elec. 70,253	% Poll 78.5
*Maginnis, K. (UUP)	26,923
Gallagher, T. (SDLP)	12,810
Molloy, F. (PSF)	12,604
Kettyles, D. (IPS)	1,094
Bullick, E. (All.)	950
Cullen, G. (NA)	747

UUP maj.	14,113
No change	

Foyle

Elec. 74,673	% Poll 69.5
*Hume, J. (SDLP)	26,710
Campbell, G. (DUP)	13,705
McGuinness, M. (PSF)	9,149
McIlroy, Ms L. (All.)	1,390
McKenzie, G. (WP)	514
Burns, J. (NLP)	422

SDLP maj.	13,005
No change	

Lagan Valley

Elec. 72,708	% Poll 67.3
*Molyneaux, J. (UUP)	29,772
Close, S. (All.)	6,207
Lewsley, H. (SDLP)	4,626
Coleridge, T. (Cons.)	4,423
Rice, P. (PSF)	3,346
Lowry, Ms A.-M. (WP)	582
UUP maj.	23,565
No change	

East Londonderry

Elec. 75,587	% Poll 69.8
*Ross, W. (UUP)	30,370
Doherty, A (SDLP)	11,843
Davey-Kennedy, Mrs P. (PSF)	5,320
McGowan, P. (All.)	3,613
Elder, A. (Cons.)	1,589
UUP maj.	18,527
No change	

Mid-Ulster

Elec. 69,138	% Poll 79.2
*McCrea, W. (DUP)	23,181
Haughey, H. (SDLP)	16,994
McElduff, B. (PSF)	10,248
McLoughlin, J. (Ind.)	1,996
Gormley, Ms A. (All.)	1,506
Hutchinson, H. (LTU)	389
Owens, T. (WP)	285
Anderson, J. (NLP)	164
DUP maj.	6,187
No change	

Newry and Armagh

Elec. 67,531	% Poll 77.9
*Mallon, S. (SDLP)	26,073
Speers, J. (UUP)	18,982
Curran, B. (PSF)	6,547
Bell, Mrs E. (All.)	972
SDLP maj.	7,091
No change	

Strangford

Elec. 68,901	% Poll 65.0
*Taylor, J. (UUP)	19,517
Wilson, S. (DUP)	10,606
McCarthy, K. (All.)	7,585
Eyre, S. (Cons.)	6,782
Shaw, D. (NLP)	295
UUP maj.	8,911
No change	

Upper Bann

Elec. 67,460	% Poll 67.4
*Trimble, D. (UUP)	26,824
Rodgers, Mrs B. (SDLP)	10,661
Curran, B. (PSF)	2,777
Ramsay, Dr W. (All.)	2,541
Jones, Mrs C. (Cons.)	1,556
French, T. (WP)	1,120
UUP maj.	16,163
No change	

1993 DISTRICT COUNCIL ELECTIONS

The elections held on 19 May 1993 used new electoral boundaries reviewed by the Local Government Boundaries Commissioner during 1991 and 1992. The twenty-six councils survived, though provisional recommendations had threatened Moyle; there were minor boundary adjustments affecting Banbridge and two neighbouring councils, Lisburn and Craigavon, and a more significant change transferring Rathfriland from Newry and Mourne. The 566 wards were reviewed, revised and increased by 16 to 582. The new wards were then grouped by the District Electoral Areas Commissioner into 101 electoral units containing five to seven members each. All the main parties improved their seat totals over 1989, except the DUP, which declined by 7 to 103. PSF gained 8 seats to recoup some of its losses in 1989; the SDLP gained 6 seats to total 127, its highest ever. Alliance made 6 gains to total 44 and the Ulster Unionists gained 3 for a total of 197. Some of the gains were at the expense of smaller parties, and others came from the sixteen additional seats, but there was a noticeable increase in the number of Independents elected. Since PR was used, seat changes reflected shifts in the party share of the vote. The most noticeable change was the increase in the PSF vote; the rise, by 1.2 per cent to 12.4 per cent, came after a decade of slow decline from its peak of 13.4 per cent in 1983. The increase was seen in Belfast, where PSF became the party with the largest share of the vote, with 22.7 per cent. The SDLP increased its share of the vote by 1 per cent to 22 per cent and Alliance did likewise by 0.8 per cent to 7.6 per cent. The DUP vote declined by 0.4 per cent to 17.3 per cent, though in Belfast and parts of the greater Belfast area it reversed this decline. The UUP, with an increase in seats and a reduction in its vote by 2 per cent to 29.4 per cent, was the exception. The election was the first District Council test of the split in the WP and the emergence of the Democratic Left. It proved disastrous for both, their combined vote being halved to 1 per cent. Independents and Others increased to 6.8 per cent, with single-issue candidates very noticeable in N. Down. Only five of the twenty-six councils had single-party control, namely, Down and Derry (SDLP),

Banbridge, Lisburn and Coleraine (UUP). Notable was the loss of DUP control of Ballymena for the first time since 1977. The annual meetings of the councils revealed more councils sharing top positions across the political divide. The overall valid poll was 56.6 per cent, an increase of 0.5 per cent over 1989. The turnout ranged from 37.6 per cent in N. Down to 80.8 per cent in Cookstown. The east/west pattern was again evident, with the eight councils closest to Belfast averaging 44 per cent and the eight in the west averaging 72 per cent.

Overall figures, 1993 District Council elections

Party	1st-preference votes	% votes
UUP	184,608	29.4
SDLP	138,619	22.0
DUP	108,863	17.3
PSF	78,092	12.4
All.	47,649	7.6
Loy./U.	17,025	2.7
Cons.	9,437	1.5
Ind. Nat.	1,762	0.3
Others	43,051	6.8
Total	629,106	100.0

Party composition of councils, 1993

Council	DUP	Loy./ U.	UUP	Cons.	All.	Dem. L.	WP	SDLP	PSF	Ind. Nat.	Others
Antrim	3	1	8	0	2	0	0	4	1	0	0
Ards	6	0	9	0	6	0	0	0	0	0	2
Armagh	2	0	10	0	0	0	0	9	1	0	0
Ballymena	9	1	10	0	1	0	0	2	0	0	1
Ballymoney	6	0	6	0	0	0	0	3	0	0	1
Banbridge	2	0	10	0	1	0	0	3	0	0	1
Belfast	9	3	15	0	5	0	0	9	10	0	0
Carrickfergus	2	0	5	1	6	0	0	0	0	0	3
Castlereagh	9	3	6	0	5	0	0	0	0	0	0
Coleraine	5	0	12	0	2	0	0	3	0	0	0
Cookstown	3	1	5	0	0	0	0	5	2	0	0
Craigavon	4	1	10	0	2	0	1	6	2	0	0
Derry	5	1	2	0	0	0	0	17	5	0	0
Down	3	0	7	0	0	0	0	13	0	0	0
Dungannon	3	0	8	0	0	1	0	4	5	0	1
Fermanagh	2	0	10	0	0	0	0	5	3	0	3
Larne	4	0	7	0	2	0	0	0	0	0	2
Limavady	1	0	6	0	0	0	0	7	1	0	0
Lisburn	3	1	16	1	2	0	0	3	3	0	1
Magherafelt	4	0	3	0	0	0	0	5	4	0	0
Moyle	3	2	2	0	0	0	0	3	1	0	4
Newry and Mourne	1	0	6	0	0	0	0	15	5	0	3
Newtownabbey	5	4	10	0	4	0	0	1	0	0	1
North Down	3	3	6	4	5	0	0	0	0	0	4
Omagh	3	0	4	0	1	0	0	5	6	1	1
Strabane	3	1	4	0	0	0	0	5	2	0	1
Total	103	22	197	6	44	1	1	127	51	1	29

SYSTEMS OF GOVERNMENT
1968-93

GOVERNMENT: TWO SYSTEMS FALL

There can be few parts of the world where two totally different systems of government have collapsed in the space of little more than two years. But this was the experience of NI between 1972 and 1974.

From June 1921 to March 1972 NI had its own Parliament and Government within the UK. The system derived from the Government of Ireland Act, 1920, which was designed to set up Parliaments in both parts of Ireland, with a Council of Ireland to look after matters of mutual concern, and possibly lead eventually to a united Ireland. Like later political approaches by Westminster, it was aimed at reconciling the conflicting desires of Ulster Unionists and Irish Nationalists. It was more Home Rule than Unionists wanted, and less ambitious than that desired by Nationalists. In fact, Southern Ireland opted for independence, and the 1920 Act became operative only in NI. Unionists, who had shown no enthusiasm for devolution, quickly came to see the advantages of a limited self-government. Ulster Nationalists refused to co-operate in promoting the new Northern state. Events tended to give permanence to partition. The Southern Irish state adopted a more separatist constitution in 1937, and became a full Republic in 1949. At that point the NI Parliament was given the right to veto any attempt to move NI out of the UK. The pre-1972 Stormont Parliament was closely modelled on Westminster. The fifty-two-seat Commons, elected by straight vote in single-member constituencies, followed the procedure and ceremonial of its Westminster opposite number, and the twenty-six-member Senate (with two ex-officio, the Lord Mayor of Belfast and the Mayor of Londonderry, and twenty-four members elected on PR by the Commons) had delaying powers very like those of the House of Lords. But in practice the upper house, with its Unionist majority, rarely opposed anything of substance originating in the Commons. Usually, two out of three MPs were Unionists, and this majority was reflected in the Senate. All the administrations set up between 1921 and 1972 were Unionist-controlled. NI continued to send MPs to Westminster – at least twelve, and thirteen when QUB had a seat – although NI matters received little attention in the British Parliament.

Some British Ministers have regarded the old Stormont system as nearer to dominion status than to simple devolution. Under a convention established in 1922, it was not possible for an MP at Westminster to raise any issue within the direct responsibility of a Stormont Minister. Thus, while the 1920 Act declared that the power of Westminster in NI was not diminished in any way by local self-government, the reality was somewhat different. Westminster Ministers considered their responsibilities in relation to NI to be limited to issues such as foreign trade, defence, major taxation, customs and excise and the High Court. The Home Secretary had Cabinet responsibility for NI affairs, and he had a few officials engaged part time in dealing with them, but until the civil rights movement developed, few Home Secretaries got beyond rare and brief token trips to NI. So it required considerable ingenuity for an NI MP to find a topic on which he could put a question to a Minister. The NI Government, normally comprising the PM and seven or eight full Cabinet Ministers and a few Junior Ministers, controlled most domestic affairs and internal law and order.

Up to the late 1960s, relations between London and Belfast were generally amicable. After 1945, Whitehall allowed NI to give more generous financial inducements to new industry than applied in GB, and finances generally were adjusted to NI's advantage. Some local taxes, such as motor duty, entertainment tax and death duties, often differed from those in GB. And although NI had been required by the 1920 Act to make an annual 'imperial contribution' to meet items of national expenditure, such as defence, foreign representation and the national debt, it was accepted in London that this must be a declining liability in face of the high costs of social services. NI had contributed about £460 million by way of 'imperial contribution' when it was finally abolished under direct rule. The principle of equality of basic social services throughout the UK implied that there could be no variation in major taxes, and NI never exercised a limited power to reduce income tax (see Economy). The general pattern of the Stormont Budget was settled in discussions between the Finance Minister and Treasury officials in London, and there was a Joint Exchequer Board to consider any disputed matters. In matters such as social legislation, including divorce, NI very often went its own way.

But the continuing split in the NI community was underlined by the impact of the civil rights movement. The long-entrenched Stormont system came under severe pressure, both from anti-Unionists and from Westminster, and increasing violence soon made it a world issue as well. The NI Government did make changes to meet some of the criticism (see Cameron Commission and Reforms), but the serious violence in the summer of 1969 and the increasing alienation of the parliamentary opposition put large question marks over the very existence of Stormont. The need for army support for the police brought a real change in the relationship between Stormont and Whitehall. An army commander took charge of anti-terrorist operations (*see* Security System section, p. 444), and a new post of British Government representative was established so that the British Government would have its own watchdog official at Stormont. The failure of internment without trial to halt the PIRA campaign, and the shooting dead by the army of thirteen civilians in Derry (*see* 'Bloody Sunday') persuaded the Heath Government that all security and law-and-order powers should be transferred to Westminster. Three NI Premiers – O'Neill, Chichester-Clark, and Faulkner – had tried to restore stability, but in March 1972 the Conservative Government suspended the NI Parliament. It was an act that pleased anti-Unionists, but horrified even the most moderate of Unionists.

For the first time in fifty-one years, NI was now ruled wholly from London (*see* Direct Rule, pp. 422–4). It got its own Secretary of State, similar to Scotland and Wales, and the first holder of the new office was William Whitelaw, a senior Conservative politician, who was assisted by a small team of junior Ministers. NI was governed under a Temporary Provisions Act, and NI legislation was brought forward by way of Orders in Council, which could not be amended on the floor of the Commons. In a bid to make direct rule more palatable, Whitelaw set up a locally recruited Advisory Commission, but Unionists boycotted it. Brian Faulkner (later Lord Faulkner), NI's last PM, who with his colleagues had resigned rather than accept the loss of law-and-order powers, said he was against NI being treated 'like a coconut colony'. The members of the last Stormont Cabinet under the 1920 Act were: Home Affairs, Brian Faulkner and John Taylor (Minister of State); Finance, Herbert Kirk; Health and Social Services, William Fitzsimmons; Development, Roy Bradford; Education, William Long; Agriculture, Harry West; Commerce, Robin Bailie; leader of Commons, Nat Minford; leader of Senate, John Andrews; Community Relations, David Bleakley (March–September 1971) and Basil McIvor (September 1971–March 1972). Outside the Cabinet were John Brooke (later Lord Brookeborough), Minister of State in Finance, and Gerard B. Newe, Minister of State in the PM's department.

In 1973 the Heath Government tried a new political initiative. A periodic referendum to test opinion on NI's constitutional status in relation to the UK and the Republic was introduced to take the border issue out of day-to-day politics (*see* Border Poll). NI was given a seventy-eight-member Assembly, elected by PR, with the object of giving minorities a bigger chance of representation and therefore participation in Government. The scheme was embodied in the NI

Constitution Act of 1973, which also abolished the office of Governor. Towards the end of 1973, talks involving the Secretary of State, Unionists, led by Brian Faulkner, the SDLP and Alliance Party brought agreement on the setting up of an Executive involving these parties. The new administration's approach was worked out at a conference in December which was attended by the Executive parties and by British Ministers headed by Heath, and Ministers from the Republic, led by Liam Cosgrave (*see* Sunningdale Conference).

The new Coalition took office on 1 January 1974 after being sworn in by the new Secretary of State, Francis Pym. Its members were: Chief Executive, Brian Faulkner (Unionist); deputy Chief Executive, Gerry Fitt (SDLP); Legal Minister and head of Office of Law Reform, Oliver Napier (Alliance); Minister of Information, John L. Baxter (Unionist); Minister of Environment, Roy Bradford (Unionist); Minister of Housing, Local Government and Planning, Austin Currie (SDLP); Minister of Health and Social Services, Paddy Devlin (SDLP); Minister of Commerce, John Hume (SDLP); Minister of Finance, Herbert Kirk (Unionist); Minister of Education, Basil McIvor (Unionist); Minister of Agriculture, Leslie Morrell (Unionist). Ministers outside the Executive were: Community Relations, Ivan Cooper (SDLP); Manpower Services, Robert Cooper (Alliance); Planning and Co-ordination, Eddie McGrady (SDLP); Chief Whip, Robert Lloyd Hall-Thompson (Unionist).

The new administration rapidly ran into trouble. While it had a majority in the Assembly, it faced violent opposition from loyalists opposed to power-sharing, and at one sitting demonstrating loyalists were ejected from the Chamber by the police. At the same time Brian Faulkner was defeated in the Unionist Council, the thousand-strong main governing body of his party, when he tried to get endorsement of the Sunningdale Agreement. Then in February 1974 a Westminster general election showed a majority for candidates of the three anti-power-sharing Unionist groups united within the UUUC, which won eleven of the twelve seats at Westminster. Finally, a loyalist strike, aimed against power-sharing and a Council of Ireland, led to the resignation in May of the Unionist members of the Executive, and the collapse of the administration. Direct rule was then resumed under the Labour Government, with Merlyn Rees as Secretary of State, and the Assembly was prorogued. Legal authority for continuing direct rule was provided by the Northern Ireland Act of 1974, which made temporary provision for the Government of NI by the Secretary of State and his ministerial team, subject to annual renewal.

The Labour Government moved quickly to try to break the political deadlock and to replace the now defunct Assembly. In July 1974 it announced that local political parties were to be given the opportunity to produce a viable constitution. For this purpose a seventy-eight-member Constitutional Convention was elected in 1975, but the project finally failed in 1976. In the aftermath of the Convention, the Government sought to widen consultation outside and inside Parliament on NI legislation. A new NI Committee of MPs was set up to allow for general debates on local policy, for example on the economy, housing, agriculture and so on. And copies of Orders were shown in advance to local parties to enable them to put forward their views. The Labour Government (after James Callaghan became PM) accepted that there was a case for more than twelve NI MPs at Westminster – a long-standing claim of Unionists. The idea of extra representation was endorsed by the Speaker's conference in 1978.

After the failure of the Convention, the British Government did not rush into any new initiative. But in November 1977 Roy Mason, as Secretary of State, put forward a tentative plan for discussion by the parties. The plan was discussed by the Secretary of State and representatives of the parties at the end of 1977 and beginning of 1978, but the initial exchanges did not suggest any agreement. At the same time the Conservative opposition was urging that the first priority should be given to local government reform – a course frequently urged by many Unionists. But the SDLP made it clear that it feared that a reform of councils would lead to Unionist domination, and remarks in Parliament by the Secretary of State indicated that he supported this view.

With the resumption of direct rule after the collapse of the Convention, the aim was to harmonise NI policy and legislation with that of the rest of the UK, and some of the departments established for the convenience of the Executive were dropped and others merged. The work of the Department of Community Relations was taken over by the Department of Education, and the departments of Environment, and Housing, Planning and Local Government were merged into a single Environment Department. By 1976 the following departments were in existence – Agriculture, Commerce, Environment, Education, Finance, Health and Social Services, Manpower Services, and Civil Service.

With the election of the Conservative Government in May 1979, it appeared at first as if its manifesto commitment to a regional council or councils for NI would be introduced. However, after the death of Airey Neave (with whom the policy was identified) at the hands of an INLA bomb attached to his car in the House of Commons car park, the policy changed. A twin-track policy was developed amid increasing external pressure from the US. First, the new Secretary of State, Humphrey Atkins, sought to establish whether a basis existed for devolution. After the publication of a White Paper, *Proposals for Further Discussion,* he called the parties to a Constitutional Conference. But by November 1980 there was still no agreement on the formation of an executive. Although in July 1981 Atkins proposed to create an advisory council of MPs, MEPs and other elected representatives, the proposal was lost in the communal tension of the H-Block hunger strike. The second track had begun in December 1980 with a unique, high-level meeting of British and Irish Ministers in Dublin. In a serious effort to improve UK–Republic relations a series of joint studies was instigated in January 1981 on security, mutual understanding, citizens' rights, economic co-operation and possible new institutional structures.

In 1981 an Anglo-Irish Intergovernmental Council was created as a forum for discussion, and provision was made for a parliamentary tier at some stage. While relations did deteriorate during the Falklands crisis, the institution for mutual contact had been established.

Despite the experience of his predecessor, James Prior, the new Secretary of State and the most senior politician to hold this post since William Whitelaw, was willing to put his reputation on the line 'to get political progress'. At first Prior investigated the possibilities of an Assembly together with local Ministers nominated by himself, with a separation of administrative and legislative responsibility on the US model. It was a concept which had surfaced vaguely from time to time, but in the end he settled on the idea of 'rolling devolution', a system where an Assembly would start off with only a consultative and scrutiny role. This could later be extended to embrace the devolution of one or more local departments, but this devolution would depend on the achievement in the Assembly of 'cross-community support'. The Secretary of State and his colleagues saw it as an infinitely flexible pattern, adding some local democracy to direct rule to start with, and allowing for an input from elected politicians. It was also seen, by the small group of Cabinet Ministers who settled NI policy, as a means of getting more political support for security policy and giving a semblance of stability which might help in the attraction of outside industrial investment at a time when unemployment was running at around 20 per cent.

The scheme that eventually emerged in early 1982 was based, as in 1973, on a seventy-eight-seat Assembly elected on PR in the twelve Westminster constituencies. (If the plan for seventeen NI seats had been approved by Parliament at that time, the Assembly would probably have had eight-five-seats – five in each constituency.) The Devolution Bill provided that the Assembly could apply to Westminster for devolved powers if 70 per cent, or fifty-five members, backed the proposals. This weighted majority was intended to guard against Unionists only being in a position to apply. The Bill also provided that the Assembly could discuss local legislation and set up scrutiny committees for each of the six Stormont departments, and an amendment allowed for a non-statutory security committee. Assembly members would get a salary of £8,700, and committee chairmen an extra £2,900. Members of the Assembly could join a parliamentary tier of the AIIC as individuals.

Predictably, the reaction of the parties was mixed. Both the UUP and DUP rejected the weighted majority and 'cross-community support' provisions as a revival of the 1973 'power-sharing', although the DUP was attracted more so than the UUP to the initial scrutiny powers. To Alliance it was a last chance for NI to solve its own problems. The SDLP regarded the scheme as 'unworkable' and an 'expensive charade' (views echoed by the Haughey Government in the Republic). PSF, contesting a Stormont election for the first time, sought to displace the SDLP as the main voice of Nationalists and win political support for its 'Brits out' approach. The Secretary of State had to face a filibuster in Parliament from about twenty right-wing Conservative MPs, some of whom were opposed to him for other political reasons and argued that the Conservative 1979 manifesto should be implemented since there was no prospect of agreement on devolution (see Conservative Party, British), and some of whom were frankly integrationist. But the measure was put through without difficulty after a 'guillotine' motion (unusual for a constitutional Bill) had been implemented, and with general support from the opposition parties. Labour's attempt to make the scheme more acceptable to the SDLP led to an amendment to provide that both Lords and Commons would be able to pronounce on 'cross-community support'. The change did not, however, persuade the SDLP that there was any real Irish dimension.

Thus, the stage was set for the election on 20 October 1982. With both the SDLP and PSF fighting on an abstentionist platform, although differing on the issue of violence, the Government's hopes for the Assembly were distinctly limited. With the SDLP getting fourteen seats (three down on the Convention and five fewer than in the 1973 Assembly), and PSF a surprising five seats, a total of fifty-nine members attended the opening session of the Assembly. The UUP had twenty-six, the DUP twenty-one, and Alliance ten, with two other Unionists, one of whom, James Kilfedder MP, was elected Speaker. The Secretary of State accepted an early invitation to address the Assembly and junior Ministers appeared at committees. But they were not responsible to the

Assembly and their appearances took on the form of a public relations exercise. The absence of SDLP members obviously made it impossible to achieve the cross-community support necessary for devolution. Ministers continued to grant SDLP access despite its abstention; even PSF had access but on a narrower, 'constituency interests' basis only. Indeed, when SDLP members were engaged in their alternative New Ireland Forum strategy, it was clearly demonstrated that neither they nor surrogates would engage the Assembly in discussions. The main work of the Assembly was, therefore, the scrutiny of Government departments and to provide advice on draft legislation. It did not have power, which remained with the Secretary of State and his Ministers, but influence, which was more difficult to evaluate.

The work of the Assembly fell into three periods. First, from November 1982 to May 1984, when the absence of the SDLP and the boycott by the UUP over the allocation of chairmanships (until February 1983) and over security policy after the Darkley massacre in November 1983 (until May 1984) gave the Assembly an uncertain future. In their absence, the most committed parties, the DUP and Alliance, worked the system as best they could.

The second phase, and its most fruitful, extended from May 1984 to November 1985 and the signing of the AIA. It was marked by the full operation of the committee system and the issue of three reports from the Devolution Committee. But in 1985, especially under the new Secretary of State, Douglas Hurd, it was clear that expectations from the Assembly were low and, instead, a UK–Republic deal was pursued, based on the 'fourth option' of the New Ireland Forum report in 1984.

The third phase was from 15 November 1985 until dissolution on 23 June 1986, and was one of protest against the AIA (see Anglo-Irish Agreement). The response outside NI to what was represented as the settlement of a historic difference between the UK and the Republic in the AIA was a general, if not effusive, welcome. Inside NI Nationalists gave it an immediate welcome which grew in strength as they witnessed Unionist discomfiture at the hands of a former political friend in the Conservative Party. Unionist rage at the role given to the Republic in the internal affairs of part of the UK crossed all classes and shades of political opinion. It was directed into protests at Belfast City Hall and at Maryfield, into fifteen simultaneous by-elections when Unionist MPs resigned their seats, into the boycott of District Council business, and other forms of showing the withdrawal of the Unionist consent from the new form of government which was portrayed as 'joint rule'. The existence of the NI Assembly as a representative body resulted in its conversion into a platform for protest. The scrutiny function of the six committees was suspended, the Devolution Committee was wound up and a new Committee on the Government of NI was set up to examine the effects of the AIA on the Northern Ireland Constitution Act, 1973, and the Northern Ireland Assembly Act, 1982. As a result the Alliance members withdrew, leaving forty-nine members attending, the NIO withdrew committee staff and cut off access to persons and papers in the departments. The Committee on the Government of Northern Ireland still issued three reports but the fate of the Assembly had been sealed. Around the time when arrangements for fresh elections would normally have been announced, it was dissolved by the British Government on 23 June 1986, and some of its protesting members were carried from the building in the early hours of the next morning by the police.

It is difficult to evaluate the earlier constructive phases of the Assembly. It did enable members to exercise a representative function which had been absent since the end of the first Assembly in 1974. The Assembly held 221 plenary sessions – about 70 per year; the various lobbies showed an awareness that it could influence decisions, and 426 witnesses gave evidence to the committees. The scrutiny committees prepared 118 reports, containing 998 recommendations of which two-thirds were accepted. They also had an input into draft legislation for NI. Its passing may have been welcomed by some, and to an extent it was inevitable, but its absence did not diminish the need to subject the direct-rule regime to a system of political and administrative accountability.

Despite the commitment of the signatories of the AIA to devolution in NI (Article 4), no new proposal has been made. The expectation by Government that, once the overarching framework of relations between the UK and the Republic was established, devolution would follow naturally, proved facile. Unionists, with two electoral mandates behind them in 1986 and 1987, could not accept devolution under the AIA framework. After the June 1987 election Paisley and Molyneaux engaged in 'talks about talks' with the Secretary of State on the principle of suspending the conference to enable inter-party talks to begin. Early in 1988 outline proposals were submitted which had not produced a detailed reply by the end of the year. The Secretary of State also held talks with other parties, including the SDLP, but without any indication that the 'widespread acceptance' criteria for devolution had been established. Further, soon after the Unionist proposals to the Secretary of State, the SDLP began a series of private meetings with PSF which set back any possibility of direct talks with Unionists. SDLP spokesmen also stated that they were not committed in principle to devolution but only in so far as it would contribute to a solution of the problem as they identified it; and that they opposed any suspension of the AIA, suggesting instead that inter-party talks run parallel with the conference and the Maryfield secretariat. Finally, in November 1988 the AIA had been in existence for three years and a review of the working of the conference (under Article 11) began.

Since the first meeting of the conference in December 1985 it had met twenty-five times: eleven meetings were held in Belfast, nine in London and five in Dublin. There had been ten meetings in the first year, four in the second, ten in the third year, and a further two meetings in the review period. After each meeting of the conference, a brief communiqué was issued outlining the main areas discussed but the sketchy details have been criticised. The Diplock courts, the administration of justice, the relationship of the security forces and the police with the Nationalist minority, flags and emblems, parades, the Irish language, fair employment and housing conditions have been among the subjects discussed. However, in the third year many of the events causing greatest concern were British–Irish issues, such as the Birmingham Six and Guildford bomb cases, the Gibraltar SAS killings, and extradition cases. At the end of the year it was clear that despite the AIA and the conference machinery, 'megaphone diplomacy' between the two countries was all too evident. In the event, the review of the working of the conference, which was expected to be brief, was extended to March 1989.

A parliamentary tier, with twenty-five members drawn from Lords and Commons and twenty-five from Dáil and Senate, was expected to hold its first meeting in June 1989, but it was postponed until 1990. Two seats were being allocated to Unionist MPs and one to the SDLP, but Unionists refused to take part since they regarded the body as inseparable from the AIA process.

DIRECT RULE

Since the introduction of direct rule in 1972 there have been ten Secretaries of State for NI. William Whitelaw (Cons.), March 1972–November 1973; Francis Pym (Cons.), November 1973–February 1974; Merlyn Rees (Lab.), March 1974–September 1976; Roy Mason (Lab.), September 1976–May 1979; Humphrey Atkins (Cons.), May 1979–September 1981; James Prior (Cons.), September 1981–September 1984; Douglas Hurd (Cons.), September 1984–September 1985; Tom King (Cons.), September 1985–July 1989; Peter Brooke (Cons.), July 1989–April 1992; Sir Patrick Mayhew (Cons.), April 1992–.

The Secretary of State keeps key responsibilities in his own hands and delegates individual departments to his ministers. Sir Patrick Mayhew,

Secretary of State since April 1992, retained responsibility for political and constitutional matters, security policy and operations, and broad economic and other policies. He is supported by two Ministers of State, Sir John Wheeler (Cons., Westminster N.) and Michael Ancram (Cons., Devizes) and two Under-Secretaries of State, Timothy Smith (Cons., Beaconsfield) and Lady Jean Denton, Baroness of Wakefield. Sir John Wheeler, who replaced Michael Mates on 24 June 1993, is responsible for law and order, information and the Department of Finance and Personnel. Michael Ancram was promoted to Minister of State when he replaced Robert Atkins on 5 January 1994, when the latter became Minister for the Environment on the resignation of Tim Yeo. Ancram retained his responsibilities for the Department of Education, community relations and political development. Timothy Smith was allocated Atkins's responsibilities for the Department of the Environment and the Department of Economic Development and the various agencies operating in each. Baroness Denton replaced the Earl of Arran on 11 January 1994, when he moved to her old job as Under-Secretary at the Department of the Environment as part of a reshuffle caused by the resignation of the Earl of Caithness, the Transport Minister. Baroness Denton, the first female appointment to the NIO, has responsibility for the Department of Health, the Department of Agriculture and their various agencies.

By the end of January 1994 and almost twenty-two years of direct rule, some fifty-four Ministers, forty-two from the House of Commons and twelve from the Lords, had served in Northern Ireland. The absence of Labour from office since 1979 meant that forty-four were Conservatives and only ten Labour. The average length of service was just under two years and three months but, as always, the average hides many differences. Richard Needham was the longest-serving Minister with six years, seven months, from September 1985 to April 1992. Brian Mawhinney with six years, three months, from January 1986 until April 1992, pushed Nicholas Scott (five years, nine months) into third place, with Lord Lyell fourth at five years, three months. Those Ministers with the shortest service were Francis Pym (Cons.) three months, Tom Pendry (Lab.) six months and Paul Channon (Cons.) seven months. The longest-serving Secretary of State remains Tom King with three years, eleven months, from September 1985 to July 1989. The second-longest serving Secretary of State was James Prior, with just under three years.

The circumstances in which James Prior was appointed in September 1981 resulted in the Northern Ireland posting being described as 'internal exile'. However, after twenty-two years of direct rule it is doubtful if the posting is different in kind, a point reinforced by examination of Ministers' careers before and after Northern Ireland experience. Ministers are required to have 'a safe pair of hands' but the political hothouse atmosphere, arising from the high news profile, two local television and radio stations, local newspapers and the penetration of RTE and the Dublin press, gives Ministers a higher public profile than jobs at a comparable level elsewhere. In the circumstances talent might well be revealed. An NIO appointment does require additional air travel, but the job is not especially demanding and does not necessarily require additional time away from home. A recent parliamentary question revealed that in the period 1 May to 31 October 1992 – 184 days – Ministers spent on average 63 nights in NI. Sir Patrick Mayhew led his team with 70, followed by the Earl of Arran, 66; Michael Mates and Jeremy Hanley tied on 64 and Robert Atkins had 50 nights. Ministers also had the statistical comfort that most would gain further promotion. Some 32 were appointed after NI experience: 20 were promoted while 12 remained at the same level. And 15 had Cabinet experience after NI even though only 2 (Whitelaw and King) had previously been in Cabinet.

NI GOVERNMENT DEPARTMENTS

In 1982 the number of Stormont departments was reduced to six – Agriculture, Economic Development, Education, Environment, Finance and Personnel, and Health and Social Services. Civil service affairs were absorbed into the Finance and Personnel Department in April, and Commerce and Manpower were merged into a Department of Economic Development in September. With the setting up of the DED, a new Industrial Development Board, linked with the department, took responsibility for attracting outside industrial investment. Since then the departments and their responsibilities have been as follows:

Agriculture   Development and improvement of agriculture, forestry and fishing industries; animal health, drainage schemes, the recreational use of water and forest. Extensive advisory services, agricultural research, education and training. Agricultural census and farm income data. Agent for MAFF in economic support for agriculture and implementation of EC Common Agricultural Policy. In 1994–5 the expenditure on agriculture allocated through the NI budget was £142 million and that which came through general UK spending on agriculture was £166 million.

Economic Development   Industrial development, employment and training of labour, and relations with commerce and industry generally. The IDB is responsible for the development of industry, for attracting new projects, for the care and maintenance of existing industry, including trade promotion, marketing, and assistance to research and development projects. It provides funds for, and liaises with, the Local Enterprise Development Unit on the promotion of small businesses. The DED is responsible for industrial science and technology, the development of tourism and mineral and energy development. It is also directly responsible for certain regulatory activities, such as the registration of companies, societies, credit unions and trade unions and the supervision of industrial assurance and unit trusts. Several of its primary duties are effected through agencies. For example, the training function is carried out through the Training and Employment Agency and Enterprise Ulster; tourism is mainly encouraged through the NI Tourist Board; industrial science through the Industrial Research and Technology Unit. Some of its other regulatory activities are performed through the Health and Safety Agency and the Consumer Council. It also has a role of mediation though the Labour Relations Agency, the Fair Employment Commission and the Equal Opportunities Commission. Since March 1992 the department has also been responsible for the Office of the Electricity Regulator (OFFER [NI]). In 1994–5 the planned expenditure was £476 million.

Education   Development of primary, secondary and further education, community, adult and special education. It has responsibility for the Schools Inspectorate, teachers' salaries and superannuation, the Youth Service, the Sports Council, the Arts Council, the Museum Service and the improvement of community relations. The main education service is administered for the department by five education and library boards; the Catholic maintained sector is administered by the Council for Catholic Maintained Schools. The examinations function is exercised by the NI Schools Examinations and Curriculum Council. In 1994–5 the planned expenditure for the department was £1,291 million.

Environment   Planning and development; housing and landscaping; water and sewerage; construction and maintenance of roads and bridges; ordnance survey and land registry; transport and traffic, including safety and licensing; fire protection; pollution control; amenity lands and parks; Government records; regional rate collection; the Development Officer service. The services are provided through a series of divisions: for example, the environment service, the planning service, the roads service, and the water service (now threatened by privatisation). A number of agencies are responsible for other services. Housing is in the hands of the Housing Executive, transport with a holding company, the rates are collected by the Rate Collection Agency, vehicles and drivers are tested by the Driver and Vehicle Testing Agency, and the Ordnance Survey is now an agency. Some agencies are concerned with urban development in Belfast and Derry, and the Laganside Corporation is responsible for a major riverside development in Belfast. There are also links to the twenty-six District Councils, which are responsible for minor environmental services including street cleaning, refuse disposal, environmental health, cemeteries, consumer protection, recreational services, dog control and entertainment licensing. In 1994–5 planned spending by the DOE was £693 million.

Finance and Personnel Control of spending by NI departments; liaison with the Treasury and NIO on financial matters; economic and social planning and research; Digest of Statistics; Ulster Savings; borrowing; loan advances; charities. The formulation and co-ordination of policy for personnel management in the civil service, central management services and computer services. The department also has functions in valuation and lands agency. It provides a legislative counsel service and monitors relations with the EC. In 1994–5 the planned expenditure was £65 million.

Health and Social Services The department is responsible for three main programmes: health and social services, social security and child support. The main functions of the Health and Personal Social Services programme are executed through four health and social services boards. The Central Services Agency administers payments in respect of the Family Health Service. In 1994–5 planned spending in this section was £1,423 million. Social Security expenditure planned for 1994–5 was £2,205 million; this spending is administered through the Social Security Agency. The Child Support Agency was set up in April 1993 under the Child Support (NI) Order, 1991. The department also has a function in social legislation on betting, gaming and lotteries, liquor licensing, clubs registration, shops, hare coursing. It is responsible for regulatory services such as the Registrar-General, the census etc. The department had a total planned expenditure of £3,628 million in 1994–5.

The head of the NI civil service is responsible for the co-ordination of the work of the six NI departments and is supported by a central secretariat. The post carried the rank of Permanent Secretary with responsibilities as chief adviser to the Secretary of State on all transferred matters. Until his retirement in 1992, Sir Kenneth Bloomfield occupied the post. He was succeeded by David Fell from the DED.

The NIO is also headed by a Permanent Secretary. It has London and Belfast divisions, which both deal with political and constitutional affairs and security. The London division of the NIO provides liaison between NI departments and the Treasury and other Whitehall departments. The Belfast divisions of the NIO are mainly concerned with the administration of reserved and excepted matters, especially law and order. Among the NIO's specific functions are criminal justice, including special powers, the prevention and detection of crime, police matters and traffic wardens, prisons and the treatment of offenders, firearms and explosives, electoral matters, political matters, constitutional matters, human rights, and international topics – including the European Community and the Intergovernmental Secretariat. The compensation for victims of crime and compensation for loss or damage under emergency legislation is now a matter for the Compensation Agency. Planned spending by the NIO in 1994–5 was £931 million.

The NI departments are formally separate from the NIO, but under the Northern Ireland Act, 1974, and in the absence of devolution, they are subject to the direction and control of the Secretary of State and his Ministers, who are responsible for the reserved and transferred matters described in the Northern Ireland Constitution Act, 1973. The planned manpower for the NI departments in 1994–5 was 23,210, and 4,902 in the NIO. A reduction of 3,000 staff was announced in April 1994 as part of the Next Steps programme.

Expenditure by NI departments has been fitted into the UK Public Expenditure Survey Cycle (PESC) since 1968 and PESC control procedures since 1972. The NI programme is in two sections: first, the NI departments administering matters transferred in the Northern Ireland Constitution Act, 1973; and second, the expenditure by UK departments, namely, NIO, M.o.D. and the Foreign Office, on excepted and reserved matters. The Secretary of State has overall responsibility for both sections of the programme. In this way NI public expenditure is integrated into the UK pattern and system of control.

Since the creation of the NIO as a separate department of state in 1972, NI has benefited from increased public expenditure. From 1972 to 1979 NI per capita public expenditure rose by 17 per cent compared to a rise of 2 per cent in Wales and a reduction of 8 per cent in Scotland. Despite the Conservative Government's commitment to cut public expenditure, the NI programme continued to expand by 2 per cent until 1985. By 1987–8 the per capita public expenditure figures for the parts of the UK, standardising on England as 100, were Scotland 129, Wales

115 and NI 150. The relative position of NI increased to 158 in 1988–9 but began to fall thereafter and in 1991–2 was 137. For the period 1994–5 planned public expenditure for NI was £7,390 million. From time to time the subvention from the Treasury becomes a political issue and in 1991–2 it amounted to £2,540 million. Figures published in 1993 showed that, when the variable security costs were excluded, there was considerable consistency over the years since 1973–4. The average subvention was £1,555 million over nineteen years with the range marked by £1,826 million in 1978–9 and £1,318 million in 1989–90.

CRITICISM AND CHANGE

At first, the temporary nature of direct rule and its annual renewal were accepted because it provided stable institutions pending devolution. Questions were raised about its legitimacy and the lack of local account-ability when functions, to a very low level, were accountable only to Parliament. As the prospect of devolution became more remote and, after 1985, available only in the context of the AIA, attitudes to direct rule began to change. The Unionist community moved away from devolution and direct rule in favour of complete integration with Britain. Nationalists prefer devolution with power-sharing, especially with the Anglo-Irish Intergovernmental Conference still in place. The result has been a more unstable form of direct rule.

First, the practical problems of direct rule became ever more apparent in Parliament, with both the SDLP and Unionists in the role of opposi-tion. The number of questions per session regularly exceeds 1,000 and the issues raised have frequently been those which local authorities might deal with elsewhere. In 1991–2 Eddie McGrady (SDLP, S. Down) was twenty-second in the top thirty MPs getting the most answers to parliamentary questions. MPs were critical of the length of time taken to answer letters, and at first Ministers refused to give timings for NI letters unlike the Secretaries of State for Wales and Scotland. Unionists were particularly concerned by the growth in number and power of quangos compared to the status of elected District Councils. Two studies, one by the UUP and another by the *Belfast Telegraph,* traced 145–150 such bodies with memberships appointed by Ministers. In 1991–2 some 121 of these were non-departmental bodies. One aspect of direct rule has attracted general criticism, namely, the legislative process and the use of Orders in Council. The Orders are debated, usually late at night, but cannot be amended. This system has recently attracted a study by the Standing Advisory Commission on Human Rights. The 'temporary' system of direct rule has provoked calls for a general review. One reform suggested by the Procedure Committee of the House of Commons in

1990 was the creation of a departmental select committee to cover NIO responsibilities in the same way as the select committees on Scotland and Wales. The proposal had been frozen pending the outcome of the current political talks process but on 16 December 1993 the Prime Minister agreed to the creation of an NI Affairs Committee. The Commons approved the decision by 324 votes to 221 on 9 March 1994. The composition of the NI Affairs Committee, approved by 312 votes to 239 on 29 March, was as follows: Conservative: James Cran (Beverley), Charles Hendry (High Peak), Andrew Hunter (Basingstoke), Richard Spring (Bury St. Edmunds), David Wilshire (Spelthorpe), Mark Wolfson (Sevenoaks); Labour: Jim Marshall (Leicester S.), Clive Soley (Hammersmith); UUP: Ken Maginnis (Fermanagh-S. Tyrone), John Taylor (Strangford); DUP: Peter Robinson (E. Belfast); SDLP: Eddie McGrady (S. Down); UPUP: Sir James Kilfedder (N. Down, Chairman).

Second, whilst the AIA had been reviewed and confirmed in 1989, it had made no progress towards the commitment to devolution contained in Article 4(b). The Secretary of State, Peter Brooke, launched a bid for inter-party talks and devolution in January 1990. He was unable to report agreement before the summer, and the autumn revealed signs of positions unravelling. The critical question was when the Irish Government would enter talks. In March 1991 Dublin agreed that the Secretary of State could decide the timing. The aim was, first, a more broadly based structure than the AIA; discussions would focus, second, on the relations within Northern Ireland (Strand One), on relations between the people of the island of Ireland (Strand Two), and, finally on relations between the governments of the UK and of the Republic of Ireland (Strand Three).

The talks between local parties began on 30 April 1991 and, despite the intervention of procedural issues raised in advance of Strands Two and Three, there were three weeks of talks before they were concluded by the Secretary of State on 3 July. Although the meetings did not resume in the autumn, the parties accepted the usefulness of the formula for talks. Early in 1992 the Prime Minister, John Major, brought the leaders together over the worsening security situation and on 9 March a plenary session of the talks was held before the general election. After the general election the new Secretary of State, Sir Patrick Mayhew, resumed the talks on 29 April with a three-month gap in AIIC meetings. Agreement on Strand One was not reached but the parties moved to Strands Two and Three from 1 July. These were the first talks between Unionists and the Irish Government since the Sunningdale Conference in December 1973, but this time they were held at Stormont.

The Strand Two talks resumed on 2 September but disagreement over the agenda and the low priority accorded to Articles 2 and 3 of the Irish Constitution led to the refusal of the DUP to attend the talks sessions in Dublin. The talks came to an impasse over the Republic's constitutional claim to NI, and moved to discuss economic co-operation. Despite intensive talks in October, the calling of a general election in the Republic on 5 November effectively ended Strands Two and Three. The final meeting was held on 10 November and, with the Anglo-Irish Intergovernmental Conference meeting on 16 November, the talks process came to an end.

Most of 1993 elapsed without any new format for talks being agreed. Despite a series of bilateral talks between the parties and Jeremy Hanley, and then with his successor, Michael Ancram, they did not progress to round-table talks. The DUP refused to meet Ancram in the autumn and at some stage in October PM Major decided to pursue a 'peace process' with Taoiseach Albert Reynolds rather than political talks with the main parties. For the British and Irish Governments this culminated in the Downing Street Declaration of 15 December. Alliance and the SDLP supported it, the UUP gave it a conditional acceptance but the DUP rejected it. PSF went through a process of consultation, then sought 'clarification', while in practice refusing a formal response and a cessation of violence. Early in February 1994, when a 'focus and direction' paper from Mayhew, containing plans for an NI Assembly, was sent first to Dublin, it further annoyed the DUP and threatened the UUP attitude to the declaration. In effect, planned institutional changes were being made to await a formal PSF/PIRA response to the declaration, at first by the time of its Ard Fheis at the end of February, and then by Easter. However, other changes were also rumoured concerning the method of legislating by Order in Council and the system of local administration.

OFFICE HOLDERS IN NORTHERN IRELAND 1968-93

KEY

————Termination of regime (e.g., Stormont, NI Executive)
    or of department

– – – – Change of administration or of Minister

NOTE

*During the life of the NI Executive, 1 January–28 May 1974, the British Ministers assisted the Secretary of State with his functions.

	Home Secretary/Secretary of State	N I Prime Minister/Chief Executive	Home Affairs	Finance	Development	Health & Social Services	Commerce	Agriculture	Education	New Departments
1968	CALLAGHAN	T. O'NEILL	CRAIG	KIRK	FITZ-SIMMONS	MORGAN	FAULKNER	CHICHESTER-CLARK	LONG	
1969	June	May / CHICHESTER-CLARK	December LONG / March PORTER		NEILL / LONG	January PORTER			FITZ-SIMMONS / P. O'NEILL	Community Relations / October SIMPSON
1970		CHICHESTER-CLARK	PORTER	KIRK	FAULKNER	FITZ-SIMMONS	BRADFORD	P. O'NEILL	LONG	SIMPSON
1971	MAUDLING	March / FAULKNER	August CHICHESTER-CLARK & TAYLOR / FAULKNER & TAYLOR	KIRK	BRADFORD	FITZ-SIMMONS	BAILIE	WEST	LONG	BLEAKLEY / September McIVOR
Direct Rule 1972	March / Secretary of State WHITELAW		LORD WINDLESHAM / June	HOWELL	LORD WINDLESHAM	CHANNON / November	HOWELL	HOWELL	CHANNON	LORD WINDLESHAM
1973	December			January	HOWELL	VAN STRAUBENZEE		MILLS	VAN STRAUBENZEE / LORD BELSTEAD	VAN STRAUBENZEE
1974										

	Secretary of State	Chief Executive / Deputy	Finance	Housing, Planning & Local Govt.	Environment	Health & Social Services	Manpower Services	Commerce	Agriculture	Education	Community Relations	Planning & Co-Ordination	Legal & Law Reform
*January 1974 Executive	PYM	Chief Executive FAULKNER / Deputy FITT	KIRK	CURRIE	BRADFORD	DEVLIN	R. COOPER	HUME	MORRELL	McIVOR	I. COOPER	McGRADY	NAPIER
May 1974 Direct Rule Resumed	— March — REES		CONCANNON	CONCANNON	MOYLE	LORD DONALDSON	ORME	ORME	LORD DONALDSON	MOYLE	MOYLE		
1975	REES		CONCANNON	CONCANNON	(Environment)	LORD DONALDSON	ORME	ORME	LORD DONALDSON	(Education)			
1976	September MASON		April REES	CONCANNON		CONCANNON	MOYLE	MOYLE	DUNN	LORD DONALDSON	CARTER		
1977	MASON		DUNN	CARTER		LORD MELCHETT	CONCANNON	CONCANNON	DUNN	LORD MELCHETT			
1978	MASON		PENDRY	CARTER		LORD MELCHETT	CONCANNON	CONCANNON	PENDRY	LORD MELCHETT			
1979	May ATKINS		ROSSI	GOODHART		ALISON	ROSSI	SHAW	SHAW	LORD ELTON			
1980	ATKINS		ROSSI	GOODHART		ALISON	ROSSI	SHAW	SHAW	LORD ELTON			
1981	September PRIOR		LORD GOWRIE	MITCHELL		J. PATTEN	BUTLER	BUTLER	BUTLER	SCOTT			

Year	Secretary of State	Finance & Personnel	Environment	Health & Social Services	Economic Development	Agriculture	Education
1982	PRIOR	LORD GOWRIE	MITCHELL	J. PATTEN	BUTLER	BUTLER	SCOTT
1983	September — HURD	June — BUTLER — BOYSON	C. PATTEN	C. PATTEN	September — BOYSON	LORD MANSFIELD	
1984		BOYSON				April — LORD LYELL	
1985	September — KING		NEEDHAM	NEEDHAM	September — VIGGERS		January — MAWHINNEY
1986		September — SCOTT					
1987		STANLEY					
1988		July — STEWART					
1989	July — BROOKE	COPE	BOTTOMLEY — July	LORD SKELMERSDALE	NEEDHAM	BOTTOMLEY — July	
1990		November — MAWHINNEY	NEEDHAM	December — HANLEY		SKELMERSDALE — December	December
1991						HANLEY	LORD BELSTEAD
1992	April — MAYHEW	MATES	ATKINS	LORD ARRAN	ATKINS	LORD ARRAN	HANLEY
1993		June — WHEELER	January — SMITH	BARONESS DENTON	SMITH	BARONESS DENTON	May — ANCRAM
1994							

THE SECURITY SYSTEM

UDR BOWS OUT AS DEATHS PASS 3,000 MARK

The near-fortresses that the security forces now occupy on the border with the Republic are a potent reminder that nearly a quarter of a century of NI violence has imposed its own geography. The sweeping away of the economic frontier in the context of the European Single Market at the start of 1993 has indeed served to highlight the dominance of security issues in the local situation and their impact on attempts to produce something like normality in local society. On 27 August 1992 the official death toll in the NI troubles reached 3,000 since 1969. It was, of course, an artificial bench mark. It took no account of the secondary deaths – the many who had died in road and other accidents that had some association with the Troubles and those who had taken their own lives as a result of pressures arising from the local situation, including members of the security forces and the ten Republican hunger-strikers who died in the Maze Prison. (It also left out of the reckoning the 112 people killed in GB, 100 in the Irish Republic and 18 in Europe up to that time.) With the killings accompanied by immense damage to property, and discouragement of investment and tourism, it is hardly surprising that precautions against bombings and shootings have been at the forefront of public debate, and, given the divided society, that there should be anxiety as well as to whether, in human rights terms, the politicians have yet got it right.

Certainly, through all the phases of the NI crisis, the effects of security issues, large and small, have been undeniable. The civil rights campaign was fuelled in the law-and-order sphere by Nationalist hostility to the all-Protestant USC, or B Specials, and the Special Powers Act, and lack of Catholic confidence in the RUC and the judiciary. The civil disturbances of 1969 brought troops on the streets. The 'Bloody Sunday' killings of thirteen civilians by paratroopers in Derry hastened abolition of the old Stormont system, but this might have been avoided if the Unionist Government had not refused to surrender all law-and-order powers in face of PM Heath's ultimatum in 1972. And when Mrs Thatcher signed the AIA in 1985, she undoubtedly looked mainly for security dividends in terms of more enthusiastic cross-border security co-operation by the Irish government and a greater readiness by Dublin to extradite terrorist suspects. On the other hand, the continuance of violence at a high level made it easier for Unionists to attack the AIA. And in the 1990s the rise of loyalist violence has revived some of the problems of the 1970s with the threat of the UFF in November 1992 to take the war to Republican areas proving no idle one. The security forces, meanwhile, eroded some of PIRA's specialist strength in bomb making, but the organisation still managed to mount substantial attacks and in 1992 switched some of its effort to London, hitting particularly at the City of London where the £800 million damage in the April bombing highlighted the absence of a state compensation scheme for victims of property damage in GB, in contrast to the situation in NI. In London, too, PIRA set off many nuisance devices, and through 'sheer ill-luck', as it put it, in November 1992 it just failed to explode two large devices, one close to Britain's tallest building, in Canary Wharf. And a mortar attack on 10 Downing Street during a Ministerial meeting on the Gulf War, whilst not causing death or serious injury, forced a major rethink of Whitehall security. Indeed, total PIRA activities throughout the UK must have cost in the region of £1,000 million in 1992, far in excess of the total criminal damage claims in NI since 1969. London was again a target at Bishopsgate in April 1993. The cost for repair of this attack on the banking and financial sector was estimated at £350 million and led to the passage of the Reinsurance (Acts of Terrorism) Act between 6 and 27 May and road checks into the City of London from 3 July. Security policy has been in a ferment in the 1990s. The controversial UDR has gone, MI5 has taken over the lead anti-PIRA intelligence role in GB, there has been closer dovetailing of RUC and army working in NI, local army strength has been raised by two battalions, and the 1991 Emergency Provisions Act provided for the first time an Act embodying all the emergency powers solely directed to the NI situation. And in 1992 the Government finally banned the UDA, a long-standing demand of Nationalists.

Many Unionists were unhappy at the disappearance of the UDR, through its merger in 1992 with the Royal Irish Rangers to form the revived Royal Irish Regiment. But the move did not attract the widespread opposition associated with the ending of the B Specials in 1970. Although the Scarman report (1972) had held that the all-Protestant USC was 'totally distrusted by Catholics', loyalists tended to remember that it had been set up by the British Government in 1920 specifically to counter the IRA, and former NI PM Lord Brookeborough regarded himself as 'father' of the B Specials. Scarman has recorded the somewhat confused role of the force in the violent summer of 1969. In July the Minister of Home Affairs, Robert Porter QC, authorised its use in riot control, with batons but without firearms. After protests from the USC, however, he allowed officers and NCOs to carry arms. On 13 August NI PM James Chichester-Clark indicated in a broadcast that the

USC would not be used for riot control, but next day an instruction was issued stating that it should be so used, but equipped, 'where possible', with batons. It was not until 15 August that USC members were expressly ordered to report with their firearms. This was after the call-out which seems to have been mandatory before the army could go on the streets in support of the RUC. In 1969 there were about 10,000 members on the USC's books. A few hundred of these were full-time, and another three hundred were mobilised for full-time duty with the RUC in 1969. Scarman found that the force was not effective when used in communal disturbances in Belfast, and that it had shown lack of proper discipline, particularly in the use of firearms, when employed outside Belfast. But the tribunal praised the USC for protecting Catholic-owned pubs in Belfast from Protestant mobs.

During the discussion in Downing Street in August 1969 between the British and NI Governments, the PM, Harold Wilson, said in a TV interview that the USC would be phased out. But after the discussions, NI PM James Chichester-Clark and his colleagues rejected the idea of abolition of the 'Specials'. The issue produced acrimonious debate within unionism, with right-wing critics of the NI Government claiming that the public was not being told the whole truth. In the end the abolition of the USC was recommended in the Hunt report, published in the autumn of 1969, and the force was eventually stood down on 30 April 1970. Later Chichester-Clark, in the 1989 BBC History Makers series, claimed that as PM he had been called out of a Stormont Cabinet meeting to be told by Callaghan that if his Government did not agree to disband the USC, the force would be abolished anyway, and his Government would not get the UDR. In the event, the UDR provided the military back-up of the RUC in most areas of NI for some twenty-two years. But it was little more successful than the B Specials in attracting cross-community support. (*See* section on the UDR/RIR, pp. 451–3.)

THE ROYAL ULSTER CONSTABULARY

In the wake of serious riots in the summer of 1969 it was clear that the British Government was intent on securing a new-look police force. There was talk of a change of uniform. Thus the Home Secretary, James Callaghan, inspired the mounting of a special committee of inquiry (*see* Hunt Report). The Cameron Commission, in its initial look at the underlying causes of the crisis, had complained of RUC mistakes, and the Scarman tribunal, in its investigation of the bitter disturbances of 1969, had recognised the 'fateful split between the Catholic community and the police'. Scarman said the RUC had been ready to do its duty as much in face of Protestant as of Catholic mobs. 'But it is painfully clear from the evidence adduced before us that by July [1969] the Catholic minority no longer believed that the RUC was impartial and that Catholic and civil rights activists were publicly asserting this lack of confidence.' Thus, while accepting that the RUC had made mistakes, Scarman rejected 'the general case of a partisan force co-operating with Protestant mobs to attack Catholic people'. Scarman held, however, that there had been six occasions during the 1969 troubles when the RUC had been 'seriously at fault':

12 August	Incursion by members of the RUC Reserve Force into Rossville Street, Derry.
13 August	Decision to put armed members of the USC on riot duty in Dungannon, Co. Tyrone, without an experienced police officer to take command.
14 August	A similar decision in Armagh city.
14–15 August	The use of Browning machine guns in Belfast.
14–16 August	Failure to prevent Protestant mobs burning down Catholic houses in Conway Street and Brookfield Street in Belfast.
15 August	Failure to take effective action to restrain or disperse mobs or to protect lives and property in riot areas during daylight and before the arrival of the army.

The burden of the Scarman criticism of the RUC was that its senior officers acted as though the strength of the force was sufficient to maintain the public peace. This meant that the army had not been called in until the Inspector-General of the RUC was confronted with the physical exhaustion of police in Derry on 14 August 1969 and in Belfast the following day. It found that the force had struggled manfully to do its duty in a situation that it could not control, and that its courage, as long hours of stress and strain took their toll, was beyond praise.

James Callaghan, who as Home Secretary was responsible for police matters in GB, took an exceptional interest in changing the RUC image. His first move was to arrange for Sir Arthur Young of the City of London Police to take over as the head of the force. In consequence of the Hunt recommendations the RUC lost much of its paramilitary character which it had inherited from the old Royal Irish Constabulary in 1922. Instead, it was remodelled on police forces in GB, and the term 'police service' became official jargon. Under Stormont Governments, the Ministry of Home Affairs handled broad police matters, but under the Police Act of 1970 a Police Authority, representative of the main sections of the community, was set up. It was given the responsibility to maintain an adequate and efficient police force, but its influence in the early years was less decisive than Callaghan had intended. Operational control of the RUC was vested in the Chief Constable, and the title 'Inspector-General' was dropped. The general rank structure was also altered to conform with practice in GB.

The size of the RUC, limited to 3,500 men and women up to 31 March 1970, had to be quickly reassessed in the light of the security demands. The regular establishment was increased to 4,940 in 1970, to 6,500 in 1974, to 7,500 in 1979, to 8,000 in 1982, to 8,250 in 1984 and to 8,489 in November 1991, when the number of the full-time reserve (created in 1970) was raised to 3,202. The part-time reserve has an establishment of 1,765. The RUC also has a substantial civilian back-up, first announced by NI Secretary James (now Lord) Prior in 1982.

At the height of the Troubles, the Army GOC was director of anti-terrorist operations, but in the mid-1970s the Government launched its 'primacy of the police' approach, designed to achieve a situation in which the RUC would be in charge of the peace-keeping effort everywhere in NI. This 'Ulsterisation' policy meant that by the mid-1980s the RUC was paramount, with the regular army providing back-up in about 20 per cent of NI, mainly in W. Belfast and in border areas, including Derry city. Elsewhere, the UDR gave support. In the late 1970s, there had been some friction between the RUC and the army, and this was one of the reasons for the appointment of Sir Maurice Oldfield (former head of MI6) as Security Co-ordinator in 1979. This post was eventually dropped in 1982. The AIA has meant that the RUC Chief Constable, by attendance at the Anglo-Irish Intergovernmental Conference, is drawn into regular discussions with British and Irish Ministers on cross-border and other common problems. This means he also has more regular contact with the Garda Commissioner, and there is also a permanent 'hot line' between the two forces.

As PM, Margaret Thatcher was annoyed at the Dublin Government's requirement that its Attorney-General should be furnished with the evidence in support of extradition applications. In 1988 she was particularly angry at the refusal to extradite Father Patrick Ryan to the UK on terrorist charges, describing it as 'an insult to the British people'. The Dublin authorities pointed to comments in the British Parliament and media as justifying their decision. But the AIA raised problems for the RUC in 1985 because bitter hostility to the agreement on the part of Unionists led to street protests, which often involved clashes between police and demonstrators. There were serious riots in Portadown, and in 1986 loyalists engaged in some 500 incidents of intimidation of RUC families, 120 of whom were forced to move home. One result of this situation was the tendency for police to concentrate their homes in areas where regular patrolling by the security forces could give them a greater sense of security. There was also Unionist anger about the requirement of the Public Order Order (effective in 1987) that seven days' notice should be given of all parades, including traditional parades, which some Orange Order interests tended to regard as sacrosanct. But the reaction was less violent than had been anticipated, and only eighteen of ninety-six illegal parades in 1987 led to disorder. But the issue of parades with a sectarian flavour through areas where the religious composition of the local community may have changed over the years is likely to continue to provoke tension.

Burden of History

Despite the reforms that flowed from the Hunt report, the RUC has had to mount a long-running campaign to secure all-round acceptability in Catholic areas. That is a struggle it has yet to win. Its major handicap is the burden of history represented by the Nationalist perception of the RUC as the creature of successive Unionist Governments in the old Stormont, rather than an independent police force. One of the main tactics to overcome this legacy has been to seek to enlarge the Catholic element in the force. But while in the early years of the Troubles this stood at around 10 per cent, when detailed monitoring began in 1990 the percentage was 7.75 for the regular force, and lower for both the reserve forces. In 1992 it was 7.78 per cent, but the percentage was around 14 for senior officers and more applications were coming from Catholics. (When Michael McAtamney, a Catholic, retired as deputy Chief Constable in March 1993, with forty-two years' service, he was the longest-serving police officer in the UK.) Efforts to mount recruiting drives through Catholic schools have sometimes come under criticism and parents of Catholic police officers have mentioned the difficulty of their sons visiting homes in Nationalist areas or maintaining friendships outside the force. Father Raymond Murray of Armagh told the Initiative '92 commission in 1993 that the RUC catered only for the British tradition. Sir Hugh Annesley, as Chief Constable, has spoken of 'strenuous efforts' to overcome the imbalance, and security chiefs have always recognised that PIRA intimidation is an important factor affecting recruitment of Catholics. In 1987 a code of professional ethics was introduced, requiring RUC officers to act impartially and without regard to religion, political beliefs or aspirations. Some of the concerns of Nationalists and human rights bodies were also addressed by the setting up of an independent Police Complaints Commission in 1988 (chairman James Grew), but NI Secretary of State Sir Patrick Mayhew in July 1992 rejected the idea of further strengthening that body. And the appointment in 1992 of a distinguished QC, Sir Louis Blom-Cooper, as Independent Commissioner for the RUC holding centres at Castlereagh, Armagh and Derry, where suspected paramilitary members are held for questioning, was a further move to deal with allegations of maltreatment of suspects. He was empowered to make unannounced visits and to report to the Secretary of State on whether a new code of practice issued in 1992 was being observed. However, the NI Police Authority said such a scheme 'would be insufficient in itself to meet the needs of the community to be reassured about holding centres'.

No 'Inner Circle'

Complaints of mistreatment of suspects in the late 1970s led to the setting up of the Bennett committee, and to TV monitoring of interrogations. But demands by human rights campaigners and the British Labour Party for video recording of questioning have been resisted by the RUC and by the Government. Other negative factors in RUC–minority relations have included RUC Special Branch errors in the choice of internees in 1971; the tensions surrounding the 1981 H-Block hunger strike; controversial shootings, including the killing of PIRA and INLA men in Co. Armagh in 1982, which were the subject of the Stalker/Sampson reports; the bitter debate over 'supergrasses' (1981–6) during which Chief Constable Sir John Hermon vigorously defended the use of 'converted terrorists' as a powerful weapon against the paramilitaries; and allegations of an 'inner circle' within the RUC acting againt Republicans and opposed to the AIA, which Sir Hugh Annesley firmly denied in October 1989. By March 1991 Sir Hugh claimed 'growing contacts' with the Catholic community, but it is not easy to measure such an advance objectively in places where – as one senior RUC officer put it – 'one man's justice is another man's harassment'.

There is an ever-changing pattern in the terrorist problems posed for the RUC. In 1985 there was the ironic situation that overall terrorist activity was at its lowest for fifteen years but the number of police officers killed (twenty-three) was the highest since 1976. This was due largely to the PIRA campaign against RUC stations, particularly in border areas. Thirteen stations were bombed or mortared and eleven officers killed, nine in a single attack on Newry station. A further twenty-eight RUC members died in 1986 and 1987, but the total death toll for the four years, 1988–91, was down to thirty-three, apparently reflecting a temporary concentration by PIRA on attacks on the army. In 1992 only three RUC members died, the lowest yearly total since 1970, but the figure rose to six in 1993. In the late 1980s there were frequent rows over the policing of PIRA funerals. In 1987 alone there were twenty-three such funerals, and RUC efforts to prevent paramilitary displays led to widespread controversy and some violent confrontations. But in 1988 there were five deaths at two W. Belfast funerals that were not closely policed (*see* Andersonstown).

In the 1990s the RUC has had to face a major upsurge in loyalist violence as well as the return of the PIRA car bomb on a substantial scale. In the 1980s Republicans accounted for 80 per cent of all terrorist murders, but in 1990 the figure dropped to 71 per cent, and in 1991 to 54 per cent, while in 1992 loyalists committed thirty-nine murders (52 per cent), with Republicans responsible for thirty-six (48 per cent). In 1993 loyalists were responsible for forty-eight deaths (57 per cent) and Republicans for thirty-six (43 per cent). Both the UFF and UVF were active at the start of 1993. The rise in sectarian murders in the early 1990s was particularly reflected in N. Belfast, NI's number one killing ground, where some six hundred people have died in the Troubles. Special squads of detectives were allocated to this area, where some twenty-five gunmen were believed to be actively involved. Greater co-operation between loyalist paramilitaries, and the emergence of a younger and more ruthless leadership of the UDA – declared illegal in August 1992 – clearly posed an increased challenge to the security forces. The RUC emerged unscathed from the Stevens inquiry (*see* Stevens Inquiry) into allegations of leaking of security documents to loyalist paramilitaries, but the convictions, for the murder of five Catholics, of an army spy within the UDA (Brian Nelson) who was uncovered by the investigation threatened a revival of army–police differences like those of the 1970s. The situation had major implications for intelligence (*see* The Secret Arm, pp. 461–6), but army–police co-operation was not seriously impaired and was helped by the alignment of RUC and army areas and the establishment of a joint Executive Committee representing both RUC and army chiefs. In 1992 the RUC strengthened its command structure by having two deputy Chief Constables – one, Blair Wallace, dealing with operations, and the other, Ken Masterson, dealing with support services. It also acquired its own spotter plane.

PIRA bombings in 1991–2 were widespread and damaging. There was considerable destruction in Belfast city centre, and the forensic science laboratory – a key institution in the anti-terrorist drive – was wrecked by a huge explosion which blasted many houses in the Belvoir Park area of the city. In the same period there were bombings of Craigavon, Bangor and Coleraine. The situation led to many more police being deployed on the ground, additional army personnel, the setting up of more permanent checkpoints and the closure of several town centres at night. But the Chief Constable claimed that four out of five major terrorist attacks planned by the paramilitaries were being prevented and there appeared, indeed, to be a growing number of admissions by PIRA that it had abandoned bombs because of security force activity. However, PIRA sustained its high level of activity during 1993. Bangor had a bomb in March, but the main concentration was three days in May: Belfast had a bomb on 20 May, Portadown on 22 May, Magherafelt and Belfast again on 23 May. The damage over the three days was estimated at £22 million, about one-quarter of the total set aside for compensation in the year. Newtownards was bombed on 5 July and hotels were targeted in Belfast, Newry and Strabane. Police remained conscious of the large reserves of explosives and weapons still held by PIRA from the Libyan shipments and the apparent ability of that organisation to bring in recruits without criminal records and from outside the traditional Republican families always subject to surveillance.

Extensive powers to deal with paramilitary racketeering were provided by the 1991 EPA, and the RUC's anti-racketeering squad, C13, has been tackling a variety of illegal operations, including drug-dealing, sales of the agricultural chemical 'angel dust', fraudulent copying of videos, and a host of methods of extortion. The Chief Constable's 1991 report offered some striking figures. In the previous five years, he said, 334 persons had been convicted of 1,210 offences involving tax exemption, extortion, mortgage fraud, video piracy and other crimes and it was calculated that the total involved in these cases was about £45 million.

The RUC has been making strong efforts to improve its public image. In August 1991 it held its first 'open day' in Ballymena, and by 1993 there were twenty-six community and police liaison committees throughout NI. In 1991, in co-operation with the Police Authority, arrangements were completed for panels of lay visitors to check the conditions in which people were held at designated police stations. In 1993 there were no deaths arising from security force activity but the RUC continued to take casualties – 6 deaths and 146 injured. (For RUC casualties *see* Security Statistics, pp. 467, 470.)

THE ARMY

After nearly twenty-five years of army involvement in the internal security operation in NI, M.o.D. chiefs in 1993 were reviewing a situation vastly different in terms of manpower resources from that in the 1970s and 1980s, when the Soviet threat still loomed large. It was then relatively easy to draw on units held in strength in Germany on a rota basis, without imposing too great a strain on individual units. But the cuts in the services led, as the Parliamentary Defence Select

Committee stressed in early 1993, to a situation where a two-year interval could no longer be maintained between tours of duty in NI. The interval had dropped to seventeen months. The select committee found that the Scots Guards had been working a 113-hour week in NI, while the 2nd Battalion, Light Infantry had been to NI four times in two years. It also reported that 30 per cent of the troops acting as infantry in NI were from the Royal Artillery. The decision of Defence Secretary Malcolm Rifkind in February 1993 to reprieve four regiments due to be axed under the Options for Change policy was largely dictated by the NI commitment, which was in effect denying the Government some of the 'peace dividend'.

The army's NI experience has had many facets. In pre-1969 days NI, with its 2,000-strong garrison, was a popular posting with the army, so it was a major surprise when, in the summer of 1969, the army found itself on the streets of NI in a peace-keeping role. For the NI Government, it was a hard decision to call for troops, since it was all too aware that once the army was involved, there could not fail to be a basic change in Stormont–Westminster relations. Ministers took their decision on 14 August 1969, after RUC officers accepted that their men were too exhausted to maintain their efforts to deal with violence on the edge of Derry's Bogside and in Belfast. Home Secretary James Callaghan, for the British Government, endorsed the request and at 5 p.m. on 14 August a company of the Prince of Wales Own Regiment went on duty in the centre of Derry. Next day 600 men of the 3rd Battalion, Light Infantry, entered W. Belfast with fixed bayonets to provide a buffer between Protestant and Catholic crowds on what later became known as the Peace Line. In many Catholic areas of Belfast the soldiers got a warm welcome because they were treated as an insurance against loyalist incursions. This situation did not persist, though, since the rise of PIRA led most Republicans to renew their natural resentment towards British forces. The Falls Road curfew in July 1970 also tended to harden Catholic attitudes against the army. The army also displayed some extra toughness in face of attacks. Army GOC and Director of Operations General Freeland warned in April 1970 that anyone throwing a petrol bomb after a warning risked being shot.

Stormont could not have any control of the army constitutionally, and it had been agreed to put the RUC under the army commander in relation to anti-terrorist operations. The army in such a situation found itself caught up in local politics. Unionists in 1969 resented what they regarded as toleration by the army of no-go areas in W. Belfast and in the Bogside and Creggan areas of Derry. But incidents involving the army had on occasion far-reaching political consequences. It was the shooting by the army in Derry of two men in July 1971 which led to the withdrawal of the SDLP from Stormont. The SDLP was acting in pursuance of an ultimatum that it would leave Parliament if a public inquiry into the shooting was refused. The shooting dead by the army of thirteen men in Derry in January 1972 was crucial in persuading the British Government to suspend Stormont (see 'Bloody Sunday'). The Heath Government wanted the NI Government to surrender to Westminster all law-and-order powers, and when Brian Faulkner and his colleagues refused to do so, they were left with only the option of resignation. As the PIRA onslaught developed, the NI campaign proved more costly in terms of manpower than the Government originally expected. There were seven major units (around 7,000 troops) involved in 1970. In 1971 this had risen to nine units (and this was a smaller commitment than the NI Government was demanding); while at the time of 'Operation Motorman' in 1972, there were some nineteen units, or 21,000 troops, in NI. By 1975 there were fifteen units, in 1979 thirteen, and in 1982 nine. Since unit strengths vary, the numbers of troops are a more accurate guide. By 1980 the figure was 11,500; in November 1981, 10,763; and at the end of 1982, 10,500. In addition, one spearhead unit stationed in GB was available to be moved swiftly to NI. Originally most army units came from West Germany on four-month tours of duty. Up to 1978 nine major units had completed six tours, and six major units had done seven tours. But in 1977 Secretary of State Roy Mason announced that there would be more long-stay units, starting with one extra in the autumn of 1978. By 1982 all but 2,000 troops (or three units) were on two-year tours of duty.

The army in NI has been temporarily reinforced to deal with two loyalist strikes – in 1974 and 1977. In 1974 the attitude of the army chiefs to the loyalist bid to bring down the power-sharing Executive stirred controversy. The power-sharing parties were deeply disappointed that the army could not provide the expertise to run the power stations and they believed more should have been done by troops to counter the erection of barricades and road blocks by supporters of the stoppage. The army, though, was obviously reluctant to put itself in a position of all-out confrontation with the loyalists once it was clear that the strike had considerable Protestant support. This approach was summed up by one senior army officer in the words, 'The game isn't worth the candle.' So, inevitably, the collapse of the Executive gave rise to some angry recriminations, some of them directed against the army. In 1977 the UUAC strike in May led to the deployment of an extra three infantry battalions, but the limited nature of the stoppage did not put any serious strain on army resources.

The PIRA ceasefire in 1975 raised very different problems for the army. The British Government had gone to the extent of co-operating with PSF in setting up a system for monitoring the ceasefire, and it was obviously gambling on PIRA deciding at last to abandon its shooting war. So Ministers were keen to avoid a situation in which the army gave PIRA an excuse to resume its campaign. The army itself described its stance as 'lowering its profile, but not lowering its guard'. But to some Conservative MPs and to most Unionists it seemed that the army was going very easy on PIRA and that their men on the wanted list were being allowed to move freely. The authorities denied, however, that people wanted for specific crimes were being ignored, and in the event the ceasefire petered out rapidly, with PIRA resuming its activities seriously in the second half of 1975.

The feature of 1976 was the introduction of the undercover SAS to fight PIRA in S. Armagh, after serious violence there. Probably fewer than one hundred SAS men were involved initially, but the move achieved a real reduction in PIRA assaults in this key border area. Later, the SAS (and undercover men from other units) were permitted to operate anywhere in NI, largely due to the growth of sectarian assassinations in the 'murder triangle', embracing parts of counties Tyrone and Armagh, and in areas like N. Belfast. The SAS has continued to be employed in difficult surveillance operations, and its most dramatic operation was the shooting dead of eight PIRA members attacking Loughgall RUC station in May 1987 (*see* Loughgall Shootings).

The year 1977 brought the implementation of the policy of 'primacy of the police', which meant that the army no longer controlled security but operated in support of the RUC. The 'primacy' policy did not mean, however, that the army came under RUC command, but that soldiers supported the police where necessary in anti-terrorist operations. There was close liaison between the army GOC and the RUC Chief Constable, and similar contacts down the chain of command in both forces. The army still retained an important role in areas where the terrorist threat was still regarded as significant – that is, along the border and in W. Belfast and in the Bogside area of Derry. In the hunger-strike situation in 1981 the army proved 'indispensable', according to the RUC Chief Constable. But as the 1980s progressed, the fall in the overall level of violence was reflected in the decline of army strength. By 1985 it was down to 9,000 – 4,000 below the 1978 level. In the wake of the AIA, however, the wave of PIRA attacks on border police stations and army posts led to an extra two battalions being moved in during early 1986. This raised army strength to ten battalions (10,000 troops) instead of eight, and this strength was still maintained at the end of 1988. The stepping up of the PIRA campaign in 1987 and 1988, with the aid of arms from Libya, led to the revival of 3rd Brigade (which had earlier operated in S. Armagh), based at Drumadd barracks in Co. Armagh, to operate as a border force from Carlingford Lough to Strabane. It became operational on 1 July 1988, with two battalions, plus SAS, and meshed in with UDR border units to increase patrolling and covert operations along the frontier with the Republic. The aim was two-fold – to disrupt PIRA operations and to prevent movements of arms across the border. During the period 1987 to 1988, tall army observation posts, complete with living accommodation, had been erected at high points in S. Armagh to make surveillance easier, often to the annoyance of local residents. The establishment of the border brigade still left Belfast and most of the eastern part of NI under 39th Brigade at Lisburn, and most of the western part under the brigade at Derry.

In 1988 the locally based Royal Irish Rangers were used for the first time during the Troubles. There had been nervousness about the idea in Whitehall for some years, and the SDLP had warned against using the regiment in NI. But army chiefs were happy with the reaction, and the Rangers–UDR merger was to follow four years later with the revival of a long-defunct unit, the Royal Irish Regiment. Also in 1988 six battalions were on extended tours of duty (two years), accompanied by their families, while four battalions were on short-term or *roulement* tours (four and a half months). At the end of 1988 estates occupied by army families became targets of PIRA, apparently in retaliation for intensive army house searches in Republican areas.

Eye in the Sky

For the army in NI adaptation has been the name of the game. Initially, it was faced largely by community conflict situations, allied to street disturbances in what the Ministry of Defence expected to be a relatively brief commitment. Twenty-four years later the challenge remains. With Libyan backing for the Republican movement, PIRA was better armed than ever before. Thus army resources remain heavily committed to the seeking out of hidden caches of weapons, some of them highly sophisticated. The old Russian RPG7 rocket was still in use, but PIRA was thought to have stockpiled American SAM-7 ground-to-air missiles which posed a special threat to army helicopters which, it was disclosed in September 1988, were permitted to make limited overflights of the border. Special measures were taken to protect the Wessex, Lynx and Scout 'choppers', flown by the Army Air Corps, which were vital in surveillance and transport, as well as the RAF Chinooks. Helicopters provided the 'eye in the sky' in the shape of binocular observation, photographic techniques, and video cameras. 'Heli-tele' came of age in 1988 when video material shot from a helicopter was admitted in evidence in a Belfast court, where men faced charges of murder of two soldiers attacked at a funeral in Andersonstown (*see* Andersonstown).

In the NI campaign, the army has acquired a vast amount of expertise in dealing with the ever-changing PIRA tactics. The extensive searches in town and country since 1969 have yielded 108.7 tons of explosives (to 30 December 1993) and nearly 11,000 firearms, plus around 1.5 million rounds of ammunition. But the authorities have been very much aware of the still-undiscovered caches of Semtex explosive and guns from the Libyan shipments, which may well provide adequate supplies for PIRA stretching into the next century. In July 1992 the RUC Chief Constable said successful shipments from Libya to PIRA before October 1987 were estimated to include: 6 tons of Semtex, 1,500 AK assault rifles, 1.5 million rounds of ammunition, 20 SAM missiles, 50 RPG7 rocket launchers, and 10 flamethrowers, in addition to general purpose and heavy machine guns. For PIRA, 1988 seemed to be a key year in bringing forward arms supplies from its dumps in the Republic, since seizures in NI soared in that year to 4.7 tons of explosives and 489 firearms, ranging from shotguns through rockets and mortars to a flamethrower, together with 105,000 rounds of ammunition. Since then, PIRA seems to have preferred to hold supplies south of the border, and recent seizures in Co. Donegal could be significant. Although most seizures have been associated with PIRA, substantial loyalist arms were uncovered in 1988, and the UDA and UVF are known to have access to caches of guns and some explosives. PIRA has set off over 9,800 explosions, but some 5,000 devices have been defused by army technical officers holding down one of the most dangerous jobs imaginable.

By the end of 1993 army deaths since 1969 were 443 and those of the UDR and the new RIR combined had reached 202. The heaviest army toll was in 1972, when 103 soldiers died; 58 died in 1973. Many have died at the hands of snipers, but losses have been greatly inflated by a small number of serious incidents: the deaths of eighteen soldiers at Warrenpoint, Co. Down, in August 1979; eleven deaths in the Ballykelly pub bombing, Co. Derry, in December 1982; eight killed when a bus was blown up near Ballygawley, Co. Tyrone, in August 1988; six killed by a bomb in Lisburn, Co. Down, after taking part in a 'fun run' in June 1988; and five deaths in a proxy PIRA bombing of the Coshquin checkpoint at Derry in October 1990. (For detailed casualties, *see* Security Statistics, pp. 467, 470.) Army sources tend to regard the PIRA effort as variable, but they are no longer as disposed to play down PIRA numbers and resources as in earlier years. During the 1970s, it was commonplace to hear a senior officer claim that the organisation had no more than a dozen or so experienced activists. One army assessment is that PIRA in 1970 had to make an average of 191 attacks to kill a single member of the security forces, while the figure was 18 attacks in 1984. But the drop in the security forces' casualties between 1990 and 1992 suggested that PIRA had decided to concentrate on major bombings, if possible in GB, for the time being. But it was apparently finding it more difficult to test its improvised weapons such as mortars without detection. Many mortars have failed, although the horizontally fired version has proved deadly, and the more recent 'barrack buster' can be destructive. In the late 1980s, PIRA introduced the 'drogue bomb', a dangerous weapon known to the army as IAAG (improvised anti-armour grenade), which consists of an explosive charge in a baked beans tin, carried by a small parachute and exploding on impact. In 1991 it brought in the coffee-jar bomb, containing 1 lb of Semtex, which has been widely used in Belfast. A magnetic device – the 'limpet mine' – was first used in Belfast city centre in June 1992, injuring two police officers and nineteen civilians. In September 1991 PIRA produced its biggest-ever bomb (8,000 lb) in a bid to destroy the army post at Annaghmartin, Co. Fermanagh, but the attack failed.

Shields and Saracens

Much special equipment has been employed by the army to cope with the varied situations encountered in NI. For the handling of street disturbances, soldiers have been issued with plastic visors fitted to their steel helmets which protect the face against bricks, stones or other missiles. On occasions, plastic shields have also been carried, sometimes with leg-guards. Flak jackets, giving protection against low-velocity weapons, are normally worn. In the early days of the violence troops were permitted to shoot at identified petrol-bombers, but political considerations forced the authorities to look for weapons that fitted in with the 'minimum force' commitment. Water cannon were frequently deployed in the 1969 riots, but the main weapons in serious street disturbances have been the rubber bullet, later replaced by the plastic bullet, and CS gas.

The rubber bullet, 14 centimetres long and 4 centimetres in diameter, weighed 142 grams. It was designed to bounce off the ground and strike at about knee level. In practice it proved highly unpredictable and there were three deaths from rubber bullets and many severe injuries. Between 1972 and 1975 it was employed extensively to break up crowds engaged in stoning or petrol-bombing and finally gave way to the plastic bullet, which was first used in 1973.

The Ministry of Defence said the plastic bullet had been introduced because it was more effective and accurate. But the new baton round – as both rubber and plastic bullets are officially termed – was developed, according to *Jane's Infantry Weapons* (1976), because the disability and injury rates of the rubber bullet were not acceptable. The plastic bullet, made of PVC, is 10 centimetres long and 4 centimetres in diameter, and also weighs 142 grams. Unlike the rubber bullet, it is fired directly at its target. In the 1981 disturbances during the H-Block hunger strike, many thousands of plastic bullets were fired by the army and the RUC, and four deaths resulted in two months. By the end of 1982 the plastic bullet had caused eleven deaths and many of its critics argued that it was proving even more dangerous than the rubber bullet. These critics have included many Nationalist spokespersons and all NI Catholic Bishops. The British Labour conference has also opposed their use, and the European Parliament has called for a ban throughout the EC. But in October 1984 the European Commission of Human Rights held that they could be used in riot situations. The security forces, supported by Government Ministers, have always argued that they cannot face rioters, who are prepared to cause death and injury, without making some effective retort. In the late 1980s and early 1990s the plastic bullet was still being employed, although more sparingly. In 1990, 257 plastic bullets were used, and 323 in 1991, mainly during violence linked with the twentieth anniversary of internment. (During riots involving loyalists in Portadown in April 1986, a twenty-year-old Protestant man was fatally injured by a plastic bullet.) Batons, 0.6 metres long, are also available to the army for street troubles.

The main army weapons in the early 1990s were the SA80 5.56 mm rifle (replacing the 7.6 mm self-loading rifle), the Sterling 9 mm sub-machine-gun, and the general-purpose machine gun, which is unsuitable for use in urban conditions. Special rifle night-sights have been developed to counter snipers operating in darkness.

On average two army technical officers engaged in bomb-disposal work were killed each year in the early years of violence. Robot devices serve to reduce the risk of examining suspect objects.

Four vehicles have been employed in the NI campaign. The land-rover, usually protected with steel sheeting and sometimes with asbestos, has been the workhorse of the mobile patrol. The Saracen armoured personnel carrier, capable of carrying ten soldiers and their equipment, has been used generally in the cities. The Ferret scout car has been a popular escort vehicle, used sometimes for patrols. The Saladin armoured car, with a 75 mm gun and two Brownings, has been largely confined to border patrols.

Although in the armed forces the army has provided the bulk of the manpower in support of the police, the Royal Marines have also served in an infantry role and, together with the Royal Navy, they have mounted coastal and lough patrols to prevent the smuggling of arms into NI. The RAF has been involved in transport and in reconnaissance, and the RAF regiment has guarded the airfield at Aldergrove and the former radar facilities at Bishop's Court.

Because of the renewed PIRA bombing campaign in 1991–3, and a sharp rise in loyalist killings, two extra battalions were sent to NI in early 1992. This raised the regular army strength to 12,000, and when the UDR was fully integrated into the army as part of the revived Royal Irish Regiment on 1 July 1992, army strength rose to 17,700. The army was then giving particular attention to border areas, since in the twelve months to May 1992, security forces came under attack six times from gunmen firing across the frontier and there were eight occasions when terrorists crossed the border into NI with explosives or command wires, whilst on four occasions they fled back across the border after attacks. In 1992 PIRA also occasionally deployed large groups of members in S. Armagh. (In 1989 a twenty-strong PIRA gang was involved in a single cross-border attack in which two soldiers died.) In an attempt to keep PIRA off balance, extra foot and mobile patrols and snap checkpoints were mounted. There was closer RUC–army co-operation through the Executive Committee. And in line with the 1991 Emergency Provisions Act, the Secretary of State announced that Belfast solicitor David Hewitt would be independent assessor of military complaints procedures in NI from 1993. He would report on the handling of non-criminal complaints against soldiers.

Ulster Defence Regiment/Royal Irish Regiment

The Ulster Defence Regiment, a locally raised and mainly part-time force to start with, and within the army structure, derived from the proposals of the Hunt committee. In essence, it was a replacement for the all-Protestant USC or B Specials which, the Government concluded, could never attract cross-community support. The UDR became operational on 1 April 1970. Early on, it did have up to 18 per cent Catholic membership, but it suffered an early image problem with Nationalists, who saw it as absorbing too many former B Specials. There were many allegations of members associating with loyalist paramilitaries, and the conviction of two UDR men for the murder of three members of the Miami Showband in 1975, in a gun and bomb attack in which two UVF men were killed by their own bomb, was a major blow to the regiment's credibility. Members were involved in other killings, usually sectarian, and some were convicted of passing security files on Republican suspects to loyalists. Its soldiers were a prime PIRA target, and 197 members and 47 former members had been murdered by the time it was merged, along with the Royal Irish Rangers, into the Royal Irish Regiment in July 1992. Four of those killed were women members, known as Greenfinches. The UDR, the largest regiment in the British army, had been on active service longer than any regiment since the Napoleonic Wars.

When the Government announced in 1991 that the UDR was to disappear in the context of the Options for Change review of the armed forces, the decision was presented as a purely military one, arising from the contraction of the forces with the ending of the Cold War. But by then only 3 per cent of the regiment's members were Catholics, and many Nationalists and the Irish Government regarded it as highly suspect. Unionists protested at the ending of the UDR, and tended to claim that the level of criminality had been exaggerated in the light of the fact that 40,000 men and women had served in its ranks over twenty-two years. Defence Secretary Tom King announced that the RIR would have up to seven home service battalions, with an additional battalion for worldwide service, and a 'significant part-time element' would be retained.

In the late 1980s the UDR provided the back-up for the RUC over 85 per cent of NI, and in June 1988 the Government seemed to be underscoring its commitment to the regiment by announcing that the Queen had granted colours to all its nine battalions, all of which would be presented before 1995, its silver jubilee. But the 1989–90 inquiry by John Stevens, deputy Chief Constable of Cambridgeshire, into allegations of collusion between members of the security forces and loyalist paramilitaries cast a large shadow over the UDR, twenty-eight of its members being arrested by the RUC in a dawn swoop. The Irish Foreign Minister, Gerry Collins, said the regiment should be stood down until the investigation had been completed. In the end, 58 people were charged as a result of the inquiry: 34 charges of having information likely to be of use to terrorists were brought against 10 UDR members and 32 members of paramilitary groups. John Stevens said there was evidence of UDR members leaking information to terrorists. He urged higher standards of recruitment to and retention within the UDR.

It appears that consideration was given within the Government to the dropping of the part-time element in the new RIR. Certainly, that element has declined sharply over the past few years. In December 1989 the part-time UDR comprised 154 officers and 3,283 soldiers, and by December 1992 it was down to 136 officers and 2,618 soldiers – a drop of about 20 per cent. The permanent cadre was 2,940 in July 1992. Undoubtedly, the part-time element has drawn particular criticism from the SDLP, but with army chiefs seeking to enlarge the proportion of Catholics, a gradual transformation could be under way. But the RIR has still to prove that it will achieve the long-term acceptability in Nationalist areas always denied the USC and UDR. In its first six months of operations, the RIR had three members murdered – two locally based and one home on leave from Cyprus. An RIR company was among the British army contingent sent to Bosnia to protect food convoys in 1992.

On 31 December 1992 the total strength of the RIR in NI was 5,700, with six home battalions in place of the nine UDR battalions. The single general-service battalion emerged in August 1993, comprising the former 1st and 2nd Battalions of the Royal Irish Rangers, which were serving in Cyprus and Germany. The RIR headquarters is at St Patrick's Barracks, Ballymena. The Duke of York is Colonel-in-Chief.

PANOPLY OF POWERS

As the NI Troubles have continued, a great panoply of anti-terrorist legislation has developed, dwarfing the local Special Powers Act, which was one of the main targets of civil rights campaigners in the 1960s. There are two main strands of anti-terrorist laws – emergency provisions and prevention of terrorism. The first Emergency Provisions Act, limited to NI, came in 1973, and replaced the Special Powers Act and the Detention of Terrorists Order.

The 1974 PTA, rushed through Parliament in the wake of the Birmingham pub bombings, gave two main powers:

1 to exclude from GB, from NI, or the UK as a whole, persons alleged to be involved in terrorism associated with NI;
2 to arrest suspected terrorists and detain them for forty-eight hours, with the possibility of extending detention for a further five days on the authority of the Home Secretary or NI Secretary of State.

The powers have been criticised as providing a form of 'internal exile'. Under (1) the NI Secretary of State excluded thirty-one people from NI between November 1974 and the end of 1987; eleven of these orders were made in 1981, the year of the hunger strike; there were no exclusions in 1985 and 1986, and one in 1987. In 1988 twenty-three of the exclusion orders were still in operation. A new PTA took effect in 1976, which retained the powers granted by the 1974 Act, but also made it an offence to contribute or solicit money for terrorism, or to withhold information on terrorism. The 1984 PTA extended the detention power to international terrorists, and it also put a three-year limit on the life of an exclusion order, although the Secretary of State could make a new order if there was fresh intelligence. The PTA gives power to proscribe organisations in GB; only PIRA was outlawed in 1974, but INLA was added after the murder of Airey Neave MP in 1979.

Following a recommendation by Lord Jellicoe, who inquired into the operation of the legislation, the 1984 PTA had a life limited to five years; that is, expiring in March 1989. Margaret Thatcher disclosed in August 1988 that the replacement Bill would include measures to tackle paramilitary racketeering and to combat fund-raising by illegal groups. Powers would be modelled broadly on existing legislation which allowed the seizure of assets of convicted drug smugglers. Defending the move against terrorist funding, Home Secretary Douglas Hurd said that terrorists sometimes ran otherwise legitimate businesses to finance their murders.

In the event, the Bill brought forward in November 1988, to become operative in March 1989, was designed as a permanent measure, subject to annual renewal. It also cut from 50 per cent to 33 per cent the maximum remission allowed to terrorist convicts. But almost as soon as it was published the European Court of Human Rights ruled, in a separate legal action, that seven-day detention for questioning was excessive. In December 1988 Hurd indicated that he required time to consider how to introduce a judicial element into the detention process and that in the meantime a temporary derogation was being sought from the ECHR. The decision was attacked by the Labour Party as a snub to the Strasbourg court. Shadow Home Secretary Roy Hattersley said measures to deal with terrorist funding should have been taken earlier, but he renewed Labour's objections to the rest of the Bill, saying that the general powers were more likely to assist terrorists than to harm them.

In 1978 the new EPA consolidated emergency powers in NI, giving wide powers of search, arrest and even internment without trial if the Government decided to reintroduce it. It listed the organisations proscribed in NI – the IRA, Cumann na mBan, Fianna na hÉireann, Red Hand Commando, Saor Éire, UFF, UVF and INLA. It provided that bail could be granted only by the Supreme Court or trial judge. A court was given power to exclude a statement by an accused person if it was satisfied that the statement was obtained by torture or by inhuman or degrading treatment. The wearing of a hood or mask or paramilitary dress in a public place was outlawed. It listed scheduled terrorist offences to which the Act applied, going back to the Offences Against the Person Act of 1861 and Explosive Substances Act of 1883. It also provided, together with the Republic's reciprocal legislation and the Criminal Law

Jurisdiction Act, 1975, that a terrorist could be tried on whichever side of the border he was arrested.

Non-jury Courts

The Diplock report in 1972 recommended that non-jury trials should be introduced for a wide range of terrorist offences because of the intimidation of jurors and witnesses. In 1973, under the EPA, the Government adopted its proposals and Diplock courts came into existence.

Following the late Sir George Baker's report in 1984 on the working of the EPA, an amending Act was passed in 1987 and the Government gave information about the operation of Diplock courts. It was shown that in 1986, 596 defendants appeared before Diplock courts, with 567 convicted. Of the total number of defendants, 89 per cent had pleaded guilty and 11 per cent not guilty; 43 per cent of those who pleaded not guilty were acquitted. It was also reported that only 17 per cent of arrests under the 1978 Act led to charges. The Government rejected a move by the Labour opposition to drop internment powers through the 1987 Act. The amending measure, which represented the first major change in emergency legislation since 1975, shifted the onus in bail applications towards the prosecution instead of the defendant. It also allowed magistrates to remand for up to twenty-eight days instead of seven, so as to reduce pressure on court accommodation in Belfast. The Secretary of State was empowered to set time limits to reduce delays in bringing terrorist-type cases to trial. (This change arose from an amendment originally tabled by Seamus Mallon, SDLP MP.) The Lord Chancellor was given power to direct that particular cases should be heard in courts outside Belfast.

The amended EPA also provided that the use or threat of violence would become an additional ground for declaring a statement inadmissible. It repealed the arrest powers in the 1978 EPA, so as to avoid duplicating PTA powers of arrest; the effect of this was to allow arrest on 'reasonable suspicion' rather than simply 'suspicion', a change widely welcomed by lawyers. The offence of collecting information likely to be of use to terrorists was extended to include information on former members of the security services, the judiciary, courts' service, and the prison service. A new system of registration of private security firms was introduced to prevent paramilitary groups operating such services.

Widening Net

In 1988, when PIRA stepped up its campaign and was clearly seen to have accumulated large supplies of arms, the Government's attention turned to extra legal powers to use against terrorist suspects. In July it brought in 'genetic fingerprinting'. The technique entails taking mouth swabs from suspects for 'DNA profiling' and the authorities claimed that samples could provide conclusive proof of guilt or innocence. In the 1990s, however, some scientists have questioned the reliability of the technique. The SACHR said it was 'firmly opposed' to the provision, since it differed from that in England and Wales, where mouth samples could only be taken with the written consent of the suspect and by a doctor, not a police officer.

After an in-depth review of security in September–October 1988, the ending of the 'right of silence' for terrorist suspects was also introduced. Its end had been recommended by Lord Colville, when he reviewed anti-terrorist laws in 1987, and Secretary of State Tom King argued that it was necessary to counter the practice of suspects refusing to answer any questions during interrogation. (Paramilitaries were told in their news-sheets: 'Whatever you say, say nothing.') Labour's NI spokesman, Kevin McNamara, protested that the change meant the overturning of 'one of the pillars of the British system of justice'. The SDLP was also critical of the change and the NI Law Society complained that it had not been consulted about a legal change 'of such a fundamental nature', which also meant 'a drift towards an inquisitorial system'.

A further move by the Government in the autumn of 1988 was to order the broadcasting organisations not to allow direct broadcasts by members of proscribed organisations or supporters of violence. The ban applied to PSF and the UDA as well as all outlawed paramilitaries. Home Secretary Douglas Hurd claimed that such appearances caused offence and also fear, but critics included the Labour opposition, SDLP, most of the press, the broadcasting organisations, and the National Union of Journalists. The NUJ failed in a court challenge and in an appeal to the Lords. The issue seems likely to be settled by the ECHR, to which a PSF challenge was referred by the NI High Court. In October 1993 the Heritage Secretary, Peter Brooke, began a review of the operation of the ban. This followed the Irish Supreme Court decision to uphold the view of the Dublin High Court in 1992 that RTE had interpreted the 'Section 31' broadcasting ban too narrowly. In February 1994 the Irish Government eased its restrictions and created expectations that the British Government might follow its lead.

The Government also moved, at the end of 1988, to make it more difficult for supporters of violence to be elected to councils. The Elected Authorities (NI) Act provided that a candidate on nomination would have to make a declaration renouncing violence. It also changed the disqualification rule for those seeking election to councils. A five-year ban on ex-prisoners would date from release rather than sentencing.

Tom King said that the introduction of the declaration occurred against a background of 'very real concern' at the way groups like PSF exploited the democratic process. (PSF had already indicated that its candidates would sign the declaration to ensure that its supporters were not disenfranchised.) The legislation did not apply to Westminster elections.

Catch-all Act

The 1991 Emergency Provisions Act broke new ground by bringing together in a single measure all the anti-terrorist provisions applying solely to NI. Thus, it picked up key provisions in previous EPAs relating to non-jury courts and proscribed organisations, but also embodied parts of the 1989 PTA. In particular, the Act was directed against racketeering calculated to benefit paramilitary organisations. Courts were empowered to confiscate the proceeds of terrorist-related activities. NI Secretary of State Peter Brooke said: 'Terrorist organisations in Northern Ireland and those who handle money on their behalf are becoming more sophisticated in the measures by which they raise and launder funds. Increasingly, persons of substance, including businessmen, are involved in this activity.' The Act gave the powers of seizure to the armed forces for the first time and created a new offence of by-passing closed border roads. There was also a new offence of possessing items intended for terrorist purposes, and a new power to allow the security forces to examine documents and other recorded data. The power to reintroduce internment was continued and, in line with the law in GB, police were given authority to take fingerprints without consent from terrorist suspects. (Labour tried without success to have three-judge courts introduced for terrorist cases – a proposal pressed earlier by the Irish Government.) During the passage of the measure, it was announced that there would be a commissioner to check on RUC holding centres and an assessor of the process of handling non-criminal complaints against soldiers, both of which measures were implemented in early 1993. The proscription of the UDA in August 1992 was imposed under the EPA, so that it applied only in NI.

The PTA has been regularly criticised by the Labour opposition, and when the then Shadow Home Secretary, Roy Hattersley, opposed the 1992 renewal and called for efforts to get all-party agreement on emergency powers, the opposition attitude was attacked as 'irresponsible' by Home Secretary Kenneth Baker. In February 1992 it was reported that, of the 7,000 people detained under the PTA over seven years, nearly 6,000 had been released without charge. In September 1991, ninety-five suspects were subject to PTA orders excluding them from GB. In early 1993, two people were excluded from NI. The

Labour Party, in March 1994, attempted to get agreement on the PTA through discussion with the Government, but details of the meeting became public and the party again voted against the renewal of the Act.

Internment without Trial

The introduction of internment without trial by the NI Government on 9 August 1971 proved to be one of the most controversial moves of the authorities to combat violence. This was partly because it was followed by an escalation of violence, and partly because it led to the serious alienation of the Catholic community from the Stormont system. The swoop in Republican areas to arrest IRA suspects came at 4 a.m. on 9 August, four days after the NI Government had decided to use the Special Powers Act for this purpose and after talks with the British Conservative Government. The action of Brian Faulkner's Government was approved by Home Secretary Reginald Maudling, who was reputed to be unenthusiastic about the move but who said later that he had feared a Protestant backlash had internment not been used. The operation, code-named 'Demetrius', came after weeks of probing activity by the army and police to finalise the list of suspects. In the event, there were 452 names of people thought to be members of the IRA, or associated with it, but some of them had fled in anticipation of internment, and the actual arrests totalled 342. Of these, 104 were released within forty-eight hours, which indicated the poor intelligence involved. Brian Faulkner, in announcing the introduction of internment, said the main aim was to smash the IRA, but the Government would not hesitate to take similar action against any individual or organisation that might pose a similar threat in the future.

The decision to intern was backed by most Unionists, although the Rev. Ian Paisley was against it on the grounds that it was also likely to be employed against loyalists. The swoop was followed quickly by serious rioting and shooting in Belfast and many other places. Twenty-three people died on 9 and 10 August, and a massive civil disobedience campaign, involving the withholding of rent and rates, was launched in the Catholic community, with the backing of opposition MPs and NICRA. The Nationalist and SDLP MPs had already withdrawn from Stormont, and the SDLP now said that it would not take part in dialogue with either a British or an NI Government until internment was ended.

Internees were held in a new camp at Long Kesh, near Lisburn (later to be known as the Maze Prison), Magilligan army camp in Co. Derry, and the ship *Maidstone* in Belfast harbour. A small number of those arrested were subjected to 'interrogation in depth', which eventually gave rise to a finding in 1978 by the European Court of Human Rights that they had been subjected to inhuman and degrading treatment, but not to torture. A month after the start of internment, a three-man advisory committee, headed by Judge James Brown QC, was set up to advise the Government on individual internees. Where they recommended a release, they required the individual to take the following oath: 'I swear that for the remainder of my life, I will not join or assist any illegal organisation or engage in any violence or counsel or encourage others to do so.' In the wake of intense violence and reports of intimidation, the Republic's Government set up five camps to accommodate refugees and dependants of internees.

Between the introduction of internment in August and the end of the year, 146 people were killed, comprising 47 members of the security forces and 99 civilians, and there were 729 explosions and 1,437 shooting incidents. Immediately before direct rule was imposed in March 1972, the number of internees reached a peak of 924. When William Whitelaw took over as Secretary of State, he declared his intention to review personally the cases of all internees. On 7 April 1972 he announced the release of forty-seven internees, and said they had not been asked to give any assurance about future behaviour. He also stated that no further use would be made of the prison ship *Maidstone*. In May 1972 a new advisory committee was set up under the chairmanship of Judge Leonard, from Oxfordshire, which was empowered to consider only applications for release from internees. By mid-August the number of men held under the Special Powers Act had been cut to 243. Whitelaw was engaged in a drive to phase out internment, and was looking for a response from the PIRA in terms of reduced violence and possibly some switch to political activity. But in this he was disappointed, and after the re-entry of security forces to the no-go areas in the summer of 1972, there was a further slow build-up in the total of those detained.

Under the Detention of Terrorists Order, the Government introduced a new system of internment in November 1972. This involved an initial 'interim custody' order, under which after twenty-eight days the person had either to be released or referred to a commissioner, who would decide whether he should be detained. At this point the term 'internee' was replaced by 'detainee' in official language. Meantime, the Diplock committee reported in favour of some form of continued detention without trial. Between November 1972 and September 1973, the commissioners authorised 453 detention orders and directed release in 126 cases. In answer to the suggestion that ex-internees frequently became involved again in violence, a Government spokesman said in

March 1973 that of the more than 800 persons released from internment or detention since direct rule, only 10 had been subsequently charged with offences. With rising loyalist violence, two loyalists were served with interim custody orders on 5 February 1973, the first to be so treated. Two months later, the number of loyalists held had gone up to twenty-two. In August 1973 the Emergency Provisions Act replaced the Special Powers Act and the Detention of Terrorists Order as the legal basis of detention, but it kept the arrangements for interim custody and commissioners' hearings, and brought in a new power to hold suspects for seventy-two hours for questioning. Between 1 February 1973 and 30 October 1974 interim custody orders were served on 626 Catholics and 99 Protestants. Shortly before Christmas 1973, 63 Catholics and 2 Protestants were released.

In January 1975 the Gardiner committee said that detention without trial could only be tolerated in a democratic society in the most extreme circumstances. 'We would like to be able to recommend that the time has come to abolish detention, but the present level of violence, the risks of increased violence, and the difficulty of predicting events even a few months ahead, make it impossible for us to put forward a precise recommendation on timing. We think that this grave decision can only be made by the Government.' In August 1975 the Secretary of State (under the Emergency Provisions Amendment Act) took back the power to make detention orders, and ended the commissioner system. The Secretary of State would, however, consider reports on detainees from legally qualified advisers. But the then Secretary of State, Merlyn Rees, was committed to ending internment quickly, and on 5 December 1975 he signed orders for the release of the last seventy-five detainees. The SACHR suggested in 1979 that the power to intern without trial should be abandoned, but Secretary of State Humphrey Atkins argued that it would be premature to drop it. He apparently supported repeal in 1980, however, but in the event the power was retained, most recently through the 1991 EPA.

With a big surge in PIRA violence in the summer of 1988, the UUP was demanding 'selective internment', and the DUP called for the introduction of internment against Republicans only. There were also some Conservative voices in favour of the former. But the SDLP was firmly against both demands, and so were leading Catholic Churchmen. The Republic was also believed to be opposing internment generally within the Anglo-Irish Conference. Margaret Thatcher said she would be 'very reluctant' to see its return but successive NI Secretaries of State have continued to talk of it as an option. But the wide range of new anti-terrorist measures in the period 1988–91 was probably considered to be the alternative to internment which was being increasingly regarded as a last resort.

THE SECRET ARM

The early 1990s have brought a new dimension to the NI Troubles – spymasters and intelligence agencies have been frequently in the news. Partly, this has been due to greater openness about intelligence issues on the part of PM John Major, who carried out a far-reaching review of NI security and intelligence-gathering in early 1992. To start with, the Security Service, MI5, was named by Home Secretary Kenneth Clarke as taking responsibility for heading anti-PIRA intelligence in GB. This meant a sea-change in organisation, since that role had been filled by the Scotland Yard Special Branch since the days when it began as the Irish Special Branch to counter Fenian activities in GB. MI5 was already responsible, however, for monitoring loyalist paramilitary movements in GB, and the Government apparently concluded that it would bring new expertise to the task under its first woman Director-General, Stella Rimington. PM Major publicly identified the Director-General for the first time, as well as the head of the Secret Intelligence Service, MI6, Sir Colin McColl. (In March 1994 it was announced that he would be succeeded by his deputy, David Spedding, in September.) The new MI5 role was not universally welcomed. Lord Holme, the Lib. Dem. spokesman, said he was 'dubious' about the change, whilst Dr Brian Feeney of the SDLP said it was 'a victory for the IRA'. There was also some suspicion in Dublin, where Fianna Fáil TDs have claimed that their former leader, Charles Haughey, was targeted by MI5.

The change immediately provoked suggestions that there was much in-fighting between intelligence organisations. When the *Irish Times* published, in April 1992, the confidential minutes of a high-level Scotland Yard meeting in December 1991, which showed that police had 'little intelligence' on PIRA's recent fire-bombing of stores in the North of England, there was press speculation that MI5 had engineered the leak to damage the Special Branch. The Scotland Yard Assistant Commissioner (Specialist Operations) William Taylor 'unequivocally rejected' any idea that MI5 had been responsible for the disclosure.

It soon emerged that there would be no downgrading of the RUC Special Branch, and that the appointment of a second RUC deputy Chief Constable would fit in with a reorganisation of intelligence-gathering overall in NI. Clearly, the Government had been impressed by a plea by RUC Chief Constable Sir Hugh Annesley in July 1992 for a new national anti-terrorist unit for the UK to provide a single intelligence focal point for the RUC, Garda Síochána, and police forces in Europe and the US. It seemed that whether or not the idea was eventually adopted in these terms, closer co-ordination of anti-terrorist information would result.

MI5, of course, continued to operate in NI. Indeed, its NI role was officially acknowledged for the first time in 1988. The NI Secretary of State was then empowered through the Security Service legislation to authorise specific burglaries or bugging by MI5 agents and the service was put on a statutory basis for the first time. The alignment of Secretary of State powers with those of the Home Secretary in this way was a clear indication of the growing importance of MI5 in anti-PIRA operations. Although a special tribunal was to be set up to deal with complaints about MI5 behaviour, the Act stated that 'no entry on, or interference with, property shall be unlawful if it is authorised by a warrant issued by the Secretary of State'. Such break-ins would be directed to securing information 'likely to be of substantial value' in helping MI5 to discharge any of its functions. Media critics of the legislation concentrated on the point that it would be difficult for any individual to lodge a complaint about the service because it would be an offence under new Official Secrets legislation for any MI5 officer or Government official to reveal anything about the operations of the service.

The measure had the effect of highlighting the significance of MI5 in local security operations, although it appears that it has been active in NI at least since direct rule was imposed in 1972, and probably for some years before that. Most likely, MI5 took a serious interest in NI in 1970, when PIRA began to gather strength and to cast about for sources of weapons and ammunition. At that time, the focus was strongly on contacts between extreme Republicans and their Irish-American sympathisers, and MI5 was in regular contact with the FBI. It was close collaboration of this kind that led to the interception of a cargo of arms and ammunition intended for PIRA which was carried across the Atlantic in 1984 by the US vessel *Valhalla,* and then transferred to the *Marita Ann* off the Irish coast. But satellite tracking could also have figured in this operation. The FBI has always been engaged in moves to frustrate US arms dealers seeking to provide materials for PIRA, although Armalite rifles and even machine guns have in fact reached PIRA from across the Atlantic.

The fact that PIRA was able to receive several shipments of arms from Libya in the mid-1980s, on which it still relies heavily, was a failure of intelligence. But it is unlikely that responsibility for this will ever be firmly pinpointed. The intelligence picture in the early days of direct rule seems to have been extremely confused. According to some experts, there could have been as many as five competing agencies in the field. The RUC Special Branch, active since the 1920s, should have been the most effective, but its out-of-date files produced for the 1971 internment operation seriously damaged its credibility. Its strength in anti–IRA activities under the old Stormont had rested essentially on a relatively small group of officers based at the Queen Street station in central Belfast, and it was ill-suited to deal with the growing PIRA and its young activists. In that situation, direct rule led to a stepping-up of the army's intelligence effort. As one army unit succeeded another in areas like W. Belfast, it handed over to its successor photographs and information on terrorist suspects, and co-ordinating officers at Lisburn were able to draw on this sizeable pool of intelligence. Lord Carver, former Chief of the General Staff, has explained the authorisation of an independent army intelligence programme as resulting from the belief that the RUC Special Branch had links with Protestant extremists.

In the early 1970s, army intelligence activity took some exotic forms. Colin Wallace, who was senior press officer at Army HQ, has spoken of 'dirty tricks' directed sometimes at politicians. Wallace was dismissed in 1975 for supplying classified documents to *Times* correspondent Robert Fisk, but in 1990 he was awarded £30,000 compensation for unfair dismissal. In the early 1970s the SAS-trained Military Reconnaissance Force set up the 'Four Square Laundry', which offered cheap cleaning but was really directed to picking up information on PIRA, mainly in W. Belfast. It was abandoned when it was detected by PIRA and one of its drivers died in a PIRA machine-gun attack. According to *Republican News,* some women selling cosmetics in Nationalist areas worked for army intelligence around the same time.

Inter-service rivalry in intelligence matters seems to have been as evident in NI as in other areas. While MI5 has been most frequently mentioned as having a co-ordinating role, and as advising Secretaries of State at crucial times, MI6 appears to have been closely involved during the 1975 PIRA ceasefire, when the controversial 'incident centres' were set up to provide for contacts between PSF and Stormont officials. Some Foreign Office officials seconded to the NIO probably had an MI6 background, and PIRA chiefs, in abandoning the ceasefire, were probably influenced by the fear that the 'incident centre' co-operation was making their organisation more vulnerable to penetration. Both MI6 and MI5 have operated in the Republic, and have reportedly had contacts within the Garda senior ranks from time to time. Occasional car crashes in the Republic involving British agents who have mysteriously disappeared from the scene have provoked comment in many areas.

Incidentally, Sir Howard Smith, who was appointed head of MI5 in the late 1970s by Merlyn Rees, had been the last UK Government representative in NI (the office disappeared after direct rule). Sir Howard was thus able to bring useful local knowledge to MI5's anti-terrorist operations at a time when army–RUC co-operation was not at its best. It was this situation that led to Sir Maurice Oldfield (ex-head of the Secret Intelligence Service, or MI6) becoming Security Co-ordinator in NI in 1979, an initiative that apparently sprang directly from Margaret Thatcher's own observations on the ground. MI5 officer Michael Bettaney, who in 1984 was sentenced to twenty-three years' imprisonment at the Old Bailey for spying for the Russians, was based in NI for a period in the early 1980s.

In *Spycatcher* Peter Wright provides some curious observations on MI5's attitude to NI in 1973. He claims that he was invited to produce 'bright ideas' to deal with what he himself termed a situation very like that in Cyprus, with a 'fierce, insoluble conflict made worse by a vacillating British policy'. But Wright admits that he fared badly with those suggestions he did put forward. The Foreign Office, he says, vetoed the idea of monitoring (via equipment in the attic of the British Embassy in Dublin) PIRA telephone communications between Dublin and the west of Ireland, and neither MI5 nor MI6 would countenance his proposal to put booby-trapped detonators on Provisionals.

It is hardly surprising that Wright's ideas found no favour in White-hall, since he was advancing them during the run-up period to the crucial Sunningdale Conference upon which both the British and Irish Governments placed high hopes. With the well-known suspicion in Irish political circles of British intelligence services, and even occasion-ally of the British Embassy in Dublin, the Foreign Office and the NIO have always been anxious to avoid any incidents in this field that could set back cross-border security co-operation. There was considerable embarrassment at Stormont when, in May 1976, eight members of the SAS were arrested by the Garda when they crossed the S. Armagh border while engaged on covert observation. Even the intervention of PM James Callaghan with the Irish Government failed to stop the prosecutions of the SAS men, who were eventually fined £100 each for having unlicensed guns. It appears that while the Irish Cabinet did not favour the charges, they had no power to stop the DPP bringing them. While the presence of the SAS in NI was only admitted in the mid-1970s, it is believed to have been active since 1969, initially in trying to uncover arms thought to have been well hidden by loyalists.

The SAS, and units trained by it, have remained a key factor in collecting information about PIRA. This has frequently entailed groups of four or five soldiers digging themselves in for several days at a time, often in extremely uncomfortable conditions, to observe locations such as disused houses in remote areas. Many seizures are attributed to such unromantic spying. This time-consuming observation is more suited to the working conditions of the army than those of the RUC. The 14th Intelligence Company is another element associated with army intelligence.

The jailing in Belfast in January 1992 of Brian Nelson, an army spy within the UDA, on twenty charges, including conspiracy to murder five Catholics, was a serious blow to the local intelligence community. Nelson, who got a ten-year term, was moved to GB to serve his sentence, but there were official assurances that this would not mean an earlier release than if he had remained in an NI prison. As a UDA intelligence officer, he was at the centre of that organisation's tactics, and it was claimed at his trial that he had saved many lives in working for the army. But Nationalists asked why the army had not acted to prevent murders of which Nelson had prior knowledge. They pointed to repeated statements by Ministers that informers could not be involved in law-breaking, and asked what knowledge the RUC had of the situation. Labour spokesman Kevin McNamara MP was concerned that NI was becoming 'an adventure playground for secret agents'.

In August 1993 Alasdair Fraser, the DPP for NI, requested Sir John Stevens to reopen his inquiry into collusion in the light of the evidence revealed by the Nelson prosecution. New files were sent to the DPP in February 1994 with a view to prosecution. The impression was left that, in future, army intelligence would no longer be a separate operation but would be subject to joint supervision by police and army chiefs, and that the new RUC deputy Chief Constable, Blair Wallace, would have the key role, as the RUC's operations boss, in directing covert as well as uniformed activities. Both the now illegal UDA and PIRA were seen as striving to root out informers, and between 1992 and 1993 PIRA shot dead four alleged informers, one of whom was accused of working for MI5. These killings were believed to have brought to about sixty the number of people inside and outside PIRA murdered for alleged spying for the security forces.

The RUC has had a large central intelligence effort, backed by computer records since the mid-1970s, and its E4A covert operators are said to have had considerable successes in tracking both PIRA and loyalist suspects, and in countering the PIRA's own intelligence agents, some of them women, who are known to operate in pubs and other public places, ready to profit from any 'loose talk' by off-duty members of the security forces. To defeat such PIRA efforts, local army units maintain lists of establishments that are at any moment out of bounds to soldiers.

The permanent border checks, with records of movements of vehicles, are also a valuable part of the intelligence network. Telephone tapping is a long-established means of uncovering terrorist contacts. In the old Stormont Parliament there were regular questions about the alleged activities of monitoring agents based in Room 22 of the old Post Office HQ in Royal Avenue, Belfast, and under direct rule there has been evidence that some journalists' conversations have been intercepted. But no official statistics are available on the practice, which has to be authorised by the Secretary of State or the Home Secretary, and which since 1985 has been subject to review by a High Court judge. In his 1991 report on telephone tapping, Lord Justice Lloyd refused to say how many warrants were issued by the NIO or Foreign Office. He said that on balance, publication would be against the public interest. But he claimed that 40 per cent of all warrants issued at the request of the police had led to arrests for serious crime or terrorism. The Government Communications Centre at Cheltenham is heavily involved in the interception of telephone and electronic communications that could have a bearing on terrorism.

The Army Air Corps helicopter operation is a further important source of information, and the use of airborne infra-red photography is believed to have helped greatly in finding buried caches of weapons. How far such operations have led to finds on the Republic's side of the border is not known, but it emerged in late 1988 that an agreement had existed between the British and Irish Governments since early 1987, allowing short overflights of the border to investigate suspect devices.

SECURITY STATISTICS

TABLE 1

Deaths, August 1969–December 1993

	NORTHERN IRELAND					TOTAL NI	OTHER PLACES			TOTAL OTHER PLACES
	RUC	RUCR	Army	UDR/RIR	Civilians	NI	GB	Republic	Europe	PLACES
1969	1	0	0	0	12	13	0	0	0	0
1970	2	0	0	0	23	25	0	3	0	3
1971	11	0	43	5	115	174	0	3	0	3
1972	14	3	103	26	321	467	7	4	0	11
1973	10	3	58	8	171	250	2	6	0	8
1974	12	3	28	7	166	216	45	37	0	82
1975	7	4	14	6	216	247	10	7	0	17
1976	13	10	14	15	245	297	2	4	0	6
1977	8	6	15	14	69	112	0	4	0	4
1978	4	6	14	7	50	81	0	1	0	1
1979	9	5	38	10	51	113	1	6	2	9
1980	3	6	8	9	50	76	0	4	2	6
1981	13	8	10	13	57	101	3	1	0	4
1982	8	4	21	7	57	97	11	2	0	13
1983	9	9	5	10	44	77	6	4	0	10
1984	7	2	9	10	36	64	5	1	0	6
1985	14	9	2	4	25	54	0	4	0	4
1986	10	2	4	8	37	61	0	0	0	0
1987	9	7	3	8	66	93	0	6	0	6
1988	4	2	21	12	54	93	1	1	7	9
1989	7	2	12	2	39	62	11	1	4	16
1990	7	5	7	8	49	76	3	0	3	6
1991	5	1	5	8	75	94	3	1	0	4
1992	2	1	3	3	76	85	4	0	0	4
1993	3	3	6	2	70	84	3	0	0	3
Total	192	101	443	202	2,174	3,112	117	100	18	235

Note Civilian figures include terrorist suspects and prison officers.
The Royal Irish Regiment (RIR) became operational on 1 July 1992, when UDR
and Royal Irish Rangers were amalgamated.

TABLE 2

Monthly record of deaths, 1972–93

	1972	1973	1974	1975	1976	1977	1978	1979	1980	1981	1982	1983
Jan.	26	17	19	8	48	13	2	2	15	7	8	6
Feb.	22	37	15	19	27	13	21	6	8	5	1	5
Mar.	39	30	26	13	17	14	7	2	4	4	8	5
Apr.	22	16	14	36	20	17	4	16	9	9	11	5
May	40	30	25	11	26	13	2	7	4	22	4	5
June	35	30	14	21	37	9	13	11	4	5	4	3
July	95	17	12	15	28	10	5	7	4	11	2	9
Aug.	55	21	14	29	20	7	6	25	11	5	3	5
Sept.	40	10	12	23	12	3	7	6	3	11	9	4
Oct.	39	8	19	31	28	6	4	11	3	8	12	8
Nov.	20	20	35	24	23	4	5	9	5	14	13	14
Dec.	34	14	11	17	11	3	5	11	6	0	22	8
Total	467	250	216	247	297	112	81	113	76	101	97	77

	1984	1985	1986	1987	1988	1989	1990	1991	1992	1993
Jan.	8	1	4	2	6	3	8	3	15	8
Feb.	4	20	5	4	5	10	0	1	18	7
Mar.	6	3	3	13	10	12	6	12	4	10
Apr.	7	4	4	14	3	4	9	7	7	2
May	9	6	10	14	5	3	1	9	2	4
June	5	3	1	9	9	4	5	8	0	6
July	5	0	12	6	11	5	8	4	5	1
Aug.	4	5	5	4	26	2	1	11	6	3
Sept.	3	3	6	6	4	3	6	8	8	6
Oct.	5	1	6	5	8	5	19	8	5	27
Nov.	2	6	2	13	4	9	9	17	10	2
Dec.	6	2	3	3	2	2	4	6	5	8
Total	64	54	61	93	93	62	76	94	85	84

Note Consolidated figures for 1969–71 unavailable.

TABLE 3

Murders by paramilitaries, 1981–93

	Republican		Loyalist	
	Murders	Attempted murders	Murders	Attempted murders
1981	69	461	12	26
1982	71	401	13	12
1983	54	286	7	13
1984	40	185	7	22
1985	42	140	5	11
1986	41	87	14	31
1987	69	176	11	23
1988	62	u/a	22	u/a
1989	39	u/a	18	u/a
1990	46	u/a	19	u/a
1991	47	u/a	40	u/a
1992	36	u/a	39	u/a
1993	36	u/a	48	u/a
Total	652	1,736	255	138

Note Consolidated figures for 1969–80 unavailable; figures for attempted murders since 1988 unavailable (u/a).

470

TABLE 4

Injuries, 1968–93

	RUC/ RUCR	Army/ UDR/ RIR	Civilians	Punishment shootings etc.	Annual injuries total
1968	379	0	u/a	u/a	379
1969	711	22	u/a	u/a	733
1970	191	620	u/a	u/a	811
1971	315	390	1,838	u/a	2,543
1972	485	578	3,813	u/a	4,876
1973	291	548	1,812	74	2,725
1974	235	483	1,680	127	2,525
1975	263	167	2,044	189	2,663
1976	303	264	2,162	98	2,827
1977	183	187	1,027	126	1,523
1978	302	135	548	67	1,052
1979	155	135	557	76	923
1980	194	77	530	77	878
1981	332	149	877	80	1,438
1982	99	99	328	89	615
1983	142	88	280	34	544
1984	267	86	513	70	936
1985	415	33	468	62	978
1986	622	55	773	82	1,532
1987	246	104	780	184	1,314
1988	218	229	600	122	1,169
1989	163	190	606	212	1,171
1990	214	214	478	175	1,081
1991	139	253	570	138	1,100
1992	148	320	598	133	1,199
1993	146	173	507	84	910
Total	7,158	5,599	23,389	2,299	38,445

Note Figures for civilians include terrorist suspects and prison officers.

TABLE 5

Record of violence, 1969–93

	Shooting incidents	Explosions	Bombs defused	Malicious fires	Armed robberies	Amounts stolen £
1969	73	9	1	u/a	u/a	u/a
1970	213	153	17	u/a	u/a	u/a
1971	1,756	1,022	493	u/a	489	303,787
1972	10,628	1,382	471	u/a	1,931	795,009
1973	5,018	978	542	587	1,317	612,015
1974	3,206	685	428	636	1,353	575,951
1975	1,803	399	236	248	1,325	572,105
1976	1,908	766	426	453	889	545,497
1977	1,081	366	169	432	671	447,018
1978	755	455	178	269	493	232,650
1979	728	422	142	315	504	568,359
1980	642	280	120	275	467	496,829
1981	1,142	398	131	536★	689	854,929
1982	547	219	113	499	693	1,392,202
1983	424	266	101	528	718	830,258
1984	334	193	55	840	710	701,903
1985	237	148	67	740	542	655,690
1986	392	172	82	906	839	1,207,152
1987	674	236	148	506	955	1,900,098
1988	537	253	205	518	742	1,388,599
1989	566	224	196	307	604	1,079,399
1990	559	167	120	333	492	1,728,685
1991	499	230	137	333	608	1,672,884
1992	506	222	149	419	738	1,665,863
1993	476	206	83	u/a	643	1,514,878
Total	34,704	9,851	4,810	9,680	18,412	21,741,760

Note   ★ Figures for April, May and June 1981 incalculable due to civil disorder.

TABLE 6

Arms finds and house searches, 1969–93

	Firearms found	Explosives found (tons)	Ammunition found (rounds)	Number of house searches
1969	14	0.1	u/a	u/a
1970	324	0.3	43,095	3,107
1971	716	1.2	157,944	17,262
1972	1,259	18.5	183,410	36,617
1973	1,313	17.2	187,399	74,556
1974	1,236	11.7	147,202	74,914
1975	820	4.9	73,604	30,002
1976	736	9.7	70,306	34,919
1977	563	1.7	52,091	20,724
1978	393	0.9	43,512	15,462
1979	300	0.9	46,280	6,452
1980	203	0.8	28,078	4,106
1981	357	3.4	47,127	4,104
1982	288	2.3	41,452	4,045
1983	166	1.7	32,451	1,497
1984	187	3.8	27,211	1,282
1985	173	3.3	13,748	812
1986	174	2.4	29,061	1,818
1987	206	5.8	19,796	2,474
1988	489	4.7	105,052	4,136
1989	246	1.4	37,700	3,027
1990	179	1.9	22,452	3,568
1991	164	4.1	18,175	2,961
1992	194	2.1	29,131	3,415
1993	196	3.9	20,066	3,264
Total	10,896	108.7	1,476,343	354,524

Note 1970–85: source, Army headquarters.
1986–93: source, RUC headquarters.

Arms finds figures indicate totals from all sources, including house searches.

TABLE 7

Persons charged with terrorist-type offences, July 1972–December 1993

	Murder	Attempted murder	Firearms	Explosives	Theft	Other
1972*	13	16	242	86	111	63
1973	71	85	631	236	186	205
1974	75	75	544	161	232	275
1975	138	88	460	100	314	97
1976	120	211	353	215	188	279
1977	131	135	301	146	203	392
1978	60	79	225	79	151	249
1979	45	39	177	40	152	210
1980	63	59	112	39	128	149
1981	48	72	155	39	158	446
1982	51	96	173	41	130	196
1983	75	60	150	48	119	161
1984	41	68	155	21	94	149
1985	24	52	105	37	65	239
1986	12	28	128	31	70	386
1987	28	21	132	22	109	156
1988	23	46	121	29	42	178
1989	31	48	130	24	41	159
1990	18	62	115	22	31	133
1991	37	83	87	24	40	120
1992	38	63	79	38	32	159
1993	15	45	91	36	52	129
Total	1,157	1,531	4,666	1,514	2,648	4,530

Note * Consolidated figures prior to July 1972 not available.

INDEX

Note Page numbers in italics refer to main entries in 'Dictionary of Northern Ireland Politics'

506

bomb, 1985, 30; landmine deaths, 20, 23, 27; mortar deaths, 30, 189, 246; three killed, 1990, 53; two killed, 1982, 24; two killed, 1993, 71
Catholic membership, 36, 87, 440
CCDC paper on, 116
code of conduct (1987), 40
complaints procedure, 30
dawn raids, 6
'Day of Action' (1986), 32
disarmed, 4, 241
E4A, 465
equal opportunities settlement, 46
on Falls Road, 4, 154–5
fatality statistics, 66
funeral policing, 38, 441–2
and Martin Galvin, 196
and Garda Síochána, 39, 126
Hendron criticises, 182
Hermon Chief Constable, 182–3
history, 437–43
holding centres commissioner, 441
homes petrol-bombed, 33
and hunger strikes, 178
Hunt inquiry, 4
informer alleged, 27
intelligence unit, 461–2
interrogation videoing urged, 58, 65, 224
irregularities in files, 28
leave cancelled (1981), 21
loyalist attacks, 19, 33, 34, 36
loyalist collusion claimed, 57
Mason enlarges role, 230
Mayhew ruling, 232
Milltown cemetery film confiscated, 43
Newman Chief Constable, 245–6
and NICRA, 248
and Orange parades, 30, 34, 65
paramilitary punishment statistics, 39
Peacocke Inspector-General, 266
and PIRA ceasefire, 276
plastic bullet death, 28
PSF office attacked by officer, 59, 287
PSF seeks licensed weapons, 67
public order laws (1987), 199
raids An Phoblacht, 55
raids UDA HQ, 329
reforms, 115, 354
reinforced, 14, 17, 24
report (1988), 43
Republic's attitude to, 203
Scarman report, 300
and SDA, 301
sex discrimination, 37, 182
Shillington Chief Constable, 302–3
shoots three PIRA, 24
Special Branch, 463
stations attacked, 4, 36, 47, 58, 59, 71, 147
stations to close, 47
Stevens inquiry, 49, 52, 314
strategy document, 52
suspensions, 34
training depot attacked, 31
and UDR, 51, 63
undercover in Republic, 27
and USC, 336
van bomb intercepted, 66
White Paper, 4
women members to be armed, 66
Young Chief Constable, 4, 357–8
Royal Ulster Constabulary Reserve, 2, 26, 38
RTE, 2, 63
Adams ad banned, 75
Late, Late Show, 59, 105

Milltown cemetery film, 43
rubber bullets, 5, 449–50
Russell, Robert, 44, 45
Ryan, Fr Patrick, 47, 204, 439
Ryan, Peter, 283
Ryder, Chris, 122

St Bedan coal boat, 22, 279
Salisbury, Marquess of, 166–7
Sampson, Colin, 312; *see also* Stalker/Sampson inquiries
Samuel, Malcolm, 171, 406
Sandelson, Neville, *299*
Sands, Bobby, 98, 120, 177, 239, 278, *299*, 310
anniversary riots (1984), 27
death of, 20
and ECHR, 114, 151
election win, 20, 178, 226, 285, 313, 350, 388
funeral, 20
hunger strike, 19
Sandy Row, *299*
Saor Éire, 104, *299–300*, 454
SAS, 184, 282–3, 324, 446
anti-PIRA intelligence, 464–5
in Armagh, 12, 277
BBC documentary postponed, 45
border crossing arrests, 13, 464
casualties, 9
Gibraltar shootings, 42, *167–8*, 281
INLA shooting, 195
Loughgall shootings, 38, *211*, 280–1
Mason introduces, 230
PIRA deaths, 26, 45, 281, 315
Savage, Sean, 42, 167–8
Save Ulster campaign, 332
Scarman, Lord, 171
Scarman Tribunal, 4, 119, 246, *300*, 437–8
on Ardoyne, 89
on Bernadette Devlin, 215
on Falls Road, 154–5
on Lynch broadcast, 212
on Paisley, 260–1
on Peacocke, 266
on PIRA, 272
'Scenario for Peace' (PSF), 286
Schull, Co. Cork, 23, 195
Scotland, 61, 94, 328, 343
Scott, Nicholas, 35, 123, 269, *300–1*, 314, 423
contradicts Haughey on AIA, 36
rejects Powell amendment, 37
replaced by Stanley, 39
Scott inquiry, 212
Scottish Nationalist Party, 60
Scottish Unionist Party, *301*, 319
Scullion, John, 342
Seanad Éireann, 159
Haughey nominations, 160, 166, 175
McGonagle member, 220
Mallon member, 22, 24, 228, 307
New Consensus, 244
NI debate, 63
Robb member, 22, 24, 296
Gordon Wilson member, 62, 354
Seawright, Elizabeth, 301
Seawright, George, 34, 35, *301*, 349
'incineration' remark, 28
murdered, 41, 197
sectarianism; *see also* discrimination; *and* Fair Employment Agency
civil service, 26
in Irish Constitution, 26
law needs strengthening, 38
Ó Fiaich on, 30